CHRISTIANITY

A Social and Cultural History

Second Edition

Howard Clark Kee
Boston University (Emeritus)

Emily Albu
University of California, Davis

Carter Lindberg
Boston University

J. William Frost
Swarthmore College

Dana L. Robert
Boston University

Prentice Hall, Upper Saddle River, NJ 07458

Library of Congress Cataloging-in-Publication Data

Christianity : a social and cultural history / Howard C. Kee . . . [et
al.]. — 2nd ed.
      p.   cm.
    Includes bibliographical references and index.
    ISBN 0-13-578071-3
    1. Church history.   2. Sociology, Christian—History.
3. Christianity and culture—History.   I. Kee, Howard Clark.
BR148.C48   1998
270—dc21
                                          97–27505
                                            CIP

Editor-in-Chief: Charlyce Jones Owen
Production Editor: Joseph Scordato
Copy Editor: Brian Baker
Manufacturing Buyer: Robert Anderson
Cover Design: Pat Wosczyk
Cover Photo: Sarcophagus of Junius Bassus, Roman prefect died 359 C.E. Detail: Christ between two
    Apostles. High-relief from upper panel. *Source:* Art Resource, NY

This book was set in 10/12 Janson by ElectraGraphics, Inc., and was printed and bound by Courier Companies,
Inc. The cover was printed by Phoenix Color Corp.

© 1998 by Prentice-Hall, Inc.
Simon & Schuster / A Viacom Company
Upper Saddle River, New Jersey 07458

Printed in the United States of America

10 9 8 7 6 5 4 3 2 1

0-13-578071-3

Prentice-Hall International (UK) Limited, *London*
Prentice-Hall of Australia Pty. Limited, *Sydney*
Prentice-Hall Canada Inc., *Toronto*
Prentice-Hall Hispanoamericana, S.A., *Mexico*
Prentice-Hall of India Private Limited, *New Delhi*
Prentice-Hall of Japan, Inc., *Tokyo*
Simon & Schuster Asia Pte. Ltd., *Singapore*
Editora Prentice-Hall do Brasil, Ltda., *Rio de Janeiro*

Contents

Preface

As is indicated by the subtitle of this book—"A Social and Cultural History"—the aim is to enable the reader to perceive how Christianity emerged from its original Jewish context and developed into a worldwide religion through engagement with the social and cultural dimensions of the world contemporary with its origins and evolution. The writers chosen to produce this work represent scholars whose academic skills embody such a contextual approach to their respective fields of specialization, ranging from knowledge of the Greco-Roman setting in which Christianity arose and spread across the Roman world (Kee and Albu), to the structuring of the church conceptually and organizationally in Europe (Lindberg), and to its spread and growth in America (Frost) and then throughout the world (Robert). The book should be helpful for those studying the history of Christianity as such, but also for those interested in the impact of Christianity on world culture down through history.

Howard Clark Kee
William Goodwin Aurelio Professor of Religious Studies, Emeritus
Boston University

Howard Clark Kee

Introduction

In the book of Acts of the Apostles, Paul is pictured as standing before the puppet king of Galilee, Herod Agrippa II, defending his role in the spread of Christianity. He reminds the king that the events which gave rise to the movement could not have escaped the ruler's notice, since "this thing did not happen in a corner" (Acts 28:26). Paul's passing remark to the king is actually a powerful understatement. What he is referring to is that what Jesus did and said, what happened to him, and what his followers were carrying out in his name were matters of public record and intended for broad public interest, not merely events taking place "in a corner." These public activities that gave rise to the Jesus movement, Paul is implying, are known to the populace at large and have involved the religious and political leaders of Palestine and Syria, of Asia Minor and Greece. Although he does not say so, the spread of the movement and its message were soon to come to the attention of the emperor Tiberius in Rome, as they already had attracted notice and responses among the civil authorities in cities from Jerusalem northward and westward across Syria and the eastern Mediterranean world. From the second century on, the Christian claims would challenge and enrage some leading intellectuals, while persuading others. The Christians would learn to use, for their own purposes, the artistic and literary styles of the changing eras down through the centuries and to develop a synthesis of Greco-Roman culture with Christian faith. In the fourth century, Christianity became the effective instrument by which the emperor Constantine gained control over the whole of the Roman empire.

1

Christianity a Public Event

To keep these public dimensions of Christianity in mind is essential for the study of its origins, development, and subsequent growth. The death of Jesus, which had such central significance for the message that his followers told about him, had taken place on a political charge—that he claimed to be king of the Jews—and it was carried out by the Roman military. From the outset, the conflict Jesus had with the religious authorities had been over his insistence that participation in the people of God was open to all humanity, regardless of ethnicity, rituals, or prior religious status. So rapid was the pace at which this message had spread throughout Palestine, gaining both Jewish and non-Jewish adherents for the new community, that within a year or two of his death, Jesus' followers had to interpret the message about him in the language and cultural forms of other Greco-Roman peoples in addition to the original Jewish hearers. This inclusive approach to religious identity—how all human beings may be related to God—raised all manner of difficulties for Christians and contributed from the outset to the struggles they experienced.

Christianity in Conflict with Established Authority

From its beginnings, the early Christian movement confronted the established religious and political leaders. In the gospel accounts of the career of Jesus, the crisis that leads to his death comes when he is called to explain his role and aims to the religious leaders in Jerusalem. He had set aside some of the laws believed to have been given by God to Moses, such as prohibition of work on the Sabbath or the avoidance of contact with non-Jews during meals. In Jesus, the Jewish leaders saw a basic threat to what most of them regarded as the ground rules for belonging to the Jewish people. Similarly, the fact that he talked so much about "kingdom" and that his followers spoke of him as king required the political leaders of Palestine to question his intentions. Was he planning a nationalist revolt against the Romans? This charge resulted in his execution because he was perceived as a threat to Roman authority in that part of the empire. How could his proclamation about the coming of God's kingdom be compatible with the sovereignty of Rome?

These issues of conflict with religious and political leadership have powerfully affected the life of the church throughout its existence. There seems to have been no general persecution of Christians until some time in the second century, but by the late third century there was an organized effort to stamp out the movement. Astonishingly, in the fourth century the Roman emperor recognized Christianity and identified himself with the church. Immediately, there arose the problem of how the church should be related to the political powers—an issue that subsequently led to the emergence of two centers of churchly power (one in Rome and one in the eastern Roman empire) and, later, to the Protestant Reformation. This has been a source of contention and conflict in Europe and America down to the present day. Church–state issues show up often in political contests and in the U.S. state and federal courts.

Christianity's Communications Strategy

Since the early Christians were convinced that they had a message for the whole human race, they had a problem of communication from the outset. In order to convey what they termed the Good News to as wide as possible a range of society, both Jewish and Gentile, Jesus and his followers had to employ a variety of media. From the beginning, Christians had to be able to use the literary forms developed by people of various cultures in order to get through to them with the Christian story. The reports of what Jesus said and did were circulated at first orally in popular storytelling form. Those who taught and preached in his name simply repeated what they had heard. Only later were these traditions about Jesus brought together in the sequential form that we have them in the gospels. Narratives about Paul and his associates were reported a generation after their time in the popular literary style of the late first and second century known as a "romance." This mode of communication was a way of attracting readers to the religious figures and experiences that were depicted. Through miracles of deliverance and disaster, and through journeys by land and sea, the gods were thought to guide the lives of those devoted to them. The Book of Acts employed and adapted this model for communicating its story about the progress of the Christian Gospel from Jerusalem to Rome, with the implicit claim of divine confirmation of this message by miracles and wonders that had taken place through the apostles.

Other traditions in the early Christian writings are recorded in styles that took Jewish hymns and psalms as their model, while some imitate formal public addresses or letter-writing patterns of the time. Still other parts of the New Testament and early Christian literature (such as the Book of Revelation and parts of the gospels and letters of Paul) are influenced strongly by such distinctive Jewish writings as apocalypses—documents that claim to be divine disclosures by God to the faithful minority of His people, warning them of conflict and suffering, while promising them ultimate vindication. Clearly, the early Christians were ready and able to use a variety of forms of communication, employing whatever means they thought best suited for getting their message through to their contemporaries. This same multimedia strategy has been adopted throughout the life of the church, with the result that its message has been conveyed through official decrees, learned philosophical discourses, epistles, and reports of visions and revelations in order to reach as wide a public as possible.

Christianity in Competition with Judaism

An essential feature of the early Christian movement was its claim that, through Jesus, it could provide the true and ultimate interpretation of the Jewish scriptures and that it was the heir to the promises God is reported in those scriptures to have made concerning the renewal of His covenant with His people. There were inevitably mixed reactions from contemporary Jews: Some were persuaded, while others fiercely resisted the movement and sought to combat the radical claims that were being made about Jesus on the basis of the biblical tradition. This infighting led outsiders to assume that what we now call Christianity was merely another form of internal debate and conflict within the Jewish religion.

In the first centuries of the Common Era, Judaism was itself undergoing radical reorganization and rethinking, following the destruction of the temple and the unseating of the priestly leadership that had guided the Jews for centuries. We shall see how the Christians dealt with these issues in a variety of ways. Some groups within the early church wanted to emphasize the continuity of the new community with ancient Israel and its traditions, while others sought to a make a radical break therewith.

Christianity's Social Structure

Throughout its history, Christianity has responded in a variety of ways to the political, social, and cultural environments that surrounded it. The responses have included hostility to the state and prevailing culture, adoption by the church of the basic structures of society and political power, and adaptation of some of the modes of human social and political life to a more acceptable form. Some leaders of the church assumed that their obedience to God demanded that they withdraw wholly from society; hence, they formed monastic communities. Yet even then, the literature produced by monks shows how deeply they were engaged with issues arising out of the wider culture. The obligation to make decisions concerning these social, political, economic, and intellectual structures was inevitable and has been a persistent factor throughout the history of the church.

The Search for Identity

Complicating the inescapable obligation to make decisions about the political powers and about the competing religions of the day were the issues of internal authority within the church. The members of the new movement had to resolve the problems of leadership, authority, and decision making within the group. As the great sociologist of religion, Max Weber, noted earlier in the twentieth century, religions typically begin as spontaneous movements launched and expanded through the powerful personality and charisma of a leader. Such a movement has no more than begun, however, before those who move into leadership roles begin to develop patterns of authority and increasingly specific guidelines for individual and group decision making. In Weber's terms, what begins as a charismatic movement soon takes on institutional forms. It must do so if it is to survive, especially as the first generation of adherents begins to die off and the continuation of the group is dependent on a new generation that must be instructed in the group's traditions and charged with the range of responsibilities essential for the survival of the movement.[1]

We shall see that before the earliest Gospel was written, and while Paul was carrying on the missionary activity reflected in his letters, the transformation from charismatic origins to institutional forms was already under way in early Christianity. The later books of the New Testament and the literature of the early centuries of the church reflect further developments in the internal structure for providing leadership and for establishing the

---

[1]This basic position is set forth in Max Weber, "The Sociology of Charismatic Authority," in *From Max Weber*, H. H. Gerth and C. Wright Mills, trs. and eds. (Oxford and New York: Oxford University Press, 1958).

norms to be observed on a range of issues by the members of the movement. From the fourth century on, Christianity moved to assume a major role in the shaping of culture and politics in the Western world. The movement was shaped by Western culture, but it has also adapted itself to other cultures around the world.

Our focus in this volume will be on a protracted process: the rise of Christianity, its shift to the role of a religion officially sanctioned by the Roman state, and its subsequent development in the western world of Europe and America, where it has experienced a mixture of relationships to the state, ranging from ecclesiastical establishment (as in the United Kingdom) to theoretically total separation of church and state (as in the United States), the consequent proliferation of religious groups claiming to be the true heirs of the Christian tradition, and the spread of Christianity across the world. Although the initial focus of this book is on the rise of Christianity in the Middle East, and its subsequent spread to Europe and America, we shall also give attention to the impact of Christianity on other cultures, such as those in Africa and the Far East in later centuries.

* * * * * * *

Thus, the insights attributed to Paul in the Book of Acts were correct. The Christian movement promised renewal of the world—not merely human society, but the whole of creation. The terms of admission to the new community were potentially universal, so there was no prior reason why the claims of Christianity should not be heard and heeded by people from any race or culture. This required a variety of strategies and formulas for communicating the message, so that—to borrow another phrase from Acts (2:8)—each person might hear the message in his or her own language. That is, Christianity had to learn how to convey its claims and hopes in symbolic and verbal modes of communication that could reach persons in spite of basic cultural and social differences. As a result of this universal outreach of Christianity, and of the range of responses that its message called forth down through two thousand years, the movement has been a diverse phenomenon from the outset. Christianity began within Judaism at a time when Jews were confronted with a range of theories as to what made them God's special people. Christians offered a radical definition of that social identity as God's people, but the detailed implications of this claim to be the people of God were understood in a variety of ways by those who came to be part of the new movement. Given the way in which Christianity, from its origins, was involved with the basic issues of social identity, cross-cultural communication, and ultimate political power, it was inevitable that there would be a range of responses by the Christians. From the outset, therefore, Christianity was fundamentally required to react, first, to the issues of identity and responsibility for those who saw themselves as God's people and, second, to the challenges that this new community faced in its relation to the wider world. Paul's earlier noted observation concerning Christian origins that "This thing did not happen in a corner" is therefore wholly appropriate.

Part I

The Context, Birth, and Early Growth of Christianity

Howard Clark Kee

Chapter 1

From Alexander to Augustus:
Cultural and Political Challenge to Jewish Religious Identity

---

To understand how Christianity began as a movement within Palestinian Judaism and then spread so quickly throughout the world requires three kinds of information: (1) that concerning the political changes which brought Jews under the power of a series of world empires; (2) that concerning the pressures on Jews to conform to the culture and customs of the dominant power; and (3) that concerning the efforts of Jews and their Gentile contemporaries to find meaning in life and a sense of group identity in the midst of these social and political changes. What did it mean to be a Jew and hence a member of a people who claimed a special relationship to God? All these factors had a powerful influence on Judaism, but they also set the stage for the rise and spread of Christianity, which had to deal with the same issues. The various ways in which these questions were posed by Jews and the answers that were sought continued to have direct effects on the shaping of Christianity. It is essential, therefore, that we look at the experience of the Jews after the time of Alexander the Great to see how that experience shaped the problems of, and pointed toward solutions among, the early Christians.

The tensions under which Jews lived in the three centuries before the rise of Christianity were in large measure the result of Alexander's change of policy from that which the Persians previously held toward conquered peoples. Alexander wanted to control the world militarily and politically and desired to force it to conform to Greek culture. As a young man, he had studied philosophy with one of Greece's greatest philosophers, Aristotle, and was convinced that that sage's view of the world was the finest imaginable. Alexander wanted to conquer the world for Greek culture. Historians refer to this process as Hellenization, a term that derives from *Hellas* (the Greek name for Greece): to Hellenize is to "Greek-ize" the world. Alexander's culturally aggressive approach became apparent after he took over the eastern Mediterranean territories from the Persians, who had governed it from the time that they seized control of the Babylonian territories in the late sixth century B.C.E. Persian strategy had been to allow subject peoples dislocated from their lands during the Persian takeover of the Middle East to return to their native regions and to live and worship there with a considerable degree of local freedom.

The Jews were among those who benefited from this policy. One of their prophets went so far as to acclaim Cyrus, the king of Persia, as messiah, or "anointed of God" (Isa. 45:1). The very fact that this pagan ruler was described as someone commissioned by God to perform a special act on behalf of Israel shows that the Jews perceived themselves to stand in a special relationship to God, both in the past and in the present. But the new situation in which the Jews found themselves after the rise of Alexander was very different from their status when they lived in their own land, before they were carried off to Babylon as captives. Earlier, they had had their own leaders: judges, kings, and priests. Now the king was a pagan, helpful as he had been in allowing them to return to the land and reinstitute the temple and its priesthood. The unavoidable questions were, What does it now mean for Israel to call itself the people of God? and What are the rules by which the Israelites must live?

Who Are the People of God?

Although interpreters down through the centuries have disagreed as to how details of the law were to be interpreted as binding on Israel in its changing circumstances, there was a wide consensus that the nation had been given special knowledge of God in three ways: (1) through patriarchal figures such as Abraham, Isaac, and Jacob, (2) through Moses, under whose reported leadership the law was given and the exodus from Egypt to the land of Canaan began, and (3) through the kings, wise men, and prophets to whom God continued to disclose his purpose to and for his people. The perennial question was, What must Israel do to preserve its purity and integrity as a nation of God's people? A second basic issue for Jews was, Who will be the agent—or agents—through whom God's purpose for his people and for the creation will be brought to fulfillment? Both these issues were to have profound importance for Christianity.

The Jews of subsequent centuries had no uniform answer to these basic questions, and the actions of the pagan powers that dominated them enormously complicated such questions of religious and social identity for those, like the Jews, who were convinced that they were, in a special sense, the people of God. A number of forces bore upon the Jews as they attempted to deal with these problems.

The Challenge of Forced Conformity to Pagan Culture

When, at age twenty-one (336 B.C.E.), Alexander the Great took over a militarily and politically subjugated Greece from his father, King Philip II of Macedon, he also set out to achieve both military and political domination of the regions to the east, where the Persians were still in control. In a series of brilliant military successes, he quickly conquered Asia Minor, with its many cities of Greek tradition. The decisive battle was at Issus, on a narrow strip of land between the mountains of Cilicia and the Mediterranean Sea north of Syria. Once Alexander was past that strategic point, the way was open for him to invade and occupy Syria, Palestine, and Egypt, as well as to conquer vast territories farther east: Mesopotamia, Persia, and parts of India.

As Alexander traveled on this relentless world-conquering expedition, he visited ancient sites and called at shrines of various deities, with some of whom he seems to have identified and even communed, treating them as manifestations of the traditional gods of Greece. In Egypt, he founded a metropolis to which his name was given—Alexandria—which became a great center of learning, rivaling or even eclipsing such ancient intellectual and artistic cities as Athens itself. It is clear that one of his major aims was not merely political domination, but to spread Greek culture. This was to pose a major problem for Jews: How could they maintain their special identity if they conformed to such pressures?

When Alexander died in Babylon in 323 B.C.E., his generals divided his empire among themselves. Two of them were able to establish enduring realms for themselves and their heirs: Seleucus in Syria and Ptolemy in Egypt. Midway between these two centers of Hellenistic power was Palestine, the land of the Jews. It was at first controlled by the Ptolemies and then by the Seleucids, both of whom pressured the Jews to adopt Greek ways of life, thought, and religion. Theaters, gymnasia, and public baths were built, as well as shrines to the Greek gods. The coinage in use in these kingdoms pictured Greek gods and addressed the rulers with divine titles. Greek was the official language, and these subject peoples' acceptance by the ruling powers was contingent on their conformity to the manner of life and the values of Greek culture. Many Jews adopted the Hellenistic modes of life and thought with enthusiasm, but others were only partially open to the pagan influences, and still others stoutly resisted acculturation. In the first half of the second century B.C.E., however, the issue of religious and cultural domination became a crisis for the Jews.

The Effort to Regain Jewish National Identity

The Seleucid king Antiochus IV (ruled 175–164 B.C.E.) was particularly eager to coerce his subjects, including the Jews, into conformity with the Greek way. He went so far as to identify himself as divine and to insist that his subjects acclaim him as "Epiphanes," which meant a manifestation of deity. Faced with understandable and mounting opposition from certain Jews who called themselves Hasidim ("pious ones"), in 168 B.C.E. Antiochus decreed that the Jews were no longer to be permitted to worship their God and ordered the erection of an altar to Zeus in the temple at Jerusalem. Altars were also constructed throughout the land, and the military was instructed to enforce the worship of the Greek gods and to require that all subjects offer the appropriate sacrifices. A priestly member of the Hasidim, Mattathias, killed a fellow Jew in the village of Modin who was making the sacrifice decreed by Antiochus the king. Mattathias then fled to the hills with his five sons to organize opposition to Hellenistic rule. One of his sons, Judah (or Judas), whose nickname, Maccabee ("hammer"), was adopted by the nationalist movement, assumed the leadership.

He drew large numbers of supporters and launched guerrilla warfare, achieving astonishing results. By 165 B.C.E., the Maccabees had gained military control of much of the land and of the temple, which was cleansed and rededicated. The brothers of Judah (whose family name was Hasmonean) assumed the dual roles of priestly and royal leadership.

Because the Maccabean rulers and their successors became increasingly secular and oppressive, however, and because they had taken the title of king even though they were not descended from David's royal line, there was growing disillusionment with them. Finally, the Maccabean dynasty turned for support to a rising power in the west: Rome. In 63 B.C.E., Roman forces under Pompey, claiming to offer assistance to their ally, but actually taking over political control, invaded Palestine, establishing the region as a Roman province. As was their policy in all the provinces under their control, the Romans allowed Jews a considerable degree of autonomy with regard to local social and economic life. The Roman governors resident in Palestine worked closely with the high priests, who had to gain approval from the Romans for their appointment and who, accordingly, collaborated with the Roman governmental authorities. At the same time, the Romans controlled parts of Palestine and adjacent areas through local puppet kings, of whom the best known was Herod, who ruled from 37 B.C.E. to 4 C.E. His mother was Jewish, and his non-Jewish father had helped the Romans establish themselves in power in this land. Herod not only rebuilt the temple in Jerusalem on a grander scale than ever; he also built Hellenistic centers throughout the land, including a city on the Mediterranean coast that he called Caesarea in honor of his Roman benefactors, which contained all the features of a Greek-style city: theaters, temples, and gymnasia. At Herod's death, his sons were placed in control of various parts of the region, including Galilee, Samaria, and the strongly Hellenized territories east of the Jordan River. One son, Archelaus, who was put in charge of Judea and Jerusalem, was so incompetent that he had to be replaced by Roman-appointed governors, of whom the best known was Pontius Pilate (26–36 C.E.).

The Range of Responses to the Challenge of Greco-Roman Political and Cultural Domination among First-Century Jews

As mentioned earlier, Jews in the time of Jesus were wrestling with the question of group identity. Rephrasing the basic questions Jews had to face in these two centuries before the birth of Jesus, we may say that they were asking:

> Who are the agents of God through whom He will work to achieve His purpose for His people?
> What are the criteria for participation in the people of God?

Should Jews accept what seemed inevitable and accommodate themselves politically and culturally to their Roman overlords? Or was it the Jewish people's destiny to be distinct from all other peoples? If so, in what way were they to be distinctive? If not, what were the areas of permissible and defensible overlap with Gentile culture and values? How was Jewish identity to be affirmed and its continuity guaranteed?

The Culturally Conformist Jews

The easiest answer to these questions was to conform to the prevailing Greco-Roman modes of life and thought in the political, cultural, social, and personal spheres. Many Jews did so, taking Greek names, sending their children to the Hellenistic schools, attending theaters and sports events, and adopting the philosophical concepts of the Hellenistic culture. A radical example of this kind of cultural adaptation is evident in a writing known as IV Maccabees,[1] which retells the struggles of the Maccabees for freedom in terms of the Stoic notion of suffering as disciplinary and morally purgative. Some Jewish males went so far as to have the marks of circumcision surgically removed, so that they could take part without embarrassment in the nude gymnastics of the contemporary Hellenistic society. They participated by the thousands in the other features of Hellenistic culture, such as theaters and the forms of often bloody public entertainment.

Combining Hellenistic and Biblical Wisdom

Far more subtle than the popular conformity to Roman culture, but of profound significance for the future of Judaism and, by extension, Christianity, was the thoughtful incorporation of Hellenistic ideas into the religious traditions of Israel. One of the clearest evidences of such influence of Hellenistic thinking on the Jews of this period was the strong emphasis in Jewish literature on wisdom. Two examples indicate how Jewish writers sought to come to terms with Hellenistic philosophy and science.

The Wisdom of Ben Sira (also known as Sirach and as Ecclesiasticus) is a conscious response to the Hellenistic claims to knowledge of the universe. The writer asserts that true wisdom comes from Yahweh, the God of Israel, and that it existed before the creation, through which it became visible to discerning human beings. Those who apprehend wisdom evince it by the purity and moral responsibility of their lives. The embodiment of wisdom is the Book of the Covenant—the first five books in the Jewish scriptures: Genesis, Exodus, Leviticus, Numbers, and Deuteronomy. These books describe God's calling and commissioning certain leaders—Abraham, Isaac, Jacob, and Moses—through whom the special relation of Israel to God was defined and established. The basic rules for the life of God's people were set forth in the Law of Moses, which came to be called the Torah. Thus, the evidence of God's accomplishment of His wise purpose in human life is to be seen in the leaders He raised up to establish and guide His people, Israel. The culmination of this process of divine ordering of the life of God's people was understood to have recently appeared in Simon the High Priest (who served in that office from 220 to 195 B.C.E.), who had restored the temple and its ritual and was thereby perceived as the supreme instrument of blessing of Israel by the Most High God. For the writer of Sirach, Jewish identity is to be found in three resources: the reading and appropriation of the Bible, the celebration of God's historical guidance of Israel, and participation in the official worship of God in the temple. Yet in making his case for the uniqueness of Israel's relationship with God, the author draws subtly on the language and insights that came from Hellenistic wisdom.

That development is even clearer in a Jewish work produced in the late first century

---

[1] The text of IV Maccabees, together with an introduction and notes, is offered in *The Old Testament Pseudepigrapha* (Garden City, NY: Doubleday, 1985), vol. 2, 532–564.

B.C.E.: the Wisdom of Solomon. Although attributed to that notable Solomon (who lived in the tenth century B.C.E.), the book is written in quite sophisticated Greek and uses the technical terminology of Hellenistic philosophy and science. Its literary style is that of the diatribe, in which the author publicly debates issues, raising questions and offering solutions. The virtues that wisdom instills are those of Stoic philosophy: temperance, prudence, justice, and fortitude. As in Ben Sira, the history of Israel is retold, but here it is recounted not so much as a celebration of the past, but as a kind of parable or metaphor of the journey of the soul that leads one to knowledge of God and His purpose.

Similarly, Philo of Alexandria, a Jewish scholar and leading figure in the large Jewish community in Alexandria in the first half of the first century C.E., retold the stories of the Jewish patriarchs and interpreted the details of the Law of Moses in allegorical fashion, as models of the journey of the soul from ignorance to revealed truth concerning God and His purpose for His people. Philo saw Hellenistic philosophy as a resource for the fresh appropriation of the Jewish biblical tradition. In the Old Testament, God instructed Moses (Exod. 25:40) to build a portable sanctuary and its associated equipment, where God was to dwell in the midst of Israel, and to do the job "according to the pattern which was shown [to Moses] on the mountain [of Sinai]." Philo interpreted this reference to the "pattern" as a statement of the Platonic notion that in the heavens there were perfect patterns or ideal models of which all earthly phenomena were imperfect, temporal copies. In this way, he perceived a complete compatibility between biblical teachings and Platonic idealistic philosophy.

Collaboration with the Roman Authorities

Jewish priestly families cooperated with Rome through the structures of local government in order to retain control of the operation of the temple and to maintain a role in guiding Jewish public life. Priests and other Jewish aristocrats participated in the local councils that Rome authorized throughout its subject territories. In Jerusalem, they met regularly in what was called (there as elsewhere in the Roman world) a *synedrion* to discharge their responsibilities of guiding the lives of their people, settling disputes, and upholding the norms of Jewish society, while leaving to the Roman administrators fiscal and political issues. The public symbol of Jewish identity for this leadership group, as well as for large numbers of Jews of the period, was the temple. Jewishness was affirmed and reinforced by required participation in the temple's rituals and celebrations. Because the temple was believed to be the place where God dwelt among His people, carrying out the proper approach to Israel's God was a guarantee of maintaining that special relationship.

Jewish Identity through Voluntary Groups

Since the days of the Maccabees, many Jews had become disillusioned by the priesthood and by the national leaders, both those who operated before the Romans took over and those who collaborated with the Roman authorities. Jews who perceived that their religious and social leaders' collaboration with Rome was compromising the distinctiveness of Israel's relationship with God became persuaded that they must maintain their personal purity in spite of the social and cultural pressures to conform to Hellenistic and Roman patterns of life.

Some withdrew into small private groups, in which they studied the scriptures and refused to adopt the manner of life that their rulers sought to force on them, thereby enabling them to remain true to their convictions. They were persuaded that God had revealed to them that in the near future He would act decisively in human affairs, crushing the pagan powers and those who collaborated with them and then vindicating and establishing in positions of power the small remnant who had remained faithful to the Jewish traditions. Scholars have given the designation *apocalyptic* to this view of God and His people, and to the revelatory style of literature through which these insights are conveyed to the community that shares such convictions. Derived from the Greek word for "revelation," the term refers both to this revelatory type of writing and also to the message that God is said to have conveyed to His chosen few about the nearness of His action in the world to defeat His enemies and to vindicate the remnant of His people who have remained faithful to His purpose. This is the point of view expressed in the Book of Daniel, in which the obedient community sees itself as the "saints of the Most High" through whom God will establish His rule on the earth (Dan. 7:11–18) and destroy the evil political powers, which are depicted as horrendous beasts. To the small community that had endured the threats and schemes of the pagan rulers and remained faithful to God's will, He has given insight concerning the victory He is soon to achieve, as well as assurance of the vindication of its faithful members, who now see themselves as the true people of God.

One apocalyptic group that arose in the later second century B.C.E. and of which only a few details were known through ancient historians, came into the clearer light of contemporary historical knowledge some forty years ago when portions of its library and the basic structure of its community center were discovered on a bluff overlooking the northwestern end of the Dead Sea in an area known to the local Arabs as Qumran. The Dead Sea Scrolls, as they have come to be known, included copies of various books of the Jewish Bible and detailed commentaries on the biblical prophets, as well as rule books for the members of the community that had its center there and writings that predicted how God would defeat their enemies. The promised process of divine triumph would result in the defeat of the Romans and their collaborators and would drive out the official priests and leaders of Judaism, whom this community regarded as hopelessly corrupt and misguided. God would enable the community of the faithful to rebuild the temple and would establish them in Jerusalem as the true and pure people of God.

Jewish Identity through Nationalistic Revolt

Another alternative for dealing with the political and cultural domination of Palestine and its Jewish inhabitants was to follow the example of the Maccabees and take up arms against the Romans. In the 60s of the first century C.E., and again in 132, there were surges of Jewish nationalism that aimed to establish once again a politically autonomous Jewish state. Unfortunately for these nationalists, the attainment of their objectives was severely hampered, not only by the superior military might and skills of the Roman forces, but also by the fact that among the Jews themselves there were various factions competing for control of the uprising. As a result, the Roman military reaction to the revolts destroyed the Jews' attempts to gain political freedom. We shall consider some of the details of these revolutionary efforts when we examine the Gospels in light of their historical backgrounds, but it is sufficient here to note that the option of political independence was not taken up until decades after the death of Jesus. Although Jesus was accused of nationalistic aims and was executed for aspiring to be "king of the Jews" (Mk 15:26), there is no evidence from the early Christian writings or from the Jewish sources that such a revolutionary effort was launched by Jews until the late 60s of the common era, a generation after Jesus' execution by the Romans.

The Pharisaic Answer to the Jewish Identity Question

The one strategy for gaining and maintaining Jewish covenantal identity that survived the failures of the others and flourished after the destruction of Jerusalem and its temple was that of the Pharisees. In the first century B.C.E., as disillusionment with the Maccabean rulers set in, a group calling themselves the Pure Ones (*perushim*), or Pharisees,[2] initially hoped to transform the ruling dynasty and the priesthood into more worthy lines of succession. After the Roman takeover, however, they turned their energies to developing a way in which they could celebrate their identity as God's people that would not make them dependent on the priestly and aristocratic collaborators with Rome, that would not require them to withdraw physically from their homes and towns (as the Dead Sea community did), and that would not be viewed as a challenge to Roman political control of the land and people. They and their offspring must know and identify personally with the biblical traditions, and the relevance of this heritage to their lives would be clear and compelling. The question was, How could these aims be achieved effectively without rousing the suspicions of the Romans that subversive or nationalistic schemes were being perpetrated?

The Pharisaic movement that developed was based on voluntary and informal gatherings in homes. There, the law could be studied and God could be honored wholly apart from the religious officials, who were widely regarded as corrupt and as collaborators with the Romans. The Pharisees interpreted the laws in such a way as to transfer to the members of their groups the purity regulations and requirements that the scripture imposed on the priests. Although initially the leaders did not have anything like our modern distinction between laity and clergy, by the later first century those promoting this movement assumed the title of *rabbi* and took on authoritative roles. Earlier, there seems to have been a spontaneity in the informal worship and in the study of the scripture in these gatherings in homes. Following the pattern developed somewhat earlier among Jews in Egypt and the Greek cities, the Pharisees called their meetings simply "gatherings," which in Greek is *synagoge*. If a home was not available or adequate for the purpose, a meeting place was chosen in a public hall or other area where assembly was feasible. In some parts of the Roman empire, such a location for the gathering of these Jewish communities was called a *proseuche*, or "place of prayer." Inscriptions from the cities of Greece and Asia Minor and literature from this period (such as that of Philo of Alexandria[3] and of the Jewish historian

---

[2] For an insightful study of the Pharisees, see Anthony J. Saldarini, *Pharisees, Scribes and Sadducees: a Sociological Approach* (Wilmington, DE: Michael Glazier, 1988).

[3] Philo's many writings are available in ten volumes, in which appear the Greek text and English translations, edited by F. H. Colson (Loeb Classical Library; Cambridge, MA: Harvard University Press, 1939–1941). Two supplemental volumes were edited by Ralph Marcus and published in the same series in 1953. The titles of Philo's treatises include On the Cherubim; The Worse Attacks the Better; The Unchangeableness of God; Noah's Work as Planter; On Flight and Finding; On Dreams; The Migration of Abraham; and Questions on Genesis and Exodus. A complete English translation of Philo's works by C. D. Yonge has been published in an updated version, *The Works of Philo* (Peabody, MA: Hendrickson, 1993).

Josephus)[4] designate them in this way. In addition to whatever prayer, worship, and instruction went on in these meetings, the high point of what occurred there was a shared meal in which the common identity of the group was celebrated.

By the time the Gospels and Acts were being written, toward the end of the first century C.E., certain formal patterns and practices had come to be associated with the synagogues. Yet the simple, informal origins of the movement have become apparent in those Palestinian cities where synagogues of the third and later centuries C.E. have been excavated. Beneath these later structures, with their evidence of set patterns for seating and designated space for worship and instruction, are private houses that show evidence of having been only slowly adapted to serve as increasingly public meeting places. The changes in architectural style from informal to formal correspond to the institutional development of the synagogue and the rabbinic roles.[5]

In ways that follow closely the pattern of change in religious movements traced by Max Weber[6]—from spontaneous origins under self-authorized lay people to carefully delineated structures of leadership and fixed patterns of instruction and worship—Judaism began to undergo a major transformation toward the end of the first century C.E. Schools came to be developed in connection with the synagogues. Instead of the earlier impulsive and unstructured exposition of the scriptures carried on in someone's living room, the methods of interpretation came to be specified and eventually written down. As the form of the meeting developed, the interpreter was provided with a dramatic symbol in the form of the Seat of Moses, from which the person designated to expound the text offered his sermon or instruction.

The results of these developments are to be seen most readily in the weighty literature produced through the synagogue movement in the period from the second to the sixth centuries.[7] Included in these ancient documents are records of debates between representatives of various points of view among the rabbis. The title *rabbi* came to be assigned to these leaders who devoted the major portion of their time and energy to interpreting the literature and institutional developments. The initial collection of these scriptural interpretations was called the *Mishnah*. It was supplemented by collections of discussions of legal questions, one assembled in Babylon and the other in Palestine, which are known, respectively, as the Babylonian and Palestinian Talmuds and which are arranged topically, dealing primarily with issues of purity. Together, the *Mishnah* and the two Talmuds provide the guidelines for the gaining and maintaining of purity for those who see themselves as

[4] Josephus's works (also published in the Loeb Classical Library) include two volumes on *The Jewish Wars* and seven on *Jewish Antiquities*. An edition of *The Jewish Wars* by G. Cornfeld contains maps, illustrations, and extensive notes (Grand Rapids, MI: Zondervan, 1982).

[5] For an examination of newer evidence and issues of interpretation, together with a newer bibliography, see my article, "Defining the First-Century CE Synagogue: Problems and Progress," *New Testament Studies* 41 (1995), 481–500.

[6] A translation of Max Weber's basic work is *The Methodology of the Social Sciences* [tr. E. R. Shils and H. A. Finch] (New York: Free Press of Glencoe, 1949). Excerpts from Weber's writings are available in English in *From Max Weber* [tr. and ed. H. H. Gerth and C. W. Mills] (Cambridge and New York: Cambridge University Press, 1977).

[7] The evolution of the rabbinic movement and its literature has been traced in the scores of volumes by Jacob Neusner, of which the following are relevant for the origins of Christianity: *The Rabbinic Traditions about the Pharisees before 70* (Leiden, The Netherlands: Brill, 1971), 3 volumes; and *Judaisms and their Messiahs at the Turn of the Christian Era*, ed. J. Neusner, W. S. Green, and E. S. Frerichs (Cambridge: Cambridge University Press, 1987). An introduction to the significant nonbiblical Jewish literature of the period is offered by George W. Nickelsburg, in *Jewish Literature between the Bible and the Mishnah* (Philadelphia: Fortress Press, 1981).

God's people. Supplementing these analyses of the law were the Targums, collections of paraphrases in Aramaic (a Semitic language found in the later biblical texts) of the Jewish scriptures, which were nearly all in Hebrew. These paraphrases, as well as the interpretive books of the law, were in wide use among Jews throughout the Middle East in the ancient world. They became the basic interpretive supplement to the Jewish Bible and have continued to fulfill this function down to the present, providing the strategy by which biblical tradition is appropriated and its relevance for the Jewish community understood.

The events of Jewish history, perceived as the acts of God on behalf of his people, came to be celebrated in a series of feasts, through which the present members of the community shared in the common heritage and gained a sense of continuity with their ancestors. The Passover meal, for example, recalled God's act of deliverance of Israel from slavery in Egypt and looked forward to the future fulfillment of God's purpose for the nation.[8] In a similar way, the sacred meal described in the supplement to the Scroll of the Rule found in the Dead Sea caves not only was an experience of present unity among this group that regarded itself as the true and pure people of God; it also was a corporate expression of the conviction that God would act through His chosen agents (the priestly and the kingly messiahs) to fulfill the destiny of the covenant community. Both in these ceremonial meals and in the increasingly structured system of instruction of the youth, effective means were adopted to ensure the transmission of the tradition of those who would take the place of the present generation. The forms of meeting, worship, and study had profound influence on the early Christian movement.

These developments within what was becoming rabbinic Judaism had their roots in earlier Jewish experience, both in Palestine and in lands such as Babylonia (Psalm 137), where Jews had been dispersed. They began to take more specific shape, however, in the second half of the first century C.E. With the fall of the temple in 70 C.E., the Roman authorities, who dreaded the collapse of one of their subject peoples as well as the emergence of another nationalist movement, seem to have encouraged the Pharisees to take a leading role in the reconstitution of their people. With the disappearance of the temple, there had to be a new focus of identity for Jews, and Pharisaism apparently provided the solution through the development of centers for group study and worship.

It is impossible to determine how systematic the development of rules, patterns, and guidelines was, although later Jewish tradition reports that there was an extended planning council which convened in the later first century C.E. at Yavneh (Jamnia), near modern Tel Aviv. All that one can be certain of is the result: the emergence in the second to sixth centuries C.E. of the basic conceptual and organizational patterns and structures that were to make possible Jewish reappropriation of the biblical tradition in a way that would ensure continuity for Jewish identity. The climax of Roman resistance to the nationalists had come with Titus's destruction of the temple in 70 C.E. The second attempt by the Jews at establishing a politically independent state, in 132–135, was better organized than the effort in 66–70, but the empire was then far more securely unified under Hadrian than it had been under Titus. The revolt was crushed, and for some time, Jerusalem was off limits for Jews. On the site of the temple, a shrine to Zeus was erected, and the city was given a Roman

---

[8] The biblical passages describing the origins of the Passover and the rules for observing this celebration include Exodus 12–13, Numbers 9:1–14, and Joshua 5:10–12. Later references appear in 2 Kings 23:22 and 2 Chron 35:18.

name, Aelia Capitolina. In spite of this second total defeat of the nationalists, the continuity of Jewish identity and commitment was effectively carried out through the emergent rabbinic pattern of interpretation and practice of the tradition.

The Context of the Christian Alternative for Covenantal Identity

In the first century C.E., before the disastrous failure of the two Jewish attempts at achieving political independence, the issues that had come to a focus during the period of Hellenistic and early Roman domination of Palestine remained unresolved, and multiple solutions were being offered. We have noted that the two major questions among those in the Jewish tradition were, Who is the one through whom God is at work on behalf of His people? and What does God require of those who are members of the people with whom He has made His covenant?

Answering the second of these questions was complicated in this period because of the considerable number of Gentiles who were attracted to Judaism and who wanted, in some way and to some degree, to identify with it. They were drawn by its strictly monotheistic base and by its rejection of any physical representation of the gods in the form of idols or statues. They also admired its strict ethical stance, including the moral demands—especially those which the Pharisaic movement placed on its adherents. In the midst of social and cultural conflicts that pervaded the ethnically and economically complex Roman empire, those who had been uprooted from their ancestral environment or who felt adrift in the alien empire were attracted to the informal Jewish gatherings, where there was the possibility of gaining and reinforcing group identity. Here was a nonpolitical group movement tolerated by the Romans. Was it possible for Gentiles to become part of such a group?

As a matter of fact, there were two ways by which Gentiles could become affiliated with the Jewish covenant community: by simply joining with those who shared in the worship of Israel's God and by becoming proselytes, which involved a process through which male Gentiles were circumcised, baptized, and received as members of the community. It is difficult to know by what stages these procedures for including Gentiles were developed, but inscriptions from the eastern Mediterranean show that there was a significant segment of non-Jews who wanted to participate to some degree in the life of these Jewish groups and, therefore, in God's people. Inevitably, the issue arose as to how completely these converts to Judaism—or Gentiles on the fringe of Judaism—were to be obliged to obey the Law as the Pharisees interpreted it. This is precisely the issue on which Jesus challenged his Jewish contemporaries: In what sense did he appear as the agent of God to prepare for the renewal of the covenant? Who were the candidates for sharing in his reappraisal of the covenant tradition? If outsiders were to become part of the community, to what extent was it obligatory for them to obey the Law of Moses? What attitude should be taken toward the Roman state? Was it to be accepted and its demands fulfilled, or was it to be overthrown? And if it was to be overthrown, by what agency? These questions, which we have seen to be at the heart of the identity crisis of ancient Israel, were the ones addressed by Jesus and the early Christians as they sought to define his role and the grounds he offered for participation in God's new people.

Chapter 2

Jesus of Nazareth and the Radical Alternative for Redefining the Covenant

Who Jesus was and what he said and did are described in a variety of ancient documents from Christian and non-Christian sources. About many details there is a regrettable lack of information and even some conflicting evidence. Yet the basic picture is clear, and there emerges a coherent outline of Jesus as an independent critic who claimed to be the agent of God, but who challenged the values, the leadership, and the institutions of his Jewish contemporaries. Through the early Christian writers who preserved and edited the Jesus traditions, it is also possible to discern how his followers and their successors, down to the present day, shaped those traditions about him in ways that were appropriate to their own changing interests and needs.

By tracing this process of modification of the material about Jesus, it is possible to achieve two useful historical goals concerning him: to see how certain features of the Jesus tradition are confirmed and illuminated by sources from outside the New Testament, and to see the development of the Jesus tradition within the New Testament period. By these methods, one can discern how the movement that began with Jesus took the forms and adopted the tactics that shifted the action from the cities and villages of Palestine to the centers of Greco-Roman culture in the wider Mediterranean regions and, eventually, throughout the world, both culturally and geographically.

The Chief Sources for Knowledge about Jesus

Christianity was to have a powerful and enduring impact on the Roman Empire, most decisively and dramatically in the fourth-century conversion of the emperor Constantine, under whom Christianity became the official religion of the empire. But evidence about the origins of the movement in the writings of historians of the first and second centuries is scarce, largely because the impact of Jesus and his followers was initially so limited in scope that the historians might have regarded it as beneath their concern. There are some references to Christianity in ancient secular historical documents, however, and they do offer sufficient detail to shed light on the more direct evidence that we have from the Christian and Jewish sources. Let us begin with the latter.

Jewish Sources

(1) Josephus

The fullest report we have concerning Jesus from outside the Christian sources comes from Josephus, a Jewish writer who shifted his role from leader of the Jewish nationalists in the revolt of 66–70 C.E. to subsequent collaborator with the Romans. His dual purpose in reporting the history of the Jews for Roman readers was to propagandize on behalf of his coreligionists. Much of Josephus' material was drawn from ancient sources that otherwise would have been lost to us, so that in spite of his apologetic aims, and because of his extensive cribbing from other historians, his work is invaluable as a historical resource.

In his *Antiquities of the Jews*, Josephus wrote (in Greek) as follows:

> About this time [during the term of office of Pontius Pilate, Roman governor of Judea, 26–36 C.E.], there lived Jesus, a wise man, if indeed one ought to call him a man. For he was one who wrought surprising feats and was a teacher of such people as accept the truth gladly. He won over many of the Jews and many of the Greeks. He was the Messiah. When Pilate, upon hearing him accused by men of the highest standing among us, condemned him to be crucified, those who had in the first place come to love him did not give up their affection for him. On the third day he appeared to them, restored to life, for the prophets of God had prophesied these and countless other marvelous things about him. And this tribe of Christians, so called after him, has still to this day not disappeared.[1]

As the passage stands, it sounds as though Josephus were a Christian. Indeed, some scholars have insisted that the paragraph is an interpolation by some early Christian writer into the original text of *Antiquities* (18.63–64). L. H. Feldman, the eminent Jewish scholar who translated and edited this document, thinks, however, that the only words added by Christians are "He was the Messiah." The rest of the statement is merely a report of what the early Christians *claimed* about Jesus. But, as such, it is extremely important. It highlights the unusual capacities that Jesus had, which are reported in the Gospel accounts of his healings and exorcisms. The passage conveys the sense of the power of his teaching and the loyalty he evoked from his followers. And it is specific about the circumstances of his death—

---

[1]The writings of Josephus have been published in Greek, with English translation, by L.H. Feldman, *Antiquities of the Jews* and *The Jewish War*, in the Loeb Classical Library (Cambridge, MA: Harvard University Press, 1927; reprinted 1965–67), 18.63–64.

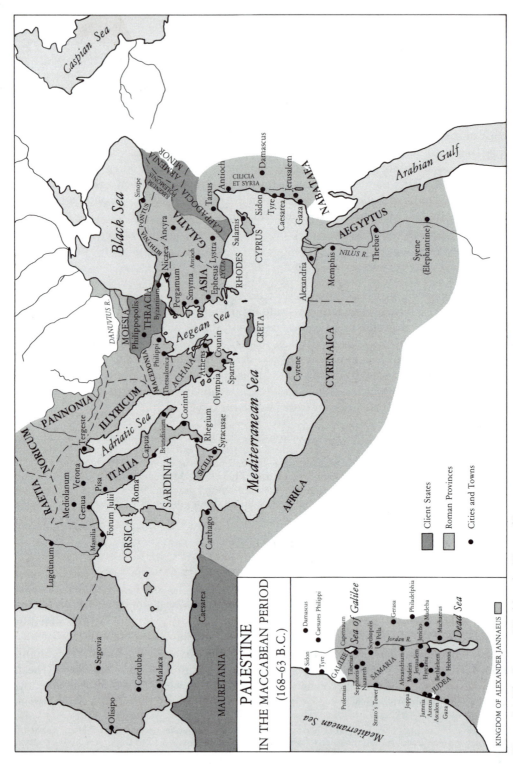

Figure 2.1 The Roman World at the Time of Jesus

both the method (crucifixion) and the identity of the one who condemned him (Pilate). Also reflected are the claims of Jesus' adherents that what he did was in fulfillment of the Jewish scriptures and that God had vindicated him by raising him from the dead. The phrase, "if one ought to call him a man," sounds as though Josephus is implying Jesus' divinity. According to the Gospels, however, Jesus' opponents insisted that he had these extraordinary powers because he was in league with Satan (Mark 3:22; Matt. 9:34). Perhaps it is this accusation that lies behind Josephus' remark. In any case, there is a series of useful parallels between what this Jewish historian reports and evidence from the Gospels.

(2) The Dead Sea Scrolls

When the Dead Sea Scrolls were discovered in the late 1940s, there was speculation and even hope that in some way these documents from the first century B.C.E. and first century C.E. would shed some light on Jesus and the origins of Christianity. The fact that John the Baptist and his followers, like this group, practiced ceremonial washings in the lower Jordan Valley and claimed to be preparing the faithful for a renewed covenantal relationship with the God of Israel suggested that there might be a direct link between the two movements and, therefore, with Jesus. The literary findings and the archaeological evidence point to the following parallels between the groups:

- The followers of Jesus and the members of the Dead Sea sect participated in a community meal of bread and wine, eaten in expectation of the coming of God's agent (or agents) in final triumph.
- Both groups were persuaded that their respective founders had given them the key to interpreting the scriptures.
- Each group had its own collections of writings that provided the insights for understanding God's purpose for and through the new community.
- Both groups were critical of the official religious leadership and expected God to replace the then-existing temple.
- Both groups believed that God would soon intervene in their behalf, defeat their enemies, and establish His rule in the world.

Apart from these general principles, however, the basis for participation in God's people for the Dead Sea community was utterly different from that of the Jesus movement. The former group was severely critical of the religious leaders because they were not sufficiently strict in holding their people to obeying the ritual and purity requirements of the Law of Moses. Jesus, however, was accused of permitting or even performing actions *violating* the Sabbath and purity laws, and of welcoming into the fellowship of his people those who, by birth or manner of life, would be excluded by Jewish legal norms. The Dead Sea community denied access to those who violated its stringent regulations. If Jesus ever had associated with that community, his break with them on requirements for admission and maintenance of status in the group would have been radical.

(3) Rabbinic Sources

Written in the second to the sixth centuries C.E., the rabbinic sources refer on occasion to Jesus, although usually without direct mention of his name. His followers are alluded to as *Minim*, which means "deviants" or "heretics." He is at times identified as "the son of Ben Stada," or "of Ben Pantheros." His mother is depicted as a disreputable person, and his father is said to be a Roman soldier. There is apparently a kind of pun here: Pantheros is close to *parthenos,* the Greek word for virgin. Instead of having been born to a virgin who did not have intercourse with a human father, as the Christians claimed, these sources held that Jesus was the illegitimate son of a Roman soldier named Pantheros. In one of the rabbinic sources, the so-called Eighteen Benedictions, which may go back to the late first century C.E., there is a curse invoked on the *Minim,* those who consider Jesus to have been the Messiah of God.[2] All that this rabbinic material tells us, therefore, is that the Christian movement was regarded as a perversion of the concurrently developing Jewish principles of the covenant people. As we examine the Gospels, we shall see what specific form these competitive claims assumed.

Roman Sources

Three Roman writers of the early second century refer in passing to the Christian movement and its origins. Tacitus (53–120 C.E.) mentions in his Roman history, *The Annals* (15.24), that the fire which destroyed a large segment of Rome during the reign of the emperor Nero (54–68 C.E.) was thought by many in the city to have been set by Nero's order. To shift the blame from himself, Nero decided to hold the Christians of the city responsible. Tacitus writes as follows:

> Neither human help, nor imperial munificence, nor all the mode of placating heaven could stifle the scandal or dispel the belief that the fire had taken place by order [of Nero]. Therefore to scotch the rumor, Nero substituted as culprits and punished with the utmost refinements of cruelty a class of men, loathed for their vices, whom the crowd styled as Christians. Christus, the founder of the name, had undergone the death penalty in the reign of Tiberius [14–37 C.E.], by sentence of the procurator, Pontius Pilate, and the pernicious superstition was checked for a moment, only to break out once more, not merely in Judea, the home of the disease, but in the capital itself, where all things horrible or shameful in the world collect and find a vogue. First, then, the confessed members of the sect were arrested; next, on their disclosures, vast numbers were convicted, not so much on account of arson as for hatred of the human race. And derision accompanied their end: they were covered with wild beasts' skins and torn to death by dogs; or they were fastened on crosses, and when light failed were burned as lamps by night. Nero offered his gardens for the spectacle, and gave an exhibition in his circus, mixing with the crowd in the garb of a charioteer, or mounted on his chariot.[3]

Apart from the gruesome fascination of the story itself, there are a number of important historical implications in the brief account. The death of Jesus was not an isolated incident in the life of a single individual, but was a climactic moment in a movement that began with his public activity and continued far and wide beyond his death. So serious were its social and political dimensions, that the Roman authorities sought to stamp it out, first in Jerusalem and later in Rome. On the basis of information elsewhere about Pontius Pilate, it is possible to fix the probable date of Jesus' death to the year C.E. 29. A little more than thirty years later, the movement had spread to the capital of the Gentile world, where

---

[2] Although the date of this material from the rabbinic sources is impossible to determine with certainty, it is likely from the time after the fall of Jerusalem to the Romans in 70 C.E. and the consequent complete break between Christians and Jews.

[3] From Tacitus, *Annals* (15:44), vol. 4, tr. J. Jackson, in Loeb Classical Library (Cambridge, MA: Harvard University Press, 1931).

there were "vast numbers" identified with it. The charges against them are not specified, except "hatred of the human race" and that they were "loathed for their vices." The first accusation probably was the result of two factors: their refusal to participate in honors to the Roman gods and the deified emperors, which would have been understood by the Romans as adding to the risk of national calamities sent by the gods; and the conviction of the members that they were the people of God, distinct from the rest of the human race. Even the principle of inclusive membership, which was characteristic of both Jesus and his followers, would not offset this sense of a favored, elect community. Their claim that they alone would survive the divine judgment that was to bring to an end the present age of the world would confirm this impression of them as hostile to the rest of humanity. The depiction of the movement as a "pernicious superstition" may reflect the claim of the Christians that, through Jesus, there was among them the power to heal, to expel demons, and to raise the dead by what they called the Spirit of God. There is no hint that their membership was limited to Jews or was primarily Jewish: They are set aside by the historian as a sect, a class, "whom the crowd styled as Christians."

The designation of the group as Christians is echoed by one other Roman historian, Pliny, and possibly by a third, Suetonius. About the year 110 C.E., Pliny was serving as governor of Bithynia, a Roman province on the south shore of the Black Sea. It was a sensitive post, since over the centuries the Romans felt threatened by the Parthians, the people to the east of this district who had periodically invaded Bithynia. In one of Pliny's letters to the emperor Trajan, he reports that the Christians, who earlier had had groups in the cities, had now become numerous even in the rural districts. As a result, there had been an alarming drop in participation in the worship of the traditional deities in the official temples. And furthermore, even under threat of execution, the Christians were refusing to offer the appropriate sacrifices to the image of the emperor, thus adding to the threat of waning popular support and hence of a decrease in divine benefactions to the Roman state. There is a deep ambivalence in Pliny's assessment of the movement. Although he denounces it as a "depraved and excessive superstition," his investigation of the practices of its members showed that they were harmless. Their custom was to gather early in the morning to sing a hymn to Christ as a god. Their sacred meal involved only ordinary food. Their common oath required them to avoid adultery, fraud, deceit, and theft. Their leaders included women known as deaconesses. They were guilty of no crime against the state, except their refusal to honor the traditional gods and the deified emperor. This, however, was sufficiently serious to lead to the execution of those members who refused to renounce their allegiance to Jesus, the Christ. The designation of the group as Christians shows that central to their existence and identity was this affirmation, and in making it, as well as in sharing the common meal, they took a firm stand as to their identity as God's people. In Chapter 5, we consider more fully the social and political import of the movement as the Romans perceived it.

The evidence from Suetonius (69–140 C.E.) is ambiguous. His *Lives of the Twelve Caesars* records an incident that occurred during the reign of Claudius (41–54 C.E.). Suetonius describes a serious conflict that developed within the Jewish community in Rome "at the instigation of one Chrestos." The response of Claudius was to drive all the Jews out of Rome. In Acts 18:1–4, there is an account of Paul's having met in Corinth a Jewish couple who had been driven out of Rome by Claudius. Originally from Pontus (like Bithynia, on the southern shore of the Black Sea), these two worked at the same craft as Paul: tentmaking. The fact that they were already Christians when Paul met them, even though they had been expelled from Rome as Jews, suggests that the source of trouble in Rome was not an otherwise unknown person named Chrestos (a common name of that day, meaning "worthy" or "respectable"), but the arrival there of the message about *Christos.* The result of the proclamation of Jesus as messiah (for which the Greek equivalent is "Christos") among the Jews in Rome had been violently divisive, so that the repercussions were known to the wider public. Claudius had reacted in a firm way by expelling the whole lot of them, both those who affirmed Jesus as Christos—which seems to have been confused with Chrestos— and those who did not. This is a significant piece of evidence, because if the reconstruction is correct, it means that the message about Jesus was being proclaimed in Rome within twenty years after the death of Jesus and perhaps two decades before Paul reached there (about 60 C.E.).

The Earliest Christian Sources

(1) Paul as a Source for Knowledge about Jesus

In the letters of Paul, there is a heavy emphasis on the importance of the death of Jesus. For example:

> God put forth [Jesus] as an expiation by his blood, to be received by faith. (Rom. 3:25)

> While we were still weak, at the right time Christ died for the ungodly. (Rom. 5:6)

> Have this mind among yourselves which is yours in Christ Jesus, who, though he was in the form of God, did not count equality with God a thing to be grasped, but emptied himself, taking the form of a servant, being born in the likeness of human beings. And being found in human form he humbled himself and became obedient unto death, even death on a cross. (Phil. 2:5–8)[4]

But Paul also makes the point that God sent Jesus into the world in human form to accomplish the salvation of his people (Gal. 4:4; Phil. 2:8). Although he does not attribute the insight to Jesus, Paul perceives the centrality of the Mosaic Laws to lie in the command to love one's neighbor, just as Jesus did (cf. Rom. 13:8–10; Mark 12:31). Similarly, although Paul describes none of Jesus' miracles, he repeatedly refers to these acts as signs that confirm the message about Jesus that he preaches (I Cor. 12:9–10; II Cor. 12:12). Indeed, Paul reminds his readers that through him and his associates, events similar to Jesus' miracles frequently took place wherever they traveled to proclaim the Gospel (Gal. 3:5; Rom. 15:18–19). The evidence about Jesus is concrete in that Paul takes for granted the life, miracles, and death of Jesus. But it is also indirect in that he assumes that his readers will see a continuity between the miracles that God did through Jesus and those that are happening through himself and his coworkers.

Another important link between Paul and the Gospel traditions about Jesus is the common conviction that God raised Jesus from the dead. Paul is persuaded that if this had

---

[4]Translation by H. C. Kee.

not taken place, then the faith of his readers would be futile, and he and his associates "are of all men most to be pitied" (I Cor. 15:16–18). Thus, even though Paul's emphases are different from those of the writers of the Gospels, he shares with them three basic convictions: that Jesus lived a life in full obedience to God, that the authorities put him to death, and that God raised him from the dead.

(2) Our Oldest Gospel Source

A careful reading of the Gospel of Matthew and the Gospel of Luke shows that they used a common source. It consisted mostly of the sayings of Jesus, which each of these writers has incorporated into his own gospel with some modifications. Although no copy of this source (which scholars call *Q*, from the German word for source, *Quelle*) has survived, it can be reconstructed with a high degree of certainty,[5] especially through Luke's use of the source, from which the quotations in the following paragraphs are drawn.

As in the Gospel of Mark (our oldest account of the career of Jesus), in *Q* Jesus is associated with John the Baptist, who went out into the desert region adjacent to the Jordan River. There John called his fellow Jews to be baptized as a public expression of their concern to be identified with the pure and obedient people of God (Luke 3:3). In *Q* John denounces his contemporaries as the offspring of snakes in his warning to them of the divine judgment that is about to fall on the world. They are not to assume that their being descended from Abraham guarantees participation in God's people: God is able to create His community of the faithful from unlikely sources (Luke 3:7–9). Jesus, however, differentiates himself from John, who seems to have become disillusioned with him when Jesus began eating and spending time with people who, by Jewish regulations, could not share in the worship of God: the blind, the lame, the deaf, and lepers. This practice contrasted sharply with that of John, who was ascetic and strict. Jesus acknowledges that his opponents call him "a glutton and a drunkard, a friend of tax-collectors and sinners." Tax collectors in the various parts of the Roman empire were local individuals who would contract to help Rome collect taxes, including those on goods transported through the region, which made them extremely unpopular and caused them to be regarded as traitors to the integrity of the Jewish people.

In the gospel tradition, Jesus was also denounced as being in league with the devil ("Beelzebub, prince of demons") when he performed exorcisms. In the *Q* source, Jesus responds by claiming that the source of his power to cast out demons is God himself (Luke 11:19–20), so that through these actions of his, God's rule over the creation is becoming a reality in their midst. Yet Jesus will not perform miracles on request as a means of proving that God is with him (Luke 11:29–32). The only "sign" that will be given is the call to his contemporaries to change their ways, just as Jonah of old had called the Gentile people of Nineveh to repent (Jonah 3:5). Jesus' wisdom will attract a favorable response from Gentiles as well as from Jewish hearers, just as Solomon's wisdom brought the non-Jewish Queen of Sheba "from the ends of the earth" to hear the truth from Solomon. Jesus claims to be a greater prophet than Jonah, and as a messenger of God's wisdom, he is greater than Solomon. He maintains that the religious leaders of his day are more concerned with rit-

---

[5]My reconstruction and analysis of *Q* are offered in *Jesus in History: An Approach to the Study of the Gospels* (Fort Worth, TX: Harcourt Brace, 1996), pp. 74–115.

ual purity than with inward moral purity, and as a result, they will reject him and his message, just as their ancestors rejected the prophets of old (Luke 11:37–53). Those who acknowledge Jesus as God's agent, on the other hand, will be acknowledged by God, and those who reject him will be judged in the presence of God (Luke 12:8).

Through Jesus, who is depicted in a unique relationship to God as "son," God's purpose and truth have been disclosed to those regarded by the religious leaders as immature and ignorant—as "babies." And these insights have been hidden from those who think themselves to be wise (Luke 10:21–22). Already, a new era has come in the history of God's people. The epoch of the Law and the prophets ended with John the Baptist. Since then (that is, in the words and works of Jesus), the good news of God's rule is being preached, although those ready to enter the kingdom must be prepared to experience violence and conflict (Luke 16:16). This new age is not something to be awaited in the future, but is already a reality in the midst of God's people (Luke 17:20–21). The rest of the human race, however, continues to live life as usual and will do so until the divine judgment falls on the world (Luke 17:22–37).

The new people of God are called to a new mode of life in which the traditional human and religious values are overturned. Instead of retaliation in kind to those who mistreat them, they are to love their enemies, to give generously to those who beg or even try to steal from them, acting in love toward all other humans as they would themselves like to be treated. In this way they will show graphically that they are indeed the children of God (Luke 6:27–36). Their daily petition to God (what has come to be known as the Lord's Prayer) should honor the divine name and the authority it embodies and ask only (1) for the daily supply of basic needs, (2) for divine forgiveness, which is to overflow into forgiveness toward others, and (3) for deliverance from the time of testing that will befall the world at the end of the age (Luke 11:1–4).

For the disciples, there is to be no certainty of a dwelling place, no time to fulfill such basic obligations as burying one's parents, no place for reflecting on what one has done in the past (Luke 9:47–62). When they are proclaiming the good news of God's rule, they can expect to meet rejection, just as Jesus did (Luke 10:16). They are to fear not those who seek to kill them, but those who try to corrupt and disqualify them for the task in which they are engaged (Luke 12:4–5). They can expect to be brought to trial before religious and political leaders, just as Jesus was, but God will sustain them in their times of testing, just as he supported Jesus (Luke 12:11–12). They are to live their lives free of anxiety, in confidence that God will care for his own people as he cares for the creation (Luke 12:22–34).

Who is to share in the life of this new community that Jesus is calling into existence by his message and activity? Building on the familiar image of a banquet, Jesus compares the invitation to share in the kingdom of God with a host who sends advance notice of a great festivity he is planning. Those first invited are too busy with ordinary, respectable responsibilities (e.g., getting married, acquiring property) to accept the invitation. It is then extended to a most unlikely segment of humanity, "the poor, the maimed, the blind, the lame," and then to the homeless living outside the city in lanes and hedges. The ailing and the outsiders do accept and share in the banquet (Luke 14:15–24). The criterion for sharing in the life of God's new people, both now and in the age to come is to be in need and, through Jesus, to look to God to fill that need.

In the Parable of the Seeking Shepherd (Luke 15:4–7), the owner of the flock goes out to find and recover the lost sheep—a clear image of God, who, through Jesus, takes the initiative in uniting outsiders and the needy as members of His Covenant People. In what was likely the conclusion of the *Q* source (Luke 22:28–30), Jesus addresses his followers as "those who have stayed with me in my trials" and promises them a share in the kingdom of God.

(3) Our Oldest Gospel: Mark

The oldest surviving narrative account of the career of Jesus is an anonymous document known since the second century as the Gospel of Mark. Since Peter figures prominently in this gospel, and since someone named Mark is associated with Peter and the other apostles in the New Testament (Acts 12:12, 25), Mark's name came to be linked very early with this report of Jesus' words and acts. Mark's Gospel is not simply a biography; rather, it is what anthropologists call a "foundation document"—that is, an account of the life and activity of the founder of a religious movement that serves to give purpose, direction, and future orientation to the members. Specifically, it serves as a source for concrete examples of what Jesus said and did to prepare his people and to define their role in preparation for the coming of the kingdom of God.

In Mark, there are compact, vivid accounts of the healings and exorcisms Jesus performed. When Jesus expels an unclean spirit from a man in a synagogue, the demon is aware that Jesus is God's agent who has come to destroy him and the powers of evil (1:24). Jesus is able to heal the relatives of his disciples (1:29), as well as throngs that follow him, seeking health or freedom from demonic control (1:32–34). At times, he links his acts of healing with the granting of forgiveness, as in the healing of a paralytic who was lowered on a pallet through the dirt roof of Jesus' house in Capernaum on the shore of the Lake of Galilee (2:1–12). For this, Jesus' claim to having been authorized by God is challenged by the religious leaders who are observing him. Ironically, the demonic spirits he expels acknowledge him to be the "Son of God" (3:7–12). The question of the source of Jesus' extraordinary power to heal the sick and to control the demons is raised by the scribes, the authoritative interpreters of the Jewish tradition, who have come to Galilee from Jerusalem to observe him. It is their conviction that he has these powers because he is in league with Satan, the adversary of God (3:22–30). His own family thinks that he is crazy and tries to remove him from public view (3:19–21, 31–35). He repeats to them and to his followers that among the new people of God, the family is radically redefined.

After initially centering his activity in Jewish towns and synagogues (Mark 1:39), Jesus begins to attract crowds that include some people from Gentile territories (3:7–8), and to perform healings and exorcisms in the Hellenistic cities and in Syrian territory to the north of Galilee (5:1–20; 7:24–37). One of the most vivid of these stories (Mark 7:24–30) describes a persistent Gentile woman who had a daughter under the control of a demon. Even though Jesus was then trying to find some privacy after his extended public appearances, the woman came directly to him, urging him to help her child. Jesus' response is to put her off by drawing a sharp distinction between "children" (Jews) and "dogs" (Gentiles, who have been denied this relationship). Her reply is vivid and powerful: "Yes, sir, but even the dogs under the table eat what the children drop." He responds favorably to her challenge, and she returns home to find her daughter cured. The traditional distinctions about access to God by Jews and Gentiles are no longer valid.

In addition, Mark tells us that Jesus makes or allows physical contact with the dead, with a woman with a bloody flux, and with epileptics, lepers, and the blind—all of whom would render him impure by the Pharisaic standards of ritual cleanliness (5:21–43; 6:53–56; 7:24–37; 9:14–29; 10:46–52). Similarly, he welcomes among his inner circle of followers and pupils (the disciples) a tax collector named Levi (2:13–17).

The challenges and responsibilities Jesus places on the disciples are spelled out in detail in Mark: His followers are to serve as witnesses of what he does and, on this basis, to proclaim the message of God's rule on earth. In preparation for it, they are to expel demons (3:14–15), just as Jesus has done. Jesus sets them the example of placing human need above the venerable Jewish stricture to observe the Sabbath when he defends his disciples' having rubbed the husks from grain and eaten some of it as they passed through a field on the Sabbath day (Mark 2:23–27), as the Law of Moses permitted (Deut. 23:24–25). The later rabbis attest that this was considered work and was therefore unlawful on the holy day of rest. Mark reports Jesus as declaring that the Sabbath was made for human beings, not the reverse, and that he, as Son of Man, is "Lord of the Sabbath." Similarly, on the Sabbath Jesus heals a man with a withered hand, which serves as the occasion for his opponents to organize a coalition of the pious (the Pharisees) and the collaborators with Rome (the Herodians) to find a way to destroy him (Mark 3:1–6).

As in Jewish apocalyptic writings, there are both unhappy and happy prospects for Jesus' followers. They must expect to suffer, to encounter opposition from the ruling authorities, and to meet with mounting catastrophes. On the hopeful side are the special revelations of God's purpose to the community of the faithful—the reassurance that God will triumph over evil and that He has provided them with the agent through whom His purpose will come to fulfillment: Jesus.

Accordingly, Jesus warns his followers that their persistence in following him may lead to their death (Mark 8:34–37). Yet he assures them that he will return to vindicate them, supported by God and His angels and in the context of the fulfillment of their hopes of the coming kingdom of God (8:34–9:1). Mark reports that Jesus informed his disciples repeatedly of his own impending death, which is to take place on the initiative of the collaborationist religious leaders, but will be carried out by the Gentile rulers on the political charge that he claimed to be "king of the Jews" (8:31; 9:31; 10:33–34). An experience of the disciples in which Jesus' outward appearance is changed recalls what happened to the leaders of Israel who were granted visions of God (Moses, Elijah, Isaiah, Daniel) to give them assurance that the difficult road they had taken would end in divine vindication (9:2–8). Meanwhile, the disciples must be prepared for suffering, rejection, and martyrdom (8:34–35).

Jesus' bold action in riding an ass into Jerusalem and entering the temple courts is implicitly in fulfilment of the prophetic promise of the coming of Israel's king (Mark 11:1–10; cf. Zech. 9:9).[6] Accordingly, his followers link him with the renewal of the kingdom of David. His subsequent bold actions in Jerusalem include disrupting and denouncing the selling of sacrificial animals in the temple and the changing of money into appropriate coinage for temple offerings (Mark 11:15–19). His Parable of the Wicked Tenants (Mark 12:1–12) is an allegory of the infidelity of those in charge of God's people (depicted under

---

[6]This link is made explicit in Matthew's version of the story (Mt 21:5).

the familiar image of a vineyard; cf. Isa. 5) and a foreshadowing of his own impending death. The outcome will be the replacement of those in charge of the "vineyard" by others: the new community Jesus is calling together.

The coming judgment on those whom Jesus portrays as the disobedient people will be dramatically symbolized by the destruction of the temple (Mark 13:1–4), which will be preceded by its desecration (Mark 13:14). Apparently, the desecration will come through the Romans, as it had through Antiochus, the Hellenistic king in Maccabean times. Jesus' followers must expect persecution and betrayal by their own families (Mark 13:9–13), but if they remain faithful, God will soon vindicate them by sending his agent, the Son of Man, to defeat their enemies and gather them together (Mark 13:21–27). All this is announced as taking place within the lifetime of the present generation, even though the precise date is known only to God (Mark 13:30–32). The temple was destroyed in 70 C.E. without the other promised events of divine deliverance occurring. But the confidence that this vindication would come and that Jesus would return as the triumphant Son of Man continued.

At the same time, Mark reports that Jesus laid down some basic rules for the life of the community of his followers. Those who fail to remain faithful to him when they undergo persecution and suffering for his sake will be put to shame by him when he comes in judgment (Mark 8:34–38). His followers must be willing to accept subservient roles within the community (Mark 9:33–35), caring for others and strictly disciplining themselves (9:42–48). The community is to include children (9:36; 10:13–16), who are to serve as models of trust. The wealthy will find it difficult to meet the obligation of renouncing their riches (10:17–31), just as they must resist the temptation to strive for positions of power (10:35–45). There are to be no divorces and remarriages among the members (10:1–12). Far from seeking to subvert the empire, they are to pay their taxes to the Roman state (12:13–17). The overarching commandment is twofold: to love God and to love one's neighbor as oneself (12:28–34). God will reward their fidelity by giving them a share in the resurrection (12:18–27).

Meanwhile, the disciples must accept the fact that Jesus' impending death is part of the divine plan (Mark 8:31; 9:31; 10:33–34). His crucifixion will serve to liberate many from the powers of sin and evil that dominate their lives (10:45). That death is prepared for symbolically by the advance anointing of Jesus for burial (14:3–9) and, above all, by the meal in which the broken bread and poured wine represent his death on behalf of the disciples (14:22–25).

To a casual observer, this last meal of Jesus would have seemed routine. Some of the gospel evidence pictures it as a Passover meal (Mark 14:12), whereas John states that it was before the Passover celebration (John 13:1). In any case, there is mention of bread and wine, which would have been standard fare for a simple meal, rather than the specially prepared Passover lamb. The meal is pictured as taking place in a large upper room of a house in Bethany, a village just east of Jerusalem. Meals like these were celebrated by families and friends, but they also served as fellowship meals to unite members of groups that met for prayer and Bible study, as did the Pharisees. Reclining around a common bowl of food placed on the floor or a low table, the participants broke off pieces of pancake-shaped bread to dip into the common food. A common cup was passed among them to provide drink, but also to reinforce the sense of belonging. All these were standard features of group meals among Jews of the period. But Jesus is pictured as adding important significance to this meal by linking the symbolism of the shared bread and wine with his own impending death.

The continuing reenactment of that meal by Christians down through the years serves to remind them that their association with Jesus will be renewed and fulfilled in the New Age that is soon to dawn.[7] In the gospel tradition, another important image for this rite of renewal of the new community is that of Jesus feeding the hungry crowd in the desert, as through Moses, God fed Israel in the barren wastes of Sinai. Mark tells two similar stories (Mark 6:30–44; 8:1–10), one symbolizing the participation of Jews in the new people and the other that of gentiles. A significant detail in these accounts is the use of what was to become the technical language of the shared meal of the Christian communities, which down to the present day is known as the communion or the eucharist: "He took, he blessed, he broke, he gave." Thus, the ritual of the meal has three temporal dimensions: It looks back to the death of Jesus, it serves as an experience of fellowship and renewal in the present, and it anticipates the final achievement of God's purpose for His people in the future age.

The closing chapters of Mark (14:26–16:8) recount in vivid detail Jesus' arrest by the authorities, his hearings before the Jewish leaders, and his being sentenced to death by the Roman procurator Pontius Pilate. There is evidence in the narrative of Jesus' own inner struggle and of the inability of his disciples to understand what is happening and why Jesus yields to these earthly powers. His execution is by the civil authorities and is based on a political charge: his claim to kingship of the Jews (Mark 15:9, 18–20, 26, 32). Just before Jesus' death comes, Mark reports two symbolic incidents: the tearing of the curtain in the temple, which suggests that access to the presence of God is now open to all, and the acclaim of Jesus by a Roman military officer as "son of God" (15:38–39).

A pious member of the Jewish council receives permission to have the body of Jesus placed in his own rock-hewn tomb. Two women followers of Jesus see the place of burial, but because nightfall is about to usher in the Sabbath, they cannot then make the traditional preparation of the corpse (Mark 15:42–47). The first opportunity for them to return and carry out this process is at dawn on what is now called Sunday. To their astonishment, the large, round closing stone has been rolled away from the opening of the tomb, the body of Jesus is gone, and a young man instructs them that Jesus has been raised from the dead and will be reunited with his followers in Galilee (Mark 16:1–8). Although the oldest copies of Mark end at this point, some manuscripts go on (as the other gospels do) to describe Jesus' post-resurrection reunion with his disciples (Matt. 28:11–15; Luke 24:13–35; John 20–21).

* * * * * * *

From the *Q* source and from Mark, therefore, we have four major lines of tradition, as follows:

1. The basic portrayal of the career of Jesus and of his words and works, which announce and demonstrate the coming age in which God's rule will triumph and which report Jesus' radical redefinition of God's people as an inclusive community.
2. The formation of the nucleus of the new community commissioned by Jesus to spread his message and to do what was necessary to enlarge the size and scope of the new covenant people.

---

[7]This renewal is implicit in Jesus' statement to the disciples that he will not share such a meal with them again until the kingdom of God has come among them. Paul makes the promise explicit in his assertion, "As often as you eat this bread and drink the cup, you proclaim the Lord's death until he comes" (1 Cor 11:26).

3. The precedent for conflict between the preceding activity and the authority of the Roman state.
4. The radical approach taken by Jesus on the issues of purity that were taking shape within the Pharisaic Jewish community and that set the stage for conflict between the two emergent movements of rabbinic Judaism and Christianity, both of which claimed to have the true way of reappropriating the Jewish biblical tradition.

The basic pattern for the subsequent development of Christianity is discernible through these earlier forms of the gospel tradition about Jesus.

A major factor heightening the tension between Jews and Christians, and even among Christians, in the first century was the movement that began shortly after the death of Jesus to take the initiative in inviting gentiles, as well as nonobserving Jews, to share in the life of the new community. On the basis of his own testimony, preserved in his letters, the man who was transformed from a violent opponent of the inclusiveness of the Jesus movement to the primary instrument for opening up participation in it to gentiles in the major cities of the eastern Mediterranean was a Jew whose Semitic name was Saul, but who was more commonly known by his Greek name, Paul. He did not set the precedent for the inclusion of gentiles, but he became its most effective agent. It is to his letters preserved in the New Testament and the biographical information that they provide about his launching of Christianity into the wider Mediterranean world that we turn in the next chapter.

Chapter 3

Paul:
Christian Encounter with the Roman World

Half the books of the New Testament are attributed to Paul, and more than half of another distinctive New Testament writing—the Acts of the Apostles—is devoted to a description of his career in spreading the Christian message from Damascus to Rome. Paul clearly served as the model figure in the activity that made possible the transition of Christianity from its original context in Judaism to the wider Greco-Roman world. Some of the writings claimed to be by Paul come from the next generation of his followers. The letters attributed to Paul in the New Testament may be grouped as follows:

1. Those almost certainly by Paul: Romans, Galatians, I and II Corinthians, Philippians, I Thessalonians, and Philemon.
2. Those probably not by Paul, but close to his style and perspectives: Colossians and II Thessalonians.
3. Those almost certainly not by Paul: Ephesians, I and II Timothy, and Titus.

The Acts of the Apostles contains material that reflects the church's image of Paul in the late first century, but it also includes historical traditions about Paul. The importance of Paul in this crucial period of transition from Jewish to gentile constituency is underscored by these later representations that depict him as the effective agent of the new changes within Christianity. Also apparent in the later writings attributed to Paul is evidence for the gradual transformation of the church from a spontaneous movement to an institution with organizational forms and defined leadership roles.

Paul's Jewish Roots

Fortunately for modern historical interests, Paul includes in his letters some information about his own life and the background from which he came to Christian faith. His credentials are solidly Jewish. He declares that he is descended from the Israelite tribe of Benjamin and that his parents were obedient to Jewish law, in that he was circumcised on the eighth day after his birth (Phil 3:4–5). In Genesis 17:9–14, this ritual act performed on a male infant is set out as the basis for participation in the covenant of God with His people. Paul was reared according to the strict Jewish tradition.

Paul identifies his way of understanding Jewish law with that of the Pharisees (Phil. 3:5). This meant that a primary concern for him had been the observance of ritual purity by all members of the covenant community, not merely by the priests, and that he was determined to stamp out any movement that laid claim to the covenantal tradition while failing to observe the rituals. In Galatians 1:13–14, Paul notes that he exceeded the zeal of many of his contemporaries by his determination to destroy what he regarded as a wholly illegitimate group calling itself the *ekklesia* (the church, or "gathered community") and claiming to be the divinely redefined covenant people. Although Paul does not specify where this group was located, he mentions that following his conversion experience, he "returned to Damascus," which clearly implies that it was in that important Hellenistic city that there was a Christian group of sufficient size and vigor to attract his attention and set off his zeal to put it out of commission.

Scholarly reconstruction of the chronology of the career of Paul indicates that his conversion to Christianity probably took place within one or two years after the crucifixion of Jesus. Therefore, the basic pattern in the earliest Christian communities of including those who were ritually or ethnically impure by Pharisaic standards had been set by Jesus and was being carried out by his followers. Their activity in persuading people about Jesus and his redefining of the covenant people was being carried forward in the thoroughly Hellenized cities of Syria and surrounding regions, of which Damascus was the largest. That there was a Christian community in such a city as Damascus shows that Paul was not an innovator in preaching the gospel to gentiles or in inviting them to share in the new community. Indeed, it must have been this feature of the movement in the year or so before his conversion that attracted his wrath and persuaded him to destroy it before it spread further.

Paul's links with the Jewish tradition go beyond his having adopted the Pharisaic reinterpretation of the Law of Moses with its emphasis on personal purity. He was strongly influenced by Jewish apocalyptic writings as well. The importance Paul attached to the return of the triumphant Christ at the end of the present age and to Christ's subduing the powers of evil (I Cor. 15:20–28) shows how central this theme was to Paul's thinking.[1] Similarly, in I Thessalonians, he describes the return of Christ and the resurrection of the faithful that will then take place (4:13–18).

Related to the apocalyptic expectation of triumphant divine intervention in history

---

[1]The importance of this idea in the thought of Paul is demonstrated in J. Christiaan Beker, *Paul's Apocalyptic Gospel: The Coming Triumph of God* (Philadelphia: Fortress Press, 1982).

was a form of mysticism in which it was believed that certain individuals were granted permission to see the throne of God as a way of assuring them that God would reward their faithfulness. In the biblical tradition, God's dwelling place among his people was associated with a chariot (I Kings 7:27–33), and God's throne is pictured as wheeled (Ezek. 1:15–21; 10:1–19). Therefore, the experience of being taken up into the presence of God was called *Merkavah* ("chariot") mysticism. Paul describes such an experience of mystical transport, which he was persuaded had been granted to him by God in order to reassure him when he was experiencing personal difficulties (2 Cor. 12:1–10).

Clearly central to Paul's thinking, both before and after his conversion, was the question of how human beings could enter into a right relationship with God. Most English translations of the letters of Paul have obscured this major factor in his understanding of God's purpose for His people by translating a crucial term in Paul's letters (*dikaiosyne*) as "justification" or "righteousness." In the argument advanced in Romans 3:19–28, for example, when Paul is contrasting faith with works, we read of the manifestation of God's "righteousness" (3:21), as though the abstract divine moral qualities were on display and have now been transferred to true believers (3:22). Legal imagery seems to be involved in Romans 3:28, where we read in some versions that someone may now be "justified by faith," as though a judicial case has been made in defense of the believer. Instead, these Greek terms Paul uses are his attempts to offer equivalents for the Semitic concepts that describe how God works to bring His covenant people into right relationship with Himself. As a thoroughly committed Pharisee, Paul had been convinced that for him and other Jews to achieve proper obedience to the Law of Moses would result in the establishment of God's rule in the world and in the maintenance of the covenantal relationship that God intended for His people.

Through the experience of meeting Jesus raised from the dead (Gal. 1:15–16), however, Paul became persuaded that the sacrificial death of Jesus on the cross was God's way of freeing human beings from the guilt they thought they would suffer when they failed to conform to the Law (Gal. 3:10–14). The Law had an interim function: to keep immature human beings under control, as a schoolmaster or baby-sitter would do (Gal. 3:23–25). But Paul became convinced that true religion had been revealed by the life, death, and resurrection of Jesus. Through the faithful trusting in God's dealing with human sin, and through God's seeking to reconcile all humanity to Himself by the death and resurrection of Jesus, God has put into operation this new understanding of who His people are and how one becomes a member of the new community. The sole requirement for admission is trust in what God has done through Christ to establish that community. According to the terms of the new covenant, all the old human distinctions are transcended: "There is neither Jew nor Greek . . . slave nor free . . . male nor female; for you are all one in Christ Jesus" (Gal. 3:28). Thus, the new community fulfills the promise to Abraham of a covenant people with the potential for including people from all the nations of the earth (Gen. 12:3; cf. Gal. 3:8). Furthermore, what God has done through Jesus to set human beings in right relationship to Himself is seen not as a novelty, but as the fulfillment of what God intended from the beginning of the human race. That purpose has now been made known through what God has done in the death and resurrection of Jesus.

Hellenistic Features of Paul's Background

The fluency of Paul in Greek and his familiarity with literary conventions of the Greek world are evident in his letters. Not only are they forceful and subtle in style; they also disclose his knowledge of Greek modes of argumentation. One such is the diatribe, in which the speaker anticipates and answers the counterarguments of his opponents. The fact that Paul's abundant quotations from the Jewish scriptures are based on the Septuagint (the common ancient Greek translation of the Jewish Bible), rather than on the Hebrew original, confirms this impression of him as strongly influenced by Hellenistic culture.

When he wants to show that all humanity stands condemned before God because of its disobedience and foolish reliance on its own corrupt, self-seeking impulses, he declares that this indictment falls not only on Jews, who had the revealed Law of Moses, but on gentiles as well. How could non-Jews know what God expected of them? Borrowing from Stoic philosophy the concept of a universal human capacity to recognize and respond to the natural laws that pervade the universe, Paul speaks of gentile possession of *conscience*. The word literally means "co-knowledge," or the universal human capacity to discern these natural laws and obey them. Paul asserts that, parallel to Jewish access to the revealed Law of Moses, gentiles can perceive through conscience what God expects of all human beings (Rom. 2:13–16).

When Paul describes how the Spirit that God sends to His people gives them both insight and strength to live obedient lives, he details the moral qualities that the Spirit produces. Among them are "kindness, goodness, gentleness, self-control" (Gal. 5:22–23), which are terms familiar from comparable recitations of virtues in Roman Stoic writers of the first century. What is evident is that, in addition to perhaps being unconsciously influenced by Hellenistic thought and culture, Paul is able to exploit these insights and concepts from the gentile culture of his time by synthesizing them with the basic orientation that came to him from his Jewish Pharisaic tradition.

Paul's Conversion Experience and Its Consequences

Although Paul does not offer in his letters an elaborate description of the experience that transformed him from a fierce opponent of the Jesus groups to the most significant agent for spreading the movement into the wider gentile world, he does give important details. He believes that Jesus appeared to him risen from the dead (I Cor. 15:8) or was revealed to him by God (Gal. 1:15–16). He is persuaded that his experience of having seen "Jesus our Lord" is as real and concrete as that of Jesus's disciples, who were convinced that the risen Jesus had commissioned them to spread his message to the world. Like Paul, they considered themselves to be "sent ones"—that is, apostles, as their self-designation in Greek, *apostolos*, indicates. When Paul "saw the Lord," he did not go to the other apostles to confirm his experience, but instead, leaving Damascus, he went off to the desert regions east of the city ("into Arabia") before returning to launch his work there. His sphere of activity soon included the wider area of the Roman province of "Syria and Cilicia," which stretched northward from Palestine to the southern coast of Asia Minor. The chief city of Cilicia, Tarsus, which is designated in Acts (9:11; 21:39) as Paul's native city, was an important center of Greek learning, rivaling Athens and Alexandria, which may help to account for his incorporation of Greek concepts into his interpretation of the Christian faith.

Based on his encounter with the risen Christ, Paul was convinced that God was now fulfilling through Jesus what he had promised to Abraham: the establishment of an inclusive covenant community. The requirement for participation in this new people was not conformity to the requirements of the Jewish law, since failure to obey even a single statute could lead to disqualification. Trust in God's promise as the ground of right relationship with Him had been established as the sole basis of human acceptance in the time of Abraham. The giving of the Law to Moses some 400 years later did not set aside the prior and primary principle of trust as the ground for human acceptance before God (Gal. 3:9–17).

Now, Paul asserts, the Spirit of God is at work among His people to free them from slavery to the law and to other powers in the universe that seek to entrap and dominate human beings (Gal. 4). The life of trust becomes the channel through which the Spirit of God produces the moral qualities of love, joy, peace, goodness, and self-control, against which there is no law (Gal. 5:16–23; Phil 3:4–11).

Paul seeks to share in Christ's sufferings through his own obedience to the purpose of God and has the hope that, like Jesus, he, too, will be delivered from death (Phil. 3:4–11).

Paul's Career as Apostle to the Gentiles

After fourteen years of preaching the message of Jesus to gentiles in his native province of Syria and Cilicia, Paul seems to have had some unspecified inner doubts and so returned once more to Jerusalem for a session with the Apostles there. Their reaction was to affirm Paul's role as one of them, but also to recognize a division of labor: In proclaiming the message of Jesus, Paul would go to the gentiles; the other Apostles would concentrate on Jews. When Peter (or to use the Semitic form of his nickname, Cephas, meaning "rock") visited Antioch in Syria, he at first met and ate freely with the gentile converts. After associates of James arrived there, however, Peter withdrew from social contact with these uncircumcised gentile Christians (Gal. 2:11–13). In response to this divisive attitude, Paul insisted that no feature of the Law—not even circumcision—was a prerequisite for sharing in the life of God's people. But Paul continued to send contributions to the Jerusalem apostolic community (Rom. 15:25–29), which seems to have chosen a term used by Jesus, "the poor" (Luke 4:18; 5:20), as the designation of its members.

Because Paul's letters were written in response to the specific, immediate needs of the communities addressed in cities across the Mediterranean world, it is impossible to arrange them in an assuredly systematic or chronological way. Although the Acts of the Apostles traces the journeys and activities of Paul in a more nearly orderly way, it is selective in what it includes and at some points is in tension with what Paul reports in his letters. For example, in Galatians 2, there are no legal obligations placed on Gentile converts by the Jerusalem leaders of the church. But in Acts 15, a consultation between Paul and the Jerusalem-based Apostles results in the imposition of minimal ritual food laws on gentiles (Leviticus 17:10–14). It may be assumed, however, that the basic pattern of Paul's career is accurately described in Acts: moving from city to city, reaching from his native Syria and Jerusalem to the capital of the empire in Rome. His initial approach was to go to places where Jews met regularly in the cities of the Roman world, to give special attention to gentiles who had been drawn to the God of the Jewish scriptures, and, on occasion, to address directly pagan worshippers or intellectuals. The author of Acts is careful to describe many occasions upon which Paul and his associates have the opportunity to explain their work and their message in the presence of religious, military, and political powers as well.

As is evident from Paul's letters, the disciples of Jesus remained primarily in Jerusalem, although some of them—Peter, for example—went to visit other cities in the eastern Mediterranean, such as Antioch (Gal. 2:11). Later he was associated with other communities of Christians in Asia Minor as well (I Pet. 1:1–2). Tradition links Peter with the church in Rome, although there is no direct reference to this in any New Testament material. The author of Acts, however, is careful to point out that, from the very beginning in Jerusalem, the intention of God was to extend the good news to all humanity—out "to the ends of the earth" (Acts 1:8).[2] The multitude depicted as converging on the house in Jerusalem when the outpouring of the Spirit of God on the disciples occurs in such a dramatic fashion (Acts 2:1–6) includes Jews and devout seekers "from every nation under heaven." The miracle by which these Jews and proselytes were able to hear the disciples' message in their own language, regardless of their native origin, is a symbolic way of showing that the good news is to reach out to people of whatever linguistic or ethnic origins. Divine confirmation of this phenomenon is offered in the address of Peter reported in Acts, which is based on an extended quotation from the Hebrew prophet Joel, who announced that God's Spirit would be poured out on all humanity (literally, *flesh*) and that whoever called on the name of the Lord would be saved. (See Joel 3:1–5 and Acts 2:17–21, 39.) Thus, Paul's mission to the gentiles is perceived as a logical development, not a dubious innovation.

This feature of inclusion is also developed in the early chapters of Acts, in which a lame man is healed by Peter at the gate of the temple (Acts 3). Lameness disqualified anyone from serving as a priest, and no lame animal could be offered in the temple.[3] In the Dead Sea Scrolls, the lame and any otherwise deformed were to be forbidden to enter Jerusalem in the new age of the restored temple. The disciples' special attention to, and careful justification for, the healing extended to this man underscore the theme that we saw in the teachings of Jesus: It is the outsiders and those on the fringe of the covenant people who are to be the special concern of the new community. In Acts 6 and 7, the role of Greek-speaking Jews is highlighted by the selection of seven men—all with Greek names!—to handle the daily distribution of food to the members of the community. One of this group, Stephen, articulates the theme that God does not dwell in houses—not even in the temple. This fits in with Jesus' regret-free prediction of the destruction of the temple (Mark 13:2). Theology Stephen goes on to denounce the collaborationist leaders of Israel who have persistently persecuted the prophets God has sent to them and who have now connived to have Jesus put to death (Acts 7:44–53). The council arranges to have Stephen stoned to death, outside

---

[2] This theme in Acts is sketched in my study, *Good News to the Ends of the Earth: the Theology of Acts* (Philadelphia: Trinity Press, 1990).

[3] See Leviticus 21:18; Deuteronomy 15:21.

the city. The leader of this mob action against one who, in the name of Jesus, challenges Israel's special relationship to God through the Law and the temple is Saul—that is, Paul (Acts 7:54–60). Acts proceeds to describe in vivid, dramatic detail the conversion of Paul and the stages that lead to his acceptance by the Christians in Damascus and then in Jerusalem, after which he goes back to Syria (Acts 9).

Alternating with the early stages of Paul's career, as told in Acts, are further indications that the Christian community is being extended to include non-Jews. Acts 8 recounts the conversion of Samaritans[4] and of a eunuch from Ethiopia, whose ethnic origins and whose physical condition would have disqualified them from participation in the covenant of Israel. Through a series of visions, Peter is brought together with a Roman military officer stationed in the Hellenistic city of Caesarea. Peter is instructed not to allow the ritual food laws to separate him from other potential members of the new community, since God is impartial. All who will may enter the covenant. After Peter tells Cornelius, the Roman centurion, about Jesus and what God was doing through him, that Gentile receives the Spirit and is baptized (Acts 10). Peter's subsequent report of this event to the church in Jerusalem makes explicit the principle of Gentile participation in the new people of God, which is then confirmed by the church leaders (Acts 11:18).

It was in Antioch in Syria, however, that Acts reports the first systematic effort being made to bring Gentiles into the community of faith (Acts 11). Barnabas was sent by the Jerusalem church to assess the situation in Antioch and recruited Paul to assist him. The results were large numbers added to the community, whose members (we are told) were for the first time called *Christians* (Acts 11:26). As in the letters of Paul, Acts tells that it is the Antioch community which commissions Paul and Barnabas to launch a mission to such regions beyond Syria as the island of Cyprus and the Roman provinces in central and southern Asia Minor (Acts 13).

Paul explains from the Jewish scriptures Jesus' role in the purpose of God and how, through Jesus, the promise that God's covenant with man will be renewed is fulfilled. The reactions are a mixture of acceptance of the message by some and violent rejection of it and its bearers by others. The cities in which this activity is carried out include Antioch-in-Pisidia, Iconium, Lystra, and Derbe. The basic pattern is to approach Jews first, in their meetings, and then to turn to interested Gentiles, especially to those who are on the periphery of Judaism ("the devout").

An important stage in the spread of Christianity is described in Acts 16, when, in response to a vision, Paul crosses from Troas to the mainland of Europe.[5] His first reported activity is at Philippi, the leading city of the province of Macedonia, which had been named by and for Philip, the father of Alexander the Great. Again, the symbolism of Paul's first European convert is significant: Lydia is a Jewish woman with a Greek name. Her livelihood is the business of selling luxury items made with an enormously expensive purple dye extracted from a type of seashell. She is a pious person, as is evident from her journeying

---

[4]Samaritans were descendants of the northern tribes of Israel, but the very different development of a temple and the priesthood in Samaria from their development in Jerusalem led the Jews to denounce the Samaritans as perverters of the tradition and to regard them as untouchable.

[5]Troas was a district on the Aegean coast of Asia Minor (part of modern Turkey), of which the chief city was Troy, famed through the poetry of Homer and regarded by the Romans as the place from which the first settlers of Rome had come, as reported by the Roman poet, Vergil, in his epic, the *Aeneid*.

to the place of prayer, where she met with a group of women. Incidentally, women, including those of means and power, were to make up an important part of the early Christian communities. Another revealing detail of this story is that when Lydia was converted and baptized, the members of her household were baptized as well (Acts 16:15). Thus, conversion was not a purely individual matter, but involved one's identity with a larger social group.

Another story in Acts 16 that is indicative of the ways in which Christianity was to penetrate the structures of Roman society and politics is that of the conversion of the jailer in charge of the prison at Philippi. Paul was placed in prison there after he reportedly exorcised a demon that was credited with enabling a slave girl to foretell the future and read fortunes. Her owners were so furious that she had lost her fortune-telling skills, that they appealed to the local judge, who ordered that Paul and his companion, Silas, be put in prison. They were stripped of their clothing, severely beaten, and thrown into prison. To guarantee that they would remain in jail, the jailer put them in an inner cell and placed their feet in stocks. Far from being discouraged by this treatment, the two Christian prisoners sang and prayed aloud on into the night while the other prisoners listened. But God was at work, the Acts narrative tells us: A great earthquake shook the prison to its foundations, the doors of all the cells swung open, and all the fetters of the prisoners were released at once.

On realizing what had happened, the jailer was ready to commit suicide for his failure to keep imprisoned those in his charge. Entering the prison with lights, the jailer fell down before Paul and Silas, asking how he might get out of the predicament. With a pun on his question how he might be "saved" from punishment by the authorities (Acts 16:30), Paul tells him how he and all in his household might be "saved" through coming into right relationship with God. Paul declares that the jailer and all those in his house must trust in "the Lord Jesus" if all are to be "saved" (16:31). During the night the jailer washes the wounds of Paul and Silas, while the latter explains God's message to him and all his household. At once, the jailer and all his family are baptized as testimony to their trust in the God whom Paul preached. On the next day the local magistrate decides to release Paul and Silas, but since they are Roman citizens, they should not have been treated so harshly and without a proper trial. After the judge apologizes, Paul and Silas agree to leave Philippi. This vivid story is an example of the way that the Christians, from the outset of their reaching out to the wider Roman world for converts, were confronted by and debated with the civil authorities of the empire. It also shows the attraction that the movement had for people at large, including government officials.

Different kinds of encounters are depicted in Acts 17. In Thessalonica, the local Jewish leaders were enraged by the success of Paul and his coworker Silas in persuading not only some male Jews, but also many devout gentiles and leading Jewish women who had been associated with the synagogue, that Jesus was God's agent sent to reconstitute His people. Before the civil authorities, the leaders accused the apostles of politically subversive claims about the kingship of Jesus. In Athens, however, Paul's public arguments in support of his claims about Jesus were depicted as carried on not only in the synagogue, but also in the public marketplace, the agora, where philosophers of various bents addressed the crowds that passed through (Acts 17:16–18).

Because Paul had a theme in his public lectures that was new to the city, he was called before the local council, which had jurisdiction over what was taught and proclaimed there.

He seized the occasion of the hearing before the council, which met on the hill of Areopagus overlooking the vast public area of the city, to make the point that the unknown god to whom a local altar was dedicated had revealed himself, not only in the ordering of the universe and in the divine presence within human hearts, but specifically through this man, Jesus, whom God had raised from the dead and who was to be judge of the world (Acts 17:19–33). In the course of Paul's speech, as reported in Acts, he quoted Greek poets and affirmed several basic ideas that Greek philosophers taught—the inner presence of God and the future judgment of human deeds, for example. The response was one of mixed scorn and interest, but a few members of the council did believe what Paul had to say. Once more, Acts presents us with a symbolic incident that points to the continuing engagement between the messengers of Christianity and the intellectual leaders of the Greco-Roman world.

In Acts 18, there is an account of a mixed reaction at Corinth to Paul's message about Jesus that was delivered to the Jewish community. The leader of the synagogue was converted, but the hostility of some Corinthian Jews was so strong, that Paul announced his intention to concentrate on winning Gentiles to faith in Jesus, using as his base of operations a house adjacent to the one where the synagogue met. The accusations against Paul brought by the Jews before the Roman governor were rejected by that official on the ground that the issue was not one of Roman law, but of the interpretation of Jewish traditions. Gallio, the governor, is known from Roman historical sources to have been in that post during the latter part of the reign of Claudius as emperor (41–54 C.E.), so that this detail in Acts provides a valuable chronological reference point for reconstructing the career of Paul. An inscription found early in the twentieth century at the Temple of Apollo in Delphi makes possible the determination of the precise period when Gallio (who was the brother of the famous Roman philosopher Seneca) was serving as governor in Corinth: between 51 and 53 C.E.

In Ephesus, the growth of the Christian community was so rapid that local merchants and craftsmen began to fear that its spread would endanger the enterprise that was the chief attraction of the city and the major source of their revenue: the temple of Artemis, the fertility goddess, for whom statues and offerings were locally prepared and sold. At a public confrontation in the city theater, where Jews, Christians, and devotees of Artemis were locked in verbal conflict, the town clerk finally quieted the masses and told them that there was no basis for their charge against Paul and his associates. These reported accusations against Paul anticipated and exemplified the two major sources of opposition that the growing movement experienced in the second and subsequent centuries: the charge of subversion of both Roman religion and civil authority brought by pagan opponents, and the hostility from some Jewish leaders who rejected the claim that Jesus was the fulfillment of the covenant promises of their scriptures.

In Acts 20, Paul's brief return visit to the churches of mainland Greece and a farewell address to the leaders of the Ephesian church are followed by a description of his return to Syria and then to Jerusalem (Acts 21). In his defense before the religious and civilian officials (Acts 22–26), Paul makes the case that (1) the message about Jesus which he proclaims is rooted in the Jewish scriptures and embodies the fulfillment of the hopes expressed there; (2) through miracles, God has repeatedly shown His support for what Paul is doing and saying; and (3) nothing which Paul and his associates proclaim is in conflict with Roman law. Accordingly, as a Roman citizen, Paul makes an appeal directly to Caesar to rule on the charges brought against him.[6] The appeal is granted, and his voyage to Rome is depicted in vivid detail, with abundant signs of special divine protection. The narrative ends with Paul awaiting trial in Rome, but engaged in missionary activity and in debate with the Jews, operating from his own rented quarters in the capital city.

Although the author of Acts includes many important historical details that have been corroborated by modern scholarship, his work as a whole is selective, stylized, and symbolic in its approach.[7] The portrayal of the spread of Christianity in Acts is on the whole historically reliable and includes considerable unique historical detail. But we are on far surer ground if we regard Acts as a schematic survey of the events it describes, written from the perspective of the late first century. More certain is the evidence that comes from the first-hand reports of Paul in his letters, although the issues discussed in Acts match those that Paul deals with in the letters.

Paul's Communications with the Gentile Churches

It is clear from the letters of Paul preserved in the New Testament that he wrote more of them than we now possess and that he received letters from the churches, to which he sent replies. In the letter known as I Corinthians, for example, he mentions his earlier letter to the community there (5:9) and the letter they had written to him inquiring about some issues within the group (7:1). Among the preserved letters of Paul are references to places and incidents reported more fully in Acts, such as the difficulties he experienced in Philippi (I Thess. 2:1) and his stay in Athens (I Thess. 3:1). In the closing sections of each of the letters is a series of notes from persons in the community to which he is writing or greetings to individuals in these churches, as well as his recommendations of those who are going to visit the community addressed in the letter. As a result of these personal notes, the reader obtains a vivid picture of the relationships within individual communities and the surprising extent to which members moved from one city to another, as was common for a considerable segment of the populace in the Roman world of the first and second centuries.

I and II Corinthians give us the fullest picture of the problems and the resources for dealing with them in the first generation of Christian churches. In I Corinthians, each chapter or group of chapters deals with a major issue that confronted a community of Gentiles who were persuaded that, through Jesus, God's purpose outlined in the Jewish scriptures was being fulfilled. The first two chapters deal with the conceptual or intellectual question whether the message Paul preached was compatible with human wisdom. Some members were siding with certain leaders in the church against the others, claiming supe-

---

[6]Citizenship in the Roman empire was by no means universal, but was instead a highly prized status that could be gained by certain subjects through their possession of commercial and property rights. It was originally transmitted by heredity only to natives of Rome and parts of Italy, but subsequently, it was conferred on persons born in other lands who had in some significant way served or supported the cause of Rome.

[7]Martin Hengel, *Acts and the History of Earliest Christianity* (Philadelphia: Fortress Press, 1979) is a significant effort to demonstrate the historical reliability of Acts. An early reference work on Acts and its historical setting is F. J. Foakes-Jackson, K. Lake, and H. J. Cadbuty (eds.), *The Beginnings of Christianity: Part One, The Acts of the Apostles* (London: Macmillan, 1922–1932), a series of five volumes. My own analysis of the setting and contents of Acts is offered in *To Every Nation Under Heaven: A Commentary on the Acts of the Apostles* (Harrisburg, PA: Trinity Press International, 1997).

rior wisdom. Paul seeks to combat this development by declaring that Christ is both the power of God and the wisdom of God. There is no place in the community for these claims about having access to superior knowledge. This issue anticipates the struggles in the late first and early second centuries on the part of the church's intellectual leaders to discern the relationship between the message that the Apostles preached and the lofty intellectual traditions of the Greco-Roman world. (See Chapter 6.)

Besides the claim to superior wisdom, some members regarded one or another of the leaders as fulfilling the most significant role in the life of the community. Paul's response in I Corinthians 3 was to declare that each leader had a distinctive task to perform and that all were essential to healthy growth of the community. Together, they made up the temple where God dwelt by the Spirit. Some members, however, were grossly proud of their individual accomplishments, either intellectually or in terms of their roles. Paul shows that the humiliation and suffering that he and the other leaders had been subjected to were analogous to the rejection that Christ had to suffer in the plan of God (I Cor. 4). Also causing major antagonisms within the Christian community was the practice of some members to turn to civil courts to settle disputes with other Christians, a procedure Paul denounced (I Cor. 6).

In I Cor. 5 Paul addresses the specific issue of the behavior of the Christians, especially those who have gone to excess in trying to show how free they are from the obligation to obey the Law of Moses. (Indeed, some are even living in an incestuous relationship.) Other debates concern whether Christians can divorce and remarry, whether couples should abstain from sexual relationships, whether the unmarried and widows should maintain their status, and whether someone who is converted should continue to be married to an unconverted spouse. On only one question does Paul have a tradition from Jesus to which he can appeal: Jesus' prohibition of divorce and remarriage (I Cor 7:10–11; Mark 10:1–12). On the other matters, Paul can offer only his own opinion. A special question is raised because Paul has no wife, although the other apostles are accompanied by theirs. The answer is that in each case the welfare and image of the community as a whole must be taken into account, as well as the distinctive roles and dispositions of the individuals involved. Some members tried to display their freedom by buying and eating meat that had originally been offered in sacrifice to pagan deities. These people would have believed that the pagan gods were shams and so would have scoffed at such religion. Paul reminds them, however, that new converts have only recently been liberated from these pagan cults and will be offended by Christians seeming to participate in such rites (I Cor. 8).

I Corinthians 9–14 deals with problems that arise from the varieties of leadership and functions within the community, including the question whether the Apostles should receive financial support from the members. Paul asserts that he has a right to receive such support as the other Apostles do from their communities, but that he chooses not to do so. He prefers to work for a living (I Cor. 4:12; 9:6) so that he can be free of all sense of obligation to any members of the community. He addresses a whole range of social issues:

- The subservient role of women in the churches.
- The fact that, at the eucharistic meal of the community (the Lord's Supper, as Paul calls it; I Cor. 11:17–22), some are drunk and some go hungry.
- The diversity of origins of the members of the community: Jew and Gentile, slave and free (I Cor. 12:13).

- The diversity of roles to be performed by the members of the community and the range of values attached to those roles: apostles, prophets, teachers, miracle workers, healers, those gifted with ecstatic speech, and the interpreters of those who "speak with tongues" (I Cor. 12:27–29).

Paul's advice regarding the divisive factors within the community at Corinth is to recognize that, like the parts of a human body, the role of each member is essential for the welfare of the whole. And the quality that is to pervade and facilitate the functioning of the "body" is love (I Cor. 13–14). What is clear in all this counsel from Paul to the community at Corinth is that there had not yet developed in the churches either a clear pattern of leadership for decision making or a set of guidelines that each community was expected to observe. It appears that Paul had different standards for different communities, since he refused to accept financial support in Corinth, but did so in Philippi (Phil. 4:15). It is not that Paul simply was inconsistent, but that his policies were adjusted to the specific conditions of each of the communities in which he lived and served. The institutional norms of structure and behavior were yet to be established in the life of Christianity. On one question, however, Paul did have a firm tradition: how the Lord's Supper is to be conducted. Here is one of the few issues on which the Jesus tradition is known and is appealed to explicitly (I Cor. 11:23–26). On the other questions he seems to have been guided by what he thought would foster the common life of the community as a whole.

A major question to which Paul had a consistent answer was: How will the present age come to an end? Paul shares with Jewish apocalyptic thought the belief that the present age is dominated by the powers of evil, although he is confident that the rule of God over the creation has already begun to be established through Jesus. When that work of subjugation of evil is complete, Jesus will return in triumph. The church's ground for confidence that this victory will take place is that God has already raised Jesus from the dead as a kind of down payment on the resurrection of all the faithful (I Cor. 15:23–24). The result will be the triumph of the power and purpose of God over the whole of the universe. This view of world history resembles the perspectives evident in the writings of Roman leaders influenced by Stoic philosophy. In the mid-first century B.C.E., for example, Cicero, in his treatise *On the Nature of the Gods*, states that the gods shape the course of nature and history and disclose the future to humans as a warning and a counsel to guide their behavior. In the first century C.E., Seneca's treatise *On Providence* affirms the divine order of the universe and how the final conflagrations that will bring an end to history will lead to the renewal of the universe, when the souls of the blest will share in peace and immortality. It was the Jewish equivalent of this understanding of divine purpose and moral responsibility that manifested itself in Jewish, and then in Christian, apocalyptic literature.

In his earlier letter to the Thessalonians, Paul expressed the same basic expectation (I Thess. 4:13–18), making clear that he was confident that he would be among those who would be alive when the cosmic event took place. In his later letter to the Philippians, which may have been written from prison in Rome, there is a clear indication that, since he is now subject to Roman governmental authorities, he may be executed by the Romans.[8]

---

[8]Paul's reference to the Praetorian Guard (Phil. 1:13) may be an indication that he was imprisoned under the elite imperial troops in Rome itself, although it could also refer to the special forces of a provincial governor in Palestine or elsewhere.

The perennial issue of when and in what mode Christ will return in triumph was dealt with in a variety of ways in the New Testament and in the ensuing centuries.

The instructions for taking up the collection for the Jerusalem Christians and for conveying the gift are quite explicit (I Cor. 16). Since this was a major factor in Paul's agreement with the Jerusalem apostles, he was determined to see that it was carried out. In doing so, he confronted the Jewish authorities, whose charges before the political powers in Palestine led to his being taken as prisoner to Rome.

As noted earlier, the overarching theme in Paul's letter to the Galatians and in his most systematic letter, Romans, is how God constitutes His new covenant people through Jesus. From this community of love, no power can separate the members of God's people (Rom. 8:38–39). God has not abandoned his historic people, Israel, but now they, too, have the opportunity to share in the life of the reconstituted covenant people (Rom. 9–11).

Jesus and Paul as Models for the Outreach of the Church to the Greco-Roman World: Luke and Acts

As we have seen, the two-volume work known as the Gospel of Luke and the Acts of the Apostles is far more than an ancient archive of information about Jesus and the apostles. From the opening words of Luke's gospel to the dramatic account of Paul's voyage to Rome in Acts, the author uses the devices and modes that were common features of popular literature of the late first and early second century of our era. The formal, stylized introductory lines of Luke are echoed in the opening of Acts. The frequent references to rulers and officials of the Roman system enable the reader to locate in time and place the events that are being described and also to perceive these occurrences on the larger stage of the early Roman empire. Although Luke's gospel is developed on the basis of an earlier Christian model (the Gospel of Mark), the style and strategy of Acts reflect what literary historians call the *Hellenistic romance*, which was a narrative type developed in this period to serve as propaganda for a religious movement or a divinity.[9]

Since the author of Luke and Acts is concerned to show the continuity with, as well as the transformation of, Judaism that occurred with the coming of Jesus, he also employs some of the literary styles of the Jewish traditions, such as the hymns and prophetic utterances that accompany the story of the birth of Jesus in Luke 1–2. In passages unique to Luke, the aged Simeon foresees that Jesus will be the instrument of God's revelation to Gentiles as well as Jews (Luke 2:32). John the Baptist announces that all humanity will see God's salvation (Luke 3:6) and demonstrates this by welcoming into his group those who would be rejected by Jewish standards: tax collectors and soldiers (Luke 3:10–14). Similarly, Jesus' sermon in Nazareth not only announces that God's good news is intended especially for the "poor"—that is, the deprived and excluded—but also recalls the precedents for non-Israelite participation in God's healing benefits through the prophets Elijah and Elisha

---

[9]A prime example of this type of literature is the *Metamorphoses* of Lucius Apuleius. Written in the mid-second century C.E., it describes how one participates in the cult of Isis, the Egyptian goddess of love and fertility. A perceptive analysis of the romance as a cultural medium is offered by Douglas R. Edwards in *Religion and Power: Pagans, Jews, and Christians in the Greek East* (Oxford: Oxford University Press, 1996).

(Luke 4:16–30). Luke reports that Jesus sent out not just twelve of his followers to spread his message, but seventy others as well (10:1–20). Twelve is the number of the tribes of Israel, and seventy is a symbolic number for the nations of the world. Jesus' actions and his parables point to the inclusiveness of the community as part of God's purpose:

- The Parable of the Good Samaritan praises the concern and kindness of a member of a religious group despised by pious Jews (10:29–37).
- The Parable of the Pharisee and the Publican contrasts the pride of the former with the humble reaching out for forgiveness by the latter (18:9–14).
- The Parables of the Lost Sheep, the Lost Coin, and the Lost Son point out that God and his agents take the initiative to restore the alienated (15:1–32).
- The story of Zacchaeus, the tax collector, illustrates Jesus' message that God welcomes all true seekers into His people (19:1–10).
- The Healing of the Ten Lepers shows how Jesus cared for those whose physical condition precluded their participation in Jewish common life or worship (Luke 17:11–19).

Women, whose status in the life of the Jewish religious community and in Roman society as a whole was often peripheral, are pictured in Luke as having a central place in the new community. This is apparent from their role in the birth and infancy stories, from the special attention Jesus gives to meeting their needs (as in the healing of the widow's son, 7:11–17), from the insight of the woman who anoints Jesus for his burial (7:36–50), from the support that women provide for Jesus and his associates (8:1–3; 10:38–42), and from the faithful presence of women during his crucifixion and in the preparation of his body for proper burial. Similarly evidencing Jesus' challenge to the social patterns of his day, Luke pictures him throughout the Gospel as stressing the blessing that is to come to the poor and the judgment that is to fall on the rich.

In at least two ways, the author of Luke prepares the reader for the possibilities and problems that will confront the community after Jesus has been taken from them: (1) In his expanded version of Jesus' examination by the political authorities, Luke notes that neither Herod Antipas (the Jewish regional ruler) nor Pilate (the Roman governor) can find Jesus guilty of any crime against the Roman state (Luke 23:6–16). This apolitical nature of the movement becomes a central theme in the Acts of the Apostles. (2) Jesus is described as promising his followers that they will be empowered by the Spirit for the work they will do in his absence (Luke 24:48). In Acts, the fulfillment of that promise occupies the center of interest for the first two chapters: The outpouring of the Spirit is portrayed as a microcosm of the worldwide role of the church in the years to come. Throughout Acts, the apostles are brought before the civil authorities, and in each case they are exonerated from any charge. One of the aims of the author of Acts is to show that neither Jesus nor Paul (nor, for that matter, any other disciple) was guilty of anti-Roman words or actions. This point would be especially important in the later first and early second centuries, as Christianity became a sufficiently large and aggressive movement to be a concern to the Roman authorities. But Jesus and Paul are portrayed as the models for effective outreach with the good news about what God has done and is yet to do. Luke and Acts offer vivid detail to make that basic point. The reworking of the tradition in each case helps to underscore the strategy that the community is to employ in following its mission to the wider world.

Chapter 4

From Charismatic Movement to Institution

The transformation of the early church from a spontaneous religious movement that emerged in various parts of Palestine and the wider Mediterranean world into an organized, structured enterprise is evident when we compare earlier with later forms of the New Testament writings—Mark with Matthew and authentic letters of Paul with those subsequently written in his name. Analogous kinds of structural changes in the early Christian movement and of adaptation to the wider Roman culture may be discerned by analyzing other writings of the New Testament as well.

From Apocalyptic Sect to Authoritarian Community: The Gospel of Matthew

Unlike the Gospel of Mark, which is written in a breathless style, moving quickly from one event in the life of Jesus to another and emphasizing throughout the imminent end of the present age, Matthew is deliberative in manner and manifests many features of a structured, ordered community lying behind his account of Jesus. The intensity and frequency of Matthew's contrasts between prevailing Jewish practices and Jesus' instruction to his followers are best accounted for as arising from the grave tensions between Matthew's community and that of emergent rabbinic Judaism in the later decades of the first century C.E. (see Chapter 1), as each sought to draw the boundaries for their conception of the covenant people.

This definitional activity is evident in both positive and negative ways in the Gospel

46

of Matthew. From its opening lines, the author keeps making the point that the birth of Jesus and each aspect of the accompanying events were in fulfillment of the Jewish scriptures (cf. Matt. 1:22; 2:5, 15, 17, 23; 3:3; 4:14). When Jesus is reported as offering his followers a summary of his teachings, the parallel with Moses' giving the Law to Israel on Mount Sinai is explicit (Matt. 5:1–2), as are the direct contrasts between what Moses taught and what Jesus teaches (Matt. 5:17, 21, 27, 31, 33, 38, 43). The conscious contrast between Judaism and Matthew's Christian community is evident in the structure of his Gospel, which is divided into five sections, just as the Law of Moses is. The phrase "when Jesus had finished" occurs five times in Matthew (7:28; 11:1; 13:53; 19:1; 26:1), in each case at the end of a major teaching section. The only item in Matthew that does not fit this structural scheme is Matthew 23, which is probably a polemical feature added to the Gospel after its original fivefold structure had already been established. Equally sharp are the differences specified between Jewish piety (alms, fasting, and prayer) and that which Jesus urges his followers to exemplify (Matt. 6:1–18). Much of this material is found *only* in Matthew, which underscores how important for his community these contrasts and controversies were. The most vehement attack on any aspect of Judaism in Matthew is the extended denunciation of the Pharisees in Matthew 23, which has no counterpart in the other gospels and which ends by blaming the Jews for the murder of all God's messengers throughout biblical history (Matt. 23:32–36) and warning that divine judgment is going to fall on them. That event of divine censure is linked explicitly with the destruction of the temple, which is a prelude to the coming of the end of the age (Matt. 24:1–3). At several points in Matthew's distinctive account of the trial and crucifixion of Jesus, the blame for his death is placed on, and accepted by, the Jewish leaders. At the same time, Pilate declares his freedom from responsibility for the sentencing of Jesus to death (Matt. 27:24–25).

Throughout Matthew, the writer pictures Jesus and his followers as engaged in discussion of precisely those issues in the appropriation of the biblical tradition that were central for Judaism in this period. Furthermore, Matthew reflects an instructional program and a decision-making process within the community that has no counterpart in the other three gospels. Jesus' commissioning of the disciples in his appearance to them after the resurrection includes his telling them to go throughout the world, making disciples from all the nations (Matt. 28:19). The term translated as "make disciples" means to give instruction or to promote the learning process, which is precisely the practice that was being developed by the rabbis of the period to train adherents in the emergent forms of Jewish life and thought. In the final verse of Matthew (28:20) the disciples are told to teach the new members of the community to observe all the commandments given to them by Jesus. What is needed, therefore, are not merely converts, but trainees to learn the truths and requirements of this new community.

Analogously, Matthew 18 describes a decision-making process within the community by means of which the appropriate behavior of the members can be determined. Disputes are to be settled between the individuals involved, but if that is not possible, officers of the church or the congregation as a whole are to hear the issues and render a decision. This process may result in expelling a member: "If he refuses to listen to the church, let him be to you as a Gentile or a tax-collector" (Matt. 18:17). The church's decisions are declared to be confirmed by God in heaven (Matt. 18:18–19). Furthermore, in Matthew 16, the disciples, as leaders of the community, are given the right and responsibility to determine the standards for admission to or exclusion from membership in the group: "I will give you the keys of the kingdom, and whatever you bind on earth will be bound in heaven, and whatever you loose on earth will be loosed in heaven" (16:19). The terms "bind" and "loose" used here (in 16:19 and 18:18) are precisely those the Jewish sources of the period employ for the comparable process within the emergent rabbinic community. Only in Matthew is there explicit reference to the community as a "church" (Matt. 16:18; 18:17). The church is not an informal community that gathers, but a social structure to be built.

Further evidence of the movement toward fixed patterns is to be found in the formalization of some of the basic practices of the earlier community. For example, the simple direct prayer of Jesus in Luke 11:2–4 ("Father, hallowed be thy name, thy kingdom come") appears in Matthew 6:9–15 with the balanced lines and formal phrasing of the Lord's Prayer as it is used in Christian liturgical form down to the present day:

> Our Father who art in heaven,
> Hallowed be thy name.
> Thy kingdom come,
> Thy will be done,
> On earth as it is in heaven.
> Give us this day our daily bread.
> And forgive us our debts,
>   as we have forgiven our debtors.
> And do not lead us into the time of testing,
> But rescue us from the Evil One.[1]

Similarly, the widespread practice of baptism as initiation into the community is linked in Matthew 28:19 with a trinitarian formula ("in the name of the Father, and of the Son, and of the Holy Spirit") absent from all the other Gospel tradition.

What is apparent in Matthew is that his community has developed patterns for liturgy, prayer, administering the sacraments, the instruction of members, decision making within the membership, polemics against the emergent forms of rabbinic Judaism, and the assignment of responsibility to its leaders. It is not in the least surprising, therefore, that the early church assigned Matthew the place of honor at the head of the New Testament, since this Gospel addressed so directly the needs of the Christian movement as it moved beyond the first generation of spontaneity into a period of consolidation, definition, and organization for both leaders and members. The urgency of these needs was heightened by the fact that, concurrent with these developments within Christianity, Judaism was taking shape in a movement that also claimed to be the true heir to the promises of the God of Israel to His future covenant people.

The Community of Mystical Participation in the Life of God: The Gospel of John

Although the mystery religions, with their promise of direct participation in the life of the gods, had flourished in the Mediterranean world for centuries, it was in the late first and

---

[1] Many later manuscripts add: "For the kingdom and the power and the glory are yours forever. Amen."

early second centuries C.E. that popular interest in them surged. The earlier policies of Greece and Rome to suppress these religious movements are evident in the classical Greek play *The Bacchae*, by Euripides (480–406 B.C.E.), in which ecstatic women devotees of this god of wine and fertility think they have been divinely enabled to kill a wild animal with their hands, only to find that they have dismembered the son of their leader. In the early part of the second century B.C.E., another group of women discovered to be engaging in orgiastic rites in honor of Bacchus (or Dionysus, as he was known to the Greeks) were forbidden by the Roman senate to continue their worship.

Yet by the second century C.E., milder forms of worship of deities such as Osiris and Isis (Egyptian divinities linked with the fertility of the land through the annual overflow of the Nile) attracted a wide following, including both the simple and the sophisticated of the Roman world. Osiris, the god of the Nile, was depicted in the popular Egyptian myth as put to death by his enemy when the flow of the Nile subsided each year. His consort, Isis, was instrumental in restoring him to life. Later, she was worshipped as the divine agent through whom her devotees could share in eternal life. The appeal of these mystery cults included the belief that, through these divinities, one might in this present life perceive the divine ordering of the universe, gain the protection of the gods, and experience direct encounters with them. Although the details of the mystery religions were mostly secret, Plutarch (46–120 C.E.) wrote an informative account of the cult of Isis, and a mid-second-century writer, Lucius Apuleius, offered a vivid story (*About Isis*) of the transformation of a man who devoted his life to her service. In this highly symbolic narrative, a man who had been turned into an ass through dabbling in magic was restored to his human form by Isis, who gave him purpose and fulfillment in his new life. In other writings of the period, Isis is identified with cosmic wisdom, so that the knowledge she provides to her followers gives them understanding of themselves and the world in which they live.

This reworking of ancient traditions along symbolic lines, with allegorical interpretations, was engaged in also by Jews. In Alexandria, for example, the prolific writer and leader of the Jewish community, Philo, interpreted the biblical laws and narratives in such a way as to picture the experiences and legal requirements of ancient Israel as symbolic vehicles for participation in the life of God through mystical visions and spiritual understanding of the Law of Moses. For example, Abraham's journey from Ur of the Chaldees to Hebron, where God met and commissioned him (Gen. 12–18), is a symbolic picture of the journey of the soul from the material realm into the realm of the divine, where a direct encounter with God occurs. The distinction between matter and spirit, as well as the concept of the discernment of ultimate reality beyond the physical world, derived from the Platonic philosophical tradition in which Jews in Alexandria were obviously being trained during the period (early first century C.E.). Philo wove together these philosophical and mystical features with his own upbringing in the Jewish biblical heritage to produce this remarkable synthesis of symbolic transformation and renewal of the older tradition.

The Gospel of John is an analogous reworking of the tradition. Jesus is the divine agent through whom the world was made, as well as the instrument through whom God's true people come to understand His purpose and to share in the true life He offers them. Instead of the feminine Greek word for wisdom, *sophia*, which is used in connection with Isis, John identifies Jesus with *logos*, a masculine Greek word meaning "word," "reason," or "rationale." Unlike the Isis mythology, however, in which she dwells in the mythical realm except in moments of mystical disclosure, Jesus is pictured as living among his own people and within the world that was created through him, bringing light of the knowledge of God to those ready to receive it (John 1:1–14).

The story of Jesus' career and the accounts of his teaching are cast in forms that distinguish them from the other gospels. Jesus' miracles are described as "signs" that manifest his divine glory (John 2:11; 20:30–31). In each case, the literal content of the narrative is intended as a vehicle of symbolic meaning for the community. The changing of water into wine at a wedding feast (John 2:1–11) is a symbol of the time of fulfillment and consummation of God's purpose for His people. The feeding of the 5,000 represents God's provision for His people during the time before that purpose is accomplished (John 6). The restoration of sight to the blind man is contrasted with the blindness of Jesus' Jewish contemporaries, who cannot see in him the instrument of God's healing purpose for them (John 9).

Similarly, many of Jesus' teachings in the Gospel of John are placed in the framework of declarations by Jesus that begin with the phrase "I am." That phrase is used in the Greek translation of the Jewish Bible (called the Septuagint)[2] as the special name of God, Yahweh, which means "I am" or "I cause to be," and which has traditionally been transliterated into English as Jehovah. Jesus declares his oneness with God, therefore, not in the abstract, but in terms of his role as God's agent to reconstitute God's people. As in the signs, the images are drawn from the biblical tradition: Jesus is the bread of life who feeds God's people (John 6:35); he is the light of the world (8:12); he is the "I am" whose call to the covenant people transcends God's call to Abraham (8:58); he is the door through which one enters the flock that is God's people (10:7), and he is the shepherd who cares for them (10:11); because he is the embodiment of the resurrection, he brings eternal life to his followers (11:25); he is the way to God, the truth about God, and the life God has prepared for His people (14:6); he is the living organism through which God's people are nourished and enabled to be productive (15:1–5). When the crowd that came to seize him in the Garden of Gethsemane asked if he was Jesus of Nazareth, he responded, "I am," and they fell back in the presence of his divine majesty (18:1–6). By this mixture of narrative, discourse, and symbolism based on the Old Testament, John sketches Jesus' oneness with God and his central role in God's purpose for His people.

As in Matthew's Gospel, John pictures Jesus in conflict with the Jewish leaders, who are excluding his followers from their synagogue meetings (9:22, 34). The crucial issue disputed between Jews and the Christian leaders is the latter's claim that Jesus is the primary agent of God. The decision about Jesus is determinative of one's destiny (9:35–41). The only moral requirements for this new community are that they are to love one another (13:35) and to bear fruit—that is, to work the works of love, even to the point of dying for others (15:1–11). The only ecclesiastical role assigned to the disciples is to pronounce forgiveness (20:22–23). In John's Gospel, there is no hint of leadership roles or of ecclesiastical structure; the major concern is with harmony and mutuality within this new community

---

[2] This number derives from the legend reported in a Jewish document called *The Letter of Aristeas*, written around 150 B.C.E., which reports that in Egypt seventy Jewish scholars began translating the Hebrew Bible at once and finished it simultaneously, with results that agreed in every detail. This was, of course, a legend that sought to show the divine sanction for the translation.

to whom Jesus has revealed God's purpose. This document probably was written near the end of the first century C.E. and represents a segment of early Christianity that had a kinship with mystical religious movements, both Jewish and pagan. It is more concerned about insight into the purpose of God and concord within the group than with its organization or outreach into the wider society.

Toward Organizational Order and Structure

When we move from the Gospel of John to the Letters of John, there are some continuities, but also some significant changes. The vocabulary and writing style of the letters are much the same as in John's Gospel, even though the content has shifted from reports of what Jesus said and did (in that Gospel) to guidelines for the internal life of the Christian community (in the letters). There is still an emphasis on love within the group, but now there is also a warning about hatred on the part of other members (I John 2:7–11; 4:7–12). In addition, there is a new feature: a warning about impending divine judgment and the need to prepare oneself for this fearsome event (I John 2:13–3:3). The symbolic language of the Gospel of John is evident in passages like I John 5:6–8, in which the references to Spirit, water, and blood could refer to the baptism and the death of Jesus, but they probably also are allusions to the Christian rites of baptism (when the Spirit comes upon believers) and the eucharist (when the body and blood of Jesus are symbolically shared by the community). This is in contrast to the Gospel of John, in which there is no account of the bread and wine at the Last Supper, but it also resembles John's admonition that sharing in the life of God's people requires eating the flesh and drinking the blood of the Son of Man (6:52–58). The sacraments of the church seem to have become somewhat more explicit by the time I John was written.

In II John, there is also a reminder of the commandment of love, but the question of correct doctrine is raised as well. Apparently some within the Christian movement were ready to affirm the divinity of Jesus, but considered his humanity to have been only a guise or an appearance. The author of this letter insists that one must affirm that Jesus came "in the flesh"—that is, in fully human form. To affirm a false doctrine concerning Christ is to forfeit one's place in God's people (II John 7–10). A similar development in the Johannine wing of early Christianity is apparent in III John. Someone named Diotrophes does not acknowledge the authority of the author of this letter and does not welcome his associates, but goes so far as to put them out of the church (II John 9–10). Clearly, this segment of Christianity that came to be identified with the name of John—even though all four of these writings are anonymous—has moved from the earlier atmosphere of mutuality toward a structure of authority and a definition of correct doctrine.

The later letters attributed to Paul (Colossians, Ephesians, I and II Timothy, and Titus) represent an even more dramatic shift toward defining true doctrine and creating a hierarchy of both leadership and membership within the Christian community. In the opening lines of the Letter to the Colossians (attributed to Paul, but probably written by one of his successors), the gospel is presented as "the word of truth," and its aim is to fill Christians "with all knowledge." The goal of this instruction is that Christians may be "rooted and built up and established in the faith" (Col. 2:6–7). Faith is no longer primarily trust in

Jesus as God's agent; rather, the emphasis falls on correct *belief* concerning Jesus. There is, accordingly, a solemn warning against vain and deceitful philosophy that rests on human ideas rather than on divine wisdom (2:8) and that fosters a false notion of piety based on ascetic rules rather than on concern for the common life of the church (2:16–23). To seek for wisdom that comes through the Christ, now exalted in heaven, is to experience true renewal in knowledge (3:1–10).

In the so-called Letter to the Ephesians (which, in its oldest existing copy, has a blank at 1:1 rather than an address to a specific church), there is a comparable emphasis on sound doctrine, which discloses "the manifold wisdom of God" (Eph. 3:10). The readers are warned against deceitful and faddish teachings that are opposed to the eternal truths disclosed to the church (4:13–14), which provide the ground of its unity in faith and practice (Eph. 2:11–12; 4:3–6). Similarly, the Letters of I and II Timothy (also attributed to Paul, but dating from the later first century) insist on teaching the one true doctrine and on recognizing and denouncing those who peddle false teachings within the church (I Tim. 1:3–7; 2:4; 6:3). This doctrine is preserved in the church through its system of instruction (Titus 1:9; 2:1), which must be guarded against infiltration by teachers of error. The educational program begins with children, continues through later life, and is based on a body of sacred scriptures (II Tim. 3:14–16), which presumably include not only the Jewish Bible, but also the earlier writings of the New Testament.

In all these letters in the later Pauline tradition, there are two types of ranking according to authority. The first is represented within Christian households, where wives are to be subject to husbands and slaves are to be subject to masters (Col. 3:18–4:1; Eph. 5:21–6:9; Titus 2:3–10). The fancy clothes and jewelry of the women (I Tim. 2:9) and the fact that members of the churches own slaves show that by the end of the first century the Christian movement had penetrated the higher levels of Roman society.

The second structure within which authority is to be defined and assigned is that of the church leadership. In contrast to Paul, who regards the various roles that are served in the communities—ecstatic speech, working miracles, prophecies, teachers, healers, and helpers (I Cor. 12:27–30)—as gifts of the Spirit, these letters describe the levels of authority of the officials of the church. The bishop, or overseer, is the highest officer of the local or regional church. Under him are elders and deacons (i.e., "servants"), who have a more menial role in the life of the community (I Tim. 3; 5:17; Titus 1). In addition, there may have been a special function for widows, perhaps resembling that of nuns in the later church (I Tim. 5:9:16), although their enrollment by the church could have been to qualify them for support from the Christian community. In either case, these details evidence the emergence of the church as a structural institution for which the architectural and priestly image in Eph. 2:11–12 is wholly appropriate: a holy temple in the Lord.

Social and Political Attitudes within the Church

Because Paul expected the imminent end of the present age and the establishment of God's rule over all the world, he was not concerned about political revolution. Accordingly, in the Letter to the Romans (13:1–7), he urged his readers to obey those in political power because he believed that power had been established by God and would be replaced in God's own time. The later Pauline tradition goes a step further and instructs Christians to pray for kings and other rulers because their maintenance of law and order makes it possible for the faithful to lead quiet, respectable lives (Titus 3:1). This same attitude of subjection to and honor of the Roman powers, as well as the effort to sustain a good reputation as law-abiding persons, is encouraged in I Peter 2:11–3:6). The public image of the Christians and their freedom from charges of insurrection are seen by these authors as essential goals for the group at the dawn of the second century. They are to be regarded by outsiders as morally upright, orderly people.

The author of I Peter (which is also a later, pseudonymous document) expects the outbreak of divine judgment and warns the Christians of trials and suffering—and even martyrdom—that they may soon be called on to undergo before the final revelation of the triumphant Christ occurs and the rule of God is established on earth (I Pet. 4:12–19). Yet they are to remain law abiding until the end. Another Christian writing from about this same time (around 100 C.E.), the Revelation of John, also expects the imminence of God's judgment, but it portrays the Roman empire as the agency of Satan and eagerly awaits its destruction by God's power. There is no hint of political insurrection in Revelation, but in an elaborate series of apocalyptic visions, John depicts the events that will lead to the final cataclysm and thus will bring human empires to an end. The faithful are to be prepared to endure suffering, confident that God will vindicate them and establish His rule over the universe.

Toward a Cultural Synthesis with the Roman World

Two of the New Testament writings at the opening of the second century display the desire of some early Christians to state their convictions in the intellectual style of the Roman world. The Letter of James shows the influence of Cynic and Stoic philosophy, and the Letter to the Hebrews employs concepts and perspectives derived from the Platonic tradition. The precedent is set for the policy of Christian thinkers to employ the ideas and the modes of expression of Greek and Roman philosophy in their interpretation of the Christian faith, a policy that was operative throughout the Roman and Byzantine periods, during the Middle Ages, and from the Enlightenment to the present.

The author of the Letter of James identifies himself by the name in Greek, ’Ιάκοβος, which is the English equivalent of Jacob. It was also the name of one of Jesus' first disciples and of his brother, who became the leader of the church in Jerusalem after Jesus' death.[3] The sophisticated language of this letter makes it unlikely that it was written by a Galilean villager, however. The author knew well the style of communication developed by the Cynic philosophers, who posed questions and then provided answers in such a way as to challenge the reader to rethink standard positions or easy assumptions. The issues with which James is dealing are not those of Paul and the Gospel writers: ritual purity, circumcision, observance of the Sabbath, the cosmic struggle between God and the powers of evil, and the relationship between Judaism and the new covenant people. Instead, he addresses the church as "the twelve tribes" (1:1), or simply as "Israel" (5:13), and builds on quotations

---

[3]Gal 1:18–19; Acts 15:12–21.

from the Jewish scriptures to make his point about how essential proper moral performance is. Even when he refers to the commandment to love one's neighbor, he derives it from the Old Testament, with no mention of Jesus' use of the precept (2:8).

For the Letter of James, the primary role of the leader of the church is teacher, and his aim is to develop wisdom (3:1–7). The good works produced by wisdom include the standard Stoic virtues of steadfastness and endurance (1:2–4). In Stoic sources, such as the third-century B.C.E. Hymn of Cleanthes and the writings of Seneca (4 B.C.E–46 C.E.), the basic principles are (1) the universal divine plan for the world, (2) human kinship with the gods through reason (*logos*), and (3) happiness attained by living in accord with the natural law inherent in the universe. This point of view is evident in James's call to his readers to be serious of purpose, to recognize the beneficence of God, and to live in accord with the perfect law (1:5–25). Questions of leadership roles or rank within the community are never discussed. Life in accord with wisdom will give stability and safety from political involvement and economic difficulties.

The so-called Letter to the Hebrews, an anonymous writing, is an intellectual discourse based on the Old Testament, especially on two themes: What is God's purpose for his people? and How can Israel have access to the presence of God? The answers are given in terms of a philosophical position similar to the Platonism adopted by Philo of Alexandria in the early first century C.E. The Platonic view of reality was that the heavens contained an eternal sphere in which a master image or an eternal model exists for every object, concept, and relationship found in the earthly sphere. The earthly counterparts are time bound, transitory, and multiple copies. The history of Israel, including the accounts of her leaders and the description of her as sanctuary, is the disclosure of the time-bound copies of God's purpose for his people. Jesus, who has now entered heaven, is the revelation of these eternal realities. His once-for-all sacrifice is a world removed from the repeated rites in the Jerusalem temple (8:1–13), which were only a shadow of what God planned for His people (10:1–22). That is the goal set for them (12:22–24), although in the interim before that transport to the heavenly reality takes place, the members' showing mutual love already manifests the qualities of the heavenly ideal. There are no ecclesiastical titles in the writing and only one possible reference to a community rite: the eucharist (13:9). This imaginative work was a forerunner of the efforts of the theologians of the church to synthesize insights from the biblical and Christian traditions with those of the wider intellectual world.

The Move in the Second Century toward Structural Unity and Conceptual Uniformity

At least three major factors impelled the leaders of Christianity in the early second century to clarify its identity and its goals for itself and for the Roman society it was penetrating:

1. The distinction between Christianity and Judaism, with which Christianity shared so many views and resources.
2. Christianity's attitude toward the Roman state, since much of the standard Christian terminology—e.g., "king," "kingdom," "universal rule"—had political implications.

3. The diversity of perceptions of Christian faith that had emerged in various parts of the empire; it was felt necessary to establish a central core of beliefs and practices.

With the reconstitution of the Jewish state by the Romans following their takeover of the land in 63 B.C.E., the leaders (high priests, kings, governors) were designated on the basis of their support for Roman policy. The Romans responded by excusing Jews from certain obligations, such as offering divine honors to the emperor, and granted them a degree of autonomy over their territories in Palestine. The two Jewish revolts against Rome—in 66–70 C.E. and 130–135 C.E.—had failed, and by the mid-second century C.E., dominant among the Jewish people were apolitical religious leaders who fostered piety rather than fomenting revolution. As long as the Christians were considered to be a group within Judaism—which was possible because they shared the same scriptures and many historic and conceptual traditions—the Roman authorities were only occasionally active in repressing the Christians. Nero had had some Christian leaders killed during the latter part of his reign (54–68 C.E.), and there may have been some persecution of Christians under Domitian (81–96). By the later years of Trajan's reign (98–117), however, since the Christians had spread widely throughout the empire and were defining themselves as different from Judaism, the Romans established the policy that Christians must publicly acknowledge the divinity of the emperor or be executed. The preserved correspondence between Trajan and Pliny, governor of provinces in northeast Asia Minor, makes this relationship explicit: Trajan and his successors would use the practice of divine honors as a way of symbolizing and enforcing loyalty.

The Christians' break with Judaism after 70 C.E. required them to emphasize the beliefs that differentiated them from the Judaic ritual definition of community and that offered instead a potential for including people in the new covenant from any ethnic or cultural background. The fact that the earlier expectation of Christians that Jesus would soon return in triumph did not take place forced them to formulate new goals for the movement and to unify organizational structures. Since they all claimed the Jesus tradition as the ground of their existence as a people of God, it had to be interpreted in ways that would foster a sense of unity. And in the face of mounting official and intellectual opposition, they had to be able to formulate their ethical norms and theological convictions in a coherent and effective way.

The body of writings that emerged from this transition period of Christianity has come to be called the Apostolic Fathers.[4] In the period from about 100 to the middle of the second century C.E., the leaders were developing intellectual and organizational structures for Christianity—and doing so with a claim of continuity that reached back through the apostles to Jesus. These preserved works include the First and Second Letters of Clement; letters of Ignatius (bishop of Antioch) to several Greek and Roman churches; a letter of Polycarp (bishop of Smyrna in Asia Minor); an allegorical treatise, the Shepherd of Hermas; the Letter of Barnabas (whose name is linked with Paul—see, for example, Gal 2:1–9; Acts 11:22–30); and the story of the Martyrdom of Polycarp. In the nineteenth century, a writing known as Didache (the Teaching of the Apostles) was found that showed close kin-

---

[4]*Apostolic Fathers,* translated by K. Lake, in the Loeb Classical Library (Cambridge, MA: Harvard University Press, 1913; repr. 1950); also in *The Apostolic Fathers,* ed. Jack Sparks (Nashville, TN: T. Nelson, 1978).

ship with the writing of the Apostolic Fathers; it seems to have used a source—the Two Ways (to life and to death)—that also lies behind the Letter of Barnabas.

Five themes run through these documents: (1) the prospect of martyrdom, (2) obedience to the church leaders, (3) differentiating Judaism from Christianity, (4) a pattern of behavior for Christians, and (5) true Christian doctrine. All these motifs are set forth along with the issues of confrontation with Rome and the expectation of the end of the present age. The Martyrdom of Polycarp obviously emphasizes the first theme. The subject of martyrdom also appears in the Letter of Polycarp, in II Clement, and in Ignatius's Letter to the Romans, in whose midst he was to be martyred under Trajan. The earliest full account of a martyrdom is the Martyrdom of Polycarp, which is a communication from a church in Smyrna (in Asia Minor) to another Christian community in Philomelium. The document (written about 155 C.E.) provides a vivid description of the ghastly tortures that Christians experienced if they refused to renounce their faith in Christ. Some were beaten until their veins and arteries were exposed. The authorities told them that if they publicly denounced Christ and acknowledged Caesar as Lord they could go free. Polycarp, a bishop, had a vision that led him to expect death by burning at the hands of the Roman authorities. When caught by them, he refused to recant his faith and offered to instruct them in the Christian way. When preparations were made for putting him to death by fire, he asked that he not be fastened, promising to remain in the fire until his death. The account says that he was filled with courage and joy, and as the burning began, he uttered public praise to God for the knowledge he had received through Christ and for the opportunity to present himself as a living sacrifice to God. After his peaceful death in the midst of such horror, his followers were permitted to collect his bones to remember and honor his faithful witness.

As bishops, both Ignatius and Polycarp emphasized obedience to the two kinds of church leaders: the bishops (who are appointed by God) and the presbytery (the group of elders who make corporate decisions for the church). Didache mentions the role of apostles and prophets in the churches, in addition to that of the bishops and deacons (those who assume more workaday tasks in the churches). The importance of differentiating Christian faith and practice from those of the Jews is stressed by Ignatius in his letters to the Magnesians and the Philadelphians. The Letter of Barnabas and the Shepherd of Hermas, however, solve the problem of this interreligious relationship by interpreting the Jewish scriptures allegorically, on the assumption that they foreshadow the fuller disclosure of God's purpose through Jesus.

The writings that incorporate the Two Ways (which may go back to the later first century C.E.) reflect the needs and procedures of the Christian communities. The Way of Life emphasizes love of God and neighbor, and offers advice to those who are joining the churches as to how they are to live and to accept responsibilities within the Christian community. Significantly, these moral instructions also show the strong influence of Stoic ethics. The effort to define and maintain true doctrine is evident in the Letter of Polycarp, but especially in the letters of Ignatius, even though the details are not spelled out. Although most of the injunctions are to affirm the truth and reject heresy, one particular theme is called *docetism*, which is the denial of the full humanity of Jesus by those who assert that he merely *seemed*[5] to take on human form. Ignatius directly denounces this view in

---

[5]The Greek word for "seem" is *doceo*.

his letter to the Smyrnaeans. It remained for the theological leaders of the church in the later first and subsequent centuries to make these issues more precise. Compounding the pressures from these matters were the growing confrontation between the church and the empire, the spontaneous movements within the church that attracted attention and followers while splitting the communities, and the small, but significant, attack on the credibility of the Christian claims by pagan intellectuals. It is to these challenges and the Christian responses that we next turn.

Themes of Apostolic Fathers

1) Prospect of Martyrdom.
2) Obedience to the church leaders
3) Differentiating Judaism from Christianity.
4) Pattern of behavior for Christians.
5) True Christian Doctrine.

(Martyrdom)

Chapter 5

Challenges to Christianity from Roman Culture

The Diversity and Vitality of Religious Options in the Empire

encountered competition.

As Christianity began its spread across the Mediterranean world, it was moving into areas of competition, rather than filling a religious vacuum in an irreligious world. The religious movements of the early empire included a wide range of options, from ecstatic cults to staid philosophical groups wrestling with religious issues, and from the imperial cult offering the emperors divine honors to small and large gatherings of devotees of various deities. These myriad gatherings met for the announced purpose of worshiping a deity or deities, but, in the process, provided a community in which participants could find a meaning for life, mutual support, and the joys of social interchange. Both church and synagogue, which were launched along planned, organized lines in the second and subsequent centuries, were examples of this social phenomenon as well as beneficiaries of the widespread yearning for these forms of group identity.

The Imperial Cult

With the official bestowing of divinity on the emperor Julius Caesar after his death, there was a growing disposition to treat the emperors as manifestations of the divine, especially in the eastern Mediterranean, where the tradition of the divinity of kings reached back into earliest antiquity. Although Nero (54–68) seems to have made some effort to promote his own status as divine, it was not until Domitian (81–96) that an emperor announced that he

58

was to be addressed as *Dominus et Deus* ("Lord and God"). That policy continued to develop until the time of Diocletian (284–305), when it reached a climax: The imagery of the worship of the sun was officially linked with honoring the emperor. In this role, the ruler of the empire became the symbol of truth and righteousness, and his function was seen to be that of bringing universal light to his subjects. Rather than merely publicizing such a policy, the emperors built grand structures in Rome and elsewhere throughout the empire to symbolize this universal authority and to provide the setting for solemn assemblies of the peoples of the Roman realms to link the power of the state with the celestial gods.

In keeping with these strategies, Trajan (98–117), in response to an inquiry from Pliny, the Roman governor of Bithynia and Pontus (provinces in northeastern Asia Minor), confirmed a policy for dealing with Christian groups, as noted in Chapter 2 (p. 23). These groups were springing up or thriving throughout the provinces in numbers large enough to diminish participation in the prescribed ceremonies and sacrifices through which subjects of Rome were to give public expression to their devotion to the emperor and gratitude to the traditional Roman gods for the peace and prosperity they enjoyed. In one of the larger cities of the area, Nicomedia, Trajan had constructed a great Temple of Rome and Augustus. Yet throughout the provinces, those who prepared the appropriate animal sacrifices were running out of customers. What was to be done? Were the Christians, with their seeming disregard or even hostility toward Roman power and its divine sources, to be sought out, apprehended, and executed?

Pliny's inquiry and Trajan's reply have both been preserved.[1] The governor had found nothing evil or subversive about the practices, worship, or food of the Christians, or even that they were engaged in illegal political activities. The crucial test came when members of the group refused to repeat an invocation to the Roman gods, to offer "adoration, with wine and frankincense" to the image of the emperor, and to curse Christ. Those who refused to perform these religious acts were executed. Trajan confirmed Pliny's policy, adding that the Christians were not to be sought out or seized without proper evidence, but when they were exposed and persisted in what Pliny called "a depraved and excessive superstition," they were to be put to death. The link between religious performance and loyalty to the state was firm. Christians, by identifying themselves with another community—the people of the new covenant—and by refusing to honor either the gods who had blessed the Roman state or the agent they had designated to preside over it, demonstrated that they were its mortal enemies. The seriousness with which the consequences of this principle were applied by subsequent emperors varied widely, but it culminated in fierce conflict. (See Chapter 8.)

Popular Associations and Cults

As noted earlier, in the ethnically, geographically, socially, and culturally complex world of the Roman empire, people with similar interests banded together in voluntary associations to preserve a sense of identity. They met in homes, taverns, or club rooms. Drawn mostly from the lower classes (which constituted the vast majority of the population of the empire), they would designate some deity or deities as their patrons and honor these gods in

---

[1] "Pliny's Correspondence with Trajan," in *Pliny* (Section 96–97), translated by W. M. L. Hutchison; Loeb Classical Library (Cambridge, MA: Harvard University Press, 1952).

formal ways as their protectors and helpers. The rallying point might be a common area of origin or occupation (like the guilds of a later era). Borrowing the term that was used for the lounging areas in the public baths, their meeting places were called *scholae*. There, the members shared their common concerns and ate common meals.

Scholae

Other social groupings that flourished in the second century were those devoted explicitly to honoring a deity. One of these was Asklepios, the god of healing. He was venerated chiefly at Epidauros in Greece and at Pergamum in Asia Minor. At a center in honor of this god on the Greek island of Cos, human anatomy was studied and training was offered for those interested in the practice of medicine. At the shrines of Asklepios, however, the sick and the wealthy took up residence for extended stays during which they would visit the shrine, hoping for evidence of the god's presence and of his healing powers. Inscriptions and texts tell of the healings said to have been performed by Asklepios at Epidauros, including recoveries from blindness, broken limbs, extended pregnancies, leeches, dropsy, tuberculosis, and disfigurement from various kinds of physical attack.

Reports of those who stayed at these shrines are similar to what may be found at modern spas: persons spending long periods there were at least as much interested in the social connections they made and in devoting time for self-examination as in recovering their physical health. For example, in the middle of the second century C.E., Aelius Aristides, who had inherited great wealth and had made an enviable reputation as a public orator in Athens and Rome, became ill and went to Pergamum, presumably in search of health. But he lingered long at the Asklepion in Pergamum and recorded his thoughts, observations, and experiences of the divine in that situation. What he found was not so much restoration of the body as renewal of the soul: great happiness in his newfound sense of the god's presence with and interest in him, and new meaning and purpose in life. Diodorus Siculus wrote of Isis in the first century B.C.E., "For standing above the sick in their sleep she gives aid for their diseases and works remarkable cures upon such as submit themselves to her; and many who have been despaired of by their physicians because of the difficult nature of their malady are restored to health by her, while numbers who have altogether lost the use of their eyes or some other part of the body, whenever they turn to help to this goddess are restored to their previous condition."[2] By the middle of the second century, however, her role as healer had been matched by the experience of her through mystical self-disclosure reported by her devotees.

In Lucius Apuleius's *Metamorphoses*, the author describes how, following years of wandering about the world and the catastrophe of having been changed by magic into an ass, he recovered both his true humanity and a sense of purpose in the world through an appearance to him of Isis in one of her temples. He addresses her directly as follows:

> O holy and blessed dame, the perpetual comfort of human kind, who by thy bounty and grace nourishes all the world, and bears a great affection to the adversities of the miserable as a loving mother. You take no rest, night or day, neither are you idle at any time in giving benefits and succouring all humans on land as on the sea; you are the one who puts away all storms and dangers from human lives by stretching forth your right hand, by which also you unweave even the inextricable and tangled web of fate, and appease the great storms of fortune, and keep back the harmful course of the stars; you make the earth turn; you give light to the sun, you govern

---

[2] In Diodorus Siculus, *Library of History*, 1.25.3. Translated by R. M. Geer, Loeb Classical Library (Cambridge, MA: Harvard University Press, 1944).

the world. You tread down the power of hell. By means of you the stars give answer, the seasons return, the elements serve; at your commandment the winds blow, the clouds nourish the earth, the seeds prosper, and the fruits grow. Birds of the air, beasts of the hills, serpents in their lairs, and fish of the sea tremble before your majesty. But my spirit is not able to give you adequate praise; my possessions are unable to provide adequate sacrifices; my voice lacks the power to utter what I think of your majesty—no, not even if I had a thousand mouths and as many tongues and could continue forever. Even so, as a good religious person, I shall do what I can: I shall always keep your divine appearance in my remembrance, and within my heart I shall enclose your most holy divinity.[3]

The mixture of personal adoration, gratitude for renewal of life, and sense of the inner presence are powerfully conveyed in this hymn to Isis. The conclusion of the story tells how Apuleius became a priest in her temple, thus locating the core of his life in the community of her followers.

Obviously, as individuals and in groups, many persons were finding meaning and a shared, enriched existence through their dedication to a beneficent deity. This growing and pervasive desire to attune one's life to the will and purpose of the gods is evident from the simplest to the highest levels of Roman society in the second and subsequent centuries. Even the emperors are reported as consulting astrologers when important matters of state were to be decided. Among the upper classes, there was widespread belief not only in the miracle-working gods and goddesses, but also in magic. To gain certain benefits, as well as to protect oneself from the attacks of personal enemies, magical rites were performed and magical formulas recited as a way of guaranteeing the desired results for one's own benefit or to the detriment of one's foes. Among documents of this period found in Egypt (known to scholars as the Greek Magical Papyri) is the following, which shows how invoking the name of a god guarantees the results desired by the one making the request:

By your name, which I have in my soul and which I invoke, there shall come to me in every way good things, good upon good, thoroughly, unconditionally you shall grant me health, salvation, welfare, glory, victory, strength, contentment. Cast a veil on the eyes of all who oppose me, male and female, and give me grace in all my activities.[4]

This is not merely a request to the god, but a demand based on the use of the divine name. Magicians claimed to know the right names and formulas that would guarantee the desired results.

Literary figures of the time were reviving and offering fresh, often symbolic, interpretations of the traditional myths and legends of the Greek and Roman deities. For example, Plutarch (46–120 C.E.) prepared an elaborate edition of the myths of Osiris and Isis that was intended to provide information and guidelines for contemporaneous worshippers of those gods, rather than to be an archive of a dead past. The question was not historical—What were the ancient gods like?—but contemporary: What can these gods do for me now? Groups of seekers were reaching out for direct experience of the gods as a way of orienting and fulfilling their own lives.

---

[3] Lucius Apuleius, *Metamorphoses* 11.25. Translated W. Adlington, Loeb Classical Library (Cambridge, MA: Harvard University Press, 1915).

[4] Translated from the Greek Magical Papyri by H. C. Kee, in *Medicine, Miracle, and Magic in New Testament Times* (New York: Cambridge University Press, 1988), p. 108.

Popular Philosophical Movements

At the highest intellectual levels in the second century, there was a surge of interest in philosophy that took as its aim the recovery and fresh appropriation of older traditions. Much of the effort assumed the form of a rebirth of the philosophical traditions of ancient Attica, of which Athens was the political and intellectual center. Assigning a name derived from *sophos*, the Greek word for "wisdom," scholars designate this period of cultural development as the Second Sophistic. Dio Chrysostom (45–115 C.E.), for example, sought to replace what he regarded as the cheap commonplaces of ideas, practices, and modes of communication of his day by a recovery of Attic culture. Similarly, Herodes Atticus (101–178 C.E.), an extremely wealthy Athenian philosopher, worked hard at reviving the heritage of Greece in philosophy, literature, and, above all, rhetoric, the art of speech that could engage and inform crowds of listeners. Even though Lucian of Samosata (120–200? C.E.) developed a delightful and effective style of comic dialogue by which he scoffed at wealth and power, belittling the gods and caricaturing the ancient myths and the great events of the past, the very fact that he chose these areas as his battleground shows how important such factors were in the culture of that era. His own goal was to enable his readers to rise above human fears and follies; his tactic was to expose what he regarded as pretentions and uncertainties in the shifting religious and philosophical trends of his time.

Seriously developed philosophical movements of this period sought to reclaim Platonic, Aristotelian, Pythagorean, and Stoic concepts and perspectives. The original Platonic preoccupation with metaphysical questions, such as how ultimate reality can be discerned behind and beyond the varied, changing, decaying physical world, was overshadowed by ethical and human issues. The Stoic principle of natural law as the primal force pervading the universe and operating within the human conscience (that is, there was a shared awareness of this universal law) was combined with the Aristotelian interest in analyzing all reality by classifying it into appropriate intellectual categories. The result was a new synthetic philosophy focused on the natural world and the place of humanity within it. The Stoics of the period were moving beyond their earlier major interest in describing the natural world and then depicting humanity's place within it to consider directly personal religious longing and experience of the gods. This shift is evident in the historical examples of individual and social moral responsibility set out by Seneca (4 B.C.E.–65 C.E.?), who emphasized the pervasive presence of God in the natural realm, and in personal experience. In his *Moral Epistles* (41.1) Seneca wrote, "God is near you, he is with you, he is in you."

The philosophy of Pythagoras (582–507? B.C.E.), with its major emphasis on the mathematical structures of the physical world, was also revived in the second century, but the emphasis shifted overwhelmingly from the structures of nature to Pythagoras's discussion of the human soul, which, he had taught, was released from the body at death to take up residence in another body, human or animal. The new version of this theory regarded the body as the prison of the soul and saw philosophy as the means of purifying the soul so that it could ascend ultimately to the celestial realms. A similar view was developed by Plutarch (46–120 C.E.), who taught that there were *daimones*, which were beings intermediate between the gods and humans, through whom the gods acted in human affairs, communicating through visions and oracles. At death, the discerning human may take up a new existence as a *daimon* and eventually ascend to the realm of the gods.

In the same period, many persons shared these philosophical ideas, but some were more skeptical about the possibilities for human happiness. The aim of the great Stoic philosopher, Zeno (336–264 B.C.E.), to seek the good was replaced by the philosophy of Epictetus (50–120? C.E.), who wanted simply to avoid everything in life that is not subject to our control, but to seek to achieve our own moral aims. Thus, one should avoid anger, desires, sorrow, and anxiety. To attain this style of life, Epictetus recommended that philosophers gain true freedom by divesting themselves of family, wealth, and permanent residences and instead wander about the earth, challenging the almost universally accepted values. Bearded and dressed in ragged clothing, these itinerant critics of society would live off the generosity of those who received and cared for them. Epictetus characterized himself in this way: "Look at me! I am without house or city, property or slave. I sleep on the ground. I have no wife, no children, no official residence, but only earth and sky and my bit of a cloak. Am I not without distress or fear? Am I not free?"[5]

At the other end of the socioeconomic scale, the philosopher-emperor Marcus Aurelius (161–180 C.E.), while affirming the essential goodness of Providence, was painfully aware of human sin and widespread wickedness in the world. He longed for a life of freedom, but expected to find it only beyond death. Yet so deep was his despair of human existence, that he was ready to accept extinction if that was what lay beyond life as he experienced it in all its frustrations and cruelty. The issues of the meaning of life, of understanding human evil and natural disaster, and of ultimate human destiny were the dominant questions in the popular consciousness, from simple handworkers to the head of the empire.

Direct Challenges to Christianity

Did Christianity give adequate responses to these profound and universal problems that dominated the popular consciousness in the second century? Answers ranging from a flat dismissal of Christianity to qualified criticisms of it were offered by central thinkers in the Roman world of this period. Included among the works of Lucian of Samosata whose critique of his contemporaries we noted earlier, was a story called "The Death of Peregrinus." Peregrinus is depicted as a wanderer in both the literal and the ideological sense. As he roamed the eastern Mediterranean world, he tried out a series of religions and philosophies, one of which was Christianity, which he encountered in its birthplace, Palestine. He met some Christians there and "picked up their queer creed" (Sec. 11–16). He succeeded in convincing them of his superior qualifications as a member of their group, with the result that he became a prophet in their movement, then an elder, and finally a ruler of one of their meetings. He not only expounded the Christian writings, but wrote some of his own. For their part, the Christians accepted his guidelines and made him leader of their sect. Lucian notes in passing that the Christians down to his own time continued to worship the man who had introduced their peculiar rites and ended by being crucified. Peregrinus was imprisoned by the local political authorities (the Roman rulers of the land) and was cared for in prison by the Christians, who, while seeking to have him released, visited

---

[5] *Arrian's Discourses of Epictetus* (4.8.31), tr. W. Oldfather, Loeb Classical Library (Cambridge, MA: Harvard University Press, 1927).

him regularly, took him food, and even bribed the jailers to be allowed to stay in the cell with him. Others, including some widows and orphans, were imprisoned because of their sympathy for him. Christian delegations were sent in support of Peregrinus from as far away as the cities of Asia Minor. Lucian remarks, "The activity of these people in dealing with any matter that affects their community is something extraordinary: they spare neither trouble nor expense." It is because "these misguided creatures" believe that they are forever immortal that they scorn death and manifest the voluntary devotion that is so common among them. "From the moment of conversion to this religion, they deny the gods of Greece, worship the crucified sage [Jesus Christ], and live according to his laws. They despise all worldly goods, regarding what each possesses as the property of the whole community."[6] Some of them adopted the garb of the philosophers: long hair, a shabby cloak, and a handbag and staff. Their support for Peregrinus continued until he discredited himself among them, perhaps by eating some kind of forbidden food. Lucian's scornful portrayal of the gullibility and strange values of the Christians builds on his low estimate of their beliefs, but it also betrays a kind of unconscious admiration of them for their devotion and courage.

A more reasoned criticism of the Christians is to be found in the extensive writings of Galen (129–199), a major figure in the development of ancient medical tradition. In his treatise *On Medical Experience*, he rejected the belief in creation shared by Jews and Christians: If God waited in time to create the world, He was either holding back from the establishment of the greatest good, and therefore morally irresponsible, or unable to accomplish the creation, and therefore limited in power. Galen deplored the degeneration of the philosophical schools of his day into warring factions that adopted fixed, exclusivist positions, rather than engaging freely in the common search for truth. Among the worst offenders on this score were the schools of Moses and Jesus—Judaism and Christianity, respectively. Galen felt that his fellow physicians who made decisions on the basis of prior theory rather than being open to trial-and-error methods of experimentation were like these Jewish and Christian dogmatists. Since only a small number of human beings had the capacity to develop or follow logically consistent arguments, most people turned (as did the Jews and Christians) from rationality to myths, parables, and miracles to support their claims to truth. Rhetoric and poetry could lead people only to conviction, not to truth. Ironically, Galen acknowledged that the Christians, in spite of the major flaws in their logical methods, did attain as high a level of morality as the philosophers, but they could not be considered true philosophers because of their irrational base and procedures. As he stated it:

> [The Christians'] contempt of death and of its sequel is patent to us every day, and likewise their restraint in cohabitation. For they include not only men but also women who refrain from cohabiting all through their lives; and they also number individuals who in self-discipline and self-control in matters of food and drink and in their keen pursuit of justice have attained a pitch not inferior to that of genuine philosophers.[7]

---

[6]*Lucian*, in Loeb Classical Library, Vol. 5, "Passing of Peregrinus," 11–16 (Cambridge, MA: Harvard University Press, 1936; repr. 1962).

[7]Quoted from the translation of an Arabic version of one of Galen's treatises, in Richard Walzer, *Galen on Jews and Christians* (Oxford: Oxford University Press, 1949), p. 65.

Their assumptions were unreasonable, he said, and their methods logically deplorable, but Christians did exhibit one of the highest of human virtues in the Greek philosophical tradition: *sophrosune*, which means "moderation, rationality, or self-control."

Severely critical of the Christians was Celsus, a Roman philosopher of the later second century whose work is known only through the extended quotations preserved in the rebuttal of him by the great Christian scholar and biblical interpreter, Origen of Alexandria (185–254 C.E.) in his huge work, *Contra Celsum* ["Against Celsus"].[8] Celsus's writing *The True Doctrine* is mentioned by Eusebius in his *Ecclesiastical History* (6.36.2)[9] as having evoked the detailed response of Origen a half century later. The elaborate nature of Celsus's attack on Christianity shows that the movement was sufficiently broad and visible—and appealing—to come to the attention of intellectuals. It is clear that Celsus knew the New Testament writings, as well as the claims that were being made in the second century by various competing Christian groups, such as the Gnostics and the followers of Marcion. His tactic was that of a scornful critic, alternating between exposing the follies of his opponents and offering his own alternative points of view. Five themes run throughout his work:

1. The Christians relied on miracle, which is to be equated with magic. The miracles Jesus is reported to have performed, including the feeding of the multitudes, are evidence that he practiced sorcery. Jesus made this accusation against his opponents, but it is applicable to him as well. He invented the story of his virgin birth and went to Egypt to learn magic. Celsus believed that if miracles of healing occurred anywhere, it was at the shrines of Asklepios, which were open to all who sought to have their needs met. These powers were not limited to Jesus, in whose behalf his followers made the preposterous claim of the resurrection of the body—his and ultimately theirs. There was abundant public testimony, on the other hand, to the healing powers of the Greek god Asklepios.

2. Christianity was a low-class movement. From the outset, Jesus appealed to the ignorant and the gullible among his contemporaries, having chosen ten or eleven infamous men of wholly undistinguished background to form the inner circle of his followers. Christianity was primarily interested in sinners, rather than in the educated or the intelligent strata of society. It failed to rely on cumulative human wisdom, treating it rather with scorn. Healing and prophecy, with which the Christians were obsessed, were trivial factors in human existence, compared with the life of the mind, which Christians ignored or demeaned. As for the boastful attitude Christians took toward Jesus and the martyrs of the early church, those who suffered and died in the cause of philosophical truth were far more noble and admirable. In this connection, Celsus tells the story of the Epicurean philosopher, Epictetus, who was being tortured by those opposed to his philosophical views. When they twisted his leg, "he smiled gently and said, 'You are breaking it.' And when [his tormentor] had broken it, he said, 'Did I not tell you you were breaking it?'"[10] For Celsus, this was true wisdom and humanity.

---

[8] *Origen: Contra Celsum;* translated, with introduction and notes, by Henry Chadwick (Cambridge: Cambridge University Press, 1965). This Celsus, whose orientation was strongly Platonic, is not the same as the Epicurean philosopher Celsus mentioned by Lucian.

[9] Eusebius, *Ecclesiastical History*, 2 vols., Loeb Classical Library (Cambridge, MA: Harvard University Press, 1943).

[10] Celsus, *Contra Celsum* 7.54.

3. Jesus could not have been divine. Celsus raised a series of questions that he was convinced completely discredited the Christian claim that Jesus was God in human form. If Jesus had really been God, he should not have had to flee to Egypt to escape his attackers or have allowed himself to be put to death. Indeed, if he was God, why did he need someone to open the tomb to let him out? When he arose from the dead, as his followers claimed, why did he show himself only to them and not to those in power who had conspired to put him to death? The prophecies it is said that he fulfilled are so general as to be applicable to a number of other human beings. In fact, Celsus insisted, the contradictory features of the Gospel showed that Jesus' followers were trying to cover up the disparities between what they claimed for him and his actual competence. He was simply powerless before the authorities of his day. Accepting a charge made by Jewish critics of Christianity in the second century, Celsus asserted that Jesus was really not the Son of God, but the illegitimate offspring of a Roman soldier, Pantheros. The Christians unwittingly betrayed the emptiness of their claim about Jesus' divinity in that they worshiped a corpse.

4. The Jewish–Christian view of God is preposterous. If the God of the Jews and Christians created the world, and did so in the realm of time, why did He wait so long to reveal himself? The result was that many human beings never had an opportunity to know Him. And why, when He chose to reveal Himself through Jesus, did He do so in such a limited sphere, thereby excluding from participation the majority of the human race? Why did the Jews and Christians claim that God created the universe for the benefit of human beings, rather than recognizing the interdependence that characterizes every feature of the cosmic order? Why did this God create the serpent as the embodiment of evil and turn it loose on humanity if He was going to hold men and women responsible for their misdeeds? Celsus was convinced that the basic difficulties with the Jewish–Christian view of God were evident in the fact that Jews and Christians differed from each other and even among their own kind as to how the world was created and who was responsible for it. Both Jews and Christians adopted the subterfuge of covering up the difficulties in their view of God by resorting to allegorical interpretation of their scriptures, which saved them from affirming the obvious, but embarrassing meaning of the texts.

5. Celsus's alternative to the Jewish–Christian viewpoint was that there is one god behind the many names. Celsus affirms that there is, and always has been, a single god accessible to humanity through reason. The name assigned to this deity is inconsequential because it derives from local factors, rather than from the cosmic source of reality. Plato's view of the world as consisting of an eternal sphere of unchanging being, of which the material universe is an imperfect and ever-changing copy, was to be affirmed and taken as the basis for understanding god, who is known through the mind, rather than the body of flesh, as assumed in the foolish Christian claim about God being incarnate in Jesus. There were, Celsus acknowledged, some admirable moral truths affirmed by the Jews and Christians, such as love of one's neighbor. But these ethical insights were already present in the writings of the Greek philosophers, just as there were oracles and prophecies at work in other religions as well. The Christians were so foolish as to employ the human, fleshly Jesus as their basis for understanding God and his purpose for the cosmos. What Celsus longed to see was for all human beings to acknowledge the one god behind and beyond the language, images, and modes of worship by which various segments of the human race approached and worshiped him. All must recognize that all were serving the one ultimate deity of the universe.

In setting out these stinging criticisms of Judaism and Christianity, Celsus made two charges that were especially important within the wider Roman culture of that time. The first was that the Christians were seditious, in that they separated themselves out from the rest of the human race, instead of affirming and working toward the basic unity of all humanity. The second accusation was that the Christians, by their refusal to acknowledge and honor the traditional gods of Greece and Rome, were raising the possibility of a divine retaliation that could work harm on the human race as a whole and on the Roman empire in particular. The security and the prosperity of the empire and its people were linked with the popular celebrations and expressions of gratitude to the god behind the gods, in which the Christians refused to participate even under threat of execution.

The most powerful and carefully reasoned ancient attack on Christianity came in the later third century through Porphyry, a pupil of Plotinus and a leading figure in the Neoplatonic philosophical movement during that period. A prolific writer, he produced a work in fifteen volumes, *Against the Christians.* Although this work was later officially destroyed when, in the fourth century, Christianity became the dominant religion in the empire under Constantine, quotations from it have survived in Eusebius's *Ecclesiastical History* and in other Christian writings in subsequent centuries. Attacking what he regarded as an anti-intellectual streak in Christianity, Porphyry observed that what Moses is reported to have said includes riddles, which are treated by Jews and Christians as divine oracles, full of hidden mysteries. He considered this way of treating the puzzling passages from the Bible as a trick to avoid the intellectual difficulties involved: "[They] bewitch the mental judgment by their own pretentious obscurity." Also, he said, they treat the prophecy of Daniel as a document from the sixth-century exile of Israel in Babylon, whereas it is actually from the Hellenistic period and was written during the reign of Antiochus Epiphanes, who was pagan ruler of Syria and Palestine in the early second century B.C.E. Modern scholarship would agree with Porphyry's shrewd perception about the date of, and circumstances surrounding, the writing of the book of Daniel, but his charge was intended to display the gullibility and anti-intellectual qualities of Jews and Christians who perceived it as originating in the earlier period.

Porphyry acknowledged the brilliance of Origen of Alexandria, probably the leading scholarly figure of the first four centuries of the church, but sought to expose him as what today would be called a charlatan and a schizophrenic. Although Porphyry admitted Origen's enormous range of linguistic competence and breadth of learning in history, science, and philosophy, as well as his repute as a teacher among pagans and Christians alike, he claimed that, although Origen was intellectual in the Greek tradition, he lived a Christian way of life that was contrary to Greek learning as well as Roman law.

If Jesus truly possessed all the learning and insight that the Christians claimed for him, Porphyry asked, why did he not make a case for himself before Pilate? Porphyry found detestable the notion that a divine being took up residence in the womb of Mary, "that it became an embryo, and after birth was wrapped in rags, soiled with blood and bile, and even worse." His estimate of Christianity as a whole was forcefully expressed in a passage quoted by Augustine. A man whose wife had turned from traditional pagan religion to

Christianity sought counsel from the oracle of Apollo as to how he might recover her from her present commitment to Christianity, to which Apollo replied:

> You may perchance more easily write in lasting letters on water, or spread wings and fly like a bird through the air, than recall to her senses an impious wife who has once polluted herself [through conversion to Christianity]. Let her continue as long as she pleases, persisting in her empty delusions, and lamenting in song one who, as a god, died for delusions, who was condemned justly by judges whose verdict was just, and executed by the worst death in iron shackles.[11]

The Issue between Christianity and the Empire: What Shapes the Destiny of Rome?

The strategy of Porphyry's attack on Christianity sounds like the infighting that was going on generally among philosophers of the period. What is surprising is that a leading intellectual would see Christianity as such a challenge that he would devote fifteen volumes to the effort to discredit it. These fragments quoted from Porphyry show how the movement was penetrating Roman society and culture at many different levels. At stake was not only the future of the church, but also the fate of the empire. How were the leaders and the people of the Roman world to perceive the future of the empire? If the populace in growing numbers abandoned the traditional rites and sacrifices in honor of the ancient gods of Greece and Rome, would the latter exact penalties, sending political or natural catastrophes? Would the decline of the official cults lead to Rome's barbarian neighbors to the north and east taking over the imperial lands?

Or was the continuing threat to the empire and the pervasive movement that refused to participate in the traditional state cult an indication that a new epoch in the life of the empire was in store? If the Christians were right, God was at work in history to fulfill His purpose for and through His people and to create a new, potentially universal community. Was that going to take place, and if so, by what stages? Before an answer to such fundamental questions could be reached, the power of the Roman state felt obligated to try to eradicate the movement (Chapter 8). Meanwhile, the Christians were having to develop a rational defense for their faith in the face of possible martyrdom (Chapter 6). And they were also having to strive for some kind of uniformity within the movement in light of the radically diverse ways in which the Christian tradition was being interpreted (Chapter 7). It is to this series of responses to challenge that we now turn.

---

[11]Augustine, *City of God* (19.23), in the series, *The Fathers of the Church*, Vol. 14, J. Defarrari, ed. (Washington, D.C.: Catholic University Press, 1947).

Chapter 6

Christian Responses to the Challenges from the Culture

By the middle of the second century C.E., the leadership and the attitudes of the church to-ward the Roman culture and the empire had changed significantly. In Jerusalem, where the movement had had its center under James, the brother of Jesus, and the other Apostles, the leaders had fled at the time of the first Jewish revolt against the Romans in 66–70 C.E. They took up residence in Pella, on the eastern side of the Jordan Valley, south of the Sea of Galilee.[1] Their fate is not reported, but the Jewish–Christian leadership in Jerusalem was replaced by Gentiles during the reign of Hadrian in 120, as Eusebius notes.[2]

The Christians continued their claim to be the true heirs of the traditions of the Jew-ish Bible, but the issue for Christians about obeying the Jewish cultic laws died out with the destruction of the Jerusalem temple and the emergence of rabbinic Judaism, with its exclu-sive claim to be the heir of the biblical tradition. Although Jerusalem continued to be an important center of the church in the eastern Mediterranean, it was at Caesarea by the sea and at Alexandria in Egypt that the vitality of the cultural life of the church was most clearly evident. Both these cities were centers of Greco-Roman culture and learning, and in both of them the Christians took on the challenge of coming to terms with that culture in ways that were both constructive and critical. In each place, the Christians developed schools for the instruction of their leaders that became major factors in shaping the life and thought of

---

[1] Quotations and references throughout this chapter are from Eusebius, *Ecclesiastical History*, tr. by K. Lake, Loeb Classical Library (Cambridge, MA: Harvard University Press, 1926, 1965).

[2] *Ecclesiastical History* 4.5.

69

Christians for subsequent centuries. The claim was that, through Jesus, God had brought to fruition the fuller and final disclosure of his plan for the human race.

In Rome and Carthage, which were the major centers of Roman culture in the western Mediterranean world, the issues that dominated the thought of the church were different:

- What were the criteria for gaining and maintaining membership within the Christian community?
- How were the sacraments of baptism and the eucharist to be understood, and who was qualified to administer and participate in them?
- What were the true teachings of the Christian church, and who was authorized to define these doctrines?

Stated in more traditional terms, How was Christian orthodoxy to be defined?

Important for the church was the developing attitude toward the Christian movement on the part of both the political and the intellectual leaders of the Roman world. Speaking for Christianity were some who had been trained in the best methods that the Greco-Roman intellectual tradition had to offer, providing reasoned explanatory justifications for what the Christians believed and taught. The Greeks called this strategy an *apologia*, which means "defense" or "rationale," rather than "apology" in the modern sense of providing an excuse. Hence, these leaders of the church have come to be known as the Apologist Fathers. Their skills and self-confidence were such that they addressed their declarations to the emperor and to their non-Christian intellectual contemporaries, rather than limiting their audience to members of the movement. Jesus was portrayed as primarily a teacher, who gave instructions to his followers that they, as apostles, passed on to successive generations. For example, the effort was made by Melito of Sardis (died ca. 177 C.E.) to show that Christianity had been free of conflict with the empire and that it had flourished since the days of Augustus, except during the mad reign of Nero and briefly under Domitian. Hadrian (117–138 C.E.) had set the example of declining to take negative action against what Melito terms "our philosophy."

Theophilus of Antioch (died ca. 185) claimed to be the sixth to have succeeded Peter in leadership of the church there, and perceived the Christian program as primarily one of instruction, including the weeding out of false teaching. By 180, a catechetical school had been established in Alexandria for the intellectual training of leaders of the church. Led first by Pantaenus, it was headed subsequently by two of the early church's greatest scholars, Clement and Origen. The major concern of these leaders was to answer constructively the intellectual and political charges that were being made against developing Christianity. As early as 125, a Christian thinker from Asia Minor named Quadratus addressed an apology directly to Hadrian, the Roman emperor. In the second half of the second century, Athenagoras of Athens wrote to the emperor Marcus Aurelius (161–180 C.E.) to reject the charge that Christians were atheists and to defend their claims that God had spoken through the prophets and definitively through His Son. The three Christian thinkers whose extensive writings provide the fullest picture of this effort to defend the Christian faith and commend it to the wider Roman political and intellectual world are Justin, Clement of Alexandria, and Origen.

Justin Martyr (100–165 C.E.)

A pagan native of the Hellenistic Palestinian city Flavia Neapolis (modern Nablus), Justin explored the major philosophical options of his day—those of the Stoics, Aristotle, Pythagoras, and Plato—before turning to an investigation of Christianity. He wandered about the Mediterranean world as a Christian philosopher, finally settling in Rome, where he founded a Christian school. His two major writings that have survived are both apologies, one addressed to Jews and the other to Gentiles.

The first of these is addressed to a Jew, Trypho, but one can infer from Justin's way of dealing with what Christians came to call the Old Testament that his line of argument is as important for showing Christians how to understand this history and literature as it is to convince Trypho about the Christian claims based on the Jewish scriptures. Justin claims that the new covenant established by Jesus as the agent of God has displaced the successive covenants with Israel described in the Bible and is now God's instrument to bring the light of knowledge of Him to all nations. Jesus was attested in this role by his works, and especially by the miracles he performed, and he is now the embodiment of the new law and the new covenant. Christians are the true heirs of the patriarchs of Israel, many of whom lived and died before such rites as circumcision and such rules as abstinence from work on the Sabbath had been instituted through Moses. Jews have abandoned the everlasting, inclusive covenant promised through David and the prophets, but it is now open to all through Jesus, the authentic offspring of Abraham.

In his "Apology to the Gentiles," which is addressed to the emperor Antoninus Pius (138–161 C.E.) and to the Roman senate and people, Justin describes Christianity as a rational search for truth and invites dialogue or debate about it on philosophical grounds. The truth that Plato conveys is derived from Moses, who preceded Plato in time and from whom Justin believes that the philosopher borrowed his ideas of the creation of the world. Justin goes on to depict Jesus as primarily a teacher who, as the divine Logos, is the embodiment of reason. That he is the divinely designated instrument of wisdom is evident from the ways in which the prophecies of ancient Israel are fulfilled in him. His predictions have taken place and his warnings of the destruction of Jerusalem have actually come to pass. In reply to the charges that Christians are morally perverted and politically subversive, Justin declares that they are law-abiding citizens, grateful for the order and stability of life that the emperors maintain and willing to pay taxes to support the Roman state. He speaks of Hadrian (117–138 C.E.), for example, as "the greatest and most illustrious emperor." Jesus' teaching is compatible with that of the ancient philosophers, and his predictions are similar to those of the Greek and Roman sibyls and the oracles of Hermes, messenger of the Greek gods, who were relied on by the Roman populace, as well as by its intellectuals and its rulers. The members of the Christian community have experienced moral and social transformation:

> We who formerly delighted in fornication now cleave only to chastity. We who exercized the magic arts now consecrate ourselves to the good and unbegotten God. We who valued above all else the acquisition of wealth and property now direct all that we have to a common fund, which is shared by every needy person. We who hated and killed one another, and who, be-

cause of differing customs, would not share a fireside with those of another race, now, after the appearance of Christ, live together with them. We pray for our enemies, and try to persuade those who unjustly hate us that, if they lived according to the excellent precepts of Christ, they will have a good hope of receiving the same reward as ourselves from the God who governs all.[3]

As Justin asserts, the Logos is fully disclosed only in Jesus: "Christ, who appeared on earth for our sakes, became the whole Logos, body and soul. What the philosophers and legislators discovered and expressed well they achieved through their contemplation of some aspect of the Logos. But since they did not have a full knowledge of the Logos, they often contradicted themselves." Paraphrasing Plato, Justin quotes Socrates that it is not easy to find the Father and Creator of all things, nor, when he has been found, is it safe to announce this to all humanity. He concludes, "Yet our Christ did all this through his own power," as the Logos who is in everyone, who assumed human nature, and who has taught these truths about the nature of reality.

A third apology of Justin (which is only a later appendix to the earlier one) is addressed to the Roman senate. In it, Justin points out the falsity of the charges of cannibalism and sexual excesses that have been brought against the Christians. He is confident that God will vindicate the faithful believers in the future day of judgment, and so he and all true Christians refuse to obey the official orders of the empire to renounce their allegiance to Christ and participate in divine honors to the emperor. Indeed, he notes that the bravery of the Christians in this regard had been an important factor that attracted him to that faith.

In a document that is very likely authentic, *The Martyrdom of the Holy Martyrs*, there is a report of how Justin and other brave Christians of this period were put to death by the Roman authorities for their refusal to sacrifice to the traditional Roman gods and to honor the emperor as divine. All those Christians who were interrogated by the Roman officials were threatened with execution by beheading. The Roman officer asked Justin, "Do you suppose that you will ascend to heaven to receive some recompense?" Justin replied, "I do not suppose it, but I know and am fully persuaded of it!" All the others on trial joined him in expressing assurance that God would take them into his presence. It was in this confidence that all of them were put to death.

Clement of Alexandria (150–211 c.e.)

Born in Athens of pagan parents, Clement was converted to Christianity and visited the major centers of Christian learning in the eastern Mediterranean world. In Alexandria, he became a pupil of Pantaenus, who was head of the catechetical school there and, about 200 c.e., succeeded him in this post. During the persecution of Christians under the emperor Decius (193–211), Clement was forced to flee Egypt, and he died in eastern Asia Minor (Cappadocia) about 212 c.e. His three major works are *Exhortation to the Greeks*, *Paidagogos* [The Instructor of Children], and *Stromateis*, which means "miscellany" or "patchwork." The strategies of these writings are (1) to challenge the Greek intellectuals on their own

---

[3]From Justin, *First Apology* 14, in *The Faith of the Early Fathers*, Vol. 1, p. 52.

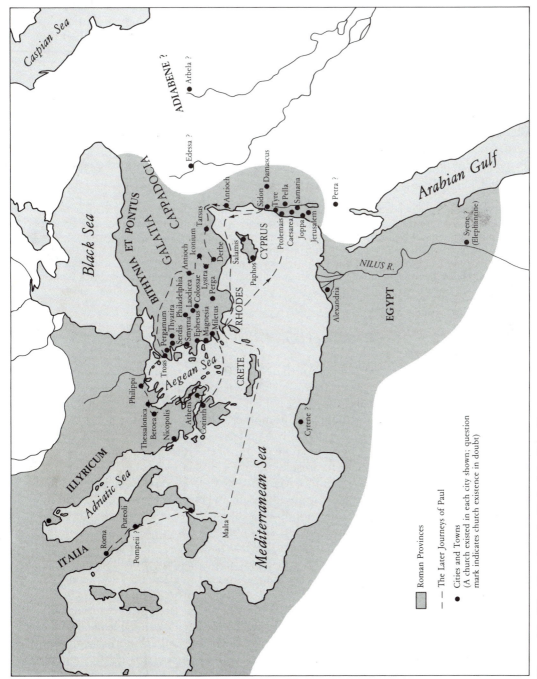

Figure 6.1   The Church at the End of the First Century C.E.

ground; (2) to offer instruction for guiding Christians from childlike to mature faith; and (3) to provide deep and challenging insights for serious Christians, behind the intentionally misleading and innocuous title "Miscellany." In the *Exhortation*, Clement declares that the Logos has become a human being to enable humans to recognize and affirm the unity and eternity of God. As Instructor, Jesus brings enlightenment to human life and thought, enabling one to attain self-knowledge and to live according to steadiness, beauty, and obedience to God. In *Stromateis*, Clement declares that faith is superior to knowledge, since it leads from what cannot be demonstrated to the universal. Yet God cannot be taught or expressed adequately in words; rather, knowledge of God is possible only through the spiritual capacity that God provides—the thoughts of virtuous men and women are produced by divine inspiration and bring full knowledge of God. The participants in the people of God stretch back through human history:

> The true church, which is ancient, is one; and in it are enrolled those who, in accord with the [divine] design, are just. . . . In substance, in concept, in origin and in eminence, the ancient and universal church is alone, gathering as it does into the unity of the one faith which results from the familiar covenants—or rather, from the one covenant in different times, by the will of the one God and through the one Lord [Jesus]—those already chosen, those predestined by God who knew before the foundation of the world that they would become right with God.[4]

Origen (185–253 C.E.)

Although Origen was named for the god of the Nile ("Origen" means "offspring of Horus"), his father was presumably a Christian, since he was killed during the persecution of the church by the emperor Severus (193–211 C.E.) when Origen was ten years old. Origen wanted to follow his father in martyrdom, but his mother kept him safe in the house by hiding his clothes. Trained in both secular and Christian learning, he quickly excelled, developing special competence in the languages and contents of the Jewish and Christian scriptures, so that at age eighteen he began to preside over the Christian school in his native city, Alexandria. Taking literally the injunction of Matthew 19:12 (to become a eunuch for the sake of the kingdom of God), Origen castrated himself. In spite of what was regarded by many as his having a physical disqualification, he was ordained as an elder by the bishops of Jerusalem and Caesarea. Among his technical accomplishments was the preparation of a set of versions of the Bible in various languages and translations, so that the reader could compare them in the finest detail. Even the anti-Christian philosopher Porphyry acknowledged the vast range and depth of Origen's learning. By means of allegorical and figurative interpretation of the scriptures, Origen was able to show the correlation, as he saw it, between Greek philosophy and the Bible. In 232 he moved to Caesarea, where he not only was a teacher, but also was constantly being consulted by local and regional leaders of the church. When he was sixty, his program of teaching and writing was so enormous that he had stenographers on hand during his lectures to record his discourses. He was among

---

[4]Paraphrased from the translation in *The Fathers of the Church*, Vol.1, p. 185 (Washington, DC: Catholic University Press, 1947).

those tortured during the persecution of the church under Decius (249–251), and died from these injuries in Tyre in 253 or 254.

Origen's greatest contributions were his detailed commentaries on various parts of the Bible and an extended apologetic response to an earlier attack on Christianity by Celsus (the *Contra Celsum*, as we noted in Chapter 5). His commentaries were on the Jewish biblical writings, as well as on the Gospels of Matthew and John. His interpretations of the text concerned its relevance for his contemporaries more than its historical context. Accordingly, much of the commentary is allegorical or philosophical in nature. For example, he used the erotic themes and language of the Song of Songs as a vehicle for conveying the possibilities of sharing in the love of God that has been disclosed through Christ. The appearance of terms in the Gospel of John that are significant in the Greek philosophical tradition provided Origen the occasion for developing deep and highly intellectual connotations for the seemingly simple language and style of that Gospel. For example, Origen interprets the opening phrase of John, "In the beginning" (in Greek, *arche*), by showing that the Greek word *arche* can mean a chronological beginning, but that it also implies a divinely intended purpose, eternal principles inherent in the universe, and the rule or standard by which the cosmos operates.

In his extended response to Celsus's intellectual attack on Christianity in *The True Doctrine* (which we examined in Chapter 5), Origen notes with some regret that he had wasted the time to comply with the request of his patron, Ambrose, to prepare a full-scale counterargument to what Origen considers to be an ill-informed and intellectually irresponsible string of charges against the faith. But he did reproduce much of the original document from some seventy years earlier, preparing this massive counterattack just before the middle of the third century, during the reign of Philip the Arab (244–249). Only then was the challenge to the intellectual integrity of the church's teaching seen to be important and demanding of a rejoinder; and only then did the church produce a scholar like Origen capable of responding effectively to this challenge.

Origen began his argument by reminding his readers of the basic disagreements and contradictions among Greek philosophers on whom Celsus was relying and of the morally debased practices of the Greek and Roman gods and goddesses. The power of Jesus is evident in the spread of Christianity throughout the Roman world in spite of official opposition to it. Although the movement began among those considered to be unlearned, its message penetrated the world, geographically and intellectually. Origen's own learning is evident in the linguistic distinction he makes between the Gospel account of Jesus' birth to a virgin (in Greek, *parthenos*) (Matt. 1:23) and the Hebrew text of Isa. 7:14 referred to by Matthew, where a "young woman" (*almah*) is predicted to bear a son who will redeem God's people. Origen notes, but dismisses, the hostile charge that Jesus had been the illegitimate son of a Roman soldier named Pantheros. The interpretation of any historical event, Origen observes, is a mixture of the literal and the figurative, as the various Greek legends of the Trojan wars evidence. The inclusion of miracle stories in the reports of Jesus' birth and public career, and earlier in the life and work of Moses, is essential for communicating with the intellectually uncritical masses, who are not reached by sophisticated arguments. The fulfillment of prophecy is, in Origen's view, a powerful element in the credibility of Christianity and one that Celsus has largely avoided. These prophecies must be seen as pointing to two advents of Jesus: one in lowliness and humiliation and one in triumph and divine vindication that is yet to come. Failure to distinguish the lofty, admirable aims of Jesus in his healings and exorcisms led Celsus to compare them with the self-serving magical stunts that professional magicians perform.

The lowly and unpretentious origins of the followers of Jesus testify to the marvelous power of this religion to transcend human boundaries, both ethnic and intellectual. Similarly, that Jesus had a human body does not deny his divine role or reduce his stature intellectually, but points to the reality of the incarnation of God in human form. No ordinary human being could have converted so many and have influenced so many human leaders—among them kings, rulers, and Roman senators, as well as the common people. If Christianity is to constitute a new human community, it cannot limit itself to the tiny intellectual elite; it must be accessible to, and understandable by, simple people as well.

God cares for all rational beings, although he holds them accountable for their way of life when they go against human nature. He warns them of divine judgment as an inducement to them to live in accord with the divine purpose. They are ever in need of divine healing and correction, which has been provided through Jesus. Celsus rightly praises the wisdom of philosophers and of other religious leaders, but he ignores the gross immorality the deities of these religions practice, such as incestuous marriages. God has left his creatures with the ability to make decisions, with the result that the demonic powers in the universe have used their capabilities to oppose God, for which they will be called to account. As for the ancient prophetic promises of wealth and prosperity, Celsus takes them literally, thereby missing the spiritual meaning by which they become promises to God's people to supply their deepest needs, both personally and within the community of faith. When God's rule comes on the earth, the human structures and systems will be replaced by the eternal order of the cosmos that Jesus announced and for which he is preparing his people through the transformation of human society.

Origen neatly epitomized what he saw as his role in life: "It is our task to try to confirm men's faith by arguments and treatises." He sought thereby "to handle rightly the Word of Truth" (II Tim. 2:15).[5] His function in the Christianity of the middle third century and his support by ecclesiastical leaders and by those seeking significant places in the life of the church show the extent to which the movement had perceived its task as both challenging and transforming the intellectual and cultural forces of the Roman world. Also essential was coping with basic differences in the perception of Christian faith and life within the church. It is to some of the major figures in this phase of the church's development that we now turn.

Irenaeus

Significant regional differences between the eastern and western parts of the empire on social and political aspects of human life led the church in the east to adopt different institutional structures, as well as different strategies, for trying to unify and systematize what it affirmed to be the truth. How was the church to organize itself to withstand mounting po-

[5]This summary of Origen's argument is paraphrased from the translation of *Contra Celsum* by Henry Chadwick (Cambridge: Cambridge University Press, 1965), 8.75.

litical, cultural, and intellectual pressures from without? How could it maintain its integrity while responding to these forces, both external (from the political powers) and internal (from the society of the region)?

A major figure among the Christians of the second century who worked on the problem of inner consolidation of faith and practice was Irenaeus. Born at Smyrna in Asia Minor (about 140 C.E.), he was made bishop of Lyons in Gaul (France) in 178, succeeding the first bishop there, Pothinus, who was martyred. It is possible that Irenaeus was descended from the Gauls (or Celts) who had invaded Asia Minor in the third century B.C.E. and that he was returning to his ancestral territory when he went to Lyons as bishop. In any case, he sought to make peace between Victor, the bishop of Rome, and Polycrates, the bishop of Ephesus in Asia Minor, over the issue of the date of Easter. So severe was the controversy, that Victor wanted to excommunicate all who failed to celebrate Easter only on a Sunday, but Irenaeus urged him and the other western bishops to withdraw the excommunication decree in recognition of the great antiquity of the eastern churches' custom of linking the remembrance of Jesus' death with the Jewish dating of the Passover.[6] What is clear from this ecclesiastical dispute between East and West is that the western bishops were more concerned about order and uniformity, whereas the eastern churches were committed to continuity with tradition. For the bishops and leading Christian scholars, reconciliation became essential. To this task, Irenaeus set himself in his *Against Heresies*, also known as *The Detections and Overthrow of What is Falsely Called Knowledge*.[7] What Irenaeus presents in this major work is not merely an attack on false teaching, but a full setting-forth of what he considered to be the essence of authentic Christian faith. It is illuminating to examine his compact summary of the faith that appears early in his treatise:

> For the church, although dispersed throughout the whole world even to the ends of the earth, has received from the apostles and from their disciples the faith in one God, Father Almighty, the Creator of heaven and earth and all that is in them, and in one Jesus Christ, the Son of God, who became flesh for our salvation; and in the Holy Spirit, who announced through the prophets the dispensations and the comings,[8] and the birth from a virgin, and the passion, and the resurrection from the dead, and the bodily ascension into heaven of the beloved Christ Jesus our Lord, and his coming from heaven in the glory of the Father to reestablish all things; and the raising up again of all flesh of all humanity, in order that to Jesus Christ our Lord and God and Savior and King, in accord with the approval of the invisible Father, every knee shall bend of those in heaven and on earth and under the earth, and that every tongue shall confess him, and that He may make just judgment of all; and that he may send the spiritual forces of wickedness and the angels who transgressed and became apostates, and the impious, unjust, lawless and blasphemous among men, into everlasting fire; and that he may grant life, immortality, and surround with eternal glory the just and holy, and those who kept His commands and who have persevered in his love, either from the beginning or from their repentance.[9]

In this statement are combined the affirmation of the oneness of God; the divinity of Jesus and of the Holy Spirit; the formulation and preservation of the faith through and

---

[6]The issue is discussed by Eusebius in his *Ecclesiastical History*, 5.23–24.

[7]See the discussion of knowledge that follows and pp. 89–92.

[8]Presumably, these refer to the variety of ways in which God has disclosed His nature and purpose to His people in earlier times, which reached their climax in God's self-revelation through Jesus.

[9]Quoted from W. A. Jurgens, in *Faith of the Early Fathers*, pp. 84–85.

from the Apostles; the continuities of God's purpose with the past through the prophets; and the miraculous birth, the death and resurrection, and the ascension and coming triumph of Christ as God's agent for the renewal of the created world. Also involved are the solemn warnings of judgment for those who reject or stray from the faith and the assurance of support and eternal blessing for those who stand firm in the faith. Like the philosophical insights about the Logos of which Origen wrote, faith has an intellectual content that is being defined with increasing clarity. It has penetrated the whole world, Irenaeus reminds his readers, and has done so in spite of important cultural and linguistic differences among various human societies. Yet this unity of faith is being threatened by those who are denying various aspects of the basic creed that Irenaeus has just summarized. In Gaul there have appeared those who teach Gnosticism, including the denial that the creation is good or that the God of Jesus is the Creator of the universe. These Gnostics relied on their expurgated version of the Gospel of Luke for their depiction of Jesus as one whose break with Israel was complete, and they share with other Gnostics the absolute break between the God of creation and the God of human redemption. For Irenaeus, God is the designer, builder, inventor, maker, and lord of the universe. The continuities between the Old and the New Testament are essential for Christian faith:

> the divine act of creation; the existence of the human race; the opening of the covenant with God to non-Israelites; sacrifice as essential to the maintenance of a relationship between God and his people; the prophetic insights and utterances as prime factors in God's self-disclosure to his people.

Reacting to those who perceive Jesus as a divine being masquerading as a human, Irenaeus insists on his full humanity, including his birth, his growth to maturity, and his literal death. The Gnostics rejected the essential features of biblical faith: creation as the work of God; the incarnation of Jesus Christ in full identification with humanity; and the eucharist as the shared symbolic meal that effects continuing renewal of the covenant people. Access to the truth of God disclosed through Jesus is possible only from the apostolic witness to Jesus in the gospels. To know the truth, therefore, one must contemplate the apostolic tradition. As Irenaeus summarizes it:

> The true gnosis is the teaching of the apostles, and the ancient organization of the church throughout the whole world, and the manifestation of the body of Christ according to the succession of bishops, by which successions the bishops have handed down the church which is found everywhere; and the very complete tradition of the scriptures, which have come down to us being guarded against falsification, and which are received without addition or deletion; and reading without falsification, and a legitimate and diligent exposition according to the scriptures, without danger and without blasphemy; and the preeminent gift of love which is more precious than knowledge, more glorious than prophecy, and more honored than all the other charismatic gifts.[10]

Thus, the unity and truth of the church are provided by the apostolic witness, the succession of leadership from the apostles through the bishops, and the fidelity to the accepted collection of scriptures, especially the four gospels. Unlike the heretics who take only one

---

[10]Quoted from W. A. Jurgens, *Faith of the Early Fathers*, p. 97.

gospel as their norm, Irenaeus insists that there are four, just as there are four winds and four corners of the earth. The one gospel message rests on four pillars, "breathing immortality on every side and enkindling life anew in human beings."[11]

4 pillars = 4 gospels.

Tertullian

Another kind of response to the mounting political and cultural pressures on Christianity in the later second century was to promote the idea that God would intervene directly in current affairs to destroy the opposition and to vindicate His own people. One Christian leader who came to share this point of view was Tertullian. Born in Carthage of pagan parents about 155 C.E. and trained as a lawyer, Tertullian was converted in 193. Thereafter, he devoted his legal skills to the defense of Christianity. His writings were in Latin, which was a new feature in Christian literature. Until that time Greek had been the primary literary language of the Christians, and Latin was the vernacular of the masses in the western Mediterranean world. In spite of his linguistic shift, Tertullian's primary concerns were to foster the instruction of Christians and to affirm the continuity of the Christian tradition in the face of new interpretations of the faith that were emerging. It is the more ironical, therefore, that in his later years he was himself strongly influenced by a speculative, charismatic movement that claimed to have received prophetic revelations which supplemented and modified the New Testament writings. The leader of this movement, Montanus, appeared in Phrygia in Asia Minor in the middle of the second century C.E., claiming that the Spirit had revealed to him that the present age was soon to end and that the New Jerusalem would descend from heaven to a valley in Asia Minor. Even though the prediction obviously was not fulfilled, the movement spread to the West and strongly influenced Tertullian in his later years.[12]

In the initial phase of his work, Tertullian addresses the two major charges that are brought against the Christians: that they do not worship the traditional gods (which is sacrilege) and they do not offer the sacrifices for the emperor (which is treason). In rebuttal, he asserts in his *Apology*, Christianity is not subversive, but offers divine instruction. Jesus is the embodiment of reason and power, the teacher of God's grace, and the enlightener and trainer of the human race, who came to renew our receptivity toward the truth. Through him all things were fashioned, and through him the divine purpose will be brought to fruition. The movement has already spread across the world, filling "cities, islands, fortresses, towns, marketplaces, the military camps, tribes, companies, the palace, the senate, the forum"—everyplace except the temples. Christians are the enemies of human error, not the enemies of the human race.

Instead of accepting the charge that Christians are morally and politically subversive, Tertullian describes in detail what they do, thereby providing the modern reader with a vivid picture of life in the churches of the second century. They gather to pray to God for strength and guidance, for the welfare of the emperor and the state, and for the triumph of peace in the world. They are also concerned for the illumination of the community through

---

[11] Quotations in the remainder of this chapter are from the Jurgens volume, *Faith of the Early Fathers.*
[12] See the discussion of Montanism in Chapter 7, pp. 88–89.

the scriptures and for calling to moral account the members of their group, to the extent of excommunicating members adjudged guilty of grievous sin. Their affairs are presided over by elders (presbyters), and the modest resources of the members are shared. Support is provided for burial of the poor, for orphans, for the aged confined to their homes, and for those deprived as the result of a shipwreck or of service in mines or imprisonment. They are ready to die for each other and share all that they have—except their wives! Their basic group rite is the Eucharist, or *agape* (from a Greek word for love), which begins and ends with prayer, includes songs, and celebrates the origins of the movement through Jesus' last meal with his followers and the symbolic anticipation of his death in their behalf.

In his *Guideline against the Heathen*, Tertullian addresses the intellectual problems that the church faced from pagan detractors, as well as from Christians dissenters from the apostolic tradition. To both types of opponents, he declares that there is no need to search for truth, because the gospel has been fully disclosed through Christ, and the rule of faith has been established: "This rule . . . was taught by Christ, and admits of no questions among us, except those which heresies bring in and which make men heretics" (13.1). The Apostles have preserved this truth, founded churches, preached true doctrine. From the one primitive apostolic church, all others are derived, and in them only what Christ revealed to the apostles may be preached. It is churches thus established that alone can decide what is true, and decisions about doctrine can be made only by those who succeeded the apostles: the bishops of the apostolic churches. Where true doctrine appears, one can be sure of apostolic origins and links. In his treatise *On Baptism*, Tertullian asserts that membership in the church is to be confirmed by baptism, which is to be performed in the apostolic tradition, preferably by a bishop, following the receipt of instruction in that tradition.

In his later writings, Tertullian gives increasing evidence of speculation about the future and of a rigorous view of Christian morality. For example, in his treatise *Against Marcion*, he reports about an event—"attested even by pagan witnesses"—that in Judea a heavenly city was visible, suspended in the sky every morning for forty days, and would vanish later in the day. This was a foretaste of the New Jerusalem coming down from heaven that John depicted in Revelation 21:9–27. Tertullian is persuaded that the fulfillment of these promises of renewal of heaven and earth is about to take place. His growing moral strictness is evident in his *On Monogamy*, in which he extols the chaste and eunuchs, as against those who have married, and in his treatise *On Modesty*, in which he says that adulterers should be permanently excluded from the community. This denial of restoration, even to repentant sinners, he seeks to justify by an appeal to a new message from the Spirit and to Hebrews 6:4, which denies readmission to apostates. In his *Apology*, Tertullian deplores the fact that Christians are being martyred, but as he puts it in a vivid and oft-quoted phrase, "The blood of the martyrs is the seed of the church" (50.12).

Cyprian of Carthage

Cyprian's personal experience, as well as his writings, point up the issues faced by the third-century church. Born of wealthy pagan parents in the opening years of that century, Cyprian had by 250 been converted, entered the priesthood, and been made bishop of

Carthage just about the time of the outbreak of persecution of the church under Decius (249–251). Cyprian was severely criticized because he fled to the hills, where he carried out his episcopal duties during the persecution. One of his major concerns was, accordingly, the restoration of those who had lapsed from the faith. In his letters to other bishops and clergy, he warned against easy restoration on terms dictated by the lapsed and stressed penitence as the essential requirement, with forgiveness to be bestowed formally by the bishop. He insisted that it is the bishops alone who provide continuity of faith and practice in the churches and are the ground of unity. His treatise *On the Unity of the Church* has survived in two versions. This in itself is an indication of the range and depth of the issue of whether authority in the church was collegial among the bishops as a group or centralized in the bishop of Rome, who was regarded as the successor of Peter, the rock on which Christ was to build the church, according to Matthew 16:18.[13] As for membership in the church, Cyprian affirmed that infants should be baptized, although, if administered by heretics, the rite was valueless. There is only one baptism into the people of God, and it is available only in the universal church. Cyprian's claim to the exclusive efficacy of baptism through the apostolic succession of the bishops and the churches and the clergy they authorized was affirmed at the seventh council of the church in Carthage, over which Cyprian himself presided in 256.

Competition for Episcopal Authority in Rome

The continuing problem of those Christians who, faced with the prospect of martyrdom, caved in under pressure and took part in divine honors to the emperor, continued throughout the third century. Hippolytus, a prolific theological writer of the first decades of the third century, was vigorous in his attacks on Christians whom he regarded as heretical in their views on the deity of Christ and on the church leaders in Rome who tolerated the heretics. But he was especially critical of the bishop of Rome, Callistus (217–222), for his policy of easy readmission of members of the church who had yielded to pressure from the empire and publicly renounced their faith. For a time he was bishop of a separatist wing of the church, having been elected to the position by his supporters, and was subsequently martyred about the year 235 C.E. The doctrinal ideas in the surviving fragments of his extensive writings affirm what had come to be regarded as the apostolic faith, so that his break with the main body of the church was not the result of his heretical theological ideas. Furthermore, in his *Apostolic Tradition*, he provided details of the process by which bishops, presbyters, deacons, and other church officials were to be ordained and of the responsibilities that they were to carry out, as well as the process by which members were to be added to the church and how the sacraments of baptism and the Eucharist were to be administered. It is the more surprising, therefore, that he would have taken such a radical step in having a small group of dissidents designate him as bishop. But the issue that was involved—readmitting those who had taken part in the emperor cult—serves as an indicator of the unresolved questions of the relation between church and state.

---

[13] Some Protestant interpreters of Mt 16:16–18 argue that it is Peter's confession of Jesus as Messiah (Christ) that is the rock on which the church is to be built, rather than Peter's role as the preeminent apostle.

Midway in the third century, another Roman clergyman had himself elected bishop of Rome. Details in Eusebius's *Ecclesiastical History* (6.43) tell how a prominent clergyman in Rome named Novatian was so eager to be bishop, that he enticed three bishops to Rome from remote parts of Italy, managed to make them drunk, and, in their stupor, led them to lay hands on him as bishop. The issues between Novatian and the official bishop were focused by the dissent over the strictness of requirements for Christians and, especially, over the question of readmission of the lapsed. Like Hippolytus, Novatian had no significant doctrinal differences with the mainstream bishops. But also like him, he insisted that Christians could not marry the second time and that under no circumstances were those who had violated their devotion to Christ through participation in the emperor cult to be accepted back into the Christian community. Although in common consciousness, the immediate issue was the restoration of the lapsed, the fundamental questions were the authority of the bishop and the basis of the unity of the church. In Chapter 7, we turn to a consideration of some of the detailed challenges to church unity, both institutionally and conceptually, that emerged in the third century.

Chapter 7

The Challenges from Within Christianity

Who Is in Charge?

Because Christianity began as a spontaneous movement and in the expectation that its hopes of a new age were soon to be fulfilled, at the outset there was no set pattern of leadership and no well-defined process for decision making within the group. The tradition apparent in the Gospels and the letters of Paul, which promised power and authority by the Holy Spirit at work among and through Jesus' twelve followers, did not point to any specific organizational structures or assigned leadership roles by which direction and specific guidelines were to be established. The only indication of a centralized leadership was the implicit role of the group of apostles based in Jerusalem, with whom Paul conferred as he carried out his mission to bring gentiles into the community of faith. He consulted first with their leader, James, the brother of Jesus, and later with the apostolic circle as a whole (Gal. 1:18–2:10). They had given corporate approval to what he was doing: They "shook hands with us on it," which symbolized their support of Paul's program of outreach beyond Judaism.

The term *apostle* is simply a transliteration of a Greek word that means "sent" or "commissioned." The group of twelve who had been Jesus' disciples (literally, "learners," as they are designated in the older gospel tradition) during his lifetime believed that he had appeared to them after his resurrection and had commissioned them to carry forward the movement he had launched with their cooperation. It was to Peter that he had appeared initially, followed by appearances to the remainder of the twelve. That was the basis of their claim to be "sent ones" (i.e., apostles). Then, as Paul put it, "last of all, he appeared also to me" (I Cor. 15:5–9). Although in the latter passage, Paul speaks of himself as "unfit to be called an apostle" because of his persecution of God's people, he does in fact regularly identify himself at the opening of his letters as "apostle." He believes that he has been commissioned and empowered by God to carry out his work of calling gentiles to faith and participation in the new community.

Originally, *apostle* did not have a technical meaning, as is evident from its use by Paul on occasion to refer to messengers or emissaries (Phil. 2:25; II Cor. 8:23). But in the final editing of the gospel tradition (Mark 6:30; Matt. 10:2; Luke 11:49), the disciples are also called apostles during Jesus' lifetime. In one text (Luke 22:30), there is an implicit link between the number of the apostles and the number of the tribes of Israel. With few exceptions, the term is limited to the circle of twelve based in Jerusalem. In his letters and in Acts, it is to the Jerusalem apostles that Paul and others appeal for confirmation of policy questions, such as the basis for gentile participation in the new-covenant people (Gal. 2; Acts 15). Elsewhere, Paul declares that the apostles are at the head of the list of those whom God has appointed for leadership roles in the churches, followed by prophets, teachers, workers of miracles, healers, helpers, administrators, and those who speak in ecstatic languages (I Cor. 12:28). Most of these roles seem to be functions essential for the ongoing life of the church, rather than official positions.

Paul identifies himself as an apostle at the opening of nearly all of his known letters. This identification is also found in the later letters attributed to Paul (Eph. 1:1; I Tim. 1:1; II Tim. 1:1), as well as in Acts 14:4, 14. In the later New Testament writings, however, the apostolic role is represented as fundamental for the church, which is described as having been built on the foundation of the apostles (Eph. 2:20). That image is given vivid expression in the Revelation of John, where the New City of God comes to earth from heaven in the new age. It has twelve gates, each bearing the name of one of the tribes of Israel, and twelve foundation stones, each with the name of one of the twelve apostles (Rev. 22:10–14). The authoritative role of the apostles is heightened in Acts, where they are depicted as making the basic policy decisions that guide the life of the whole church. It is astonishing, therefore, that after the fall of Jerusalem to the Roman armies in 67–70, nothing more is heard of the apostolic circle other than the single report in Eusebius's *Ecclesiastical History* (3.5.3; 4.6.4) that the church fled to Pella east of the Jordan and that the original Jewish bishops of Jerusalem were replaced in the second century by those of Gentile origin. The word "bishop" derives from the Greek term, *episkopos*, which means "overseer." Paul mentions it only once (Phil. 1:1), but in the later letters produced in his name, there are detailed guidelines for selecting a bishop (I Tim. 3:1–7; Titus 1:7–9). These guidelines include fidelity in marriage and parental responsibilities, being temperate in drinking, and being amiable and free of greed, as well as having an aptitude for teaching and being orthodox in doctrine. The qualification that a bishop must not be a recent convert shows that these texts deal with a considerably later stage in the development of Christianity. Although Acts does not mention bishops, Paul's farewell to the leaders of the church of Ephesus (20:17–35) is addressed to the elders (*presbyteroi*), who are instructed to serve as overseers (*episkopoi*) of the church, which is God's new flock. What seems to have happened is that the elders replaced the apostles as the policy-making council in the churches. They are associated with the apostles in the decision-making function in Acts 15 ("apostles and elders"), even though the term "elder" is never used in Paul's own letters.

Another leadership role that was developing in the first century and a half of the church was that of deacon (*diakonos*). The word means "servant" and is used by Paul to refer to secular civil servants (Rom. 13:3–4) and to Christ's role in fulfilling the purpose of God to form a new, inclusive Covenant People (Rom. 15:8). Paul also uses the term to refer to his own role in carrying out the ministry to which God has called him and his coworkers. Yet in Paul's letters there are references to those persons who have provided financial support for him and the churches as deacons, including a woman, Phoebe, in one of the churches near Corinth (Rom. 16:1). In the later material attributed to Paul, however (I Tim. and Titus), qualifications and responsibilities for both elder and deacon are spelled out. The elders are to be in charge of the churches, even while they are to be responsible heads of their families, but they are subject to trial and expulsion if they misbehave. Deacons, who may be male or female, are to be morally upright and fiscally responsible. Emphasis on good management tends to confirm the inference that may be drawn from the brief mention of the apostles' appointment of seven "who serve (*diakonein*) tables" in Acts 6 when there was a problem of unequal distribution of common funds: A deacon was someone with financial and physical responsibilities for the life of the community.

Clearly, there was no set, uniform definition of these leadership roles in the church during the first century of its existence. From the later first century onward, the bishops of major metropolitan centers, such as Antioch, Alexandria, Carthage, and Rome, not only had large constituencies, but also derived prestige from the fame and fortune of their seats of power. Obviously, those powers were modest and limited at the outset, but became increasingly significant as the size and influence of the movement grew. Fortunately, literature has survived that reflects and even characterizes the episcopal role in the early centuries. Like the New Testament, these sources also evidence significant changes that took place in the leadership patterns within early Christianity.

One of the earliest bishops of whom direct knowledge is available is Ignatius, bishop of Antioch in the opening years of the second century. He wrote letters to the churches of Asia Minor and to Rome as he passed through on his way to martyrdom in Rome in the latter years of the reign of the emperor Trajan (98–117 C.E.). In each letter, he calls for submission by the members to the bishop and the elders and requests respect for the deacons. In poetic imagery, he writes to the Ephesian church that the bishop and the presbytery are attuned like strings of a harp so that Christians led by them may sing with one voice to God and Jesus Christ. There is to be unity of faith and practice of the Eucharist under the presidency of the bishop. In his letter to Polycarp, bishop of Smyrna in Syria, Ignatius says flatly, "Let nothing be done without your approval." The members are to be subject to the bishop, the presbyters, and the deacons. A council convened at Smyrna will elect the successor to Ignatius for the church in Antioch.

Also surviving from the early second century is a letter from Polycarp to the church at Philippi in northern Greece. In it, he offers counsel to the deacons and the elders, much of which consists of quotations from the gospels, the letters of Paul, and other parts of both the New and Old Testaments. This practice indicates how basic for Christian belief and behavior the Bible had become by that time. Significantly, the apostles are referred to as venerated figures from the past. Even so, other writings from the second century evidence the eagerness of churches in various parts of the empire to claim continuity with, or even to have been established by, one of the apostolic figures. Thus, Peter is associated with Rome, Mark with Alexandria, John with Ephesus, and Matthew with Antioch. There is no firm evidence to establish or refute these claims. Significant, however, are the foundational role of the apostles in this later tradition and the efforts to guarantee continuity of belief and practice by establishing legitimating links with the apostolic period of the past through the presiding roles of the bishops in the present.

Additional evidence for the appeal to the authority traced back to the apostles is *The Teaching of the Twelve Apostles*, which we have already examined (Chapter 4). Dating from the second century, this document may incorporate earlier Christian moral traditions. The ongoing development of these traditions is evident in Hippolytus's *Apostolic Tradition*,[1] written about 215, in which he describes ways Christian charity may be practiced, how nuns are to be chosen and supported, what attitudes are to be assumed toward Judaism, how the Eucharist is to be celebrated, and what is the essence of Christian character. That the sanction for these guidelines claims to be the teaching of the apostles shows how important these roots were to the authorization of subsequent developments in Christianity.

The Relationship of Christianity to Emergent Rabbinic Judaism

The failures of two attempts by Jewish nationalists to establish an autonomous Jewish state (in 66–70 and 130–135 A.D.) were concurrent with the moves within Judaism toward institutionalization of the synagogue movement and the emergence of its rabbinic leadership. We have already examined this development (pp. 14–17), which began a process of reinterpreting the Law of Moses with the aim of transferring the requirements for cultic purity from the priests and the temple to the pious laity and the houses or halls where they gathered for prayer and worship, for study of their scriptures, and for fellowship. Gaining and maintaining group identity were central for the adherents of the movement; nationalistic hopes, and even specific messianic expectations of a divinely endowed deliverer, were absent. Accordingly, there was an abandonment of the prophetic traditions announcing God's intervention and of the apocalyptic literature in which the elect community was warned of the sufferings through which it was to pass and was assured of its impending vindication by God. The importance of this Jewish move toward defining the group's community identity was heightened by the appearance and remarkable growth of the Christian church.

In the churches of the eastern Mediterranean world, there were two conflicting reactions to the problem of the relationship with Judaism. The first was the strategy of Marcion, which (as we have noted) was to repudiate the Jewish scriptures, as well as those parts of the New Testament evidencing Jewish influence. The church was to regard itself in a wholly new way as the people of God. The second reaction was just the opposite: Within the church in these centuries, there were also those who wanted to affirm the continuity

---

[1] Excerpts appear in W. Jurgens, trans. and editor, *The Faith of the Early Fathers*, vol. 1 (Collegeville, MN: Liturgical Press, 1970).

between Israel and the church by claiming that Christians were the true heirs of the Jewish biblical tradition.

Given the anxiety that pervaded the church in Asia Minor because of the martyrdoms resulting from Trajan's policy of forcing the Christians to take part in the imperial cult, it was natural that the church there would be drawn to a Jewish resource that dealt with the problems arising when a community of one faith lives under the threat of destruction by a state of another faith. As noted earlier, that resource was the Jewish apocalyptic literature. The Revelation of John is the most fully developed instance of this literary style and outlook on the world within the New Testament, but apocalyptic elements are also present in the Gospel tradition and in the letters of Paul, as we have observed. We examine some of these adapted Jewish documents and some early Christian parallel writings in the next section.

An issue that arose between the eastern and western churches during this period may seem to the modern reader to be insignificant, but it exemplifies the eastern leaders' eagerness to keep continuity with Jewish tradition and the western churches' sense of the importance of Christian distinctiveness and ecclesiastical order. The issue concerned the date of Easter.[2] In the western churches there had developed a pattern of forty days for the observance of Lent, a period of pious self-examination that culminated in Good Friday as the day of penitence, which commemorated Jesus' death. This was followed by Easter Sunday as the celebration of his resurrection. The moveable Passover adopted in the eastern churches spoiled this ecclesiastical symmetry and led to a denunciation of that policy. A cynical reader of the extensive surviving literature on the subject might conclude that the controversy was more of a power struggle than a substantive issue. In any case, it was a symptom of the ambivalence of the church about its relationship to Judaism.

Predicting the Future: Oracles and Revelations

Characteristic of Jewish apocalyptic writing are the convictions that all history and the whole creation are ultimately governed by God, but that the powers of evil which have seized control in the present are to be defeated in the age to come. Meanwhile, the faithful must suffer during the transition, but will be vindicated by God when his rule triumphs. Insight into this process and the outcome has been reserved for the faithful and is now being conveyed in the veiled, symbolic form of the apocalypse. The messenger through whom this divine wisdom is provided for the community is in each case someone reported in the Jewish Bible to have had a direct, personal relationship with God—for example, Enoch, who walked with God and was taken by God (Gen. 5:24); Isaiah, who saw God enthroned (Isa. 6:1); and Elijah, who did not die, but was taken up to God (II Kings 2:1)—or someone who was closely associated with God's disclosure of a new status for Israel. Examples of the latter are the prophet Baruch, who was the scribe of Jeremiah and who announced the new covenant (Jer. 36:32), and Ezra, who prepared the people of Israel for a new kind of life on their return from exile in Babylon. To each of these biblical characters, a newer secret rev-

---

[2]The problem was that the date of Jewish Passover (which was the occasion for Jesus' Last Supper) was based on the phases of the moon, and could fall on any day of the week—not merely on Easter Sunday. Eusebius discussed the issue in his *Ecclesiastical History* 5.23–24.

elation has been given of God's purpose for his people that is embodied in an apocalyptic writing preserved down to the present. From the first century C.E., certain early Christians simply took over these apocalyptic writings, interpreting them in relation to God's people in a Roman-dominated world. Others supplemented the writings by minor additions or modifications, or composed new works that they attributed to these ancient messengers of God to Israel.[3]

Two prime examples of the ways the apocalyptic literature grew are in writings attributed to Ezra and Enoch. In addition to the biblical book of Ezra (or two books of Ezra that are found in some versions of the Old Testament), there are later Christian additions, so that modern scholars distinguish six stages of the books of Ezra (sometimes known as Esdras). Furthermore, there are also a Greek apocalypse of Ezra, the Question of Ezra, and the Vision of Ezra. In the versions of this material known as Fourth Ezra, there are explicit references to Jesus as Son of God, as well as the pronouncement of judgment on those who formerly considered themselves to be God's people: the Jews. The imagery in the Ezra Apocalypse points unmistakably to Rome as the enemy of God's people. Similarly, the Enoch literature includes sections from the period before Christ, parts of which were found in manuscripts among the Dead Sea Scrolls. One part of the literature (the Similitudes of Enoch) dates from about the time of the birth of Jesus and speaks of "that son of man" who will be God's agent to defeat the powers of evil and to establish the new age. It was inevitably picked up by the early Christians and linked with the role of Jesus. Enoch 1:9 is quoted as though it is scripture in Jude 1:14. The schematic view of history found in the apocalyptic writings, which divided time into a series of ages under the control of various earthly powers, resembles, and may even derive from, the scheme of the successive ages of humanity sketched by Hesiod in his poem, *Works and Days* (ca. 700 B.C.E.). In this work, the golden age, followed by the ages of silver, bronze, and iron, is the period of the ideal human community, to which the wise and moral are called to aspire. The impact of this apocalyptic tradition on both Christianity and Judaism in the early centuries of the common era—whatever its origins may have been—was thus deep and varied. The Greco-Roman phenomenon of the oracles consulted by commoners and rulers for insight in making important personal and national decisions also clearly influenced both Judaism and Christianity during the same period. Two examples of this cultural influence are the *Shepherd of Hermas* (mentioned in Chapter 4) and the *Sibylline Oracles.* The revelation concerning the future of God's people seems to have been modeled after the Cumean Sibyl, where, at a cave on the coast of Italy north of Naples, women known as Sibyls, said to be inspired by Apollo, gave answers to questions addressed to them concerning personal affairs or matters of state. In a poem known as the *Fourth Eclogue* by Virgil, the Sibyl predicts the unprecedented prosperity of Rome that will take place as the result of the birth of a child who will become the agent of renewal.[4] The Christian Sibyllines announced the coming of Christ, the spurning of him by the Jews and the acceptance of him by the Gentiles, the judgment that will fall on Rome, and the coming of God's reign over the world.

The most dramatic manifestation of the apocalyptic view of Christianity in the sec-

---

[3]These writings are translated and edited with introductions in J. H. Charlesworth, ed., *The Old Testament Apocrypha* (New York: Doubleday, Vol.1, 1983; Vol. 2, 1985).

[4]The complete text of the *Fourth Eclogue* is in H. C. Kee, *The New Testament in Context: Sources and Documents* (Englewood Cliffs, NJ: Prentice-Hall, 1984), pp. 162–163.

ond and third centuries came through Montanus of Phrygia, a section of Asia Minor referred to in the only complete apocalypse in the New Testament, the Revelation of John. Montanus and his two associates, the prophetesses Priscilla and Maximilla, claimed to be the instruments of the Holy Spirit. Some time after 170, they announced that the return of Christ was about to occur and that the New Jerusalem predicted in the Revelation of John was going to descend near some villages a dozen miles outside Philadelphia on the Aegean coast. In spite of fierce opposition by the ecclesiastical authorities and the failure of this prediction to come true, Montanism took hold in the villages of Asia Minor. It also spread to the churches of the West, where it took root in Gaul, but especially in North Africa.

This opposition on the part of the church leaders fits well with the apocalyptic tradition evident in Daniel: The official religious leaders were regarded by the Montanists as part of the political coalition that opposed God's real work. The official opposition served only to encourage the enthusiasm of the supporters of Montanus's prophetic pronouncements. As we have observed, it was Tertullian who, in his later years, adopted the Montanist point of view, especially concerning the central role of the Spirit in the life of the church, which he regarded not as a structure ruled by the bishops, but as a free community of those guided and empowered by the Spirit. He viewed the Spirit's work as leading to a strict moral life for clergy and laity alike, including the refusal to readmit those put out of the church on moral or political charges. In Tertullian's hands, the details of apocalyptic interest in prophetic fulfillment were eclipsed by insistence on the purity of God's people.

Knowledge of the Truth: Gnosticism

In contrast both to the nationalist movements that had set the Jewish people against Rome and to the apocalyptic groups that awaited God's intervention in history to destroy the empire and establish God's rule over the earth, there arose among the Christians of the second century groups that sought liberation from the world through knowledge. They came to be known as the Gnostics, from the Greek word for "knowledge," *gnosis*. The Gnostics saw themselves as characters in a cosmic drama beyond the physical world of appearances. Proper knowledge of ultimate reality would enable them to escape from this material realm of deceit and appearance and to return to the eternal sphere from which they had originally come. The ability to understand this origin and destiny came through a special kind of knowledge of God: gnosis.

The two components from which the Gnostic view of the origin and destiny of humans was formed were the philosophical concepts of Platonism as they had been reformulated in this period and an allegorical understanding of the creation stories in the opening chapters of Genesis. Similarly, in the first century C.E. Philo of Alexandria had drawn heavily on Plato's *Timaeus* for his interpretation of the creation. In the fourth century B.C.E., Plato had made a sharp distinction between the eternal world that was knowable and unchangeable and the physical world that could be known only imperfectly and tentatively: The latter was an ever-changing and temporal copy of the former. God had formed the world at a point in time, and in it human souls were a mixture of immortal and rational elements, which came from God, and material, temporal features. The human body was created by lesser gods (i.e., the stars). God was the intelligent and efficient cause of the structured world, which is always in a state of change. Thus, Being (God in his changeless essence) is the cause of Becoming (the world in its constant condition of change and decay). It is this basic view of God and the world, woven in with details of the Genesis stories of creation, that lies behind the myth set forth by the Gnostics to account for the creation and for evil.[5] Also articulated is the Gnostic hope of deliverance from the present world. The Gnostics had a sense of group identity, evident in an esoteric style of expression that communicated to the inner members, and in the ritual by which that identity was gained. The specifics of the myth can be reconstructed from two kinds of sources: (1) the criticisms of the Gnostics in the writings of the leading teachers and writers of the church, such as Justin Martyr, Irenaeus, Clement of Alexandria, Origen, and Hippolytus of Rome; and (2) the Gnostic writings that have been preserved, especially the manuscripts from a Gnostic library found in Upper Egypt in 1945 at Nag Hammadi.[6] The fullest account of the Gnostic myth is in "The Secret Book According to John,"[7] in which four stages of the scheme of cosmic redemption are depicted:

1. The eternal, solitary principle expands into a spiritual universe filled with divine power.
2. Out of this spiritual universe is created the material universe, including the stars, the planets, the earth, and hell. In the process of the formation of the material world, a nonspiritual being, Ialdabaoth, steals divine power and uses it for his own purposes.
3. In the creation of Adam and Eve and their begetting of children, the thieving Ialdabaoth is deceived, so that in spite of the death of Abel and the corruption of Cain, Seth is imbued with spirit and thus becomes the progenitor of the Gnostics, in whom the spirit can work.
4. Gradually, the divine recovers power in the universe when the Gnostics are summoned by a savior and return to God and their destined place in the spiritual universe. Wisdom is the agent through whom this knowledge is dispensed and the renewal accomplished.

In the elaboration of this myth in other Gnostic writings, it is Ialdabaoth who is responsible for the creation of the material universe. In the *Gospel of Truth*,[8] creation is corrupted by error and therefore is unable to discern its origins. Jesus, who is God within and exists within God the Father, comes as a teacher, and by suffering on the "tree" (the cross), overcomes the produce of the tree of the knowledge of evil. He discloses God only to the members of the elect community. The material world will vanish, but to the enlightened group, the Father gave the secret name of the Son whom he produced to be the messenger of truth to the elect. Only those who possess this great name can utter it and have access to reality. All who came from the place of eternal repose will return to it, having escaped sorrows and hell and attained truth and perfection. Yet it is in that state, spiritually speaking, that the true children of God already dwell.

Valentinus, born in lower Egypt about the turn of the second century C.E. and educated in Alexandria, migrated around 140 to Rome, where he became the intellectual leader of the Gnostic-oriented Christians. The school of thought that arose in his name flourished in both the eastern and western churches down to the seventh century. By using the alle-

[5] This sketch of the Gnostic myth and teachings depends on the illuminating analysis of Gnosticism by Bentley Layton in his study and translations, *Gnostic Scriptures* (Garden City, NY: Doubleday, 1987). These writings are in Coptic, an ancient form of Egyptian still used among Christian groups there.

[6] James M. Robinson, ed., *The Nag Hammadi Library* (San Francisco: Harper and Row, 1977).

[7] In B. Layton, ed. *Gnostic Scriptures* (Garden City, NY: Doubleday, 1987).

[8] In Layton, *Gnostic Scriptures*.

gorical method of interpreting scripture, Valentinus and his followers were able to remain within the church, even though the substance of the Gnostic teachings was incompatible with the New Testament claims that the God of Jesus was also the God of the creation of the world and that Jesus would return to restore and renew the world. Examples of the allegorical interpretation appear in the Gnostic Gospel of Thomas, where eating flesh and drinking blood are perceived as partaking in the Word and Spirit. In the Gnostic writings, Jesus does not invite anyone to share in the eucharistic meal: He *is* the Eucharist. As God anointed Jesus, so He anointed the Apostles, and the elect are anointed through the Spirit and the light, which Jesus brings to his own and which is essentially self-knowledge.

A parallel development of Christianity along Gnostic lines took place in Syria, where the central figure for conveying the hidden truth to the elect was the apostle Thomas, who was portrayed as the twin of Jesus. This may have been meant literally or figuratively, but the point was that the relationship between Jesus and Thomas was a model of the links between Jesus (who was thought to dwell within his own people) and the inner life of the faithful. Other writings from this tradition include the Acts of Thomas, the Book of Thomas the Contender, and the Gospel of Thomas. The basic features of the Gnostic myth appear in the Hymn of the Pearl,[9] which builds on Jesus' parable of the man who seeks the costly pearl (Matt. 13:45–46) to describe the journey of the soul. The soul enters the physical body, but gains release following a series of inner experiences leading to heightened self-knowledge and comes finally to the eternal repose. Similarly, the formless collection of sayings of Jesus in the Gospel of Thomas are a summons to the elect to free themselves from family ties or sexual identity, and from physical bonds or obligations, in order to gain unity and enlightenment from within through true self-knowledge. Jesus is the All; his kingdom is spread over the earth, but is discernible only to those who have found the light of true knowledge through him.

Simon Magus was credited by some ancient critics of the Gnostics with having founded the Gnostic sectarian movement. He is mentioned briefly in Acts 8 as a Samaritan magician who was converted to Christianity, but who tried to buy the rights to the bestowal of the Holy Spirit that was accomplishing such wonders according to the narrative in Acts. There are reports in the writings of Justin, Irenaeus, and Hippolytus of Rome that during the reign of Claudius (41–54 C.E.) Simon Magus went to Rome, where he lived in association with a Phoenician woman named Helen. It is told in these Christian sources that he died in a failed attempt to duplicate Jesus' experience of death, entombment, and resurrection. From these later sources, we hear that Simon claimed to be the supreme god, with Helen as the primary concept emanating from him. She had appeared in history as Helen of Troy and was reincarnated as Simon's companion of the same name. Simon had taken on bodily form to rescue her and symbolically to redeem all the elect from involvement in physical existence and the material world. Trust in him—or them—assures salvation. It is likely that the stories of Simon and the claims made in his behalf were created well after the New Testament period. It is difficult to know whether they arose as competition with, or a caricature of, the claims Christians were making about Jesus. But the extent to which they were taken seriously shows how ready segments of the populace in these early centuries of the Christian era were to accept claims of celestial visitors and heavenly messages.

[9]In Layton, *Gnostic Scriptures.*

In at least two ways, Gnosticism offered a serious challenge to Christianity. At the intellectual level, it represented a basic alternative to the Platonic philosophical tradition used by Philo and drawn on by Clement and Origen to provide a rationally coherent framework in which to understand the origins of the world, the human race, God, and the future. Philosophers in that tradition, such as Plotinus, sought to maintain the notion that the eternal model of the world was discernible in the imperfect, transitory copies composing the material world. Later Platonists, however, assumed that an independent principle of evil was responsible for this world, subject as it was to corruption and decay. The Gnostics not only took this position about the material universe, but denied that knowledge of God was attainable by humans apart from the special revelations granted to the elect. Although rejecting the proposals of the Gnostics, Christian thinkers in this and subsequent centuries—most notably, Augustine in the later fourth century—would deal with these twin issues of how God may be known and how one can account for evil.

At the level of social identity, Gnosticism posed the problem of how one might find identity as a member of God's people. The apparently widespread positive responses to Simonian, Valentinian, and other forms of Gnosticism among Christians and others served to show the mainstream Christian leaders and writers that they must emphasize the full humanity of Jesus and the earthly, human sphere in which they were persuaded God was to achieve the divinely intended goal of the establishment of His rule on earth. In the older Christian tradition of evangelism, all humans were invited to faith in Jesus as the Messiah regardless of ethnic, social, financial, or intellectual status. Was Christianity ready to become an esoteric, intellectualistic movement like the Gnostics? If not, what were the alternatives for its mode of group identity? What was required was a clear image of the church as a human society, complete with guidelines for admission and maintenance of membership and with defined structures of leadership. Down to the present, these have continued to be the perennial issues the church has faced.

Which Are the Authoritative Scriptures?

By the turn of the first century C.E., the Judaic rabbinic leadership had made firm decisions that defined the movement in distinction from Christianity, which increased the urgency for the church to make comparable decisions. Which of the writings were to be used for study and instruction and considered authoritative for depicting their respective histories, formulating their present obligations, and sketching their views of the future? According to later tradition, at Yavneh in the last decade of the first century, the Jewish leaders designated as authoritative the Hebrew writings known by Christians as the Old Testament. The version of the Jewish scriptures in most common use among Christians in this period and subsequently was the so-called Septuagint, the widely used Greek translation of the Jewish scriptures, which later was translated into Latin and other languages.[10] It is from the Septuagint that nearly all the quotations from the scriptures are to be found in the New Tes-

---

[10] Protestant Christians, following the lead of Martin Luther, adopted the rule of Jewish orthodoxy, which recognized only the Hebrew scriptures as authoritative. These were called the Old Testament, and the other Jewish writings were designated as Apocrypha.

tament. Because the various parts of the New Testament were produced in sites scattered across the Mediterranean world, and because some of its parts had not yet been written by the end of the first century, there was no immediate possibility or necessity to create a Christian counterpart to the official list of Jewish scriptures.

That necessity began to emerge, however, as the result of several factors in the life of the church in the second and third centuries.[11] One of these, which we have noted earlier, was the proposal by Marcion to recognize only his version of Luke and the letters of Paul as authoritative for Christians. He rejected the Old Testament and purged any favorable references to it in Luke. For Marcion, Christianity became the antithesis of Judaism. Montanus, as we have observed, sought to supplement the basic Christian teachings through the prophetic utterances he and his associates claimed had been given them by the Spirit of God. The church had to face the possibility of ongoing supplements to the Gospels and other early Christian writings that would alter or even supplant the older documents. The Gnostics, as we have seen, effectively transformed the Jewish scriptures by means of their allegorical interpretation of them, which they derived from their reading of Plato. For the church to tolerate these movements in diverse directions would make it impossible to define itself, the criteria for membership in it, or the ground of its faith.

By the middle of the second century, therefore, there began to appear among various Christian writers lists of writings from what we now call the New Testament that were declared to be based on the teachings of the apostles and, consequently, to be authoritative. The effective list came to be known as the canon, which derives from a Greek word meaning "rule" or "authoritative measurement." The New Testament writings referred to by three Christian writers from different parts of the Roman world at the end of the second century illustrate this emerging consensus. Theophilus of Antioch, who died about 190, quotes as scripture: the four gospels, the letters of Paul (including I and II Corinthians, Romans, Philippians, Colossians, and the so-called Pastorals[12]). Clement of Alexandria testifies to the authority of the four Gospels, the fourteen epistles of Paul (among which he includes the letter to the Hebrews), Acts, I Peter, I John, and Revelation. He expresses doubts about the other so-called Catholic Epistles,[13] however. Indicative of the fluid state of the question about the New Testament canon are Clement's reference to some non-New Testament writings as "inspired" and his statement that there are three versions of the Gospel of Mark: the canonical, the spiritual, and the secret, which was supposed to be accessible only to a small Christian group. Similarly, earlier in the second century, Justin (100–180) had spoken of the Gospels as the "memoirs of the apostles." He expressed a preference for the first three Gospels, while using in his theological constructions the Logos or "Word" that appears only in the Gospel of John. It is Irenaeus of Lyons, however, who discussed directly the importance of what he regarded as the core of the New Testament: the four gospels, the number of which he compared with such basic features of the world as the four winds, the four points of the compass, and the four elements. Furthermore, he stated that the unchanging faith of the church rested on scripture and tradition, and by "scripture," he

---

[11] The finest survey of the origins of the New Testament canon is that of Bruce M. Metzger, *The Canon of the New Testament* (New York and Oxford: Clarendon Press, 1987), and is followed here.

[12] The Pastorals include I and II Timothy and Titus, all of which purport to have been written by Paul.

[13] II and III John, II Peter, and Jude.

meant these authoritative New Testament writings in addition to the Jewish scriptures, for which the Christians now claimed to have the key to proper understanding. His list of "scripture" included not only the Revelation of John, but also the Shepherd of Hermas.[14]

One of the earliest and most important pieces of evidence of the development of a canon of the New Testament is an eighth-century copy of a document from the late second century found in Rome in the eighteenth century. Called the Muratorian Canon, in recognition of Muratori, the Italian scholar who found and published it, this document discusses Christian canon on the basis of "what is recognized and received," thus highlighting the consensus of the churches and their leadership on the issue of the canon. By the early fourth century, Eusebius—whose *Ecclesiastical History* we have repeatedly referred to and whose role in the establishment of the church through the emperor Constantine we shall consider later—prepared a list that included the four Gospels, Paul's epistles, I Peter, and I John. Eusebius gave differing opinions on Revelation, but admitted it to the canon. He debated the inclusion of James, Jude, II Peter, and II John and rejected a whole series of writings that were apparently being taken as authoritative or being used in various parts of the church, which he grouped as follows:

- *Spurious works that are orthodox but not canonical:*
    Acts of Paul; Shepherd of Hermes, Apocalypse of Peter, Barnabas, Teachings of the Apostles (Didache), Gospel according to the Hebrews.
- *Fictions by heretics:*
    Gospel of Peter, Gospel of Thomas, Gospel of Matthias, Acts of Andrew, Acts of John.

Similar confirmation of the central core of agreed-on writings for the New Testament canon and the items over which uncertainty continued may be found in two of the oldest (fourth century) manuscript copies of the Bible: Codex Sinaiticus and Codex Vaticanus. The former contains the four Gospels, fourteen letters of Paul (including Hebrews), Acts, seven catholic epistles, and Revelation. But Barnabas and the Shepherd of Hermas are also in these copies of the "New Testament." By the last third of the fourth century, Athanasius of Alexandria attempted to close the canon. In an official communication to the diocese under his supervision, he listed as canonical what are today the twenty-seven books of the New Testament. In subsequent centuries, however, various individual and corporate decisions differed in some details, even though the common core remained as it had been since the middle of the second century.

As significant as the official actions about the canon of the New Testament, however, is the evidence for the enduring popularity in certain regions of the church of writings that never gained canonical status. Examples of these are:

- *Letters and reports of preaching:*
    The Preaching of Peter
    Correspondence between Paul and Seneca (Roman philosopher and advisor to emperors)
- *Acts of the individual Apostles:*
    Acts of John, Peter, Paul, Andrew, Thomas
- *Gospels addressed to special groups:*
    Gospel of the Nazoreans, of the Ebionites, and of the Hebrews

---

[14]See p. 55.

- *Gospels linked with an Apostle or early follower of Jesus:*
    Gospel of Philip, of Thomas, of Nicodemus, and of Bartholomew
    Gospel of Mary
- *Secret revelations:*
    Sophia Jesu Christ (Wisdom of Jesus Christ)
    Pistis Sophia (Faith-wisdom)
- *Infancy Gospels:*
    Protevangelium of James (Early Gospel); Infancy Gospel of Thomas.[15]

Other apocryphal Gospels and acts have been described in our analysis of the apocalyptic and Gnostic developments of Christianity within the early centuries, such as the Gospel of Thomas and the Gospel of Truth, which claim to offer additional revelations about Jesus. The Acts type of writings seek to highlight the supernatural features of the experiences of the apostles, just as second- and third-century Roman literature sought to highlight and expand the miraculous features of wise men and philosophers. Philostratus's *Life of Apollonius of Tyana* vividly portrays the journeys of an itinerant philosopher across Syria and Persia to India.[16] Astonishing events are depicted in connection with his travels and teaching, with the clear aim of suggesting divine approval of the content of his teachings. Jesus and the apostles are similarly portrayed in these apocryphal writings as performing astounding public actions as a way of proving that God is behind their message. In some of them, Jesus strikes down his detractors, as when (in the Infancy Gospel of Thomas) he puts to death one of his playmates who mocks him. Peter outdoes Simon Magus in public stunts before crowds in Rome. As the Christian communities grew in numbers and rose in cultural status, there sprang up Christian equivalents of the romantic, novellike stories of their founder and his original associates. Only rarely and in scattered places, however, did any of these apocryphal documents come to be treated as authoritative, except in cases like the Gnostics, who held a writing such as the Gospel of Truth to be essential for understanding the whole of the Jesus tradition.

The Canon as a Primary Instrument of Unity

By the end of the third century, there was as yet no center of authority for the churches scattered across the Roman empire. The high mobility of the populace, the mounting political and intellectual pressure on the Christians, and the strains produced from groups within the church who were espousing ideas incompatible with those held by the majority of Christians made it essential to develop fixed norms on the basis of which decisions could be made about Christian faith and life. Vital for the Christians in this period was the formulation of an official list of sacred writings that could be appealed to for settling these burning issues. Before there was any firm consensus on this issue, however, the growth of

---

[15]These noncanonical materials are conveniently brought together in English translation in the two volumes edited by W. Schneemelcher (English translation ed. R. McL. Wilson), *New Testament Apocrypha* (Philadelphia: Westminster, 1963, 1965).

[16]Philostratus, *Life of Apollonius of Tyana*, ed. F. C. Conybeare, Loeb Classical Library (Cambridge, MA: Harvard University Press, 1918, 1960). See my analysis of the phenomenon of miracle in *Medicine. Miracle and Magic in New Testament Times* (Cambridge: Cambridge University Press, 1986).

the Christian movement and the clear threat of a split within the Roman Empire between centers of power in the eastern and the western Mediterranean began to place a stress on the church as well. The shaky state of the imperial system led many to revive the charge that it was the reaction of the gods against the Christians' refusal to participate in divine honors to the emperor that was causing the profound unrest in, and uncertainty about, the future of the empire. By the second half of the third century, this state of affairs had resulted in major periods of persecution of the Christians. It is these developments and the unforeseen outcome of the empire's turning to Christianity for unity and stability that we discuss in Chapter 8.

Chapter 8

Conflict between Church and Empire

In spite of Nero's attack on the Christians in the 60s, the issue of the relationship of Christians to the Roman empire did not come into clear focus until well into the second century. Until that time, the Christian movement had been widely regarded as a Jewish sect, and its disputes with Judaism were seen by the Roman authorities as intra-Jewish. The Jews had long benefited from imperial policies that classified their religion in the officially permitted category, and Christians throughout most of the first century seemed to be a variant version of that tolerated group. Major factors in the respect Judaism enjoyed among the Romans were the antiquity of its laws and the fidelity with which its adherents sought to obey them. There were, however, hostile attitudes toward Jews as well. The first-century B.C.E. author and senator Cicero said of the Jews that "The practice of their sacred rites was at variance with the glory of our empire, the dignity of our name, and the customs of our ancestors."[1] Earlier, Jews had been regarded as allies of Rome, but by the late first century C.E., the nationalistic uprising of the Jews in Palestine, followed by the revolt under Bar Kochba in the second century, made them suspect in official Roman eyes. As a result, despite their benefiting from the officially favorable policy toward the Jews, the early Christians did suffer an ongoing suspicion that they might instigate subversion or political revolt.

---

[1] Cicero, *In Defense of Flaccus* (28.69); from Cicero, Marcus Tullius, *Speeches*, Loeb Classical Library (Cambridge, MA: Harvard University Press, 1937).

Christianity Regarded as a Branch of Judaism

The Roman confusion of Christians with Jews in the first century is readily understandable. Judaism was highly diverse, both in Palestine and in the wider Roman world in which Jews had lived for centuries. Although nearly all Jews identified with the cult that was carried out in the splendid Jerusalem temple of Yahweh, the physical remoteness of that shrine for most Jews had led them to develop the practice of holding meetings in homes or public halls where they could gather to read their ancient writings, to worship, and to study the implications of these scriptures for their own lives. Until the late second century C.E., when the interpretations of the Law began to be organized into the collection known as the Mishnah, the pattern of worship and study in the synagogue seems to have been informal, with local peculiarities. As noted earlier (p. 12), in some areas, such as Egypt, there had been efforts to bring together insights from pagan philosophy and the biblical tradition, as exemplified by the extensive writings of Philo of Alexandria. Elsewhere, the intellectual level was more modest, with the primary concerns being to foster social identity for Jews in a pagan environment. Outwardly, the Christians' gatherings for reading the scriptures and informal worship in what they called *ecclesiae* (churches) must have seemed nearly identical with those of the Jews: Both groups studied the Jewish scriptures and prayed to the God of Israel, both were concerned to define their relationship to God as His covenant people, and both declared the universal power of God over the universe and human history.

The political criticism of Rome and the potential for hostility toward the empire in Jewish and Christian apocalyptic literature were apparent and could be regarded by the Roman authorities only with profound suspicion. The fact that the Jews had twice revolted against Rome in this period and, on other occasions, had sided with Middle East nations determined to regain control over the eastern provinces of the empire increased suspicion of the Jews. The Christians' steadfast refusal to take part in the sacrifices to the Roman gods on behalf of the empire and its leaders became the major issue between the church and the Roman state.

By the middle of the second century, several factors helped to set Christianity apart from Judaism in the eyes of the Romans. The Jews, following the crushing defeat of their forces under Bar Kochba in the second revolt against the Romans, abandoned the nationalist cause and turned instead to sharpening the definition of themselves as God's covenant people. The criteria for separating themselves from the Gentiles were strict observance of circumcision and of food and Sabbath laws and the maintenance of ethnic purity through marriage within their community. The Christians did not observe these requirements, and their numbers included a growing majority of Gentiles, some from intellectual circles and even some from families involved in the Roman political structure. The burials of Christians in the catacombs of Rome began to display distinctive Christian art at this time. Just as Judaism was organizing itself into what became the rabbinic system, the Christians were developing regional hierarchical structures that were presided over by a bishop, with presbyters (elders) and deacons under his supervision. There was no mistaking that this movement was different from Judaism. The major distinction, however, was that, whereas the Jews, as a substitute for offering sacrifices in the name of the emperor, agreed to pay to Rome the equivalent of the tax they had paid to the temple in Jerusalem before its destruction, the Christians would not under any conditions share in the emperor cult. To bear the name of Christian, therefore, was evidence of attitudes hostile toward Rome.

The Central Issue: Christian Nonparticipation in the State Cult

The expectation that there would be universal participation in the rites on behalf of the emperor became increasingly important by the beginning of the second century. The first clear evidence of this expectation is in the famous correspondence between the emperor Trajan and Pliny, governor of the province of Bithynia in Asia Minor. Further evidence of the importance of the state cult appeared in the policies of the emperors. As noted earlier, Domitian (81–96), for example, insisted that he be addressed as *dominus et deus* ("Lord and God"). Most of the peoples conquered by the Romans were polytheistic and seemed to have recognized the similarities between the roles of their gods and those of the Romans. It was possible for them to find Roman equivalents for the deities of their own religions. Accordingly, these subject peoples were quite willing to take part in the divine honors on behalf of the emperor. Because the Romans believed that the maintenance of political, social, and moral order was directly dependent on continued devotion to their gods by all subjects of the empire, the refusal of the Christians to participate in this politico-religious rite was seen as subversive.

The Christians' acclamation of Jesus as Lord (in Greek, *kyriou;* in Latin, *dominus*) forced them to decide which person was to be acknowledged by them as such: Christ or Caesar? Failure to offer a libation to the genius, or guardian spirit, of the emperor was a clear sign of disloyalty. The belief in the divinity of rulers that was widespread among the Greek kings combined with the Roman concept of divine support for rulers to construct an idea of sacrifice on behalf of the monarch. This idea was almost universally accepted during the period, and it served to bind the diverse peoples ruled by Rome in support of the emperor. The refusal of the Christians to share in this mixture of devotion and patriotism set them apart as suspect and despicable. Both Christian apocalyptic writings and the Christian Sibylline oracles foretold in cryptic, symbolic language the downfall of earthly empires before the establishment of God's rule on the earth. Jewish opponents of Christianity drew to the attention of the officials the import of these predictions of doom promulgated by the Christians.

Yet from the beginning of their movement, the Christians had insisted on their gratitude for the order that Rome maintained and on their commitment to obey Roman law. Paul advised the Roman Christians to be subject to the governing authorities as having been placed in power by God (Rom. 13:1), to pay taxes, and to honor the rulers as "ministers of God" (13:6–7). The author of Acts makes the point repeatedly that neither Paul nor the other Christian leaders were ever guilty of violation of Roman law. The author of the First Letter of Peter calls his readers to be subject to human institutions, including governors and emperors, who are to be honored by Christians (I Peter 2:13–17). Yet Christians remained under suspicion because of the more or less secret nature of their gatherings and their implicitly anti-Roman hopes for the triumph of God's kingdom over the earthly powers.

In 135 the defeat of the Jewish nationalists led to the transformation of Jerusalem and its temple into a fully Roman city with a shrine to the chief Roman god, Jupiter. Nerva (96–98) seems to have reversed the anti-Christian policy of Domitian. The policy of Trajan (98–117), as outlined in his response to Pliny, was to allow the Christians to continue their movement, so long as they were not called before the Roman authorities, in which case they could choose between making the sacrifice on behalf of the emperor or death. Similarly, Hadrian (117–138) ruled that action was to be taken against Christians only as lawbreakers, and that they were to be protected against informers or unfounded accusations.

The Christian apologists of the second century sought to show that their teachings were in harmony with true philosophy of the Greek tradition (Plato and the Stoics, especially) and that Christians were the soul of the world, devoted to the service of humanity. In an anonymous treatise of this period addressed to someone named Diognetus, its author declares that "What the soul is in the body, that are the Christians in this world." They preserve the body, and even though hated by the body, as flesh hates the spirit, they love and preserve the body.[2] By the second half of the second century, however, the success and increased visibility of Christianity resulted in its heightened vulnerability, with the result that a number of its leaders were challenged by the imperial authorities and executed.

The oldest and most detailed report of these martyrdoms describes the death of Polycarp, bishop of Smyrna in Asia Minor. He is reported by ancient tradition to have been a disciple of John the Apostle and to have lived from about 70 until his martyrdom in 155 or 157. The Roman proconsul offered to release him on condition that he would acclaim the emperor as lord and offer sacrifice, to which he replied, "I have served God eighty-six years, and he has never done wrong to me. How, then, could I blaspheme the King who saved me?"[3] Polycarp insisted that he was a Christian and therefore could not swear by the guardian spirit of the emperor. When he was about to die, he looked up to heaven and praised God for the knowledge of Himself and His people that God had provided and for the privilege of being granted a place among the martyrs. His final petition was that his death might be a sacrifice acceptable to God.[4] The author of this account of Polycarp's martyrdom notes that he was the twelfth in that region to die for his witness as a Christian.[5] An ancient and probably reliable account of the death of the second-century leader Justin and several of his Christian associates reports that the crucial issue in their interrogation by the Roman officer was that they declared themselves to be Christians and therefore refused to offer the required sacrifice to the emperor. All were beheaded forthwith.[6]

By the turn of the third century, the growing tendency in the Roman Empire to combine features of various religious traditions (called by modern scholars syncretism) was evident in the highest place: the imperial family. Septimius Severus (193–211), of African origins, had sought to legitimate his role as caesar by claiming that Marcus Aurelius (161–180)

[2]"Epistle to Diognetus," in *The Apostolic Fathers*, tr. K. Lake, Loeb Classical Library (Cambridge, MA: Harvard University Press, 1912–1913).

[3]"Martyrdom of Polycarp," in *Faith of the Early Fathers* (tr. W. Jurgens (Collegeville, MN: The Liturgical Press), pp. 30–31.

[4]"Martyrdom of Polycarp," p. 14.

[5]"Martyrdom of Polycarp," p. 19.

[6]"Martyrdom of the Holy Martyrs," in *Ante-Nicene Fathers*, Vol. 1 (Grand Rapids, MI: Eerdmans, n.d.), pp. 305–306.

had adopted him as son. But he also was eager to lend an aura of divine sanction to himself by having himself identified in ceremonies and on coins with Sol, the god of the Sun, and his wife, Julia Domna, as the Moon. It was further claimed that Julia Domna was Cybele, a deity in Asia Minor known as the mother of the gods. Her son, Caracalla (198–217), called himself "Lord" and "Ruler of the World" and sought to unite all humanity religiously in devotion to the Egyptian god, Serapis, who combined features of Zeus and Osiris as sovereign and healer. A little later, Julia Mamaea, mother of Severus Alexander (222–235), was designated as mother of all the gods. In these circumstances, the refusal of the Christians to adopt any kind of synthesis between their religion and those of the rest of the empire seemed to the authorities all the more odd, annoying, and subversive.

In spite of the efforts of some emperors, such as Commodus (176–192), to relax the opposition to Christians, and even though there was a significant number of conversions of women within the imperial establishment, pressures against the church continued to mount. In 202, Septimius Severus decreed a prohibition of conversions to Christianity. An empirewide persecution of the Christians began, with reports of martyrdoms from Antioch, Corinth, and Alexandria in the east to Rome and Carthage in the west. Although most political leaders were scornful of the movement, Julia Mamaea set up an extended conversation with the great Christian scholar Origen (185–254), the outstanding intellectual figure in the church at that time. A later Roman historian reported that in Severus Alexander's imperial chapel there were statues of great religious figures of the past, including Orpheus (the mythical Greek musician), Abraham, and Christ. Severus Alexander, whose origins were in Syria, was killed on the banks of the Rhine by Maximinus (235–238), who tried to combat the imperial policy of quiet support for the church by a campaign of martyrdom for its leaders.

A Latin writer of the late second or early third century, Minucius Felix, reports the description of Christianity by one Caecilius as the pronouncement about the universe and its powers by "people ignorant of learning, unlettered, unacquainted with even the meanest arts" and as a "sham philosophy." He calls the Christians "a gang of discredited and proscribed desperadoes . . . gathered together from the lowest dregs of the populace." They are "ignorant men and credulous women—and women are naturally unstable—and have formed a rabble of impious conspirators; at their nocturnal gatherings, solemn fasts, and barbarous meals; the bond of union is not any sacred rite but crime. They are a secret tribe that lurks in darkness and shuns the light, silent in public, chattering in corners."[7]

Intensification of Roman Opposition to Christianity and the Christian Response: Martyrdom

In the middle of the third century, the Christians' view of the impending overturn of the present order had a resurgence in the west as well. Tertullian (150–230) in Carthage became more and more interested in the pronouncements of self-styled new prophets and their revelations about the future. In his later years, he became persuaded by the visions and

---

[7] Quoted from J. Stevenson and W. H. C. Frend, eds., *The New Eusebius* (London: SPCK, 1987), pp. 177–178.

predictions of the end proclaimed by Montanus and developed his own version of the apocalyptic expectation of the destruction of the present order and the establishment of the Kingdom of God. Hippolytus of Rome (170–230?), who was probably originally from Antioch, also emphasized the themes that Christians had borrowed from Jewish apocalyptic writing, with the result that the Roman authorities suspected that the leaders of the church were organizing to subvert the state.

Instead of the martyrdoms cooling the fervor of the Christian movement, however, this violent imperial effort at suppression succeeded in increasing the zeal and commitment of its members. Irenaeus, although eloquent and learned in combating what he believed to be the heresies taught by his contemporaries in the name of Christianity, continued to affirm his expectation of the New Age and saw the death of the Christian witnesses as evidence that it was soon to come. Although Origen did not share the apocalyptic expectation of Irenaeus, he wrote a treatise, *Exhortation to the Heathen*, in which he described anyone who died for the faith as entering mystical union with Christ in his suffering and death.[8]

Origen prized martyrdom because it showed publicly who the true believers were: Only the martyr was the authentic follower of Christ.[9] Quoting extensively from the Psalms and the Old Testament prophets, and even more from the Gospels and the letters of Paul, he developed the case that God has already stored up in heaven a reward for those who have shown their fidelity to Christ by accepting death as his followers. Just as God ordered Abraham to leave his native land to journey to the unknown land of promise, so Christians are called by God to leave this world and prepare to enter the kingdom of heaven. Belief in the heart is not enough: It must be matched by confession in public. From the days of Trajan onward, this public affirmation or denial of oneself as a Christian had been the crucial factor in deciding whether one accused of membership in the movement was in fact a Christian and therefore doomed to be executed by the Roman authorities. Refusal to take part in the imperial rites, and especially the failure to take an oath by the fortune or genius of the emperor, was considered to jeopardize the support of the empire by the gods. The true Christians rejected any conformity or even compromise on this issue, Origen insisted. Central for identification of the individual as a member of God's new-covenant people was the passage in the gospels in which Jesus calls his disciples to take up the cross and follow him (Matt. 16:26–27). God will render to each according to his or her response to that demand. The faithful will be enthroned and will receive multiple awards in the presence of God. True blessedness is to affirm this basis of the covenant in spite of scorn of neighbors and officials, because it will be acclaimed by the heavenly throngs of the saints and the angels. The special significance of a martyr's death is "that it is endured for the sake of Christianity and piety and holiness," according to Origen. The first baptism was with water; the second is with the blood of martyrdom. Jesus' instructions about accepting death at the hands of the authorities are addressed to the inner core of his disciples, rather than to the masses. Accordingly, no one should be surprised that large numbers of professing Christians submit to imperial pressure and offer the required pagan sacrifices, thus avoiding martyrdom.

[8] Tr. in Henry Chadwick, *Alexandrian Christianity* (Philadelphia: Westminster Press, 1954).
[9] Henry Chadwick and J. E. Oulton, eds., *Alexandrian Christianity*, Library of Christian Classics (Philadelphia: Westminster Press, 1977), p. 371.

The mixture of the astonishing courage of their convictions on the part of many Christians with the intellectually impressive defense of their faith offered by brilliant thinkers of the caliber of Origen forced many thoughtful Romans to reassess their attitudes toward this strong and surging religious movement. There is no hint of an official attitude that assumed, "Just keep quiet about Christianity, and it will go away." Instead, the emperor Valerian (253–260) renewed the attack on the Christians, going so far as to prohibit them from gathering in their places of worship or even in cemeteries for burial of their members. The antagonism toward the church was heightened by the fact that, at precisely this time when the empire was undergoing major financial and military crises, the churches were stable and economically prosperous even though some bishops and ordinary Christians alike were driven into exile or put to death. Typical of the range of responses of Christians to the crisis created by the emperors is that of Cyprian, the bishop of Carthage. As noted earlier, at first he simply fled from Carthage while maintaining communications with the Christians in the provincial capital. For this escape, he drew criticism among the more radical opponents of Rome, but he seems to have justified his action on the ground that he was providing stability and leadership for the faithful in a time of crisis. Later, however, he was exiled by the authorities, and in 258 he was beheaded in Carthage, the first bishop there to undergo a martyr's death.

The Climax of Imperial Hostility to Christianity and the Beginning of Transformation of the Empire

At the end of the third century, Diocletian (284–305) made another attempt to regain order in the empire. In the more than 100 years before his accession to power, major social, political, and economic changes had occurred. The once-dominant military and political roles of the senators (the traditional elite with respect to wealth and power) were shifting increasingly to the *equites* (knights), a group whose economic status and political power were far below that of the senators. It was now a frequent occurrence that persons of low position in the Roman social order proved effective in the military or in an administrative role and were designated as knights and given central posts under the emperors. The latter divided the provinces so that the number of persons to whom the emperor could assign the role as head of a province was doubled, and hence, the circle of the emperor's personal power was enlarged. The military system dominated the empire and was controlled by the emperor.

As an aid to fostering stability and tranquility in the realm, Diocletian adopted the practice of having titles and names of the Greek and Roman gods and mythological figures applied to himself and to his major officials. Accordingly, he took the name of Jupiter for himself. Because the extent of the empire was so vast, he imposed men of his choice to control both the eastern portion of the empire, where he was resident, and the western provinces as well. To preserve the old tradition of heredity in the imperial rule, he adopted two men as "caesars" and married his daughters to them: Constantius, to share with Maximian (Diocletian's chief colleague) responsibility for rule in the West, and Galerius, as his own major aide in the East. Maximian was identified with Hercules, who in mythology was the strong man who triumphed over beasts that symbolized the powers of evil. Then, in 305, Diocletian and Maximian abdicated, after naming as "caesars" Severus in the West and Maximin in the East. Aiding them were Constantius and Galerius, who were designated by Diocletian as "augusti." Constantius was in charge of Spain and Gaul, but took the initiative in suppressing a rebellion in Britain. Galerius had commanded the armies along the Danube, where the threat of invasion by Germanic tribes was recurrent, but in 298 he shifted to the eastern borders when the Persians tried to regain control of the Syrian and Asia Minor provinces. Further evidence of the effort to exploit Roman religious traditions to achieve unity and order is reflected in the coins Diocletian issued, which honored "The Genius of the Roman People." These imperial figures also adopted the practice of wearing clothing or displaying symbols, such as the radiant crown of the Sun God, which suggested their links with the gods.

A major tactic for getting the public to pledge allegiance to the empire was Diocletian's decree requiring everyone to offer the sacrifices and oaths in behalf of the emperor, including the Christians. When an omen consulted by the emperor failed to give an unambiguous response, Diocletian concluded that it was the consequence of the nonparticipation by the Christians, with the result that the gods were showing their displeasure. In the spring of 303, the church in Nicomedia, a leading city on the neck of land that joins Europe and Asia Minor, was destroyed in the presence of civilian and military officers. Apparently, Diocletian hoped to establish a major city there to serve as the capital of the eastern empire, or even of the empire as a whole. Although he did not live to see the fulfillment of this hope, a city in the same vicinity, Byzantium, *was* to become the center of the empire and ultimately to be named Constantinople (modern Istanbul), in honor of the one who made it the seat of Roman power: the Emperor Constantine I. Diocletian's decree ordered that all churches were to be destroyed throughout the empire, as well as all copies of the Christian scriptures. Any Christians who served in governmental posts were to be dismissed, and any who had special legal privileges were to lose them immediately. They could not serve as witnesses in the courts in most types of civil cases. Although there was not to be mass murder of all adherents to the faith, in Nicomedia alone 268 Christians were put to death as a consequence of this decree. Although Diocletian shared control of the realm with other "caesars" in the West, the attack on the Christians was not matched in those provinces where the movement was not perceived as so great a threat to Roman control. But the basic issue was posed for the Christians: Could Christianity and the empire coexist?

In the early years of the fourth century, Constantius (250–306), a military leader under the Emperor Maximian, was taken ill in Eboracum (in what is now York, in England). He sent for his son, Constantine, who was with Galerius in the eastern empire. Described by some ancient Roman sources as the child of a commoner or even of a prostitute, Constantine's intelligence and administrative skills continued to stand him in good stead when the army in Britain proclaimed him ruler of the western provinces. In 307, Severus was deposed and fled to Ravenna, where he was soon put to death. Maxentius, who succeeded him, had himself declared *princeps* ("leader") and assumed control of Rome and southern Italy. Meanwhile, Constantine had married the daughter of Maximian and took from him the title of Augustus. The coalition between Galerius and Maximian in the east was broken by the latter's defection. Galerius's efforts to impose order on the empire failed, as can be inferred from the fact that at one point there were six who bore the imperial title. Initially, Galerius sent a colleague, Licinius, to try to regain control of the northwestern provinces from Constantine, but soon these two were allied against Maxentius. The latter's struggle for power led to his brief designation as emperor (306–312). In 312, Constantine led his troops across the Alps into northern Italy, where, in spite of fierce opposition from Maxentius's army, he was victorious and found that city after city opened its gates to him. The Milvian bridge, north of Rome, was the scene of the final decisive battle in which the vastly more numerous Roman troops were defeated by Constantine, who entered Rome as victor.

One legend tells that Constantine had sought the help of the God of the Christians when he undertook his invasion of Italy and that it had been promised to him. There are reports of his placing on the shields of his troops a chi-rho, formed by combining the first two letters in the Greek word, Christos, and a symbolic representation of Christ. When Constantine was declared emperor in Britain, he released all the Christians in the province under his control, granting them full freedom of worship. In Rome, he was confirmed as senior Augustus by the Roman senate. His policies included the restoration to the Christians of property the government had seized from them. Even Maximin (309–313), who came to power in the east, agreed to religious freedom for the Christian subjects there as well.

The Beginning of the Transformation of the Church under Constantine

In many ways, Christianity had been victorious in this struggle for power and popular commitment within the far-flung empire. But in gaining imperial support—or, as some cynics might say, through being used by Constantine to take over the empire—the Christians were confronted with a series of problems they would not have anticipated a century earlier. Foremost was the relation between church and state: How were the lines of responsibility to be drawn between the ecclesiastical and the political authorities? A prior question was, Who will now make the decisions about the leadership of the churches? About the defining of areas assigned to a bishop? About the exercise of authority within that framework? Since the new emperor had claimed support of the God of the Christians in gaining victory over his enemies, was he to be the center of decision making within the church? If not, how and by whom were these crucial decisions to be made?

A major problem within the church that we have mentioned earlier was how to treat those who, under pressure from the pagan leaders of the empire, had violated their Christian obligations by offering prayers or sacrifice to the Roman gods. Were these lapses on the part of formerly professing Christians simply to be forgiven or overlooked? Some members proposed that the solution for restoring those who were regarded by the faithful as traitors was a repetition of their baptism. What did that imply about the efficacy of their original baptism if they now needed to pass through the cleansing waters again?

These kinds of issues did not originate in the time of Constantine. They had been more or less submerged within the church as it sought to present a united front against its antagonists. Once that pressure from the central government was removed, however, the unresolved intra-Christian issues rose rapidly to the surface. The matter of restoring or excluding those who had betrayed their Christian commitment under pressure came to a head in North Africa, specifically in Numidia, the province to the west of Carthage. The leaders of the church there had a mixed record on the issues of betrayal of the faith and surrender of the scriptures. When Constantine, on advice of an ecclesiastical counselor, supported Caecilian to become bishop of Carthage, immediately the stories surfaced about this man's having yielded to pressure from the Romans during the period of persecution. One of those involved, Menurius, claimed that Caecilian had fooled the officials into thinking he had so yielded. In any case, the Numidians, led by one Donatus, denounced Caecilian and the bishops who had consecrated him, on the ground that they had all been traitors to the Christian faith. As troublesome as the basic issue of dealing with those who were regarded as traitors was the larger question of with whom responsibility rested to adjudicate such disputes. In 316, in Milan, Constantine took a step of grave consequence when he ruled that Caecilian was properly the bishop and ordered the confiscation of the property of the followers of Donatus. This action not only raised doubts about the emperor's earlier proclamation of freedom of conscience in religious matters; it also failed to remedy the situation of the church in Numidia, which continued to reject Caecilian. At a council of the church convened in Arles in France, an effort was made to force clergy to accept the appointments and assignments made through these theoretically universal conventions of clergy. The powerful hand of the emperor could no longer be ignored, however: The church–state issue was not resolved, but in fact intensified.

The high esteem in which the martyrs continued to be held by the church following the assumption of imperial power by Constantine produced two kinds of literature. First, it produced a large body of material in which the martyrs were depicted in vivid narrative style, including details of their courage, suffering, and death. Known to modern scholarship as *The Acts of the Martyrs*, this material is readily available in various translations. Although the details are no doubt heightened and even romanticized, they still give a clear picture of the issues that confronted Christians under pressure from the empire and of the enormous faith and strength that enabled martyrs to refuse to conform to the demands of the political authorities. A vivid example of this type of literature is the *Letter of Phileas*. This man, who was noted for his vast secular learning, wrote a letter describing the martyrdoms that took place in Alexandria in the early years of the persecution under Diocletian. He noted the precedents from the lives of earlier martyrs and the instructions given in the sacred writings. The martyrs followed the example of Christ, who "humbled himself unto death, even death on a cross" [Phil. 2:8]:

> What words could be adequate to the courage and the heroism they showed under every torture? Everyone was allowed to insult them as he liked: some beat them with cudgels, some with rods, some with scourges, some again with thongs, some with whips of rope. And though the spectacle of their indignities kept changing, it constantly involved the utmost viciousness. Some were affixed to wooden horses with their hands tied behind them, and then had their limbs torn apart by pulleys. Then the torturers at a signal got to work on their entire bodies, and then not merely on their sides (as in the case of murderers), but they tormented them with instruments on their belly, the thighs, and the cheeks. Others were fastened by one hand and hauled up from the portico, and no pain could have been more intense than the stretching of

the joints and limbs. Others were tied to columns facing inwards with their feet on the ground, the weight of the body forcing the bonds to tighten.[10]

After describing additional forms of torture to which the martyrs were exposed, Phileas goes on to depict the results of this treatment at the hands of the civil authorities and the hostile populace:

> In this way some passed on under the tortures, putting their adversary to shame by their courage; others were locked up in prison semi-conscious, and not many days afterwards, overcome by their agony, attained perfection. Others with care and a sojourn in prison recovered their health and became ever more confident. At any rate, the order was given that they had a choice either of participating in the unholy sacrifice and going free, and thus obtaining from their persecutors a tainted liberty, or else not sacrificing and paying the penalty of death. Here they did not hesitate, but gladly went to their death. For they were aware of what the sacred scriptures had prescribed for us. It said: "Whoever sacrifices to other gods shall be utterly destroyed, and you shall have no other gods before me" (Exod. 22:20; 20:3).[11]

The editor of this letter notes that Phileas, whom he characterizes as a "lover of wisdom as well as a lover of God," had sent the message to fellow members of his diocese while he was in prison, urging them to be faithful unto death, even while his own martyrdom was about to be accomplished.

This type of literature effectively served the aims of those within the church who wanted to give a primary focus to the saints. In both life and death, the saints embodied total commitment to the Christian faith and values and therefore came to be regarded not only as models for the faithful in any era, but also as those whose works of love and grace in some way benefited their less worthy followers of the time. The cult of the saints and martyrs can be seen as already developing in this collection of stories about those committed even to death.

Another kind of literature that emerged during the period came from the hand and archives of Eusebius of Caesarea in Palestine. Born in Caesarea, which by that time was an important center of Christian learning and Roman culture, Eusebius took as his second name that of his teacher, Pamphilus, who had succeeded to the post held earlier by Origen of Alexandria. During the years before and after the accession to power of Constantine (300–325), Eusebius wrote his *Ecclesiastical History.*[12] This encyclopedic work not only is the first of its kind; it contains hundreds of quotations—many of them fairly extensive—from ancient pagan and Christian writers whose works would otherwise have been lost. It describes the origins, growth, and spread of the church, with detailed references to leading figures from the first to the early fourth century. As was appropriate and politically timely, the *Ecclesiastical History* sees the hand of God at work through what has occurred and portrays its own epoch as one in which a new purpose of God is about to be achieved. Modern critics of Eusebius think it was to benefit his own standing with Constantine that he

---

[10] Quoted from *Acts of the Christian Martyrs*, tr. and ed. by Herbert Musirillo (Oxford: Oxford University Press, 1972).

[11] Quoted, with some modification, from Musirillo, *Acts of the Christian Martyrs*, pp. 260–265.

[12] In Loeb Classical Library; vol. 1, tr. K. Lake; vol. 2, tr. J. E. L. Oulton (Cambridge, MA: Harvard University Press, 1949, 1953).

shaped his account of the church's transformation from a beleaguered sect to an instrument for achieving imperial power. What is certain is that this weighty work served the emperor as an apologetic for his exercise of power in relation to the new circumstances of the church and that it has served scholars since the fourth century as a rich resource of knowledge of the development of Christianity in the first three centuries.

By the time that Constantine had first assumed power in the west, however, his one-time ally, Licinius, was in control of the imperial regions to the east. It was to this military and cultural challenge that he had now to direct his attention.

The site of the Dead Sea
community at Qumran, where the
Dead Sea Scrolls were produced.
(Howard C. Kee)

The ruins of Sebaste,
the capital of Samaria,
where descendants of
the northern tribes of
Israel lived, worshipping
God in their own
nearby temple on
Mount Gerizim.
(Howard C. Kee)

The site of the temple in
Jerusalem from the
Mount of Olives. Only
the massive retaining
wall remains of this
monumental structure
built by Herod the Great.
(Israel Government
Tourist Office)

The Tholos at Delphi in Greece, to which seekers came from all over the Mediterranean world to obtain answers to their problems through the oracle of Apollo there. (Howard C. Kee)

The Acropolis at Athens, with the Parthenon (temple of Athena) above and the Areopagus (Hill of Ares) in the foregound, where Paul addressed the Athenian council. (Agora Excavations, Athens)

A fourth-century C.E. synagogue pavement in Galilee, which shows by the Greek inscriptions and the signs of the zodiac how heavily influenced Palestinian Judaism was by hellenistic culture. (Israel Government Tourist Office)

A Christian sarcophagus portraying Jesus being baptized by John the Baptist, with the Spirit descending as a dove. (Howard C. Kee)

The Roman forum was the seat of imperial power; the senate met in the rectangular, nearly windowless building. (Howard C. Kee)

The sacred treasures, which are being carried in triumph from the Jerusalem temple following the fall of that city to the Romans in 70 C.E., is portrayed on the Arch of Titus in Rome. (Howard C. Kee)

A portrait of Christ as a triumphant figure from the Catacomb of Domitilla, the underground burial chambers which were named after a convert to Christianity who was a member of the family of the emperor Domitian. (Howard C. Kee)

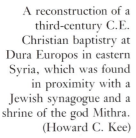

A reconstruction of a third-century C.E. Christian baptistry at Dura Europos in eastern Syria, which was found in proximity with a Jewish synagogue and a shrine of the god Mithra. (Howard C. Kee)

An illuminated manuscript of the Bible, Codex Purpureus (sixth–seventh century C.E.) picturing the wise and foolish virgins described in Jesus' parable (Matthew 25). (Giraudon/Art Resource)

Chapter 9

The Christian Empire and Arianism

The Greco-Roman World in 324

In 324 the rival emperors Constantine and Licinius declared war on each other, with the victor to win sole lordship of the Roman Empire. Religion and politics were inextricably linked in this contest. Licinius stood for the ancestral gods of pagan Rome, the gods who had protected and nurtured the state throughout its illustrious history. Before the campaign, Licinius performed the time-honored sacrifices to these gods, and he carried their images into battle as Roman emperors had done for centuries. Constantine's standard-bearer, in vivid contrast, held the golden banner with the new Christian symbol at its top, a jewel-encrusted wreath surrounding the chi-rho monogram signifying Christ. The two armies met at Adrianople in Thrace. (See Figure 9.1.) In the fierce combat, Constantine himself was wounded in the thigh before his well-disciplined forces finally defeated their more numerous enemy. The Christian victors credited their standard, called the *labarum* in late fourth-century sources, with miraculous aid against the pagan foe.

Licinius fled and holed up in the ancient city of Byzantium on the Bosphorus, an impregnable fortress that Constantine failed to take in a two-and-a-half month siege. Losses at sea forced Licinius to leave this haven and risk a land battle at Chrysopolis, where once again the labarum presided over his defeat.

Constantine was now master of the empire that he would rule until his death in 337. What was his empire like? In the early fourth century, the Greco-Roman world was very

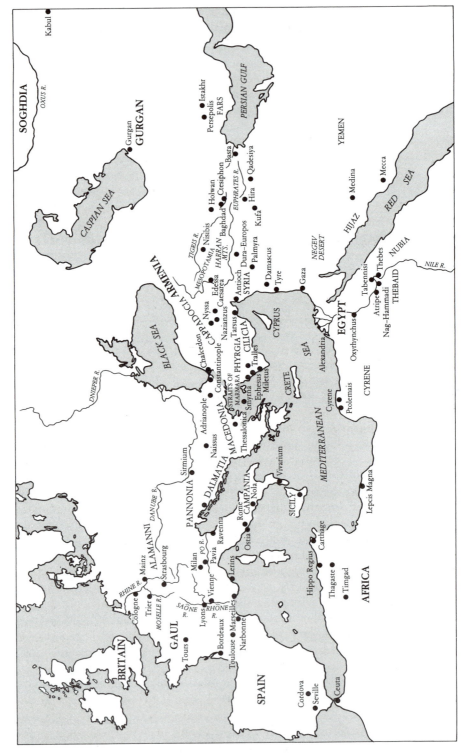

Figure 9.1   The Greco-Roman World Circa 324 C.E.

different from the old realm of Augustus or even of Marcus Aurelius, which the chaos of the third century had swept away. Devastating plagues, military revolts, and civil wars had produced nearly a hundred years of political instability, massive inflation, and fiscal collapse. Germanic and Persian invasions had capitalized on a weakened state. This instability on the frontiers strangled trade. To push back the invaders and control civil unrest, emperors had nearly doubled the size of the army. Only an oppressive taxation could support this expanded army, as well as a growing central and provincial bureaucracy. The principal financial support came from the land tax levied against the free and slave tenant farmers who had now replaced the slaves on the old plantations. But there were no longer enough peasants to till the soil. Perhaps one-third of North African fields went out of cultivation, and the remaining farmers were tied to the land to assure a continuing supply of produce and taxes. In an increasingly rigid society, tenant farmers everywhere felt the oppressive burden of their proscribed lives and increasing taxation. Did they also sense the widening gap between themselves and the wealthy? The senatorial aristocracy may have been as much as five times wealthier in the fourth century than in the first century C.E. If the century of chaos did not precisely represent a class war, as some historians have claimed, at the very least it exposed heightened social tensions and a rejection of old Roman values. The breakdown was more than military or economic; it was spiritual as well.

The old empire was distinguished by its urban life, and this had not entirely changed. The great cities of the east (including such venerable centers as Alexandria, Ephesus, Antioch, and Jerusalem) were still especially strong, even if civic responsibility was declining as men of wealth and privilege attempted to renege on their old civic duties and withdraw from public life or transfer allegiance from the town to the imperial power. Private spiritual quest replaced civic duty for some; for others, personal greed and the acquisition of vast wealth seemed to cut them off from the celebrated old Roman virtues.

Out of the third-century disorder came the rigid political, economic, and social policies of Diocletian and Constantine, radical revisions of the Roman Empire. Arguably the most profound changes were yet to appear with the creation of a new capital, a new wave of barbarian invasions, and perhaps especially with a thorough Christianization of the society. In an age of anxiety, religious fervor ran high. Transformed by Christianity, this passion would create a new society. If the year 324 saw the restoration of *pax Romana*, the celebrated Roman peace, still there would be no return to old Rome.

Having finally conquered the eastern provinces with his victory over Licinius, Constantine entered into the center of this empire's wealth and resilience, a significantly Christianized Asia Minor. Who were the Christians in 324, and where did they live? Christianity was still largely an urban movement. Christian communities existed in most of the towns throughout the empire, where the poor, manual workers (including slaves) and merchants were the major converts. As early preachers had traveled from city to city, they had founded urban churches, and the parish system had yet to move into the countryside. For this reason, the term *pagani*, designating the country people, came to mean non-Christians. Many peasants, conservative by nature, offered passive resistance to the new religion they confronted only in the towns and whose preachers spoke only Greek or sometimes Latin, but not the native languages of the countryside. The army, recruited from the peasantry, was predominantly pagan as well, although soldiers wrenched from their native communities seem to have converted rather easily to the prevailing religion of their commanders and colleagues. Wealthy and powerful families, meanwhile—and particularly the senatorial aristocracy—remained largely devoted to ancestral rituals.

The typical Christian, then, was an urban resident of modest means. Geography still played an important role, too. Christianity was strongest in the eastern provinces, closest to the land where Christianity was born and where Greek-speaking missionaries would have the greatest impact. Christian communities were already flourishing in North Africa and Egypt, but some towns in the western provinces (notably in Gaul, Illyricum, and Spain) were still without bishops. And Rome itself remained a hotbed of aristocratic devotion to traditional deities.

In the newly won east, Constantine could witness, more dramatically than in the west, where paganism was dominant, the power of the Christian community in an otherwise alienated world. While pagans were withdrawing from the civic life in towns all over the empire or transferring their loyalty from the local town to the imperial power, Christians were shifting their allegiance to supporting the church and nurturing the poor and needy. The bishops of these cities were building local organizations with stable and potent administrations destined to survive the collapse of the imperial structure in the west and to exercise considerable power and influence in the east throughout the Middle Ages. Christianity had its own distinctive flavor in the east, too, where Greek rather than Latin was the common tongue that linked peoples of various native languages and dialects and where traditions of ancient philosophy and law, and of Hellenic literature and culture, were still strong. Christianity was absorbing this culture and its ideals and forging a moral unity that would create the sensibilities of a new age.

Constantine's Christian Capital

To celebrate his victory over Licinius, Constantine at once began plans for a new Christian capital untainted by pagan rites and dedicated to the Christian God. Rome and its rowdy populace had become a liability to recent emperors. Impossible to defend against a siege, the venerable city was also strategically unimportant, far from the empire's eastern heartland. For Constantine, Rome's connection with pagan ritual provided additional problems, especially since the pagan senators, so wealthy and powerful, could continue to thwart his majesty just as they had acclaimed the rival emperor Maxentius during the civil wars.

Constantine chose the old city of Byzantium to replace Rome. The new capital would soon attract stories about its foundation that were modeled on the myths of Rome's creation. Like Aeneas, the legendary Trojan hero whose gods guided him to Italy, Constantine is supposed to have been advised by oracles that protected him from choosing the wrong site. He allegedly looked at Thessalonica, Chalcedon, and even Troy itself, Rome's mythic parent, before turning to Byzantium. Within about seventy years, the residents would discover that the city was situated on seven hills, like Rome, and they would divide it into fourteen regions, also in imitation of Rome. With characteristic modesty, Constantine named the city after himself, Constantinople, and gave it the title "New Rome."

Constantine's city was a brilliant choice that would assure the survival of the Christian empire. Strategically placed close to both the Danube and eastern frontiers, it straddled Europe and Asia and also commanded the sea routes that linked the eastern with the western parts of the empire. For its fleet and merchant ships, it boasted a calm inland harbor, the famed Golden Horn. Although the city was easily accessible, its position along the Bosphorus was highly defensible, requiring land walls on only one of its three sides. Constantine pillaged the empire, including Rome, for antiquities befitting the new capital. The imperial city needed a senate, too, mostly as an adornment rather than a potential rival. Some senatorial families were induced to move from Rome with gifts of property in the new city. Late sources even report that Constantine used clever coercion, sending Roman senators away on campaign against the Persians and, in their absence, moving their wives and families to Constantinople, where the senators eventually joined them. Much of the senate, however, came from families of recent wealth, the new group of administrators unfettered to senatorial traditions and so ripe for social and religious change. Many doubtless converted as an act of conscience; for those who did, conversion to Christianity proved a good career move.

Constantine consecrated his Christian capital on May 11, 330, the anniversary of the city's principal martyr, Saint Mocius. Constantinople would become the greatest city in Christendom and the monastic center of the empire, throughout its history housing 325 monasteries and nunneries inside the city and in its suburbs. The city was a Christian reliquary that would boast the tool that Noah used to build his ark, the head of John the Baptist, the stone of Jesus' tomb, the crown of thorns, the Virgin Mary's belt and robe, and countless other precious remains. Constantine himself commissioned the great church of Holy Wisdom, Hagia Sophia, and many other sacred buildings, including the Church of the Holy Apostles, with its twelve symbolic tombs and a thirteenth for himself.

The Arians

Constantine's city would be a monument to Christian victory over paganism, but could the emperor forge harmony within the Christian community itself? This question haunted Constantine's days and nights when a struggle among Christians threatened the faith as pagan persecutions never had.

United in the promise of salvation, early Christians had not troubled to hammer out coherent doctrine, but communities in different regions of the empire were developing their own theological concepts and beliefs that sometimes conflicted with the assumptions made by other Christians. How should these conflicts be resolved? Each urban center, with its own bishop, was more or less autonomous. Churches boasting descent from apostolic founders claimed special authority, but there was still no firm hierarchy of administration for settling disputes or determining and enforcing incipient doctrine. The Arian controversy would compel the Church to move toward creating both universal dogma and government.

Arius (ca. 250–336) was a Christian priest in Alexandria, Egypt, which had long been the cultural center of the Hellenized, intellectual east, where Christianity was forging an alliance with Greek philosophy. In attempting to understand the nature of Jesus, Arius began with the Platonic idea of God's eternal oneness. Since there cannot be two gods, he reasoned, Jesus the Son must be a creation of the Father, not coeternal with Him, and therefore not fully God. "There was a time," Arius preached, "when he [Christ] was not." Nor is Christ fully human, but he is a bridge between God and the world of human beings. Arius took his ideas directly to the people, working his dogma into popular ballads that were sung, his opponents claimed, "on the sea, at the mill, and on the road."

His bishop, Alexander, and the young deacon and future bishop Athanasius were alarmed by the number of supporters Arius attracted. "Ario-maniacs," they called them, stricken with an "Arian plague." If Christ was not fully human, how could he suffer and die on the cross? If he was not God, how could he promise salvation? Neoplatonism had led to a disdain for the physical world, but the essence of Christianity was the affirmation of God's presence in the created order and among men and women. The Christian God became man and intervened in history to save humankind. If Christ was less than fully God or less than fully human, the sacrifice was meaningless. Behind Athanasius stood the people of Asia Minor, whose doctrine supported the complete equality of God the Father and God the Son.

The church lacked a structure for resolving such a fundamental conflict. And so it was the emperor who summoned the first general council of bishops to Nicaea in 325. Constantine seems mainly to have longed for consensus—an end to dissension that threatened the unity of his empire and of Christendom. Awed by the emperor's presence, the bishops allowed him to dominate the council and agreed to the solution that Constantine's western advisors offered him. The council produced the Nicene Creed, which affirms that Jesus Christ is fully God and fully human, consubstantial (*homoousios*) with the Father. A term current in the unphilosophic west, the *homoousion* was distasteful to the intellectual sensibilities of the east, including Constantinople and the territories of Asia Minor, Syria–Palestine, and Egypt; but the emperor's advocacy assured its promulgation.

If the decisions of this first ecumenical (i.e., general) council were important, equally critical was the emperor's role at Nicaea. He convened and chaired the council, he proposed a doctrinal formulation that the council felt obliged to accept, and he authorized civil penalties for parties deemed heretical, banishing Arius and his unreformed partisans. Under Constantine's domination, the church was subsumed by the jurisdiction of the Christian empire. By permitting imperial dominance, the council set a crucial precedent for the future relationship between church and state, forming the foundation for the Eastern Roman Empire.

Constantine died in 337, after having been baptized by the Arian bishop Eusebius of Nicomedia. The Roman senate decreed him a god; posterity would call him a saint, the Great, and peer of the apostles. He deserves the last title at least, because his conversion assured the survival of Christianity and its place as a world religion. The eventual success of Christianity may seem to have been inevitable to us today, but comparative evidence suggests otherwise. In fourth-century Persia, there were many Christian churches; the exotic appearance of one Persian bishop even created a stir at Nicaea. Yet no Persian king ever converted, and Christians remained a minority there. On the other hand, Christian territories in Syria, Egypt, and North Africa became predominantly Muslim after a few centuries of tolerant Muslim rule. Within the Roman Empire, imperial protection, which began under Constantine, offered the Christian religion a safe haven and open encouragement. Some critics have argued that this was ultimately bad for the church because self-interest and inertia brought nominal and indifferent converts and undermined the ethical and religious fervor of the church. But the church flourished under Roman emperors after Constantine, and the Roman Empire soon became nearly synonymous with Christendom.

At Constantine's death the empire was divided among his three sons, who took opposing sides in the Arian controversy. The Arian Constantius ruled in the east, surviving his brothers to become sole emperor from 353 to his death in 361. By the time the Arian Valens ascended the eastern throne in 364, Arianism was the dominant religion in the East, at least among the wealthy and powerful families.

The most charismatic leaders of the day, however, were devoting their energies to the orthodox cause. Arius's old opponent, Athanasius, bishop of Alexandria off and on (whenever the orthodox were in power) until his death in 373, used his considerable strength in vigorous support of the Nicene doctrine. He galvanized public opinion with a blockbuster saint's life, *The Life of Antony*, the first work in this genre that would be so popular throughout the Middle Ages.[1] In Athanasius's pages, the Egyptian ascetic becomes a champion of orthodoxy and a mighty spokesman against the Arian heresy.

Three leading figures, who came to be known as the Cappadocian Fathers, inherited Athanasius's cause and assured its intellectual victory. In the fourth century, Cappadocia, in eastern Asia Minor, was not a wild and barren place; rather, it was a center of considerable culture. Basil of Caesarea, his friend Gregory of Nazianzus, and his brother Gregory of Nyssa used their knowledge of Greek philosophy to Hellenize Christian tenets and to reconcile Nicene doctrine with Greek learning. Gregory of Nazianzus, bishop of Constantinople for a brief, but critical, moment in 381, won the capital to orthodoxy with his eloquent preaching. Basil was a capable administrator as well as an intellectual, and he worked to elevate orthodox priests to bishoprics and to buttress the orthodox structure of the ecclesiastical organization. He also created an influential monastic rule, the code under which monks would live, that stressed restraint, order, and obedience. Monastic movements in Egypt and Syria, more and more linked to the orthodoxy of Basil and Athanasius, became passionate foes of the Arians.

In the west, too, the most dynamic religious leader, Bishop Ambrose of Milan, lent his support to Nicene orthodoxy. Arianism attracted no such advocates in this critical period, and when the ardently orthodox Theodosius came to the throne in 379, the time was ripe for outlawing Arianism altogether and seeking peace and unity within the church and empire. Theodosius made Christianity the only official religion of his realm. After banning pagan sacrifices, he closed famous pagan monuments at which the ban had been ignored. During his reign, zealots took a violent offensive against paganism. The archbishop of Alexandria rounded up a posse of monks to demolish the great Serapeum, shrine of the Egyptian god Serapis and one of the wonders of the ancient world. Theodosius congratulated the perpetrators, who had also destroyed the temple's magnificent library. In 381 the emperor convened the second ecumenical council. This Council of Constantinople affirmed a modified Nicene Creed. Theodosius promptly disestablished the Arians and handed over all their church property to the orthodox. Without official sanction or brilliant supporters, Arianism limped along for a half century or more, its numbers of adherents gradually, but steadily, declining. Forced to hold clandestine services outside the city walls, split into sects that haggled over the minutiae of their doctrine, and harried by orthodox emperors, Arians slowly disappeared from the Roman Empire.

---

[1] See *The Life of Antony and The Letter to Marcellus*, trans. and intro. by R. C. Gregg (New York: Paulist Press, 1980). Recent scholarship has suggested that a monk in Antony's monastery wrote the original version of this *Life* in Coptic.

The Arian Germans

It is perhaps ironic that just as the Arians of the empire were dying out, the heresy was winning fresh converts on the Gothic frontier. For centuries, the German presence had been building along the empire's northern borders. When pressure from the Mongolian Huns forced the Visigoths to cross the Danube into Roman territory in 378, these Germanic tribes would confront the orthodox Romans with their own brand of Arian Christianity.

It was a meeting of two very different societies. The Germans did not live in cities, nor did they have a written culture that linked various peoples to a common heritage. Instead, the Germanic tribes were kinship groups united by blood and custom. Most Germans lived by hunting and herding. Many farmed the land, settling in small villages separated from one another by dense forests. The men were warriors who valued women strong enough to tend the land and to maintain the home while the warriors were off fighting, perhaps as soldiers in the Roman army. By the fourth century, many tribes had significant contact with Rome, not only through military service, but also through the exchange of German slaves for prestigious Roman wares. Increasingly familiar with Roman civilization, Germans came to admire its handiwork, its grand architecture and art, its ceremony and luxury, and the religion they associated with that culture—Christianity.

Before these invasions, many Goths knew of Christianity not only from Roman military service and commerce, but also through Roman Christians who lived among them. One such family was that of Ulfila, who claimed descent from Roman prisoners captured during a mid-third-century raid on their village in Cappadocia. When Ulfila was born, about 311, the family was still Christian, and so he was raised Christian in a pagan society. Still, he also grew up as a Goth who spoke the Gothic language. Dispatched to Constantinople as a hostage or ambassador, he espoused the Arian Christianity that was dominant there in the final years of Constantine's reign. It was almost certainly the Arian leader Eusebius of Nicomedia, the same bishop who baptized Constantine, who consecrated Ulfila bishop to serve the Christians in Gothia, the old Roman province of Dacia (now Romania). For seven years Ulfila preached Arianism there, until a persecution of Christians forced him to flee with his community to Roman Moesia. He probably was never able to return to Gothia, but at his death in about 383, he left behind a tradition of Gothic Arianism and a translation of the Bible into Gothic, for which he first had to devise an alphabet. One fifth-century source claimed that Ulfila refrained from translating the Books of Kings (that is, I and II Samuel and I and II Kings) because he was unwilling to expose the savage Goths to bellicose scripture that might seem to condone warfare. In fact, we do not know whether he translated the Old Testament at all, since only later fragments remain of Old Testament books in the Gothic Bible. Still, this assertion provides early testimony for the expectation that Christianity ought to play a significant role in civilizing the barbarians.

The process was slow. To train priests and to preach Christian doctrine, to eradicate or Christianize pagan customs in the countryside, and perhaps especially to inculcate Christian ethical values were complex tasks. Like the Christianization of the Roman peasantry, genuine conversion of German farmers and villagers would take centuries of effort. The nobles, on the other hand, quickly declared themselves and their tribes to be Christian. German kings saw the immediate advantages in adopting a religion that could unify their people by diffusing tensions among tribes, eradicate the power of tribal priests and chiefs, affirm divine authority for their rulership, and also win Roman military aid.

Arianism made a further political and social statement by asserting independence from the Huns, who rejected Christianity, and also from the orthodox Romans. Christianity was the religion of Roman civilization, but Arian Christianity was distinctively German, too. Over time, it would influence western Christianity even as the two strains merged to create medieval Catholic Christendom.

Chapter 10

Pagan Reaction and Christian Victory

The Pagan Response

In the second half of the fourth century, Greco-Roman paganism was by no means dead. Constantine might embrace Christianity, and Theodosius might even outlaw polytheism. Still, many subjects of the Roman Empire considered paganism to be interconnected with all elements of their ancient heritage. For some of the old aristocracy, paganism *was* the traditional and civilized way of life, and they actively resisted any loss of this integral part of the social fabric. Unwilling to abandon their art and literature, these patriotic Romans further argued that to abandon pagan rituals within state ceremonies could imperil the Roman state.

Pagan rivals challenged the authority of Constantine's sons to rule. In 350 Constans died fighting the pagan usurper Magnus Magnentius, who was finally defeated by Constantius in 351. At Constantius's death ten years later, the Christian future of the empire must have seemed secure until his cousin and successor, Julian, cast off the pretense of being a Christian and sacrificed oxen to the gods in public thanksgiving for his accession to the throne.

The last pagan emperor of Rome, Julian was also the first emperor to have been born at Constantinople, his uncle Constantine's new capital. No opulent and carefree youth was in store for this child of the imperial family. Soon after his birth, his mother died. Then, when he was only six, in the uncertain period following the death of Constantine, his father and most other family members were massacred. Julian always held Constantius accountable for the murders. Indeed, the ultimate beneficiary of the dynastic battles was this same Christian cousin, who later (in 354) executed Julian's half-brother Gallus for treason. Small wonder that Julian finally moved against Constantius in 360 and that civil war was averted only by the emperor's death by fever in 361.

Even if Julian had personal, philosophical, cultural, and patriotic reasons for loathing Christianity, he could not escape the influence of a religion whose success he attempted to emulate in restoring paganism. He saw clearly that the high moral tone of Christianity attracted converts from the old cults and that the organizational structure of the church nurtured Christians and promulgated the faith. He attempted, therefore, to create a pagan church with its own structure and hierarchy, and he tried to enforce pagan charity and a morally pure priesthood in imitation of Christian virtue. Understanding that persecution had only strengthened the church, he promulgated a policy of official tolerance while eliminating any advantages for Christians. Still, his idiosyncratic and archaic movement failed to attract converts, in part because his strange personality repelled potential allies. Bitterly disappointed by this failure, he led a reluctant army on campaign into Persian Mesopotamia, hoping that a stunning victory would dazzle his subjects and bring them around to paganism. At about age thirty-one, Julian might have expected that a long lifetime of persuasion would turn the tide against Christianity. Instead, he fell victim to a fatal lance during a skirmish with Persian forces and was buried at Tarsus. The great pagan rhetorician of Antioch, Julian's admirer and ally Libanius, pretended that the people revered Julian after his death as if he were a kind of pagan saint. In the oration to the emperor's memory, Libanius asserted that the late emperor was answering prayers directed to him. In fact, Julian seems to have been virtually unmourned, and his quirky personal vision of restored paganism died with him.

Julian had been preaching his philosophy in the Christianized east, but from a distance, even the more pagan west had virtually ignored him. Enormously wealthy, Roman senators devotedly pursued *otium*, the cultivated leisure that they could enjoy on their country estates far from the bother of Rome. Much as they cherished *otium*, however, they valued tradition even more and willingly pursued the active civic careers and weighty responsibilities that their ancestors had shouldered, accepting government office or acting as emissary between emperor and senate. Many still held to classical paganism, which enjoyed a venerable link with Roman ceremony, might, and social habit. Among the leaders of this senatorial class, the patrician Symmachus provides a noble example. Governor of Lucania and proconsul of Africa, he held the title of urban prefect of Rome in 384. His father, grandfather, and father-in-law had all been urban prefect before him. Well born and well connected, he was a superbly cultivated pagan and an excellent spokesman for the senate.

During his prefecture, he clashed with the emperor and especially with the powerful and brilliant Ambrose, bishop of Milan, where the imperial court was residing. The immediate cause of the dispute was the Altar of Victory, a gift of Augustus to the senate of Rome. Christian emperors beginning with Constantius had removed the altar from the senate house, only to see it returned in answer to the senators' pleas. On behalf of the senate, Symmachus drafted a respectful plea that the emperor once more return the altar on which the senators made their prescribed sacrifices, the traditional rituals that assured the survival and political success of the Roman Empire. The response came from Ambrose, himself born to secular power in the senatorial ranks. Drafted as bishop, he became a tough and fervent Catholic. The fiery and brilliant preacher who would convert Augustine demanded that the emperor refuse Symmachus's plea. The unyielding bishop, the Christian emperor he controlled, and the pagan aristocracy were on a collision course.

Rome witnessed the last hurrah of pagan spring rites in 394, when forbidden cult rituals were revived and performed with ostentatious opulence. Once again, Rome saw processions for Magna Mater and Isis, along with sacrifices to Jupiter and Saturn, Mithras and the Unconquered Sun, and Ceres and Proserpina. With all the ancestral rites, the younger Nichomachus Flavianus, scion of a great pagan family, married a daughter of Symmachus, further allying two families at the head of the revolt. Then the Roman senatorial pagans rode out under pagan standards to defend their antiquarianism, patriotism, and the old ways. With statues of Jupiter looking down from the cliffs above and the image of Hercules paraded among the troops, the last Roman army to march under pagan standards met defeat at the Frigidus River when (so reported the Christians under emperor Theodosius) a miraculous wind blew up, tearing the shields from the hands of the pagan soldiers and hurling their spears back against them. The same wind at Theodosius's back drove him down from the mountain pass where he was trapped and on to victory. In purely political terms, the results were clear: Imperial forces had smashed an insurrection of the Roman aristocracy. Christian writers interpreted the contest from another perspective: In their eyes, divine forces had crushed the last pagan resistance along the Frigidus.

Christianity and Classical Culture

Symmachus and his friends closely associated paganism with Greco-Roman culture. Their Christian neighbors agreed. Must these Christians therefore abandon classical literature and art as incompatible with their religion? Given the necessity of choosing, would a Roman aristocrat abandon Christianity or the Greco-Roman cultural heritage? There was some danger that Christians themselves might force that choice. Tertullian had asked, "What has Athens to do with Jerusalem?" The church father Jerome feared that a passion for Ciceronian rhetoric, which sometimes seduced him away from biblical study, would lead to his eternal damnation. In a nightmare, the heavenly judge charged him with this sin. To Jerome's desperate defense, "I am a Christian," the terrifying answer came back: "You are a Ciceronian, not a Christian!"

Augustine (354–430), the famous North African bishop with whom Jerome carried on a meticulously civilized and sometimes rancorous correspondence, convinced the western empire that Christians could use pagan learning so long as they granted scripture the foremost importance in this synthesis. There need be no conflict if the Christian used Ciceronian eloquence in defense of the faith. In the Hellenized east, the three Cappadocian Fathers had already envisioned a Christian culture that accepted and transformed their ancient intellectual heritage. Basil of Caesarea, Gregory of Nyssa, and Gregory of Nazianzus—the champions of orthodoxy—encouraged the use of pagan philosophy and literature, the best products of ancient Greece, which Christianity was absorbing as part of its own culture.

Cities and Bishops in Late Antiquity

As demonstrated by the struggles with paganism and classical culture, the emerging leaders of both church and society were influential bishops such as Ambrose at Milan (374–379), John Chrysostom at Antioch and Constantinople (398–407), and Augustine at Hippo in North Africa (391–430). Although they might be unwillingly conscripted, despite initial resistance, such men earnestly and capably filled the vacuum created by the withdrawal of the old aristocracy and the great landowners, who abandoned the responsibility of onerous public service. The bishop tended to his Christian flock, preaching, overseeing the distribution of alms, and caring for the needy. His tireless work in the community deserted by civil authorities made a great impact on contemporaries. After cataloging the many volumes of Augustine's works, his biographer Possidius reflected on the man himself: "Yet I think that those who gained most from him were those who had been able actually to see and hear him as he spoke in church, and, most of all, those who had some contact with the quality of his life among men."[1]

Increasingly, as civil administration failed, the bishop was called to more and more duties, becoming arbiter of private quarrels and patron of people in the town and surrounding countryside. In 387, for instance, the people of Antioch rioted to protest an increase in taxes. When they reflected on the nasty consequences of their civil disobedience, it was the bishop whom they dispatched to Constantinople to plead (successfully) for the emperor's forgiveness. In a violent age, it was the bishop who could win mercy or dispense justice, even when the adversary was the emperor. In 390 the bishop Ambrose excommunicated Theodosius for his angry massacre of 7,000 people in the circus at Thessalonica after the citizens there had assassinated a barbarian military commander. Before Theodosius could receive communion again, Ambrose forced him to accept public penance. Cowed by the bishop, the emperor stood before all without imperial regalia, admitting the superior authority of the church. It was a precedent that theologians would not forget. To decide cases involving clergy or ecclesiastical matters, Theodosius further permitted the church to create its own courts, which would begin to develop their own law, called *canon law*.

Inevitably, there arose a tension between spiritual and civic duties. The bishop became courtier and administrator within a complex hierarchy. Some Christians were asking whether *any* person could live an upright life amid the cares and decadence of the city. Perhaps the only way to salvation lay in radical asceticism divorced from civilization.

Monasticism and Holy Men and Women

A young Egyptian, Antony (ca. 250–356), heard the message of the gospel: "If you will be perfect, go and sell all you have, and give it to the poor, and you shall have treasure in heaven: and come and follow me" (Matt. 19.21). So he gave away his inheritance and fled to the desert, becoming one of the first Christian hermits. ("Hermit" comes from the Greek *eremos*, meaning "desert.") Antony lived to a ripe old age, attracting a famous biographer, Athanasius, and countless imitators.

---

[1] Peter Brown, *Augustine of Hippo: A Biography* (Berkeley, CA: University of California Press, 1967), p. 433.

How did he live? According to Athanasius, he struggled with himself daily, seeking to make the body subject to the soul. If he could not suffer actual martyrdom, which was the most desirable lot, at least he could deny the body its physical wants and thus become as spiritual as possible. Moving deeper and deeper into the desert, Antony experienced mystical ecstasy, as his soul fought its way upward to a blinding beam of light. By his hard-won holiness, he performed socially valuable acts of exorcism, casting out demons and healing physical and spiritual wounds, as Jesus had done. He spoke only Coptic, so his religious dogma was inscrutable to most observers. The passionately orthodox Athanasius, however, assured his readers that Antony loathed all heretics—Meletians, Manichaeans, and especially Arians. Even the emperor Constantine heeded Antony's teachings of the ascetic life that Antony had learned from scripture.

Antony's own example and Athanasius's influential *Life of St. Antony* led many people to conversion and imitation. Translated from Greek into Latin, the *Life* reached a large audience. Many of its readers felt compelled to follow Antony's example, prompting the famous quotation from Adolf von Harnack, an unsympathetic modern critic: "If I may be permitted to use strong language, I should not hesitate to say that no book has had a more stultifying effect on Egypt, Western Asia, and Europe than the *Vita S. Antonii.*" To be sure, the *Life* encouraged a dramatic rejection of the classical ideal of an educated, rational mind in a healthy, athletic body. Antony expressed a radical anti-intellectualism, as when he confronted smart-aleck philosophers with the taunt, "The person who has a sound mind doesn't need to know how to read and write." By a brutal denial of the physical world with its profane knowledge, and by a punishment of the body, Antony simply turned his soul to the perception of God, actively rejecting pleasure in this life in the hope of winning salvation after death. Antony's life looks ahead to a powerful strain in medieval Christendom.

Antony's ideal had many imitators, often poor and simple folk who found it a dramatic way to defy society and seek personal salvation. In Syria and Mesopotamia, ascetics became particularly notorious for their extreme mortifications. Some wore heavy iron chains; others wore almost no clothing and lived like animals in the open air, grazing on grass and avoiding shelter; still others lived in trees or in tiny cages, depending on neighbors for meager food and support. Near Damascus, Symeon the Stylite (389–459) lived for forty years on top of his narrow pillar, sixty feet high. There he performed brutal acts of self-punishment, such as touching his feet with his head 1,244 times in a row or standing for hours on end with his arms outstretched in prayer while crowds gathered to venerate him and even to worship the worms that fell from his body. Though he was illiterate, his advice was sought by country people, bishops, and the emperor himself. The government even required his ratification of the ecclesiastical councils of Ephesus (431) and Chalcedon (451).

The austere sanctity of such men dazzled the late antique world. People felt that these holy men performed acts of value to the whole society by praying for ordinary Christians and healing their bodies and spirits and by keeping demons at bay. People who saw Symeon high on his pillar believed that, through their hero, they were glimpsing the divine.

Such passions presented a dilemma for the church and for the bishops whose authority the hermits rivaled and sometimes defied. The hermits were following biblical injunctions thoroughly compatible with a messianic, apocalyptic community. While these solitaries scorned the world, however, the bishops were busily organizing within the world a Christian community that they themselves would order and control. Could they expand this community to embrace even its most antisocial members? At the same time, could they place ascetics firmly within the hierarchical structure of the organized church? Hermits like Antony often claimed direct mystical experience of God, without the mediation of priest or church. Could such men disregard the church or even replace priests and bishops as spiritual leaders of Christendom?

The solution came through the creation of monastic orders, where men and women might lead ascetic lives in common under the authority of an abbot or a bishop. When other hermits sought him out, Antony himself had organized hermits' colonies into semi-monastic communities. The true founder of Christian monasticism was another Egyptian nearly contemporary with Antony, but living far to the south in the district around Thebes. Pachomius (ca. 292–346) was a soldier who brought to his task the ideal of strict discipline and military obedience. He converted to Christianity at about age twenty and at his death left ten monasteries in Egypt, including a convent for women, all governed by his brief written rules for a life of common prayer and strenuous manual labor. The great austerity of Pachomian monasticism, bred in the desert in an age of heated religious controversies, provided a harsh standard that individuals were free to exceed. By the end of the fourth century, 7,000 monks were living in his monasteries. After Jerome translated Pachomius's Rule into Latin in 404, Pachomian monasteries began to spring up in the west.

A wide variety of monastic arrangements soon evolved in various parts of the Christian world. Asia Minor saw a relaxation of austerities, with greater emphasis on communal activities and charitable works. After himself living six years as a hermit, Basil of Caesarea wrote the *Long Rules* that have influenced eastern monasticism until the present day. Persuaded by his sister Macrina to renounce his chair of rhetoric, Basil embraced the ascetic life and traveled to Egypt, where he experienced austere Pachomian monasticism. Still, he did not altogether abandon his philosophical training, which had taught him to seek virtue through disciplined moderation, avoiding extremes of asceticism. A central feature of the Basilian rule is its insistence that the ascetic life should serve not only the individual who practices it, but also the church and community. Basilian monks operated hospitals, orphanages, and schools for both boys and girls. By working for the Christian community, these ascetics provided an active example of the Christian life.

In the west, meanwhile, the appeal of asceticism was considerably weaker, and the monastic movement was slow to emerge. Cold and snowy winters deterred people from living the hermit's life in the wilds of northern Europe, where fierce animals prowled dark forests and Germanic tribes also threatened. Irish ascetics gained notoriety by flaunting their disregard for the elements. In his *Ecclesiastical History* (early eighth century), the Venerable Bede wrote of Brother Drycthelme of Melrose, who habitually broke the ice over a nearby river so that he could stand in its chilly waters, answering stunned onlookers with a laconic "I've seen colder." For most of the west, however, only a moderate and protected monastic life could assure survival.

Various models appeared. Fashionable senators and aristocratic ladies converted their palaces or country estates into ascetic communities. About 540, for instance, the Roman senator Cassiodorus turned his Italian villa into a cultural center called the Vivarium, where men of learning copied religious and secular texts. Bishops such as Augustine housed their clergy in communal centers. Martin of Tours in Gaul (ca. 335–397) and Patrick in Ireland (early fifth century) combined asceticism with missionary activity. Amid this great variety, it was Benedict of Nursia (ca. 480–ca. 547) who created the rule that would become the standard for the west.

Benedict wrote his rule for his monastery at Monte Cassino, founded in 529, but it soon spread through the west. Here was a rule ideally suited to its age, offering humane and simple regulations for ordinary country people. Roman in its emphasis on order and organization, on obedience and respect for law, Benedict's rule stressed moderation and self-discipline. The day and night were organized around periods of common prayer, called the Work of God, chanted in choir. There were times for private Bible study, and monks were taught to read. Benedict also prescribed daily manual labor that balanced the hours of prayer and devotional reading, because he believed that idleness was the enemy of the soul. All the monks should have adequate sleep, however, and two good meals a day, so that no one would indulge in extravagant self-punishment. The rule allowed flexibility for adaptation to various climates and seasons, for women as well as for men, for scholars or farmers. Within a self-sufficient monastery in Gaul, Italy, or Britain, all monks of varied skills and abilities might find a home where they could live their whole lives through, without wandering from place to place, a practice Benedict roundly condemned. In times of war, pestilence, and famine, medieval men and women would find a haven of peace, stability, and order in the Benedictine cloister, where the abbot was enjoined to treat his tightly knit community as if he were the father of this family.

With ascetics safely in their monastic communities, the early institutional church had to face a similar problem with spontaneous popular cults centered on the tombs of local martyrs. Just as people venerated the holy men, so they also worshiped local saints as human beings whose devotion and courage had brought them into direct contact with the divinity. They could thus intercede with God on behalf of a suppliant, or the saint's relics could work miracles and heal the sick. Some scholars have suggested that the rise of the cult of saints demonstrates popular resistance to the solidifying power of the bishops and emperor: The people wanted to maintain personal access to spiritual authority. Others have speculated that these cults represented a survival of the traditional Roman patron–client relationship: The people still needed a private protector in treacherous times. Whatever the impulse that produced such popular movements, the church acted quickly to absorb the phenomenon, as it had the ascetic movement.

By the early fifth century, the church's institutional hierarchy was already complex and carefully defined. In each city a bishop held authority over local priests, including those of the surrounding countryside. The bishop of a larger city was called a *metropolitan* (known in the west today as an archbishop) and exercised authority over all clergy of his province. The highest rank belonged to the patriarchs, bishops of the most venerable Christian cities: Rome, Constantinople, Jerusalem, Antioch, and Alexandria. Quite distinct from the clergy, the laity were expected to follow the teaching of their priests and bishops and obey the precepts of the institutional church.

Women's Roles in the Chain of Command

Attitudes toward laymen and women were shaped by the prevailing attitudes of the society in which Christianity was flourishing. The bishops accepted the social, political, and economic order more or less without questioning and generally agreed that the church should authorize and protect that natural and God-given order. Augustine argued this view most coherently:

> The Catholic Church, most true Mother of Christians. . . . it is You who make wives subject to their husbands . . . by chaste and faithful obedience; you set husbands over their wives; you join sons to their parents by a freely granted slavery, and set parents above their sons in pious domination. You link brothers to each other by bonds of religion firmer and tighter than those of blood. You teach slaves to be loyal to their masters . . . masters . . . to be more inclined to persuade them than to punish. You link citizen to citizen, nation to nation, indeed, You bind all men together in the remembrance of their first parents, not just by social bonds, but by some feeling of their common kinship. You teach kings to rule for the benefit of their people; and You it is who warn the peoples to be subservient to their kings.[2]

It was a tidy and compelling system. Although Roman women—especially aristocratic women—had won a measure of legal rights and social prominence, the church fathers preferred a more restrictive model, often citing precedents from the Hebrew Bible or the example of Jesus and his male disciples. Following this standard, women were forbidden to hold the priesthood or other positions of authority within the church. Yet Christianity did open new doors to women, even if the hierarchy of the church was keeping other doors firmly closed. Wealthy women found a prestigious vocation in patronage to the bishops and the urban poor. They might win both honor and salvation by supporting ecclesiastical and monastic institutions. Religious vows of celibacy could free them from family obligations and bestow greater independence than they had enjoyed before.

Imperial women provided role models for Christian women, and the church voiced strong approval of their dutiful piety. In the official paean at the death of Flacilla, first wife of Theodosius I, Gregory of Nyssa praised her acts of charity to the poor and needy, to widows and orphans. An ecclesiastical historian, Theodoret of Cyrrhus, testified that she visited the sick and maimed in the hospitals of Constantinople, personally feeding them soup and giving them medicine.

Men like John Chrysostom, archbishop of Constantinople from 398 to 404, continued to assail women as the heiresses of Eve, vain and dangerous snares for men, unfit in God's eyes for spiritual leadership. He approved of only the modest and obedient women who served God by donating their fortunes to the church. He did support the right of one recent widow, the heiress Olympias, to resist the new marriage arranged for her by the emperor Theodosius II. Chrysostom ordained her a deaconess in order to thwart the emperor's plan. In the bargain, Olympias won autonomy, and the bishop became trusted advisor for the disposition of her wealth. Theodosius's own sister, Aelia Pulcheria Augusta (413–453), proclaimed perpetual virginity for herself and, by her asceticism, assured that she would share her power with no husband and his ambitious kin. In her last years, she concerned herself with the rights and care of holy women.

Ordinary women, by contrast, had constrained and limited options. Enjoined to become subservient wives and devoted mothers, many poured their energies into these traditional roles. Syrian saints' lives reveal other women empowered by their faith to explode

---

[2]Brown, *Augustine of Hippo*, p. 225.

societal stereotypes, shunning marriage, family, or even religious community to become solitaries in men's clothing or pilgrims to the holy shrines. A few women found voices of their own, like the fourth-century pilgrim Egeria (or Aetheria), who left an enthusiastic and distinctively personal journal of her tour to biblical sites.

Articulate Christianity

Egeria's Latin itinerary joined growing volumes of Christian literature. Although Greek and Latin were the languages of the urban upper classes, we must not forget the diversity of early Christendom and the variety of cultural influences at work. Outside the cities, farmers and laborers spoke their own native languages. The old Roman Empire had made little effort to integrate these people into the political structure, and Christianity was slow to preach to them in their own tongue. Early records do substantiate such efforts in the eastern Mediterranean, where Syriac had become the language of Christian communities during the first and second centuries C.E. and had developed a rich Christian literature. When the eloquent John Chrysostom preached in Greek to a packed congregation in the cathedral at Antioch, a bilingual deacon would offer simultaneous translation to the farmers and humble workers who knew only Syriac.

By Chrysostom's time, a Christian rhetoric had already been developing for several centuries in both Greek and Latin. In the Latin west, Jerome (ca. 340–420) combined rigorous training in classical thought and literature with biblical scholarship and Christian asceticism. His crowning achievement was the translation into Latin of both the Hebrew Bible and the Greek New Testament. Jerome's Latin Bible, usually called the Vulgate version, became the authoritative text for the European Middle Ages.

Jerome's correspondent, Augustine of Hippo (354–430), also used pagan learning to support Christian teaching. His supremely influential spiritual autobiography, *The Confessions*, explored the moral struggles within the developing soul of a man living in the last years of Roman North Africa. Converted to philosophy through Cicero's *Hortensius*, then to dualist Manichaeism, and finally to orthodox Christianity through bishop Ambrose of Milan, Augustine was a contemplative conscripted into the priesthood. As a bishop who had to act as patron and protector of his flock, he came to accept coercion as a proper ingredient in opposition to heresy and in defense of the social order. He had used every power at his command to crush the Donatists, rigorists who wanted to restrict the church to the elect alone and banish sinners who had denied their faith when threatened with persecution. In his later years, Augustine similarly opposed Pelagius, the British or Irish monk who came to Rome about the year 400 and attempted to demolish the social habits of the Roman world and enforce a stern morality. Pelagius inherited the old moral ideal of the autonomous human mind and spirit, as seen, for instance, in Stoicism. He held that original sin did not condemn humans to imperfect lives; on the contrary, all could draw on their own willpower to lead perfect lives if only they would. Those who did not should be exiled from the Christian community. Augustine, on the other hand, found the human race essentially weak; only through divine grace could any men or women find salvation. This idea was taking hold in late antiquity and anticipated the medieval spirit. Augustine's victory over Pelagianism, confirmed at the Third Ecumenical (or universal) Council at Ephesus

(431), assured that ordinary good Christians had a place within the fold. Christianity was not to be a tiny sect of righteous ascetics within a pagan world, but a religious community that embraced all sinners and worked within the imperfect world in which it grew.

Christianization of Late Antique Art

As Christians were finding a distinctive Greco-Roman voice, so, too, Christian art was developing its own style, evolving from its classical heritage. In the fourth century, the wealth that used to go to public buildings was channeled into imperial palaces and aristocratic estates. By the fifth century, such riches went into the construction of magnificent Christian basilicas adorned with shimmering mosaics, silk tapestries and vestments, silver candelabra and liturgical vessels, and perhaps an ivory throne for the bishop.

Mosaics made of stone paved floors in ancient buildings and porticoes. Late antique artisans discovered that lighter and more brilliant glass cubes could be fitted into wall mosaics perfectly suited to the new architecture. Rough cut or smooth, dyed a rich purple or even made of gold, set at various angles to catch and reflect the light, mosaics seemed to expand the sacred space and to radiate a divine essence. The so-called Mausoleum of Galla Placidia at Ravenna, dating from the middle of the fifth century, has preserved the earliest surviving mosaic decoration in complete harmony with its setting. Over the entrance door of this tiny space, the Good Shepherd is a traditional bucolic figure from the Hellenistic age transformed into a potent symbol of regal and spiritual glory. Christian art had found its ideal medium.

The Council of Ephesus

Only a generation earlier than the construction of the Mausoleum, the council at Ephesus (431) had hammered out a formula for defining the relationship of human and divine natures within Jesus Christ. The story behind this controversy illustrates social struggle within the fifth-century Church—a struggle of bishop against bishop and of bishop against monks and imperial women.[3]

On a purely theological level, the arguments seem relatively straightforward. Nestorius, patriarch of Constantinople (428–431), claimed that two *separate* natures, the divine and the human, coexisted in Jesus. Here he was following the rationalist school of Antioch, which contended that God could not suffer in the flesh; Jesus the man was only the chosen vessel of the godhead. Cyril, patriarch of Alexandria, adhered to the Alexandrian mystical teaching that the divine and human natures united in Jesus, who was God become man. There were important theological reasons for Cyril's argument: If Jesus did not suffer on the cross as God, could his sacrifice truly bring salvation? What meaning could his death hold if only the man Jesus died? Cyril found support from Rome, from the empire's growing number of monks, and from another unexpectedly powerful source, the women of Con-

---

[3] This discussion follows Kenneth G. Holum, *Theodosian Empresses: Women and Imperial Domination in Late Antiquity* (Berkeley: University of California Press, 1982).

stantinople, led by imperial and aristocratic women who were not influenced by doctrinal reasons alone.

The contentious Nestorius had alienated the people by assailing their much-loved circus races, theater, and mimes. In other attempts to enforce order, he demanded that monks leave their public ministry and stay in the monastery, where they could no longer encourage the populace to resist the oppression of unprincipled authorities. A hard line against heretics and various dissidents brought him headlong against Cyril, raising again the question of the relative authority or independence of their respective bishoprics. Could the patriarch of Constantinople overrule the patriarch of Alexandria? Finally Nestorius met his match in Pulcheria, sister of the reigning emperor Theodosius II and a woman dedicated to holy virginity. Cyril saw that with her support he could bring Nestorius to defeat.

Like Chrysostom before him, Nestorius was eager to put women in their proper place. Women had traditionally attended evening psalms and prayers, as well as night vigils for the dead. In Nestorius's view, these were plainly invitations to promiscuity, and he acted swiftly to lock women out. The prominent women of the imperial city did not submit meekly to his will. Down from the women's gallery of the Great Church rained shouts of anger from Heleniana, a noble woman whose piety and benefactions were beyond dispute. The bishop had already alienated the most powerful and influential lady in the city in a confrontation only five days after his ordination. The empress Pulcheria was accustomed to take communion with her brother and priests of the Great Church, but that Easter Sunday Nestorius personally blocked her entry into the sanctuary, proclaiming that "only priests may walk here." Seeing only a daughter of Eve, he could not bear the sacrilege of a woman's presence in the Holy of Holies. Considering herself to be living the life of a religious virgin in the footsteps of Mary, the empress asked, "Why? Have I not given birth to God?" Nestorius drove her away with the incensed charge, "You? You have given birth to Satan!"

The lines were drawn. Strongly implying that Pulcheria had not kept her vow of chastity but had been sexually promiscuous, the new bishop refused to honor Pulcheria as the bride of Christ in his prayers for the imperial house and systematically withdrew other dignities from her. The attack broadened to an assault on the Virgin Mary, and here Nestorius made a fatal mistake: He canceled a popular festival dedicated to Mary that had become an occasion during the liturgical year when virgins and religious women were honored. Mary was not the mother of God, claimed Nestorius, but only the mother of Jesus the man, *christotokos* but not *theotokos* (Christ-bearer, not God-bearer).

To decide the question, Theodosius summoned the bishops to the Third Ecumenical Council at Ephesus in 431. The emperor expected that his bishop would be vindicated, but he seems to have been outsmarted by his sister, who may have chosen the battleground. Ephesus was not only a haven for pro-Cyril forces, but also the ancient cult center of the virgin goddess Artemis/Diana and now devoted to the cult of the *theotokos*. Cyril's allies packed the city with supporters, including dissident monks from Constantinople. It took only a day for the overwhelmed council, meeting in a church dedicated to the Virgin Mary, to excommunicate Nestorius and declare Jesus fully God and fully human. Proclaiming victory for the *theotokos*, women swinging censers led the crowd that escorted Cyril from the council. A reluctant Theodosius finally ratified the council's decision, yielding to his sister's influence and Marian piety.

Nestorian churches survive to the present day in Turkey and India. Throughout most of the fifth-century Roman Empire, however, a reaction set in against Nestorianism, a reaction so potent that many Christians moved to the opposite extreme expressed by monophysitism, a Greek term meaning "the doctrine of a single nature." Whereas Nestorians believed that Jesus had two separate natures, human and divine (with an emphasis on the human), monophysites stressed his predominantly divine nature.

The Council of Chalcedon and Chalcedonian Orthodoxy

Monophysites were strongest in the eastern provinces, Syria and Egypt, where Semitic tradition reinforced visceral reactions against any multiplicity of gods or divisions within the godhead. The doctrines of the Trinity and the incarnation were difficult enough; to divide the nature of Jesus further fragmented and diluted God, in the view of eastern Christians, who inherited their biblical tradition and cultural orientation directly from the Jewish communities out of which they arose. The Greco-Latin churches in the west, on the other hand, responded to the Christian message through their own background in the thought-world of classical antiquity. The texture and tone of the distinct communities were bound to be different, although they shared a common faith. Monophysitism emphasized the cultural gap, broadening it even further, as it became an outlet for the cultural and political separatist tendencies of Egypt, Syria, and Armenia.

Far from the world that bred monophysite ideas, the bishop of Rome could not understand the fuss, and he was unsympathetic. In Constantinople, bishop and emperor had to be more sensitive to the spirituality that produced monophysitism. At the Fourth Ecumenical Council, held at Chalcedon in 451, monophysitism was nonetheless condemned. Chalcedonian orthodoxy adopted a doctrine of salvation through a savior who is perfect man and perfect God.

Since Persia had captured (and would soon execute) most of the Armenian bishops, who had recently rebelled against Persian domination, the Armenian church had no representatives at Chalcedon and would ultimately reject the council's decisions. In Egypt and Syria, Chalcedon provoked rebellions and talk of secession. Indeed, some scholars have argued that these provinces yielded easily to Islam in the seventh century because of their continuing disaffection with Chalcedonian orthodoxy imposed by Constantinople. In the intervening years, some emperors would attempt to find consensus or compromise; others would persecute the recalcitrant or exile them to Persia. None of these tactics succeeded, and most Syrian and Egyptian Christians remain non-Chalcedonian to the present day.

Barbarians and the Fall

The Nestorian and monophysite controversies of the fifth century raged in a world radically transformed by the unforeseen collapse of the imperial government in the west. On the death of Theodosius I in 395, the empire had irreversibly split in half, with one son (Arcadius) holding the east and the other (Honorius) taking nominal control of the west. Although the concept of imperial unity survived, the division emphasized differences of language, military and material resources, and social custom. The east survived the barbarian threat, but the west fell prey to Germanic tribes that crossed the Rhine and Danube frontier and ravaged the provinces. In 378 the emperor Valens fell to the Visigoths at Adrianople, and Vandals ravaged North Africa. Finally in 476 the last Roman puppet emperor, Romulus Augustulus, was deposed as an unnecessary nuisance, and the fragmented west was in the hands of various Germanic kings and princes.

The powerfully symbolic end of the Roman imperium in the west was the pillaging of Rome by Alaric's Visigoths in 410, a cataclysmic event that sent shock waves throughout the Mediterranean world. Rome had stood inviolate since a Gallic sack 800 years before. Why, asked the Roman world, had their ancient capital fallen so soon after the conversion to Christianity? Were Christians to blame because they had abandoned civic duties, preferring the monastery to the army or the farm, endowing churches instead of public buildings? Had the Christians sacrificed civilization in selfish folly while looking only to their lives in the next world? Had they alienated the ancestral gods who had protected Rome, and was Rome's destruction the sign of divine vengeance?

The brilliant and visionary Christian response came from Augustine, who would live to see a tribe of 80,000 Vandals cross Gibraltar and descend upon his native North Africa like a virulent plague, besieging his city of Hippo even as he lay dying in 430. Augustine's *City of God* looks beyond ruined Rome and doomed Hippo, beyond Babylon and the corrupt cities of this earth, to describe a celestial Jerusalem, the heavenly city where the chosen people would at last find a home.[4] All human history has inexorably led to the grandeur of the Christian community on earth, destined to be united by God's grace and love. Into his vast scheme, Augustine absorbed both the Jewish and the Roman past. Adam's fall has condemned human beings to experience the woes of this life; Christianity has in fact blunted evil in the world, even touching the barbarians and making them (Augustine claimed) remarkably merciful in their destruction of Rome as they spared churches and Christians who sought haven in them. Human beings' propensity for sin has made the Roman state essential for the preservation of an orderly environment in which people may pursue their quest for the City of God. The bonds of human society have their useful place because the state controls its sinful people through laws divinely revealed and vigorously enforced.

The *City of God* systematically demolished paganism and, in the process, came to terms with the classical heritage as a building block for a Christian future. Augustine's Christian masterpiece moves with epic grandeur from the ancient world into a new Christian age, throughout the voyage articulating the sensibility that would define and shape medieval society.

---

[4]See Henry Bettenson, trans., *Concerning the City of God against the Pagans* (Baltimore: Penguin, 1972).

Chapter 11

West and East after the Fall

Emergence of Medieval Christendom

What did the map of the Mediterranean world look like after the fall of Rome? Two distinct cultures emerged out of the vast migrations that shook the late antique Roman world (Figure 11.1). The eastern empire survived intact. It would in fact endure another thousand years, until the Ottoman Turks stormed Constantinople in 1453. Boasting healthy cities with thriving trade and industry, the more populous east could gather sufficient wealth in taxes to support a strong army and to pay off barbarians. The east also had energetic leaders who acted decisively to protect the capital. Alarmed by Alaric's sack of Rome in 410, men at the court of Theodosius II began in 413 to construct new walls that would protect the city from Attila's siege. Because the population had outgrown Constantine's walls, the Theodosian walls extended the city limits to the west, as well as guarding the coastline. Later in Theodosius's reign, a second land wall was added, so that there were two such walls fortified with towers and separated by a terrace. Just beyond the outer wall, workers dredged a deep ditch that could be filled with water when enemies threatened, thereby making Constantinople the most defensible city in Christendom.

The city's hard-pressed empire, surrounded by enemies, would need all the defenses it could muster. To its east were the Persians, ancient rival of Greco-Roman peoples. To the north, groups of Alani, Indo-Iranian nomads, joined forces with assorted Goths and Huns for an attempt on Constantinople that was repelled at last by the new walls. Vast numbers

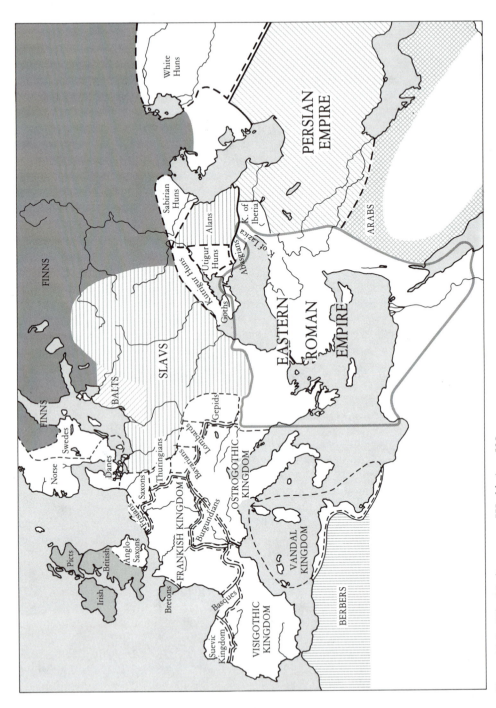

Figure 11.1   The Mediterranean World circa 528 C.E.

of Slavs swarmed along the Danube frontier, occupying what is now eastern Europe and southern Russia, and swept into the Balkans. In the sixth century, Slavs and Bulgars raided the countryside around the capital, to be stopped only by the massive walls. When 100,000 Avars (an Asian people related to the Huns and Turks) arrived in 558, their sophisticated political development under a strong khan allowed them to subjugate millions of Slavs and ultimately to engineer the great Avar-Slav-Persian siege of Constantinople in 626.

The battered eastern empire survived all these assaults because the capital remained untaken and the succession of emperors unbroken. Eastern sources, however, dated the fall of the western empire to 476, when the last formally designated emperor was deposed. From the eastern imperial viewpoint, this marked the significant breaking point. Modern observers tend to see an ongoing process of invasion, instability, and fragmentation into various Germanic states after the breakup of Attila's realms at his death in 453.

Of all the Germans, the Vandals earned a reputation as the most violent and fearsome. Crossing the straits from Spain into North Africa, Vandals took the rich farmlands of the coast, the breadbasket of Rome. In an instant they disrupted that critical source of grain and also destroyed the intellectual primacy of North Africa within the western church. From their capital at Carthage (439–533), they persecuted Catholics and ruled a defiantly Arian state, even building a fleet through which they controlled the Mediterranean Sea along with western Sicily, the Balearics, Corsica, and Sardinia. Not content to shatter Roman hegemony over the Mediterranean, they assailed Rome directly in 455, committing atrocities much more brutal than those of Alaric in 410.

Other Germanic peoples established less destructive kingdoms in old Roman territory—a Visigothic realm in Spain, Ostrogothic in Italy, Burgundian in the valleys of the upper Rhone and Saône rivers (the region still called Burgundy), and Frankish in Gaul, while Anglo-Saxon tribes took control of Britain. When Germans settled in Roman provinces, they followed varying models of *hospitalitas*, the system by which chiefs and armies received a portion, usually one-third, of revenues from land. Gradually chiefs and kings claimed the land itself. Because Germans settling on Roman territory composed a small share of the total population—perhaps as low as 5 percent—slowly assimilated Germanic chiefs and Roman elite tended to preside as landlords over peasants who were largely native "Romans." Many peasants saw few changes in their lives under the new regime; perhaps a Germanic landlord replaced their old Roman master and armed Germanic forces patrolled their lands. The newcomers usually absorbed the language and much of the culture of the natives, with whom they intermarried. The great cultural change occurred beyond the countryside, with the demise of cities that had controlled the economy and distinguished the culture of Mediterranean antiquity. Besieged and pillaged by invaders, then shunned by Germanic farmers and herders who preferred their habitual village life, cities virtually disappeared from the west. With them went the cosmopolitan society of the ancient world, along with its characteristic economic and cultural life, to be replaced by the predominantly peasant society that marked the medieval west.

This new society emerged from the combination of three elements: Roman cultural heritage, Germanic customs, and Christianity. The most influential of these was Christianity, which molded divergent cultural elements and offered a common world view and model for behavior. Many factors allowed for diversity of time and place, including such variables as geography or the relative strength and numbers of the indigenous peoples and

Germans. To study one specific example, let us look at the Ostrogothic kingdom of Italy, where Theodoric dreamed of a glorious civilization of cultured Romans and virile Goths coexisting and complementing one another's strengths. But religious antipathy between Catholic and Arian became the lightning rod for cultural and ethnic animosities that would blow the society apart.

Ostrogothic Italy

In 476 the army in Italy finally dismissed the boy emperor Romulus Augustulus and proclaimed their leader Odoacer as his replacement. Odoacer ruled until 493, when he fell before Theodoric's Ostrogoths, who had moved on to Italy following raids into the eastern empire. Technically, Theodoric assumed power as subject-king of Byzantium, formally acknowledging his allegiance to the emperor in Constantinople and receiving in return an authentication of his own rule. In fact, Theodoric exploited this prestigious connection in his grand experiment, quite self-consciously creating a new composite civilization of Germans and Romans. For a brief time, the experiment seemed destined for brilliant success, but charges of Roman treason triggered Gothic reprisals before Theodoric's death in 526. When the Roman emperor of the east, Justinian, found a pretext for intervention, his armies fought to wrest Italy from Ostrogothic hands. By the time the last sizable Gothic force surrendered in 553, Italy lay in ruins, easy prey for barbaric Lombards. The promising Ostrogothic reign had lasted only sixty years.

While Theodoric ruled, he was zealous to preserve the best of Roman culture, which he admired. He courted the favor of the Roman senate; in his theoretical separation of Roman and German, the senate played an honorable and useful role. Theodoric celebrated this survival and transmission of culture by carrying out an impressive program of building and repairing palaces, amphitheaters, aqueducts, baths, and city walls. His mausoleum stands today in Ravenna, a monument to a grand program. A mid-sixth-century source known as *Anonymus Valesianus II* praised Theodoric for bringing peace and prosperity, offering the traditional games and grain dole for the people, keeping the laws of former Roman emperors like a new Solomon, offering gracious treatment to the Pope and Catholics, and choosing from the old Roman senate such fine statesmen as Boethius and Cassiodorus to assist him.

Cassiodorus (ca. 485–ca. 550) was a particularly fine example of a talented and immensely learned Roman aristocrat in Gothic service. Secretary to Theodoric by 514, he was to hold office under three Ostrogothic kings. By about 538 he withdrew from the court, at first with the ambition of founding a university of Christian studies at Rome, but then retreating to his country estates, where he lived in monastic seclusion until his death at an advanced age. Profoundly conscious of the old culture that was fast dying, he lamented the loss of books burned during barbarian incursions. To save, even in abridged form, whatever knowledge he could rescue, he wrote works fusing Greco-Roman wisdom with Christian piety—works that would inspire learning throughout the Benedictine monastic houses in the medieval west. In the face of declining literacy, Cassiodorus stimulated generations of monks to spell correctly by insisting that "every word of the Lord written by the scribe is a wound inflicted on Satan." He honored pragmatic knowledge such as grammar and rhetoric as the products of a world created by God and so linked to the Creator. But he believed that theoretical study is also valuable in drawing the mind away from carnal affairs to the world of the spirit. So, for instance, he praised music, which leads the ear and soul to the divine, and astronomy, which draws the human mind to contemplation of the celestial realm.

The learned and pious Cassiodorus, philosopher, theologian, and monk, was the last of his kind, his works a precious and tantalizing remnant of the old erudition and culture nourished within the Gothic-Roman synthesis. How did this promising civilization die? According to an anonymous contemporary source, the devil entered Theodoric and made him suspicious and cruel. Modern critics are tempted to make a similar assessment by reckoning that religious tensions in Italian society finally erupted into violence.

The native Romans were orthodox Christians. The Ostrogoths, on the other hand, cherished their Arianism as an important element of their culture. Like their long hair and distinctive jewelry, it made an essential statement about their heritage and special character. Their institutional lives focused on Arian churches in the center of Gothic communities. Few Goths cared about or understood the fine points of dogma that separated their churches from the orthodox. Rather than studying discourses on the Trinity, Goths showed a fondness for stories of the Old Testament featuring warriors and battles. To most Goths willing to abandon their pagan ways, Arianism was simply the new tribal religion or perhaps the national religion of their Gothic state—Christianity grafted onto Germanic rituals and beliefs. Had it been given the time, political Arianism may well have died out in the long run, since its theological base among Goths was not intellectually or spiritually firm. As they were assimilated into Christian Roman society, individual Ostrogoths (even Theodoric's mother, Hereleuwa) were converting to orthodoxy, just as their Visigothic kin were doing in Spain.

Most Ostrogoths seem quite deliberately to have seen Arianism as a version of Christianity that bound them to their kin and set them apart from the Romans. A natural consequence of this distinction was further hostility between the two peoples as religious differences exacerbated other tensions. Romans who hated a second-class status in their homeland concentrated their animosity on the heretical status of their rulers. The Goths, for their part, feared treason motivated by religious passions.

Religious change in the eastern empire triggered the feared explosive reaction. So long as the monophysite Anastasius held the imperial throne (491–518), the orthodox Roman aristocracy had neither reason nor opportunity to join cause with the east. In those years, Theodoric acted as protector of the orthodox church. When the militantly orthodox Justin succeeded to power, however, influential senators at Theodoric's court entered into an incriminating correspondence with Constantinople. Were the two parties joining to foment revolution against Theodoric? Soon Justin began to harry Arians in the east, and the suspicious Theodoric snapped. One famous victim of his rage was the aristocrat Boethius, who wrote the *Consolation of Philosophy* while in prison awaiting execution for treason. Like Cassiodorus, Boethius had sought to preserve classical culture as he witnessed the demise of the ancient world. He had labored diligently to translate Greek works into Latin and to write handbooks and commentaries. His final philosophical treatise, the *Consolation*, is heavily informed by Christianity's message that human beings must seek fulfillment not in earthly pleasure or wealth but in pursuit of God. Boethius's final legacy inspired readers throughout the Middle Ages, including Dante, and provoked numerous commentaries. King Alfred translated the *Consolation* into Old English in the ninth century, and Notker translated it into Old High German in the tenth.

The execution of Boethius signaled the end of Theodoric's dream of Gothic-Roman synthesis. Literature produced at his court had praised Theodoric as a Christian king who united two peoples in harmony before God. In his capital at Ravenna, the great church of St. Apollinare Nuovo featured mosaics celebrating this harmony. The west end of the nave showed a procession of Theodoric and his entourage; balancing this on the east was Christ enthroned in company with his angels. On both sides of the nave, stately processions of martyrs and saints linked the earthly and heavenly kings. Images of Christian rulership blessed with peace and prosperity dominated the church. But this fragile culture disappeared in Theodoric's persecutions and the long Gothic–East Roman wars that followed. Only the persistent myth of Theodoric as ideal Christian–Germanic–Roman ruler would survive to influence another Christian prince of like vision, Charlemagne.

Justinian and the Eastern Empire: Dreams of a Single Empire (527–565)

Perhaps the Gothic Wars were inevitable, given Roman-Gothic tensions and Theodoric's violent reprisals. They were also an integral part of the program of Justinian, the tireless East Roman emperor driven by the conviction of his sacred mission to free Roman territories from barbarians and Arian heretics and to restore the frontiers of a single Roman and orthodox Christian empire.

Justinian inherited an empire that had weathered the storms of the fifth century, from barbarian incursions to religious controversies. Thanks to the prudent fiscal policies of the emperor Anastasius (491–518), the imperial coffers were full. The prospects for the state seemed limitless to Justinian, nephew of the emperor Justin (518–527). A Macedonian swineherd turned soldier, Justin had come to power through the army. Justinian, too, hailed from the westernmost territories. Latin, not Greek, was his native language. His eyes were trained west, so that he was determined to restore the ancient boundaries of a Roman Empire united by a single faith.

To pursue his dream, he first had to buy peace with the Persians, whose heartland had recently shifted from Iran and central Asia to Mesopotamia, on the borders of Justinian's empire. The Persians also had a new ruler, the formidable Chosroes I. Religious tensions heightened the rivalry of strong neighboring foes, as the Persians embraced a zealously intolerant Zoroastrianism led by a powerful priesthood. Byzantine diplomacy, on the other hand, had brought Christianity into Lazica and Caucasian Iberia, creating spiritual, and hence political, allies at Persia's doorstep. Yet Justinian chose to pay increasing tribute to Persia rather than exploit potential eastern inroads, because he was willing to accept peace at any cost in the east so that he could direct all his military resources to reconquest in the west.

At first the gamble seemed remarkably successful. Justinian's troops crushed the Vandal kingdom by a surprise attack in 533 and then took the Spanish coastline from the Visigoths. Ostrogothic resistance, however, was crushed only after more than twenty years of costly campaigns that depleted Justinian's resources of men and provisions. The destruction in Italy was devastating. During successive sieges, the aqueducts serving Rome were cut, closing down the great public baths that were prominent features of classical civilization. Surrounding territories reverted to marshes that would be drained only in the twentieth century. The price of reuniting Christendom was indeed dear. Nor would the union last. Depopulated and economically ruined, Italy proved easy prey for the Lombards, who swept down the peninsula only three years after Justinian's death. Its wealth exhausted, the eastern empire could not hold the hard-won lands.

If Justinian dreamed of removing Arians from the west, he also longed to root out heresy from the eastern provinces. More than any of his predecessors, he exercised control over the church, and aimed at absolute domination. Here Justinian's background and instincts as a westerner impeded him. When left to his own devices, he exhibited a personal intolerance for monophysites. This theological aversion was reinforced by political considerations: Abandoning monophysitism would encourage renewed contacts with Roman senators and assure their support in the Gothic war. Actions against monophysites, however, risked dangerous consequences in the eastern provinces. With this thorny problem, as with many others, Justinian was immeasurably assisted by his wife Theodora, daughter of a bear keeper in the circus and former prostitute and exotic performer. Theodora was savvy in the ways of the world. When a lover abandoned her in Alexandria, she had reportedly been rescued by monophysite leaders, who persuaded her to give up her scandalous life. She became a monophysite supporter, perhaps out of appreciation for their help in her survival and rehabilitation, but also because, unlike her husband, she had lived in Egypt and Syria and understood both the religious temperaments of the east and the importance of respecting eastern religious expression if these valuable territories were not to be irretrievably alienated. To Theodora it seemed self-evident that the orthodox emperor must find some accommodation with monophysites.

Under Theodora's influence, Justinian duly suspended the persecution of monophysites and attempted conciliation. In 533 he reverted to the emperor Zeno's policy. Zeno's *Henoticon*, or "Edict of Union" (482) had recognized the rulings of only the first three ecumenical councils and avoided expressions of "one nature" or "two natures," thus trying to skirt the burning issue. In 533 Justinian issued his "new *Henoticon*," allowing monophysites to preach their doctrine. He even permitted a monophysite, Anthemius, to assume the patriarchate in 535. Hoping to mollify the anti-Nestorian monophysites, he convened the Council of Constantinople in 553 to anathematize the Three Chapters, pronouncements of Chalcedon that had approved three Nestorian-leaning theologians. Despite such conciliatory moves, the orthodox emperor failed to find a compromise that would satisfy any of the parties in the dispute, orthodox or monophysite. Disaffection only increased.

Even while he dictated various compromises, Justinian ever remained the complete autocrat. A devout student of theology, he successfully championed the imperial claim of supremacy over ecclesiastical powers. But not all the bishops surrendered quietly to his demands. Italy provides a particularly interesting example of this resistance from the west.

Once Justinian reclaimed Italy, he sought to express his sovereignty there through imperial portraiture, as Roman emperors had customarily done. In the great church of San

Vitale in Ravenna, as elsewhere, he wiped out traces of Theodoric's presence and replaced them with emblems of his own power. This plan produced the famous mosaics of Justinian and his court, and opposite them, Theodora and her entourage. Justinian wears silks with Persian motifs signifying the absolute autocracy of a Persian king of kings, while his consort appears equally regal in her diadem and jewelry heavy with pearls, emeralds, and sapphires. Theodora and Justinian occupy a place of honor in the church, on facing sides of the apse, linked by the apse mosaic of Christ, angels, and saints. Here is a potent association of imperial authority and religious devotion expressed by an iconography that fuses sacred and imperial powers and serves to sanctify the imperial ideology. Such a political statement in a sacred building might shock an American Christian raised in the tradition of church–state separation, but it seemed entirely appropriate to a Christian emperor for whom empire and church were mutual protectors, with the emperor styled as Christ's regent on earth.

This mosaic is often admired as the most beautiful and dramatic expression of Justinian's imperial domination, but does the bishop who consecrated the church in 547 or 548 in fact have the last word, challenging Justinian's primacy? The scene is a grand procession, a notable moment in the liturgy. Does not the bishop, Maximian, at least seem to be jockeying for position with the emperor? Their dark robes set the two apart from the other central figures. Although Justinian's robe overlaps Maximian's slightly, the bishop's feet are plainly farther forward than the emperor's, and so the bishop appears to be standing ahead of Justinian. Only Maximian is identified with his name inscribed over his head. The emperor who would be supreme autocrat in the church, as well as in the society at large, must unwittingly share prominence with the local bishop who oversaw the mosaic's workmanship.

But this was, after all, distant Ravenna, for decades at war with Justinian, naturally offended by his policy of autocracy from afar. Were there signs of disaffection in the east as well? Indeed, no one has attracted extremes of adulation and vituperation more than Justinian. Perhaps the examples best known today come from the pen of Procopius, who sang the emperor's praises in works describing foreign wars (*History of the Wars*) and magnificent monuments to God's glory (*Buildings*) and yet who vilified him in the *Secret History*.[1] The *Secret History* describes a mad, demonic Justinian, a hypocritical devotee of assassination and robbery, who looked and acted like the notorious Roman emperor Domitian. This Justinian is a demon who stalked the imperial palace by night, his severed head tucked under his arm, and a monster who extorted taxes to hand out as bribes to barbarians. Such wild charges express the frustration of a man disillusioned by Justinian's policies, maybe personally harmed as well, and seething at the impossibility of open criticism against an autocratic regime.

Procopius was not alone in his anger. The civil unrest that had plagued Roman cities escalated during the fifth and sixth centuries and erupted with great violence during Justinian's reign. Procopius described the hooliganism of "skinheads" in the Circus Factions, associations of sports fans that had survived from the earlier Roman period. Young men affected Persian-style beard and mustache, shaving their hair to the temples and then wearing it long in the back in the fashion of the Huns. They appropriated Hunlike clothing, too,

---

[1]See Averil Cameron, trans. and ed., *History of the Wars, Secret History, and Buildings* (New York: Washington Square Press, 1967).

with long flowing sleeves that concealed the weapons they used to rob and kill, terrorizing the city. An anonymous sixth-century dialogue, *On Political Science*, blames the Circus Factions for corrupting the youth of the empire and ultimately weakening the army; instead of hooliganism (or, incidentally, monasticism as well, which harbored vast numbers of draft resisters, according to this same source), armed service to the state should consume the energies of young men.

Rebellion came to a head with the Nika Revolt of January 532, when the Circus Factions united to protest hated officials and extortionate taxation. Nerves were on edge in Constantinople because the disorganization of transport and economic uncertainty in the provinces had caused temporary disruption of the food supply to the capital. Amid the riots and fires, it was Theodora who persuaded Justinian to fight back and not to flee. In a surprise sally, his soldiers entered the hippodrome to slay 30,000 demonstrators and put down the rebellion.

The factions had burned great stretches of the city. Before the embers were cool, Justinian resolved to turn this tragedy into a brilliant opportunity. He had already embarked on an empirewide program of building fortifications, monasteries, palaces, bridges, cisterns, aqueducts, baths, hospitals, and especially churches, like the monastery of St. Catherine on Mount Sinai. But the Nika revolt offered the orthodox emperor the grandest stroke of all: to rebuild Hagia Sophia, the Great Church that would reign over orthodox Christendom for nine centuries. More than 100 feet across and 180 feet high, the Great Church's vaulted interior would be much more massive than churches of Europe and would soar to heaven (so witnesses marveled), reaching even the choirs of the stars. At its dedication only five-and-a-half years later in 537, Justinian exclaimed, "Solomon, I have surpassed you!" The architects were master mathematicians and theoreticians who perfected the dome style. Under the spell-binding influence of Hagia Sophia, this element would characterize eastern churches for the future, as would a near indifference to the exterior appearance of the building. In contrast with classical temples such as the Parthenon, with graceful exteriors fitted to their own peculiar landscapes, eastern churches would follow the example of Hagia Sophia in emphasizing the interior space, which was a model of God's universe intended to guide the worshiper to contemplation of the divine.

The surviving capitals and marble floors convey something of the original grandeur. Because the interior decorations are lost, except for post-Justinian mosaics, we must imagine the total effect of the spacious interior gleaming with silver altar screen and silk draperies, and smoky with incense, candles, and lamps. On a rare sunny day along the Bosphorus, light would flow from the circle of windows in the dome, which (in Procopius's words) "seems not to sit upon solid masonry but to cover the space beneath as if suspended from heaven by a golden chain."

The people of Constantinople crowded eagerly into Hagia Sophia, just as they did into their other churches, even pressing against the sanctuary barrier. Only the sanctuary itself was inaccessible to the masses, but the church otherwise invited all initiates to the full revelation of the mysteries. Some modern scholars have assumed that women were relegated to special balconies. It seems, however, that instead, special aisles on the left of the nave were reserved for women. Men sat separately on the right. One gallery above was reserved for the empress and her entourage. The emperor had his own throne in Hagia Sophia, located in the southern aisle, where he could witness the grand, public celebration of the liturgy. In Justinian's day, a series of processional movements structured the liturgy, beginning with the First Entrance of the clergy and congregation singing together with the bishop as they streamed into the church. The Ravenna mosaics of Justinian and Theodora are meant to portray just such a procession.

The Great Church was not Justinian's only legacy. He also planned the reorganization and preservation of the legal code, which had fallen into a confusing disarray. By the sixth century almost no one in the east could read Latin, the language of the laws. As a concession to his Greek-speaking people, Justinian ordered all new laws written in Greek. An even worse problem than the language barrier was the tangled mass of the law. Under the pagan jurist, Tribonian, Justinian's commission organized the vast code into manageable form, resolving inconsistencies. The old Roman law was pagan, but its principles of justice were not fundamentally at odds with Christianity. Only occasionally do we see in Tribonian's Code a softening of penalties, which may reflect the influence of Christianity. Justinian's New Laws (the Novels), however, expressed more clearly the merging of the traditional pagan legal system with the Christian ethic of the medieval empire. The New Laws, for instance, restricted the death penalty, often substituting mutilation, which was considered more humane. Other laws improved the position of slaves so that they could more easily win emancipation. This was not an especially courageous stand, because slavery was not very important in the sixth-century empire. Laws improving the lot of women may be more telling. Perhaps Theodora's influence, as much as that of Christianity, prevails in Justinian's laws reclaiming and protecting prostitutes, granting women the right to keep the property that had been their dowries, and allowing them guardianship of their children. The law increasingly intruded into the most private lives of imperial subjects, inspired by a Christian ruler eager to regulate the morality, conduct, and orthodoxy of his people.

The presence of non-Christians in his realm particularly incensed Justinian. He abused the few surviving Samaritans in Palestine until they rebelled, and then he crushed their revolt. The Jews he treated a little better. After two centuries of Christian rule, there were still pagans throughout the empire, even among the court at Constantinople, as Tribonian attests. Justinian destroyed the last pagan temples in Egypt, and he struck at the intellectual core of paganism by closing the Platonic Academy of Athens, whose scholars fled to the Persian king. In western Asia Minor alone, an early center of Christian communities, the emperor's emissary Bishop John of Ephesus found 70,000 pagans, mostly in the countryside. Despite great efforts at conversion, pagans would persevere there into Arab times, when they took the name Sabians to win status as "people of the book." Evidence from the later sixth and seventh centuries proves the continuing activities of pagan magicians, diviners, and rainmakers. Canons of the Council in Trullo (691–692) mention pagan festivals of the Brumalia and the new moon. In the eighth century, the cult of Kybele still lived in Caria, and a sacred stone outside Melitus was venerated into the tenth century.

Still, Justinian persisted in imposing strict control over all people within his realm, suppressing resistance wherever he could. His autocratic rule stretched to the breaking point the emotional and financial reserves of the eastern empire. Drought, swarms of insects, and bubonic plague also took their toll. In Constantinople alone, during one three-month bout of plague in 543, as much as one-third of the entire populace died—as many as 1,000 a day. (Procopius says that 10,000 perished daily.) Plague recurred in waves; by the year 600 the population of the eastern empire may have been only 60 percent of its pre-plague figures. It seemed an empire ill equipped to handle the stresses that lay ahead. Despite pockets of resistance to autocracy, however, the empire had a strong spiritual center and a consistent sense of itself as the God-given Christian empire, ruled by a sacred emperor who was God's regent on earth. This certainty of communal identity and sacred mission would play a monumental role in the survival of the empire.

Rome: From Episcopate to Papacy

Whereas Justinian and his successors dominated the eastern church, a radically different situation prevailed in the west, where the collapse of Roman civil authority left the bishops in charge. Within this highly visible episcopal structure, the bishop of Rome held nearly uncontested power and prestige. No emperor resided in Rome, as in Constantinople, to challenge the bishop's political or spiritual control, nor were there western patriarchates to compete with Rome.

Medieval tradition traced the lineage of the Roman bishop (called "pope" from the Latin *papa*, meaning "father") back to Peter and the scriptural authority of Matthew 16:18:

> And I tell you, you are Peter and on this rock I will build my church, and the powers of death shall not prevail against it.

At least as early as Stephen (254–256), Roman bishops had claimed supremacy over all other bishops by invoking the doctrine of Petrine Succession: the belief that they inherited Peter's authority and importance. The prestige of Leo I (440–461) moved the papacy to greater heights. By 445, the emperor Valentinian III ordered all western bishops to submit to Leo's authority. Although this order applied only to the west, where not all complied, reverence for Leo was so great that the predominantly eastern bishops at Chalcedon in 451 greeted his legates with the salutation, "Peter speaks through Leo." His courage and leadership became legendary; according to tradition, he won mercy for Rome from two barbarian armies—the dread hordes of Attila the Hun and the Vandal Gaiseric.

Leo consistently stressed the principle of Petrine Succession, and later popes followed his example. In the early centuries papal power remained primarily local, and popes did not even attend the first eight ecumenical councils, although they would convene and preside over all later ones. Growing papal prestige found a worthy recipient in Gregory I (ca. 540–603), known as Gregory the Great, whose influence extended far beyond the borders of Italy.

Born in Rome during the Gothic wars, Gregory lived through the brief East Roman imperial dominance and the Lombard invasions. These were nasty and violent years for Italy. As a member of a senatorial Christian family, Gregory received the aristocratic education of the day, but there was much less classical culture available to him than to Boethius and Cassiodorus only two generations earlier. In these few intervening decades, Italy had entered the Middle Ages. While he studied Latin grammar, law, and music, Gregory never bothered to learn Greek, even though he spent six years in Constantinople as a papal envoy. This ignorance—even disdain—illustrates the breach between East and West as surely as it marks the gap between Gregory's world and classical antiquity.

Gregory began a civil career and rose to become city prefect of Rome, but like many of the best men of his day, he was drawn to the church. In 575 he converted his palace into the monastery of St. Andrew, one of seven monasteries he would found out of his ancestral inheritance, and withdrew to the life of a Benedictine monk. In such troubled times, a man of Gregory's practical talents could not stay in seclusion, however, and he reluctantly resumed public life, this time under the church's auspices. In addition to his experience in Constantinople, Gregory served as deacon, managing the church's estates and charities. Conscripted as pope, he stepped in to fill the void at a moment when the city was threatened by plague, famine, and Lombard invasions. The civic administration of Rome had collapsed, and so it was Gregory who concluded the truce of 598 with the Lombards. Ransoming captives, providing food and water, and founding hospitals for the sick, he organized the church to meet the social and political needs of his people, who came to consider the church their state. Not surprisingly, Gregory's claims of Roman primacy carried great weight in the west, where there were no rival patriarchates, and helped transform the Roman episcopate into the medieval papacy. But this only sharpened discord with the east, where the Patriarch of Constantinople countered by taking the title of Ecumenical or Universal Patriarch.

Meanwhile, Gregory became recognized as one of the four fathers of the western church, along with Ambrose, Augustine, and Jerome. Gregory's much-loved *Dialogues*, lives of Italian saints and martyrs written in a simple, conversational style, enthralled medieval audiences with credulous accounts of wonders. He was an influential interpreter and popularizer of Augustine for the Middle Ages, following his master especially in creating a distinctively western theology of penance and purgatory. The latter became another of the issues dividing western and eastern Christendom, the emerging Catholic west and Orthodox east.

According to legend, Gregory also created a dynamic Latin liturgy, the Gregorian chant. This plainsong remains in Roman Catholic ritual to this day as one of the elements distinguishing it from the eastern rites. A prominent feature of the eastern service was the *kontakion*, developed in Justinian's time by the monk Romanos from sources in Syriac hymns and Greek rhythmic prose homilies. Chanted by a cantor, with a choir or the congregation singing the refrain, these rhythmical sermons, full of dialogue and drama, as well as paradox and word play, enlivened many services until the Council in Trullo (691–692), whose Canon 19 mandated the preaching of a *prose* homily at all major liturgical functions.

In fact, Gregory did not invent western religious song, as tradition held, but merely initiated some liturgical reforms. In another respect, however, Gregory's true influence ranged far beyond Italy. Through his patronage of Benedictine monks, he helped the young order survive rough times to become, for centuries, the west's only monastic order. When Gregory commissioned Benedictine monks to extend the bounds of Christendom far to the north, he gained not only souls for the faith but also loyal supporters for the papacy. Gregory's friend, the monk Augustine, and thirty companions traveled to the Anglo-Saxons in Britain, where little of Roman culture, including Christianity, had survived nearly two centuries after the Roman retreat in 406–407. At Kent, Augustine converted King Ethelbert, whose Christian Frankish wife had perhaps prepared the way. Then Augustine set up his own see at Canterbury, beginning the slow and not altogether steady process of Christianization from the top reaches of society downward. With Christianity came Latin learning, writing, and law, altering the society of medieval Britain even as it changed the social expression and spirit of Christianity in the west.

Christian Culture: Christianity as a Central Expression of Medieval Life

In important ways, late sixth-century Christendom was no longer the classical world. On the one hand, conversions had extended the bounds of Christendom beyond the frontiers of the Roman Empire, from Britain to Armenia, Georgia, and Albania. Abyssinia converted in the early fifth century, Nubia in the early sixth. Arians such as the Spanish Visigoths gradually embraced Roman Christianity. As the physical horizons of the Christian world expanded, on the other hand, so its cultural sensibilities simplified into the nonclassical views of medieval life.

In the west, a rather uniform Roman high culture disappeared with the creation of tribal societies, virtually erasing the boundaries between aristocratic and popular culture. The despoiled capital, its ancient monuments ruined and decaying, had a population of perhaps only 30,000, reduced from several hundred thousand. Where once cultured aristocrats fostered the classical tradition of Greek and Roman literature and learning, now bishops and monks read the scriptures and wrote biblical commentaries and saints' lives in Vulgar Latin. But Gregory the Great embodied the vision of the papacy and the new vigor of medieval Christendom.

Major cities of the east, especially the capital, nurtured the survival of a secular elite who studied ancient Greek literature and wrote elegant letters for their cultivated friends or histories modeled on Thucydides (for example, Procopius's *History of the Wars*). These archaizing works had a very limited audience. Even in the east, society was being redefined by its Christian outlook as the church absorbed the culture and made it its own. New kinds of literature appeared, naturally steeped in Christian language and values, and accessible to people whose secular education was modest.

One such work from the age of Justinian is the *Chronicle* of John Malalas, an Antiochene who spent his last years in Constantinople.[2] The *Chronicle* owes much to Eusebius's Christian chronicle and is itself an influential representative of the genre of popular historical writing, the world chronicle. Malalas wrote in a simple style close to that of the spoken language, a Greek dialect with some Latin and eastern expressions. His view is Christian and apologetic, showing much biblical influence on language and content. Like others of its genre, the *Chronicle* begins with Adam and Eve, assuming that all peoples claimed descent from Ham, Shem, or Japheth and that all events of this world, directed by God, led inexorably to Christ's incarnation and the Last Judgment. Stories in the Hebrew Bible provide the benchmarks for structuring the most ancient events of world civilizations. For more recent history, Malalas organized his chronology around the reigns of Roman emperors from Augustus to Justinian.

Malalas is famous for his errors, such as having Nero die of illness at the age of sixty-

---

[2]See E. M. Jeffreys, M. J. Jeffreys, and R. Scott, et al., *The Chronicle of John Malalas: A Translation*, Byzantina Australiensia 4 (Melbourne: Australian Association for Byzantine Studies, 1986).

nine. Mostly, however, he tells us information we would love to have regarding all periods and places of the Middle Ages—gossip, fiction, anecdotes, and historical details—all as the average sixth-century east Roman of fairly good education viewed them. Imagine a twentieth-century tabloid with a primitive Christian overlay, and you will understand the tone, value, and limitations of the *Chronicle*. Malalas was determined to entertain, and the *Chronicle* shows what fascinated the ordinary east Roman. Malalas recorded portents, signs of Persian–Roman tensions, riots among the Circus Factions in Antioch, and flooding in Edessa. In this partisan provincial view, the great fire in Antioch, with its subsequent earthquake and banditry, receives a disproportionate emphasis. The *Chronicle* is an excellent source for social history. For example, there are valuable tidbits about Justinian, such as the confession that he "did not speak the Roman language [that is, Greek] correctly." From Malalas we learn that the emperor was always more comfortable with Latin. The *Chronicle* reveals how a sixth-century Antiochene viewed the world: When it lists rulers elsewhere, it gives the ominous sense of God's people being surrounded by potentially dangerous aliens. In such a world, Malalas's credulous piety remains the ordering principle.

Another telling example from the age of Justinian is the superstitious and otherworldly *Christian Topography*, written in about the 530s by Cosmas Indicopleustes (i.e., sailor to India). Cosmas probably hailed from Alexandria, where he settled in a monastery upon retiring from the life of a merchant who had sailed throughout the Mediterranean, Red Sea, and Persian Gulf. His precious book is the only Christian topography extant, combining descriptive geography, cosmography, and scriptural exegesis. Much of the geography is quite accurate, based on personal observation in lands as far ranging as Ethiopia and Christian Abyssinia, and from the Sinai Desert to India. For all his practical experience, Cosmas cheerfully confessed his lack of formal education, and in fact he considered the absence of rhetorical training an asset, since rhetoric would be out of place in a book "for Christians, who had more need of correct notions than of fine phrases." The resulting grammar is loose and colloquial but usually clear and forceful and even eloquent when Cosmas was writing about his faith.

Cosmas ordered his experience and beliefs from a Christian worldview. As he rejected "pagan" grammar, so he also rejected pagan science. Like many pious Christians of his day, he assumed that the universe created by God could be understood only through the interpretation of Christian scripture. So he refuted the Ptolemaic concept of the earth as a globe and deduced instead that the earth must be shaped like the sanctuary of the tabernacle of Moses, which was a copy of the earth; the tabernacle itself was modeled on the universe, which had the earth as its base and God's heaven at its vaulted top. Ancient Jewish and Akkadian concepts of the universe had clearly influenced Cosmas. He tells the reader that he got his ideas on creation from Mar Aba, who was then the Nestorian Katholikos (metropolitan bishop).

The views of Cosmas and Malalas nicely illustrate the changing tastes and passions that we identify as medieval. Christianity became an essential, inextricable part of the culture of medieval men and women, east and west. These people created their own evolving Christian mythologies to express their worldview. From the second century onward, they venerated martyrs and their relics, looking back to the time of the persecutions as a heroic age when martyrs were the athletes of Christ. By the end of the fourth century, the popular imagination revered martyrs as protectors and healers, intercessors with God. The bodies of saints or anything they had touched remained sacred. The passion for relics increased, as did the enthusiasm for pilgrimages to places where they were preserved, especially the Holy Land or Rome.

The apostles continued to be revered, too, and by the fifth century the angels were also, especially Michael. Both Rome and Constantinople built churches in his honor, and Michaelmas, his feast day on September 29, became one of the most popular in the medieval west. When the Third Ecumenical Council at Ephesus authorized the title "Mother of God" for Mary, she could with official sanction receive much of the fervor once granted to the ancient mother goddess, as Christianity absorbed and modified some of the pagan impulses it could not obliterate. With Christendom entering the Middle Ages, the religion was secure in its position as the central expression of medieval life. Christianity was molding all the elements of society into the distinctive tastes and passions that identified the medieval world.

Chapter 12

The Eastern Empire and the Struggle Against Islam

Byzantium after Justinian

Justinian's failed attempt at reunion served only to separate western and eastern Christendom and to alienate each from the other. In the generations after Justinian's death in 565, his empire seemed less and less Roman, less and less classical. By the time of his death, it was appropriate to call the eastern empire by the name now commonly used for its medieval continuator: Byzantium.

It is important to remember that the people we call Byzantines recognized no radical break from their Greco-Roman heritage. They continued to call themselves *Romaioi*, "Romans." Their empire they called *Basileia ton Romaion*, "Empire of the Romans." They spoke these names in Greek, having lost virtually all contact with the Latin language. Modern historians have seen this change as but one sign of a new era that began with Constantine's conversion to Christianity and his movement of the capital to Byzantium (renamed Constantinople) and ended when the city fell to the Turks. Many historians thus date the Byzantine empire from 330 to 1453. Others count Justinian as the first Byzantine emperor; still others begin with Heraclius (610–641). Far-reaching transformations marked the century from Justinian's accession to Heraclius's death. The eastern empire had to make radical adaptations to survive and flourish once again, and religious issues played a dominant role in these changes.

Justinian had not been able to resolve the religious tensions of the Christological controversies. From its earliest years, Christianity had attempted to be ecumenical, to be inclusive. But in an age of religious fervor, the prevailing Greco-Roman heritage within Christianity could deem as heretics those people whose radically different cultures had developed outside the Roman mainstream.

The continuing Nestorian and monophysite disputes illustrate this problem. Late antique Syria harbored many monophysites, and a Nestorian community survives there even now. The Armenian church, originally reacting against the Nestorianism of its ancient oppressor, Persia, embraced monophysitism and remains monophysite today, as does the Coptic church of Egypt and Ethiopia.

Religious dissatisfaction, as in Armenia, sometimes had political roots. So it could also have political consequences. Three of the five great patriarchates (Alexandria, Antioch, and Jerusalem) were lost to Islam in the seventh century. Did the religious alienation of Egyptians and Syrians from Constantinople incline them to capitulate first to the Persians and then to the Muslims, rather than resist? That is the standard view, although in fact we have little historical data from that period of chaos.

Heraclius and His Tragedy

Shaken by natural disasters, religious controversies, and foreign invasions, the eastern empire was vulnerable to lawlessness and revolution. In 602, for the first time in 300 years, a usurper had successfully snatched the throne. This emperor, Phocas, seems to have inaugurated a reign of terror, although we must use contemporaneous sources with great caution because nearly all the accounts that survive come from his enemies, supporters of the man who dethroned him eight years later. Heraclius (610–641), son of the governor of Africa, sailed from Carthage to Constantinople and founded a dynasty that would last for five generations. He rescued an empire fallen into dire straits. Lombards had overrun Italy; Avars and Slavs had swept across the northern frontier into the Balkans; in the East, the Sassanid Persian empire was gaining strength. These pressures would culminate in 626 with a combined Avar-Slav-Persian siege of Constantinople.

Enmity between Greeks and Persians had a long history, stretching back 1,100 years to Darius and Xerxes and the Persian Wars recorded by Herodotus. Under a strong Sassanid king, the Persians might have found victory at last and crushed the Byzantine empire if it had not been for the energy and military brilliance of Heraclius. He built up the fleet, strengthened and reorganized the army, radically altered provincial administration, and counted heavily on the religious passions and convictions of his Christian subjects. Without a doubt, Heraclius and his people viewed their Persian Wars as a religious crusade. Standing firm in their collective assumption that they lived in a God-given Christian empire, Byzantines shared a potent religious–political theory: the belief that their Roman Empire was the last of the world empires and would survive until the apocalypse, to surrender only to God. Until that moment, God would protect their city and their empire from ultimate harm, although they stood poised on the brink of disaster.

In fact, even as Heraclius wrested his empire from Phocas, the two superpowers were preparing to fight to the death. The year 611 marked the beginning of Persian aggression aimed at the Byzantine heartland. In lightning campaigns, the Persians took Antioch and

Damascus and held all Syria. They set their sights next on Palestine, and after a twenty-day siege, they took the holy city of Jerusalem. There it became clear that the Persians saw this as a religious war. With determined ferocity, they destroyed Christian monuments, including the Church of the Holy Sepulcher built by Constantine and his mother Helen, which was despoiled of its treasures and then burned. Eager to be free of Christian domination, the Jews of Jerusalem took the Persian side. Some sources report that 60,000 Christians were slaughtered in the melée, and the patriarch of Jerusalem, Zacharias, was taken prisoner to Persia. One of the most precious relics of all Christendom, the Holy Cross on which Jesus was believed to have died, was also carried off to Ctesiphon. The loss of the holy city with its sacred monuments and relics was a disaster beyond reckoning.

In 618 or 619 (the records for this chaotic period are extremely spare and confusing), a third patriarchate fell as a Persian army stormed Alexandria, exposing all Egypt to Persian domination. This was a severe economic loss because Egypt supplied the grain for Constantinople. Of the four eastern patriarchates, only that capital city was not yet in Persian hands, and the disappearance of its provisions considerably weakened Constantinople's defenses. In 626 the Persians reached the Bosphorus, took Chalcedon, and camped opposite the capital. By chance, a great Avaro-Slav horde had also reached the city on a raid from the north and began a siege with Persian support.

Since 622 the emperor Heraclius had been in an almost constant campaign, allied with Caucasian tribes and the Khazars, waging distant battles on the old frontiers and into the heart of Persia. For this crusade, the patriarch had finally surrendered the church's treasuries, lending them to the state at interest. Heraclius was winning dazzling victories, but he was obliged to leave the capital with few defenders, and the Persians resolved to imitate Heraclius's tactics and strike at the enemy's vital core. The siege of 626 presented the double assault by land and sea that Heraclius had most feared. For eleven days the patriarch Sergius sustained the religious fervor of the people with passionate sermons, night vigils, and solemn processions. In this desperate moment, when all might have seemed lost, the Byzantine navy managed to turn the tide. Byzantine maritime supremacy overwhelmed the Slav fleet, compelling the land army to retreat in complete disarray. Although historians have ascribed victory to the naval forces, the inhabitants of Constantinople credited the direct intercession of the Virgin, who defended her people and her shrine at Blachernae.

Heraclius had sent forces to the city, but he himself remained at the eastern front. There he struck the final blow, virtually annihilating the Persian army in a battle near ancient Nineveh in 627. The following year the Persian king Chosroes was deposed and murdered. His successor sued for peace, returning the lost provinces of Egypt, Syria, and Palestine. The Byzantine victory was complete. Never again would Persia threaten Byzantium.

After a six-year absence, Heraclius returned to Constantinople in triumph. The patriarch Sergius met him on the coast of Asia Minor, leading senate, clergy, and people, who greeted their victorious emperor with olive branches, lighted candles, hymns, and acclamations of joy. After a brief respite, Heraclius cleared Asia Minor of Persians, and then in 630 he traveled with his wife, the empress Martina, to Jerusalem, where he restored the Holy Cross to its place of glory amid great celebration. A contemporaneous Armenian historian, Sebeos, has left an eyewitness account:

There was much joy at their entrance to Jerusalem: sounds of weeping and sighs, abundant tears, burning flames in hearts, extreme exaltation of the emperor, of the princes, of all the soldiers and inhabitants of the city; and nobody could sing the hymns of our Lord on account of the great and poignant emotion of the emperor and of the whole multitude. The emperor restored [the Cross] to its place and returned all the church objects, each to its place; he distributed gifts to all the churches and to the inhabitants of the city and money for incense.[1]

These joyous ceremonies symbolized the victorious conclusion of the first great holy war of Christendom. Flush with God's evident approval of Christian Byzantium, and angry with the Jews for their support of Persia, Heraclius ordered all Jews of the empire baptized. His realm would be a true city of God, untainted by non-Christians or heretics, so that even the Nestorians who had taken refuge in Persia had to flee to sanctuaries deep in Asia.

For Byzantine Christendom, the intoxicating joy was brief. Even as Heraclius celebrated, his victory was being duly recorded in the Koran, the holy book of the emerging religion that would nullify Heraclius's triumph in the emperor's own lifetime. It was Heraclius's tragedy to live as a contemporary of Muhammad (ca. 570–632), prophet of Islam. In 622, the very year when Heraclius began his counterattack against the Persians, Muhammad fled from Mecca to Yathrib, later called Medina, "the city of the prophet." This marks the Muslim year of the Hegira (or *hijrah*), Year One in their reckoning of time.

Welcomed in Medina, Muhammad began to establish a community there and to lay the foundations for a religiously based state. He then returned to Mecca as conqueror and set about destroying its idols and all remnants of polytheism. His religion he called Islam, "submission" to God, its fundamental nature revealed in the Koran. Monotheism and discipline characterize Islam, showing the influence of Judaism, Christianity, and even Persian Zoroastrianism. Muhammad may have been reacting in part to monophysite teachings about Christ when he stressed the unity of the one god Allah, whose prophets (himself included) were holy men, but not themselves divine. By the time of Muhammad's death, the diverse Bedouin tribesmen and wealthy merchants of all Arabia had accepted his creed of submission to Allah. The social and political effects of this union were enormous, as the hostile energies formerly directed against one another were channeled outward in holy war, the Islamic jihad.

Desperately exhausted by their wars, Persia and Byzantium proved easy prey for Arabs united in a fresh religious passion. Within ten years of the Prophet's death in 632, Persia and the eastern provinces of Byzantium had yielded to Islam. Syria succumbed in 636, after the decisive military defeat at Yarmuk. Jerusalem surrendered following a two-year siege in 637 or 638, although only after Christians succeeded in removing the Holy Cross to Constantinople. Mesopotamia was conquered along with Persia. Devastated by the relentless and completely unanticipated Arab advance, Heraclius died in 641, a pathetic and broken man. Within a year or two, Muslims occupied Alexandria, burning the famous libraries, with irretrievable loss of ancient learning and literature. The disorganization of the Byzantine army in Egypt and the apparent weakness of its resistance to Islam have provoked continuing speculation that religious disaffection with Constantinople was taking a

---

[1] A. A. Vasiliev, trans. (following K. Patnikov and F. Macler), *History of the Byzantine Empire*, vol. 1 (Madison, WI: University of Wisconsin Press, 1952), p. 198.

political toll. Imperial intolerance of religious diversity can only have undermined the will of both Egypt and Syria to defend their ties to the orthodox empire.

Never again would a Roman Empire hold Egypt. Once the Arabs claimed that rich province, they moved into North Africa and assailed Mediterranean islands, working irreparable damage to many remnants of classical civilization. The Colossus of Rhodes, a statue of Helios that was one of the wonders of the ancient world, was sold to Jewish merchants, who carted it away on 900 camels. Arabs crossed the Straits of Gibraltar in 711 and swept across Spain in a mere seven years, passing over the Pyrenees into the kingdom of the Franks, where they would finally be stopped by Charles Martel at the battle of Tours (732). Meanwhile, a contemporaneous proverb proclaimed the Mediterranean—once a Roman sea—now a Muslim lake.

The Aftermath: Crisis of Church and Society

Very limited sources have survived from the troubled seventh century, making it difficult to assess that period. The documents that do exist are predominantly religious in orientation, written by men attempting to find a spiritual interpretation of the catastrophe. Just as the Byzantines believed that good fortune or success demonstrated divine approval of the empire, so they felt that disasters were signs of God's wrath, perhaps even signifying the impending end of the world. One Mesopotamian monk, horrified not only by the Muslim conquest of the region, but also by the easy accommodation some Christians made to Muslim rule, wrote the so-called *Revelation of Methodius of Patara*, which argued that recent events fulfilled New Testament prophecies; very soon the Antichrist would come, followed by the Son of Man and the Last Judgment. Greek and Latin translations of the Syriac *Revelation* brought these ideas to a large and receptive audience. With the unforeseen tragedies of the Muslim advance, Byzantium became a society in turmoil, questioning its identity as God's chosen realm and the very survival of its civilization.

There were numerous signs that the empire had changed significantly since the age of Justinian, when it was still characterized by its thriving urban life. As late as the sixth century, the eastern empire was dotted with cities that were self-administering units with control over the surrounding countryside. For 200 to 300 years, since the barbarian threat, these cities had been walled towns, small by our standards. But the walls enclosed wide streets laid out in a regular pattern, with shops under colonnades, a forum ringed by public buildings and decorated with statues and fountains, public monuments, a theater, and perhaps a hippodrome if the city was large enough. And, of course, there were churches throughout the city—so many churches, in fact, that their upkeep was becoming a financially oppressive responsibility.

Only in the Balkans had cities collapsed under assaults from Huns and Ostrogoths, and later from Slavs, who had learned to storm walls but had no interest in living within them. Ruined cities dotted the Balkan landscape. Elsewhere in the eastern empire, people continued to enjoy the amenities and culture of Greco-Roman urban life. Everyone—women, men, children, and even clergy—seems to have spent plenty of time at the baths. Although amply criticized by the church, the theater, hippodrome, and wild beast fights remained popular. City folks lived very public lives, lingering with friends in taverns or listening with admiration to the speeches of rhetoricians.

With the disruptions of the sixth century, city life declined. Drought, plague, locusts, earthquakes, and urban violence all took their toll. In Asia Minor the Persian invasions further weakened cities, and the Arabs delivered the final blow. Archaeological evidence suggests that Byzantine cities surviving into the seventh century dwindled in size and population. Nearly every remaining city (*polis*) was transformed into a *kastron*, a heavily walled fortress. Most cities built around a hill (*acropolis*, the high city) withdrew to the hillside alone, abandoning territory outside the old *acropolis*. Even a once-flourishing coastal city such as Ephesus saw its harbor silt up and let its baths fall into decay, becoming a tiny and isolated settlement, walled and landlocked. By the seventh century, when Byzantines spoke of "the city," they usually meant Constantinople. Only in Constantinople did the hippodrome still exist, and even there it operated no more than a few days a year for imperial ceremonies.

The capital produced imperial art; elsewhere, art became notably provincial in style. Much of public life disappeared with the loss of theaters and civil basilicas that housed both courts of law and commercial centers, with the colonnades where the people had gathered. Public activity continued almost exclusively in the church, which became more and more important as the site of social contact, ritual, and entertainment. Otherwise, social intercourse contracted to focus on private life within the family.

The extent of this fortification and ruralization of the empire is still being debated among scholars, but beyond doubt, the character of Byzantine society changed radically during this period. With the collapse of civic life in the provinces, intellectuals clustered in Constantinople, where the bureaucracy required men with a classical education in ancient Greek letters. Outside the capital, secular training at the primary school level continued, so that basic literacy survived. Even in public schools, children first learned to read the Psalter, and echoes of the Psalms resound throughout Byzantine literature.

The church took over more and more aspects of education, just as it accepted an increasing role in other areas of Byzantine life. Public doctors of Greco-Roman cities, for instance, were no longer paid by the city in which they practiced, but instead were retained by the church and worked in church-supported hospitals, where the sick might stay and receive round-the-clock care, clean beds, and good meals. These philanthropic institutions were an original creation of Byzantine Christianity. Tensions often arose between the monks' twin goals of loving both God and neighbor. To resolve this conflict, the *typika* (foundation documents) of some monasteries specifically forbade the monks themselves from serving as physicians or servants in contact with the patients. Hospitals outside the monastery's inner walls, however, might be staffed by doctors and other caretakers whom the monastery supported.

The Icon and Iconoclasm

Rapid changes in the society and challenges from threatening enemies brought a crisis of identity and faith. Various signs point to this spiritual conflict. It was marked, on the one hand, by a rising number of anti-Jewish texts, which were really expressions of Christian self-doubt. The documents featured staged debates between Christians and Jews, in which the Christians answered various arguments against their religion and defended it from attack. In these texts, the Jews were inevitably confounded or even converted, but the real audience was Christian, and the real successes lay in alleviating anxieties and resolving uncertainties of Christians.

The most far-reaching sign of this societal tension lay in the attack on, and defense of icons. Icons are images or pictures of Jesus, Mary, or saints. They portray the holy person in a distinctively stylized pose, as a frontal image of an isolated figure hovering in empty space. Typically, the saint faces the worshipers with both eyes visible so that viewers can have full access to the holy person, the prototype the images lead them to emulate. Icons are meant to be symbols rather than realistic representations—symbols of divinity and spirituality, richness and power. As representations of a holy person, they attracted the veneration of Christians. They are still venerated by the faithful today. Even for persons outside the orthodox tradition, Byzantine icons provide a unique and compelling entry into the spirituality of Byzantine society.

Byzantine Iconoclasm: Icon Smashing

At the moment when Byzantium needed to concentrate all its resources against Islam in order to survive, the empire began diverting energies to an internal battle over the icons. In fact, this conflict proved both a symptom of crisis and a provocation of further tensions that reached dangerous proportions. Just as monophysitism had done in previous centuries, so iconoclasm threatened to tear Byzantine society apart.

Iconoclasm (icon smashing) was the imperial policy during two periods, 726–787 and 815–843. The struggle pitted the Greco-Roman love of figural representation against Old Testament prohibitions of idolatry. These ideals represented two very different sensibilities. Often displaying a visceral antipathy to icons, iconoclasts accused iconophiles (icon lovers) of worshiping idols, and they called them iconodules (icon slaves). Iconophiles vigorously denied this charge and insisted that they were simply venerating holy images of the divinity and saints; to destroy the images was to assail the saints themselves.

At least as early as Clement of Alexandria (ca. 150–ca. 215) and Tertullian (ca. 160–ca. 240), some Christians had expressed a theological distaste for pictorial representations of divinity, from time to time exciting outbursts of violence against holy pictures. Yet the cult of the images flourished during the sixth and seventh centuries, perhaps in part because people cherished intercessors with God during particularly difficult times as popular piety increased. In 691–692 the Quinisext Council (so called because it continued the work of the fifth and sixth ecumenical councils, but sometimes also called the Council in Trullo, or Trullan, from the domed hall where it met) debated the issue of images and the popular depiction of Christ as a lamb, encouraging the representation of him in his human form. Canon 82 concludes: "Through his figure we perceive the depth of the humiliation of God the Word, and we are led to remember his life in the flesh, his suffering and his saving death, and the redemption which comes from it for the world." In encouraging the production of icons, the council decreed that the image of Christ in his human form helps the viewer understand the full impact of the incarnation, of God's suffering and death for humankind.

Almost simultaneously with this decree, the emperor Justinian II made a very public show of support for the idea it promulgated. In a daring move, he replaced the imperial portrait on the obverse (front) of an issue of gold coins with a portrait of Christ, inscribed "King of Kings." Justinian relegated his own portrait to the reverse, with the inscription "Slave of Christ." Since such a valuable gold piece was likely to be seen not by ordinary Byzantines, but by wealthy traders who might well circulate it beyond the borders of the empire, this new coinage may have been partly intended as a provocative act against Islamic neighbors. In fact, the coin instigated a chain reaction in the Arabic world, ultimately resulting in the removal of the caliph's image from coinage, to be replaced by religious slogans in Arabic script.

Evidently, such a bold image troubled Justinian's successors, too, for they dropped his controversial design and returned to a traditional portrait of the emperor on coinage. Does this rejection point to the questioning of images in imperial circles? If so, it would support a recent scholarly thesis that labels iconoclasm an "imperial heresy," initiated and supported primarily by a few emperors. At any rate, the iconoclast impulse, smoldering for centuries, erupted with Leo III in 726. Some Byzantinists have felt that Leo was stimulated by the actions of the Caliph Jazid II, who may have initiated an iconoclast policy in 723–724, ordering all Christian churches in the caliphate to remove their icons. The evidence points to mutual influence, as well as hostility, within the iconoclast movements of the caliphate and the Byzantine empire. In Leo's own day, enemies charged that he was semi-Muslim. Although Leo persecuted Jews and fought Arabs, both these Semitic peoples had an impact on his thought. He seems to have grown up in Syria and lived for many years in Asia Minor, where he learned Semitic prejudices against images, prejudices that Islamic societies would nurture. Should Christianity adopt these widespread religious impulses or maintain a distinctive alternative? For Leo and other Byzantines, iconoclasm paradoxically attempted a kind of accommodation to Islamic ideals alongside the fierce competition with this religion that was Christianity's most threatening rival. Islam claimed to be the legitimate heir to Christianity and to supersede it, just as Christians believed that their religion had inherited and superseded the traditions and special role of Judaism. Military victories appeared to confirm Islamic claims to possessing God's favor. The resulting challenge to Byzantine identity was profound. It is only natural that Islamic ideas would influence a Christian society struggling to redefine itself as a religious people and political entity in the wake of enemy successes and natural catastrophes.

Leo III began cautiously, encouraged by the bishops of Asia Minor, who opposed the iconophile tendencies of the patriarch Germanos I. The people of Asia Minor harbored strong iconoclast sentiments, whereas support for venerating icons came from European provinces of the empire. While Leo wavered, a providential earthquake persuaded him that the persistence of icons in his realm was angering God. The emperor laid the groundwork for his revolution by delivering sermons against the icons; but when he ordered his agent to remove the mosaic figure of Christ from its honored place above the Chalke Gate, the ceremonial entrance to the palace in Constantinople, a riot ensued and the imperial agent was killed. Women, rather than the usual adolescent males of the old Circus Faction melées, made up the large majority of rioters. A protest erupted in Greece, where a rival emperor even emerged to dispatch a fleet against Constantinople.

The emperor easily defeated the usurper, but he could not win over the patriarch or the pope, Gregory II. In letters to Rome, Leo explained that as God's designated chief pontiff, he himself must take the responsibility for executing this policy. Gregory found himself in a bind. The iconoclast agenda did not sit well with him, but he could not afford to lose imperial protection needed against the Lombards. The best defense of icons came from outside the Byzantine empire, but from the east rather than the west. The greatest theologian of the age, John of Damascus (ca. 675–ca. 750), argued on behalf of the iconophiles. A Christian Arab who was treasury official for the caliph, John wrote three treatises in defense of images, maintaining that they were not idols but symbols, mediators between heaven and earth, like the saints themselves. He employed a Neoplatonic argument that the appreciation of visible beauty leads necessarily to the appreciation of absolute beauty—that is, to the true knowledge of God. The incarnation justifies the material form of the image. It might even be argued that the incarnation makes the icon a uniquely Christian object of veneration, as suitable for Christianity as it is inappropriate for Judaism or Islam.

Led by the emperor Constantine V (ruled 741–775), the brilliant military man and theologian who succeeded his father Leo III, the iconoclasts responded with a subtle theology of their own. From the primitive, instinctive attack on images as idolatry, they moved to Christological arguments, declaring that iconophiles were either Nestorians or monophysites. That is, either the artist was portraying only the human nature of Christ and thus sliding into Nestorianism by separating the inseparable divine and human natures of the divinity, or the artist was pretending to portray both the human and the divine, confusing them into one as the monophysites did. In fact, iconophiles were successful in throwing this theological argument back on Constantine, seeing an element of monophysitism in iconoclasm that emphasizes Christ's divinity and distant majesty.

In 754 Constantine summoned a council he called the Seventh Ecumenical Council, which ordered icons destroyed and prohibited their veneration. In Hagia Sophia, as throughout the empire, images were smashed or plastered over, often replaced by mosaics of the cross or pictures of the emperor and his family. Constantine initiated vigorous persecutions, especially against monks, and even some executions. Not all scholars agree that these persecutions were direct retribution against iconophile monks; some insist that Constantine's personal aversion to the monastic ideal must be considered a separate issue. But it is likely that there was a link between the veneration of the holy man and the veneration of the icon that individualized and privatized worship and salvation, threatening imperial authority. Monks may have played a considerable role in the support of icons, thus contributing to the hostility of a military emperor who resented the empire's large numbers of monks (perhaps 100,000 at the time), who drained the potential ranks of soldiers and farmers, defied the usual Byzantine social order of the nuclear family, and resisted imperial control. Constantine confiscated prominent monasteries in Constantinople and turned them into army barracks. To humiliate monks, he commanded some to be paraded in the hippodrome, each forced to hold the hand of a woman while the crowd shouted insults. At Ephesus the provincial governor summoned all the monks and nuns of his territory and ordered them to choose either marriage or blinding and exile. To escape persecution, pious people fled to the Caucasus or the north shore of the Black Sea, or even to Rome.

It was a woman who restored icon veneration to Byzantium. Constantine V had arranged for his son and heir, Leo IV, to marry the Athenian Irene, perhaps as a conciliatory gesture to European territories. She was herself an iconophile, like most of her Greek compatriots. Under compulsion, before her coronation and marriage in 768, Irene swore a solemn oath never to accept icons. She was under suspicion, however, when her husband died suddenly in 780. A much later source reported that Leo had found two images hidden under cushions in Irene's apartments.

Irene carefully prepared the way for the true Seventh Ecumenical Council, which met at Nicaea in 787. Its full acts are extant. The bishops found few biblical endorsements of icons, and so they relied heavily on unwritten tradition and quotations from the Church Fathers, using the arguments articulated by John of Damascus. To the charge that images were pagan idols, they replied that Christians worshipped only the personalities represented in the images; iconophiles offered the icons not worship but veneration and honor. To the charges of Nestorian or monophysite tendencies in the creation of the icon, they answered that the artist paints just the body, but the soul and personality are reconstructed only in the mind of the viewer.

For her role in the restoration of icons, the orthodox church still reveres Irene as a saint. She also coveted the secular designation as emperor. After years of rivalry with her son Constantine VI, she had him blinded in 797 and took for herself the masculine imperial title, *basileus*, becoming the first woman to rule Byzantium in her own right, not as co-ruler or regent. Her ambitions ranged far: She hoped to marry Charlemagne. His envoys were in Constantinople when Irene was deposed in 802.

The forces of iconoclasm were by no means spent. Military disasters under iconophile emperors (especially Irene) seemed convincing signs of God's disfavor with the icons. Iconoclast emperors on the other hand, most notably Constantine V, had won stunning victories against the Arabs. In reinstating the decrees of 754, a second iconoclast council of 815 protested that "female simplicity" had restored the adoration of "dead figures" and "lifeless icons." The synod inaugurated a second period of vigorous iconoclasm linked to internal reform of the empire. In 843 this period, too, ended with the restoration of icons by a woman, the empress Theodora, regent for her six-year-old son after his father, the emperor Theophilus, died in 842. During her regency, Theodora imitated Justinian II by striking gold coins with a bust of Christ on the obverse. From that time on, Byzantine coins always contained some image of Christ, the Virgin, or a saint.

Can it be coincidental that icons were both times restored by women? Some Byzantinists have argued that the significant operative factor was not the woman herself but rather the weak imperial control during a regency. These critics see iconoclasm as a statement of imperial dominance over the church and society, a dominance shattered without a strong man at the helm. Others believe that women were more often than men the ardent venerators of images, and so it was natural that a woman in power would restore the images. According to this view, women sought out sacred mediators (often Mary and female saints) to intercede with a God of overwhelming power and majesty. There is evidence that mothers encouraged their daughters to kiss and fondle icons, just as some children today play reverently with dolls. Family icons seemed almost like honored family members, even being named occasionally as godparent to a child, and women might feel a special intimacy with these images.

On this particular question of female support for icons, the debate still rages. It seems likely, however, that the icon question did polarize Byzantine society along certain lines, pitting women and monks against the army and the emperor, and setting the Greek religious and cultural outlook against the Asian and Semitic. Later iconoclasm, at least, developed antimonastic tendencies and served as an outlet for antimonastic sentiments. Although both sides developed theological arguments to support their views, the controversy over icons was primarily a societal issue, one symptom of a clash of cultural values and the resulting struggle for dominance during a period of great stress.

The course of the controversy reveals much about Byzantine society, including the depth of Byzantine piety, the lingering intensity of the Christological conflicts, and the complexity of their philosophical underpinnings, as well as the inseparability of religion, politics, and culture. We can see that the emperor usually exercised great control over the patriarch and the religious policy of the empire, but it is also clear that some forces were beyond even the emperor's control. Despite obvious hostilities toward monks, in the end the monks held the people's confidence, so that they could prevail against the throne, the army, and the central authorities of the church. And despite the considerable constraints on women, they, too, could stand against imperial will and even become the agents of the restoration of the icons. Finally, the iconophile–iconoclast conflict illustrates the intricate workings of a Christian society that was by no means monolithic or unchanging.

Iconoclasm exacted a heavy toll in its destruction of Byzantine art. To grasp what was lost in Constantinople and Asia Minor, we need only look at the dazzling late antique and early Byzantine art of Ravenna, which was beyond the range of icon smashers. Some media never recovered from the long hiatus in production; for example, the techniques for sculpting statues disappeared among Byzantines forever, and religious statuary never returned to the empire. The political repercussions were equally far reaching. Iconoclasm weakened the empire by magnifying internal dissent at a time when all resources were sorely needed to combat the major external threat, Islam. The conflict also strained relations with the west, motivating the pope to turn elsewhere for support. As central Italy was wrenched away from the Byzantine sphere of influence, Byzantium's field of vision narrowed, and the concept of universal empire receded into the background.

The consequences of iconoclasm, however, were not all bad. Out of that period came a renewed consensus of Byzantine self-definition as a Christian empire in which distinctively Christian art and sensibilities could flourish. Constantinople was clearly the cultural, economic, and political core of this Christian realm. Abounding in relics rescued from Syria and Palestine, the capital attracted pilgrims unwilling to risk the dangers of visiting sacred sites under Muslim domination. By the late ninth century, pious visitors to Constantinople could also witness the relics of new iconophile martyrs and miracle-working images that had multiplied to counteract iconoclasts' claims. Constantinople had become the world's greatest Christian treasury, a holy city.

Schism between Eastern and Western Christendom

The iconoclast–iconophile controversy struck another in a series of blows against the unity of Christendom. Constantinople was once again trapped between eastern and western religious convictions. Even during the Persian campaigns, Heraclius had tried to find a compromise that would mollify the monophysite provinces over which they were struggling and yet not alienate the west. His solution was monothelitism, the concept that Jesus Christ had "one will." The emperor wanted monophysites to agree that Jesus had two natures if the orthodox would concede that he had one will. But by the time Heraclius published his statement of this dogma, the *Ekthesis* (or "Exposition of Faith"), in 638, Syria and Palestine were already unexpectedly lost to the Muslims, with Egypt soon to follow. The *Ekthesis* succeeded only in alienating the pope, who condemned monothelite teaching as heresy. This act naturally resulted in great hostility between pope and emperor. Constantinople was caught between a rock and a hard place. It is doubtful that any compromise could have mollified either east or west, or reconciled them to the center, represented by Constantinople. The religious sensibilities were profoundly different, and the breach was widening.

Heraclius's successor continued his monothelite policy but also tried a new tack in search of harmony in the church and peace with the pope. Constans II proclaimed the *Typus* (or "Type of Faith"), forbidding "all Orthodox subjects being in immaculate Christian faith and belonging to the Catholic and Apostolic Church, to dispute and to quarrel with one another over one will or one energy or two energies or two wills." In other words, the topic was banned without exception; even written discussions were removed from public view—including Heraclius's *Ekthesis* from the walls in the narthex of Hagia Sophia. And what was the papal response to the imposed ban? At the Lateran Synod, in the presence of Byzantine clergy, Pope Martin condemned "the most impious *Ekthesis*" and the "vicious *Typus*" and proclaimed as heretics any people associated with those documents. A furious Constans II, himself of course included in that attack, ordered the imperial authority in Ravenna to arrest Martin and deliver him to Constantinople, where he was convicted of attempted sedition, humiliated, and imprisoned. Later exiled to far-off Cherson, on the south coast of the Crimea, Martin soon died there after dispatching pathetic pleas for bread.

Despite the animosities aroused by that incident, the emperor and patriarch negotiated successfully with Martin's successors to end the schism. Peace seemed assured with the Sixth Ecumenical Council of 680 in Constantinople, where monothelitism was condemned and Chalcedonian orthodoxy affirmed. Byzantium was writing off the eastern provinces lost to Islam. In 691 Emperor Justinian II summoned the Quinisext, or Trullan, Council and charged it with completing the work of the Fifth and Sixth Councils. Its decrees contained provisions to which the pope protested—for example, those forbidding fasting on Saturdays and allowing priests to marry. These tenets were unacceptable in the west, and Pope Sergius I refused to sign. Justinian tried to follow earlier tactics and have Sergius arrested by imperial forces in Italy, but the plan backfired when the army protected the pope. An honorable meeting in Constantinople between Justinian and a later pope, Constantine, seemed once again to forge a peace.

An increasing number of issues, however, divided eastern and western Christendom. Not the least of these concerned icons. Pope Gregory II had tried to sustain cordial relations despite his firm disapproval of imperial iconoclast policy, but Leo's iconoclast edict of 730 and his deposition of the iconophile patriarch compelled Gregory's successor, Gregory III, to condemn Byzantine iconoclasm. Leo responded by imprisoning the papal legates, and religious dissension led to political enmity. The popes finally made a complete break from Byzantium to find new supporters in the Franks (754). Popes such as Paul I (757–767) routinely referred to the Byzantines as *nefandissimi Graeci* ("most villainous Greeks") in asserting papal claims to autonomous spiritual and political power.

It is a tragic irony for Christianity that the onslaught of Islam did not unite Christendom against a common religious and political enemy; instead, the Muslim expansion only exacerbated hostilities between the eastern and western churches. Increasing isolation, combined with prejudice on both sides, bred contempt. Finally, in 1054 a theological disagreement and severe personality conflicts led the bishop of Rome and the patriarch of Constantinople to excommunicate each other. The outcome was a permanent schism between the Roman Catholic and the Greek Orthodox churches.

Mutual animosities prevented the west from acknowledging the important role played by Byzantium in the struggle against Islam. A long-standing goal of Muslim armies, Constantinople proved the roadblock to Mediterranean conquest. The turning point in the Muslim advance came after fifteen years of annual raids in Asia Minor when the Muslims besieged the city by sea (674–678). The city was saved by the fleet's secret weapon, Greek fire, a liquid probably containing naphtha, sulphur, and saltpeter, which was so potent that it ignited spontaneously and burned even on water. Along with the defeat of Muslim forces in Asia Minor, this victory checked the Muslim advance and prevented Muslim armies from taking the direct northern route to the west along the efficient Roman roads that had linked Rome to her provinces for more than 700 years. Byzantium thus sheltered the west from the full brunt of the assault until the Franks were strong enough to withstand a weakened Muslim onslaught. Charles Martel's victory near Tours (732) was made possible by the Byzantine stand, which, arguably, preserved Christendom from Islamic occupation.

Chapter 13

The Early Medieval Church in the West

The Franks and Merovingian Gaul

In contrast to the sophistication of Byzantium's theological debates and the epic importance of its struggles with Persia and Islam for the very life of Christian civilization, the story of Frankish Christianity seems small and secondary—a minor episode set in the backwoods. Yet out of this savage Germanic society would develop a durable and mighty medieval realm. It is customary to credit the Franks with the salvation of Christendom from the invading Muslims. As we have seen, this victory was possible only because the Byzantines provided such a formidable defense in the east. Still, the Frankish resistance was critical to the survival of Christian Europe. How did the Franks assume this role of leadership in Christendom? How did the longing to forge a moral Christian society culminate in a renaissance under Charlemagne? The answers to these questions reveal much about the bridge between late antiquity and medieval Christendom.

In our Roman sources the Franks appear first in the mid third century as a confederation of tribes with their homeland in the lower Rhine valley (most of modern Belgium and southern Holland). Historians must rely heavily on archaeological data to piece together bits of these peoples' past because written materials for the early period are so sparse. We have only two major documents. The Salic Law, the first written Germanic code, issued by the Frankish king Clovis in the early sixth century, provides ample evidence of the violence of the age. Near the end of the same century, the remarkable historian, Gregory, nineteenth

163

bishop of Tours, completed a *History of the Franks* that confirms this picture in terrifying detail.

Gregory of Tours (538 or 539 to 594 or 595, not to be confused with his notable contemporary, Pope Gregory the Great) belonged to the Gallo-Roman aristocracy. Among his distinguished ancestors were senators, bishops, saints, and even an early Christian martyr of the year 177. Gregory claimed that all but five of the previous bishops of Tours were his relatives. In Gregory himself we can see how the old Gallo-Romans and the Franks were merging into one Christian people. This bishop of noble lineage had no contempt whatsoever for the upstart Franks, although he scorned Arian Germans.

Thoroughly orthodox, Gregory was a man who shared the religious sensibilities of his contemporaries, both Frankish and Roman. At his mother's urging, he wrote saints' lives filled with miracles, including some he had supposedly witnessed himself. His most famous biography, on the life and miracles of St. Martin of Tours, inspired readers throughout the Middle Ages with tales of Gregory's fourth-century predecessor, whose tomb attracted pilgrims seeking miraculous cures for their ailments. This same spirit pervades his *History of the Franks*, which was so shaped by religious convictions that some critics have called it *The Ecclesiastical Histories*.[1] The work begins, like any good chronicle, with the creation of the world, revealing debts to the earlier church histories of Eusebius, Jerome, and Orosius. Gregory brought the account up to his own day, stopping only a few years before his death.

Gregory had received the best education available in sixth-century Gaul, but this modest training did not prepare even so talented a man to write a taut and coherent narrative. On the contrary, the chaos of his Latin syntax mirrors the chaos in his society. Nevertheless, despite a confused chronology and episodic style, a certain coherence comes from Gregory's profound belief that the church and its bishops were working tirelessly to civilize the Franks and their brutal princes. The *History* gives us an invaluable view of a vicious age for which the bishops were beacons of light in ominous darkness. Life in such a world was wholly unpredictable, although astrological portents could foretell a tyrant's death and relics might heal an ailing Christian. Very much a man of his time, Gregory believed deeply in these signs and cures.

From Gregory we glean precious details about the early Merovingian kings, descendants of King Merovech, for whom the royal dynasty is named. A son of Merovech, Childeric I, helped the Romans against Visigoths and Saxons. He also worked with the Gallic church, although he and his kin were still pagan. In this way, Childeric set the stage for his son Clovis (ruled 481–511), who founded the Frankish state through military victories against other Germans and assassinations of rival Frankish kings and through his conversion from paganism to Christianity. In an immensely significant move, Clovis converted to Catholicism instead of Arianism. If Gregory was correct, the king finally surrendered to the influence of his Christian wife Clotilda, a Burgundian princess, who wanted their firstborn son to be baptized. Writing nearly 100 years later, Gregory credited her with the following argument to woo Clovis away from paganism:

> The gods whom you worship are useless. They haven't been able to help themselves, let alone others. They are carved out of stone or wood or some sort of metal. The very names that you

---

[1] See Lewis Thorpe, trans., *Gregory of Tours: The History of the Franks* (New York: Penguin, 1974).

have given them were the names of men, not of gods. Take Saturn, for instance, who is supposed to have slipped away in flight from his own son so he wouldn't be exiled from his kingdom; and Jupiter, that really foul perpetrator of all sorts of lewd acts, who defiled other men and enjoyed humiliating female relatives and couldn't even refrain from sleeping with his own sister, as she herself said: . . . *Jovisque/et soror et coniunx* ["Both sister and wife of Jupiter"; *Aeneid* 1, 46–47]. What could Mars and Mercury ever do? They may have been endowed with magic arts, but they certainly didn't deserve to be called divine.

You should instead worship him who created at a word and out of nothing heaven and earth, the sea and all that therein is [*Psalms* 146:6]; who made the sun to shine; who adorned the sky with stars; who stocked the waters with fish, the earth with beasts, the sky with birds; at whose nod the fields are graced with fruits, the trees with apples, the vines with grapes; by whose hand the human race was created, and by whose dispensation all that creation in compliant devotion serves the man whom He created.[2]

The rhetoric is obviously Gregory's own. He had read selections from the *Aeneid* when he was a student, whereas Clotilda surely was a stranger to classical literature. Would Clotilda have mentioned the Greco-Roman deities and not the Germanic gods? Whatever her real arguments may have been, Clotilda's pleas slowly took effect until, again according to Gregory, the king remembered them in the midst of a difficult battle with the Alamanni, and swore fealty to the Christian god if only he would provide victory as a sign of his power. After routing the enemy, Clovis was baptized along with 3,000 Franks by Bishop Remigius of Reims (St. Rémi). It is difficult to overemphasize the impact of that conversion on medieval Christendom. Clovis's Catholicism provided a convincing pretext for warring against rival Arian Germans and conquering their territories. From distant Constantinople, the emperor Anastasius dispatched an embassy in 507, apparently sending his Christian brother the insignia of an honorary consul. The Byzantine emperor could not have known that Clovis was forging a close union with the papacy that would eventually rival, and then replace, Byzantine protection of papal territories and privileges.

At the death of Clovis, his four sons ruled together, crushing the Burgundian kingdom and winning Provence from the Ostrogoths in exchange for military aid. Within a half century, the Merovingian kings were the most powerful monarchs of the west, despite continuing migrations of Germans and the arrival of Avars into the middle Danube region (Hungary) and Slavs into the Balkans, Bohemia, and Moravia. The sons of Clovis ruled most of Gaul and some of Italy and Germany, held power over other tribes in Germany, and claimed control over southeast England. Clovis's last surviving son, Chlothar I, died in 561. Gregory of Tours reported the words of this proud ruler as he lay on his deathbed: "Wa! What kind of king is it in heaven, who kills off great kings like me?"

The Merovingians left an important legacy. Other Germans fell under the influence of the Franks and renounced Arianism to embrace Catholic Christianity. The Burgundians converted in 517, a few years before they became part of the Frankish kingdom. Throughout the sixth century, while Justinian was assailing Arian kingdoms of the Ostrogoths and Visigoths, individuals in Italy and Spain continued to abandon Arianism at a steady rate. King Recared of Visigothic Spain converted in 587, confirming this act at the Third Council of Toledo in 589. By the mid seventh century, the process was complete. The last to convert were the Lombards, and their tardiness provided a political opening for the Franks:

---

[2] Gregory of Tours, *History of the Franks* (II.29). Unpublished translation by Emily Albu.

When Arian Lombards in Italy threatened papal territories, the Franks became champions of popes, eventually ousting the Lombards from papal lands.

Paganism in Gaul

The west became nominally Catholic, but paganism was slow to die, especially in the countryside. In his *Book on the Glory of the Confessors*, Gregory of Tours described pagan rites performed in late fourth-century Gaul, outside Autun:

> They say that in this city there was a statue of Berecynthia [Kybele, the great goddess] as the history of the passion of the holy martyr Symphorian explains. When pagans were drawing her about in a cart, according to their wretched custom, to assure the salvation of their fields and vineyards, the bishop Simplicius was nearby. Not far away, Simplicius saw them singing and dancing before this statue. And groaning to God for the people's folly, he said: "I entreat you, Lord: enlighten the eyes of these people so that they know that the idol of Berecynthia is useless." And when he made the sign of the cross against it, at once the statue fell down to the earth. And the animals that were drawing the cart in which the statue was carried were cast down on the ground and could not be budged. The huge crowd was stupefied, and the whole throng exclaimed that the goddess had been hurt. Victims were sacrificed and the animals were beaten, but they could not be budged. Then four hundred men of that foolish multitude, gathered together, said to one another: "If the statue of the deity has any power let her stand herself up without any help, and order the oxen, who are immobilized on the ground, to get moving. Surely, if she cannot move herself, it is clear that there is no divinity in her." Then, approaching and sacrificing one of their animals, when they saw that their goddess could by no means move, they abandoned their error of paganism . . . and they were consecrated by baptism.[3]

Despite dramatic confrontations like this one and the continuing vigorous protests of the Christian clergy, pagan rites associated with the protection of crops survived into Gregory's own lifetime and long after. A seventh-century sermon by Saint Eligius of Noyen (588–659) warned his congregation against pagan practices they were still observing, such as wearing charms to ward off evil, consulting the moon's phases for auspicious times to undertake a new venture, and engaging in ancient ceremonies at temples or sacred rocks, fountains, trees, or crossroads. It seems that Eligius's parishioners, too, were purifying the crops with magic rites.

The protection of the crops was central to the existence of the medieval peasantry, who abandoned ancient rituals only with the greatest reluctance or merely transformed them into Christian rites. An excellent example comes from the legend of Radegund, a historical figure from Merovingian Gaul and wife of Clovis's son, Chlothar I. Gregory reports that Chlothar took the Thuringian princess Radegund as part of the booty after he invaded her land and massacred the Thuringian army. His eventual marriage to the princess did not stop Chlothar from arranging for assassins to murder her brother. Radegund turned to God, took the habit of a religious, and built a nunnery for herself in Poitiers. For her prayers, vigils, and charities, she became so famous that the common people looked upon her as a saint.

[3] Gregory of Tours, *Liber in Gloria Confessorum*, chap. 77, in Joannes Zwicker, *Fontes Historiae Religionis Celticae* (Berlin, 1934), p. 180. Unpublished translation by Emily Albu.

Later folklore wove a dramatic tale of her desperate flight from Chlothar and his angry pursuit. During her escape, it was said, the queen came upon a peasant sowing his field. She urged him to tell anyone who inquired that no woman had passed through that field since he had sowed the oats. At once the oats grew so tall that the queen could hide in the grass. When the king arrived and interrogated the farmer, the peasant's truthful answer tricked him into abandoning the chase. The Christian saint Radegund, venerated for bringing miraculous fertility to the field, came to replace the ancient grain goddess. In modified form, the ancestral rites connected with the February sowing continued, with worshipers carrying to church little sacks of grain dedicated to Radegund. Finally, in 1627 the bishop of Poitiers authorized a festival for February 28, dedicated to Saint Radegund of the Oats.

In such ways some irradicable pagan habits survived among the Franks, assimilated into Christianity. While churchmen were often willing to accommodate these customs, they saw no satisfactory compromise with the notoriously bad behavior of Merovingian princes, who had readily accepted the name of Christian but were slow to adopt Christian morality. It was a vexing problem for bishops such as Gregory of Tours, who understood the civilizing role the church should play and tenaciously worked for its success.

Of all the vile Merovingian princes whom Gregory chronicled, the worst was Chilperic, son of Chlothar I by his third wife, Aregund. Gregory found him monstrously cruel, so greedy and arrogant that he proclaimed him "the Nero and Herod of our time." Chilperic's domestic affairs were as violent as his public crimes. He repudiated his wife and later had her murdered, in order to acquire the rich dowry of a second wife, the Spanish princess Galswintha. Soon he had Galswintha strangled so that he could keep her dowry and marry his favorite concubine, Fredegund. Chilperic himself was murdered in 584, after a life of unimaginable evil. By Gregory's admission, he was a man of stunning contradictions. This murderer of wives, for instance, actually championed the rights of women to inherit land on occasion, against the restrictions of the Salian law. He also fancied himself a theologian and opposed the dogma of the Trinity, arguing vigorously with Gregory that no one should speak of three persons when describing God. Gregory's firm insistence on the orthodox formulation, backed by other eminent churchmen, finally persuaded Chilperic to rescind his decree outlawing Trinitarian language.

The domain of Chlothar I and Chilperic seems an unlikely center for a Christian renaissance, but the Church relentlessly stressed Christian values prescribing a kinder and gentler morality. Gradually, these teachings had an impact, until committed and strong Carolingian rulers (the dynasty named for Carolus Magnus, or Charlemagne, who ruled from 768 to 814) would create a Christian empire out of the chaos their Merovingian forebears had wrought.

The Carolingians

This emerging Christian realm was far different from the old Roman Empire, with its urban centers and Mediterranean commerce (Figure 13.1). In the seventh century the Muslims had come to control the sea, holding many islands, the southern Mediterranean shore, and Spain. Like all of northwestern Europe, Gaul lost most ties with Roman ways of urban commerce and sea trade and turned to agriculture instead. To support this agrarian life, the

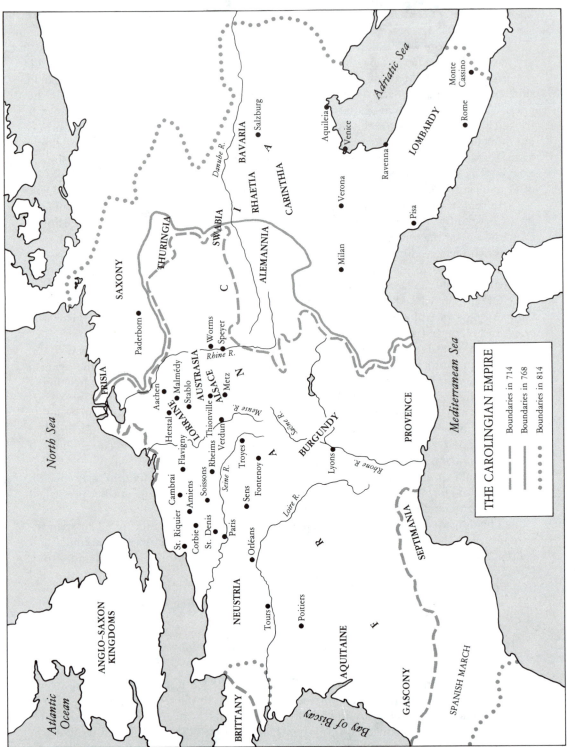

Figure 13.1   The Carolingian Realm

Franks needed political stability, but at the same time as Muslims were extending their control, the kingdom of the Franks was deteriorating, and any central authority was collapsing. The administrative agencies of Merovingian kings slipped into the hands of household officials, called mayors of the palace, who were wooing the Frankish aristocracy to their side.

One of these mayors of the palace, Pepin II of Heristal (mayor from 687 to 714), consolidated Frankish power under himself. Pepin's son Charles Martel (717–741), famous for his victory over the Muslims in 732, extended this authority, while also tightening his grip on church and society. Martel's policy replaced local control of the church with a centralized, hierarchical episcopal structure that he kept firmly under his thumb. It was Charles who appointed and deposed bishops. When he needed revenues or lands to distribute to his followers as a reward for service, he systematically confiscated ecclesiastical holdings. The pope scolded him for these impertinences but never severed the mutually beneficial bond.

Martel's son, Pepin III (also known as Pepin the Short) (747–768), finally used this alliance to remove the last Merovingian, Childeric III, from the throne. Pepin dispatched two envoys, the abbot of St. Denis and the bishop of Wurzburg, to Pope Zacharias I (reigned 741–752) to ask "concerning the kings in Francia who had no royal power, and whether this was fitting or not." The pope agreed that this situation did not promote order and justice, and he sent a papal legate, the Anglo-Saxon Benedictine Boniface, to anoint Pepin as king in 751 before an assembly of Frankish nobles at Soissons. No Frankish king had ever been anointed before. This act signified divine approval of the king's rule and, at the same time, granted him a kind of priestly authority. In return, Pepin deeded to Zacharias's successor, Pope Stephen II, estates in central Italy that the papacy would hold for more than 1,000 years, until the kingdom of Italy absorbed them in 1870. Pepin personally conducted campaigns in Italy to wrest these lands from the Lombards and present them to the pope. This so-called Donation of Pepin alienated not only the Lombards, who had been allies of Pepin's family in the struggle against the Arabs, but also the Byzantines, who still claimed Italy as part of their Roman Empire. In distant Constantinople, however, the emperor Constantine V was too preoccupied with iconophiles and Muslims to intervene in the west. He had been unable to protect the pope from Lombard threats, and to make matters worse, his iconoclasm made him a heretic in the pope's eyes. When the Franks offered aid against the Lombards, therefore, Pope Stephen formally broke with Byzantium and declared Pepin "protector of the Roman church" (754).

About this time (ca. 754–767), the Donation of Constantine was forged. It pretends to be a charter issued by the fourth-century emperor Constantine I when he moved the capital to the East in 330. The document granted to the papacy spiritual and temporal power, specifically including authority over Rome and Italy. Ever since Lorenzo Valla exposed the document as a fake in 1440, critics have claimed that the Donation's forger had a broad political motive. Most scholars placed the document in the context of the papal-Frankish alliance, assuming that the forger's primary goal was to discredit Byzantine claims to Italy and to pave the way for the deal between Pepin and the pope. Some historians argue that it was fabricated especially for the occasion of Pepin's anointing. Most recent research, however, suggests that the forgery had a more private and localized purpose. Because it features the supposed endowment of the Lateran Palace to Pope Sylvester, it may well be the invention of a lower cleric of the Church of the Savior (St. John Lateran). Frustrated because the rival church, St. Peter's in the Vatican, was siphoning off pilgrim business from his own church, he merely wanted to produce a dramatic confirmation of the historical importance of St. John Lateran. This anonymous cleric could not have foreseen the larger implications of the controversy exacerbated by his forged document, which successive popes used to authenticate their claims to secular rule in Italy.

The Celtic Church and English Monasticism

Thanks to Pepin's ousting of the Lombards, the pope became an influential temporal prince, sometimes more important as a politician than as a theologian or spiritual leader. English Benedictine monks played a critical role in forming the powerful alliance that strengthened both popes and Frankish kings. Alliances of these three parties would shape both the history of Europe and the history of the church.

By the third century, Christianity had reached the Celts of Roman Britain and spread from there to Ireland (Figure 13.2). This Celtic church outlived the departure of Roman troops in 407. Its history is difficult to trace in detail, but its center gradually shifted from England to Ireland, which the Roman Empire had never dominated. Just as Celtic culture in Ireland had evolved independently of the Roman, so the Celtic church developed in its own way, although it never lost contact with the church on the continent or severed ties with papal Rome. Throughout the Mediterranean world, Christianity had been growing as an urban religion, governed by bishops in cities. The church had a distinctively different development in the rural, tribal communities of England and especially Ireland. Like the pastoral society it penetrated, the Celtic church remained decentralized.

Rural monasteries held special importance in this nonurban church. Leaving their own foundations, significant numbers of monks traveled great distances to construct new outposts of Christianity among the pagans. In his sixth-century missions to Scotland, for example, St. Columba (ca. 521–ca. 597) established a monastery on the island of Iona, which in turn sent out other missions to Christianize Northumbria. One of these missions reached the island of Lindisfarne, founding a bishopric and a monastery that became the core of English religious life. St. Columbanus (died 615) spread Celtic monasticism in the opposite direction, taking it to the continent. His foundations include Luxeuil in Burgundy and Bobbio in northern Italy.

Monks directed the monastic Celtic church, and abbots ruled over it, even holding authority over the bishops, who fulfilled liturgical functions but had little administrative control. Other peculiarities of this Celtic church included retaining the old method for calculating the date of Easter and dictating a unique tonsure for monks. The common "tonsure of St. Peter" was a shaven head with only a circle of hair shaped like a crown. The Celtic tonsure seems to have been a semicircle of hair at the top of the head from ear to ear, with the hair behind it growing long. This unique tonsure may have been a remnant of old practices; it was the ancestral hairstyle of elite males such as the Druids in Celtic society. Celtic monks became famous for their idiosyncratic and extreme behavior, for mortifications such as flagellations and fasts lasting as long as four days. Some lived their lives as hermits, like their Syriac brothers in the spirit, and others accepted voluntary exile and

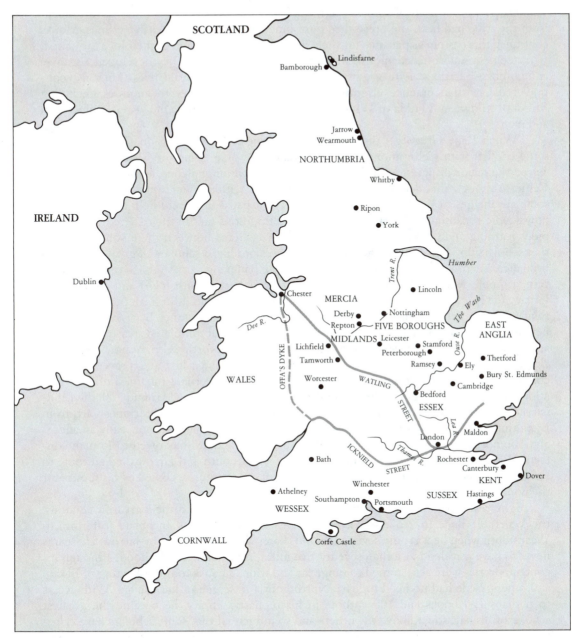

Figure 13.2   English Monasteries

wandering. This custom of aimless pilgrimage may also recall Irish tradition; banishment from the tribe had been the prescribed punishment for the most offensive crimes. Monks continued this custom as penance for their sins or as a dramatic sign of their love for Christ.

Celtic monks often demonstrated a flair for the dramatic. They developed a strange and bombastic Latin style that matched their sometimes flamboyant lives. They also contradicted Christian practice elsewhere by allowing great power to abbesses, including Brigid of Kildare and Hilda of Whitby, two who ruled over double monasteries of women and men.

When Pope Gregory I dispatched Benedictine monks as missionaries to England, some conflict with Celtic monasticism was inevitable. The Synod of Whitby in 664 resolved the major disputes, with the Roman tradition winning a complete victory over the Celtic. Although this decision suppressed traditions with ancient roots, it also brought some advantages to English monks, who found that papal ties could help free them from unwelcome constraints of local barons. The two traditions met in their shared passion for pious learning and classical culture, and the disagreements between them stimulated further scholarship. The dynamic marriage of cultures produced scholars of great energy and brilliance, such as Benedict Biscop, born Biscop Baducing, an Anglo-Saxon nobleman turned monk, who founded St. Peter's monastery at Wearmouth (674) and St. Paul's at Jarrow (682). Staunchly Benedictine, he introduced Roman liturgical practice in his religious houses and nurtured the Northumbrian cultural renaissance by risking five journeys to Italy to collect manuscripts, art, and relics. Biscop's accumulated treasures immediately influenced the impressive manuscript production of Northumbrian monasteries, including missals for the celebration of the mass, books of psalms and prayers, biblical commentaries, and collections of laws, letters, and sermons. Perhaps the finest of these creations is the richly illustrated Gospel book of Lindisfarne. Produced around 700, the Lindisfarne Gospels contain portraits inspired by eastern and western Mediterranean art, from Byzantium to Greece and Italy. This is a brilliant manuscript, but it is not really an anomaly. The northern monasteries quickly repaid the cultural debt they owed to Roman contacts. When the stern and able abbot Ceolfrid of Wearmouth and Jarrow died en route to Rome (713?), he was bearing a deluxe manuscript of the scriptures, copied by his monks for the pope.

The resources of Ceolfrid's monasteries were well spent on their greatest alumnus, the Venerable Bede (672/673–735). His parents brought him as an oblate (offering) to Wearmouth when he was only seven years old. Later he moved to nearby Jarrow. He seems never to have traveled more than seventy-five miles from that neighborhood, although his contemporaries were accustomed to range far and wide. Thanks to the collecting of Biscop and others, Bede had no need to leave Northumbria in search of knowledge. With access to perhaps 200 books and 100 authors in his monastic library, he became the greatest scholar of his day, so far above the others and so influential that some scholars have called the years from Pope Gregory I to the coronation of Charlemagne (604–800) the Age of Bede.

Bede's vast literary output encompasses a variety of writings, including scriptural studies, prayers, and hymns in Latin verse, as well as textbooks to instruct scribes on proper spelling, grammar, and even handwriting. Bede's learned biblical commentaries drew on the works of great predecessors whom he admired and knew well, including Augustine,

Ambrose, Jerome, and Gregory the Great. Bede also had a creative mind of his own. He popularized the idea of reckoning time from the birth of Christ, instead of from the foundation of Rome or from the regnal year of German kings, and he introduced the term *anno Domini*, "in the year of the Lord," abbreviated A.D. He is best remembered, however, for tracing his spiritual and cultural heritage in two works, the *History of the Abbots of Wearmouth and Jarrow* and his masterpiece, the *Ecclesiastical History of the English People*.[4] The *Ecclesiastical History* delivers more than its title promises, for it contains much secular information on early Britain, culled from many sources, which Bede conscientiously identified for his audience while he compared and analyzed them for their reliability. His critical judgment earned him the title Father of English Scholarship, History, and Literature.

Few scholars were as deeply admired as Bede was in his own lifetime and beyond. He lived a simple and pious life. Finding holiness, humility, and scholarship utterly compatible, he would not let his talents and revered status exempt him from the usual duties of monks. Alcuin (a student of Bede's disciple, Egbert) reported Bede's disclaimer: "I know that angels visit the congregation of brethren at the canonical hours, and what if they should not find me among the brethren? Would they not say, 'Where is Bede?'"

Bede's gentle holiness seems all the more remarkable when viewed in the context of his own day. The warrior ideal of Germanic society had by no means disappeared. It is useful to remember that the Lindisfarne Gospel and Bede's *History* are roughly contemporary with *Beowulf*. Set in the period of the Germanic migrations, this heroic poem glories in the splendid halls of great princes and in the blood of combat. Although scholars point out its Christian allegories and theological themes, the poem testifies to the persistence of the pagan spirit in Bede's day and beyond.

The Anglo-Saxon passion for missionary work, however, continued the Christianization of England that would result in a tenth-century renaissance, the Anglo-Saxon monastic revival. Meanwhile, Anglo-Saxon teachers carried the learning of Wearmouth, Jarrow, and Bede to the Frankish realm, where the close attachment of the English Benedictines to Rome would have far-reaching consequences.

An early missionary to the continent was the Northumbrian monk Willibrord, who crossed the English Channel to Christianize pagans on the Frisian Islands and in the territory that is now the Netherlands, Belgium, and Luxembourg. With the support of the Frankish king Pepin II and the pope, he became the first bishop of Utrecht. One of Willibrord's assistants in Frisia was another Anglo-Saxon Benedictine, Wynfrith, who had been raised in English abbeys and baptized as Winfrid (ca. 675–754). When he was ready for his own mission, Winfrid traveled to Rome to receive the blessing of Pope Gregory II, who gave him the new name of Boniface (719) after the Roman martyr. In Thuringia, Frisia, Bavaria, and Hesse in central and southern Germany, Boniface won many converts among the poor through his emphasis on Christian charity. During another sojourn in Rome in 722, Boniface was consecrated bishop, swearing fidelity to the pope. His enthusiastic support of papal authority continued the English Benedictine tradition. When he founded the monastery of Fulda, which would be his base, he even put it under papal control.

Meanwhile, the widespread missionary activity of Boniface met continuing success.

---

[4]See James Campbell, ed., *The Ecclesiastical History of the English People and Other Selections from the Writings of the Venerable Bede* (New York: Washington Square Press, 1968).

When he chopped down the famous Oak of Thor at Geismar, a pagan cult center, Boniface won new converts among pagans who were impressed that such a courageous act of sacrilege brought no retribution from their gods. Boniface continued to demolish pagan temples and replace them with Christian churches. He founded the bishopric of Mainz, which would become the chief see of Germany. As he organized southern Germany into Christian dioceses, he planted numerous Benedictine monasteries throughout the countryside, all with links to England and reverence for papal authority. Gregory III made him archbishop in 732 and papal legate in 739.

It was the pope who arranged Boniface's connection with Charles Martel, Carolingian Mayor of the Palace. The alliance fit nicely with Martel's plans to expand eastward into Germany; religious and political expansion could work hand in hand. After Martel's death in 741, his successors, Carloman and Pepin III, invited Boniface to reform the Frankish church. With their encouragement and under their protection, he held reforming councils, confronted heretic priests, ousted worldly bishops, and regularized monastic rule, using the Roman model for uniformity in liturgy and religious practice. At the same time, he preached peace and Christian obedience to the civil authorities—the Carolingian princes and their agents. As papal emissary in 751, Boniface anointed Pepin king, with divine sanction. (His brother Carloman had become a monk.) Pope Stephen II crossed the Alps in winter to repeat the consecration, anointing Pepin, his queen, and his sons.

These two anointings, taken together, represent an important stage in the alliance of the papacy, English monasticism, and Frankish kings. To Boniface belongs the greatest credit for cementing this bond and for influencing each of the three related elements: a strengthened papacy controlling a reformed and reorganized church; Benedictine foundations that shared a single rule—indeed, after the work of Boniface, the only rule in Britain, Italy, France, and Germany; and the Carolingian dynasty, now advanced to royal status. On his missions to monastery and court, Boniface never wavered in loyalty to the Roman pope and the Roman cultural heritage. Thanks in large part to Boniface, with the Christianization of northern Europe came its Romanization as well. Under the united western church fostered by Boniface, the cultural and religious groundwork was in place for the creation of the Carolingian renaissance.

On June 5, 754, in a dawn attack by a group of pagans, Boniface was martyred in Frisia with his companions. Having devoted the last thirty-five years of his life to conversion and the organization of the church, he left behind a remarkable legacy as a brilliant evangelist, statesman, and administrator. Boniface well deserves to be remembered as apostle to Germany; in truth, he was one of the most important people of the early Middle Ages.

The letters of Boniface reveal a great deal about Germanic social customs, which were at variance with Christianity, and show how far the two had to go before they could meet on common ground. He wrote about the Germans' love of extravagant dress, the dangers women pilgrims faced on their pilgrimages to Rome, the survival of pagan practices, and sacrifices to the pagan gods. Boniface reported that Christians among the Germans were even selling slaves to pagans for use in human sacrifice. He found it necessary to persuade the people not to eat horse meat. He lamented the laxity and immorality among clergy. Pope Gregory III urged Boniface to forbid widowers to remarry "if you are able." The question of remarriage was minor compared with other domestic issues on which the two cultures clashed. German and ecclesiastical law were worlds apart in matters of polygamy, incest, and divorce—all of which were accepted elements in German society. A half century after Boniface's martyrdom, Charlemagne finally forbade incest and decreed penalties for both men and women who committed adultery. Royal pronouncements did not put an immediate stop to old customs, of course, but the values of state, church, and society were slowly moving toward conformity.

Charlemagne and the Carolingian Renaissance

Charlemagne (also called Charles I or Charles the Great) (ruled 768–814), son of Pepin III and grandson of Charles Martel, was the Frankish king whose vision and energy converted the legacy of Boniface into Europe's first medieval renaissance. For a century Charlemagne's family had been leaders in the political, economic, and religious revitalization of the west. These efforts culminated in the reign of Charles the Great, who fashioned western Europe into a single Christian empire.

When Pepin III died in 768, Charlemagne and his younger brother Carloman shared the kingdom uneasily until Carloman's timely death in 771. Charles proved himself a brilliant monarch, by turns savage and civilized. His military conquests of Muslims in northern Spain and of Lombards, pagan Saxons, and Bavarians more than doubled the size of the realm, as his fighters killed tens of thousands who resisted. The Saxon campaigns proved particularly brutal when Charlemagne showed no patience toward a people particularly loath to surrender their paganism. But at last the subjugated territories yielded rich booty for the royal coffers, giving Charles a measure of independence from his barons. At the same time, the campaigns offered the center of the kingdom a period of stability and recovery essential for an agrarian economy. Charlemagne lavished loving attention on the details of governing, controlling the forces of anarchy—the warrior chiefs with their rich estates and violent ambitions. In this way, he worked to establish a unified central administration and to create a civilized state. To him this meant a Christian realm, with church and state mutually supportive of each other.

With Charles's imperial coronation by Pope Leo III in Rome on Christmas Day 800, the western church formally renounced its ancient dependency on Byzantium. No longer did the papacy acknowledge the Byzantine emperor as nominal master and protector of Italy. The eastern empire responded with outrage, but the pope's recognition of Charles as Holy Roman Emperor sealed the bond of the ecclesiastical and political units in the west. The coronation explicitly linked old imperial Rome and new Christian Rome, with the authority of both devolving to Charles.

It was no easy matter for Charlemagne to Christianize his empire. Christian ideals linked to Roman traditions merged slowly with Germanic ideals, but the impact of this union on the Germanic peoples and on western civilization was to prove immense. Pagan Germans lived in Europe's deep forests, which separated one tribe from another and fragmented Germanic societies. These pagans considered it an act of terrible impiety to cut down trees, which were sacred, and to offend the gods and spirits of the forests. Likewise, they would not build bridges or mills over rivers for fear of disturbing the river spirits. The rivers' power remained unharnessed, just as the land remained uncleared. Christianity changed all that. Christian saints' lives repeatedly report the cutting down of some sacred tree or another as proof of the pagan spirit's inefficacy and sign of the power wielded by the Christian god and his agents. Charlemagne's first campaign against the pagan Saxons saw the felling of Irminsul, the sacred oak tree. When the pagans realized that no ill consequences befell the Christian perpetrators, many accepted baptism. The course of western history changed dramatically when the Germans came to believe that God had given humankind dominion over the earth. At last the Germans could use rivers and forests; all people could graze animals in the forests, burn logs on the hearth, and build homes of wood. Men no longer had to wander as nomadic hunters; they could enjoy a settled economy instead. As the forests were destroyed, so agriculture increased. Until very recently, the western world has viewed this as a uniformly positive step in the progress of civilization. Now, of course, new questions about the global effects of deforestation have challenged the conviction that human beings own natural resources, and so may exhaust them at will. Civilization as we know it, however, was unthinkable among the Germans before Christianity overcame their pagan prohibitions.

Conversion of the Germans to Christianity produced dramatic consequences, yet the assimilation of Christian ideals of poverty and humility proceeded slowly. Once tribal chiefs were baptized, the entire tribe was expected to follow. Charlemagne himself seems to have regarded baptism as a mandatory sign of loyalty to him. He even decreed in 785 that conquered Saxons who refused baptism (or violated Christian law in any way—for instance, by eating meat during Lent) should face the death penalty. Charlemagne's ecclesiastical advisor, Alcuin of York, argued against this policy, but his master would not back down. Still, baptism was only a first step.

German warriors might accept Christian baptism, but would they adopt Christian beliefs and values? The ideals of poverty and love of enemies, for example, are difficult for many people to accept even now after two millennia of Christian tradition; these concepts were virtually incomprehensible for fierce warriors whose status came from bloodshed and the spoils of war. The Christian emphasis on poverty, universal brotherhood and sisterhood, and love of enemies was nearly impossible for German warriors to understand. The concepts of sin and repentance were equally difficult for them to grasp.

Charlemagne understood what few of his contemporaries could. His genius lay in envisioning a Christian society made over in the image of Augustine's *City of God*. He followed a deliberate program of religious and moral renewal, consciously inaugurated and supported by earlier Carolingian kings, especially by his own father, Pepin III. Under Charles, these policies bore succulent fruit. The program aimed at no less than a spiritual regeneration of the entire society, the creation of a truly Christian community. Moved by this religious and moral impetus, Charles initiated specific and pragmatic policies. As a first step, he wanted to improve literacy so that people could read the scriptures. He especially wanted to provide basic education for the clergy. This required a school system for parish-level education for men on the front lines of teaching and preaching. The priests needed to understand their responsibilities and their faith; for their own study and for teaching others, they also needed adequate libraries with liturgical and biblical texts.

From this simple goal came far-ranging results: Schools were founded throughout the kingdom, and manuscripts were copied to fill their libraries. Carolingian scribes created a new style of writing, the Carolingian minuscule, from which our modern typefaces come. It was a uniform and highly legible script that all literate people could decipher—a lower-case script (hence, the word "minuscule") that was compact and therefore made economic use of precious vellum.

Once Latin had been the common tongue of the west, but the people of Charlemagne's day spoke a variety of vernacular languages. By the late eighth century, Latin posed a problem not only for native speakers of German but also for those in Gaul whose spoken language was developing away from classical Latin and toward what we know as Old French. It was difficult for both groups to understand the Bible and the Latin liturgy. In his missionary efforts, Boniface had encountered a Bavarian priest who did not know the simplest word endings for Latin and so was mistakenly baptizing "in the name of the Fatherland and the Daughter and the Holy Spirit." Anglo-Saxon and Irish monks of Charlemagne's court had texts for teaching Latin to nonnative speakers. Through accurate Latin, priests could teach true doctrine, and the various peoples of the Carolingian empire could communicate with one another. Uniform and correct Latin, comprehensible to all who knew the language, was therefore an important priority. With a common Latin education and manuscripts available to many, once again there arose a whole class of people who could write and also read each others' writing, creating their own literature that rivaled the production of the ancient world. Scholars compiled biblical commentaries and collections of canon law, and some also wrote secular verse and epics.

Charlemagne's modest beginnings of scholastic renewal led to a classicizing revival, as scholars turned to ancient texts in order to understand standards of correct grammar, spelling, and style. Inevitably, some also found literature they wanted to preserve and imitate. This effort rescued classical learning, which was by then in danger of extinction as existing manuscripts decayed or were burned in monastery fires or otherwise lost. Carolingian manuscripts are critical links in the transmission of Latin literature. Without this renaissance, much of our precious legacy from antiquity would have perished. The phenomenon has often been studied through the eyes and sensibilities of classicists, who have focused on the new literature created in imitation of classical style and on the preservation of ancient culture. This was an incidental result, however, of the renewal whose primary impetus was the desire to infuse society with Christian sensibilities and to mold Christian behavior. Although the study of Latin benefited from the revival, a certain loss counterbalanced the gain. By forcing ecclesiastical Latin back into the classical mold, Carolingian scholars unwittingly assured the artificiality of that Latin and the demise of Latin as a living vernacular language.

To set in motion the phenomenon he envisioned, Charlemagne wooed learned men from all over Europe to his court at Aachen (Aix-la-Chapelle), where Anglo-Saxon, Irish, Italian, and Visigothic scholars found some stability, refuge from Muslim (and later, Viking) incursions, and the promise of royal patronage. The brightest men of the age became enthusiastic supporters of this self-conscious religious movement aimed at purifying society. From Visigothic Spain came Theodulf, distinguished theologian and a talented poet. From the Lombard district of Italy came Paul the Deacon, who later returned to the monastic life at Monte Cassino, where he wrote a *History of the Lombards*, which remains our primary source for understanding the rise and success of his people.[5] From the abbey of Fulda came Einhard, who wrote the famous biography of Charlemagne modeled on the work of the an-

---

[5] William Dudley-Foulke, trans., *History of the Langobards* (Philadelphia: University of Pennsylvania, 1907, 1974).

cient Roman historian Suetonius.

The most influential figure in the transfer of learning to the Carolingian centers was the Anglo-Saxon missionary Alcuin of York (ca. 730–804), student of Bede's disciple Egbert. Born in Northumbria and educated at the cathedral school in York, Alcuin became teacher and then headmaster there. When he was about fifty years old, he met Charlemagne on one of his visits to the continent. Charles persuaded him to head the palace school at Aachen, where Alcuin became the king's religious and educational advisor. Alcuin's students at Aachen were scholars and courtiers—even Charles himself and his family. The academic program at the school under Alcuin encompassed the trivium and elements of the quadrivium, with the emphasis always on biblical and ecclesiastical application of this learning. It would be difficult to overstate the Christian orientation of the program Alcuin directed. Christianity was its core, and the service of Christianity was its purpose. Alcuin and his school assisted the Christian program, for instance, by editing and correcting biblical and liturgical texts and by creating a uniform lectionary. The aim was not merely to educate people of the secular and ecclesiastical court, but also to provide tools for clerics and parish priests throughout the realm.

As we have seen, the educational reforms Alcuin oversaw had modest aims: to enable people to read Latin, write the Psalms, know correct grammar and the rudiments of mathematics, master the chant, and understand Christian texts. The pursuit of these goals nonetheless brought Roman Christianity to the people of northern Europe. Alcuin thus completed the work of Boniface and the other Anglo-Saxon missionaries. For the last eight years of his life, he retired from the court to oversee the Abbey of St. Martin at Tours. There he wrote his own epitaph: *Alchuine nomen erat, sophiam mihi semper amanti* ("Alcuin was my name and wisdom always my love"). For Alcuin, as for Charlemagne, this wisdom was Christian.

The Carolingian renaissance nurtured art and architecture as well as literature. The court school produced beautifully illuminated manuscripts, including masterful Gospels. This Carolingian art, like the Carolingian literature and learning, adapted classicizing forms in the service of Christian sensibilities. To rival Roman grandeur, Charlemagne imported marble columns and bronze statues from Rome and Ravenna and displayed them in his royal capital. Not content only with pillage, he set up a foundry at Aachen that cast bronze doors and gallery railings, and he patronized mosaicists and painters. Such artists could decorate the grand public art of Charles's ambitious building program. As we might expect, the most important public buildings of the period were churches. Carolingian princes built many palaces; scholars have counted 100 in the period from 768 to 855, but those same few decades produced at least 27 new cathedrals and 417 monasteries.

Classicizing monuments looked to the past for their inspiration and sometimes achieved a timeless majesty. Still, it is important to keep in mind the fundamentally Germanic character of the Carolingian realm. Charlemagne himself worked assiduously to learn Latin. His biographer, Einhard, poignantly described the emperor's habit of keeping writing tablets under his pillow so that he could practice his letters on nights when he could not sleep. The art of writing Latin did not come naturally to a Frankish king, even if he was the author of the Carolingian renaissance. In his later years, Charlemagne appreciated the Germanic cultural heritage of his people and collected songs celebrating the Franks.

The greatest masterpiece of the Frankish epic tradition in fact arose from legendary material surrounding Charles's own exploits. Composed as late as 1100, the *Song of Roland* contains some memory of Charlemagne's struggle against the Muslims of Spain. Crossing the Pyrenees upon returning from one campaign, the rear guard of Charlemagne's army was surprised by an enemy ambush, and many Franks were massacred. Three hundred years after the event, the epic still held the remembered consciousness of the close proximity and threat of the Muslim world. Of Charlemagne's many campaigns, some checked Muslims in Spain by the establishment of strongly fortified borderlands known as marches.

These enemies who were kept at bay by Charles and who were remembered by later generations as treacherous infidels were in fact the heirs of a rich cultural tradition. Centuries earlier, monks and scholars had fled from Africa to escape the Vandal threat. The North Africans had exercised a strong influence on Visigothic kings, converting them to Christianity. The cultural mix had produced the most learned man of the early seventh century, Isidore of Seville, bishop of that town and thus head of the Spanish church. Isidore wrote a vast collection of historical and theological works and became an important transmitter of ancient thought to the Middle Ages. Until the twelfth century, the western church used his statements of doctrine, collected in the *Book of Sentences*, as its principal theological textbook. Isidore's *Etymologies* was an encyclopedia that summarized Greco-Roman wisdom for the medieval world. Isidore and others produced a lively intellectual heritage that was permitted to survive and even flourish under the Muslims. Latin, Greek, and Arabic learning intermingled in this cosmopolitan society in which ancient philosophy, science, and medicine prospered. Although not nearly as brilliant as the Ummayad emirate to the south, Christian and Islamic Spain nevertheless proved to be civilized compared to its Frankish neighbor.

Feudalism and the Dissolution of the Frankish Realm

In the Frankish realm, a social revolution was occurring with the evolution of feudalism. The disappearance of the Roman imperial structure and the centralized state had left a power vacuum. Local lords, no longer checked by the imperial administration, rose to fill the void. Without governors to shield them from mayhem, free farmers had to surrender to these lords, who offered defense in exchange for property and service. Lesser lords swore fealty to greater lords, granting them military service in return for patronage and protection. The *Song of Roland* illustrates the values of this military elite who prized loyalty, courage, and martial prowess. When abbots or bishops were the property holders, the church became part of the feudal process, which it hoped to civilize. In the feudal ceremony itself, when one man swore allegiance to another in the presence of priests, holy relics, and the Bible, all the people in the community witnessed the visible and inextricable connection between religion and politics in feudal society.

By the year of Charlemagne's coronation, the process of feudalization was well under way. Scholars have estimated that by 800 perhaps as many as 60 percent of the people in western Europe were serfs bound to the land and their feudal lords. Increasingly, free people were submitting to more powerful military men. Charlemagne could manage the feudal lords, but his grandsons could not. During the ninth century, weak control by Carolingian kings left the land vulnerable to attack by Muslims, Magyars, and Vikings.

Viking pirates sailed in their longboats from the fiords of their mountainous homeland and terrorized Europe from the eighth to the eleventh century. Unleashed by domestic upheaval and a land too poor to sustain a growing population, expert sailors who traded in fish, wine, salt, metals, and furs turned to more profitable brigandage. The east-facing Swedes raided as far as the Black Sea, conquering Slavs and founding a monarchy at Novgorod and Kiev. In the west, the Danes and Norwegians ranged as far as Iceland and beyond. They repeatedly assaulted France and the British Isles, sailed around Spain, and entered the Mediterranean in 859. Even Italy knew the wrath of these marauders. Viking ships penetrated rivers, threatening inland towns and especially the monasteries and cathedrals whose wealth held special attraction for hostile pagans.

The first recorded Viking attacks were against the great northern monasteries at Lindisfarne (793), Jarrow (794), and Iona (795). Some scholars have suggested that Vikings were especially attracted to monasteries not so much for the treasures they yielded as for the opportunity to express their fanatical paganism and hatred of Christianity. They pillaged monasteries with systematic violence, stripping them of their treasures, sometimes burning the libraries, and exercising particularly bloodthirsty vengeance on monks.

Still, even Viking terrorism yielded some advantage for the larger Christian community. Vikings chased scholars and their rescued books to the Carolingian court, where Charlemagne nurtured the resulting convergence of resources. In 911 a descendant of Charlemagne, the French king Charles the Simple, ceded the land at the mouth of the Seine to a Viking named Rollo, who accepted baptism as a sign of loyalty to the king. This territory—the land of the Northmen, Northmannia, or Normandy—served as a buffer against rival pagan bands and attracted others who readily accepted Christianity as a condition of settlement. Ultimately, the Viking raids brought Scandinavia into closer contact with Christian Europe. This meeting of hostile worlds would eventually Christianize the last outposts of northern European paganism.

Meanwhile, Muslims to the south of the Frankish realm began a fresh assault, invading Sicily and southern Italy. They attacked St. Benedict's abbey of Monte Cassino and forced the monks to flee for their lives. Muslim raiders even made a foray up the Tiber in 846, threatened Rome, and sacked the basilica of St. Peter, still outside the city walls. From bases in Muslim Spain, Saracens plundered the southern coast of Gaul and sent raiding parties as far inland as Burgundy. By the end of the ninth century, the Asian Magyars, or Hungarians, threatened from the east. Soon they were raiding Lombardy, Bavaria, Saxony, and Burgundy. They ravaged villages and monasteries, selling their prisoners as slaves across the eastern frontiers.

All these raids of Vikings, Muslims, and Magyars took their toll on the Carolingian kingdoms, increasing their instability and giving further impetus to the feudal forces that were fragmenting the realm. The empire began to collapse almost at once upon Charlemagne's death, because only the tremendous personal strength of the great king had held it together. Military barons were not the only ones who imperiled the unified state: Churchmen did so as well. Abbots and bishops vied with other lords to seize authority over vast estates. Feudal struggles and enemy raids tore Frankish society apart from within and without.

The disintegration of the Carolingian empire proceeded apace under Charlemagne's only surviving son and heir, Louis the Pious (814–840), and Charlemagne's grandsons.

Louis was deeply religious and well educated, but no soldier. At Louis's death, the empire was divided among his sons, Charles Lothair and Louis the German, who embarked upon a course of fratricidal warfare.

Given the swift decay of the Carolingian kingdoms, it is no wonder that later generations venerated the memory of Charlemagne. For a while, he had fashioned a uniform Christian culture for western Europe. True, his program provoked some idiosyncratic responses, pedantic treatises, and quarreling among intellectuals. Still, his vision resulted in a remarkably consistent and radiant culture. Carolingian scholars created a virtual canon of authors to be read for a Christian education, including ancient Roman poets and grammarians. This canon linked Christian European culture with the old Roman world. The Church Fathers also occupied a cherished place in that canon, and Charlemagne's schoolmen adapted their writings for medieval readers. The legacy of this Carolingian tradition—classical and Christian—was a shared language and script, a literate class enjoying the vitality of cathedral and monastic schools, and a tradition of royal patronage of Christian culture. At the same time, the culture that flowered in Carolingian schools differed significantly from that of the classical world it emulated. Pope Leo's coronation of Charlemagne in the year 800 signifies the shift of power from the Mediterranean to the North, marking the end of the ancient world. Soon Charlemagne's empire would fragment into the localized communities that characterized medieval European civilization.

Was Charlemagne's program a success? How Christian was the society he inspired? The scriptural, Christian view from Charles's court and schools reveals the determination to initiate a Christian renaissance. At the same time, aristocratic warriors and rustic peasantry present a different picture, marked by a lively persistence of magic, sorcery, and paganism. Still, Charlemagne's program produced notable results. Under his aegis, church and state were acting together to order Christian education and preaching. The state undoubtedly benefited directly, because this process produced literate clerics who could assist with the secular administration. On the other side, even as clerics learned to manage the church's vast resources, the church also became more civilized through monastic and educational reform.

Later centuries revered Charlemagne as the archetypal Christian ruler. In legend he became a pilgrim who returned from Jerusalem laden with holy relics and a victorious warrior in the crusade against the Saracens of Spain. Admiring the power of his image and myth, many European princes strained to trace their descent from Charlemagne, the ultimate Christian hero of the Middle Ages and the creator of a Christian European culture.

Chapter 14

The Flowering of Medieval Christendom

Byzantium after Iconoclasm

While the Carolingian empire was fragmenting and disintegrating under Charlemagne's heirs, the Byzantine east was entering a period of political expansion and cultural renaissance in the wake of the iconoclast controversy. The battle over the icons had threatened to tear apart Byzantine society. The dangerous intensity of the crisis, however, also stimulated intellectual and religious ferment that led to a revival sometimes called the Macedonian Renaissance (from the dynasty that ruled from 867 to 1057, founded by an Armenian peasant whose family had settled in Macedonia or Thrace). Through this struggle, Byzantium reclaimed its classical heritage and gave definitive shape to its Christian identity.

When Irene became Empress-Regent in 780, she set about defending the icons with the assistance of her learned iconophile patriarch, Tarasius. The two encouraged research and the copying of theological manuscripts that would provide textual support for the veneration of icons and evidence of the icons' power. The iconophile authorities published new sources, including sermons and correspondence of Tarasius and the lives of iconophile saints and martyrs. The educated elite rallied around the defense of icons. During the second iconoclastic period (815–843), animated debate between the two sides led to vigorous scholarship. Enthusiasm spilled over from theological into secular interests such as mathematics, astronomy, and grammar. In Constantinople, the center of this revival, perhaps 2,000 or, at most, 3,000 men at any given time constituted the intellectual elite. Although only these few were highly educated, the general literate public expanded dramatically. In the monastic schools monks received a good education, while private tutors taught the women of elite families at home.

Along with this broad revival of learning came a renewed influence of the Greco-Roman tradition in art and literature. Byzantium had never abandoned the classical past, but the iconoclast emperors adopted a secularizing policy that revived classical learning. As icon smashers struggled to extricate themselves from religious images, they replaced the images with ancient models whose proportion and restraint they admired. This revival gained a momentum that continued after the restoration of icons. Byzantium would always remain a distinctly Christian state, but classical decorum restrained and ordered an intense religious inspiration, combining with Christian passion to produce the greatest art of Byzantium.

With the controversy resolved in favor of the icons, the production of religious art resumed throughout the empire. Artists adorned Hagia Sophia with lavish mosaics and decorated new churches according to schemes rooted in late Roman art. Most of these new churches were small. Travelers from the west were continually surprised to find major eastern churches considerably smaller than the cathedrals they had seen back home. Hagia Sophia remained the exception. Aside from this one glorious monument, the Byzantines preferred a church whose interior they could grasp as a whole and view as a single icon, with images of God, the Virgin, angels, martyrs, prophets, and saints hierarchically arranged on various surfaces.

The eleventh-century monastery church in Phocis, Greece, dedicated to Hosios Loukas (St. Luke), shows the typical scheme. The floor plan exhibits the usual Byzantine pattern from the posticonoclastic period, a cross with equal arms, inscribed in a square. A dome crowns the intersection of the arms. The plan boasts structural integrity and balance, requiring no external supports or buttresses. From the outside, most Byzantine churches do not look remarkable, but to walk into such a church is to step into a holy space and see a miniature of the larger universe. The dome is the heavenly realm, adorned with Christ Pantocrator ("Ruler of All"), who looks down on the faithful. The dome mosaic from Hosios Loukas is lost, but the mosaic from the Church of the Virgin at Daphni, also in Greece, presents a contemporary masterpiece. On nearby ceilings stand the archangels, and the twelve apostles support the dome. The worshipers look up, straining to see heavenly figures. Dominating their view, straight ahead on the vault of the apse, sits the loving intercessor between the congregants and God: the Virgin Mary, holding the baby Jesus. Scenes from the life of Christ occupy the curved corners where the dome meets its square base. Saints, martyrs, and prophets line the walls, each in his or her proper place, signifying the church on Earth. All these holy images announce the presence of the divine at the liturgy, which daily represents Christ's Passion.

The holy liturgy, like the sacred building and its icons, became stabilized in the period after iconoclasm. Religious life revolved around this liturgy, and Byzantines cherished its unchanging form, with liturgical cycles imitating the temporal cycles in endless repetition. In the fifteenth century, when Ottoman Turks threatened the city, Byzantines rejected union with the western church and possible rescue from Islamic invaders, in no small part because this earthly salvation would have required them to adopt the western liturgy and abandon their own.

Byzantium had emerged from the icon controversy a strong empire, sure of its identity as a Christian state. The social and cultural principles of the iconoclasts prevailed. Although monks had controlled intellectual life in the earlier period, in the ninth and tenth centuries Byzantine culture became more secular. The emperor retained his power as a sacred figure, God's regent on earth and the authority who appointed patriarchs and dominated ecclesiastical affairs. Monks could pray for mankind and mediate between humans and their God, perform the sacred liturgy and administer the sacraments, or deliver social services, but the emperor was master of the Byzantine church, patriarch, and monks.

The so-called Macedonian dynasty capitalized on the unified purpose and culture of Byzantium, nurturing the cultural renaissance. Constantine VII (913–957) himself was a notable scholar who directed various important compilations, including a precious record of court ceremonial and a treatise on the neighbors of Byzantium, friend and foe. Constantinople was then the greatest city of Christendom, the site of the imperial and patriarchal courts and center of international trade controlled by the emperor and his agents. The capital stood utterly without peer in the empire. Since the seventh century, the empire had changed from an urban to a rural economy. Provincial cities had disappeared, and the society shifted from a monetary economy to a barter system. No stable class mediated between the civil aristocracy in Constantinople and the independent peasants, who had by then replaced slaves as the basis of countryside economy. Although the empire was almost continuously at war from the seventh through the ninth centuries, Byzantium employed no professional army, so the free farmers were soldiers, too. Barely better off than the poorer peasants, these soldier–farmers had to supply horses and fight in long campaigns, as well as farm.

This posticonoclastic Byzantine state had a very different social structure from that of the old Roman Empire. The public life of urban civilization had disappeared, replaced by village society. In medieval Byzantium the most important social units were the nuclear family and the *oikos*, the household. Religious life was increasingly isolated as well, as smaller establishments replaced large monasteries. In general, smaller social units tended to benefit the emperor, whose power met no rival until the early tenth century, when the provincial aristocracy began to rise again. This occurred when the peasant warriors accepted serfdom under wealthy neighbors in exchange for protection from burdensome taxes and military service. The church, too, began ceding monastic lands to local aristocrats, who were to administer them on behalf of the church. These tendencies presented unwelcome dangers to the emperor and the central administration, which could not condone the alienation of taxes and manpower or the volatile rivalry of feudal lords.

As the aristocracy was rising to challenge imperial authority, external threats continued to exert pressure on the Byzantine state. Strong Macedonian emperors such as Basil II (976–1025) devoted their lives to the state's defense, but the growing struggle between the landed military aristocracy of the provinces and the civil aristocracy of the capital would produce disastrous consequences after Basil's death. Soon Italian mercenaries would replace the Byzantine navy, proud victor over Muslim ships in the seventh century and the terror of Muslim and Russian fleets in the tenth. Because an essentially rural society put little stock in maritime ventures, Byzantium would surrender valuable commercial control to Jewish, Muslim, and, especially, Italian merchants. Potentially the middlemen in the booming commercial revival of the twelfth century, the empire instead lost revenues to enemies who gained tax concessions and harbor rights in exchange for naval protection.

During the Macedonian period of military expansion and glory, all this devolution was in the dark future. Meanwhile, Byzantium was winning military victories, most notably over the Bulgars, along with religious victories in the conversions that brought the Slavs into the spiritual and cultural sphere of the empire.

Byzantine Missions to the Slavs

The ninth-century missionary successes of the Byzantines owe much to two brothers, Constantine (who took the monastic name Cyril just before his death) and Methodius. Growing up in Thessalonica, they received a bilingual education in Greek and Slavic. Since the migrations of the fifth and sixth centuries, the Slavs had been scattered widely over eastern Europe: west to the Elbe River, south into the Balkans and Greece, east beyond the Dnieper River, and into the northern forests of Russia. West Slavs would come under the influence of the Latin and Germanic west, while East Slavs and most South Slavs would enter the sphere of Byzantium, in no small part thanks to Constantine and Methodius.

The rivalry for the souls of central Europe both exemplified and aggravated tensions between eastern and western Christendom. Constantine and Methodius began their mission with Patriarch Photius and Pope Nicholas in a conflict that climaxed with mutual excommunications of the two leaders (863–867). In a meeting place between east and west, Franks and Byzantines were vying with one another to convert the Slavs. The territory was variously called Moravia or Bohemia; the natives called their land Čechy and themselves Czechs (Češi). In 845 fourteen of their nobles journeyed to Regensburg to accept Christian baptism from their western neighbors. It looked as if Bohemia/Moravia would soon enter the western religious alliance.

The Moravian prince Rastislav (846–870), however, sought Byzantine ties in order to counter the Frankish-Bulgar alliance against his realm. Enter Constantine and Methodius, sent on a cultural and diplomatic embassy by the Byzantine emperor. For their mission into still un-Christianized territories, Constantine had created a new Slavonic alphabet, now called Glagolitic. (Today most Slavic peoples use the Cyrillic alphabet, named after Constantine–Cyril but composed later.) He had also translated both the Bible and the liturgy into the vernacular language of the converted. To defend this translation, Constantine invoked the biblical precedent of the apostles preaching in many tongues on Pentecost (Acts 2:5) and also St. Paul's teaching (I Cor. 14:19):

> Since you have learned to hear, Slavic peoples,
> Hear the Word, for it came from God,
> The Word nourishing human souls,
> The Word strengthening heart and mind. . . .
> Therefore St. Paul has taught:
> "In offering my prayer to God,
> I had rather speak five words
> That all brethren will understand
> Than ten thousand words which are incomprehensible."[1]

---

[1] Roman Jakobson, trans., "St. Constantine's Prologue to the Gospel," *St. Vladimir's Seminary Quarterly* 7, no. 1 (1963), pp. 17–18.

The distinctive feature of Orthodox missions was this concession that the believer must understand the Word of God, the *Logos*. Sometimes the Byzantines enforced the use of Greek when they controlled Slavic lands, but the principle articulated by Constantine remained the church's official stance. The Christian west, on the other hand, insisted that the vernacular was not an acceptable medium for preaching the gospel. During their mission to Moravia and their stay in Venice, Constantine and Methodius debated with Franks, who held what Byzantines called the "heresy of the three languages," that is, the conviction that Christians should spread God's word only in the languages inscribed on Jesus' cross: Hebrew, Greek, and Latin. Constantine and Methodius, by contrast, affirmed that East Slavs and Armenians, Persians and Egyptians, Georgians and Arabs, all properly praised God in their own languages.

By this policy of translation, Orthodox Christianity settled profoundly in people's lives and in the indigenous cultures. The Slavic liturgy has continued among eastern and southern Slavs until the present, and in Moravia it lasted until the eleventh century, when the lingering influence of Latin Christendom finally prevailed. This vernacular tradition reaped a rich harvest. A literature in Slavonic developed within 100 years of the conversion, whereas vernacular literatures appeared only later in the west. But there were problems for Orthodox Christians, too. The use of various languages created national churches and further weakened the unity of Christendom, already divided into an eastern and a western branch. Without Greek, eastern European Christians had no direct access to the classical heritage, while a common use of Latin gave the western church greater cohesion along with the precious bonus of accessibility to Latin classical culture.

Because they permitted native peoples to retain their own languages for the liturgy, Constantine and Methodius enjoyed an advantage over rival missionaries from the west. In their mission, the brothers also received support from a surprising quarter: the papacy. While they were in Venice, Pope Nicholas I invited them to Rome. They took with them the alleged relics of St. Clement of Rome, a first-century martyr. When they presented these relics to Nicholas's successor, Adrian II (867–872), he threw the weight of his support behind the Slavonic liturgy. Constantine–Cyril died in Rome shortly thereafter, but Adrian consecrated Methodius as archbishop of Sirmium and granted him jurisdiction over much Slavic territory, including Moravia, Pannonia, and Slovakia. There Methodius met continued resistance from Frankish missionaries, who promoted a Latin liturgy and also a Latin version of the Nicene Creed, to which they had added the controversial *filioque*. By the interpolation of this word, the revised creed affirmed that the Holy Spirit had proceeded from the Father *and the Son*. The eastern Church maintained that the Holy Spirit proceeded only from the Father. Methodius's new protector, Pope John VIII (872–882), indicated his disapproval of the *filioque* clause, but the Frankish missionaries ignored the pope's views.

Byzantine Christianity exercised a lasting influence on the East Slavs, called in medieval times the *Rus*, whose modern heirs are the Russians, Ukrainians, and White Russians. In their movements from the sixth to the ninth centuries, these peoples had pushed east as far as the Volga River and north almost to the Baltic Sea, establishing important settlements at Novgorod and Kiev. Viking invasions in the early ninth century brought the Scandinavians into contact with the East Slavs, who called them Varangians. Their contact produced the first East Slavic state, which Oleg (873?–913) founded by uniting Kiev and

Novgorod under his rule. In 988 the ruler Vladimir converted to eastern Christianity and forced his people to accept baptism.

Under Vladimir's son Yaroslav (1015–1054), the principality of Kiev achieved its greatest power and brilliance. Yaroslav extended the boundaries of the Kievan state and also established the independence of the Rus church from Constantinople. The Rus church had its own leader, called a metropolitan, who reigned from Kiev, the political and ecclesiastical capital of the state. Yaroslav imported Byzantine artisans to decorate the many churches he built, including St. Sophia Cathedral at Kiev, modeled on Hagia Sophia of Constantinople. Attempting to imitate in wood the domes of Byzantine churches, the builders of Kiev created the onion domes that characterize Russian churches. Byzantine influence is also visible in the painted or enamel icons that decorate these churches.

Byzantine clergy dispatched to Kiev established schools for training priests, but these schools also trained young men from the aristocracy, and convents educated some women. Missionaries translated parts of the Bible and other ecclesiastical writings. These influenced Kievan writers, who produced a native literature featuring sermons, saints' lives, and religious treatises. The masterpiece is the *Primary Chronicle*, which focuses on the conversion of the Rus to Christianity and their struggles against the pagans surrounding them. Through this treasure of medieval literature, the East Slavs expressed their national identity within a Christian framework.

Despite religious links to Constantinople, the Rus of Kiev maintained political links with the west as well. Yaroslav's daughter Anna married the French king Henry I. (She may have been the only literate lay person at the French court during her day.) Yaroslav's family also had marriage ties with the ruling families of England, Germany, Norway, Poland, and Hungary, along with Byzantium. Although Kiev declined after Yaroslav's death, eastern Christianity continued to influence the civilizations of the East Slavs.

The spectacular expansion of Byzantine Christianity after the ninth century brought cultural advantages to the Slavs in Russia and the Balkans. The Cyrillic alphabet made possible the birth of Russian literature, and Russian art and architecture were inspired by Byzantine models. So great was the influence, that Moscow eventually became known as the Third Rome, after the New (second) Rome, Constantinople.

Byzantine missions to the Slavs brought those peoples within the realm of eastern Christian influence, but ironically, these same missions helped the Bulgars challenge Byzantine claims to universal supremacy. A mighty Bulgarian empire had taken command of the Balkans in territories wrested from Byzantium. This empire boasted an administration rendered efficient by the introduction of Greek and then Cyrillic as the official written language. Its unique Slav–Bulgar culture was dominated by warlord khans who aspired to Byzantine grandeur. Byzantium and Bulgaria engaged in a bloody struggle that finally ended in victory for the last ruler of the male Macedonian line, Basil II, called the Bulgar-Slayer (976–1025).

In 866 the Bulgar khan Boris accepted a Christian mission founded by Constantine and Methodius, and Bulgaria soon became a Christian state. In the tenth century, Bulgaria hatched a native-born Christian heresy, Bogomilism. Perhaps influenced by Armenian Paulicians dispatched to the area around Philippopolis, this sect was the creation of a Bulgarian called Pop Bogomil. Byzantines connected the heresy with Manichaeans, followers of the fourth-century Mani, who had taught that two creative urges, good and evil, were at work in the world. Like Mani, the Bogomils claimed that the physical world was entirely the work of the devil. The human spirit, an angel imprisoned in the flesh, longed to escape the Earth and flee to God. Since matter is evil, Christ could not have been truly material and born of a human mother (so Bogomils rejected the cult of Mary), but he will return at the Last Judgment to overturn Satan and his allies, who include all those who have wealth or power, either temporal or religious. In this Bogomil scheme, the church and its prelates are agents of the devil. Our information comes mostly from the tenth-century orthodox Bulgarian priest, Cosmas, who has Bogomils hurl the following challenge to orthodox priests:

> If you are holy, as you claim to be, then why do you not lead lives in accordance with the letter of Paul to Timothy: A bishop must be "above reproach, the husband of one wife, temperate, honest, dignified and hospitable . . . not a drunkard, not quarrelsome and no lover of money, but gentle . . . and must manage his own household well." But you priests do the opposite; you indulge in secret vices, of which no one may reform you.[2]

Cosmas insisted that the Bogomils had a political and social agenda as well as a spiritual one: "They teach their own people not to obey their masters, they revile the wealthy, hate the king, ridicule the elders, condemn the boyars, regard as vile in the sight of God those who serve the king, and forbid every serf to work for his lord."[3]

If it was in fact a movement of social protest against authority, Bogomilism seems to have condemned especially the claims of Byzantine ecclesiastical supremacy. It may thus have provided a spiritual ideology to support the national movement of Bulgars against Byzantium, although many modern scholars are quick to point out that Bogomil leaders do not seem to have supported militant acts against the enemy. Still, Bogomils expressed the national Bulgar animosity toward Byzantium. For example, they believed that, while church buildings are the work of Satan and the places where devils dwell (and therefore, the good Bogomil must never go to church), Satan himself lives in the grandest church of all, Hagia Sophia in Constantinople.

Bogomils sent missionaries to neighboring peoples, even into the heart of enemy territory. In a famous confrontation, Basil the Bogomil entered the imperial palace in Constantinople and tried to convert the emperor Alexius Comnenus (1081–1118), who finally burned the heretic before a huge crowd in the hippodrome. In their native Bulgaria, Bogomils seem to have attracted only a small following. By their aggressive proselytizing, however, they eventually influenced the twelfth- and thirteenth-century dualist heresies of the Cathars, Albigensians, and Patarins.

Rome versus Constantinople

An arguably greater threat to Christianity than Bogmilism was the widening rift between eastern and western Christendom. The last ecumenical council accepted by both churches

---

[2] Janet Fraser, trans., from Martin Erbstösser, *Heretics in the Middle Ages* (Leipzig: Edition Leipzig, 1984), p. 48.

[3] Robert Browning, trans., *Byzantium and Bulgaria: A Comparative Study across the Early Medieval Frontier* (Berkeley, CA: University of California Press, 1975), p. 164.

was the seventh, in 787. Even before this, councils had produced rulings rejected by one part of Christendom or another. For example, the west refused to confirm the decrees of the Council in Trullo (or *Quinisext* Council), which met in Constantinople in 691–692. Its official acts affirmed the Chalcedonian position that Constantinople enjoyed equal privilege with Rome. The council also permitted deacons and presbyters to marry, condemning the Roman prohibition of these marriages. In Orthodoxy today, priests still may marry. The council further attacked Roman customs, such as fasting on Saturdays during Lent and the artistic depiction of Christ as a lamb, popular in the west. The *Quinisext* Council insisted that Christ be shown in human form to emphasize the incarnation. These points of difference may not indicate major doctrinal divisions, but the acts of the council demonstrate insensitivity and hostility to western practices. When the pope rejected these decrees, Justinian II dispatched a legate to Rome with orders to deliver him to Constantinople to stand trial. In both Ravenna and Rome, the legate's mission so incensed the local militia that soldiers would have lynched him had the pope not urged clemency.

In fact, the doctrinal distinctions remained minor. Could priests marry, or should they remain celibate? Must the liturgy be in Latin, or may it be celebrated in vernacular languages? There was, of course, the *filioque* dispute, and only the western church believed in purgatory, an intermediate state between heaven and hell where souls cleansed themselves of lesser sins before they could enter heaven. All these issues were fiercely debated. But cultural, sociological, political, and personal differences (more than doctrinal ones) led to schism. Although Byzantines remained devoutly Christian, the Byzantine church enjoyed limited political and economic influence. The emperor ruled in Constantinople, where he selected the patriarch and sometimes deposed him. The Roman church, on the other hand, filled the vacuum left by the collapse of the western Roman Empire. The pope exercised strong authoritarian control, often claiming secular power and rivaling secular princes.

Tensions arose from Roman claims to universal primacy and also from arguments about influence over newly Christianized eastern Europe. A mutual intolerance and distaste for rival cultures intensified existing hostilities. Finally, of course, easterners and westerners simply could not speak with one another. The language barrier aggravated the many cultural barriers. Only an elite handful of Byzantines knew Latin, and few westerners understood Greek. Liudprand, bishop of Cremona, left a diary of a famous encounter between the rival cultures during his embassy to Constantinople. Sent by Otto I to the court of Emperor Nicephorus I (963–969), Liudprand loathed all aspects of the civilization he encountered, from the resinated wine to court ceremonial and from the "piglike" emperor to customs officials who confiscated the silks Liudprand tried to smuggle out of the empire. For their part, the Byzantines insisted that they were the true Romans. "Listen!" demanded one imperial official, "the silly blockhead of a pope does not know that the sacred Constantine transferred to this city the imperial sceptre, the senate, and all the Roman knighthood, and left in Rome nothing but vile slaves, fishermen, confectioners, poulterers, bastards, plebeians, [and] underlings."[4]

Reciprocal disaffection and lesser religious differences led inexorably to the schism of 1054. Disagreements arose in southern Italy, where eastern and western claims collided.

---

[4]F. A. Wright, trans., *The Works of Liudprand of Cremona* (New York: E. P. Dutton & Co., Inc.), 1930.

Arguments focused on the old dogmatic and liturgical problems—the *filioque*, Roman fasting on Saturdays, married versus unmarried clergy, questions of primacy and jurisdiction, and especially the use of leavened or unleavened bread for communion services. Hoping to foster understanding and cooperation, Pope Leo IX dispatched Cardinal Humbert of Silva Candida to Constantinople. The rigid personalities of the papal legate and the imperious patriarch Michael Cerularius assured disastrous results. Failing to wring concessions from the patriarch, the legates deposited a bull of excommunication on the high altar at Hagia Sophia. Michael Cerularius responded in kind, and the Latin envoys barely escaped with their lives. Only in 1965 was the mutual excommunication lifted by pope and Greek patriarch.

The Ottonian Empire and the Church

While Byzantium flourished in the ninth century, western Europe was reeling from the attacks of Vikings, Magyars, and Muslims, as noted (179–181). Without the unifying power of Charlemagne, Carolingian principalities disintegrated, but the Carolingian ideal of a Christian state did not die. In Germany, where Charlemagne's line ended in 911, the Ottonian dynasty succeeded the Carolingian as protectors of Christianity. In 919 Henry the Fowler, duke of Saxony, was elected king by the German nobles and greater clergy. Beginning with Henry's reign, the kingdom of Germany rose to supreme importance in western Europe for much of the next three centuries.

Henry's son, Otto I (936–973), checked feudal anarchy by using the financial and military resources of the church. He waged successful campaigns against the Hungarians/Magyars and moved into Italian territories, where he seized a rich stash of holy relics and also won royal power in 951. To symbolize his role as Charlemagne's heir, he had himself crowned king in Aix-la-Chapelle (Aachen). At Rome in 962, Pope John XII crowned him emperor. To express the mutual dependency between pope and emperor, Otto I and John XII drew up an agreement, the *Ottonianum*, defining papal obligations to the emperor and imperial protection of papal interests. Otto perfected the practice of earlier medieval princes who controlled the church by appointing bishops and abbots who owed them feudal homage. This process, called "lay investiture," produced a crisis between church and state in the eleventh century. Initially, the *Ottonianum* brought back the potent union of church and state that Charlemagne had nurtured. Otto I confirmed the vital importance of that union: "We believe that the protection of our Empire is bound up with the rising fortunes of Christian worship" [Tardif, *Cartons des rois*, no. 357; *Diplom. regum et imperatorum Germaniae*, I, Otto I, no. 366]. Otto and his heirs brought peace to northern Italy, resulting in the revival of cities, notably Venice.

A contemporary, probably a relative, of Otto has left us a precious literary record of the era. Hrotsvitha lived in the convent at Gandersheim, whose history she wrote. Her account describes visions and prophecies that inspired the foundation of the convent by the Lady Oda and her husband, Duke Liudulf, great-grandparents of Emperor Otto I. Pope Sergius provided sacred relics for the new foundation, the intact remains of two bishops of Rome, Anastasius and Innocent. Borrowing imagery from the gospels, Hrotsvitha described how humble swineherds saw a "dazzling radiance" of lights from the woods, pointing out the spot where the convent should stand. Here her narrative owes some inspiration to the biblical account of shepherds and the starry light that guided the wise men to the site of Jesus' birth. The pristine wooded spot, home to fauns and monsters, also borrows elements from Vergil's account of the site where Rome should rise. Such a mingling of classical and biblical elements characterized Carolingian literature, and the Ottonians inherited this tradition.

Gandersheim's cofounder, Liudulf, was an aristocrat in military service to Charlemagne's grandson, Louis, king of the Franks. Louis married a daughter of Liudulf and Oda. From its beginnings, therefore, aristocratic and royal connections set Gandersheim apart from the usual convent. Its abbesses came from the ruling family. In 947 Otto I invested the abbess with complete authority, free from episcopal or royal control. Gandersheim enjoyed the direct protection of the papal see and had a representative at the imperial assembly. The convent and its properties constituted a small principality with its own courts, army, and mint. There, unmarried royal women could wield power and meet intellectual challenges while living spiritually satisfying lives. The dynasty benefited, too, because these women did not marry princes whose new kinship to the royal family might make them dangerous rivals to the throne.

Except for the servants, all the women at Gandersheim were of noble birth. Some were nuns who had surrendered their fortunes and taken vows of perpetual chastity. Others, perhaps including Hrotsvitha herself, were canonesses who could keep their wealth and maintain their own servants and libraries. Canonesses were free to entertain guests and to come and go as they pleased; they could even leave the nunnery to marry without penalty or disgrace. Hrotsvitha had perhaps spent some time at Otto's court. She had literary aspirations and wrote plays that are the first to survive after the demise of ancient classical theater. Hrotsvitha claimed that she was inventing Christian dramas to rival the sublime Roman playwright, Terence.

Hrotsvitha was a talented woman, and she enjoyed rare advantages of education and birth. For most women with monastic ambitions, however, the tenth and eleventh centuries were a difficult age. In that period, few convents were endowed, and women's religiosity received little encouragement. The great monastery at Cluny, itself created in the tenth century, founded dozens of monasteries for men but only one for women, a retreat for wives whose husbands had become Cluniac monks. Gandersheim provided a unique refuge for women of privilege.

The Ottonian line ended with the premature death in 1002 of Otto III, son of a Byzantine princess, at age twenty-one. Powerful nobles opposed the troubled succession of his cousin, Henry II of Bavaria (1002–1024), who also died without heir. His successor, Conrad II (1024–1039), inaugurated a new dynasty. Conrad's son Henry III (1039–1056) died leaving the infant Henry IV as his heir. A minor as ruler invited difficulties; enemies felt free to flex their muscles and test the authority of regents and young ruler alike. The reign of Henry IV spawned the so-called investiture conflict, which challenged the theocratic basis of imperial power and ultimately weakened the German throne.

Meanwhile, the lands farther west, ravaged by Viking raiders and reduced to feudal estates designed for self-defense, were edging toward a revival that later generations would call the last medieval renaissance or the renaissance of the twelfth century. Rapid changes occurred after 1000, as the population increased, settlers cleared land for farms and villages, commerce revived, and urban life reappeared. Serfdom waned in France, Spain, Italy, and western Germany. Women and men enjoyed the freedom to travel on pilgrimage or crusade. Philosophers scrutinized Christian theology, and the church entered into major reform.

Normandy, France, and England

While the German empire was thriving, Carolingian France suffered from Muslim and Viking threats. In 911 a desperate Carolingian king, Charles the Simple, ceded land to a Viking chief named Rollo. Charles hoped that Rollo and his Northmen would protect Paris from raids by rival Viking bands. For his part, Rollo received land that would form the core of the future duchy of Normandy, along with its principal city, Rouen. In return, Rollo and his Vikings accepted Christian baptism. Within a few decades, the versatile and highly adaptive Northmen, or Normans, had abandoned their old language and religion and had become nearly indistinguishable from their French neighbors, whose language they spoke and whose institutions they adopted. For an increasingly sophisticated administrative machinery, their courtiers issued documents written in the Latin of France. Men who had pillaged monasteries and cathedrals and destroyed their relics saw their sons and daughters fervently embrace Christianity. According to Norman legend, Rollo's own son, Duke William Longsword, piously harbored monastic ambitions. Rollo's great-great-great-grandson, Duke William I (1035–1087), controlled the feudal system in his duchy and limited warfare while supporting the church-sponsored peace movement. He took an active role in church councils and ecclesiastical appointments.

This William became known as the Conqueror after he took England in 1066. Like France, England had suffered from the chaos of the Viking incursions, with the attendant damage to culture and religious tradition. Under Alfred the Great (ruled 871–899), Britain finally began its revival. Alfred engineered military and political successes, as well as cultural, spiritual, and religious reforms. It was Alfred who molded Britons and Anglo-Saxons into a united people, but the reconciliation of Vikings and Anglo-Saxons fell to Cnut, king of England (1016–1035) and, from 1030 until his death, king of Norway, too. Cnut fashioned a strong state. Despite some abuses in the English church, Christianity flourished in preconquest England. Benedictine monasteries fostered learning and provided educated men for both church and government. The conquest of 1066 returned the island state to the European realm and to greater western Christendom.

The "Pornocracy" and Monastic Reform

By the time of the Conqueror, Christendom had seen hard times and then a brilliant revival. Under St. Nicholas I (858–867), the papacy was a powerful institution. Twenty-five years after his death, it had plummeted to a debased condition sometimes called the "pornocracy." When a pope died, Italian nobles and Roman factions vied to choose his successor, sometimes selling the office to the highest bidder. Other bishoprics often suffered similar fates, being considered by local nobles as prizes for the best schemers. In the case of Rome, because of its claims to supremacy, the scandals had broad consequences. The outrageous behavior of some popes shocked the sensibilities of Christians far and wide. Consider, for instance, Pope John XII (955–964), who succeeded his father at age eighteen. A contemporary chronicle alleged that he wore himself out with sexual excesses before he turned twenty-eight. When King Otto found it politically expedient to depose John, he discovered no dearth of moral pretexts, including the charges that he had castrated a cardinal, toasted the devil's health, and called on Venus and Jupiter to help the dice fall in his favor.

Reform began in the monasteries. In the early Middle Ages, Benedictine monasteries had been precious centers of Christian living and education. Monasteries such as Bobbio in northern Italy, St. Gall in Switzerland, Luxeuil in France, and Wearmouth and Jarrow in England were beacons of civilization that preserved both classical and Christian learning. Charlemagne protected monasteries, but after his death, Viking, Magyar, and Muslim raids took a deadly toll. The invaders destroyed some establishments, and others fell into the hands of feudal lords who used monastic resources and sold offices to men without spiritual commitment. No longer havens of religious observance and intellectual efforts, the surviving monasteries often exploited the very societies that devout monks were supposed to protect with their prayers. But in 909 William the Pious, duke of Aquitaine, gave land in Burgundy to monks, who built the abbey at Cluny. Duke William promised the new monastery complete autonomy from any lord except the pope alone. This freedom from secular control would soon catapult Cluny into the center stage of the monastic reform movement.

The monastery and its foundation charter came to exert vast influence. Following the Rule of St. Benedict, the earliest monks at Cluny strove for spiritual perfection through obedience to their abbots and careful liturgical practice. Cluny came to inspire clerics throughout the west in the movement toward celibacy and against simony (the buying and selling of offices or sacraments). Within a generation, neighboring monasteries sought Cluny's help to reform along Cluniac lines. Even Monte Cassino, the mother Benedictine monastery, entered Cluny's sphere of influence. Cluny's fifth abbot, Odilo (994–1048), established the right of Cluny's abbot to appoint and oversee the abbots of all Cluniac foundations. This made Cluny almost an order. Cluny's rise to power and influence culminated in the sixty-year reign of Abbot Hugh (1049–1109). At his death, from England to Spain and Italy, and from France and Germany even to the Holy Land, hundreds of monasteries submitted to the jurisdiction of Cluny. The list grew to include nearly 1,200 houses. Sometimes the monks objected to unwelcome discipline, but support came from powerful secular rulers such as Alfonso VI of Leon-Castile, who had married Constance of Burgundy, a niece of Abbot Hugh. With such mighty allies and reforming zeal, the Cluny movement expanded beyond monasticism, becoming a voice for larger issues of church reform.

As benefactors showered Cluny with gifts, new wealth led to corruption. Late in the eleventh century, Cluniac monks adopted opulent lifestyles that threatened monastic discipline and spirituality. Abbots traveled with huge retinues, like the great feudal lords they were; the monks wore only the finest clothes and ate sumptuous meals. Men disillusioned with Cluniac decadence created new monastic orders. The Cistercians best exemplify the reforming spirit of the twelfth century. In 1098 monks fled Molesmes in Burgundy and founded a new monastery in the wetlands of Cîteaux. There they sought a simple and austere life on the frontiers of civilization, working uncultivated soil and living lives unencumbered by feudal gifts. By searching out wilderness, they led the way in the land reclamation of the twelfth century. In the Low Countries, Cistercians built dikes and reclaimed land from the sea. In the eastern reaches of the German empire, they drained swamps. In Burgundy they planted vineyards, and on England's rocky soil, they built sheep runs.

The first Cistercians braved illness and deprivation. In 1112, however, Bernard of Clairvaux entered Cîteaux with thirty of his noble friends and kinsmen, and their arrival energized the movement. In the twelfth century, Cîteaux founded hundreds of monasteries and exercised great influence on European society, nurturing the high ideals of the age. The Cistercians formed a closely knit organization that could wield considerable influence, although by the end of the century, wealth began to corrupt Cistercian monasticism as it had done Cluniac.

How did monks live? Monastic life varied considerably according to time and place. The early Cistercians, for instance, placed great emphasis on the physical labor of bare survival. For all monks, the liturgy held central importance. Seven times daily and once during the night, monks met to chant the psalms and offer prayers for benefactors, deceased abbots, and the monks' relatives, as well as for the welfare of the people and the blessing of the crops. To pray for God's blessings was a critical function of monks in medieval society. Because the liturgy played such a crucial role in monastic life, monks lavished wealth and attention on the accumulation of liturgical art and vestments and sacred vessels. They cherished precious reliquaries, gospel books, and thuribles for burning incense.

When they were not in prayer, monks performed various roles. One monk, the cellarer, supervised the peasants or lay brothers who tilled the soil. The aristocratic choir monks did not cultivate the fields themselves until the early Cistercians insisted on doing their own work. Monks kept herb gardens and prepared medicines from them. The almoner fed and nurtured the neighboring poor. The cantor sang the liturgy and cared for the liturgical repertory. The sacristan looked after the sacred vessels, candles, altar cloths, vestments, and incense. A few monks copied manuscripts and wrote their own works. And the novice master trained the recruits, often children presented by their parents as oblates, although some men and women entered monastic life in adulthood. For younger offspring of the feudal aristocracy, the monastery offered careers; in turn, it served the kings and feudal lords by training administrators and scribes.

In a society that lacked the concept of governmental responsibility for social welfare, monks performed social services and ran schools and hostels. Rarely did Benedictine monasteries care for sick laypersons. Only in the mid-twelfth century did hospitals appear in most western towns and many villages. Laypersons built and staffed some hospitals, while bishops or monasteries supported others. In this period, religious orders arose specifically to assist pilgrims and provide nursing care. The Knights of St. John of Jerusalem (also known as the Knights Hospitalers) organized a huge hospital for pilgrims and crusaders in the Holy Land. Although this development came late to westerners, Byzantine hospitals were part of the philanthropic system supported by state, monastery, and bishopric from the fourth century on. At one time Constantinople alone had forty hospitals, including the well-documented institution at the Monastery of the Pantocrator, staffed by male and female physicians trained in various medical specialties.

In yet another area, the monastic influence on society moved beyond prayer to action: Monks inspired the peace movement of the church. According to the monastic theory of the Three Orders—those who work, those who pray, and those who fight—each order provided services for the others. In his biography of St. Gerard of Aurillac, Abbot Odo of Cluny expounded the belief that warriors were duty bound to defend the helpless and the church. The idea was expanded by bishops in a series of councils, beginning near the end of the tenth century in Burgundy. There in southern France, part of the old Carolingian Empire, chaos reigned, with local lords even attacking churches and peasants in their fields. The council put the poor, priests, and monks under ecclesiastical protection; it safeguarded places, too—peasant fields and sacred buildings. Any men who attacked these persons or places risked anathema; that is, the Church denied them any contact with Christians. In 1027 another council enjoined warriors to observe the Truce of God and refrain from fighting during specified periods or suffer excommunication. To keep the Lord's Day holy, no one could attack an enemy from Saturday evening until Monday morning. Soon councils increased the days of truce, adding Thursday, Friday, and Saturday in commemoration of Christ's Passion and then including major saints' days and the seasons of Advent (the four weeks before Christmas) and Lent (the six weeks before Easter). By the mid-eleventh century, Duke William of Normandy had thrown his support to the Peace of God and Truce of God, forcing his vassals to support the movement.

These precepts may not have held up often in practice, but they influenced public opinion of Christian behavior. In advancing ideals of a just society, the church also moved to limit slavery by opposing the enslaving of Christians. This was a rather late and fitful development, however. Early Christians had inherited the justification for slavery from the Greco-Roman past. Slaves (along with women and children) were considered intellectually inferior to free men. Following Aristotle, St. Augustine argued in *The City of God:* "The justice of masters dominating slaves is clear, because those who excel in reason should excel in power." Slavery thus continued into the early Middle Ages. In fact, our word "slave" comes from the name "Slav," suggesting the common practice of trading war captives from Slavic territories. Monasteries kept slaves, including sometimes female weavers and domestics. The number of slaves declined in the later Middle Ages, however, partly in response to condemnations of the church, such as the ruling by a London council in 1102 forbidding "the ignoble trade whereby men are sold like beasts."

Papal Reforms and the Investiture Conflict

The religious revival of the eleventh century, begun in monastic reform, finally reached the papacy itself. Some support came from Otto I and his successors in the German empire, who fought against simony and clerical marriage and protected church lands from lay lords who would usurp them. But emperors would not threaten their own interests by surrendering lay control; the monks and reform-minded bishops would have to turn to the pope for leadership.

After a century of depravity, the papacy responded at last to the spiritual movement. Some evidence suggests direct influence from Cluny. There was, for instance, the partnership of Abbot Odilo of Cluny (994–1048) and the German Emperor Henry III in supporting reforms. Pope Gregory VII (1073–1085) had been at Cluny, as had Urban II (1088–1099), formerly a Cluniac monk and prior. These popes worked to provide moral guidance and direction in codifying church law and doctrine, strengthening the hierarchy of bishops, authorizing the college of cardinals to elect and advise popes, enforcing priestly chastity, and excluding women from the priest's household as wives or companions.

Despite papal censure, in the eleventh century most priests were probably living with women. Critics called these priests "Nicolaites," from condemnations in the Book of Revelation (2:1–17) assailing false Christians who practiced heathen debauchery. To compel priests to be celibate, reform propaganda focused on the sacramental argument that priests who celebrated the Eucharist should not profane themselves by engaging in sexual activity. Privately, the popes had pragmatic material concerns that married priests were using church resources to care for their wives and children, and even bequeathing churches to them. Priests' sons often inherited the parish ministry of their fathers. Compelled to care for their families on stipends meant to support only one man, some parish priests sold sacramental services, so that people had to pay for baptisms, masses, marriages, and absolution of sins. The reformers felt that they could remove the need for this simony by eliminating married priests. For their part, many clergy resisted the papal commands, claiming marriage as their ancient right. Some angry priests even threatened to murder bishops who were trying to enforce the papal decree.

The reforms began in earnest with Pope Leo IX (1049–1054), a humble man whose high moral character lent authority to his decrees. Under Nicholas II (1058–1061), the Lateran Council of 1059 authorized the college of cardinals as the sole body to elect new popes, removing the quarrelsome Roman factions from this process. But the critical figure in sustaining the reform and directing it to a new revolutionary phase was Pope Gregory VII (1073–1085), for whom the papal reform movement of the eleventh century is often named Gregorian. Gregory held the deeply felt conviction that God commanded people through the pope, who was God's regent on earth, free of all judgment except God's. In Gregory's view, only a pope could wear the Roman imperial insignia or have his feet kissed by all princes. For their part, secular princes had a sacred duty to maintain peace and order and, in this way, to facilitate the Christian journey to the heavenly city. Kings must act righteously; if they did not, the people need not obey them. This was a revolutionary theory, especially along with its corollary: that God granted to popes the duty to oversee the kings' behavior and depose them if necessary.

Did the king have power over his subjects, or did the pope? In 1075 Gregory convened a council at Rome that published decrees against Nicolaitism and simony and issued the first decrees against lay investiture, with penalties for all parties to the transaction. Guilty clerics were to lose their office, laymen to face excommunication. The most powerful rulers of the Christian west rebelled: the French king Philip I, the German emperor Henry IV, and William the Conqueror, king of England and duke of Normandy. Henry responded with the greatest anger. Although he and his predecessors had strongly supported the reform movement, this latest step threatened his Holy Roman Empire, a huge realm governed only with the administrative help of churchmen, most of whom he had chosen and invested. He could ill afford to relinquish this right or the authority over his subjects. He flaunted his intransigence by appointing three bishops to Italian sees over which the pope claimed authority. Gregory and Henry exchanged angry letters. Finally in 1076 at the Diet of Worms, Henry and most of his bishops proclaimed themselves freed of obligations to Gregory.

The lines were drawn. Gregory excommunicated Henry and the bishops loyal to him.

He released the German nobles from obeying their king and encouraged insurrection. Pleased to display their piety by ridding themselves of a mighty lord, the nobles eagerly supported the pope's wishes. They even elected a new king, the German prince Rudolf of Rheinfelden, whose authority Gregory confirmed. Threatened with the defection of his princes, Henry played out the drama brilliantly in his famous journey to the northern Italian castle at Canossa, where the pope had taken refuge. In the middle of a bitter winter (1076–1077), Henry crossed the Alps and then waited before the castle gates, seeking forgiveness. According to tradition, Henry stood barefoot in the snow for three days. This scene of Henry's submission is commonly interpreted as a victory for papal power. In fact, the king outmaneuvered the pope, whose priestly duty compelled him to forgive the penitent sinner and lift the sentence of excommunication. This freed Henry's allies to rally around him again and angered the pope's German supporters, who felt betrayed.

On the one hand, the papacy had demonstrated its power over secular rulers, who would rarely venture serious rebellion for another 200 years. On the other hand, the questions of lay investiture and the rights and duties of Christian kings remained an open wound. Successive popes and Henry's heirs continued to quarrel. Gregory even excommunicated Henry a second time, in 1080, but now public opinion shifted to support Henry, who kept the loyalty of his lords. This enabled the emperor to invade Italy and take Rome. Gregory VII died in exile in 1085, and his successors retaliated by pressing Henry's sons to rebellion.

The quarrel with the German emperor took center stage in European affairs, but the papacy struggled against the kings of England and France as well. William the Conqueror practiced lay investiture in England and relied on bishops as crucial barons. His sons, William Rufus and Henry I, continued to quarrel with the papacy until 1107. The French king, Philip I (1060–1108), profited from the sale of church offices and also feared an independent church in his realm. Philip's bigamous marriage, however, provoked his most bitter contest with the papacy, consigning investiture to a less conspicuous role.

The English king Henry I agreed to terms in 1107. At last, in 1122, the papacy and the German emperor—then Henry V, son of Henry IV—reached the same compromise with the Concordat of Worms. According to this agreement, canon law would dictate the selection of bishops by the clergy, but the emperor or his delegate won the right to be present. Although lay rulers would no longer invest the bishop with the episcopal ring and staff, they would continue to invest a bishop or abbot with the symbols of their temporal power. The emperor's continuing right to accept or refuse feudal homage from the new bishop offered some power of veto. This compromise failed to resolve whether king or pope ruled supreme, but it brought a formal end to the contest.

Fifty years of struggle created serious social and political consequences. In Germany the winners were the feudal aristocracy, who gained vigor while the emperor and pope feuded. Along with acquiring rights from the emperors, the nobles also came to exercise tighter control over the peasants and serfs in their domains. The investiture controversy was directly responsible for the localism and feudal independence that weakened and divided Germany in the late Middle Ages. Not until the nineteenth century did a strong, united Germany emerge. In France the consequences were quite different. Because each cathedral chapter (the organization of priests who administered the cathedral) claimed the right to elect its own bishop, the great nobility found it increasingly difficult to award these posts to their relatives. Bishops came more and more from the minor nobility, who posed a smaller threat to the French crown.

From the long struggle popes learned that they could humble even emperors. The conflict had also compelled popes to centralize church government and to consolidate their own power within the ecclesiastical hierarchy. But all this reform had a dark side: a hardening of attitude and practice toward dissent, whether by defiant king, noble, or cleric, or by heretic, Muslim, or Jew. In no part of Europe did Jews make up more than five percent of the population, but even these small numbers threatened medieval concepts of a homogeneous Christian society. Jews were easy scapegoats in times of trouble; when religious passions rose, Jews could become their victims. So, for instance, in 1096 mobs of German crusaders slaughtered Jews in one Rhineland town after another before heading east. Some bishops tried to protect the Jews, but to no avail.

For good and ill, the controversy energized all of western Christendom, compelling the laity to take sides in matters of Christian policy and belief. This broad participation awakened an intense piety that found expression in the First Crusade (1095–1099) and in the religious enthusiasm of the twelfth century, with its focus on love as the ultimate worthy pursuit. In the new emotionalism of that century, troubadours sang of "new love" or "true love," which we sometimes call courtly love, a rapture that could be both carnal and spiritual. Religious passion produced outpourings of love for God and a rebirth of the cult of the Virgin.

Popular Religion

Even before the Third Ecumenical Council had authorized her title as Mother of God (431), Mary had enjoyed special honor among Christians. The cults of other saints arose or flourished near their relics, but all Christendom venerated Mary. It is true that Constantinople claimed to possess her robe and Chartres the nightdress she wore when she gave birth to Jesus. Other sites displayed fragments of her veil and even drops of her milk. Christians came to believe, however, that she had entered heaven, leaving no relics. Mary's universal appeal made cult centers spring up everywhere.

The eleventh century saw increasing interest in Jesus the man, and so in his human mother. Prayers addressed him as "God, son of Mary." The movement met resistance from ecclesiastical leaders who had inherited the deep-rooted notion that women represented Eve and that feminine influence was treacherous. But in popular expressions of piety, Christian worshipers sometimes elevated Mary to a loftier emotional level than the Trinity, inspiring Gautier de Coinci (ca. 1177–1236), a Benedictine friar who wrote fanciful and pious songs to Mary, to proclaim, "God changed sex!" Twelfth-century monks began insisting on Mary's immaculate conception. The influential Bernard of Clairvaux (1090–1153) attacked this new idea, but without success. The people praised Mary as queen of heaven, *Regina coeli*, and by the early twelfth century, artists were depicting her as crowned by her son. The thirteenth century was yet to witness the climax of her cult, when Mary aroused spiritual passion just as the courtly lady inspired her lover's devotion. In the metrical patterns of Latin church hymns, Peire Cardenal (ca. 1180–ca. 1278) wrote a song to the Virgin, using words commonly heard in troubadour lyrics to a beloved lady:

Vera vergena, Maria,	True virgin, Mary,
vera vida, vera fes,	true life, true faith,
vera vertatz, vera via,	true truth, true way,
vera vertutz, vera res,	true virtue, true thing,
vera maire, ver' amia,	true mother, true friend/lover
ver' amors, vera merces;	true love, true mercy:
per ta vera merce sia	grant by your true mercy
qu'eret en me tos heres!	that your heir inherit me![5]

The church was compelled to embrace this enthusiasm. Within Bernard's own Cistercian order, all churches came to be dedicated to the Virgin.

Great church festivals arose to commemorate events in Mary's life: the Annunciation, the Visitation (to her cousin Elizabeth, mother of John the Baptist), Candlemas (recalling the Virgin's purification, the day when candles are blessed for sacred use), the Assumption, and eventually, the Immaculate Conception (celebrating Mary's freedom from the taint of original sin). Interest spread to include her family, notably embracing the cult of her mother, St. Anne.

Eastern Christians revered Mary with increasing enthusiasm, too. After the demise of iconoclasm, Byzantines took a fresh look at the Virgin, stressing her humanity and accessibility. Beginning in the tenth century, the theme of her intercession finally found a distinctive iconography that was more passionate and more loving than earlier, static forms. The oldest known images in the new style are votive icons from tenth-century Cappadocia in central Asia Minor, where they are frequently found on the south wall of churches. The pose became common. The famous Vladimir icon of the twelfth century shows this maternal sentiment as human love meets the divine.

The increased spirituality of the age, along with broadened horizons and commerce, encouraged pilgrimage. Western Christians found a new incentive to visit holy sites, which began to offer indulgences to shorten the time the pilgrim would have to spend in purgatory. The first recorded pilgrim to the northern Spanish shrine of St. James, in the cathedral city of Santiago de Compostela, arrived in 950. St. James came to symbolize the *Reconquista*—the gradual reconquest of Spain from the Muslims—and became a popular pilgrimage center, along with the Italian sites of Rome, the Church of St. Nicholas at Bari, and Gargano. Westerners even risked journeys to relic-laden Constantinople and Jerusalem.

Relics were precious sacred items and also valuable assets to a shrine or church. A vigorous trade developed in inventing, altering, and stealing relics. Sometimes duplicate relics caused embarrassment or confusion. Toulouse already claimed the body of St. James when a Spanish bishop found the saint's bones in the early ninth century. To counter conflicting assertions, a twelfth-century guidebook to Compostela insisted that the bones proved to be immovable, so the high altar of the cathedral was built above the intact remains. In another case, three monasteries claimed to hold the body of the Welsh St. Teilo, who had ruled them all. It was decided that each had genuine relics because the saint had prevented violence among his communities by producing three authentic sets of himself.

---

[5] René Lavaud, ed., *Poésies Complètes du Troubadour Peire Cardenal* (Toulouse, France: Edouard Privat, 1957). Unpublished translation by Emily Albu.

Saints and their relics, pilgrimage and hope of heavenly reward worked their way deep into the consciousness of medieval men and women. Christianity offered hope for the life to come and meaning in their harsh and precarious earthly lives, touching virtually all elements of their everyday existence. From birth to death, the lives of peasants revolved around the village church, where infants were baptized, couples were married, and the bereaved prayed for the souls of their dead, who were buried in the church cemetery. The central event in religious experience was the liturgy of the Eucharist, the re-creation of the Last Supper. In the medieval west, people called this service the mass, from the priest's dismissal at its close, *"ite, missa est"* ("go, [the meeting] is dismissed"). Every Sunday and holy day, all the people in the village stood at mass. Especially pious folks might attend daily, although they did not necessarily stay for the entire service in Latin, a language understood by few. Great Christian festivals—Easter, Christmas, and Pentecost—and the numerous saints' days dominated the calendar and defined the passing of time. Inside the church, people met to reconcile differences, solemnize oaths, or ratify treaties. Circuit judges held court on the church porch. Fairs, usually opened on church festivals, flourished in the churchyard, as did feasts to celebrate baptisms, weddings, and funerals. The priest was an important member of the community. Often the only literate person in the village, he played a critical role as protector of the peasants by making their contracts with merchants and tax collectors.

For medieval people, Christianity offered a sense of security, belonging, and meaning. But most could not read and so had scanty exposure to details or subtleties not preached by clergy in vernacular homilies. In a traditional society that passed on beliefs and customs from one generation to the next, most of Christendom shared a profound faith—but one that had regional variation in folk practices and often deviated significantly from official teachings. The rituals of popular religion sometimes preserved and cherished elements of pagan rites. For instance, folks often put salt on the tongue of a child at baptism in order to chase away demons; pagan Roman sacrifices had used salt, which had also symbolized purity to the Jews. And though clergy often repeated the statement of Pope Gregory I permitting a woman to enter the church immediately after childbirth, ancient superstitions and Old Testament laws of purification conspired to keep the "unclean" woman away for forty days; only then could she enter for the ritual of "churching," or the "benediction of a woman entering church after childbirth." Sometimes magic and ritual directly challenged Christian practice, as when young people defied interdict to perform masked dances in the village cemetery.

Economic Recovery of Europe:
The Rise of Towns and Commerce

Village life in medieval Christendom changed only slowly from one generation to the next. In the eleventh century, however, Europe was entering a period of revolutionary social change leading to the rise of towns and the origins of a new commercial class. From the tenth to the fourteenth centuries, no major plague assailed Europe. In the century after 1080, mild weather blessed England, France, and Germany. The more hospitable climate led to prosperity and growth in population.

Some of the new towns grew up around cathedrals or monasteries to offer services to the religious establishments. Whatever the reasons for the town's origins, it began to attract peasants seeking respite from the burdens of their old lives. Gradually a law evolved promising freedom for the serf who stayed in the town for a year and a day. In addition to freedom, towns offered more diversity than the countryside. By the late eleventh century, many towns had Jewish residents who settled near one another and near their synagogue. Merchant guilds and craft guilds appeared, offering men and sometimes women the opportunity for commercial profit. As might be expected, hostilities often developed between the peasants and townspeople, and the church might have been wary of the town at first, too. But early Christianity had been an urban phenomenon, and the church proved it could adjust to the changing social setting. No longer were nobles and princes the only ones who could provide generous endowments for buildings and acts of charity: The growing wealth from crafts and business provided new benefactors.

The Meeting of Christians, Muslims, and Jews in Spain, Norman Sicily, and the Holy Land

While the Christian flock was expanding from within, the borders of Christendom were growing, too, with the *Reconquista* in Spain. This heroic era demanded military men, and it catapulted some, like El Cid (Rodrigo Díaz de Vivar, 1043–1099), to fame and glory. The expectation of military expansion provided only a small part of the motive for fighting. For Christian Europe, the Spanish reconquest offered an exhilarating crusade, forerunner of the crusades to Jerusalem. Troubadour lyrics promised a "washing place" nearer than the Holy Land, a battleground where sins were washed clean in the blood of Christian struggle against the infidel.

The Spanish frontier provided the opportunities for social mobility that traditionally accompany a frontier society. Throughout the Islamic occupation, Spain had also enjoyed a long history of tolerance among Mozarabs (Arabized Christians) for their Muslim lords. The Christian liberators, however, brought a zealous hatred for the infidel. With the capture of Toledo in 1085 by Alfonso VI of Castile (1065–1109) and the end of Muslim rule in most of Spain and Portugal by 1200, Mozarabs pleaded for toleration, but to no avail. The invading conquerors transformed the chief mosque of Toledo into a cathedral. Active Cluniac influence led the newly arrived Christians to substitute the Roman rite for the native Mozarabic liturgy, which was condemned. The attitudes of Christian and Muslim hardened.

Indigenous Spanish traditions suffered, but still the Iberian peninsula remained fertile soil for the meeting of Christian, Muslim, and Jewish culture. Islamic intermediaries preserved Greek learning for the Latin west. An important school of translation flourished in Toledo, giving special attention to scientific and mathematical documents. A famous abbot of Cluny, Peter the Venerable, commissioned Spanish scholars to make a Latin translation of the Koran and other Muslim texts. Important contributions also came from Jewish scholars, who knew Latin, Hebrew, and Arabic. Until his family was forced to wander to escape persecution, the greatest commentator on the Torah, Moses Maimonides (1135 or 1138–1204) spent his childhood in Córdoba. The fertility of the cultural mix in Spain, where the three major religions of the medieval west had intimate contact with one another, enriched even European music. Spanish Moors introduced new forms of song and new instruments into western culture.

In southern Italy and Sicily, Normans nourished similar cross-cultural contacts, with similar results. The Norman kingdom of Sicily imitated Byzantium and imported Byzantine artisans to build churches and create mosaics. Sicilian kings ruled and even dressed, not like the dukes of Normandy, but like the Byzantine emperors they aspired to be. Eastern and western Christendom, Judaism, and Islam met in Sicily, and their meeting further expanded the mental and cultural horizons of western Europe and stimulated intellectual awakening, theological development, the rise of universities, and enlightenment. Shipwrecked on Sicily in 1184, a Spanish Muslim named Ibn Jubayr marveled at the varieties of religious expression freely tolerated at the court. He reported that all the pages were Muslims, who prayed to Allah without royal reprisals. When Roger II found his concubines and pages praying to Allah after a frightening earthquake, he allegedly said, "Let each of you pray to the God he adores; he who has faith in his God will feel peace in his heart."[6]

At the end of the eleventh century, a revitalized western Christendom exuded energy and self-confidence. Cluniac and Cistercian reforms had made monasteries the cultural centers of Europe, nurturers of spirituality and rich ceremony, art, and architecture. The moral revival of the papacy had bred a political resurgence that strengthened the church bureaucracy and centralized authority. In 1095 Pope Urban II summoned both his moral and his political authority to call for a crusade to recover Jerusalem from the Turks. Knights and princes, peasants and churchmen mustered to take the cross.

Crusaders to the east found a Byzantine empire weakened by the civil unrest that followed the reign of Basil the Bulgar-Slayer and the subsequent death of Basil's brother, Constantine (1028), who left no male heir. Shattered by internal quarrels, in one year (1071) Byzantium lost Bari, the final outpost in Italy, to the Normans and suffered a more ominous defeat against Seljuk Turks on the eastern frontier. Following their victory at Manzikert, Turks overran Asia Minor, the heartland of Byzantium, and camped across the Bosphorus from Constantinople. A capable military ruler, Alexius Comnenus (1081–1118), finally ascended the throne by coup d'état and methodically began to push the frontier back across Asia Minor. When Alexius requested the aid of western mercenaries, however, he got—against his will—the First Crusade. In battles to restore the Holy Land to Christendom, east and west would meet again, intensifying old hostilities.

---

[6]R. J. C. Broadhurst, trans., *The Travels of Ibn Jubayr* (London: Jonathan Cape, 1952). This work is the chronicle of a medieval Spanish Moor who journeyed to the Egypt of Saladin, the holy cities of Arabia, Baghdad (the city of the caliphs), the Latin kingdom of Jerusalem, and the Norman kingdom of Sicily.

Sarcophagus from the Lateran Palace in Rome, featuring the labarum. (Alinari/Art Resource)

A gold plaque from a sixth-century reliquary, showing Symeon the Stylite on his pillar confronting the devil in the form of a monstrous snake. (Reunion des Musées Nationaux)

Twelfth-century mosaic from Hagia Sophia in Constantinople, with Constantine I (right) presenting his newly consecrated capital to the Virgin Mary and Justinian I offering the great church. (Hirmer Fotoarchiv)

The Good Shepherd, a fifth-century mosaic from the Mausoleum of Galla Placidia in Ravenna. (Alinari/Art Resource)

A mosaic from the church of San Vitale, showing the Emperor Justinian I and members of his court with Maximian, bishop of Ravenna, and churchmen. (Alinari/Art Resource)

Ivory throne from Ravenna, from the sixth century. (Marburg/Art Resource)

A sixth-century mosiac from the church of San Vitale in Ravenna, showing the Empress Theodora and her entourage. (Alinari/Art Resource)

Interior of Hagia Sophia in Constantinople; the large disks are Turkish additions. (Hirmer Fotoarchiv)

Majestic and austere Christ Pantocrator from the dome of the eleventh-century church at Daphni in Greece. (Marburg/Art Resource)

A ninth-century mosaic from Hagia Sophia, showing the enthroned Mother of God and Child. (Courtesy of Dumbarton Oaks Center for Byzantine Studies, Washington, D.C.)

Christ crowning King Roger II of Sicily, from the Martorana Church, Palermo, twelfth century. (Scala/Art Resource)

Chapter 15

The Bloom of the Twelfth Century

The cathedrals of Europe continue to fascinate, awe, and inspire almost everyone who sees them. Students of medieval life and society especially view them as the figurative, as well as the literal, centerpiece of medieval culture. The cathedral symbolizes the identity of the church with the whole of medieval society. The harmonious proportions of length, width, and height; the brilliantly colored windows and the light they allow to play upon the frescos, statues, and carved stonework; the interior space; the graceful lattices of flying buttresses; and, not least of all, the soaring towers—a whole symphony in stone—together symbolize medieval society's aspiration toward the heavenly city.

By the late twelfth century, the storm and stress of western Christendom's pilgrimage from St. Augustine's fifth-century penning of *The City of God* to the age of the cathedrals had abated. The violence and chaos of the first feudal age, with its spasmodic social order, internal cruelties exacerbated by Viking invasions, hardscrabble existence in the great forest wildernesses, and declining population, had sown the seeds for the second feudal age. Medieval life now began to hold its own and even had a quickened pulse. What seem to us simple advances—the balanced and sharp scythe, the horse collar, the iron plowshare and other iron farm implements—spurred agricultural advance and population growth. Water and wind mills, as well as an effective harness for draft animals, relieved some of the strains on human muscles. New building techniques increased the number of masonry structures, such as bridges and buildings with windows. But lest we wax too romantic about the high Middle Ages, recall that as late as the seventeenth century, Thomas Hobbes (1588–1679) described life as "nasty, brutish, and short." Recall also that soap did not come into much use until the twelfth century. Camelot was more smells and garbage than sanitized fairy tale. Kings and nobles traveled from castle to castle not only because, without effective communication systems, they had to appear personally in their lands, but also because they and their retinues used up an area's produce and left piles of refuse.

Most people did not have the luxury of moving on. They lived mainly on cereals and cabbage in small, dark, and damp homes. An open fire for cooking provided some heat in the winter, but mostly it provided smoke that filled the chimneyless huts from the roof down to about head height. Infant mortality was astoundingly high. Most medieval people never had the opportunity to contemplate having a "midlife crisis," because they had fully shouldered adult responsibilities of family and work by the age present-day youth learn to drive. The key to survival was strength. By our standards, most lives were extremely insecure, marginal, impotent, and brief.

The cathedral and the faith it symbolized broke into the threatening space and time of this world of feeble struggle and pointed beyond it to the security and stability of the heavenly city. Medieval humankind, at the mercy of natural and social forces largely beyond its control and understanding, yearned for peace and rest. The great architect of medieval mentality, the north African bishop, St. Augustine (354–430), had already expressed this in his *Confessions:* "You made us for yourself, and our hearts are restless until they rest in you." Augustine had continually hammered home the theme that this world is not our true home and that we are pilgrims on the way to the heavenly city. But the great medieval theme of pilgrimage carried within it seeds of alienation and introspection that easily took root in a harsh world. If this world was at all to be a suitable vehicle for human pilgrimage to the beyond, it would have to be linked to and patterned on the heavenly city. Thus, in ritual, art, architecture, and political and religious thought, people strove to create an image of an eternal world within a world of change.

The Cathedral of the Intellect

One of the most exciting discoveries for the medieval thinker was logic, because it was an instrument for imposing order on a chaotic world. The medieval person perceived nature as a realm of supernatural forces, demonic and otherwise, over which he or she had no control. Politics, economics, law, language, and society itself were similarly disordered and intractable to comprehension. But logic, however little at first, began to open a window to an orderly and systematic view of the world. The whole process of simplification and arrangement of material revealed the powers of the mind and provided a sense of order behind the bewildering complexity of apparently unrelated observations and experiences.

Gerbert of Aurillac (ca. 940–1003), later Pope Sylvester II (999–1003), is reputed to be the first teacher of logic in medieval Europe. Gerbert, a master at the cathedral school in Reims, set forth a substantial part of the logical works of Aristotle and Boethius. From Gerbert through the twelfth century, intellectuals labored to digest Aristotle's logic. By the thirteenth century, Aristotelian logic had become the main feature of undergraduate studies at both Paris and Oxford. The ideal of ordering all knowledge into a coherent whole stimulated the development of universities, comprehensive expositions of knowledge known as *summae*, and a particular method of thinking that came to be known as scholasticism because it developed in the schools.

The incredible blossoming of creative thinking in this period has prompted historians to call it the renaissance of the twelfth century, even though the period included is from about 1050 to 1250. Three men in particular personify the intellectual and cultural ferment of the period: St. Anselm (1033–1109), Peter Abelard (1079–1142), and St. Bernard of Clairvaux (1090–1153). Each in his own way was vitally involved in every aspect of his culture, and all three forcefully put the lie to the modern prejudice that scholasticism was an ivory tower abstraction from "real" life.

St. Anselm

Anselm was born in Aosta, a small town at the foot of the St. Bernard pass on the Italian side of the Alps. Little is known of his family—probably nobility of declining fortune. In his early twenties, Anselm left Aosta and never returned. After some time in southern France, Anselm was drawn to the monastery of Bec in Normandy by the intellectual renown of its prior, Lanfranc. He went to Bec, not to become a monk, but to learn the new disciplines of grammar and logic. His conversion, at the age of twenty-six, to the Benedictine rule (the norm for medieval monasticism, derived from St. Benedict of Nursia in the sixth century) did not at all diminish his questing mind. The last sixteen years of his life were in public and political service as the archbishop of Canterbury, a post he had desperately tried to avoid.

Anselm became archbishop of Canterbury in circumstances beyond his control in every respect. He was visiting England on business for his monastery. His reputation for piety and knowledge was well known. The most secular ruler of England up to that time, William Rufus, had kept the archbishopric open as a means of using its revenues for his own purposes. During Anselm's presence in England, however, William Rufus believed he was mortally ill and that, in light of an impending eternity, it was time to make amends with the church and appoint an archbishop. The bishops and the king's councillors chose Anselm, but he refused. A great scene ensued in the king's chamber, with councillors, friends, bishops, and the king alternately entreating and threatening Anselm to consent. Finally, they thrust the bishop's staff into his hand, but he refused to hold it. Failing to wrench open his hand, they held the staff by force against his closed hand and literally carried him off to the church. The king, by the way, recovered, only to be assassinated a few years later.

Anselm is not remembered because of the unusual story of his entry into the episcopacy, however. Rather, the story is remembered because of Anselm. A thinker and logician of unparalleled power and originality, Anselm is regarded as the "father of scholasticism." He replaced the static mentality and the social holding operations—the "survival mentality"—of previous generations with a rousing search for new avenues and possibilities for understanding and living life. To be sure, peasants in their huts, knights on their chargers, and many of his fellow monks in their cells did not know, or if they did, could not follow, all his logic. But he symbolized a new energy and a new questing that vitalized succeeding generations. This is apparent in his theological program: *fides quaerens intellectum* (faith seeking understanding).

Anselm expressed the quest to know and to understand in arguments for the existence of God and the necessity of the incarnation. But none of his arguments were mere intellectual exercises: "Does God exist?" and, if so, "Does God care for us?" were existential questions in the midst of human suffering and perceived assaults by the devil. Anselm's first effort to prove logically the existence of God, his *Monologion,* failed to satisfy his desire for a logical and aesthetic exposition. Just as theoretical physicists today sense that a theorem remains unrefined and inadequate if it is not aesthetically simple, Anselm desired a simple argument that did not need other proofs for its support. After much prayer and meditation, he was suddenly inspired by what is known as the ontological argument.

Anselm's ontological argument in his *Proslogion* briefly states the conception provided by faith that God "is that than which nothing greater can be conceived." Even the fool (Ps. 14:1) who says that there is no God understands this statement. Thus, what is understood must exist at least in his understanding. But "that than which nothing greater can be conceived" cannot exist merely in understanding, for then it would not be that than which no greater can be thought, for it is greater to exist in fact and not merely in the mind. Hence, that than which no greater can be conceived exists both in the mind and in reality. The subtle simplicity of this argument is that conceptions of God that do not include God's existence are inferior conceptions. Although the argument has often been criticized, it has never ceased to fascinate logicians and philosophers.

Theology also includes biography. Anselm's arguments for the existence of God developed in the context of his meditative life as monk and teacher in the monastery of Bec. He began his famous treatise on why God became incarnate in a person, *Cur deus homo,* just before he went into self-imposed exile in 1097 because he would not consent to William Rufus's exploitation of the church. While in Italy, waiting for papal support, Anselm withdrew to a mountain village to escape the summer heat, and there he finished his treatise.

Becoming archbishop of Canterbury wrenched Anselm out of his meditative monastic environment and thrust him into the political and social world of feudalism. A key concept in the hierarchical feudal society was that an offense is commensurate with the status of the person offended. Thus, an offense by one peasant against another was proportionately magnified if the peasant turned against his lord, a knight, a baron, or the king. To impugn or deprive a person of his or her honor was extremely serious in Anselm's society; it was a fundamental crime against the social order. In feudal language, honor included a person's estate, lands, title, and status.

For feudal society, the absolute head of the social hierarchy was God. If the maintenance of a king's honor was necessary for the preservation of his kingdom, of a baron's honor for his barony, and so on down the social scale, how infinitely much more important for the preservation of the entire social world was the maintenance of God's honor. An offense to the king could be satisfied and his honor restored by a punishment commensurate to the offense. But how could the offense to God caused by human sin be satisfied? Christ.

Anselm's response centered the satisfaction of God's honor within God Himself. For this reason, his theory of the atonement is sometimes called "theocentric." For God merely to forgive the offenses of humankind would diminish His justice and honor and thereby undermine the stability of the universe itself. For God to reclaim His honor by just punishment of humankind's offenses would annihilate humanity and condemn all to eternal punishment. The solution to the maintenance of both God's honor and mercy was for God himself to become a human being and thereby to satisfy the offenses of humankind.

Without venturing into the complicated and controversial issues of the extent to which theological expressions of doctrine both reflect and form the aspirations, fears, and hopes of an era, we can see that some aspects of Anselm's thought appear to express new perspectives for his time. The feudal imagery of his *Cur deus homo* has been noted. The work is also of interest for its omission of a mainstay of the religious thought of prior generations: Satan's legal claim on humankind. Since the famous "cosmocentric" theory of the atonement set forth by Gregory the Great (d. 604), Christian theologians spoke of a constant, mortal struggle to atone for the devil's claim on humankind by heavy penances and abundant alms. The constant conflict and battle within feudal society against the forces of chaos and evil were not limited to the warrior class; those who prayed (i.e., the monks) were understood to be the front line in the struggle for life against death. This religious orientation posited that rigorous monasticism is the preferred path to salvation. Anselm's religion, too, is severe, but it opens the door to a more relaxed and hopeful religion. God Himself has made the offering to Himself that remits all human sins. Redemption is no longer only for the few elite, the spiritual knights of monasticism, but is available for all. This should by no means be mistaken for the heady liberation that came with the sixteenth-century Reformation's proclamation of salvation by grace alone, apart from works. There began, however, a new hopefulness in Anselm's time. And it is probably not an accident that it was then that the practice of indulgence (ecclesial remission of the temporal penalties of sin) arose. As abused and venal as the practice became, it nevertheless expressed the sense that the treasury of grace is available to all.

Abelard

The stormy life and thought of Abelard, so poignantly told in his autobiography, *The Story of My Misfortunes*, expressed the new hope and humanism of the twelfth century. Born in Brittany, the eldest son of a lower noble, Abelard gave up his inheritance to pursue the studies attracting so many of the younger generation. From the beginning, he was recognized as both exceptionally brilliant and extremely difficult to get along with. For example, he irritated his teachers in Paris by setting himself up as a lecturer in competition with them and attracting their students. And he dismissed his renowned teacher, Anselm of Laon, by comparing him to a fruit tree with verdant foliage but no fruit. He also claimed he was irresistible to women, a claim that brings us to the relationship for which Abelard is most famous—or infamous, as the case may be: his affair with Heloise. Her uncle and guardian, Fulbert, a fellow priest with Abelard at the Cathedral of Notre Dame, commissioned him to teach the apparently attractive and intelligent young woman philosophy and Greek. By the time Uncle Fulbert realized that more was being conjugated than Greek verbs, Heloise was pregnant. Fulbert's rage found expression through a gang attack on Abelard, that in Abelard's words, "cut off the parts of my body whereby I had committed the wrong of which they complained."[1] The event also cut short his teaching career at Paris. Following the birth of their son, Heloise became a nun.

---

[1] Betty Radice, trans., *The Letters of Abelard and Heloise* (New York: Penguin Books, 1974), p. 75.

Abelard retired to the monastery of St. Denis in 1119, where he assumed the office of abbot. There he incurred the wrath of ecclesial authorities by his teaching on the Trinity. His opponents condemned him unheard at the Council of Soissons (1121) and forced him to burn his book, which they also condemned. Soon after, he fled the monastery to escape the anger of the monks over his argument that the patron saint of the monastery was not Dionysius the Areopagite, convert of St. Paul (Acts 17).

Abelard next established a small house of prayer outside Paris. Dedicated to the Paraclete (i.e., the Holy Spirit), this place of worship attracted large numbers of students. About 1135, Abelard once again began teaching philosophy and theology in Paris. In the years that followed, he wrote a number of important treatises on Christian theology, ethics, and methodology. St. Bernard's formidable opposition to his theological contributions led to Abelard's second condemnation, in 1141 at the Council of Sens. By now, Abelard had had enough of "misfortunes," and he retired, a sick man, to a monastery under the jurisdiction of Cluny. There he died in 1142. Heloise was buried next to him in the Paraclete cloister on her death in 1164.

Abelard was out of step with contemporaneous authorities. The rest of his age fell into step with him, however, or perhaps he had perceived before others the steps they yearned to take. At any rate, Abelard's life and theology manifested a new understanding of love destined to dominate Western thought until its banalization in Hollywood movies and "true confessions" journalism: romantic love. In fact, it was Heloise who did not want the marriage pushed on her by Abelard. "God knows," she wrote to him later from her nunnery, "I never sought anything in you except yourself; I wanted simply you, nothing of yours. I looked for no marriage-bond, no marriage portion."[2] Heloise shared Abelard's low view of marriage as no more than the legalization of the weakness of the flesh, a view transmitted to their time from early Church Fathers such as Jerome and Augustine. They also shared the "ethic of intention" set forth in Abelard's *Scito te ipsum* (Know Thyself). For Heloise, marriage could add nothing to their relationship, for she believed that it would interfere with Abelard's true calling as a philosopher. She wrote to him: "Wholly guilty though I am, I am also, as you know, wholly innocent. It is not the deed but the intention of the doer which makes the crime, and justice should weigh not what was done but the spirit in which it is done."[3]

It may be suggested that Abelard's experience of the love of Heloise, with its heady joy and love songs, as well as its profound pain and loss, influenced his understanding of the Atonement. For Abelard, the significance of the incarnation shifted from satisfying the claims of either the devil or God to the example and teaching of love manifest in Jesus. Abelard's so-called moral-influence or anthropocentric theory of the Atonement became widely popular in nineteenth-century Protestant liberalism. Abelard's worldly and humanistic inspirations displaced the monastic and feudal inspirations of Anselm's theology. However, the guardians of the old order were not ready for this attention to personal fulfillment.

Abelard and Heloise typify one of the important cultural developments of the period: the discovery of the individual. Although few of their contemporaries were as self-con-

[2] *Ibid.*, p. 113.
[3] *Ibid.*, p. 115.

scious about self-knowledge, there was a flowering of vernacular poetry and song concerned with friendship and romantic love, as well as with religious introspection.

Abelard's most influential contribution, however, was his philosophical and theological method set forth in his *Sic et Non* (Yes and No). A milestone on the road leading away from unexamined reliance on past authorities, *Sic et Non* shifted theology from meditation to a science. Abelard proposed a series of 156 doctrinal questions with quotations from the Fathers of the Church in support of both a "yes" and a "no" to them. He approached contradiction among, and even within, these authorities by a critical methodology for determining the authenticity, reliability, intentionality, and historical context of the text in question. When resolution of contradiction by these means was not possible, the strongest witness with the greatest support was to be preferred. Abelard's strong impulse toward an intellectual systematization of the faith was carried forward by Peter Lombard's (d. 1160) *Four Books of Sentences.* Lombard provided the opinions (*sententiae*) of various authorities on the subject under discussion. Lombard's *Sentences* became the basic instructional text in theological studies for the next few centuries.

The new theological orientation that sought to comprehend all of life by means of intensive rational reflection corresponded to contemporaneous themes of personal responsibility, an ethics of intention, personal and subjective interpretations of doctrine, reason, and centralization attendant on the beginnings of urban and commercial development.

At the same time, contact with Jewish and Islamic culture and thought stimulated an expanding awareness of the world. The scholars of Muslim Spain introduced Christian thinkers to aspects of Aristotelian philosophy that had been lost to the West. The works of Islamic philosophers such as Avicenna (lbn Sina, 980–1037) and Averroës (Ibn-Rushd, 1126–1198), and those of the great Jewish philosopher Maimonides (Moses ben Maimon, 1135–1204), were translated into Latin. Peter the Venerable (ca. 1092–1156), abbot of Cluny, commissioned the Latin translation of the Koran (1141–1143). The classical philosophical writings provided by Arabic and Jewish thinkers stimulated learning and the development of universities in the West. On the other hand, the first Crusade, initiated at Clermont by Pope Urban II in 1095, created a reservoir of mutual antagonism between Christianity and Islam that has lasted until today.

In spite of the great cultural and intellectual contributions to Western culture by Islamic philosophers and scholars, Christians reacted to Islam with profound fear, anxiety, and hatred. To a great extent, this reaction was rooted in the perception that Islam was the first serious challenge to the Christian faith. The early church had explained away the religious challenge of pagan religions and Judaism by claiming that they were forerunners and only partial expressions of the final revelation of God in Jesus Christ. Islam came into existence well after the rise of Christianity, however, and therefore could not be explained away as its forerunner. To medieval Christians, Islam was an even greater scandal, because it incorporated elements of Judaism and Christianity into its faith. Christians, unwilling to give up their claim to superiority over all other religions, thus resorted to attacking Islam militarily and theologically as the incarnation of the devil and all heresies. The purpose of the Latin translation of the Koran was to provide material to refute, rather than to understand, Islam. Unfortunately, the medieval Christian response to Islam has strongly biased Western understanding of Islamic peoples up to the present.

St. Bernard

It is ironic that St. Bernard, who pursued and hounded Abelard with a fervor worthy of later inquisitors, refined, further than did Abelard himself, the introspective conscience that St. Augustine bequeathed to the Western church. Bernard (1090–1153), born to a noble family near Dijon, seemed destined to be a religious giant from his youth. By the age of twenty-two, he persuaded thirty other young noblemen, including his brothers, to join the Benedictine renewal movement that had just recently developed into an order in its own right: the Cistercians (named after its foundation in Cîteaux). The rigor of the Cistercians had already brought the order to the edge of extinction when Bernard's impact so transformed it that the Cistercians also became known as the "Bernardines." Bernard played such a role in the affairs of his time—selecting popes, haranguing kings, preaching crusades, advising clergy, reforming the church, and rooting out heresy—that he has been called "the uncrowned ruler of Europe." However, to his own and subsequent generations, Bernard was known as the "father" and teacher of medieval mysticism. Thus, two centuries later, Dante (1265–1321), in his *Divine Comedy*, has St. Bernard, as the representative of mystic contemplation, lead him in Paradise to the Virgin Mary.

Bernard's emphasis on personal experience, individual conscience, and spirituality did not depart from the love of logic that stimulated the age, but rather reflected a self-conscious and systematic searching of the soul. The resulting self-knowledge and humility before God focused the mystic's goal of finding God in oneself, of ascending to God by descending into oneself. The ascent to God proceeds through logical steps, beginning with self-love and moving through self-knowledge to union with God. Logic investigates the internal movements of the soul and states of mind.

Bernard's tremendous spiritual influence derived not only from the power of his personality and perception, but from the readiness of his age to look inward, a readiness that also informed and received Anselm's emphasis on meditation and Abelard's call to know oneself. The romanticism and humanism of this twelfth-century renaissance were graphically expressed in its changing art. Images of the crucifixion shifted from representations of divine power and majesty to depictions of extreme human suffering. The heroic images of Christ the king, a crowned and royally clothed warrior on the cross with head erect and open eyes expressing power, slowly changed to images of a humiliated, dishonored man, eyes closed, whose head and arms slump under the pain and whose naked body shows his wounds. Likewise, Virgin and Child images changed from the enthroned Byzantine images of *theotokos*, Mary the God-bearer, whose child holds up his right hand in benediction and clasps a symbol of dominion such as an orb or book in his left hand. The new art depicted a mother feeding her child who no longer clasps symbols of authority. Maternal tenderness and infant vulnerability come to the fore. The stage was set for the Christian romance incarnated in St. Francis. Anselm's faith seeking understanding, Abelard's quest for self-knowledge, and Bernard's love seeking spirituality focused, in the person of Francis, on the symbolism of the wandering, homeless beggar. The virtue of poverty was transmuted from the vigor of Benedictine renunciation of pride to the romantic embrace of material impoverishment. The prelude to this story is the transformation of social life in relation to urban and commercial development.

Church and Society

Sociologists of knowledge provide a helpful clue to understanding the church's role in the development of the hierarchical social structure of medieval society. In *The Sacred Canopy*, Peter Berger posits that every human society is involved in an ongoing task of structuring or maintaining a meaningful world for itself.[4] Society strives to shield itself from chaos, formlessness, meaninglessness, and the terror of the void by structuring a meaning that can deal with the marginal situations of life. The Viking, Magyar, and Saracen invasions from without and the knightly raids and brutality within contributed greatly to the natural marginality of medieval life. Faced by the constant possibility of personal and cultural collapse into lawlessness, humankind has perpetually grounded social structures in the cosmos and thereby given ontological status to institutions. Religion provides a cosmic frame of reference with answers to the questions of origin, identity, purpose, meaning, and destiny.

The model of religion as world-building is fruitful for understanding the church's contribution to a political order that derives peace and justice in the world from the sacred and that legitimates and sanctifies social structures through the sacraments and the jurisdiction of the church. Through the agency of its pope, bishops, priests, and monks, the church brings divine order to human society; divine law then finds expression in historical legal codes. From this perspective, the long development from the Middle Ages to contemporary Europe is the struggle to construct a world in the face of the chaos and pressures in the West, beginning with the collapse of the Roman Empire and then the collapse of the Carolingian (from the reign of Charlemagne, d. 814) rule.

Medieval prelates developed the biblical image of the Christian community as a body (e.g., I Cor. 12; Eph. 4; Col. 3) into a metaphor for society, the *corpus Christianum*. Their Latin word *ordo* signified the immutability of human social existence grounded in God's created order. By the tenth century, the concept of social order was refined by dividing it into three orders: workers (*laboratores*), prayers (*oratores*), and warriors (*bellatores*). In France, Bishop Alderberon of Laon dedicated a political poem to King Robert in which he wrote:

> But the city of God, commonly thought to be a single whole, has in reality three Orders: the men who pray, the men who fight and, thirdly, they who work. All three Orders coexist; none can dispense with the others; the services of each enable the others' tasks and each in turn assists the others.[5]

Theologians, politicians, and moralists emphasized the cooperation and harmony among these three orders under the rubric that there can be no order (*ordo*) without the orders. After all, a Godhead believed to be a Trinity sanctioned this social organization. The complementary functions of the social orders (spiritual welfare, defense, and supply and maintenance) assisted all in their earthly life to conform to the divine plan, the ultimate end

---

[4]See Peter Berger, *The Sacred Canopy: Elements of a Sociological Theory of Religion* (Garden City, NY: Doubleday & Company, 1967).

[5]Cited in Georges Duby, *The Making of the Christian West* (Geneva: Editions d'Art Albert Skira, 1967), p. 61.

of which was, in the words of Thomas Aquinas, "the enjoyment of God." On the other hand, it is not difficult to imagine how this "divine" design impressed upon the collective consciousness contributed to a static view of society and to the sanctioning of social inequalities and exploitation: "For the knight and learned clerk live by him who does the work." By the sixteenth century, the fables of Adam and Eve's children, assigned their social status by God on the basis of their beauty and ugliness or goodness and badness, expressed this darker side of the orders of society.

The three orders, sometimes called estates, formed the "feudal" foundation for social relations that lasted, in varying degrees, up to the French Revolution. The term "feudal" is the invention of modern historians to describe a social pattern more complicated than the three orders would suggest. The term itself derives from the Latin *feudum*, meaning a fief: something over which one has rights and control. Nearly all wealth in the agrarian Middle Ages rested on landholdings and their produce. And the granting of a fief by a lord to a vassal was the backbone of the social structure. However, common phrases such as "feudal system," "feudal law," and "feudal custom" are misleading if they are read to mean that the European Middle Ages were uniformly organized everywhere. With this caveat in mind, it is possible to make some observations about the feudal system.

Feudal relationships facilitated cooperation in war. The lord protected his vassals and their lands, and his vassals served in his army. Vassals also provided counsel to the lord when summoned to his court. Swearing fidelity and doing homage expressed the relationship between lord and vassal. In this ceremony, the vassal placed his hands between the lord's hands and swore to be faithful and to carry out the services required of him. Eventually, vassals could fulfill their obligations by substituting money for personal service. The church was fully involved in the feudal system, both in terms of its own fief holdings and lordship, and in the obligations of bishops to provide men and material to their lords, both secular and religious. To avoid such feudal obligations, monasteries sometimes sought exemption from obedience to the local bishop through a direct relationship with the pope. The word "lord" also applied to God; thus, the French *seigneur* was used of the feudal lord and is still used to address God. The posture of prayer with the hands held together that is so common today is a development from the posture of a vassal doing fealty. Portrayals of covenants with the devil used the same posture. By the twelfth century, these ideas of lordship and vassalage also described relationships between men and women. In courtly literature, the man as vassal pledged service to his lady (lord). Hymns to both God and the Virgin Mary also began to use this language.

The Rise of Cities

The hierarchy of the three orders and the language, customs, and relationships of feudalism in which function determined social classification had a place for everyone and everyone for a place—almost! By the twelfth century, a new "class" was arising: the merchants. That feudal structure, society, custom, theology, and ethics had no place for the merchant is epitomized in the dictum of canon law that "a merchant is rarely or never able to please God."

However, feudalism itself provided conditions conducive to the rise of a merchant class. The relative peace and agrarian developments allowed the growth of population, roads, trade, and cities. In turn, the initially itinerant merchants began to congregate around settled places for both protection and the increase of commerce. There is no doubt that the symbiotic development of towns and a new commercial class constituted a social revolution that formed the basis for Europe's gradual transition from a rural, agricultural society to the urban, industrial society we know today.

For the medieval person and community, however, this transition was fraught with anxiety as well as promise. The town exemplified the shift occurring at the time from an exchange economy to a money and profit economy. The development of money as a tool to be used for the creation of more money and goods, rather than just a treasure to be displayed, created changes in every aspect and corner of society. The anxieties accompanying these changes directly related to the impersonalism and moral uncertainty involved in a profit economy.

Impersonalism related directly to the growth of the towns. The quality of interpersonal relationships experienced in the small village, where common tasks and dialect undergirded solidarity and identity, diminished markedly as a town grew in size and the number of specializations increased with a market economy. Anonymity may be heady at first, but the initial euphoria evaporated with the loss of personal and material support. Anonymity was a function not only of the size of towns and cities, but also of the use of money, an impersonal medium of exchange. The rise of both formal education and prostitution in the cities may be related to this anonymous, impersonal medium of money used by youth away from family, home, priest, or village. Since up to half of any given urban population consisted of immigrants from the countryside, personal encounters with urban impersonalism and complexity were widespread. The loosening of social ties and the relaxation of tradition and religion in the cities became a matter of increasing concern.

It took money to live in a city. Yet, the cities grew because they were the places where early capitalism could thrive. That made the cities attractive to outsiders, who hoped to make their fortunes there. But the new money economy was as unsettling as it was attractive. Instead of trading goods crafted or grown by a neighbor, one exchanged money for something from a stranger. And with enough money, anything could be had—privileges, positions, prostitutes, and even penance to make one feel better about whatever had been bought. The combination of the city and money did not make everyone feel better, however: It left many feeling uneasy and guilty. The traditional morality valued humility and attacked pride, and it found idealized expression in the monastic striving for spiritual poverty. Traditional morality was not prepared to cope with the avarice and poverty arising with the growth of cities.

The religious reaction to the new profit economy was twofold: severe judgment of those engaged in urban and financial life, and projection of this judgment, with its attendant guilt and anxiety, on the only available outsiders to the Christian community—the Jews. Already by the twelfth century, avarice had displaced pride in popular perception as the chief vice infecting both society and church. The satirical version of the traditional acclamation "Christ conquers, Christ reigns, Christ rules the world" substituted "money" for "Christ." Artists depicted avarice as a person, usually accompanied by demons, desperately clutching money bags or burdened by the terrible weight of money hanging from the neck or pressed on the back. Writers described merchants as liars who would do anything for gain. Morality tales expressed public as well as ecclesial hostility to usurers. One such tale from Dijon described a usurer's head split open when the stone purse from a statue of a usurer fell on him.

The profound ambivalence toward the new profit economy related not only to the vice of avarice, but also to the fact that a profit economy uses money as an instrument of growth. Throughout the Middle Ages, Christian moralists rejected loaning money at interest (termed "usury"). The "dirty work" of moneylending prohibited to Christians was foisted upon Jews and became an important factor in the complicated story of Christian anti-Jewishness. The consequent pogroms against Jewish communities not only expressed religious bigotry, but also projected Christian anxiety and self-hatred concerning the new use of money onto the Jews. The Jews served as scapegoats for Christian difficulties with the new profit economy.

The Church and Poverty

The rise of cities and a profit economy, along with the aspirations and values they created, collided head-on with the fundamental religious values of the prior millennium. For a thousand years, the church had posited poverty as the favored path to salvation. Jesus succinctly stated that it is harder for a rich person to enter heaven than for a camel to go through the eye of a needle. Clement of Alexandria's (ca. 150–ca. 215) famous sermon titled "How Is the Rich Man to Be Saved?" posed the problem of salvation for the wealthy. Almsgiving to the poor and needy provided the answer. A selection of biblical and early church texts formed an ideology of poverty that had profound social as well as theological significance for the Middle Ages. This ideology served as a cognitive and ethical map for society until the rise of the urban profit economy.

The architect of the theological perspective dominant through the Middle Ages was St. Augustine (354–430). His doctrine of charity became the heart of medieval theology. Charity or love directed to God enjoys God for his own sake and loves self and neighbor for the sake of God. Cupidity, or sin, is love directed away from God with the intent of enjoying oneself at the expense of one's neighbor and God. For Augustine, love not only makes the world go 'round; love sustains the entire cosmos and is the essential ingredient even in sin, which is misdirected love. In Book Fourteen of *The City of God*, Augustine stated: "Two cities have been formed by two loves: the earthly by the love of self, even to the contempt of God; the heavenly by the love of God, even to the contempt of self."

At the risk of oversimplification, the complex theology of Augustine may be thought of diagrammatically in terms of ascent. For Augustine, the hierarchy of being culminates in God, the highest good, being itself. All beings below the eternal, absolute, immutable God are relative, temporal, transient, and incomplete. Augustine graphically expressed this in his metaphor of the traveler. In our journey to our true home, God, we are in danger of enjoying the journey itself and thereby forgetting our destination. The world, in other words, may be used to aid us on the way of love up to God; but it becomes a hindrance if enjoyed, for then our love misdirects us down and away from God to the earth. The earthly city is a foreign land; here we are pilgrims, travelers on our way to the heavenly city, our true homeland. Here is the root of the great medieval themes of pilgrimage, renunciation, alienation, and asceticism. Thus, alienation and order are intimately related in the fundamental theology of the West. And the story of medieval development may be described as the effort to realize, in society, the right relationship between alienation and order.

Love of the earthly city leads to disaffection from the heavenly city, and love of the heavenly city frees one from the earthly city. Here the biblical suspicion of riches (e.g., Mk. 10:25; Mt. 5:3 and 19:24; Lk. 18:25; James 5:1–3) receives systematic theological articulation. Pride and avarice are the major vices; humility and almsgiving the major virtues. Although Augustine modifies Tertullian's (d. ca. 225) claim that God always justifies the poor and damns the rich, he does view poverty as the favored status for the Christian. This precept found its most startling expression in St. Francis of Assisi (1181–1226), whose life was not merely an imitation of the real poor of his time, but rather, his own stylization of this apostolic model.

The monastic movement both interiorized and projected upon society the human condition of pilgrim and wayfarer. The earlier Benedictine rule emphasized stability: The monastic community in ascetic withdrawal from the world provided a glimpse of divine order through its own highly ordered life and liturgy. In response to the social tensions of the early Middle Ages, the monasteries posited that every pilgrim who appeared at the door of the monastery must be received as though he or she were Christ himself. Beyond this hospitality to individuals, the Benedictine effort was oriented to the tension between the powerful and the weak—a predominant phenomenon in pre-urban, agricultural, and feudal society. The major vice was perceived to be pride associated with power and status. The Benedictines, themselves largely from the noble, fighting class, sought protection from the sin of pride through spiritual warfare against worldly power. Their emphasis on voluntary poverty was thus not material, but spiritual in nature. In fact, Benedictine monasteries were frequently comfortable and occasionally magnificent. This was not seen as a contradiction, because their function was prayerful struggle against the violent forces of their age. Knightly violence was ritualized and thus restrained by the monastic liturgy that spiritually sanctioned Christian warfare.

In the eleventh century, economic and social changes began to influence Christian ideals. Avarice rather than pride became the major vice, and thus, material poverty became more highly regarded than spiritual poverty. Mendicant (from the Latin for "begging") movements associated with men such as Waldo and Francis from the new merchant class emphasized the abandonment of material wealth and literal rather than spiritual pilgrimage. As the Benedictines sought protection for themselves and their society from pride, so the mendicants sought protection for themselves and their society from avarice. As the Benedictines sought within a feudal context to develop a moral theology in response to power and violence, so the Franciscans and mendicants sought within an urban context to develop a moral theology in response to the profit economy and to aid townspeople toward a vision of Christian citizenship. The future of the monastic movement belonged to the Franciscan and mendicant movements because, instead of Benedictine withdrawal from the world into monasteries outside the cities, they established themselves in the cities and moved about with the people.

The theological construct of poverty made charity a condition of salvation. Later scholasticism gave this ideology an epigrammatic formulation in the phrase "faith formed by charity." Even before such theological precision, the early church developed a theological and social perspective that included a symbiotic relationship between rich and poor. The second-century writing, "The Shepherd," portrayed the relationship between rich and poor by analogy to the relationship between a vine and an elm tree. The huge elm itself bears no fruit. And the vine, when limited to the ground, bears only poor fruit that is easily crushed underfoot. But when the elm supports the vine, the vine is able to bear rich fruit for both of them. Biblical passages, especially from the popular apocryphal books, Tobit and Sirach, provided support for the redemptive significance of charity.[6] In these passages, almsgiving and charity are presented not only as an investment in heaven, but even as a remedy for sin. Charity delivers from death. Sirach, so esteemed by the Latin church that it came to be known as Ecclesiasticus, provided what must certainly be one of the more memorable passages on the subject of alms: "As water extinguishes a blazing fire: so almsgiving atones for sin" (Sirach 3:30).

The symbiosis of rich and poor expressed in terms of alms and intercessory prayer allowed begging to become a recognized, even religious, form of life in medieval society. From within the perceived immutability of the feudal structure, the powerful ninth-century archbishop of Reims, Hincmar, subscribed to the formula recounted in the *Life of St. Eligius:* "God could have made all persons rich, but he willed that there be poor in the world so that the rich would have an opportunity to atone for their sins."[7] Such perspectives created an obstacle to what we today might consider realistic understandings of poverty and its causes.

Popular Piety

In spite of arising outside the feudal structures of society, the medieval merchant began to carve a niche for himself in the *corpus Christianum* by relating to the existing theology of poverty. The cities and guilds also created space for themselves by direct expressions of community building through sacred oaths and charters ritually commemorated in festive anniversaries. These new expressions of medieval life found sustenance in their understanding of human community originating in Adam and Eve and renewed in Christ. The kinship of the *corpus Christianum* transcended individual genealogies. The theology and piety of sacraments, as well as an ecclesiology that transcended space and time in encompassing the suffering church in purgatory, the militant church on earth, and the triumphant church in heaven, shaped and channeled the Christian family. Because piety (*pietas*) means dutiful conduct toward the family and relatives, as well as toward God and country, the church's sacraments covered the major rites of passage in human life, from birth to death, and related them to the maintenance of the whole society.

The church's intensive interest in the sacraments began very early in its history, even though the number of sacraments was not doctrinally limited to seven (baptism, confirmation, penance, Eucharist, marriage, orders, extreme unction) until the Council of Florence

---

[6]The Apocrypha—"the hidden things"—are those books excluded by the Hebrew Bible, but included by the Greek-speaking Jews in the Septuagint (LXX). The apocryphal books included in the Latin Vulgate were rejected by the Reformers of the sixteenth century.

[7]Michel Mollat, *The Poor in the Middle Ages: An Essay in Social History*, trans. by Arthur Goldhammer (New Haven, CT: Yale University Press, 1986), p. 44.

in 1439. Already in the twelfth century, however, Peter Lombard assumed that there were only seven sacraments. The word "sacrament," from the Latin *sacramentum*, translates the Greek term for "mystery." The Latin term originally meant an oath—in particular, a soldier's oath of allegiance and its accompanying tattoo of identification. Thus, in the early church, the language itself conveyed the sense that the nonrepeatable sacraments (baptism, confirmation, and ordination) impressed an indelible mark on the soul.

Whereas baptism initiated a person into the community, the Eucharist nourished the community as it progressed in its pilgrimage toward the heavenly city. The early church had expressed its understanding of the Eucharist in both realistic and symbolic terms. Sacramental realism could speak of converted Jews drinking the blood of Christ they had once spilled and of communicants eating and drinking the real body and blood of Christ. At the same time, the Eucharist was understood symbolically as the church's perpetuation of the memory of the once-and-for-all sacrifice of Christ. During the Carolingian era, popular piety and crude faith in miracles strengthened and intensified the realistic understanding until it became generally accepted that the bread and wine somehow change into the body and blood of Christ as the result of their consecration by the priest.

There were a number of influences on this development. The contemporary mentality conceived the divine as increasingly transcendent, yet viewed ordinary Christian life as surrounded by myriads of mysteries and miracles. Thus, there was popular pressure to develop the Lord's Supper into the wonder of wonders so that it would not be diminished by comparison with common miracles. The period so emphasized God as the omnipotent, mysterious, arbitrary power, that even the incarnation of God in Jesus was perceived in terms of divine majesty and judgment. The real, human person in Christ faded into the background, and the institutional church was perceived to be the safest means of apprehending God. The growing perception of Christ as the divine judge had a number of ramifications: Contact with God increasingly focused on the point at which the mystery of Christ's incarnation and death was most present and palpable—the Eucharist. Sociologically as well as religiously, the clergy gained power as those who alone could make Christ present in the Eucharist. And hope and reliance increased in those who might be able to mediate between Christ and the community—the saints and Mary.

A series of eucharistic controversies from the ninth to the eleventh centuries led to the supremacy of the realistic view of the Eucharist. The Synod of Rome in 1079 stated that "the bread and wine, which are placed on the altar, through the mystery of the sacred prayer and the words of our Redeemer are substantially changed into the true, proper, and life-giving flesh and blood of our Lord Jesus Christ."[8] Although the doctrine of transubstantiation had not yet developed, the church asserted the real change of bread and wine into Christ's body and blood. The sacrament so awed the laity, that they began to adore the host and withdraw from the cup. The latter practice developed by popular demand because of the great fear of dishonoring the sacrament by spilling the consecrated wine. By the time of Thomas Aquinas (1225–1274), lay communion using only the bread was a widespread practice that found its explanation and legitimation in the doctrine of "concomitance." This doctrine asserted that the whole body and blood of Christ are present in either consecrated

---

[8]Hubert Jedin and John Dolan, eds., *The History of the Church, III: The Church in the Age of Feudalism*, Anslem Biggs, trans. (New York: Crossroad, 1987), p. 468.

element. A decree of the Council of Constance in 1415 officially established the centuries-old desire of popular piety to abstain from the consecrated wine and commune by using only the consecrated bread.

While baptism incorporated a person into the pilgrim community of the church in its process of traveling to its true home with God in the heavenly city, and the Eucharist nourished the pilgrims during their voyage, the danger of shipwreck on earthly delights was omnipresent. In response to this danger, the church offered what medieval theologians called the "second plank after shipwreck": the sacrament of penance. Through this sacrament, the church provided not only the absolution of guilt, but also the means for satisfying the socially disruptive and religiously offensive actions of persons. Although historians have suggested Germanic and feudal roots for the idea of atoning for crimes by rendering satisfaction, the theological basis for penance is also important. The theologians of the early church had conceived of penance as a way of making satisfaction to God, and this concept was incorporated into the understanding of the sacrifice of Christ in Anselm's (d. 1109) *Cur Deus Homo*.

The term "penance" (from the Latin *poena*) means not only punishment, but also compensation, satisfaction, expiation, and penalty. On the basis that the penalty for sin must be satisfied, there developed the doctrine of purgatory and its purifying fire, the pastoral and disciplinary life of the church, and the indulgence system for commuting penitential impositions too severe for completion outside the monastic regimen. Thus, when the austere eleventh-century reformer, Cardinal Peter Damian (1007–1072), imposed a 100-year penance on the Archbishop of Milan for simony, he also indicated how much money would commute each year of penance. Although the intent of the indulgence system was to adjust satisfaction for sins to changing social conditions, by the late Middle Ages it became such an abused instrument for clerical social control and for raising revenue, that it evoked Luther's *Ninety-five Theses* on penance and indulgences and thus contributed to the Protestant Reformation.

By the twelfth century, private penance before a priest consisted of three parts: heartfelt repentance (contrition), oral confession, and satisfactory work. A further development eased the sacrament by making attrition (i.e., fear of punishment) a possibility when contrition was lacking. The Fourth Lateran Council (1215) codified the close connection of penance to the sacramental means of grace—the Mass—and mandated that every Christian had to make a private confession and partake of the Eucharist at least once a year. As a rule, the penitential works were expressed in terms of the triad of almsgiving, fasting, and prayer. Here, once again, may be seen the intimate connection between social conditions, ecclesial social control, and the raising of revenue, as well as the symbiotic relationship between rich and poor.

The sacrament of penance intimately affected the lives of the laity, but the church was unable to move much beyond a monastic and clerical penitential piety. The superiority of clerical life posited by the vows of poverty, celibacy, and obedience did not allow the development of lay piety, but instead imposed upon the laity the piety of the clergy. In the course of the Middle Ages, the originally inspiring piety of the monastic life became an increasingly oppressive subject of criticism.

The burden of individual and collective acts of satisfaction for sin became focused in collective rituals of asceticism. In some cases, these efforts skirted heresy—for example, the penitential bands of men known as flagellants who spread through Italy in 1260 scourging themselves. In other cases, ascetic movements such as the Franciscans and Dominicans became institutional organs of the church. But the collective ritual of ascetic penance par excellence was Lent. Its communal ascetic rigor was such that it spawned a wild collective prelude known as "carnival." The term derives from the *dominica carnevalis*, "farewell to flesh Sunday," that marked the transition to the meatless asceticism of Lent. Carnival consisted of the days or week preceding Shrove Tuesday, the day before Ash Wednesday, which is significantly termed in French, "fat Tuesday," *Mardi Gras.*

The object of carnival was to expose the sins of the community. Carnality, represented as a fat figure carried in procession, was tried, condemned, and executed by fire at the end. The obligatory overindulgence in food and drink is vividly expressed by the dedication of Shrove Tuesday in Nantes to St. Dégobillard—St. Vomit! Sexuality and obscenity were equally on display:

> Prostitutes, whatever their status during the rest of the year, were essential; bears, cocks and other symbols of lechery abounded in the iconography; massive representations of the penis, plain in Naples or disguised as enormous sausages in Königsberg, were carried in procession through the streets. Since the object of the performance was to expose that which was concealed, it was natural that conduct to which shame was attached should be a favorite target for exposure.[9]

Violence and hostility were also displayed, more or less symbolically and more or less anonymously through mask and costume. Even today, one is liable to assaults by rotten eggs and bags of flour in parts of France during Mardi Gras. This was also when the hierarchical and patriarchal culture could be overturned, at least momentarily, and women ruled and beat men. For a fleeting moment, carnival turned the world upside down.

---

[9]John Bossy, *Christianity in the West 1400–1700* (Oxford: Oxford University Press, 1985), p. 43.

Chapter 16

The Harvest of the Medieval Church

The thirteenth century began to harvest the bloom of the twelfth-century church and culture. As the cathedrals were beginning to be topped off by their remarkable spires, the papacy reached the heights of its power and influence, and universities extended the frontiers of human understanding and knowledge. Protest movements also arose, but they in turn stimulated responses such as the Franciscan and Dominican movements, further generators of social, spiritual, and intellectual renewal.

Innocent III and the Zenith of the Papacy

Innocent III (reigned 1198–1216), the ablest of the medieval popes, effectively based his great personal, intellectual, and political abilities on the centuries-long development of papal ideology that began with Constantine's fourth-century recognition of the church as a legal corporate body within the terms of Roman law. That settlement set the stage for the medieval conflict between rulers and the bishops of Rome. Emperors conceived of themselves as divinely ordained rulers of a Christian commonwealth in which the bishops were members. The bishops of Rome, however, understood the state to be coterminous with the church, of which the emperor was a member. To strengthen their position, the bishops appealed to the Petrine basis (Mt. 16:15–19) for the Roman church: "On this rock [Peter] I will build my church."

However, to impress upon the emperor the authority and prestige of St. Peter and his heirs, the Bishop of Rome needed legal documentation. The translation and embellishment of a Greek document, the Epistle of Clement, provided the first step. Purported to be a letter by Pope Clement I written to St. James, brother of Jesus, the letter claimed that St. Peter himself passed his authority on to Clement. The letter traced to Peter both the succession of Roman bishops and the juridical usage of the passage in Matthew 16 regarding the binding and loosing of sins. On this foundation, Leo I, himself a superb jurist, used the Roman law of inheritance to assert that the pope is Peter's heir in regard to his powers, though not to his personal merits. Leo's formula of the pope as "the unworthy heir of St. Peter" expressed the Roman tradition that the heir legally takes the place of the dead person in terms of estate, assets, rights, and duties.

Leo further developed papal primacy by applying the Roman legal term for imperial monarchy to the papacy. He distinguished imperial and papal claims by positing that a unique divine act established the papal monarchy, whereas only historical developments supported imperial monarchy. Pope Gelasius I (reigned 492–496) gave classic formulation to Leo's program. The Gelasian theory, sometimes called "the great charter of the medieval papacy," distinguished sacral power from royal power by use of the Roman distinction between *auctoritas* and *potestas*. The authority of the church was *auctoritas* (legislative), whereas the authority of the emperors was *potestas* (executive). In Roman law, legislative authority was superior to executive authority. Thus, the church as legislative institution gave power to the emperor as executive. The conversion of Clovis (496), the king of the Franks, and the developing relationship between the papacy and the Franks confirmed this political theology.

By the mid-eighth century, the Frankish Merovingian (from Merovech, grandfather of Clovis) dynasty had a reached a low point, and in Italy the Lombards (sixth-century invaders of northern Italy) were making substantial inroads upon the empire. Pope Stephen II (reigned 752–757) used the former situation to resolve the latter. In 754, he arrived in Frankish lands and negotiated with the king, Pepin, whose usurpation of the Merovingian rule the church had legitimated only three years earlier. In return for papal prohibition of the choice of a Frankish king outside the line of Pepin, Pepin agreed to drive the Lombards out of papal territory. At St. Denis in 754, the pope anointed Pepin as patrician (i.e., supreme magistrate) of the Romans.

Pepin fulfilled his part of the bargain by crushing the Lombards and donating the lands to St. Peter (i.e., to the papacy) in a solemn document, the Donation of Pepin, deposited at the tomb of St. Peter. The "documentary" basis for the Donation of Pepin was the Donation of Constantine, which portrayed the conversion of Constantine and legitimated the superiority of Rome over Constantinople, the new capital of the empire. The legend vividly portrays the emperor lying prostrate without imperial garments and emblems before the pope in contrition for his sins. In gratitude for papal absolution, Constantine gives the pope his imperial insignia, the lands of the empire, and the right to create consuls and patricians. The pope then returns the imperial regalia to Constantine and allows him to establish a new seat of government in Byzantium; the pope will keep Italy as a papal patrimony. The story thus accounts for the displacement of Rome by Constantinople as a direct result of papal permission and also for the papal right to make emperors. Pepin's Donation confirmed that of Constantine and manifested Frankish veneration for St. Peter and Peter's successors.

Pepin's son Charlemagne (ruled 768–814) fully lived up to the role of patrician of the Romans. He added more territory to the papal patrimony and came to the defense of Pope Leo III (795–816) when Leo was charged with lechery and perjury by the Roman aristocracy. In 800, Charlemagne went to Rome, where Leo took a solemn vow of innocence of all charges against him. Leo based his oath on the ancient, but hitherto unused, principle that the pope could not be judged by anyone (I Cor. 2:15: "The spiritual man judges all things, but is himself to be judged by no one").

In this context, Leo took the initiative to crown Charlemagne Roman emperor. Leo had worked out this highly orchestrated event partly in collusion with Charlemagne, but also partly to his surprise. Before the celebration of the Christmas mass—held at St. Peter's rather than at the customary Santa Maria Maggiore because of the pope's sensitivity to the Frankish veneration of Peter—Charlemagne had agreed to take the title of emperor. He understood this to mean king over several nations, at best a parity with the emperor in the east. But the coached crowd responded to Leo's crowning with the acclamation, "Emperor of the Romans." With one stroke, Leo extricated the papacy from the east and placed the center of the Christian world in Rome rather than either Constantinople or Aachen, Charlemagne's capital. The Roman empire was now identified with the papal ideology of a Christian empire held together not by ethnic or historic ties, but by the faith enunciated by the church of Rome. The further significance of the papal crowning of an emperor was that the pope could either withhold the crown until a candidate pleased him or take it away if the emperor displeased him. Throughout the Middle Ages, popes more or less successfully exerted this authority over the emperors of the Holy Roman Empire.

The mid-ninth-century collection of doctrines, decretals, and laws—including the Donation of Constantine—known as the Pseudo-Isidorian Decretals further strengthened papal supremacy. This exhaustive collection, a forerunner of canon law, was attributed to Isidore of Seville, a Spanish archbishop contemporary with Gregory I (d. 604). The Pseudo-Isidorian Decretals expressed a papal ideology of supreme judicial authority, limited archiepiscopal rights, clerical freedom from secular control, and the right of clerical appeal to the pope. The collection supplied what the papacy had up to now lacked: laws in the form of decrees allegedly issued by the papacy in the first centuries. The first pope to make effective use of the Decretals was Nicholas I (858–867), who bent Lothair II, king of Lorraine, to his will by threat of excommunication. Nicholas also used this threat to depose archbishops and the patriarch of Constantinople.

Following Nicholas, a succession of weak and corrupt popes made the church increasingly dependent on secular powers. The subsequent renewal movement in the church came to be called the Gregorian reform, after one of its leading exponents, Hildebrand (ca. 1021–1085), who became Pope Gregory VII in 1073. Gregory proceeded with vigor against immorality and lay interference in ecclesial appointments (the investiture struggle). His most famous stand was against Emperor Henry IV, who finally submitted to the pope in 1077 at Canossa.

Gregory's theoretical contribution to the concept of papal monarchy rested on his knowledge of the Pseudo-Isidorian Decretals and his ecclesial administrative experience prior to being elected pope. He declared the universal monarchy of the papacy in his famed *Dictates*, a summary of papal rights. These rights included claims to absolute power over the church and the secular world, as well as the assertion that "the Roman church has never erred and will never err." In both theory and praxis, Gregory exceeded the prior ideology of papal supremacy. He moved beyond the power to bind and loose sins to the power to depose rulers; he connected the power to open and close the gates of heaven to the right to judge on earth.

Innocent III also believed that the whole world is the province of the pope and that Christ had commissioned Peter to govern not only the universal church, but also the secular world. A gifted lawyer, administrator, and leader, Innocent expressed his conviction that the church was superior to the empire by his image of the monarchy being related to the papacy as the moon is to the sun. The first to employ the title Vicar of Christ, Innocent III proceeded to actualize his vision of a centralized Christian society under papal jurisdiction.

Innocent levied the first general income tax on European churchmen to provide for papal diplomatic and military ventures. The death of Emperor Henry VI in 1197 and the consequent struggle for the throne between rival claimants gave Innocent the opportunity to intervene and arbitrate among them. In his bull (a papal edict so-called because of the lead papal seal, *bulla*, attached to it) *Venerabilem*, he claimed that, although an emperor is elected by the imperial electors, the appointment of the emperor comes within the sphere of papal authority *principaliter* (principally) and *finaliter* (finally)—*principaliter* because the translation of the empire from the Greeks to the Romans was due to the pope, and *finaliter* because the blessing, coronation, and investiture of the emperor came from the pope. Innocent allowed the German feud over the election to continue for three years in order to deplete the power of the German crown. Then, in 1200, he decided in favor of Otto IV. Otto in turn recognized the boundaries of the papal states, surrendered the remnants of royal authority over the German church, and promised not to intervene in Italy.

However, once he felt secure, Otto again took up the perennial policy of the German kings to claim Italy for himself as patrician of the Romans. In turn, Innocent recognized the only son of Henry VI, Frederick II, as Otto's replacement. He then organized a great coalition of the papacy, Frederick II, and Philip Augustus of France against Otto and his ally, King John of England. This is the first great example of the clash of international alliances in European history. Otto was crushed at the battle of Bouvines in 1214.

Innocent paralleled his triumph in the "imperial business" with the English and French kings. In a dispute concerning traditional English royal authority over the church, Innocent forced King John to accept the papal appointee to the see of Canterbury and to become his vassal, thus making England a fief of the papacy. One of the interesting sidelights of this story is that John accepted Innocent's conditions in 1213 because he was unsure of the support of his barons. When, in 1215, these rebel barons compelled John to issue the *Magna carta libertatum*, which restricted the crown's feudal and sovereign rights, Innocent stood by the king and declared the *Magna carta* null and void.

Innocent also placed France under interdict (cessation of the administration of the sacraments), to compel its king, Philip Augustus, to be reconciled with his wife, Ingeborg of Denmark. In general, however, Innocent's reign benefited Philip's monarchy by, among other things, allowing Philip to cloak his expansionist policy in the south of France in the dubious morality of a crusade against heretics. The occasion for this crusade was Innocent's effort to win the hearts and minds of the heretical communities in southern France known as the Albigenses or Cathari. Missions by outstanding preachers to these communities had little effect, and when a papal legate was murdered in 1208, a crusade was launched against the heretics.

The shift of the crusading mentality from infidels to heretics was facilitated by the capture and sack of Constantinople during the Fourth Crusade. This sorry spectacle of "holy war" of Christian against Christian poisoned relations between east and west for generations to come. But if a crusade could turn against Christian allies, then certainly it could be directed against heretics, the cancer within that threatened not only the unity, but the faith, of Christendom.

The French barons responded enthusiastically to Innocent's preaching of a crusade against the Albigenses. The consequence was a great bloodbath and land grab. The battle of Muret (1213) broke the resistance of the southern nobility, and by the 1220s the French crown assimilated the wealthy Languedoc lands of southern France. Because the papacy did not trust the local officials in southern France to purge the remnants of heresy, Innocent sent papal legates to establish courts to deal with the heretics. The Inquisition (ecclesial courts for the discovery and punishment of heresy), officially established in 1233, developed in this context.

Although Innocent reorganized the church, humiliated kings, and took up the sword against heretics, he also realized the importance of law and piety for the well-being of Christendom. He commissioned a collection of canon law that was the first since Gratian's *Decretum* (ca. 1140). Completed in 1210, it was sent to the University of Bologna to be the authentic text for teaching. Innocent recognized the value of piety in the religious movements of Dominic (the Dominicans) and Francis (the Franciscans) for the renewal and reform of the church. The institutionalization of asceticism through papal approval of these orders was a major factor in the development of the thought, religion, and culture of the centuries that followed. Finally, his summoning the Fourth Lateran Council in 1215 established one of the most important conciliar meetings between those of Nicaea (325) and Trent (1545–1563). The council set the number of sacraments at the seven still recognized; made transubstantiation the orthodox doctrinal teaching on the eucharist; limited confirmation and ordination to bishops; mandated at least annual penance and communion; legislated moral and educational reform; placed limits on the cult of relics and pilgrimages; and prohibited Jews from appearing among Christians during Holy Week and mandated their wearing of yellow identification badges.

Tares among the Wheat: Heretical and Protest Movements

Compared to his predecessors, Innocent alone realized in practice the papal ideology that had developed up to his time. More than any other pope before him, he focused the power and wealth of the church on the goal of a centralized Christian society. It may be, however, that his very success added to the growing unease and anxiety of some elements of this society, who wondered how the wealth and power of the church correlated with its Lord, who had said, "My kingdom is not of this world." More and more people listened to preachers who identified the apostolic life with actual poverty. These preachers often were associated with such radical poverty movements as the Humiliati, the Waldenses, the Beguines, and the Cathars.

The Humiliati originated in Milan and spread to other cities of Lombardy in the late twelfth and early thirteenth centuries. They recruited members from the monied, favored class, who then embraced the apostolic life of poverty. They exercised poverty in moderation, but also in explicit opposition to the new lifestyle of well-being around them. They opposed ostentation and every form of what they perceived to be avarice and greed, prohibited every kind of usury and interest taking, and distributed their surplus income to the needy.

The Waldenses originated with the religious conversion of Peter Waldo (Valdez), a wealthy merchant of Lyons, who embraced apostolic poverty. These "poor men of Lyons" spread quickly throughout southern France, northern Italy, the Rhineland, and southern Germany. Valdez himself, some time around 1173, was moved by the story of St. Alexis (a favorite medieval tale about a fifth-century wealthy Roman who gave up everything for a life of mendicancy and almsgiving) and by Jesus' counsel for perfection in Matthew 19:21 ("sell all you own, give the proceeds to the poor, and follow me"). Valdez then provided for his wife, placed his daughters in an abbey, distributed his wealth, and became an itinerant and mendicant preacher. His followers produced vernacular translations of parts of the Bible for preaching purposes, embraced voluntary poverty, and sought ecclesial recognition at the Third Lateran Council in 1179. The papacy granted them preaching rights only on condition of local clerical approval. Such approval was not forthcoming, but the Waldenses preached anyway and thus were excommunicated in 1184. They then organized themselves apart from the church, appointed their own ministers, and developed a theology and piety at variance with the church, including Donatist tendencies (the doctrine that the validity of the sacraments depend on the worthiness of the minister). Viciously persecuted through the centuries, they survived to become what is today the Waldensian Church.

The Beguines were a movement of pious women active in the cities of the Low Countries, the Rhineland, and northern France. They led a semireligious communal life and actively served the sick and needy. Their male counterparts, the Beghards, were mainly from the cloth industry, in which they worked as weavers, dyers, or fullers. The Beguines did not reject private property, but the Beghards did, while maintaining a common purse to support their activities. Their names supposedly derived from that of Lambert le Bègue, a revivalist preacher at Liège. Their social doctrines, religious mysticism, and especially their sympathy toward the Spiritual Franciscans led to their condemnation by the Council of Vienna in 1311.

The most notorious of all these groups were the Cathars (from *katharos*, meaning "pure"), or Albigenses (after the town of Albi), whose opponents associated them with the ancient heresies of dualism and Manichaeanism. Their origins are obscure. The church regarded them as a major threat, both for their heretical theology and for the austerity of their lives. The group gained adherents because of its sharp contrast with the lax clerical life of the time. The theology of the Albigenses seems to have been strongly dualistic, positing the evil of the physical world, which caused them to embrace extreme asceticism. The Albigenses believed that they, not the church, truly followed Christ. They believed that they were the true *pauperes Christi*—the true imitators of the apostolic life—because they did not possess houses, land, or any personal possessions, just as Christ and his disciples had nothing. They charged that the Catholic clergy sought only things of this world, and that even the most high-minded clergy were fallen because individual poverty practiced within a wealthy corporation was no poverty at all.

Successive councils in 1165, 1184, and 1215 condemned the Albigenses. After Innocent III's unsuccessful attempt to convert them, a crusade was mounted against them, and in 1233 Gregory IX charged the Dominican inquisition with their final extirpation. They had largely disappeared by the end of the fourteenth century.

Why did peasants, workers, merchants, and nobles, including women, join the Albigenses? The poor may have sensed the chance to exchange their corrupting and distressing involuntary poverty for a morally and spiritually sanctioned voluntary poverty. Women, whether prostitutes or noblewomen, may have seen an offer of equality that the patriarchal and priestly Roman church could not make. For others, there may just have been the comfort of an ultimate spiritual security. It seems that economic insecurity and social friction contributed to religious heterodoxy: the unorganized and unprotected poor flocked to the antichurch of the Albigenses. The more successful participants in the new commercial society, both businessmen and usurers, tended to remain faithful to the traditional church.

Weeders before the Harvest: Franciscans and Dominicans

Francis (ca. 1181–1226) and Dominic (1170–1221) responded in innovative ways to the social crises that stimulated the rise and attraction of various heretical movements. The social construction of reality to which the early medieval church had contributed so much now showed ever more dangerous signs of stress. Theology had worked to legitimate and reflect a culture based on a patrimonial peasant economy that was almost totally agricultural. The population had remained fairly stable, with kinship and social communities the norms for personal relationships. Gender, age, and hierarchical position indicated and prescribed social roles. Church and state were closely related, and even in their antagonisms, shared the vision of a Christian commonwealth. The center of the system was the king, who controlled the mobility of his subjects and preserved balanced relations with the church. The latter provided the ideology for the king's role by pronouncing and affirming the values of stability, tradition, and order in the doctrine of the three estates or orders (workers, prayers, and warriors, as discussed earlier). The monastery itself incarnated the ideal of *stabilitas*. Theology and ritual maintained the equilibrium between the earthly and heavenly cities through the sacrifice and penance of the people and by the proxy of monks and priests.

The social changes that accompanied the growth of population, the development of technology, urban growth, and the profit economy were in kind as well as degree. Personal roles as businessman, citizen, and worker became increasingly differentiated, and the keynote of life shifted from cooperation to competition. An increasing number of people needed to prove themselves rather than play assigned roles. New social experiences exposed them to situations for which their religion offered no meaningful patterns. Their disorientation was not merely material suffering, but a sort of cognitive dissonance; that is, it became increasingly difficult to coordinate personal and social experience with the teachings of the church. That is why the newly rich, such as Valdez and Francis, suffered disorientation as much as the poor did. Mobility in any dimension—horizontally in space or vertically in a social hierarchy—raises new problems for the displaced person. Such significant changes called into question the religious construct of society. Religious authorities faced adaptation or obsolescence.

The urban, economic development then led to social experiences for which the church provided no meaningful patterning. What relevance had a religion of stability to a life of mobility, competition, and uncertainty? If God is the reinforcer of social order and conformity and of the unity of religious and political structures, then what happens to those who fall between the cracks of the new social realities? How can God have any regard for the marginal person who is in physical and social transition?

The church's response to these issues tended to reaffirm traditional practices such as the piety of pilgrimage, building churches, monastic patronage, eucharistic ritual, and indulgences. Furthermore, the Cluniac and Gregorian renewal movements intended to purify, not change, the church and its theology.

In contrast, the heretical movements raised a crucial note of disobedience in the promulgation of their new apostolic lifestyle. A renewed search for community and for identification with the divine through personal commitment to asceticism sought to resolve the crisis. Both Francis and Dominic incorporated contemporary concerns into their commitment to apostolic poverty as the means of a new communion with God. In contrast to the Benedictine monasteries of the earlier Middle Ages, which spurned towns as iniquitous, the mendicant orders of the Dominicans and Franciscans rooted themselves in the centers of urban development. The Benedictine movements had emphasized humility, obedience, and stability; poverty to them was understood in terms of poverty of the spirit. The mendicant orders, as their name indicates, lived by begging and emphasized material poverty. As a consequence of their desire to imitate the early church and the wandering, preaching, poor Christ, they understood their place to be in the cities and towns. Their effectiveness rested on the fact that they displaced the older monastic ideal of rural stability by urban itinerancy; they were able to go to where distressed people longed for their message of the life and poverty of Jesus.

The Dominicans, or Order of Preachers, were founded by the Spanish priest, Dominic Guzmán (1170–1221). His inspiration to found an order of itinerant preachers derived from his accidental confrontation with the Albigensian movement. In 1203, Dominic accompanied his bishop on a royal mission to Scandinavia to arrange a marriage for the king's son. On the way they stayed in Toulouse, where Dominic engaged the Albigensian innkeeper in a nightlong religious conversation and converted him back to the Catholic faith. The experience made Dominic aware of both the prevalence of the Albigensian heresy and the need for persuasive preaching to counteract it. Dominic perceived that it would be possible to preach true doctrine with credibility only by equaling the ascetic austerity of the heretics. Thus began a new style of Catholic evangelizing that embraced voluntary and absolute poverty as a means of promoting an itinerant preaching mission. The difference between Dominic and his contemporary, Francis of Assisi, is that Dominic embraced poverty as a tactic to get a hearing, whereas Francis embraced poverty as an end in itself.

Dominic's years of preaching in southern France bore little fruit because, in the meantime, the pope decided to restore order and true religion by means of a crusade rather than preaching. In 1215 Dominic went to Toulouse, where he received the support of the bishop and also attracted followers. In 1216, Pope Honorius III officially recognized Dominic and his followers as an order according to the Rule of St. Augustine, which was more flexible than the Benedictine Rule. In the next few years Dominic traveled tirelessly, establishing friaries (from *frater*, brother) and organizing the order. He urged his preachers to live entirely by alms in their own communities as well as on the road; everywhere, the gospel was to be preached in itinerant poverty. Furthermore, by example and by argument, he insisted that the order always remain flexible so that it could respond to needs as they arose. In 1220 Dominic set out to preach to the pagans in Hungary, but fell ill and, on his return to Bologna, died.

Dominic's original impetus to preach the Gospel to the Albigensians convinced him of the necessity for a learned ministry. The establishment in Dominic's own lifetime of his order in the intellectual centers of Paris and Bologna was significant for his goal of academic discipline to support preaching. The intellectual focus of the Dominicans (by 1228, three years of theological study were required for permission to preach publicly) formed outstanding scholars, such as Albertus Magnus (ca. 1200–1280) and Thomas Aquinas (ca. 1225–1274), and led to the papal appointment of the Dominicans as inquisitors in 1232.

The most radical exponent of the new evangelical piety of the twelfth and thirteenth centuries was Francis of Assisi (ca. 1182–1226). More than any other individual of his time, and perhaps since, Francis lived out the ideal of "naked, following the naked Christ" (*nudus nudum Christum sequi*) and "poor, following the poor Christ" (*pauper pauperum Christum sequi*). These twelfth-century formulas, adapted from ancient tradition, associated the individual Christian with Christ in a common nakedness, or poverty, of both worldy goods and worldly cares.

Francis vividly enacted this ideal when, nearly twenty-five years of age, he stood before his angry father and the bishop's court of Assisi and stripped himself naked, gave his clothes to his father, and declared that from now on he would speak only of his Father in heaven.

Whereas for Dominic, poverty was a means for credible preaching, for Francis, poverty was the goal and expression of the imitation of Christ. Francis's emphasis on a life of the utmost poverty confounded not only his merchant father, but others as well. Francis rejected the new merchant world of profits and accumulation of wealth—the world of his father—as something so corrupt that he henceforth refused even to touch money, which he regarded as excrement. He urged his followers to flee money as if it were the devil. The Rule of St. Francis, established in 1223, strictly commanded all friars "never to receive coin or money, for themselves or for any other person." The thirteenth-century *The Mirror of Perfection* recounts how Francis commanded a friar who had absentmindedly touched money to pick up the coin with his mouth and to place it with his mouth upon a pile of dung.

Although this attitude toward money would at first seem unlikely to enhance the recruitment process, it nevertheless worked wonders. Whether Francis touched some deep emotional springs of piety or the nerves and anxieties of the urban, profit-oriented society, his ideal of nakedly following the naked Christ stimulated a remarkable response from his contemporaries. Francis soon became the reluctant head of an organization that, in perceiving the whole world as its parish, grew by the early fourteenth century to encompass all Europe, with numbers reaching perhaps as high as 28,000. Francis also established a female branch known as the Poor Clares, after Clare of Assisi, the first woman converted to the poverty ideal by Francis. For those unable to embrace the full rigor of Franciscan poverty, a third order was established that permitted remaining in secular life while practicing certain elements of the ideal.

Why were Francis and his mendicant order so appealing? Certainly, the medieval person was deeply concerned about achieving salvation and was also concerned that, since the early church, poverty had been presented as the preferred path to Christ. The Franciscans showed that this path could have an orthodox expression. Francis himself reputedly received the stigmata, the very wounds of Christ, the highest expression of medieval piety. However, other motives may be surmised as well. Rebellion against fathers and the rejection of social respectability were not limited to Francis (nor to his age!). The fact that well-to-do families supported the friars, but were horrified by the prospect of their children joining them, may have imbued the poverty of the friars with the appeal of high romance. And for the intellectuals and aspiring teachers of the time, the friars, both Dominican and Franciscan, offered an escape from the heavy debts and obligations incurred even then by a university education, as well as escape from the rat race for promotions and financial support. The desire of scholars to live and work in a university community dovetailed nicely with the needs of friars to educate their new recruits.

Dominican and Franciscan scholars addressed the social and ethical problems confronting urban life. They legitimated private property as necessary and good for the development of an ordered state. They applied their new moral theology to economics and developed a theory of just price in relation to supply and demand, and they conceived of money as a rational medium of exchange rather than a seductive evil. These contributions, as well as their work on business ethics in general, made it possible for the urban Christian, previously marginalized by feudal social mores and religion, to be reintegrated into Christian society. Furthermore, as mendicant orders, the Dominican, and Franciscans provided merchants with a meritorious subject for philanthropy. They provided not only a key to the justification of profits, but also an honorable and much preferred option to the penance and opprobrium that earlier had accrued to businesspersons.

The mendicant friars supplied city dwellers not only with a new ethic and an outlet for charity, but also with an urban ideology that explicitly recognized and praised the city as an integral part of the well-ordered society. Their urban ideology was then crowned by the creation of not only urban, but merchant saints, and thus "marked the coming of age of Europe's commercial economy." The great despiser of money, Francis of Assisi himself became such an urban merchant saint. In the 1260s, in one of his annual sermons to his city, the archbishop of Pisa, Federigo Visconti, exclaimed: "How pleasing it must be for merchants to know that one of their cohorts, St. Francis, was a merchant and also was made a saint in our time. Oh, how much good hope there must be for merchants, who have such a merchant intermediary with God."[1]

The Rise of the Universities

Universities developed symbiotically with the urban and mendicant developments. Earlier organized studies depended on the monasteries and cathedral schools, reflecting their everyday tasks of calculating liturgical calendars; composing books on the lives of the saints,

---

[1] Lester K. Little, *Religious Poverty and the Profit Economy in Medieval Europe* (Ithaca, NY: Cornell University Press, 1978), pp. 213–217.

hymns, and lectionaries; and ongoing computing and corresponding with individuals regarding rents, crops, and lands. The foundational studies for the development of a "free man"—the seven liberal arts—had long been established. Alongside the development of the professional curricula of theology, medicine, and law in the universities, the arts faculty continued to emphasize the *trivium* (grammar, dialectic, and rhetoric) and the *quadrivium* (arithmetic, music, geometry, and astronomy). We have already mentioned the excitement generated by the discovery and use of logic and its impetus to early scholasticism. By the twelfth century, there was growing enthusiasm for ordering knowledge into a coherent whole—a *summa*. In theology, the great example is Peter Lombard's *Four Books of Sentences*, endorsed by the Fourth Lateran Council in 1215. This work became the leading theological textbook until it was replaced by the *Summa theologica* of Thomas Aquinas in the sixteenth century. Lombard's contemporary, Gratian, working in Bologna, initiated the science of canon law with his *Decretum* (ca. 1139), which sought to harmonize the legal resources of the time. Gratian's "Concordance of Discordant Canons" (*Concordantia Discordantium Canonum*) dealt with nearly 4,000 texts and with conciliar and papal decrees. The advances in the study of theology and law symbolized by works of Aquinas and Gratian began to attract students from all parts of Europe to those places—initially, Bologna and Paris—where these subjects had the best known teachers (Figure 16.1).

The cities not only were conducive to the development of universities, but also strove to attract them. Scholars not only provided an appealing aura to a town; they also provided technical know-how and advice for merchants and a pool of servants for government and the church. The cities provided a freedom of life and intellect not possible in the rural monastic schools. Cities offered living possibilities for the increasingly large numbers of teachers and students flocking around renowned masters. And the urban social arrangements of charters and guilds provided models for the first university corporations. Indeed, the word *universitas* can mean "corporation" or "guild." Thus, for their mutual support and protection, students formed corporations (student unions) and were granted monopolies by the city government similar to those of other guilds. Teachers later followed their example. A student who completed a satisfactory apprenticeship to a teacher received a certificate of membership in the guild of teachers (i.e., became a "master"); hence the degree system.

The Discovery of Aristotle

The core of the new ideas in the Latin West in the thirteenth century flowed from the discovery of the complete writings of Aristotle. Renewed contact with Aristotle's philosophy occurred in Syria, Constantinople, Sicily, and, above all, Spain. In all these areas, the mixed population of Christians, Muslims, and Jews stimulated intellectual exchange. Toledo exemplified these developments as the leading center for the translation of ancient Greek writings into Latin. This was a sensational event, because the full body of Aristotle's philosophy had implications for every facet of medieval life, from esthetics to politics to theology. For example, the traditional ecclesial claim of superiority over the secular world based on the Augustinian view of the state as a consequence of sin was challenged by the Aristotelian view of the state as a positive and creative force. Not surprisingly, rulers wanted to hear more about this. In the realms of philosophy and theology, Aristotelian thought

Figure 16.1   European Universities (12th–16th centuries)

brought new challenges to everything from epistemology to sacramental theology. In short, Aristotle—whose influence was so great that it became commonplace to refer to him simply as "The Philosopher"—affected nearly everthing people thought and experienced about God, the world, and humankind.

Once again, the mendicant friars contributed excitement and innovation, in this case to the universities. The Dominicans and Franciscans, with their vision of the world as their parish and of education as the tool for its conversion, unleashed an intellectual energy that transformed universities from trade schools for clerks into centers of intellectual ferment and creativity. Such intellectual giants as Albertus Magnus (ca. 1200–1280), Thomas Aquinas (ca. 1225–1274), and Meister Eckhard (ca. 1260–1327) among the Dominicans and Bonaventure (ca. 1217–1274), Duns Scotus (ca. 1265–1308), and William of Ockham (ca. 1285–1347) among the Franciscans made theology the "queen of the sciences."

Thomas Aquinas and the Cathedral of Intellect

Thomas Aquinas has long been regarded as one of the most brilliant and clearest thinkers of the Middle Ages—indeed, even of Western Christianity in general. The range of his thought and the phenomenal synthesis he achieved in relating reason to revelation give his architectonic system an esthetic quality. "St. Thomas's thought has often been likened to a Gothic cathedral, and at the risk of banality, their common sweep and proportion, balance and harmony, may be reiterated."[2]

And yet Thomas was no disembodied intellect. By all accounts, he was of massive physical proportions, although the story that a semicircle had to be cut out of the table to accommodate his girth is only legend. It was undoubtedly his stature, along with his quiet and gentle nature, that led his fellow students to dub him "the dumb ox." His teacher, Albert the Great, was far more perceptive than Thomas's fellow students when he told the class, "You call him a Dumb Ox; I tell you this Dumb Ox shall bellow so loud that his bellowings will fill the world."[3]

Albert was right, although Thomas's "bellows" would be measured not in decibels, but in a sort of Richter scale of conceptual intensity. One occasion when both occurred was during a great court dinner given by King Louis IX (St. Louis, 1214–1270). Attending the dinner out of respect for the authority of the king and the command of his Dominican superiors, Thomas soon became absorbed in his own theological reflections in the midst of the glitter and hubbub of the royal dinner. Suddenly, during a lull in the conversation, goblets and plates jumped and crashed in response to Thomas's huge fist smashing down on the table, accompanied by his bellow, "And *that* will settle the Manichees!" King Louis's response was to send two of his secretaries to Thomas's place to take notes of his refutation of the heretical community Dominic had set out to convert by theological argument a generation earlier.[4]

---

[2] Gordon Leff, *Medieval Thought: St. Augustine to Ockham* (Baltimore: Penguin Books, 1965), p. 213.
[3] G. K. Chesterton, *Saint Thomas Aquinas* (Garden City, NY: Image Books, 1956), p. 71.
[4] *Ibid.*, pp. 97–101.

Thomas was born into the great feudal family of Count Landulf of Aquino, who was related to the emperor and to the king of France. As befitted his family's position and prestige, Thomas was sent at the ripe old age of five to the famous Benedictine monastery of Monte Cassino, where he was to be trained to become its abbot. The conflict between the pope and the emperor, Frederick II, on whose side the Aquinos were aligned, prompted the father to move his son to Naples for the study of the liberal arts in the Studium Generale founded by the emperor. As a teenager, however, Thomas decided to enter the newly formed begging order of the Dominicans. His father and warrior brothers were furious that Thomas would turn away from a respectable ecclesial career customary for the younger sons of nobility. No doubt, the family concern was not just for what they perceived to be an immature decision by Thomas, but also for their good name, which they did not want to see connected with ecclesial riffraff. The family response was as straightforward as it was feudal: They imprisoned him in the family castle for fifteen months. As if this were not enough, his brothers attempted either to dissuade him from his decision or to render it impossible by scandal. This they did by putting a courtesan in his room. The story is that Thomas sprang up, snatched a burning log from the fire, and chased the poor woman out of the room, slamming and barring the door after her and burning a huge black cross into the door with the blazing brand.

Thomas's determination to become a Dominican did not weaken, and he joined the order in April 1244. He studied with St. Albertus Magnus (Albert the Great) at both Paris and Cologne. Albert introduced Thomas to the newly discovered philosophy of Aristotle. In 1252, Thomas returned to Paris to become lecturer at the Dominican convent of St. Jacques. In 1259, he lectured in various Italian cities, until he was recalled to Paris in 1269. Soon on the move again, he went to Naples in 1272 to set up a Dominican school. He died in 1274 at the Cistercian monastery of Fossanuova on his way to the Council of Lyons. The archbishops of Paris and Canterbury condemned several of his propositions in 1277, but in 1278 the General Chapter of the Dominicans endorsed his teaching. He was canonized in 1323 and declared a Doctor of the Church (i.e., official teacher) by Pope Pius V (a Dominican) in 1567. In 1879, Leo XIII's encyclical *Aeterni Patris* made Thomas's works mandatory for all students of theology. In 1923, on the sixth centenary of Thomas's canonization, Pope Pius XI reiterated his teaching authority.

Thomas was and continues to be so influential in the life and thought of the church not only because he addressed the crisis of intellectual faith of his time clearly and forcefully, but also because he did so in a way that opened faith to dialogue with philosophy, revelation with empirical reason, and religion with science. Thomas slaked his contemporaries' great thirst for reality without giving in to their influential cries that one could drink at only the bar of reason or only the bar of faith, but not both. For Thomas, there is only one truth, not two mutually exclusive truths. He expressed this conviction in his watchword that grace does not destroy nature, but fulfills it; that is, there is a continuity between reason and revelation.

Like Anselm before him, Thomas also began from the position of faith seeking understanding. Both insisted on the importance of reason. But whereas Anselm developed the rational necessity of concepts already given by revelation, Thomas thought there are truths, such as the existence of God, that can be developed by applying reason to the data provided by sense experience. Thomas began with what is and reflected on what that means for faith.

And for Thomas, what *is* in reality is not first in the mind, but rather, what is in the mind first *exists* in reality.

On this basis, Thomas regarded Anselm's ontological argument as invalid and put in its place rational proofs for the existence of God that began with an examination of God's nature. Thomas's arguments for the existence of God are heavily indebted to Aristotelian philosophy, especially the relationship between effects and their causes. Everything that exists has a cause, except the cause behind the series of causes. Aristotelian reasoning enabled Thomas to conclude that there is a first unmoved mover: God. That God is a personal Trinity is, however, not a knowledge achievable by reason, but granted by revelation. Here, again, revelation does not destroy reason, but fulfills it.

Thomas applied his conviction of the continuity of nature and grace, and the natural and the supernatural, to all areas of life. Here we can only sketch how this continuity influenced his understanding of human nature and salvation.

Thomas accepted the Greek philosophical understanding of human nature as being oriented toward self-fulfillment. The Greek term here, *eudaemonism*, sometimes translated to mean "happiness," should not be interpreted to mean that the purpose and meaning of life is simply to have fun. Rather, when the term is broken down, it is seen to mean the driving divine power (*daemon*) toward the well (*eu*)—that is, health, wholeness, and the fulfillment of one's essential nature. For Thomas, this pagan beginning finds its true fulfillment only in the blessedness of knowing not just oneself, but God. The God-given supernatural or theological virtues of faith, hope, and love are necessary to complete the natural virtues of courage, moderation, wisdom, and justice and thereby enable the blessedness of knowing God.

Following the commonsense philosophy of Aristotle, Thomas agreed that virtues are acquired through practice and thus become a "habit." The supernatural virtues, however, unlike the natural virtues, are not innate to humankind, but must be infused into the person through God's grace, mediated by the church's sacraments. Once infused, the supernatural virtues are, analogously to the natural virtues, to be "acquired" or "realized." In this sense, the person who is in a state of grace does good works that please God and thus cooperates in his or her salvation. The scholastic phrase that expresses this process is *facere quod in se est*—to do what is within one. The significant point is that salvation is understood as occurring within one through the actualization of faith formed by acts of charity. Thus, the person who did his or her best to cooperate with the aid of grace would receive the reward of eternal life as a just due. Later scholastic theologians would be even more optimistic about human capability to cooperate with God in salvation and would suggest that good works done in the state of nature would also be rewarded by God with an infusion of grace as an appropriate due.

Although Thomas's philosophical–theological work is rightly regarded as a great achievement in the face of the Aristotelian challenge of the day, he was not (as was Luther) the initiator of a paradigm shift in theology and church history. He certainly modified significantly the received Augustinian Latin paradigm, but he did not replace it. Also, despite his considerable accomplishments, Thomas's theology is finally a court theology that safeguards the papacy.

Although Thomas's synthesis of reason and revelation, and his conviction that faith could not be endangered by reason, provided a certain intellectual freedom to medieval thinkers, the sixteenth-century reformers would regard this accomplishment as the source of the fundamental distortion of faith into human moral efforts. From a historical point of view, the age of Thomas was the watershed of the medieval era. The greatest of the medieval popes, Innocent III, died in 1216. The ideal Christian monarch, Louis IX of France, died in 1270, and three years later so did Henry III, the English servant of the papacy. The close friend of Thomas, the great Franciscan theologian and mystic, St. Bonaventure, also died in 1274. The creative synthesis constructed in this period covered all realms of life, including not only revelation and science, but sacerdotal authority and individual religious experience. The hierarchical church authority, the sovereign state, and the links between them could not be maintained, however. Even the advances in the development of canon law, reinforced by the Thomist claim that the state is subject to an eternal and absolute order of values, could not stand before the growing view that the law has no other sanction than the absolute will of the state. In little more than a generation after Thomas, Philip of France turned the Thomist hierarchy upside down in his subjugation of Pope Boniface VIII. Perhaps partly because of the tremendous intellectual achievement of Thomas and partly because of the later Roman Catholic endorsement of Thomism, it has become a common fallacy to regard thirteenth-century thought as the age of Thomism.

Chapter 17

"The Haywain," or "All Flesh Is Grass": The Withering of the Medieval Bloom

The medieval aspiration of the *corpus Christianum*, the Christian commonwealth, appeared to reach fulfillment in the great Thomist synthesis. But this achievement was short lived if not illusory. A brief review of the innumerable factors that contributed to the religious and moral hardening of Christendom's arteries will provide the context for the attacks on the heart of the church's authority: the papacy.

Charles of Anjou, brother of Louis IX of France, invaded southern Italy under papal auspices with the grand scheme of creating a new Mediterranean empire. But Sicilian rage against the oppressive occupation led to the massacre of the French garrison at Palermo on Easter Monday, 1282. The revolt, known as the Sicilian Vespers because it began at the hour of vespers, led to a protracted war involving France, Sicily, Naples, Aragon, and the papacy. Of all the parties involved, the papacy lost the most by siding with the French and overusing to ill effect the powers of excommunication, interdiction, deposition of rulers, and crusades.

Papal authority also suffered from abusing its power in other financial and territorial issues. Questions and even open criticism of papal activity, spurred further by the critical spirit of inquiry arising in the arts and law faculties of the universities, reached an intensity previously unknown. Furthermore, the urban laity, now increasingly part of a new social class, began to perceive the papacy with suspicion and even animosity. The new laity, the nucleus of the Third Estate, began to conceive of itself as citizens with intrinsic rights and duties, and not simply as subjects of papal authority. The Aristotelian orientation of the age redirected the attention of scholars and citizens from preoccupation with the heavenly city

240

to interest in the earthly city, the natural, and the human. The obvious disparity between the theoretical exposition of the *corpus Christianum* and the reality of papal activity further prepared the way for the development and reception of new political theories. The papacy's claim to be an institution of government rooted in the supranatural began to be challenged by an emerging concept of the state as a body of citizens.

Statism (nationalism was a later development), frequently attributed to the spread of Roman law and Aristotelian philosophy, included assemblies of estates (representatives of churches, nobles, and towns) and was one of the first signs that people were beginning to put their own particular interests above those of Christendom as a whole. The erosion of the ideal of the *corpus Christianum* was further abetted by the displacement of Latin by vernacular literature. Latin, the universal language, had symbolized the idea of a universal European Christian community. Now the Latin monopoly was being broken by the rapid rise of vernacular literature of every type, including hymns, songs, and translations of the Bible. Although this development was not a direct consequence of the declining credibility of the papacy, it impinged on the domination represented by the papacy as a universal government.

The credibility of the papacy was, however, directly affected by another development of the time: the growth of subjectivism. From the beginning, papal ideology had distinguished person and office. Popes were always acknowledged to be "the unworthy heir" of St. Peter; what was crucial was the objective and universal validity of the institution of the papacy itself. Now there was growing concern about the person of the pope. Anxiety about the pope as a person was, ironically, the basis for the Franciscan argument for papal infallibility.

In the latter half of the thirteenth century, the Spiritual Franciscans, a minority group of the Franciscan order, vehemently upheld Francis's ideal of absolute poverty in opposition to the more lax interpretations of the Conventual Franciscans, who used property and money held in trust for them. This so-called *usus pauper* was embodied in Pope Nicholas III's decretal, *Exiit qui Seminat* (1279). Influenced by the apocalyptic theology of history advanced by Joachim of Fiore (d. 1202), the spokesperson for the Spiritual Franciscans, Peter John Olivi (d. 1298) proclaimed that the final age of history had begun with Francis. Olivi and others harshly criticized the wealthy church and its existence as a state. They called for a return to the poverty of the primitive church and warned that the Antichrist would appear in the papacy. Olivi's argument for papal infallibility intended to *limit* the sovereignty of future popes and thus to prevent the prophesied Antichrist from altering the endorsement of the Spiritual Franciscans by Celestine V (1294). This zealous revival of the ideal of absolute poverty to the point of Christian anarchy against all institutions, including the papacy, contributed to a mood of apocalyptic suspicion about the total ecclesial institution.

Boniface VIII and the Decline of the Papacy

Following the death of Pope Nicholas IV in 1292, the College of Cardinals had been deadlocked for twenty-seven months due to conflicting factions within the college of the powerful Roman noble families of the Orsini and the Colonna. The compromise candidate, from outside the college, was the esteemed pious and ascetic hermit, Peter of Murrone (ca. 1215–1296), who took the name of Celestine V. Celestine was hailed by the Spiritual Franciscans as "the angelic pope" because of his reputed goodness and piety. At the time of his election, he was nearly eighty years old and yielded to the pleas of the Cardinals with great reluctance. It was immediately apparent to all, including the new pope himself, that he was unequal to the responsibilities thrust on him. Crowned pope on August 29, 1294, he abdicated on December 13. His abdication was a sensation at the time and earned him a place in Dante's Vestibule of Hell—the place of futility.

Celestine V supposedly heard heavenly voices urging him to abdicate. After consulting with Cardinal Benedict Gaetani, Celestine declared the legal validity of papal resignation and laid down his office. The fact that Gaetani was then chosen pope prompted the rumor that Celestine's "heavenly voices" were really the whispers of Cardinal Gaetani. Gaetani, now Boniface VIII (1294–1303), fearing that both his opponents and the adherents of Celestine would unite against him, placed Celestine in custody until his death in 1296.

Born about 1240 at Anagni, Boniface was of Roman noble lineage. He had studied law at Bologna and went into the service of the Curia, eventually being made a cardinal and a legate to France. Although an able administrator and canon lawyer, he was vain (he distributed statuettes of himself and claimed, "I am pope, I am Caesar"), arrogant, extremely ambitious to increase his own family fortune, and temperamental. By experience and temperament, Boniface represented the papal legacy of Gregory VII and Innocent III that political facts could and should be altered by papal ideology. Unfortunately for both Boniface and the papal office, the world context had shifted markedly since Innocent's triumphs.

When Boniface attempted to increase his family's estates at the expense of other noble houses—in particular, the house of Colonna—he ran into his first difficulties. The Colonnas raided the convoy transporting Boniface's (actually, the papal treasury's) funds. In return, Boniface preached a crusade against the Colonnas, destroyed their castles, dispersed their lands among his relatives, and forced the Colonnas to flee to the French court. Two of the Colonna family were cardinals, and although now deposed by Boniface, they continued to call for a general council to try the pope for his ostensible part in removing Celestine from the papacy.

Boniface proved equally adept at alienating the kings of England and France. In 1295, Philip IV of France (1285–1314) and Edward I of England (1272–1307) were preparing for war over the duchy of Gascony. The friction between the two countries finally sparked the outbreak of the Hundred Years' War in 1337. Both kings moved to supplement their war chests by taxing the clergy. In 1296, Boniface challenged the kings by his bull *Clericis laicos*, which forbade clergy to give up ecclesial revenues or property to any ruler without prior consent of the pope. The bull further forbade the laity to exact or receive taxes from the clergy. Neither Edward nor Philip was intimidated. Philip responded by banning the export of precious metals from France, thus cutting off the flow of money from France to the papal court. He also expelled all foreign merchants from France, thus affecting papal finances. Boniface had met his match. He tried to mend relations with the king by explaining that the bull did not invalidate feudal clerical obligations and that, certainly, "voluntary" gifts could be made to the king by the clergy upon the king's "friendly suggestion." And if there was a case of necessity, then the king, who was the judge of such things, could proceed to taxation without papal permission. Finally, to appease Philip's anger and show his strong affection for the French monarchy, Boniface canonized Philip's grandfather, Louis IX, in 1297.

Boniface's next miscalculation was stimulated by the great jubilee year. On the basis of the popular belief that special graces and indulgences could be gained in Rome at the turn of a century, Boniface proclaimed the first jubilee indulgence in February 1300. This afforded him a great show of papal pomp to salvage his damaged reputation. Huge crowds flocked to Rome, but Boniface failed to notice the singular absence of princes and rulers in these crowds. Thus, he mistook appearances for reality and assumed undiminished universal support for the papacy. Boniface's renewed self-assurance was once again shattered by the French king.

Informed in 1301 that Philip had imprisoned the bishop of Pamiers, Bernard Saisset, on charges of defamation of the crown, treason, sedition, simony, and heresy, Boniface charged the king with violating the freedom and immunity of the church and reinstituted the bull *Clericis laicos* for France. Furthermore, Boniface summoned the French bishops to Rome to take measures to reform the king and the kingdom. The bull *Ausculta fili* (Listen, son) of December 1301 summoned Philip himself to Rome to answer the charges. Undaunted, Philip had *Ausculta fili* destroyed and a forgery, *Deum timi* (Fear the Lord), put in its place that distorted the papal claims. Philip ("the father of the big lie") executed a brilliant propaganda coup by circulating the forged bull along with his response to the pope, which began, "Your utter fatuity may know that we [the king] are not subjected to anyone." The royal chancery also drew up a list of charges against Boniface that included blasphemy, simony, heresy, the murder of Celestine V, and fornication. At the same time, popular pamphlets and academic treatises attacking Boniface in particular and the papacy in general fanned public opinion.

In response, in 1302 Boniface issued one of the most famous and debated decrees of the medieval papacy, *Unam sanctam:* "The true faith compels us to believe that there is one holy catholic apostolic church, and this we firmly believe and plainly confess. And outside of her there is no salvation or remission of sins, ... We therefore declare, say, and affirm that submission on the part of every man to the bishop of Rome is altogether necessary for his salvation."[1]

One of Philip's royal ministers is said to have remarked, "My master's sword is of steel, the pope's is made of verbiage." Philip was no slouch at verbiage either. He focused his wrath on achieving the deposition of Boniface. The French king and his advisors used the new ideas of representation and participation of the Third Estate in important public matters. In June 1303, all three estates met in a large assembly that was stage-managed to include speeches against the pope by eminent leaders and the king himself. The assembly resolved that the pope should be tried by a general council. The resolution was then disseminated throughout France. Against Boniface's papal ideology, the king had forged new weapons of government propaganda and the claim to be executive spokesman for the nation.

Philip knew that Boniface's only remaining weapon was excommunication, and he

---

[1] Ray C. Petry, ed., *A History of Christianity: Readings in the History of the Early and Medieval Church* (Englewood Cliffs, NJ: Prentice-Hall, 1962), pp. 505–506. Only the concluding sentence received dogmatic sanction by the Fifth Lateran Council in 1516.

moved quickly to prevent its publication. A troop of soldiers led by William Nogaret, the king's advisor, and Sciara Colonna stormed the papal palace at Anagni the night of September 7, the night before the excommunication decree was to be published. Boniface refused to resign and offered instead his life. This was acceptable to Colonna, but Nogaret's wisdom prevailed: A dead pope was of little use to him or his master. The pope was liberated the next day by the local populace, but he soon died a broken man.

"*Unam sanctam* was the sonorous, proud and self-confident swan song of the medieval papacy."[2] The centuries-long development of the ideal of a universal Christian commonwealth within the confines of the church, the ark of salvation captained by the papacy, had run aground on the particularist rocks of language, culture, and statism. Papal ideology since the Donation of Constantine had focused exclusive attention on the empire and the emperor and had neglected those rulers whom Gregory VII had called mere "kinglets" (*reguli*). These kinglets, however, had become aware of a new national sense and outlook over which the papacy had little or no ideological means of control. Philip's triumph over Boniface concluded one phase in the history of the papacy and initiated another.

Avignon and the Western Schism

Traumatized by the shocking attack on Boniface, the papacy attempted both to appease France and to restore its own shattered prestige and role. Boniface's successor, Benedict XI (1303–1304), revoked the papal censures of Philip, but demanded the punishment of Nogaret, the king's servant. Benedict, however, died before this plan could proceed. The next pope, Clement V (1305–1314), the archbishop of Bordeaux and thus a subject of the English king Edward I, was French by upbringing and outlook. He was supposedly not a partisan in the conflict between England and France or a partisan of the papacy because he was not a member of the Curia. This politic choice, whether or not influenced by Philip, foundered on the personal weakness of Clement, who was a sickly hypochondriac. Unwilling to expose himself to the rigors of crossing the Alps, Clement continually put off his journey to Rome. He soon ensconced the papacy at Avignon, which, although on the empire's side of the Rhône river, was under the influence of France. Thus began what became known in Petrarch's phrase as the "Babylonian captivity" of the church (1309–1377), during which all the popes were French. Clement himself created twenty-eight cardinals, twenty-five of whom were French. France was declared exempt from *Unam sanctam*. A French pope with a French curia lived in a French-speaking city on the French frontier. The papacy, which, under Innocent III, had subdued kings and emperors, was now widely perceived to be captive to the French.

The reign of Clement had an ominous beginning. At his crowning in Lyons, a wall collapsed during the solemn procession and killed several dignitaries; Clement himself fell from his horse and lost the most precious jewel from his tiara, which had been knocked from his head. More fateful than this, however, was Philip's desire to gain even more from his conflict with Boniface VIII. Philip demanded that Boniface be exhumed, put on trial,

---

[2] Walter Ullmann, *A Short History of the Papacy in the Middle Ages* (London: Methuen University Paperback, 1974), p. 275.

and publicly burned for all his supposed heretical and immoral activities. Not surprisingly, the papacy wanted to avoid such a public humiliation at nearly any cost.

Philip's price was high: the dissolution of the Order of Templars and the transfer of their immense wealth to the royal coffers for "safekeeping." From the time of the Crusades, this order of knights had acquired many privileges, immunities, and great wealth, especially in France. Philip's propaganda experts once more earned their keep: They charged that the order had become a den of iniquity based on obscene rites with the devil and that its members were sodomites and blasphemous heretics. The Templars in France were arrested and, after sufficient torture, confirmed the charges against them. The tendency to retract such extorted testimony when questioned by papal commissioners was effectively minimized by burning some fifty Templars. Clement V avoided the threatened trial of Boniface VIII by congratulating Philip on his zeal in pursuing the Templar heresy and by dissolving the order and distributing much of its wealth to the French treasury.

In hindsight, it might be assumed that the humiliation of the papacy from Boniface VIII to Clement V would have sobered papal claims and tempered papal efforts to subordinate rulers. It seems, however, that the inertia of papal ideology was greater than the roadblocks thrown in its way. Pope John XXII (1316–1334) became embroiled, to the further detriment of the papacy, in conflicts with the claimant to the imperial throne, Lewis the Bavarian, and with the Franciscans. In the former case, Lewis ignored papal strictures, invaded Italy, and had himself acclaimed emperor by the Roman people and crowned by their representative Sciarra Colonna—the very man who had assaulted Boniface in Anagni twenty-five years earlier. In the latter case, John "settled" the dispute between the Franciscans and other orders over the absolute poverty of Christ and the Apostles by declaring the Franciscan claim heretical. Among the more noteworthy and influential Franciscans who rejected the pope and fled to Lewis the Bavarian for protection was the English philosopher William of Ockham (ca. 1285–1347).

One of the consequences of all these events was the first critical study of the concept of the church and its theological and legal bases. The French Dominican, John of Paris (ca. 1250–1306), argued in his treatise *On Papal and Royal Power* that secular government was rooted in the natural human community and that therefore not only was royal authority not derived from the papacy, but that the popes had no authority to depose kings. A far more radical treatise was the 1324 work *The Defender of the Peace*, by Marsilius of Padua (ca. 1275–1342). Marsilius, a former rector of the University of Paris, made it clear that it was the papacy which was destroying world peace. The solution was to limit the authority of the papacy by the laws governing all human institutions, laws that derived from the whole community. Not only did Marsilius stress the principle of popular consent as the basis for legitimate government; he also denied that the papacy was divinely established. These attacks on the papacy, which went to the heart of its legitimacy as an institution, used arguments from Aristotle and Roman law.

Dante (1265–1321), who had been exiled from Florence in 1301 for supporting the opponents of Boniface VIII, assailed the papacy and popes not only in his *Divine Comedy*, but also in his treatise *On Monarchy*. In the latter, he argued that the papacy should abandon all temporal authority and possessions and that temporal peace required a universal monarchy under the emperor. Papal condemnations and excommunications could no longer either control rulers or silence critics.

The Avignonese papacy further alienated Christians throughout Europe by a building craze that left splendid palaces and monuments for modern tourists, but severely taxed the faithful in order to build them. The poet Francesco Petrarch (1304–1374), who had lived in and around Avignon for some years, described the luxury and worldliness of the papal court as "the sewer of the world." A bureaucratic mentality further clouded the spiritual vision of the papacy. Instead of responding to the philosophical, theological, and literary critiques against it, the papacy developed increasingly efficient administrative machinery for collecting more and more taxes, shuffling its thousands of pages of documents concerned with benefices, indulgences, and politics, and administering its webs of patronage.

Gregory XI (1370–1378) heeded the calls to return the papacy to Rome. On January 17, 1377, the papacy reentered Rome and took up official residency at the Vatican. It remains a disputed question how much influence the entreaties of St. Catherine of Siena (d. 1380) and St. Bridget of Sweden (d. 1373) had on Gregory's decision. He is reputed to have sought mystical enlightenment for difficult problems, and thus, they probably at least strengthened his resolve to return the papacy to Rome.

Ironically, the end of the "Babylonian captivity" of the church led almost immediately to the great Western schism of the church. Gregory XI died on March 27, 1378. His body was barely cold when Romans began rioting in the streets, demanding the papacy remain in Rome and that a Roman or at least an Italian be chosen pope. While the cardinals struggled in conclave to resolve their own internal factions regarding the papal election, Roman mobs milled around outside, shrieking their will. It was not a pleasant scene. All but four cardinals voted for the efficient, hardworking bureaucrat who was administrator of the Avignonese curia, Bartolomeo Prignano. He was neither Roman, Italian, nor French, but a Neapolitan. (Naples was closely related to France through the house of Anjou.) Although a respected administrator, he was essentially a civil servant with no experience in policy making. He took the title Urban VI (1378–1389). In spite of the riotous behavior during the election, there is no indication that the cardinals were intimidated by the mobs. Indeed, the very choice of Prignano may indicate the cardinals' resistance to threats. This is important to note because soon after the enthronement of Urban, the cardinals decided they had made a serious mistake and used the supposed pressure of the mobs to invalidate the election.

In the weeks following his election, Urban exhibited a behavior extreme even in the context of his immediate predecessors. The cardinals soon came to the conclusion that Urban was unfit to be pope. They then impugned their own election process on the basis that it had taken place under conditions of duress and fear. One by one, they slipped out of Rome and gathered at Anagni, where they declared to all Europe that Urban had been uncanonically elected and that the papacy was to be considered vacant. In September they elected Cardinal Robert of Geneva, who took the title of Clement VII (1378–1394). Urban did not accept the cardinals' request that he abdicate. Instead, he excommunicated Clement, who returned the favor. The sorry spectacle of pope excommunicating pope and vice versa would continue for nearly forty years (1378–1417).

There had been antipopes before in the history of the church, but this was the first time that the same legitimate College of Cardinals had legitimately elected two popes within a few months. Urban VI and his successors, Boniface IX (1389–1404), Innocent VII

(1404–1406), Gregory XII (1406–1415), and Martin V (1417–1431), remained in Rome. Clement VII and his successor, Benedict XIII (1394–1423), returned to Avignon. It is difficult today to appreciate the depth of the religious insecurity and the intensity of institutional criticism this schism caused. If, as decreed by *Unam sanctam*, salvation itself was contingent on obedience to the true pope, it was crucial to know who was the true vicar of Christ. But how could this be decided? And now not only were there two popes, each claiming to be the sole vicar of Christ; there were also two colleges of cardinals and so on down the line, even to some parishes that had two priests. Europe itself split its allegiance: Clement VII was followed by France, Scotland, Aragon, Castille, and Navarre; Urban VI was followed by much of Italy, Germany, Hungary, England, Poland, and Scandinavia.

Public opinion was hopelessly confused. Even the learned and the holy clashed over who was the true pope. St. Catherine of Siena worked tirelessly to secure universal recognition of Urban. She called the cardinals who elected Clement "fools, liars, and devils in human form." On the other hand, the noted Spanish Dominican preacher, Vincent Ferrar, was equally zealous for the Avignon popes and labeled the adherents of Urban "dupes of the devil and heretics."

The major victim of this protracted struggle was the church. The prestige of the papacy sank to a new low; papal primacy was called into question, and so was the universality and validity of the church's sacraments. The rise of renewal movements in England under Wyclif and in Bohemia under Hus further complicated efforts to restore the credibility of the church.

John Wyclif (ca. 1330–1384) was an English philosopher and theologian whose ideas for renewing the church led to his condemnation by synods of the English church and, finally, by the Council of Constance in 1415. For a time he served the English crown, which certainly took an interest in his claim that the state could lawfully deprive corrupt clergy of their endowments. Pope Gregory XI, however, was not amused and condemned Wyclif in 1377. Wyclif also argued that papal claims to temporal power had no biblical warrant, and he appealed to the English government to reform the whole church in England. The extent to which he influenced the Lollard movement for a biblically based Christianity and the English Peasants' Revolt (1381) is problematic.

Wyclif's ideas were widespread among the lower English clergy and spread to Bohemia after the marriage in 1382 of Richard II of England to Anne, the sister of King Wenceslaus IV of Bohemia. The Bohemian reformer John Hus (ca. 1372–1415) translated some of Wyclif's writing into Czech. Hus, rector of the University of Prague, was a fiery preacher against the immorality of the papacy and the higher clergy in general. In spite of a safe-conduct from the Emperor Sigismund, the Council of Constance condemned and executed Hus in 1415. Both Wyclif and Hus were signs of growing national consciousness. After Hus's execution, the University of Prague declared him a martyr and national hero.

Conciliarism

From the beginning of the schism, there were efforts to resolve it. It was proposed that both popes abdicate to allow a new election. Neither the Roman nor the Avignonese line favored this. Other solutions included the establishment of a tribunal, with each pope to ac-knowledge its verdict, and the withdrawal of allegiance by government supporters of the popes, thus preparing the way for a new election. The universities favored and advanced the recovery of the ancient principle that in an emergency (e.g., the case of a heretical pope) a general council would decide what to do. This royal way of the ancient church had al-ready been suggested by two German professors at the University of Paris, Henry of Lan-genstein (d. 1397) and Conrad of Gelnhausen (d. 1390). Other scholars concurred with their solution.

Finally, in June 1408, cardinals of both popes met and resolved to summon a general council to meet at Pisa. Both popes were invited to attend, but they refused. The Council of Pisa (March through July 1409) met anyway and was well attended by cardinals, bishops, hundreds of theologians, and representatives of almost every western country. Among the participants were distinguished scholars of conciliarism, such as Pierre d'Ailly, chancellor of the University of Paris, and Jean Gerson, his successor. Their argument that supreme ecclesial power was located in the council was accepted. The council proceeded to depose both popes as notorious schismatics and heretics and then elected a new pope, Alexander V (1409–1410), archbishop of Milan and a cardinal of the Roman line. The deposed popes re-fused to recognize the validity of the Pisan council, however, and thus there were now three popes.

The scandalous situation was further aggravated after the death of Alexander V by the election to the new Pisan papacy of a man reputed to have engaged in piracy during his pre-vious military career. Baldassare Cossa had been such a successful commander of papal troops, that Boniface IX had made him a cardinal in 1402 and then a papal legate. Cossa took the title John XXIII and reigned from 1410 until 1415, when he was imprisoned and deposed by the Council of Constance. His title and efforts to manipulate the council were redeemed approximately 450 years later by John XXIII (1958–1963) and Vatican II.

Without being unduly concerned about the means, John achieved his initial goal of expelling the pope of the Roman obedience from Rome. However, political and military events in central Italy forced him to take shelter with his curia in Florence and to seek a protector. He turned to the king—later (1433) emperor—of Germany, Sigismund.

Sigismund had already endorsed the line of popes established at the Council of Pisa and thus was a natural source of assistance for John XXIII. However, Sigismund was also greatly concerned for the unity of the church. He had been persuaded by the writings of conciliarists, especially those of Dietrich of Niem (1340–1418), who asserted that in an ec-clesial emergency the emperor should follow the model of the ancient Christian emperors and convoke a general council. Dietrich further argued that a general council had plenary powers, including the rights to depose a pope and reform the church. Although not yet em-peror, Sigismund decided to act on the arguments that a general council is superior to the pope and that the emperor, as first prince of Christendom and protector of the church, has the duty to call a council when needed. He successfully arranged to organize such a coun-cil on German soil at the city of Constance. John could not afford to jeopardize Sigismund's support and oppose his plans.

John convoked the Council of Constance (1414–1417) in 1414. The council was to deal with three main issues: the great schism, the extirpation of heresy, and reform of the church in "head and members." The council was one of the greatest ecclesial assemblies of the premodern church. The active participation of Sigismund stimulated a large and representative attendance and overcame threats to the validity of the council.

Pope John initially hoped that the council would depose the popes of the Roman and Avignonese obediences and legitimize him. He soon discovered, however, that there was a consensus that all three popes should resign. John's own plans for the council were further jeopardized by the conciliar decision to vote by nations rather than by persons, with each nation having one vote. This procedure counterbalanced the preponderance of Italian prelates on whom John was counting.

The decision to vote by nations had a significance beyond the immediate politics of John's efforts to win conciliar endorsement. It was a democratizing event, because, in the separate deliberations of the nations, now not only the prelates, but also representatives of cathedral chapters and universities, theologians, canonists, and representatives of princes, had a voice. Furthermore, the idea of a nation as a unit, an idea taken over from the universities, contributed to the already developing sense of nationalism that was undermining the old idea of a universal Christian commonwealth under the headship of the papacy. The further consequences of this nationalism were to be seen in the Reformation and the rise of national churches.

John soon perceived that the polity of the council did not favor him. His concern was heightened by the circulation of a lengthy document that detailed charges against him. Hoping to get to a safe haven in order to dissolve the council, John fled at night in disguise. Sigismund not only rallied the confused council; he also managed to have John captured and held in protective custody in the vicinity of Constance.

An important consequence of John's flight was that, in his absence as papal convenor, the council thought it necessary to give itself judicial standing. This is the context of the famous decree, *Haec sancta* (1415), which clearly placed the authority of the council over that of the pope. *Haec sancta* sanctioned conciliar theory as the official teaching of the church. It set forth the character of a general council as a lawful assembly representing the universal church. The power of the council was held to derive directly from Christ, the authority of the council therefore extended over every officeholder in the church, including the pope.

John XXIII was deposed for abetting schism by his flight from the council and also for notorious simony and a disgraceful life. The Roman pope, Gregory XII, agreed to resign on the condition that the council allow him to reconvoke it and authorize it as a council. This was accepted without the council's either acknowledging any prior illegitimacy or implying that Gregory was the true pope. The Avignonese pope, Benedict XIII, was adamant in his determination to remain pope. Gradually, however, his Spanish support eroded, and in 1417 he, too, was deposed as a schismatic, perjuror, and heretic. He continued to claim to be the legitimate pope until his death in 1423, even though he no longer had any significant following. On November 11, 1417, Cardinal Odo Colonna was elected pope by the college of cardinals and six representatives of each of the five nations present at the council. He took the title of Martin V in honor of the saint of the day. The great Western schism was over.

The council declared heretical the renewal movements of the time led by Wyclif and Hus. Wyclif escaped the punishment of the council by having already died. Hus was executed at the stake, an action that ignited fires in Bohemia still burning at the time of the Reformation.

Concerned that reform of the church would falter without conciliar direction and support, the council passed the important decree, *Frequens*, in 1417. The decree provided for frequent general councils, the next one to be held in five years, a second in seven years, and thereafter every ten years "in perpetuity." The decree ended by stating that it is lawful for the pope to "shorten" the period, but on no account to put it off.

Martin V closed the council in April 1418. He did not, however, confirm or approve it, an omission probably little noted because of the profound relief over resolving the schism. His successor, Eugene IV (1431–1447), approved it in 1446 insofar as it was not prejudicial to the rights, dignity, and supremacy of the papacy. Pius II (1458–1464), in his bull *Execrabilis* (1460), prohibited any and all appeals to a council over the pope; any such appeal was to be regarded as heresy and schism. This principle would later be applied against Martin Luther, who initially hoped that the church would be reformed through an ecumenical council.

Some of the decrees of the Council of Constance became parts of special agreements between Martin V and particular nations. This was the beginning of papal agreements with nations, called concordats, which further indicated the displacement of the ideal of a universal Christian commonwealth by the independence of individual nations. The papacy, hitherto claiming sovereignty over all peoples, was now reduced to one government among many national governments, and it bound itself in a contractual manner to them. This, too, had significance a century later in the Reformation.

The Councils of Basel (1431–1449)
and Ferrara–Florence (1438–1445)

The immediate aftermath of the Council of Constance may perhaps be described in terms of battle fatigue. The spiritual and physical anxiety and stress occasioned by the long schism and the energy required for its resolution left confusion and uncertainty. The church was now entering a period of transition in which the old hierarchical papal institution had not yet become merely a memory and the new conciliar orientation was still an innovation. Was the *corpus Christianum* to be reformed and renewed from below or from above?

While the weary participants in the conciliar–papal struggle understandably hoped for a respite, a new problem arose. Islamic expansion seriously threatened the eastern empire. In 1371 Bulgaria became a vassal state of the Turks, and by 1389 the Turks ruled the entire Balkan peninsula. The seriousness of the Greek situation was indicated by the circuit around Europe made by the Byzantine emperor, Manuel II Palaeologus (1391–1425), in an effort to arouse support from the west. Sigismund invited Byzantine representatives to the Council of Constance, but the combination of the death at the council of Manuel's major representative and the press of western issues precluded help for Byzantium. Desperate for western political and military assistance, Byzantine envoys approached Martin V, requesting a council of union between the Roman and Byzantine churches. It was suggested that the east was even willing to accept the Roman papal primacy, faith, and ritual. Conciliarists and the papacy now competed with each other to court Byzantine favor.

In the meantime, Martin V, in accord with the decree *Frequens*, convoked a council at

Basel for 1431. By December only a few participants had arrived, and in February Martin died. His successor, Eugene IV (1431–1447), was against the council from the start and dissolved it on the basis of insufficient attendance and the argument that the appropriate setting for discussions on reunion with the Greeks was an Italian city. Because the ideal city for papal leverage, Rome, was in too much disorder for a council, Eugene convoked a council to meet in Bologna in 1433. By now, however, the Council of Basel had already had its first session and, offended by the action of Eugene, sharply protested the action of the pope. Those at Basel, supported by Germany, England, France, Scotland, and Burgundy, threatened to depose the pope. In 1433 Eugene formally recognized the Council of Basel, which had become practically a European parliament. Basel reaffirmed the superiority of a council over the pope and then further alienated Eugene by a number of decrees, including curtailing papal finances.

The mutual hostility between Eugene and the council increased when Eugene transferred the council to Ferrara in order to advance his agenda regarding reunion with the east. A minority of the council acceded to the pope's decision; the majority declared Eugene deposed. In turn, the pope declared those remaining at Basel heretics and schismatics. The election of an antipope, Felix V (1439–1449), had little significance because he lacked support from the nations. The French had already embodied no less than twenty-three decrees of Basel into national law in the Pragmatic Sanction of Bourges (1438), an action that supported the older claims of the French national church to a privileged position in relation to the papacy. Gallicanism, so called from those *libertés de l'Église gallicane*, continued to assert the autonomy of the French church until the definition of papal infallibility at Vatican I (1869–1870).

A local epidemic in Ferrara prompted the council to move to Florence, where a union with the eastern empire was negotiated and signed in 1439. The Byzantine emperor himself and all members of his legation signed it. But it was not acceptable in Constantinople, where, in spite of the Turkish threat, the centuries of east–west strife were indelibly etched. Byzantium fell to the Turks in 1453, and its legacy was appropriated by Russia. Tsar Ivan III (1462–1505) had married the niece of the last eastern emperor and claimed succession to the "Roman" empire, arrogating the imperial double eagle as the symbol of its continuation. The Tsars and Russia also inherited the eastern antipathy to the papacy that has continued until today.

Meanwhile, the authority of the Council of Basel eroded when its leading spokesmen deserted their own camp and joined the forces of the very papacy they had vigorously attacked. One of these men, the secretary of the council, later became a hard opponent of conciliarism when he was elected Pope: Pius II. These one-time conciliarists increasingly sensed what the representatives of rulers also saw in the conciliar movement—the danger that the governed everywhere would become the masters of their kings and princes, as well as of their pope. With the demotion of the papacy to the status of one monarchical government among others, it dawned on other monarchs that conciliarism was a two-edged sword. As rulers realized that the means developed to control the papacy could be a weapon against them, they raised gloomy predictions of sedition and anarchy. Thus, as never before, the papacy and monarchs became disposed to conclude concordats with each other. The possibility of democracy drove all theocratic monarchs, including the papacy, toward cooperation for the sake of mutual preservation. The papacy's own effort to overcome the challenge of conciliarism and to consolidate its patrimony in Italy diverted its energy and attention from the widespread cry for reform of the church in head and members.

In less than a century, this cry would become the full-throated roar of the Reformation that blew away the last vestiges of the *corpus Christianum* and the papal efforts to realize a universal headship over Christians. Although that roar would include a cacophony of voices, its first sighs and murmurs came from (1) those alienated by poverty, the profit economy, and the stress of urban growth, augmented by terrors of famine, plague, and war, (2) the anger of the frustrated renewal movements of Wyclif and Hus, and (3) the individualism of the Renaissance. Altogether, by the end of the Middle Ages, people were in one way or another being thrown back on themselves, while the external supports of their Christian commonwealth were undermined.

Famine, Plague, and War

Western Christendom's spiritual insecurity, uncertainty, and anxiety during the papal schism had already been initiated by the famines and plagues that swept through Europe by the mid-fourteenth century. The increased food production of the twelfth and thirteenth centuries contributed to a steady population growth, but the population outgrew the agricultural output that had made its growth possible. By 1320, nearly all of northern Europe suffered under a terrible famine precipitated by a conjuncture of major crop failures caused by years of unusually bad weather, considerable price inflation, and urban dependence on the immediate countryside for food due to the lack of long-distance transportation. Weak and malnourished, the population was hit by an outbreak of typhoid fever in 1316 that killed an estimated 10 percent of the population of Ypres within a few months. The malnourished population of Europe was ripe for the Grim Reaper, who soon appeared in the form of the bubonic plague.

The spread of the bubonic plague to Europe was facilitated by improvements in the design in Italian ships that enabled them not only to sail faster and farther, but to sail year-round, even up the dangerous Atlantic coast of Europe. The rats that carried the fleas that bore the disease thereby reached all of Europe's ports. Originating in the Far East, the plague brought by Genoese ships reached Sicily in October 1347. Within months, nearly all Italy was infected; by late spring 1348 the disease attacked southern Germany, and in June 1348 it entered England. The dense and filthy urban environments provided good breeding grounds for the black rat that carried the disease-bearing fleas, and the thatched roofs of so many houses made fine launching pads for the fleas to jump on persons below. The lethal nature of the plague was not limited to transmission by flea bites, however; the pneumonic form was transmitted from person to person by coughs and sneezes.

Modern mortality rates for the bubonic form transmitted by flea bites ranged from 30 to 90 percent before the discovery of antibiotics. Because there are no population figures for fourteenth-century Europe, it is not possible to give an accurate account of the mortality rate due to the plague. It is estimated that the plague killed 30 percent of the population. Local variations must also be taken into account; some areas were passed over, whereas others were completely wiped out. The horror of the devastation was increased by the gruesome nature of the disease itself: first a large, painful boil called a *buba*, followed by black spots or blotches caused by bleeding under the skin, and then the last stage of violent coughing up of blood. A more graphic description reads: "All the matter which exuded from their bodies let off an unbearable stench; sweat, excrement, spittle, breath, so fetid as to be overpowering; urine turbid, thick, black or red."[3] Family and friends deserted the sick, leaving them to die alone and in agony.

It is difficult for us today to realize the profound personal and social impact the plague had on those who survived. The plague was inexplicable and swift. People did not know where it came from or what it was. The widespread and intense fear of imminent death—exacerbated by religious anxiety over purgatory and hell—broke down customs and norms. The result was often panic, bizarre behavior, and the projection of guilt and fear upon others outside the group. People began flagellating themselves in frenzied orgies of penance for the personal and communal sins believed to be the cause of the plague. A variation on the theme blamed the Jews for the disease, with the consequence that thousands of Jews were murdered across Europe. Not a few survivors of the plague lost all confidence in their tradition and faith, which had not prepared them for a disaster of such magnitude. A profound pessimism ensued, illustrated by the dance-of-death motif that entered art, as well as by more realistic representations of suffering. The rational view of an ordered world was severely tested, if not destroyed, by such an experience of arbitrary disaster. If God acted in such inexplicable ways, then perhaps the way to God was not through rational theology and the sacramental, institutional church, but through direct, intensely personal mysticism. Widespread efforts arose to achieve personal, rather than institutionally mediated, access to God. The other side of this coin of the loss of traditional meaning was to lose oneself in gross sensuality. In short, the plague left the survivors with guilt and insecurity, compounded by a crisis of faith.

As if natural disaster were not enough, the human community managed to turn on itself through the Hundred Years' War (1337–1453), which was both a dynastic struggle between the English and French monarchies and a feudal struggle within France itself. The expansionist policy of the French king, Philip VI (1328–1350), sought to absorb the English duchy of Aquitaine. Edward III of England (1327–1377), the eldest surviving male heir of Philip IV (Edward's mother, Isabella, was Philip's daughter, whereas Philip VI was Philip IV's nephew), decided that his rightful sovereignty over Aquitaine could be achieved by assuming the title of King of France. The feudal or civil war aspect in France derived from the French barons' attempt to thwart the centralizing policy of the French crown by aligning themselves with Edward on the basis that he was a more legitimate overlord. Economic factors also played a role in terms of the wool trade between England and Flanders, a fiefdom of the French crown. The disruption of the wool trade threatened the prosperity of the Flemish citizens, and thus, they supported Edward. The war, really a series of sporadic raids and sieges, was fought almost entirely in France, with England winning most of the battles.

Although the natural disasters of famines, epidemics, and plagues claimed more victims than war did, war brought vast destruction and the disintegration of economic and social life. The French taxation for the Hundred Years' War was a tremendous burden on the

---

[3]John McKay, Bennett I. Hill, John Buckler, eds., *A History of World Societies,* 2nd ed., vol. I (Boston: Houghton Mifflin, 1988), p. 430.

peasants, who exploded in rage and rampage in 1358. Mobs swept through the countryside, murdering nobles, raping their wives and daughters, and destroying their estates. In revenge, the nobles viciously suppressed the peasants and mercilessly slaughtered thousands, guilty and innocent alike. A similar revolt in England in 1381 combined economic and religious grievances against noble and clerical rulers. The popular preacher John Ball (d. 1381) immortalized its revolutionary sentiment of social equality in the famous couplet, "When Adam delved and Eve span; Who was then the gentleman?" In England, too, the revolt was ferociously crushed. Similar rebellions occurred in Italy, some of the north German cities, and parts of Spain.

The "Babylonian captivity" of the church and its consequent schism, accompanied by famine, plague, and war, combined to plunge late medieval Europe into crisis. In place of the old Augustinian order of the City of God embodied in the ideal of a universal Christian commonwealth, the *corpus Christianum*, headed by the papacy, there now appeared to be only universal disorder, death, and devastation.

The Crisis of the Late Medieval Era

Embittered by the crises they had gone through, many described life as a kingdom of death and desolation. The *Apocalypse* woodcut cycle of 1498 (based on the biblical book of Revelation) by the German artist Albrecht Dürer (1471–1528) provided the age with a graphic symbol of its distress and fear. The best known woodcut of this series, *The Four Horsemen*, represented pestilence, war, famine, and death.

The rupture of social and personal life that occasioned these images had actually begun in the cities of the twelfth and thirteenth centuries. The derangement of human relations initiated by this new urban environment and accelerated by the mass death and destruction of the fourteenth century called into question the medieval Christian conviction that death is not an end of life, but a passage into a new life. In the mass death of the plague, when parent deserted child and child deserted parent, when friends, neighbors, and servants abandoned the sick, and when public authorities did not know what to do, the worst experience was not death itself, but the death of the self.

The traditional religious rites and customs of death—the funeral procession and meal that enacted the separation of the dead from the living while symbolically reconstituting the family and the continuity of society—collapsed totally in the face of the plague. The old rules of mourning that channeled and reduced the trauma of death rarely endured during the mass death of the time. The new fear of the contagious dead ruthlessly uprooted the socialization and "domestication" of death by common custom that had provided a certain rapport with the past and with one's ancestors.

As a consequence of the plague as well as migrations, it was no longer possible to mourn the dead according to traditional rules. If one was fortunate enough even to have a deathbed, there certainly would be no relatives and friends gathered around it. Nor would there be rest for the deceased among ancestors in the cemetery or the church. The survivors more and more understood themselves to be like orphans. The end of the Middle Ages was characterized by widespread melancholy—today we call it depression—that has been interpreted as an unconscious protest not just against the horror of death, but against the solitude and abandonment that death thrust on the townsfolk of the fourteenth and fifteenth centuries.

A consequence of this shock to faith and to feudalism was a new search for the self that ranged from the egoism manifest in Boccaccio's *The Decameron* (1353) to personal and national narcissism. The disturbing discovery of the death of the self is nearly contemporaneous with the development of new funeral practices and the writing of wills and testaments. In the hierarchy of contributions to the price of passage from this world to the next, a concern to endow as many masses as possible for oneself after death displaced the earlier emphasis on charity to the poor. A "mathematics of salvation" exalted the multiplication of intercessions that directly favored the passage of the deceased into the beyond. It also indicated not only the church's ability to adapt to a new situation, but also the growing influence of a market mentality with its orientation toward the calculation of accounts. Between the mid-fourteenth century and the beginning of the sixteenth century, the mass became the essential preparation for the journey to the beyond. At the moment when the relations between the living and the dead were interrupted, the mass ritually established powerful bonds between this world and the next.

The development of masses for the dead, with the essential ritual action providing direct and efficacious aid to the deceased, complemented the development of the doctrine of purgatory and increasing emphasis on the saints and the Virgin Mary. The multiplication of masses for the dead stipulated in merchants' wills reflected both these merchants' views of purgatory as a place for those snatched from life without benefit of time to amend their ways or prepare for death, as well as their extension of calculated self-interest to the afterworld. In purgatory, abandoned or orphaned souls found a refuge with a new family. Purgatory also mitigated the fear of damnation by the opportunity it offered to purge the offenses incurred during life and to benefit from the prayers and intercessions of the Mass.

Likewise, the cult of the saints and the Virgin of Consolation increased during this time when people were losing their relatives on a soul-numbing scale. In the communion of saints a new family was recognized, and heaven became populated with a multitude of familiar intercessors. It has been suggested that the appeal to Mary was primarily a quest for protection against misfortune on the basis of the iconography presenting her cloak as a shield against the arrows of the plague. Equally, if not more important, was the appeal of Mary as the Great Mother and Consoler at whose feet those bereft of family might find a tender welcome.

Humanists among the new orphans created by the disasters of famine, plague, and war sought new ancestors among the ancient Greeks and Romans, aiming at a rebirth, or renaissance, of society. The focus on the individual that arose from the matrix of the disasters, fears, and anxieties of the late Middle Ages led to a new awareness of the human being as a natural, and even secular, phenomenon to be developed and praised. The long, complex story of Western individualism includes these new attitudes toward humankind and the world. Both time and space became "humanized," that is, organized from the individual's viewpoint. Linear time regulated by clocks and linear space in art entered urban and mercantile areas to organize nature from the perspective of the spectator. The initial sparks of self-consciousness present in Abelard's quest for self-knowledge were fanned to life by a driving ambition to realize to the fullest every aspect of human potential.

The popes themselves were drawn into this same orbit of individualism as the office-holder began to take the place of the office. That is, the papacy itself as an office or institution of government began to recede behind the personal character of the individual pope. However, the personal characters of the Renaissance papacy raised more issues than they resolved. Sharp and tough minded, they set out to smash the conciliar movement's strictures on papal authority. Their success may be seen in that, apart from the Council of Trent (1545–1563), held to counter the Reformation, there was not another council until Vatican I (1869–1870), which, in its declaration of papal primacy and infallibility, finally answered the Council of Constance. Late medieval people, of course, could not see that far ahead. They could see, however, the great gulf between the biblical image of the shepherd guiding the flock toward the heavenly city and the Renaissance popes who exploited the flock for their own advancement in the earthly city. A woodcut of the sixteenth century portrayed the mercenary spirit of the papacy by picturing the pope and curia counting money in one panel and Jesus driving the money changers from the temple in the other panel. The papacy became an Italian Renaissance court, and the pope was increasingly perceived to be nothing more than an Italian prince whose problems and interests were now local and egoistic rather than universal and pastoral. Two particularly notorious popes exemplify the depths to which the papacy sank at this time: Alexander VI (reigned 1492–1503) and Julius II (reigned 1503–1513).

A Spaniard by birth, Rodrigo Borgia was made a cardinal by his uncle, Pope Callistus III, in 1456 and won the papacy largely through bribery. It is no surprise that continuing familial and financial concerns dominated Alexander VI's reign, rooted in nepotism and simony from its beginning. He is one pope to whom the title "father," if not "holy," may be literally applied. His many mistresses bore him at least eight known children, the most famous of whom are Cesare Borgia and Lucrezia Borgia. The former is infamous for his ruthless exaction of total obedience as his father's military leader, as well as for his immorality, murders, and possibly the assassination of his brother. He is the model for Niccolò Machiavelli's *The Prince* (1513). Lucrezia served her father's plans by a series of ambitious political marriages marked by extravagant wedding parties in the Vatican palace. One of her husbands was murdered by order of her brother Cesare. At one point, when absent from Rome for a political and military campaign, Alexander appointed his daughter regent of the Holy See.

Alexander's own involvement in sexual promiscuity, alleged poisonings, and intrigue made the name "Borgia" a synonym for corruption. He was denounced in his own time by the influential and fiery Dominican preacher Girolamo Savonarola (1452–1498). When Alexander could not persuade Savonarola to discontinue his attacks by offering him a cardinal's hat, he proceeded against him and was at least partly responsible for Savonarola's execution in Florence. Alexander's political efforts to strengthen the papal state abetted French intervention in northern Italy, which helped initiate a new period of power politics with Italy as the focus of international struggles. The sordidness of Alexander's life aside, he also patronized great artists whose legacy may still be enjoyed by the visitor to Rome.

Julius II continued patronage of the arts by his support of Raphael, Michelangelo, and Bramante. As a result of Julius's generosity, we still have, among other works, Michelangelo's statue of Moses, the paintings in the Sistine Chapel, and Raphael's frescoes in the Vatican. Julius's enthusiasm for rebuilding St. Peter's led to the indulgence that later occasioned Martin Luther's *Ninety-five Theses*. In his own time, the art by which Julius was primarily known was the art of war; Raphael painted Julius mounted and in armor.

Julius continued the political and military efforts of the Borgias to control the Papal States and to expel all foreigners from Italy. He himself led his troops with such strength and drive, that he became known as *terribilita*, the terrible man. So much of his reign involved warfare, that more and more of the laity began to wonder in disgust what this pontiff had to do with the Prince of Peace. The great humanist, Erasmus, who witnessed Julius's triumphal martial entry into Bologna, angrily criticized and satirized Julius in the *Praise of Folly* (1511), *The Complaint of Peace* (1517), and *Julius Exclusus* (1517). The last of these, in dialogue form, spread rapidly all over Europe and portrays Julius appearing before the gates of heaven on his death. For all his threats and bombast, Julius cannot force his way into heaven.

On the eve of the Reformation, the question was not *whether* the church should be reformed, but *when* it should be. The successor to Julius II was a son of the famous Florentine political and banking family, the Medici. He took the title Leo X (1513–1521) and was pope during the early years of the Reformation. The words with which he reputedly opened his reign indicate how little prepared he was to respond to the widespread desire for reform of the church: "Now that God has given us the papacy, let us enjoy it."

Chapter 18

The Reformations of the Sixteenth Century

Little did Leo X know, as he was preparing to enjoy his spoils, that his papacy would soon be the lightning rod for a reform movement unleashed by a young student struck to the ground by a lightning bolt in 1505. The thunderstorm that prompted Martin Luther (1483–1546) to become a monk was but a foretaste of the storm that would shake late medieval Europe to its foundations and permanently alter western Christianity. These destructive and constructive energies were fed by the highly charged atmosphere of life on the eve of the Reformation.

Aspects of Everyday Life on the Eve of the Reformation

Everyday life in the sixteenth century was difficult at best. Poor diet, little sanitation, and repeated outbreaks of the plague, as well as various other diseases, not to mention everyday violence, feuds, and warfare, prompted people to think of themselves as old if they reached the age of forty. Although the population of Europe recovered from the devastations caused by the plague of the mid-fourteenth century, the disease still posed a real danger for the future. The Swiss reformer, Ulrich Zwingli (1484–1531), nearly succumbed to the plague, and in 1527 the plague struck Luther's area. In Wittenberg, those who could, fled; the others died or were cared for in Luther's home, which he turned into a hospice. Even love could not close a person's eyes to the omnipresence of death in the midst of life, for at this time syphilis appeared on the continent. The shortness of life was never far from people's minds.

The vast majority of the population engaged in a daily struggle for survival. The struggle became critical when there was a crop failure or shortfall owing to any number of natural causes, such as drought, too much rain, or early frost. Although the larger towns constructed granaries for storing surpluses from good harvests, opportunists would hoard food and inflate prices in times of need. Furthermore, surplus food in one area was not readily available to another area that was in need, because, apart from rivers, transportation networks were primitive. Grain prices could fluctuate as much as 150 percent in a year. Speculators who profited from these events were the targets of vigorous sermons and tracts by Luther and other churchmen who condemned such "usury" and called for increased government control of commerce.

Most people in the sixteenth century toiled on the land from sunrise to sunset, with occasional relief in the festivities of major holy days and the ritual breaks occasioned by marriages and funerals. In some areas, the peasant was a virtual slave, whereas in others he was a small landholder. The diversity of conditions in the German area alone makes generalization about peasant life difficult. In any case, the life of the peasant was hard and, not infrequently, hardening. The upper class frequently depicted the peasant as stupid, coarse, loathsome, untrustworthy, and prone to violence. For the nobles, such self-serving descriptions rationalized and legitimated oppression of the peasants.

Not all writers and lawyers supported such prejudice against the peasants; some reproached the lay and ecclesial nobility with the adage that true nobility derives from virtue, not from blood. Nevertheless, long before the Reformation, the adverse economic and social status of the peasant was legitimated by blaming the victim. The Noah story (Gen. 9:20–27) was used in medieval Germany for the same purposes as in slaveholding America: to foster the belief that subjugated people bore the curse of God.

When pushed to extremes, the normally conservative peasant could react violently. Usually, peasants acted out their rage against their conditions by turning against each other, but a picture from the period shows four peasants slaughtering an armored knight with axes. Far more serious than individual acts of violence were outbreaks of communal peasant rebellion against the oppression of their lords. Peasant uprisings in 1493, 1502, 1513, and 1517 culminated in the great Peasants' War of 1524–1525. The nobility believed that these were orchestrated conspiracies; in fact, they began as spontaneous revolts generated by much the same kind of rage and frustration that stimulated the African-American riots that swept through American cities in the 1960s. The long-repressed peasant anger against the lords, including the ecclesial lords who were great landholders, helps explain the enthusiastic reception of Luther's early writings that attacked church authority and extolled Christian liberty.

In spite of social problems, this was also a period of expanding lay education. By the eve of the Reformation, the efforts of monarchs, princes, and wealthy merchants expanded the number of European universities from twenty to seventy. Prince Frederick the Wise, for example, founded the University of Wittenberg in 1502. Perhaps 3 to 4 percent of the population could read by the beginning of the sixteenth century. The thousands of published Reformation pamphlets and sermons were thus designed to be read *to* the illiterate as well as *by* the literate. "Faith," as Luther stressed, "comes by hearing."

The educational system Luther encountered as a youth certainly worked in his case, but he did not find it at all edifying. Knowledge was literally beaten into the students. Unprepared students had to wear a dunce cap and were addressed as an ass. A student speaking German rather than Latin in class was beaten with a rod. Even music, Luther's favorite subject, was presented in a utilitarian fashion to train youths for church choirs. In short, the education of children was at best dull and at worst barbaric. Luther later recalled that one morning he was caned fifteen times for not mastering the tables of Latin grammar.

Those who mastered enough Latin went on to more advanced education. A university education opened doors for commoners to careers in medicine, law, and the church. The late medieval university consisted of an arts faculty and three professional faculties of medicine, law, and theology. *The* authority, "the father of those that know," was Aristotle. Emphasis on Aristotle's writings on logic taught students how to think. The typical mode of higher education was the disputation. The teacher would assign a set of theses to the students, who then had to defend them according to the rules of logic. The disputation format also served as the final examination for a degree. Today's oral examination of Ph.D. students in our universities, during which they have to defend their dissertation, is but a pale reflection of the rigorous exercises common to the medieval university. It is of interest that the disputation is precisely the form in which Luther cast his *Ninety-five Theses*, as well as many of his other Reformation writings. In many ways, the Reformation was a movement from within the universities.

By all accounts, the insecurity of the late medieval period derived not only from physical conditions, but also from the rapid social changes that called into question the values and traditional truths people had lived by. The church further irritated these insecurities by promoting a type of pastoral care designed to make people uncertain about their salvation and thus more dependent on ecclesial intercessions. Visitors to medieval cathedrals and churches can still see today the representations of Christ on the throne of judgment with a sword and a lily on either side of his head. The lily represented resurrection to heaven, but the sword of judgment to eternal torment was more vivid in the minds of most people.

Everywhere in everyday life, images served to remind the medieval person of eternity and how to achieve it. As Gregory the Great (d. 604) had said, "images are the books of the laity." Medieval churches presented the Bible and the lives of the saints in stone, stained glass, and wood carvings. The "books of the laity" were also evident at the town fountain and the town hall and were carved in the doorways and painted on the walls of homes and public buildings. Wherever people walked, worked, and gathered for news and gossip, religious images reminded them of their origin and destiny.

A whole set of practices and exercises developed to assist people in avoiding hell. As if people needed reminders of their omnipresent sense of mortality, the artwork of the day presented the theme of the "dance of death," complete with a skeletal Grim Reaper and manuals on the "art of dying." The relics of saints were avidly collected and venerated, with the conviction that they were efficacious in reducing sentences to purgatory rather than hell. Luther's own prince had one of the largest relic collections of the area—more than 19,000 pieces.

The place where every real or imagined sin was ferreted out was the confessional. There the priest pried into every aspect of people's lives, especially their sexual lives. The list of sexual sins in the confessional manuals of the day was so complete, that even sexual thoughts were categorized according to their particular danger of damnation. Whether sexual relations within marriage were serious sins was debated, but there was agreement that at least in principle they were sins. Part and parcel of this orientation was the elevation of celibacy and the cloister as the supreme forms of a God-pleasing life. The corollary to this view was a demeaning of marriage and family as necessary evils for the propagation of the community. It is no wonder that the Reformation attack on mandatory celibacy for the clergy, as well as its renewed appreciation of the human value of sexuality, was so well received by the laity.

Everyday life on the eve of the Reformation also included elements regarded today as superstitions: belief in witches, magic, and astrology. But before we look too quickly down our collective modern nose at late medieval superstitions, we might recall that most of our daily newspapers include horoscopes and that the "health and wealth" gurus use contemporary media to appeal to the same fears and desires that motivated the medieval person to seek out supernatural healers and diviners of the future.

Martin Luther and the Beginnings of the Reformation

Luther's reform movement was initiated not by the moral indignation of a Savonarola or an Erasmus directed against the Renaissance papacy, but by his own personal anxiety about salvation—an anxiety that, if the popular response to him is any indication, was widespread throughout Europe. The crises of famine, plague, and war, exacerbated by the rapid and confusing social changes caused by technological developments, urban growth, displacement of the feudal economy by the profit economy, and the perceived corruption of the church, fueled this anxiety. Cynics played on the traditional image of the church as the ark of salvation by comparing it to Noah's ark without benefit of shoveled stalls. The medieval animal epic, Reynard the Fox, stated succinctly: "Little crooks are hanged; big crooks govern our lands and cities." The fable ends with the moral, "Money counts, and nothing else."[1] Reynard's point is that if you want to get to the top, you should imitate him.

By the late fifteenth century, the population had largely recovered from its decimation by famine and plague, but the social effects were still being felt. The labor shortage due to the plague lured many peasants to the cities with the hope of making better lives for themselves. But this flight from rural areas jeopardized the livelihood of landowners, who therefore took whatever steps they could to keep their workers on the farms. In many cases, these steps were oppressive. Serfdom was established or, where already present, strengthened. Laws such as the English Statutes of Laborers arose throughout Europe, mandating that laborers were not to abandon their employers. These laws prescribed severe punishments for vagrancy and begging. In southern Germany especially, there was a movement to replace local laws and customs by Roman law in order to squeeze as much labor and goods as possible out of peasants and day laborers. The ecclesiastical landlords were particularly adept at this practice because they were already familiar with Roman law in the form of canon law. This is one of the reasons for the widespread anticlerical anger on the eve of the Reformation.

Technological developments also stimulated the insecurities of the age. The inven-

---

[1] Gerald Strauss, ed., *Manifestations of Discontent in Germany on the Eve of the Reformation* (Bloomington, IN: Indiana University Press, 1971), pp. 91, 96.

tion of movable metal type, inexpensive paper, and good ink led to a media explosion. More books were printed between 1460 and 1500 than had been produced by scribes and monks throughout the entire Middle Ages. The printing press made possible the rapid and reliable dissemination of new ideas, including religious ideas. Luther himself was a prolific author. Before 1520, he had already produced eighty-two writings that appeared in 607 editions. Assuming a printing of 1,000 copies each, more than 500,000 pieces were in circulation. This was only the beginning of a flood of writings that, thanks to the printing press, allowed Luther, and then other reformers, to transmit their messages.

The development of sump pumps and smelting led to a boom in mining and metallurgy. One effect of this technology was a massive increase in silver production that in turn stimulated inflation because much of the silver was made into coins. Another effect, in combination with the invention of a stable gunpowder mixture, was the development of guns and cannon. Indiscriminate death and destruction were now possible beyond the medieval person's wildest nightmares. When this technology was coupled with national and religious fanaticism, those nightmares all too often became reality. There was money to be made in arms, and so a fledgling military-industrial complex grew and bore its deadly fruit. In turn, these developments hastened the demise of an entire medieval class of people, the knights. Along with other factors, this led to the Knights' Revolt of 1523.

All these various crises found their focal point in the crisis of the church or, in broader, modern terms, the crisis of society's fundamental values. The erosion of security in so many aspects of late medieval life came to a head in the loss of certainty about the meaning and goal of life itself. The church had been the guarantor of the symbols of certainty, but the many late medieval vicissitudes of the church contributed to the perception that the church itself was in crisis.

The crisis of the church affected the credibility of religion in every area of life. Scholars have puzzled over the great surge of popular piety in the late Middle Ages. Why did people throw themselves into such a piety of achievement? Perhaps because in times of crisis people tend to yearn for the "good old days" and try harder to emulate what they think they were. No other period celebrated so many religious festivals and processions or threw itself so wholeheartedly into the construction of churches. Mass pilgrimages, frequently sparked by some perceived miracle usually associated with the Lord's Supper, caught on like wildfire. The dark side of this devotion erupted in mass attacks on Jews and persons thought to be witches. Miracles seemed to multiply everywhere in the empire. The veneration of saints reached its peak. Saints were depicted life size, individualized, and garbed in contemporary dress. Saints were aligned with the arrangement of society and made patrons for every human exigency. Insecure about salvation, people attempted to guarantee it by capturing mediators between themselves and God.

Death seems never to have been more realistically considered than in this era and hardly ever so anxiously feared. Even today, we are still fascinated by the bizarre paintings of the Dutchman, Hieronymous Bosch (ca. 1450–1516), with their weird, rapidly breeding hybrid creatures associated with lust and fertility, but which in the end symbolize sterility and death. Artistic realism also blossomed with popular manuals on the art of dying, depictions of the "dance of death," and deeply moving representations of Christ's passion. Relic collections abounded. Luther's contemporary, Cardinal Albrecht of Brandenburg, believed that his collection was worth 39,245,120 years off purgatory. The extraordinary prosperity of the indulgence trade was fueled as much by the desires of believers as by the financial interests of the church. If this seems surprising, think of the similar appeal and success of modern media evangelists who promise to satisfy contemporary desires to control God and conquer insecurity. Late medieval Christendom has been characterized as having "an immense appetite for the divine."[2]

Theological and Pastoral Responses to Insecurity

A characteristic of late medieval theology and pastoral practice was that its very effort to provide security led an insecure world only to more insecurity and uncertainty about salvation. One of the key scholastic ideas that led to this uncertainty about salvation was expressed in the phrase *facere quod in se est* (do what lies within you). That is, striving to love God to the best of one's ability—however weak that may be—will prompt God to reward one's efforts with the grace to do even better. The Christian's life of pilgrimage toward the heavenly city was increasingly perceived, literally and not just theologically, as an economy of salvation. The "mathematics of salvation" concentrated on achieving as many good works as possible in order to merit God's reward. In religion, as in early capitalism, work merited reward. Individuals were to be responsible for their own life, society, and world on the basis stipulated by God. The concern of the theologians was to provide an avenue to security through human participation in the process of salvation. The result, however, aggravated the crisis because it threw people back upon their own resources.

As Thomas Aquinas was fond of saying, grace does not do away with nature, but completes it. So the famous scholastic phrase, "Do what lies within you," means that salvation is a process that takes place *within* us as we perfect ourselves. Put another way, we become righteous before God as we do good works. But to an anxious and insecure age, the question became "How do I know if I have done my best?"

The answers came primarily from the parish priests, who were frequently unversed in the subtleties of academic theology. The most common answer, "Try harder," is the clue to that great surge in popular piety mentioned earlier. When in doubt about your salvation, examine yourself to determine whether you have done your best, and then put more effort into achieving the best you can. To encourage more effort, pastoral practice consciously stimulated anxiety and introspection by citing the church's translation of Ecclesiastes 9:1, "No one knows whether he is worthy of God's love or hate."

Catechisms—simplified expositions of basic theology, usually in question-and-answer format, used by the priests in daily pastoral practice—provide an important clue to the religious sensibilities of the people. Dietrich Kolde's (1435–1515) *Mirror of a Christian Man* indicates the deep religious fear and anxiety of the people up to the eve of the Reformation and thereby provides the context for understanding Luther's reform movement.

Kolde's *Mirror* was very popular. First printed in 1470, it appeared in nineteen editions before the Reformation. Kolde's work was probably the most widely used Catholic catechism before and during the early years of the Reformation. The significant point of

---

[2]Lucien Febvres's phrase, cited by Bernd Moeller, "Piety in Germany Around 1500," in Steven Ozment, *The Reformation in Medieval Perspective* (Chicago: Quadrangle Books, 1971), p. 59.

this catechism for our purposes is the author's expression of the people's widespread lack of certitude about salvation. Kolde summed up this anxiety when he wrote, "There are three things I know to be true that frequently make my heart heavy. The first troubles my spirit, because I will have to die. The second troubles my heart more, because I do not know when. The third troubles me above all. I do not know where I will go."[3]

Luther's first steps on his own quest for certainty about his relationship to God were not unlike those of many before him and countless others since: He entered "seminary." In Luther's case, it was the Augustinian monastery in Erfurt. Again, not unlike the situation of countless other seminarians, both past and present, Luther's decision greatly upset his father, who was by this time making a decent living at what we might call the medieval equivalent of a mining engineer. He had sent Martin to Erfurt University with the ambition that he would earn a law degree, return home to the town of Mansfeld, and perhaps eventually become mayor. Luther had barely begun his law studies when his father's dreams were shattered by the same lightning bolt that knocked Martin to the ground as he walked to Erfurt after a visit home. In terror, Martin implored St. Anne, the patron saint of miners, for help, shouting, "I will become a monk."

And become a monk he did! In July 1505, he entered the Black Cloister (so called because the monks wore black) of the Observant Augustinians in Erfurt. The Black Augustinians' rigorous pursuit of spiritual benefits more than matched in intensity the pursuit of material benefits practiced by Luther's father and other budding entrepreneurs in the world. It was no less the business of monks to earn spiritual currency for themselves and others than it was the business of the early capitalists to earn material currency.

In the monastery, Luther threw himself wholeheartedly into efforts to achieve salvation. Between the six worship services of each day, which began at 2:00 A.M., Luther sandwiched intense prayer, meditation, and spiritual exercises. But this was just the normal routine that Luther soon surpassed in his zeal to mortify his flesh and make himself acceptable to God. It has been suggested that his long periods of fasting, self-flagellation, and sleepless nights in a stone cell without a blanket against the damp cold characteristic of the area all contributed to the illnesses that plagued him for the rest of his life. Nevertheless, Luther could not believe that God was placated by his efforts to do what lay within him. And so, Luther came to hate "the righteous God who punishes sinners. . . . Nevertheless, I beat importunately upon Paul at that place, most ardently desiring to know what St. Paul wanted."[4]

"That place" is the passage in Romans 1:17, "For in it [the gospel] the righteousness of God is revealed through faith for faith; as it is written, 'He who through faith is righteous shall live.' " Up to this point, Luther, like so many of his contemporaries, had heard the gospel as the threat of God's righteousness and wrath because medieval theology and pastoral care presented the righteousness of God as the standard that sinners had to meet in order to achieve salvation. Years later, Luther wrote, "But every time I read this passage, I always wished that God had never revealed the gospel—for who could love a God who is angry, judges, and condemns?"[5]

[3] Denis Janz, *Three Reformation Catechisms: Catholic, Anabaptist, Lutheran* (New York and Toronto: The Edwin Mellon Press, 1982), p. 127.

[4] *Luther's Works*, ed. by Jaroslav Pelikan and Helmut T. Lehmann. 55 vols. St. Louis: Concordia Publishing House and Minneapolis: Fortress Press, 1955–1986, vol. 34, pp. 336–337.

[5] *Ibid.*, vol. 5, p. 158.

Then Luther discovered, through his intense study of the Bible, assisted·by the linguistic tools provided by the Renaissance humanists, that the righteousness of God is not a demand to be met by achievement, but a gift to be accepted by faith. This discovery is the source for the Reformation watchwords of *sola gratia* (grace alone) and *sola fide* (faith alone). Luther's conversion was the realization that salvation is received, not achieved—that salvation is not the goal of life, but the *foundation* of life. It is an indication of the power of this discovery that the theology faculty at the University of Wittenberg, which he had joined in 1512, instituted a curriculum reform that replaced scholastic theology with the studies of the Bible and St. Augustine. The Bible displaced the authority of Aristotle—hence the other major Reformation watchword: *sola scriptura* (scripture alone).

What Luther discovered and what so moved his faculty colleagues and students was an understanding of God and salvation that overthrew the anxiety-ridden catechetical teachings of priests such as Kolde. Luther's biblical study led him to the conviction that the crisis of human life is not overcome by striving to achieve security by what we do, but by the certainty of God's acceptance of us *in spite of* what we do. The burden of proof for salvation rests not on a person's deeds, but on God's action. This conviction delivered Luther from what he called "the monster of uncertainty," that is, dependence on his own achievements, and affirmed God's promise of salvation.

The Diet of Worms

The indulgence controversy propelled Luther into the public arena. The popular mind, abetted by some preachers, had twisted the meaning of indulgence from that of the remission of a church-imposed temporal penalty to that of a ticket to heaven. Hard-sell medieval indulgence sellers offered direct access to heaven even for those already dead and in purgatory. One of the Dominican monk Johann Tetzel's sales jingles was "As soon as the coin into the box rings, a soul from purgatory to heaven springs." Crowds of anxious contemporaries believed that they could buy salvation from him. He was good at his job, but then, he was also rewarded handsomely.

Tetzel's routine would have been the envy of Madison Avenue. His advance men announced his arrival some weeks before he came to town. They also compiled a special directory of the town that listed the financial resources of its citizens. Tetzel then entered the town accompanied by a fanfare of trumpets and drums and a procession complete with the flags and symbols of the papacy. After a vivid sermon on hell and its terrors in the town square, he proceeded to the largest church and gave an equally vivid sermon on purgatory and the sufferings not only awaiting the audience, but presently endured by their dead relatives. After the next sermon picturing heaven, his audience was sufficiently prepared and eager to buy indulgences. There was something for everyone, because Tetzel had a sliding scale of prices depending on the person's financial resources.

Luther's prince, Frederick the Wise, did not allow Tetzel in Wittenberg because he did not want competition with his own relic collection and its associated indulgences. Luther's parishioners overcame this inconvenience by going out to Tetzel. Luther was appalled when they returned and said that they no longer needed to go to confession, penance, and the Mass because now they had tickets to heaven.

This was the immediate context for the *Ninety-five Theses* of October 31, 1517, the traditional date for the beginning of the Reformation. In these theses, Luther attacked not the church's doctrine of indulgences, but the abuse of that doctrine so evident in the activities of Tetzel. In fact, the *Ninety-five Theses* were a typical academic proposition for debate among university colleagues. The theses were written in Latin, and most Wittenbergers could not even read German. Thus, the popular image of Luther as the angry young man pounding incendiary theses into the church door is far more romantic fiction than reality. Then how did this document for debate cause such an uproar? Luther sent it to Tetzel's superior, Albrecht, the archbishop of Mainz, with the naive thought that Albrecht did not know that his hireling was abusing the authority of the church. Someone in the archbishop's office sent the document on to Rome. The resulting explosion startled and frightened Luther as much as anyone else.

Luther had unknowingly touched the nerve of a far-reaching political and ecclesiastical scam. Pope Leo X needed funds to build St. Peter's to impress his secular rivals, and Albrecht provided such funds in return for the archbishopric of Mainz. Albrecht, legally under age to hold an archbishopric and not even ordained, belonged to the ambitious House of Hohenzollern. The Hohenzollerns wanted the office of Archbishop of Mainz because it included membership in the electoral college that elected the Holy Roman Emperor. The electoral college consisted of seven electors: the archbishops of Mainz, Trier, and Cologne, the Count Palatine of the Rhine, the Duke of Electoral Saxony (Luther's Prince Frederick), the Margrave of Brandenburg (Albrecht's brother!), and the King of Bohemia. With two votes of their own, the Hohenzollerns reasoned that they might be able to swing the impending imperial election. Thus, the Hohenzollern "bought" the archbishopric for Albrecht. The special papal dispensation that allowed Albrecht to become archbishop cost a very substantial amount of money, borrowed at an exorbitant interest rate from the famous Fugger banking house of Augsburg. To pay back this huge loan, Albrecht, now archbishop, received the right from Leo X to sell indulgences, with half the proceeds going to finance the building of St. Peter's in Rome. It is no wonder that Albrecht hired the best indulgence salesman he could find: Tetzel.

Events accelerated rapidly. In the summer of 1518, the papacy informed Luther that he was a heretic and summoned him to Rome. Local pride and German law, however, saved Luther from what would surely have been his execution had he gone to Rome. By this time, Prince Frederick realized that student enrollment had increased markedly at Wittenberg University, his pride and joy that he himself had just founded in 1502. He was not about to let his prize professor and academic drawing card go off to be burned at the stake. Besides, German law said that its citizens should be tried in its own courts. Thus, papal representatives agreed to interview Luther in Germany. But his interview with Cardinal Cajetan in Augsburg in October 1518 did not satisfy either party. Luther would not recant, and the cardinal would not discuss the theological issues.

The next step in the rapidly escalating "Luther affair" began with a debate in Leipzig in July 1519. Surrounded by armed students and colleagues, Luther journeyed to Leipzig University, where he confronted Johann Eck, one of the most clever debaters of the day. Eck prodded Luther with charges that he was a Hussite and a Bohemian, tantamount to being called a communist in the 1950s. After some consideration, Luther burst out that many of Hus's views condemned by the Council of Constance were indeed Christian, which indicated that a church council, as well as the pope, may err. The audience was shocked. Luther confirmed the implications of the teachings he had been developing over the past years: Christ alone is head of the church, and when the institution of the papacy usurps this headship, it is the Antichrist.

Luther, now center stage, gained the attention of humanists and German nationalists, as well as clergy and theological professors. In June 1520, the papal bull *Exsurge Domine* gave Luther sixty days to recant or to be excommunicated. If Luther failed to recant, his very memory would be erased. This, of course, was easier said than done, for by now much of Germany had rallied to his side. When the bull was posted in Germany, it was defaced. When the book burnings that normally accompanied such a bull took place, gleeful students gave papal and scholastic writings to the enforcers of the bull, who then burned them as Luther's works. Eck himself added fuel to the fires by adding his own private "enemies list" to those condemned.

The sixtieth day of grace granted Luther by the bull fell on December 10, 1520. On that day Luther's colleague, Melanchthon, led the faculty and students out of the university for a truly revolutionary act: They marched to the place where the personal effects of plague victims had been burned and there publicly and solemnly burned the constitutional foundations of medieval Europe—the books of canon law. Luther himself threw the papal bull on the fire. After singing the Te Deum, the faculty returned to the university. The students, however, carried on boisterous demonstrations against the pope for the next few days until the town authorities stopped them. The actual bull of excommunication, *Decet Romanum*, appeared on January 3, 1521.

The papacy urged the recently elected emperor, Charles V, to issue a mandate against Luther. But the German constitution and Charles's coronation oath upheld the right of Germans to trial by an impartial panel of judges. Thus, Charles promised Luther a safe passage to a hearing at the Diet to be held at Worms. In spite of the friendly reminders that Hus, too, had been given a safe-conduct to Constance but then was executed, Luther made a triumphal journey to Worms. There, before the emperor, princes, and lords—a whole world away from his monastic cell and classroom—Luther did not receive a hearing. Rather, he was presented with a pile of his writings and asked to recant their errors. Luther's brief answer included the following memorable lines: "Unless I am convinced by the testimony of the Scriptures or by clear reason . . . I cannot and I will not retract anything, since it is neither safe nor right to go against conscience. I cannot do otherwise, here I stand, may God help me. Amen."[6]

The evening the Diet closed, the emperor gathered a rump Diet of conservative princes and bishops and issued the Edict of Worms (1521), which proclaimed Luther an outlaw. All subjects of the realm were forbidden to have any dealings with him, but were to seize him and deliver him to the authorities. Luther's followers and supporters were to be treated likewise, and their property was to be confiscated and given to the one carrying out the edict. Fortunately for Luther, he had a number of powerful supporters, including his own prince, Frederick the Wise.

[6]*Ibid.*, vol. 32, pp. 112–113.

The Reformation and Social Change

Medieval people certainly made distinctions between ecclesial and civil rights and responsibilities, but they had no conception of the modern separation of church and state. They took for granted that theological change had social implications and consequences. It is not surprising that Luther's translation of the Bible into German was so influential that it contributed significantly to the development of the modern German language, but his translation had other social and political effects as well. Coupled with Luther's theological emphasis that all baptized Christians are equally priests before God, his emphasis on making the Word of God accessible to all deprived the elite class (the priests and some rulers) of control over words as well as the Word. The printing press facilitated this challenge to authorities.

Furthermore, Luther's emphasis on the normative religious authority of the Scriptures, which convinced him that all Christians should be able to read the Bible, preferably in its original languages, became an important step toward universal education. Luther also made it clear that Christians should be educated not only for deepening their faith, but also for serving the community. God would preserve the church, "but in the worldly kingdom men must act on the basis of reason—wherein the laws also have their origin."[7]

Luther also appealed to religious and civil leaders to reform the structures of social welfare. As mentioned earlier, late medieval society faced extensive and often severe poverty. Pre-Reformation laws to compel able-bodied beggars to work were largely ineffective because the medieval church had developed an ideology of poverty as a virtue. By viewing the poor person as blessed by God and an object for the meritorious work of almsgiving, this ideology obscured the social causes of poverty. Luther's rejection of charity as a means of salvation undercut that ideology. Because salvation was now understood to be a free gift apart from works, there was no longer any need to have poor people as God-given objects for the practice of charity and the benefit of businesses. In attacking the theological idea that poverty is a virtue as well as an opportunity for the rich to do good works of almsgiving, Luther and other reformers such as Zwingli and Calvin exposed the social roots of poverty and contributed to the development of social welfare programs directed to systemic, and not merely individual, change.

Nearly every town that adopted the Reformation enacted legislation that included the provision for a "common chest" to support social welfare. The common chest—literally a large chest kept in the town's major church and usually fitted with several locks—contained relief funds for the poor, account books, and lists of the area poor. The funds initially came from the large endowments of the church that had accumulated during the Middle Ages, supplemented by offerings of money and goods; later, taxation regularized funding. Elected representatives, usually one from each quarter of the town, each had a key to one of the locks on the chest. Every Sunday the representatives, along with the pastor and the church deacons, met to assess the needs of the town's poor and to provide for the distribution of money and goods to them. The legislation establishing the common chest not only concerned remedial work, such as relief of the poor, low-interest loans to poor workers and tradesmen, subsidies of education for poor children, and dowries for daughters of the poor,

[7] *Ibid.*, vol. 46, p. 242.

but also addressed social structures and policies, such as job training, to try to prevent poverty. The first common chest was instituted in Wittenberg in 1522 and soon became a model for similar programs in the major cities of Germany and Scandinavia. The organizational genius for social welfare programs in the Lutheran areas was Luther's coworker, Johannes Bugenhagen (1485–1558). Bugenhagen traveled tirelessly throughout northern Germany and Scandinavia, developing legislation for reform of the church that included educational and welfare policies.

As these examples suggest, Luther never advocated that Christians withdraw from the world. Indeed, the very point of his understanding of the gospel is that, because salvation is the foundation rather than the goal of life, the Christian is free to serve others with the time and energy previously expended on achieving salvation. That is, trust in God's promise of salvation liberates one from constantly checking one's spiritual pulse. The Christian can turn his or her attention from otherworldly achievements to this-worldly activities.

Thus, Luther vigorously distinguished between the kingdom of God and the kingdom of the world. He hammered incessantly on this distinction because he wanted to call Christians to political action in an age that conceived of religion primarily as withdrawal from the world—even kings preferred to spend their last days in a monastery! The medieval person could not conceive of having a vocation in the world, because "vocation" had a narrow religious meaning and politics was "dirty." Luther hoped to free Christians for service in a world shrouded in political ambiguity by distinguishing between human, civil righteousness measured by justice and equitable laws and the righteousness before God that is a free gift.

Luther's distinction, but not separation, between life in the world governed by reason, law, and works and life before God governed by grace alone was put to the test by a contemporary radical reformer, Thomas Müntzer (ca. 1489–1525). Initially influenced by Luther, Müntzer came to believe that civil authorities should play a central role in Christianizing society. In his famous "Sermon Before the Princes" (1524), preached to the Duke of Saxony and his advisors, Müntzer exhorted the princes to act as the servants of God's wrath on all the ungodly.

The princes not only were not convinced by Müntzer's message, but considered it dangerous. Müntzer then fled from one city to another. When he returned to Saxony, he became involved in the Peasant's War not because he was a social revolutionary, but because he saw the war as the occasion for the final battle of God against all the ungodly. He exhorted others to join the battle: "The time has come, the evil-doers are running like scared dogs . . . show no pity. . . . Don't let your sword grow cold . . . . It is not your fight, but the Lord's."[8] By this bloody purification of the world, Müntzer hoped to usher in a genuine theocracy that would realize completely the medieval aspiration for a Christian commonwealth. In May 1525, Müntzer preached encouragement to the peasant troops at Frankenhausen before their bloody slaughter by the troops of Duke George of ducal Saxony. But his utopian exhortations were no match against the duke's firepower. Müntzer himself fled, but was found hiding in a bed feigning illness. Under torture, he recanted and was executed.

The Müntzer episode reaffirmed to Luther that the world must be governed by rea-

[8]Peter Matheson, trans. and ed., *The Collected Works of Thomas Müntzer* (Edinburgh: T. & T. Clark, 1988), pp. 141–142.

son and law, not by religious ideology. From Luther's point of view, all efforts to govern the world by the gospel of free forgiveness would lead either to unrestrained chaos and destruction or to a demonic crusade against all perceived "evil empires." To Luther, the identification of any political program, regardless of its intrinsic merit, with the will of God would subvert both politics and the gospel. It would subvert the political process because the claim to absolute righteousness precludes the ambiguity present in all social life, as well as the art of compromise necessary in social relations. Group and national self-righteousness lead people to see political opponents as followers of the devil (i.e., the "ungodly") who have no right to live. The identification of a political program with the will of God would subvert the gospel, forcing citizens to conform to a religious norm and making salvation dependent on a particular political affiliation and program, i.e., on the good works of politics. For Luther, faith alone grants the security to live within the human insecurity of relative political structures and to avoid the defensive sanctification of past, present, or future goods and values. For Luther, faith alone enables the person to be human and to let God be God. Luther's efforts to improve education, social welfare, and the political process reflected his conviction that all systems of justice and politics are only relative and instrumental for the humanization of persons. He attempted to de-ideologize politics by declaring that God, not the party and not the church, is sovereign in history.

The Peasants' War

The Peasants' War presented Müntzer with what he believed was the context for the coming divine separation of the elect from the godless, but Müntzer was by no means the instigator of the war. Neither was Luther, although he was blamed for it after the defeat of the peasants. In Germany, the peasant protest against political and economic injustice coalesced in a peasant league known as the *Bundschuh*, after its logo of the peasants' laced shoe as a contrast to the nobles' fancy boots.

A moderate peasant appeal known as "The Twelve Articles of the Peasants" (1525) presented the godly common people as wanting only such legitimate rights as community authority to choose, appoint, and, if necessary, depose their pastor; proper and biblically regulated taxation; the abolition of serfdom; common access to game and fish; free firewood from the forests; release from excessive services; cessation of oppression by the lords; equitable rents; a return to the old laws of custom in place of the new imposition of Roman law; the return of expropriated common lands; and the abolition of the "death tax" that oppressed widows and orphans.

Luther replied to "The Twelve Articles" with his *Admonition to Peace*, which called on the rulers to amend their oppressive ways before a rebellion arose that would destroy all Germany. At the same time, Luther insisted that rebellion is never justified and especially not when identified as a Christian action. This was a position he had publicly expressed years earlier, and it was widely understood.

However, Luther was no more effective in stopping the rebellion than Müntzer was in leading it to victory. Peasant rage exploded in a number of areas. Once the princes recovered from the initial shocks of the war, they ruthlessly crushed the peasants. As many as 100,000 peasants may have been killed in Germany in 1525! In spite of this great tragedy, the Reformation did not lose peasant support. Evangelical preachers continued to go out to rural areas, and the Reformation continued to spread in Germany.

The Swiss Connection: Zwingli and the Reformation in Zurich

The Swiss Reformation went public with the "Affair of the Sausages." During Lent, 1522, the Swiss Reformer Ulrich Zwingli (1484–1531) was at the house of Christopher Froschauer, a printer preparing a new edition of the epistles of Paul. To refresh his tired workers, Froschauer served sausages. The public breaking of the Lenten fast flouted medieval piety and ecclesial and public authority. The Zurich Town Council arrested Froschauer, but not Zwingli, who himself had not eaten the meat. Zwingli, who held the eminent post of peoples' priest at the Great Minster in Zurich, could have smoothed everything out. Instead, he made a public issue of this incident by preaching a sermon, "On the Choice and Freedom of Foods," which he soon enlarged into a printed pamphlet. Almost certainly influenced by Luther's earlier treatise on Christian freedom (1520), Zwingli argued that Christians are free to fast or not to fast because the Bible does not prohibit the eating of meat during Lent.

How had Zwingli reached this point of public opposition to ecclesial and political authority? A precocious farm boy from an alpine village, Zwingli was already studying the classics in Basel at age ten. He then went on to the universities of Vienna and Basel, where he studied theology, philosophy, and the classics. He received his master's degree from Basel in 1506 and then became the parish priest at Glarus in the Swiss canton of the same name. Here he had time for his passionate interest in the classics, the church fathers, and the Bible, with enough time left over for his avocational interest in women.

However, his growing tensions with the magistrates of Glarus were not over his personal morality, but over his public denunciation of the mainstay of the Swiss export business—mercenary soldiers. France, Spain, and the papacy sought Swiss pikemen, renowned for their skill and ferocity, for their armies fighting over Italy. As chaplain to the Glarus contingent of soldiers, Zwingli witnessed the carnage of battle and experienced the pain of informing families of the dead. Both Zwingli's pastoral concern and his patriotic nationalism motivated him to oppose the mercenary practices he believed were eroding the moral and social fabric of the Swiss, not to mention their very existence as a people as they killed each other in the pay of opposing armies.

The magistrates of Glarus granted Zwingli's request to transfer to the nearby parish of Einsiedeln in April 1516, where he functioned as a chaplain to the many pilgrims who flocked to its shrine of the Black Virgin. In his off-hours, he pored over the newly published Greek New Testament compiled by Erasmus. Zwingli soon became a celebrity for his expositions of the Bible in worship and sermons. His Erasmian erudition and biblical fervor served him well in his denunciation of the Franciscan indulgence seller, Bernard Samson, the Swiss counterpart to Tetzel. Zwingli preached Samson right out of town.

Zwingli's reputation for biblical preaching led to his nomination for the post of people's priest at the Great Minster in Zurich in 1518. Detractors raised the issue of Zwingli's womanizing, but their charges were ineffective because the other priest vying for the post lived openly in concubinage and had six children. In light of this specific example and the generally widespread practice of priestly concubinage in the late Middle Ages, it is not surprising that one of the first reforms initiated in the Swiss Reformation was the right of the clergy to marry. Only months after the Affair of the Sausages, Zwingli, then living with the widow Anna Reinhart, led ten other Swiss priests in a petition to the Bishop of Constance *To Allow Priests to Marry, or at Least Wink at their Marriages* (July 1522). The priests signing this petition declared that chastity is a rare gift of God and that they hadn't received it. Zwingli married Anna in a public ceremony in 1524 shortly before the birth of their child. In 1525, the Zurich magistrates mandated that clergy living in concubinage either end the relationship or marry. A marriage court was also established that clarified marital relationships by expanding grounds for divorce to include extreme incompatibility, desertion, physical and mental illness, and fraud.

On the basis of his humanist and biblical studies, Zwingli formulated the reform principle that scripture judges everything. What did not conform to biblical teaching did not command obedience. The test, whether traditional ceremonies and teachings promoted the gospel of redemption by Christ, quickly raised questions about all areas of life beyond sex and sausages. The effort to provide biblical norms for all of life also led to "neighborly" spying and court-enforced attempts to oversee the city's moral life.

The town magistrates called for a public disputation between the advocates and opponents of reform in the Zurich town hall in January 1523. Zwingli prepared his *Sixty-seven Articles*, the charter of the Zurich Reformation, for this event. The articles affirmed salvation by grace alone, insisted on the full and final authority of scripture, and rejected the pope, the mass, good works for salvation, monastic orders, a celibate clergy, penance, and purgatory. Zwingli's proposals meant nothing less than the dismantling of medieval ecclesiology. Zwingli carried the day against the old order, and the Zurich clergy were ordered to confine their preaching to scripture.

Zwingli's reform movement spread rapidly throughout Switzerland and south Germany. Congregations in Constance, Ulm, Frankfurt, Augsburg, Lindau, Memmingen, and Strasbourg were won over to the Zurich Reformation. The conversion of the Swiss canton of Bern in 1528 was particularly important not only for the immediate establishment of Zwinglianism in the Swiss Confederacy, but for the future reform of Geneva under the auspices of William Farel and John Calvin. Basel, also of political importance, followed Bern into the Zwinglian fold.

In the meantime, however, the rural and conservative Catholic cantons of Switzerland allied to oppose the Reformation. In 1529 the threat of Zwinglian expansion pushed the Catholic cantons of Uri, Schwyz, Unterwalden, Zug, Lucerne, and Fribourg into an alliance with the ancient enemy of the Swiss Confederacy: Austria. The execution of a Zwinglian preacher as a heretic in Schwyz led to a military confrontation at Kappel. The obvious strength of the Zurich forces and the common Swiss distaste for Habsburg meddling in the affairs of the Swiss Confederacy prompted an armistice in June 1529. At least temporarily, Swiss nationalism superseded religious differences.

Religious friction continued, however, and Zwingli believed that the southern cantons were still allied with Austria. At the same time, the German Lutherans were menaced by Charles V, who, by greatly reducing French and Turkish threats, felt free to turn his attention to the Luther affair. He intended to eliminate heresy from his lands. At the Diet of Speyer in April 1529, the emperor demanded that the previous Diet's (1526) allowance of territorial and urban discretion regarding the Reformation be rescinded. In response, four evangelical states and fourteen free imperial cities submitted a formal *Protestatio* (hence the name "Protestant") that decreed that the agreement of 1526 be maintained until a national assembly and ecumenical council could be convoked to settle the religious issues. The signatories to the *Protestatio* included Lutheran (e.g., Electoral Saxony) and Zwinglian (e.g., Strasbourg) areas. In this context, the German Lutheran prince, Philip of Hesse, decided that the time was ripe to create an international political and military alliance between the Lutherans and the Zwinglians for their mutual protection against the emperor and for the spread of the Reformation.

Philip knew that his dream of a Protestant alliance was unrealizable unless the mutual antagonisms of Luther and Zwingli over their respective understandings of the Lord's Supper could be reconciled. So Philip invited the two sides to meet for a religious colloquy at his Marburg castle in October 1529.

It is a tragic irony that the Lord's Supper, the sacrament of Christian unity, has divided rather than united Christians in various periods of church history. This was especially the case in the sixteenth century: To be right about the sacrament was to be right about God and salvation. Neither Luther nor Zwingli thought the other was right about the sacrament. Although they agreed in rejecting both the mass as a sacrifice and the doctrine of transubstantiation, they disagreed—vehemently!—over their understanding of the Lord's Supper.

By 1524, Zwingli, influenced by the Platonic dualism of flesh and spirit advanced earlier in connection with the sacrament by Erasmus, began to interpret the "is" of "This is my body" as "signifies." In his 1503 *Enchiridion*, which went through numerous editions and translations, Erasmus developed a spiritual or memorial understanding of the Lord's Supper that strongly influenced Luther's former colleague, Karlstadt, and, through Karlstadt, Zwingli. One of their favorite biblical verses was John 6:63: "It is the spirit that gives life, the flesh is of no avail." Karlstadt and those he influenced used this verse to justify differentiating between the bread eaten by the communicant and the Christ received by faith. Indeed, Karlstadt's interpretation of the words of institution of the Lord's Supper posited that when Jesus said "This is my body," he was pointing at himself. This led one contemporary wag to suggest that when Jesus said "This is my blood," he must have had a nosebleed.

After falling out with Luther, Karlstadt not only had five tracts on the Lord's Supper printed in Switzerland; he also visited Zwingli. Erasmus had attacked Luther, too, in 1524. Thus, Luther's controversies with Karlstadt and Erasmus strongly colored his view of Zwingli. Luther's insistence that Christ is really present in the sacrament appeared to Zwingli to be a relapse into the Catholic doctrine of transubstantiation. A further sense of the magnitude of Philip's task in reconciling these two reformers is provided by an overview of their positions on the subject prior to 1529.

In 1525, Zwingli developed his distinction between the "natural" body of Christ before the crucifixion, the "glorified" body of Christ ascended to heaven, and the mystical body of the church. Influenced by humanist linguistics, Zwingli argued that only the recognition of the Bible's figurative use of words—in particular, the metaphorical explanation of the Last Supper—could make the Bible plain, reasonable, and humanly intelligible. Christ's own words were intelligible only if the bread and wine were symbols to which the recipient brought faith and hope in God. To Luther, this meant that Zwingli had shifted the focus of the Lord's Supper from God's promise of salvation present in the eucharistic action to the active memory of the congregation. Luther saw this shift as another way of putting the burden of proof for salvation on the believer rather than on God.

Luther's argument against Zwingli found expression in the phrase that "the finite is capable of bearing the infinite." This meant not only that ordinary bread and wine may communicate the presence and promise of God, but that all creation may serve the Creator. Here is the theological foundation for Luther's profound appreciation of nature and art as vehicles for communicating the Gospel.

Those reformers who so emphasized the transcendence of God that they denied that the finite is capable of supporting the infinite began the process toward the modern world's exclusion of the sacred altogether. The first steps in this process may be seen in the iconoclastic reactions of reformers from Karlstadt to Zwingli and, in part, on into Calvin, who strove to purify the church by removing as much art as possible. These reformers stripped the churches of all images and color, and in Zurich they literally nailed shut the organs. Later, the word "puritan" expressed this trend. Some theorists think that these reformers struggled so successfully against the possibility of idolatry, that the holy was transformed into the morally good and that righteousness received ascetic connotations—all of which was finally banalized in the phrase that "cleanliness is next to godliness."

In early 1527, Zwingli completed his *Amica exegesis* (Friendly Exposition) in which he tried to combine independence and conciliation. Zwingli warned that Luther was perilously close to the Catholic doctrine of transubstantiation. But let the conflict end, wrote Zwingli, for the future could be bright if Luther would only recognize his mistakes. Luther's response to "this insolent Swiss," as he called Zwingli, appeared in his April 1527 tract, *That these words of Christ, "This is my body" still stand fast against the Fanatics*. His opponents, Luther wrote, were both crazy and possessed by the devil, not to mention blasphemous in their appeal to reason and common sense. In May, Zwingli responded in his "Friendly Answer" that, among other things, Luther incorrectly read scripture and conceded too much to Rome, and that God had not revealed to Luther the meaning of the Lord's Supper. So it went!

The antagonism between Zwingli and Luther was aggravated by what we may call nondoctrinal factors. One was Zwingli's humanistic fascination with classical figures of speech, which Luther thought only obscured biblical interpretation. Another nondoctrinal factor that contributed to mutual misunderstanding was that Luther lived under a benevolent and sympathetic prince, whereas Zwingli lived in a city that had a representative style of government. For Zwingli to carry out his desired reforms, he had to explain his position in a way that would be intelligible and persuasive to ordinary people. This plus Zwingli's humanistic leanings help to explain why Luther saw him as a rationalist. On the other hand, for Zwingli to agree with Luther's understanding of the Lord's Supper, which many Catholics saw as basically orthodox, would have been a political disaster in the Swiss context.

The Marburg Colloquy opened on October 1, 1529. By October 4, the Lutherans and the Zwinglians agreed to fourteen of fifteen articles prepared by Luther. They could not agree, however, on the Lord's Supper. Both sides repudiated transubstantiation as well as the belief that the Eucharist is a sacrifice for the living and the dead, and they insisted on communion in both kinds (bread and wine). But the Lutherans continued to hold that Christ is really present in the Eucharist for all recipients, whereas the Zwinglians maintained that Christ's presence is only in the hearts of believers. Although the two parties left Marburg with the intention of practicing Christian charity toward each other, they failed to achieve either a confessional or a military alliance.

In less than a year, the Imperial Diet met at Augsburg, where the Lutherans presented their confession of faith, the Augsburg Confession, which is still the basic confessional document of Lutheran churches. A confession with Zwinglian affinities, written mainly by the Strasbourg reformers Martin Bucer and Wolfgang Capito, known as the Tetrapolitan Confession because the four cities of Strasbourg, Constance, Memmingen, and Lindau subscribed to it, was also presented at Augsburg, but was not accepted. Zwingli, himself not invited to Augsburg, was determined to be heard and thus sent his hastily composed *Fidei Ratio*. Since this writing had no effect on Charles V, Zwingli composed a pamphlet, *Fidei Expositio*, for Francis I in the hope of winning the French king's support against the emperor and Rome. There is no evidence that Francis ever read this impressive defense of Zwingli's faith, and the pamphlet had no influence on the course of events.

A Zurich-inspired economic blockade of the Catholic cantons that refused to admit Protestant preachers increased Protestant–Catholic tensions. In retaliation, the Catholic cantons surprised Zurich with a vastly superior military force. Zwingli, himself armed, accompanied the Zurich forces into this second battle of Kappel in 1531. During the rout of the Zurich forces, Zwingli was seriously wounded and left on the battlefield. Later recognized by the Catholic forces, he was given a mortal blow, and the next day he was quartered (the punishment for traitors). Then the parts of his body were burned with dung so that nothing of Zwingli would be left to inspire other Protestants.

Unlike Zwingli, the Swiss Reformation was not exterminated; where established, it was allowed to remain. Catholic minorities were not to be disturbed in Protestant lands, whereas Protestant minorities were not to be tolerated in Catholic lands. The division of Switzerland offered a foretaste of the fate of Europe. Almost a quarter century later, in 1555, the Peace of Augsburg legally ratified the confessional divisions of the empire by aligning the religion of an area with that of its ruler. Later, this was described by the motto *cuius regio, eius religio* (whose reign, his religion). The Peace of Augsburg included the safety valve of allowing persons to emigrate to territories amenable to their confession of faith.

Chapter 19

The Radical Reformers

The radical reformers were, and still are, a difficult group to define. From the beginning, these reformers and their adherents were lumped together under labels that nearly always were pejorative. Their contemporaries called them enthusiasts (from *en theos*, "God-within-inism"), spiritualists, fanatics, and Anabaptists (or rebaptists). The last label indicated the belief that only adults able to make a profession of faith could be baptized. Because the first generation of these reformers already had been baptized as infants, an adult baptism was literally a rebaptism. The heterogeneous origins, leaders, and visions of reform further complicate discussion of the radical reformers. The umbrella term "radical" covers such disparate groups and persons as the Zwickau prophets, who apparently rejected infant baptism and initiated the Wittenberg disturbances of 1521–1522; Karlstadt (p. 273); Müntzer, who called for the execution of the godless; the equally, if not more, disruptive leaders who took over the city of Münster and precipitated a bloody debacle there; the dissenters in Zurich who were a thorn in Zwingli's side; and such men as Menno Simons, whose heirs form the still-existing peace church known as the Mennonites. (See Figure 19.1.)

A number of outstanding Anabaptist leaders contributed substantially to the vitality of the movement, but none of them enjoyed the widely acknowledged leadership positions of reformers such as Luther, Zwingli, and Calvin. The Anabaptist groups also lacked a clear confessional norm or statement, aside from the brief Schleitheim Confession of 1527, which not all of them accepted. Such ambiguity both dismayed and delighted their contemporaries (and modern historians), who picked and chose among the multiplicity of opinions, groupings, divisions, and leaders to form their own judgments. These judgments,

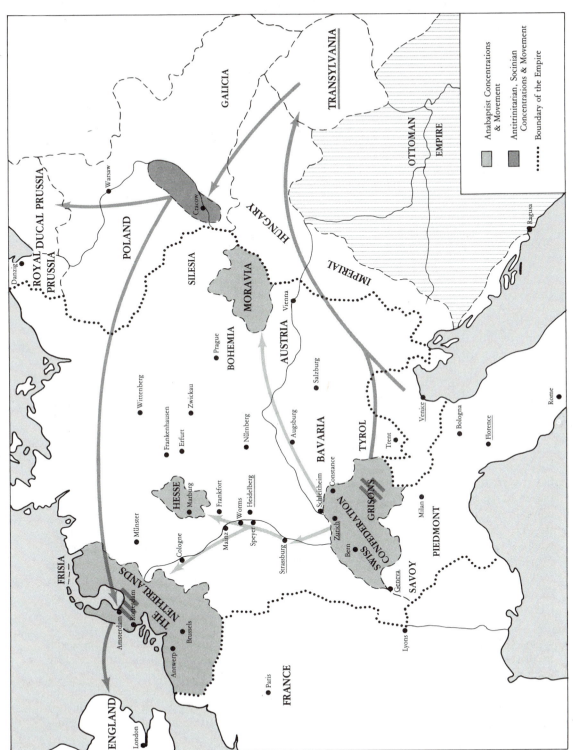

Figure 19.1 The Left Wing of the Reformation

whether formed by Lutheran, Zwinglian, Calvinist, or Catholic, were united in perceiving the Anabaptist groups as a threat to sixteenth-century society.

A major locus of Anabaptist development was Zurich. We have already seen that Zwingli's reform program depended on persuading the authorities and existed in the face of threats emanating from Catholic cantons. In the sixteenth century, nearly everyone believed that a community without a common ideology not only was at the mercy of one that was united (e.g., the Turks), but also was subject to a civil war that could imperil its very existence.

Zwingli therefore saw the rise of the Zurich Anabaptists as a clear and present danger. He regarded these evangelicals as quarrelsome, envious, backbiting, and hypocritical extremists who lacked charity and undermined government. Their opposition to infant baptism, their open-air preaching, and their constant street discussions and harangues brought the gospel into disrepute. Indeed, Zwingli saw them as social revolutionaries whose teaching would overthrow society and religion alike.

The immediate controversy centered on infant baptism, but behind it lay a very different view of Christianity. Other reformers, such as Luther and Calvin, agreed that there was but one catholic (i.e., universal) church with one creed. They understood the visible church as coextensive with the local community wherein people must live and worship in harmony. The Anabaptists, however, focused not on the whole community, but on local congregations of voluntary members who regarded themselves as altogether set apart from the state. For them, the one true church consisted only of true believers, whose status could be ascertained by tests of conduct and belief. Those not meeting their standards for church membership were expelled and banned. The Anabaptists posed a radical alternative to the state churches of Lutherans, Zwinglians, and Roman Catholics. The alternative churches of the Anabaptists scrutinized members to eliminate the unworthy and worshipped and associated in separate, voluntary communities.

The Anabaptist development in Zurich is instructive for understanding the widely held perception of this reform movement. Zwingli and the Zurich magistrates perceived a threefold danger in the Anabaptist movement. First, they were seen to be deliberately and consciously disruptive of the social and religious tenets of the town and therefore they posed a danger to both Swiss unity and the success of Zwingli's reform. In Zurich, as elsewhere, the success of the reform movement depended on the support of the magistrates. Fearful of possible aggression from the Catholic cantons, Zurich and other reformed cantons believed that only a community united in religion could defend itself and maintain its freedom. Insofar as the Anabaptists hindered this union, they were seen as abetting the Counter-Reformation.

Second, the Anabaptists turned Zwingli's own weapon, scripture, against him, much as had Karlstadt and Müntzer against Luther. Much to their chagrin, the reformers began to discover that the lay assertiveness and independence they encouraged against the Catholic Church could be turned against them as well. The dissidents insisted that they were only carrying to its logical conclusions Zwingli's own commitment to the Bible as the norm for faith and life. When the Anabaptists read the Bible, they found no warrant in it for infant baptism, but only for baptism as a sign of adult faith and regeneration. When they read the Sermon on the Mount, they believed that it literally meant believers must separate from the world. Just like Luther, Zwingli experienced the shock of having his own followers read very differently the biblical text he had labored to make available. Both Zwingli and the Anabaptists accepted the same Bible and agreed that tradition and human authorities must give way before the Word of God. And they agreed that the Bible was perfectly clear if read under the guidance of the Holy Spirit in faith and love. Of course, when their followers did not agree with them, Luther and Zwingli insisted that this was precisely what the "fanatics" did not do. So Zwingli viewed the Anabaptists' alternative reading of scripture as an expression of ignorance, malice, and contentiousness.

Third, the Anabaptists were seen as politically, as well as religiously, exclusivistic and thus a civil liability. In refusing to accept the normal obligations of citizenship (oaths, the tithe, military service), the Anabaptists were held to be forming states within the state. Their refusal to take oaths was a very serious element in this perception because the oath was a major part of the glue that held late medieval society together. Citizens swore oaths to the common good and defense of the town, to the guilds to which they belonged, and to the truth. Perjury, with its assumed certainty of divine punishment, was abhorred. Without the public oath, indispensable in any court of justice, the ordinary daily administration of public life was in danger of breaking down. The Swiss confederation itself was traditionally dated from an oath-swearing in 1291 that was annually renewed.

The refusal to bear arms was equally serious. In sixteenth-century Switzerland, there was no paid standing army. Every man was responsible for defense and was expected to appear armed and ready when called on by the government. The citizen soldier was the support and guarantor of public order and independence. The walls of the towns were to be guarded according to a set pattern. Every male was liable for military service, and military preparation was a normal, expected duty for which boys trained from an early age. For a man to refuse military service was, in effect, to renounce his citizenship. Townsmen resented Anabaptist pacifism as a shirking of indispensable duty and as a placing of extra burdens on themselves. A further fear was that if the Anabaptist movement spread, there would be no one to shoulder arms for defense.

The Anabaptist refusal to pay tithes and interest was also seen as a rejection of civic responsibility. The Anabaptists made it clear that the tithe was refused not because it was an economic imposition, but because it was perceived as an instrument of control by the Zurich government over the parishes within its jurisdiction. For Zwingli, the tithe was a key to the centralized territorial church that he wanted to reform, but not to dissolve. The refusal of tithes, like iconoclasm and attacks on the mass, represented the disintegration of the old religious order. To some at least, the rejection of tithes appeared very similar to the Catholic Church's unpopular insistence on exemption from taxation and civil law court proceedings. Similarly, the Anabaptist insistence on a church of true believers, with excommunication and the ban, led people to associate the Anabaptists with elements of Catholicism.

Beginnings in Zurich

In 1522, a group of future Anabaptists began to meet in the home of Klaus Hottinger for Bible study. The most attractive and influential member of this group was Conrad Grebel (1497–1526), the reputed founder of Anabaptism. Grebel, from a patrician family and educated at Vienna and Basel, at first actively supported Zwingli, but then became one of Zwingli's ablest and bitterest critics. Grebel became deeply disappointed by the magistrates' slowness in "cleansing" the churches and by the fact that the mass was still said. Grebel acknowledged that Zwingli had pointed the way to reform, but now he called Zwingli a false prophet.

After Christmas 1523, Grebel's calls for changes in society and religion led to an uproar. The dissidents interrupted sermons, became involved in iconoclasm, and ended up smashing the baptismal font in the Zollikon church. A public discussion, held on January 17, 1524, was dominated by Zwingli, and the majority in Zurich felt that Zwingli had answered the dissidents' charges and objections. The magistrates ordered the baptism of all unbaptized children within the next eight days under penalty of expulsion from Zurich. Furthermore, all unauthorized preaching was to cease, and the broken baptismal font was to be repaired.

In response to these orders, a small group of dissenters gathered on January 21 at the house of Felix Mantz (ca. 1500–1527). Among them were Grebel and George Blaurock, a married ex-priest who was later martyred in Innsbruck in 1529. The company joined in prayer, and then Blaurock called upon Grebel to baptize him. After this, Grebel and Blaurock baptized fifteen others at what was the first recorded adult baptism. At this very time, the city was drawing up an order requiring Grebel and Mantz to abstain from further propaganda. A couple of days later, Grebel followed his continued preaching by distributing bread and wine—a clear act of defiance because no town decision had yet been made concerning the mass. By the end of January, it was reported that eighty adults had been baptized.

Zwingli and the Zurich magistrates warned and threatened the dissenters and then imprisoned some and expelled others. Nevertheless, the new teachings spread with remarkable rapidity. Soon a small group paraded through Zurich with ropes around their waists and willow rods in their hands, crying, "Woe to you, Zurich" and "Freedom to Jerusalem," and calling Zwingli "the old dragon." These new prophets proclaimed that only forty days remained for Zurich to repent. Blaurock went so far as to call Zwingli the Antichrist. In early November, Zwingli confronted Grebel, Mantz, and Blaurock in a debate on baptism, but the debate soon degenerated into a shouting match.

The town magistrates decided to deal more severely with those they regarded as "the wild men in the streets." Balthasar Hubmaier (1481–1528) was arrested, tortured, and allowed to leave upon recanting. Others were imprisoned. Grebel, Blaurock, and Mantz reappeared in March 1526 to renew their attacks on Zwingli as a false prophet and to demand separatist worship. Because threats did not silence them, they were imprisoned. They were soon free, however, because someone had left a window open in the prison.

At the same time, Zwingli's dream of a reformed Swiss Confederacy was evaporating before the advances of Catholic opponents. Convinced that the Anabaptists were weakening the cause of the reform, Zwingli and the magistrates moved against the dissidents with new severity. Grebel missed martyrdom by dying of the plague in August 1526. His father, Jacob Grebel, a town councilor who symbolized both the Anabaptist opposition to Zwingli and the patrician resistance to the more democratic guilds on which Zwingli depended, was less fortunate. On October 30, 1526, Jacob was beheaded on charges of treason. By mid-December, Mantz and Blaurock had been recaptured and delivered to Zurich. By this time, rebaptism was mandated punishable by death by drowning—a grim parody of believer's baptism. Mantz and Blaurock were steadfast during their hearings and professed the divine ordinance of adult baptism. Since Blaurock was not a citizen of Zurich, he was whipped out of town. Mantz was executed by drowning on the day he was condemned, January 5, 1527, thus becoming the first Protestant martyr at the hands of Protestants. The Anabaptist understanding of themselves as the continuation of the early suffering church led them to rejoice in martyrdom and to neglect or refuse opportunities to leave quietly when possible.

Anabaptist Multiplicity

Zwingli may have been one of the first, but he was certainly not the last, to learn that the sparks of dissident evangelicalism could not be extinguished by drowning people. Both Protestant and Catholic authorities soon confronted a variety of Anabaptist movements in Switzerland, Austria, the Netherlands, and Germany. Popular Anabaptist preachers and leaders continued to arise from both evangelical and Catholic clergy and laity. Their professions in word and life of brotherhood and egalitarianism appealed to the oppressed both during and after the Peasants' War. The dissident movement spawned radically different expressions of the ideal of restoring the early church that ranged from an absolute pacifism to an apocalyptic crusade to usher in the kingdom of God. In every case, however, the establishment authorities perceived the Anabaptists as seditionists—underminers of the social order.

It is easy to understand the nervousness of the authorities when they were confronted by those radical dissident movements and persons such as Thomas Müntzer and the Anabaptists at Waldshut under Hubmaier, who linked up with local expressions of the Peasants' War and who appeared to be able to stimulate mass revolutionary loyalties. The teeth of the authorities were put on edge even by the more representative Anabaptist teachings expressed by Michael Sattler (ca. 1490–1527).

Sattler, an exemplary leader of the Swiss and southern German Anabaptist movements, moved from being prior of a Benedictine monastery in Breisgau to becoming an Anabaptist in Zurich. After expulsion from Zurich, he took refuge in Strasbourg and then moved to the Black Forest to continue his missionary work. He was so esteemed by the dissidents that he was chosen to preside at their 1527 conference at Schleitheim on the German–Swiss border that developed perhaps the most representative statement of Anabaptist principles, the Schleitheim Confession.

In seven articles, the Schleitheim Confession set forth a consensus on baptism contingent on repentance and amending one's life; the ban or excommunication of those who break the commandments; the Lord's Supper as a memorial meal for the baptized; a radical separation of believers from the evil world; the pastor as the model of the godly life; the absolute rejection of bearing arms and holding civic offices because the Christians' citizenship is in heaven and their weapons are spiritual; and the prohibition of oaths.

For his leading role in developing this confession, Sattler was arrested, tried, horribly tortured, and executed by the Austrian authorities. The historical context surrounding the Austrian Catholic tribunal does not excuse their action, but does provide some insight into the rulers' anxieties about the spread of Anabaptism. At the time, Austria was confronted by a Turkish advance that threatened to enter the whole empire through the gates of Vienna. At his trial, Sattler stated:

> If the Turks should come, we ought not to resist them. For it is written [Matt. 5:21]: "Thou shalt not kill." We must not defend ourselves against the Turks and others of our persecutors, ... [I]f warring *were* right, I would rather take the field against so-called Christians who persecute, capture, and kill pious Christians than against the Turks. . . .[1]

The suspicion that even the pacifist Anabaptists were really only wolves in sheep's clothing and potentially radical revolutionaries was confirmed, if it ever needed confirmation, in the minds of the authorities by the wild events at Münster in 1533–1535.

The Münster Debacle

Anabaptist aspirations for the restitution of the pure church and the social unrest epitomized by the Peasants' War found explosive expression in Münster, an episcopal city near the Dutch border. There was already a widespread religious dissident movement in the Netherlands. Influenced by the extravagant visions and prophecies of Melchior Hofmann (ca. 1495–1543), these people were known as Melchiorites. Sometimes called "the father of Dutch Anabaptism," Hofmann, a furrier by trade and a lay preacher by conviction, declared that everyone should accept baptism into the pure church of Christ in preparation for the return of Christ and the end of the world in 1533. Proclaimed the prophet Elijah, Hofmann went to the city of Strasbourg, which he prophesied would be the New Jerusalem. The magistrates of Strasbourg declined the honor of being the locus for the end of the world and imprisoned Hofmann until his death in 1543. Nevertheless, Hofmann's preachings and writings continued to influence others, some of whom transposed his prophecy of the New Jerusalem from Strasbourg to Münster. Hofmann's ideas about the triumph of the godly, written while in prison and smuggled out in his tract *Concerning the Pure Fear of God* (1533), included his vision that the ungodly would be exterminated *before* the end of the world, that *before* the return of Christ the saints would rule the earth through cooperation between the prophet (the second Jonah) and a pious ruler (the second Solomon), and that the "apostolic messengers" could not be hurt or defeated. In one way or another, these themes found expression in the Anabaptist takeover of Münster.

By 1532, Münster had become an "evangelical city" under the fiery leadership of Bernard Rothmann, a priest turned Lutheran preacher and then Anabaptist. Thousands of Anabaptist refugees flocked to the city in search of haven from persecution in the Netherlands and areas surrounding Münster. The townspeople divided into three factions: a small number of Catholics who still supported the expelled bishop, conservative Lutherans who were the majority in the town council, and the Melchiorites, who won the backing of the town guilds. In the summer of 1533, simmering tensions in the alliance of the guilds with the magistrates boiled over. Rothmann, under the influence of the Melchiorites, became increasingly radical in politics and religion, and both opposed infant baptism and innovatively

---

[1] George Williams and Angel Mergal, eds., *Spiritual and Anabaptist Writers*, Library of Christian Classics, vol. XXV (Philadelphia: Westminster Press, 1957), p. 141.

celebrated the Lord's Supper with unconsecrated bread. The town council, due to the strength of the radicals, no longer had sufficient authority to expel or even discipline Rothmann. Alarmed Catholic and Lutheran families began to flee the city, but this population loss was more than made up by the influx of Anabaptists.

In the February 1534 elections, the radical party won the town council. Münster had already been declared the New Jerusalem by Jan Mathijs, a baker from Haarlem, who believed, as had Müntzer, that the godless had no right to live. On February 25, Mathijs announced his intention to put to death all who refused to join the new rebaptismal covenant. Persuaded by a colleague to allow people to leave rather than to execute them, Mathijs announced he had received another revelation allowing the expulsion of the godless. All who remained were forcibly rebaptized in the marketplace. A blacksmith who dared to challenge Mathijs was killed instantly by Mathijs himself. Not long after this, Mathijs himself was killed when he led a sortie against the army assembled by the bishop besieging the city. It seems Mathijs had received a vision that God would make him invulnerable to the weapons of the godless.

During the six weeks Mathijs ruled Münster, he instituted the ideal of Anabaptism everywhere: a society based on the life of the primitive church, as recorded in Acts and an early church writing, the Pseudo-Clementine Epistle IV, which claimed that all things should be held in common. The property of the expelled citizens was confiscated; food was made public property; real property was declared to be in common, although people could continue using what was theirs, with the stipulation that all house doors had to be kept open day and night; the use of money was outlawed; and twelve elders were appointed to oversee the stockpiling of goods and their distribution to the needy.

After Mathijs's death, Jan of Leiden took up the prophetic mantle. After repulsing a major attack by the bishop's army in May, the Münsterites believed that they were God's chosen people. After another major victory in August, Jan had himself anointed and crowned "king of righteousness" and "the ruler of the new Zion." He stated that to oppose him was to oppose the divine order; he ruthlessly crushed his, and thus the Lord's, opposition. Church, state, and community were to be one and the same regenerated body. The regenerate church could consist only of the righteous; sinners were to be punished by death. Sinners were identified by their blasphemy, seditious language, disobedience to parents and masters, adultery, lewd conduct, backbiting, spreading scandal, and complaining!

Jan's most controversial and notorious innovation was the introduction of polygamy. Some 200 townsmen were killed or executed for resisting Jan's vision of the New Jerusalem, rationalized as an emulation of the Old Testament patriarchs. Although Jan found justification in the Old Testament for polygamy, nonbiblical factors also influenced his decision. Already married, Jan wanted to marry the young widow of Mathijs to bolster his own claim to leadership. Furthermore, there was a disproportionate number of women to men in the city as a result of male attrition from battle and expulsion. Polygamy provided the means not only of increasing the population in preparation for the return of Christ (the eschatological number of the saints, according to Rev. 7:4 was to be 144,000), but also of subjugating all women to male authority. In his book on the restoration of the primitive church, *Restitution* (1534), Rothmann added that sexual dependence on one woman lets her lead a man about "like a bear on a rope" and that women for too long have "everywhere been getting the upper hand" and now should submit to men as men submit to Christ and Christ to God. In political perspective, Jan was ensuring control over the majority of the population.

As might be expected, many women did not respond warmly to this new state of affairs. Those women who objected to polygamy were imprisoned. Jan himself beheaded and trampled the body of one of his fifteen wives in the marketplace in front of the rest of them. That seemed to have quieted their murmurings!

In spite of Jan's proclamation of the New Jerusalem and accompanying revelations, the siege of the city inexorably took its toll on the bodies and spirits of its inhabitants. Appeal after appeal to Anabaptists outside the city to bring armed relief were frustrated by the besiegers. People were reduced to eating vermin and, finally, even the dead. In June 1535, the city was betrayed by two deserters who revealed the weakest gate to the army. After a fierce battle, the city was taken on June 25, and nearly all the inhabitants were slaughtered. Rothmann was apparently killed in battle, but the other three leaders, including Jan, were condemned and then tortured with red-hot irons. Their bodies were suspended in an iron cage from the tower of St. Lambert's church as an example to all. The Anabaptist kingdom of Münster was materially destroyed, but it lived on in the minds of religious and political authorities as the logical consequence of Anabaptist dissent. In the minds of the establishment, both Protestant and Catholic, there was a clear revolutionary continuum from Thomas Müntzer to the city of Münster.

The Anabaptists aspired to communal solidarity as a holy people defined by believers' baptism and celebrated by the community-constituting act of consensus in the Lord's Supper. The effort to expand this theocratic ideal to the limits of the urban space in Münster led, however, not to the peaceable kingdom, but to the annihilation of the community itself. The result discredited militant millenarian (the belief in a 1,000-year reign of blessedness; Rev. 20) communalism. After this, there were no further Anabaptist attempts to restore the world to primitive Christianity. Rather, future Anabaptist developments were marked by withdrawal from the world. Under the leadership of Menno Simons (1496–1561), whose brother was killed in the Münster debacle, the Anabaptist remnants were gathered into voluntary communities separate from the established civic and religious world.

What Menno did for the Dutch and northern German Anabaptists, Jacob Hutter (d. 1536) did for the disparate Anabaptist refugees in Moravia who had sold house and goods to form communistic colonies. Hutter was able to develop and stabilize the faltering communalism expressed by the Anabaptists in Zurich, Münster, and elsewhere into a Christian communism that shared goods and production. In this development, we may see a certain continuity with the aspirations of medieval monasticism, as well as an advance beyond it. Medieval monasticism was marked by ascetic contempt for the world that, until the Franciscan movement, contrasted with the corporate wealth of the order itself. Furthermore, although the monastic movement shared a common life and a common goal, each monk was primarily concerned for his own salvation. The Mennonite and Hutterite Anabaptist advance beyond medieval religious asceticism and individualism consisted in developing a covenanted community of families that claimed to be *the* church itself, outside of which there is no salvation. The household of faith was marked by a communism of love and production, pacifism and suffering, separation from the world, trust in its ultimate vindication as the true household of faith, and confidence that until the final end of the world, human freedom and fulfillment are possible only in the brotherly love of evangelical communism.

Persecuted throughout Europe, the Mennonite and Hutterite Anabaptists eventually found homes in North America. Their faithfulness and perseverance under dreadful tortures and oppression contributed to the gradual development of the idea of religious toleration and liberty. And their insistence on a voluntary, separate church contributed to the modern development of religious pluralism and constitutional separation of church and state.

Chapter 20

"The Most Perfect School of Christ": The Genevan Reformation

In 1556, the fiery Scottish reformer John Knox (1513–1572), a refugee in Geneva from the wrath of Mary Tudor, wrote to a friend: "[Geneva] is the most perfect school of Christ that ever was in this earth since the days of the Apostles. In other places, I confess Christ to be truly preached; but manners and religion to be so sincerely reformed, I have not seen in any other place."[1] This extravagant praise of Geneva should not obscure the fact that the city not only welcomed refugees, but also created them. The central figure of both processes was John Calvin, himself a displaced person from France.

John Calvin (1509–1564)

John Calvin (Jean Cauvin) was born in Noyon, a cathedral city about sixty miles northeast of Paris. His father, an attorney for the cathedral chapter and a secretary to the bishop, obtained a modest church benefice for John that subsidized his education. At fourteen, Calvin set out for Paris, where he engaged in general studies at the Collège de la Marche and then theological studies at the Collège de Montaigu, where Erasmus had preceded him and Loyola was to follow. In 1528, at eighteen, Calvin received his master-of-arts degree. His mastery and skill in the prevalent forms of Latin argumentation, as well as his religious and ethical seriousness, may be behind the legend that his classmates nicknamed him "the

[1]John T. McNeill, *The History and Character of Calvinism* (New York: Oxford University Press, 1967), p. 178.

accusative case." A friendlier description of Calvin's student days comes from his friend and biographer, Theodore Beza (1519–1605), who explained Calvin's penchant for lying in bed in the mornings as time for reflecting on his diligent late-night studies.

In 1528 Calvin moved from Paris to Orléans and then to Bourges, where, at the insistence of his father, he completed a degree in law in 1532. At Bourges, Calvin had the opportunity to pursue his lively interest in the classics, including the study of Greek. That his pursuit of law was largely a matter of filial obedience is evident in the fact that, on the death of his father, Calvin returned to Paris to study the humanities. In 1532 he published his first work, a learned commentary on Seneca's *On Clemency*, an expression of his enthusiasm for the classics.

Calvin himself provided scant autobiographical information regarding his conversion to Protestantism. He certainly shared the humanists' desire to return *ad fontes* (to the sources) of culture, including the scriptures. Late in his life, Calvin did speak of his "sudden conversion," which scholars posit took place sometime in 1533–1534. He publicly attested to his conversion by his return to Noyon in May 1534 to surrender the ecclesial benefices he had held since he was twelve. Unlike many French reform-minded humanists who remained publicly in the Roman church, Calvin made a clean break. Throughout the rest of his ministry, Calvin would sharply criticize those "Nicodemites" (after Nicodemus in John 3:1–10), who could not bring themselves to live publicly what they believed inwardly.

Journey to Geneva

Calvin left Paris because of the Cop affair. Nicholas Cop, a friend of Calvin's from their student days, was elected rector of the Sorbonne. In his inaugural address, delivered on November 1, 1533 (All Saints' Day), Cop attacked the theologians of the Sorbonne, citing as his support not only the works of French humanists and Erasmus, but also a sermon of Luther's. The theologians responded by charging that Cop was a Lutheran propagandist, and the king called for the arrest of the Lutherans. Calvin, suspected of being a coauthor of the address because of his close association with Cop, fled. Cop managed to escape to Basel. Calvin found security at a friend's home in Angoulême, where he began to write what would soon become the most significant single statement of Protestantism: the *Institutes of the Christian Religion.*

Calvin completed and published the first edition of the *Institutes* in 1536 in Basel, where he had sought refuge in January 1535 from the intensifying French persecution of Protestants. Intended as an evangelical catechism for the education and reform of the churches, the work quickly earned Calvin an international reputation. Analogous to Luther's catechisms, the first edition consisted of chapters on the law, the creed, the Lord's Prayer and the sacraments of baptism and the Lord's Supper, arguments against the remaining Roman sacraments, and a discussion of Christian liberty. In great demand, the *Institutes* was repeatedly republished, expanded, and also translated into French. By the 1539 edition, Calvin conceived of the work as a text for the training of ministerial candidates. Calvin's final revision of 1559 extends to more than 1,500 pages in modern English translation. The *Institutes*, prefaced by a letter to Francis I, the king of France, pled for a fair hearing of the evangelical faith. The letter is a defense attorney's masterpiece of vindication for French Protestantism, and it clearly exhibited Calvin's leadership qualities to Protestants everywhere.

The letter did not change Francis's heart, however. His brief general amnesty for French religious exiles was prompted rather by his need for support on the eve of his third war with the emperor Charles V. Taking advantage of this opportunity for a safe return, Calvin made his way back home to settle family affairs. Then, with his brother Antoine and his sister Marie, Calvin set out for the free imperial city of Strasbourg, where he intended to settle down to a life of scholarship. On the way to Strasbourg, they were forced by imperial troop movements to detour via Geneva. It turned out to be one of history's most remarkable detours.

Calvin arrived in Geneva in July 1536. He planned to stay only overnight before continuing his trip to Strasbourg. But someone recognized him and tipped off an old acquaintance of his from Paris, William Farel (1489–1565). Farel, a fiery preacher, had been laboring for some months to bring Geneva to the Protestantism already espoused by Bern, Basel, and Zurich. Farel saw Calvin as literally a godsend to the cause and exhorted him to stay and join in the work of reforming Geneva. Calvin refused, explaining that he was a scholar, not an administrator or a preacher, and that he lacked the temperament for such a task because he generally did not get along well with people. As Calvin later wrote of himself, "Being of a rather unsociable and shy disposition, I have always loved retirement and peace. So I began to look for some hideout where I could escape from people. . . . My aim was always to live in private without being known."[2]

Farel denounced Calvin's selfish desire and proclaimed that God would curse Calvin's scholarly life if he did not stay in Geneva and carry out God's assignment. Calvin was overcome by this "dreadful adjuration." As he said of the event: "Farel kept me at Geneva not so much by advice and entreaty as by a dreadful adjuration, as if God had stretched forth his hand upon me from on high to arrest me."[3] Thus, Calvin yielded to a responsibility he had neither sought nor wanted: "In spite of my disposition [God] has brought me into the light and made me get involved, as they say."[4]

The Reformation in Geneva

The Reformation in Geneva was intimately allied with the city's political emancipation. Geneva exemplified the revolutionary potential of the Reformation, a fact not lost on the French crown, which henceforth suspected Protestants of political subversion. In the early sixteenth century, Geneva was struggling for independence from the House of Savoy, the dominant power south of the city between France and Italy. The traditional ruler of Geneva was a prince–bishop who by this time was little more than an extension of the House of Savoy. To the north of Geneva, the powerful Swiss cantons of Catholic Fribourg and Protestant Bern wanted to draw the city into a Swiss alliance. In 1525, Savoy lost its satel-

---

[2]B. A. Gerrish, "John Calvin," in B. A. Gerrish, ed., *Reformers in Profile: Advocates of Reform, 1300–1600* (Minneapolis: Fortress Press, 1967), p. 151.

[3]Williston Walker, *John Calvin: The Organizer of Reformed Protestantism, 1509–1564* (New York: Schocken Books, 1969), p. 158.

[4]Gerrish, *op. cit.*, p. 152.

lite Lausanne to an alliance with Bern and correctly surmised that Geneva might follow. Although Duke Charles III of Savoy coerced a reaffirmation of Genevan allegiance to its bishop and the House of Savoy, Genevan exiles negotiated a treaty with Fribourg and Bern that brought the city into the Swiss orbit in February 1526. In 1527, the Genevan Council of the Two Hundred was instituted; it formally assumed the legislative and judicial powers previously exercised by the duke of Savoy. Executive functions were exercised by the Little Council, which consisted of twenty-five members, sixteen of whom were appointed by the Council of Two Hundred; the others (four syndics, the city treasurer, and four from the previous year's Little Council) were elected annually by the General Council of the citizenry.

Savoy attacked Geneva in 1530, but Bern and Fribourg intervened. In 1533, Bern energetically missionized Geneva for Protestantism, and the resultant religious riots, iconoclasm, and rise of "heresy" in the city collapsed its alliance with Catholic Fribourg. Through public disputations and fiery sermons, Farel led the vanguard of Protestants against the old church. He gained the pulpit of the cathedral and persuaded the Council of Two Hundred to suppress the mass on August 10, 1535. In May 1536, a general assembly of citizens ratified reform measures and affirmed their will "to live according to the gospel and the Word of God." Bern had defended and liberated Geneva from Savoy, but Geneva resisted Bernese attempts to substitute itself for the ousted prince–bishop and the House of Savoy. Bern formally recognized Genevan sovereignty in August 1536, although Bern continued to be a power for Geneva to respect.

When Calvin arrived in Geneva at the age of twenty-seven, Farel and his colleagues were just beginning to implement the recent mandate for reform. The Roman church had been expelled, but a new Protestant structure was yet to be created. Farel believed that Calvin had been divinely sent to Geneva for this task. Apparently, not everyone was privy to Farel's insight, for in formalizing Calvin's appointment as reader in Holy Scripture, the secretary of the Little Council missed his name and wrote down "that Frenchman."

Calvin's first attempts to reform Geneva not only failed, but led to his expulsion from the city. It was axiomatic to him that church worship and discipline belonged in the hands of church leaders, not politicians. The citizenry, which still included a large population of Catholics, was not pleased with the discipline and doctrinal uniformity that Calvin and Farel sought to impose. In November 1537, the general council refused to enforce the confession of faith to which Calvin insisted the whole population adhere. Next, the Council of Two Hundred denied Calvin and Farel the right to excommunicate those who did not adhere to the faith. The town had not gotten rid of a Catholic prince–bishop in order to replace him with Protestant ones! And in February 1538, the annual election put syndics in office that were hostile to Calvin. In mid-March the Council of Two Hundred warned Calvin and Farel not to meddle in politics, but to stick to religion. The council also mandated the liturgical practice sanctioned by Bern that unleavened bread must be used in the Lord's Supper. On Easter Sunday 1538, Calvin and Farel preached in the two main Geneva churches, but refused to administer communion, in defiance of the order of the magistrates. In short, they excommunicated their entire congregations. They were not against the use of unleavened bread *per se*, but against the right of the civic authorities to dictate ecclesial matters. An uproar ensued, and the Genevan council dismissed Farel and Calvin and gave them three days to leave Geneva.

Farel settled in Neuchâtel, and Calvin, at the urging of Martin Bucer (1491–1551), the leading reformer of Strasbourg, settled there. Having finally arrived at his original destination, Calvin spent three of his happiest and most productive years (1538–1541) as a university lecturer and pastor to a French refugee church in the city. While in Strasbourg, Calvin learned a great deal about church organization from Bucer, a former Dominican, who himself had received his initiation into the evangelical movement from Luther at the Heidelberg Disputation in 1518.

From Bucer, Calvin learned how to integrate civic and religious life through the church offices of doctor or teacher, pastor, lay elder, and lay deacon. By this time, Strasbourg had become signatory not only to the semi-Zwinglian Tetrapolitan Confession, but also to the Lutheran Augsburg Confession. Bucer's irenic and ecumenical leadership included Calvin in international Protestant–Catholic ecumenical efforts to avoid the division of Christendom that finally happened with the Council of Trent.

Calvin also learned from the humanist Jean Sturm (1507–1589), whose educational labors made Strasbourg one of the foremost educational centers in Europe. Sturm's humanist ideals, which included learning Greek, Latin, and the classics, as well as religious and moral education, informed Calvin's own later educational efforts in Geneva.

Not least of Calvin's joys in this marvelous reformed city was his marriage to Idelette de Bure, the widow of an Anabaptist he had been instrumental in converting. In response to the efforts of Farel and Bucer to push him toward marriage, Calvin made it clear that his model of womanhood focused on modesty, thrift, and patience with his ill health, rather than on a "fine figure." But Farel, whose priorities in such matters did not exactly coincide with Calvin's, mentions that she was also beautiful. Farel himself married a young refugee widow when he was 69, much to Calvin's disapproval. In any case, Idelette remained Calvin's faithful companion until her death in 1549.

During his stay in Strasbourg, Calvin reworked his Institutes and expanded the original six chapters to seventeen. He also compiled a book of French psalms and a liturgy for his congregation and wrote an exposition of Paul's letter to the Romans, as well as a treatise on the Lord's Supper. Most important of all, he responded to Cardinal Jacopo Sadoleto's appeal to the people of Geneva to return to the Roman church.

Sadoleto was a humanist and a distinguished cardinal who had participated in the drafting of a famous Catholic report calling for thorough moral reform of the church in preparation for a reform council. He took advantage of the unstable situation in Geneva to affirm Roman authority and tradition against Reformation innovations. Sadoleto's long entreaty was addressed to the Little Council. The magistrates could find no one capable of making a suitable reply to this dangerous challenge to Geneva and thus appealed to Calvin, who responded to Sadoleto with one of the most noteworthy defenses of the evangelical faith. On the two major issues of the Reformation, Calvin sided fully with Luther in arguing that the ultimate authority in Christian life and the Christian community is scripture, and not the church, and that justification is by faith and trust in a merciful God, apart from human achievements.

Calvin's eloquent defense of the evangelical faith won him new respect in the city. In mid-1540, the new magistrates pled with Calvin to return to Geneva and resume his work of reformation. Calvin responded that he would rather die a hundred times than go back to Geneva. Once again, Farel, who was not invited back, threatened God's wrath on Calvin if he did not accept this call. Calvin yielded and was back in Geneva in September 1541. This time the secretary noted not only his name, but that he was "to be forever the servant of Geneva." He was appointed the pastor of the ancient cathedral of St. Peter and was provided with a decent salary, a large house, and annual portions of 12 measures of wheat and 250 gallons of wine.

Geneva under Calvin, 1541–1564

Although the Geneva government had implored Calvin to return, his progress in winning the town to his vision of the church rightly constituted and truly reformed was neither smooth nor rapid. His eventual triumph over numerous opponents by 1555 and his creation of a model of Protestantism that continues to influence churches the world over are remarkable because he worked solely by moral suasion. Calvin never enjoyed the political power and material resources of the deposed Catholic bishop of Geneva. Nor did Calvin have at his side the hundreds of priests, monks, and canons available to the old church. By Calvin's death, there were only nineteen pastors in Geneva, all employees of the municipal government. To an astute observer of Geneva in 1541, it would have appeared highly unlikely that Calvin could carry out a thorough reform of the city. Yet Calvin's reform of this recalcitrant city was so thorough that it may legitimately be called a revolution. How did he accomplish such a reform?

A clue to Calvin's success in Geneva is that he himself wrote the city's political and ecclesial rules. He had not been trained as a lawyer for nothing! As one of the conditions for his return from exile, he claimed the right to draft the institutional and legal form of the church. Within six weeks of his return, he submitted his *Ecclesiastical Ordinances* to the magistrates. With a few minor amendments, the government enacted them into law. Within the next two years, two further sets of laws regarding justice and political offices were enacted that further formed the constitution of the Geneva city-state. Whether or not Calvin was the author of these later laws, as some scholars believe, there is no doubt that the magistrates looked to him as a legal and moral resource for drafting them. In short, Calvin's success in Geneva was related to his firsthand and intimate knowledge of who made decisions and how those decisions were made.

The *Ecclesiastical Ordinances* organized the Genevan church by setting forth four categories of ministry—doctors, pastors, deacons, and elders—and creating institutions for the work of each. The doctors were to study scripture and to teach. Their theological scholarship was to maintain doctrinal purity and to prepare ministers. Pastors were to preach the Word of God, administer the sacraments, and instruct and admonish the people. Candidates for the office of pastor were examined in doctrine and conduct, and they had to be approved by the ministers and the Little Council. The pastors of Geneva and its dependent villages met weekly to discuss theology and doctrine. Deacons were responsible for the supervision of charity, including relief of the poor and overseeing the hospitals. They were elected once a year in the same manner as the elders.

The doctors and the pastors together constituted the Geneva Company of Pastors, also known as the Venerable Company. The Company of Pastors met quarterly for purposes of administration and mutual discipline. Although of limited legal authority, the Venerable Company held a notable place in the moral structure of Geneva.

The function of the elders was to maintain discipline within the community. Against Calvin's wishes, the elders were political appointees chosen from and by the magistrates. In all, there were twelve elders, of whom two were chosen from the Little Council, four from the Council of Sixty, and six from the Council of Two Hundred. Selected for their wisdom and piety, they represented different parts of the city. They were to watch over the lives of the people, admonish the disorderly, and, when necessary, report errant people to the Consistory, a kind of ecclesial court.

The Consistory was the principal organ of church discipline; it included the twelve elders and the pastors. Its presiding officer was ordinarily one of the syndics. The main concern of the Consistory was the systematic supervision of the morals of the people of Geneva. This was the source of Geneva's reputation for austerity. The Consistory had the power to excommunicate those who, in its eyes, had committed serious offenses.

It is not surprising that the Consistory was the most controversial institution of the Reformation in Geneva. It became the focal point for opposition to Calvin, but it was also a crucial vehicle for expressing his authority. The latter point warrants emphasis because those living in contemporary pluralistic and secular societies easily forget how threatening the charge of unauthorized innovation was to the Reformers. From the early church to the early modern period, innovation was equivalent to heresy. The very reason Calvin had been implored to return to Geneva was that the Genevans were threatened by Sadoleto's accusation of innovation and his appeal to traditional authority. The Consistory was Calvin's means for instilling respect for his authority, even if at times this approximated a moral reign of terror.

Calvin's Consolidation of His Authority

Opposition to the not-so-secret ecclesiastical police in Geneva crossed class and economic lines to include magistrates as well as common citizens. In turn, the Consistory did not shrink from judging prominent citizens. In January 1546, Pierre Ameaux, a member of the Little Council, publicly criticized Calvin, who perceived the criticism not as a personal attack, but as an attack on his authority as a minister. He persuaded the Council of Two Hundred to impose on Ameaux the punishment of a public penance that included a walk around the town dressed only in a penitential shirt and begging for God's mercy. The effect was a public proclamation of Calvin's authority.

More serious threats to Calvin's authority came from the patrician families of the Perrins and Favres, respected Genevan families who had been among the strongest advocates for bringing Calvin back to Geneva. Neither Ami Perrin nor François Favre, his father-in-law, was in favor of the Consistory's inquisitorial practices. When Calvin censured François's wife for lewd dancing at a wedding and excluded François himself from the sacrament for immoral behavior, Ami Perrin publicly questioned the competence of the Consistory. The Favres fled town, and Ami left on a diplomatic mission to France. When they returned to Geneva, both François and Ami were imprisoned, the latter because he was also suspected of being in collusion with France to invade Geneva. Bernese intervention obtained the release of Favre, and Perrin was acquitted. Calvin labeled Perrin and his followers "Libertines," alleging that they did not want discipline because it would expose their loose living and faithless lives.

One of these Libertines, Jacques Gruet, also from an old Genevan family, not only criticized Calvin, but was found to have appealed to the French king to intervene in Geneva. Believing Gruet to be part of an international plot against Geneva, the magistrates tortured and then beheaded him with the consent of Calvin. In December, a Libertine mob gathered to intimidate the Council of the Two Hundred. Calvin himself ran into their midst proclaiming, "If you must shed blood, let mine be first." Unnerved, the mob subsided.

The continuing influx of religious refugees into Geneva provided a source of political support for Calvin, for they were generally of high social and intellectual status and obviously grateful for the haven Calvin provided them. Not all of these newcomers agreed with Calvin's theology, however. A famous example of such opposition was Jerome Bolsec, who, although generally sympathetic to reformed theology, sharply criticized Calvin's doctrine of predestination. Consequently, he was banished from Geneva for life. In revenge, in 1577 Bolsec published a scurrilous biography of Calvin that continued to be an arsenal for anti-Calvinist polemics for the next two centuries.

The Servetus Case

Growing opposition to Calvin provided the context for the infamous Servetus case. Michael Servetus (ca. 1511–1553), from Aragon, became a public figure through the publication of his *Seven Books on the Errors of the Trinity* in 1531. Protestant and Catholic theologians alike condemned Servetus's attack on the fundamental doctrine of the Trinity. The next year, Servetus responded with his *Two Dialogues on the Trinity*, which maintained that in its doctrinal development, the church had fallen away from Jesus. Although Servetus was not renowned for his discretion, he finally realized that the better part of valor incuded anonymity and a different profession. He went to Paris, where he studied medicine and anatomy. In the annals of medicine, he has a certain fame for being one of the first to discover the pulmonary circulation of the blood, a discovery probably prompted by his concern to show that the Spirit entered the blood system through the nostrils.

Servetus could not abstain from theological publication and controversy, however. He began a pseudonymous correspondence with Calvin, who recognized him from his writings. When Servetus sent Calvin his newest endeavor, *The Restoration of Christianity*, Calvin sent back his own *Institutes*, which Servetus promptly returned filled with insulting marginal comments. Calvin then sent all this correspondence to a friend in Vienne who passed it on to the Inquisition in Lyons to assist in the capture of Servetus. In August 1553, Servetus managed to escape and fled toward Italy. On the way to seeking asylum in Naples, he stopped in Geneva.

In his writings and in his correspondence with Calvin, Servetus presented infant baptism as diabolical, denied original sin and likened the Trinity to a three-headed Cerberus. Jesus was not the eternal son of God, but a human become divine. Servetus presented himself as another archangel Michael, leading an angelic host against the Antichrist. To Calvin, this was the "impious ravings of all the ages," and he wrote that should Servetus ever appear in Geneva, he would not leave alive. In Geneva, Servetus disguised himself and attended Calvin's church. He was spotted and immediately arrested. Servetus was tried, found guilty of spreading heresy, and sentenced to death by burning. Executed on the morning of October 27, 1553, Servetus died with the prayer, "Jesus, Son of the Eternal God, have mercy on me." To the end, Servetus would not pray in Trinitarian language to "the eternal Son of God."

In an unsuccessful "humanitarian" gesture, Calvin sought to commute the punishment from burning to beheading. Farel rebuked Calvin for such undue leniency! Following the execution of Servetus, Calvin wrote his *Defense of the Orthodox Faith*, in which he declared that in cases of heresy the glory of God must be maintained regardless of all feelings of humanity. But Sebastian Castellio, the Genevan schoolmaster forced out of town in 1544 by Calvin, responded that "To burn a heretic is not to defend a doctrine, but to kill a man." However, Castellio's plea for religious toleration, *Concerning Heretics, Whether They Are to be Persecuted* (1544), was far ahead of its time, for Calvin and Geneva received congratulations and applause from all quarters for execution of the arch-heretic. The modern world reserves its wrath and persecution for political heretics.

The Servetus affair was a turning point for Calvin. His opponents were unable to use the Servetus case against him, and those leading Libertines who tried were discredited. Soon Geneva was firmly in Calvin's control. As a consequence, restrictive and disciplinary elements in the city were enhanced, the Consistory became more of an ecclesiastical court, and the ministers were consulted on the choice of elders. There were, however, personal trials for Calvin: His sister-in-law was discovered in adultery with his own servant, and later his stepdaughter Judith was also caught in adultery. Both women were expelled from Geneva. Nevertheless, Calvin's influence continued to grow with the combined circumstances of the defeat of his enemies and the continuing influx of religious refugees. In 1559 Calvin founded the Geneva Academy, now the University of Geneva, which attracted students from all areas of Europe and became the training ground for influential Protestant leadership throughout the continent. In the same year, Calvin was made a citizen of Geneva.

It is a mistake to conclude that Calvin turned Geneva into a theocratic police state. Rather, for most of Calvin's career, he had to struggle to maintain authority. Indeed, there were times when Calvin's authority was so fragile that Genevans called their dogs "Calvin." In common with other reformers, Calvin recognized that the success of his movement rested in no small part on respect for his leadership and authority. What is remarkable is not his efforts to consolidate authority, but that in this process, he did not succumb to favoritism to win support. Neither prominent citizens nor his own family were allowed to be above the law. In this, Calvin provided a model of democratic equality under the law that modern states would do well to emulate.

Chapter 21

The Protestant Mission and Evangelism: The "International Conspiracy"

Nearly 5,000 religious refugees flocked to Geneva, attracted by the stature of Calvin and driven from their homelands by persecution. From nearly every province in France, as well as from England, Scotland, Holland, Italy, Spain, Germany, Poland, and Bohemia, they took Calvinism with them when they returned home. The Geneva Academy furthered the spread of Calvinism by training missionary pastors. Frequently disguised as merchants, these pastors slipped into countries where Calvinism was outlawed and established churches patterned after the church in Geneva. The Geneva church functioned as the international headquarters for this missionary movement, a kind of Protestant Vatican. Served by an extensive news bureau and communication network centered in Geneva, the missionary churches submitted their theological disputes and questions to the Geneva church for resolution and clarification. Calvinism ultimately prevailed in England and Scotland, whereas it survived only in a minority status in France.

The Reformation in England

Historians have sometimes portrayed the English Reformation as an act of the state in response to popular anticlericalism and the wishes of the crown. English resentment over perceived clerical abuses provided fertile soil for Lutheran preaching and doctrine, which entered England about 1520. The first Lutheran sympathizers began meeting at the White Horse Inn in Cambridge, whose university would provide most of the future leaders of

English Protestantism. From Cambridge, the movement spread to Oxford. Lutheran ideas also influenced London merchants and their colleagues in the English business colony in Antwerp. There, outside the control of the English king and his bishops, Protestant Bible translators and publicists worked with enthusiasm. Largely through the influence of Thomas Cromwell (ca. 1485–1540), the chief political agent behind Miles Coverdale's first complete English translation of the Bible (1535), and Archbishop Thomas Cranmer (1489–1556), the king was persuaded to put the Bible in all the churches—a step that could not be retracted.

Even Henry VIII's Catholic reaction of his last years could not halt the Protestant advance. The religious phraseology in middle-class wills of the time indicate the decline of saint worship and the advance of Protestant convictions. These convictions were present even in the court and among the tutors of Henry's son, Edward VI. With the death of Henry in 1547, the English Reformation had six years of development under Edward VI and his advisors. During this time, Cranmer presented the English people with his prayer books (1549 and 1552), the second of which was a distinctly Protestant expression of worship and theology.

The Reformation in England took root during the energetic reign of Henry VIII (1491–1547), who became king in 1509. His father, Henry VII, had victoriously concluded the English civil war, the War of the Roses, and had established the Tudor dynasty. Like his father, Henry VIII took his Catholicism very seriously and in 1521 published a tract against Luther titled *Assertio Septem Sacramentorum*, for which Pope Leo X awarded Henry the title "Defender of the Faith." Henry's defense of the seven sacraments indicates not only his lifelong zealousness for the Catholic faith, but also a theological and literary skill rare among heads of state. Thus, Henry's ultimate break with Rome was not theological, but personal and political. Henry VII, bent on providing stability, prestige, and power to the fledgling Tudor house, pursued his goal through long diplomatic wrangling for an alliance with Spain, cemented by the marriage of Catherine of Aragon to his first son, Arthur. But five months after the marriage, the young Arthur died. In order not to lose his new connection to one of the oldest and most powerful houses of Europe, Henry immediately proposed that his second son, Henry (VIII), marry the young widow. Since Leviticus 18:6–18 prohibited marriages within close relationships, a special papal dispensation for the marriage of Henry and Catherine was obtained from Pope Julius II.

Henry and Catherine were married in 1509. Of Catherine's numerous pregnancies, only one child survived—Mary Tudor, born in 1516. By 1525 the queen was forty, and there appeared no hope for further children. In the meantime, Henry was involved with a variety of mistresses and then became infatuated with Anne Boleyn, a lady at court and sister to one of his earlier mistresses. His growing desire to be rid of Catherine and to remarry, however, was motivated not just by his intense attraction to Anne, but primarily by a hope for the stability of the Tudor reign and England itself. He needed a male heir to avoid the specter of civil war over the succession if his daughter succeeded him.

Henry appealed to Pope Clement VII to annul his marriage to Catherine on the basis that it was invalid to marry a deceased brother's widow (Lev. 20:21). This put the pope in an extremely difficult situation. Doctrinally, it would be awkward, to say the least, for the pope to grant Henry's request because that would impugn the decision of a previous pope to allow the marriage and would raise the question of papal fallibility, already sharply put by Luther. Perhaps more to the point, the pope this time (1527) was the virtual prisoner in Rome of the Emperor Charles V, Catherine's nephew.

Henry's rage at Cardinal Wolsey for failing to sway the pope to his cause led to Wolsey's downfall and his replacement by Thomas More (1478–1535) in 1529 as lord chancellor. Thomas Cromwell finally achieved the king's desire by appealing to the universities of England and Europe for a decision on the case and suggested that the crown displace the pope's headship of the church in England. The dispensation for Henry's annulment was granted by the English court in 1533.

The pope responded by annulling the annulment and excommunicating Henry. In turn, Henry replied with the Act of Supremacy (1534), which appointed the king and his successors "Protector and only Supreme Head of the Church and Clergy of England." This decisive break of the English church with Rome was accompanied by a loyalty oath to the king that led to the beheading of Thomas More in 1535 for refusing to sign it. The Act of Supremacy was a constitutional break from papal authority, not an introduction of Protestantism. Although Henry used the anticlerical—especially the antipapal—sentiments of his people to his advantage, he reaffirmed Catholic dogma in the Statute of Six Articles in 1539. The Six Articles maintained transubstantiation, communion under one kind for the laity, clerical celibacy, the sanctity of monastic vows, the necessity of auricular confession, and private masses; and it declared the denial of any of these to be heresy.

Henry further consolidated his position as head of the English church by suppressing first the smaller, and then the larger, monasteries in 1536 and 1539. The dissolution of the monasteries effectively eliminated the last refuge of the papistry in England and thus smoothed the way for Protestant development to some degree. Furthermore, it enriched the king's treasury, and the sale of monastic lands to wealthy laity ensured the self-interest of the laity against the reintroduction of monasticism.

Passions, Politics, and Piety

Although Henry's passions provide raw material for plays and movies, few historians would use them to explain the English Reformation. Nevertheless, Henry's wives and their children have a legitimate place in the story of the development of English Protestantism.

On January 25, 1533, Henry secretly married Anne Boleyn, pregnant with Elizabeth, who would be born in September. It was crucial to Henry that his expected heir be born legitimate. In March the Parliament's statute restraining appeals to Rome was passed, and this made possible Henry's divorce from Catherine. Anne was crowned queen on June 1, 1533. Unfortunately for her, Henry's passion rapidly waned because their child was a girl, and Anne's future pregnancies ended in miscarriages. As long as Catherine lived, Anne was secure as queen, because the repudiation of her marriage would imply the validity of Henry's marriage to Catherine. Catherine, however, died in 1536. On May 17 Cranmer declared Anne's marriage void, and on May 19 she was beheaded on charges of adultery.

On May 30, Henry married Jane Seymour, a lady of the court. In October, Henry at last had a son—Edward—whose birth cost his mother's life. Henry next married Anne of Cleves on January 6, 1540, at the prompting of Thomas Cromwell to establish a political alliance with the duchy of Cleves against the emperor and on the basis of a flattering portrait of her. When she arrived in England, Henry was immediately displeased with both her and Cromwell. By the end of June, Henry had divorced her, and Cromwell was on the way to the scaffold for this and other advice the king did not like. In August 1540, Henry married Catherine Howard, who seems to have lacked discretion about her behavior in the court. Her reputed adultery led to her beheading in February 1542 on the charge of treason. Catherine Parr, the king's last wife, whom he married in June 1543, had the good sense to remain in both his political and marital beds, and thus, she outlived him. Henry himself died on January 27, 1547, and the Tudor succession, according to earlier legislation and the king's will, passed to his children Edward, Mary, and Elizabeth, in that order.

Edward VI came to the throne at the age of nine; always sickly, he died in 1553. Edward, or, more accurately, his advisors, established the Reformation in England. His uncle, Edward Seymour, the earl of Hertford, appointed lord protector and duke of Somerset, immediately ended all persecution of Protestants and led the Parliament in repealing most of the treason and heresy laws, including the Six Articles. This in turn not only stimulated the return of those Protestants who had fled under Henry VIII; it also attracted continental reformers, most of whom were of Zwinglian persuasion. Such prominent reformers as Martin Bucer of Strasbourg and Peter Martyr Vermigli of Italy were invited to Cambridge and Oxford universities, respectively.

The architect of English Protestantism, however, was Henry's archbishop of Canterbury, Thomas Cranmer, whose Protestant orientation found significant expression under Edward. Clerical marriage now flourished. Cranmer himself had been married since 1532 to Margaret Osiander, niece of the German Lutheran theologian, Andreas Osiander. Cranmer's revision of the *Book of Common Prayer* (1552) set the tone of an English Protestantism that avoided extremes in doctrine and liturgy. In 1553, Cranmer produced a statement of faith for the English church that represented a compromise between Lutheran and Calvinist theologies. These Forty-two Articles were the foundation for the later Thirty-nine Articles that defined the Church of England under Elizabeth I and that continue to inform the Anglican Church today. The reform of the English church moved rapidly—perhaps too rapidly, for it depended on the continuing health of Edward.

The anxiety that Protestant reforms would be undone after Edward's death by the ascent to the throne of Mary Tudor, a staunch Catholic, led Edward and Somerset's successor, John Dudley, the duke of Northumberland, to conspire to exclude Mary from the succession on the grounds that, as the daughter of Catherine, she was illegitimate. In her stead they proposed Lady Jane Grey (1537–1554), the Protestant grandniece of Henry VIII and daughter-in-law of Northumberland. Unfortunately for the innocent, youthful Jane, the plan ran aground on the passionate loyalty of the English to the Tudor succession. Queen for a day, or, more precisely, nine days, the plot cost Jane Grey and the leadership of Edwardian Protestantism—John Hooper, Miles Coverdale, Hugh Latimer, Thomas Cranmer, and Nicholas Ridley—their lives. Knox fled to Geneva, where he bided his time for a fiery return.

Mary Tudor and the Catholic Reaction

The accession of Mary Tudor to the English throne severely threatened the English Reformation. Yet, ironically, Mary's overwhelming concern for the Roman Catholic faith served to strengthen the Protestant cause. By her marriage to Philip of Spain, she identified Catholicism with the unpopular, foreign Spain; by her reliance on her cousin Reginald Cardinal Pole and his efforts to introduce the Counter-Reformation, she became more unpopular; by attempting to restore monastic lands to the church, she alienated the landed class that had bought them; by persecuting Protestant leaders without proceeding to eradicate Protestantism itself, she created an army of martyrs who were celebrated in the influential book *Acts and Monuments*, by John Foxe; and by exiling some 800 leading Protestants to Frankfurt, Geneva, and Strasbourg, she created an army of zealous Protestants trained in continental Protestantism eager to return and recapture England for the evangelical faith.

Mary Tudor was queen only five years (1553–1558), but her brief reign left an indelible antagonism in English minds toward all things Catholic and Spanish. The daughter of Catherine of Aragon, she was reared Catholic and, from a purely nontheological perspective, had to be Catholic to be the legitimate heir to the throne. She became queen solely because she was Henry's daughter and the English were loyal to the Tudor crown. She failed to understand this, and the consequences were disastrous. Her failings consisted primarily of her obsession with her Catholicism and her Spanish descent. Initially welcomed by her people, she died hated by nearly all.

From Mary's perspective, her vocation was to save her people from mortal sin by restoring them to papal obedience. She chose to accomplish this by a foreign policy that allied England with Spain. The Hapsburg emperor Charles V was more than willing to help and decided that his son, Philip II of Spain, should do his bit for the empire and Catholicism by marrying Mary and bringing England into the Hapsburg orbit. The English were not at all pleased, for although they were by no means wedded to the recent Edwardian turn to Protestantism, they hated foreign intervention and still retained a residual dislike of papal and clerical rule. As Mary's plans advanced, she and her counselors were always sniffing conspiracy and rebellion in the air. In the first months of 1554, Sir Thomas Wyatt led a rebellion of some 3,000 men into London. They were overcome and the leaders executed. Elizabeth Tudor almost suffered the same fate, but was instead imprisoned in the Tower.

Since Parliament balked at Mary's plans to restore Catholicism, she proceeded, ironically, to use her father's break from Rome to restore Rome to England. She acted as supreme head of the church to remove Protestant clergy from their churches, usually on the grounds that they had broken the vow of celibacy. The Mass was restored, and with the return of Cardinal Pole, the old heresy laws were reinstated, accompanied by ferocious new treason laws. In addition, Parliament at last agreed to repeal all the antipapal and anti-Roman legislation passed since the days of Henry. Thus, a legal basis was provided for the Marian persecutions.

The Spaniards, including Philip II and Charles V, were against persecution for policy reasons. But Mary and Cardinal Pole, perhaps sincerely believing that they were saving English souls from damnation, inspired heresy trials that led to the burnings of nearly 300 dissenters, who became martyrs for the Protestant faith.

In September 1555, Philip returned to Spain, leaving Mary childless and disconsolate. War between Spain and France broke out, and in providing assistance to Philip, Mary lost Calais, the last remnant of England's medieval empire on the continent. From a practical point of view, Calais was no loss, for it had been expensive to maintain and served no purpose to the English. From a symbolic point of view, however, its loss was a blow to English pride and eroded the last vestiges of loyalty to Mary. In November 1558, Mary died. Cardinal Pole died twelve hours later. With their deaths, the Catholic reaction was over. Mary had succeeded in destroying the two things most dear to her: the old religion and the Spanish alliance. Elizabeth learned from her sister's failure.

Elizabeth I

The forty-five year reign of Elizabeth Tudor (1558–1603) appeared to some as a heaven-made match between monarch and people. Under Elizabeth, England turned Protestant, became a leading nation of Europe, won a world empire, and experienced a cultural renaissance.

Elizabeth came to the throne at the age of twenty-five, already wise beyond her years. Just as Mary had to be Catholic to be a legitimate ruler, so Elizabeth had to be Protestant, because she was the daughter of Anne Boleyn. Her diplomatic skill, evident in all she did, was at times tested by the pressure on her to marry for the sake of the realm, a pressure exerted not only by various lovers, but by Parliament as well. Her brother-in-law, Philip II, offered his services, but Elizabeth was too smart to repeat Mary's mistake. Her passionate, but spoiled and undependable lover, Robert Dudley, earl of Leicester, was surrounded by public scandal that included the death of his wife under mysterious circumstances. Elizabeth was strongly attracted to him, but ruled her heart with her head, putting her reign above her personal feelings.

Elizabeth, fluent in French, Latin, Italian, and double-talk, was able not only to keep many ambitious men living in hope and in her service, but also to control the factions in her court and countryside. To Protestants, the "virgin queen" was a heroic Judith; to Catholics, she was a Jezebel, a servant of infamy, and the refuge of evil men. Elizabeth's religious policy sought a middle way between extremes. Her *via media* intended to provide England the peace necessary for development after the Edwardian and Marian upheavals. She knew by both experience and observation the dangers inherent in rapid religious change. She claimed she would rather hear a thousand masses than be guilty of millions of crimes done by some who suppressed masses. Elizabeth held both Catholics and radical Protestants in check by fostering an Anglican settlement in doctrine and discipline. Hence, John Knox observed that Elizabeth was "neither good Protestant nor yet resolute papist."[1]

Elizabeth appointed Matthew Parker, a moderate, as archbishop of Canterbury. Parker, a follower of Martin Bucer, was married and knew well many of the Marian exiles now returning to England. It was from these Marian exiles that Elizabeth had to choose most of her bishops, all of whom were more radical in religion than she.

Parliament guaranteed the success of Elizabeth's policy. In April 1559, Parliament passed an act of supremacy that recognized the queen as head of the English church. All royal officials, judges, and clergy, on pain of losing their office, had to take a loyalty oath acknowledging the supremacy of the crown over the church. To uphold the authority of any foreign prince or prelate was high treason, punishable by death. Mary's Catholic legislation

[1] L. W. Spitz, *The Renaissance and Reformation Movements* (Chicago: Rand McNally & Company, 1971), p. 525.

was rescinded, and Edward VI's second *Book of Common Prayer* was reintroduced with some modifications. The retention by the prayer book of images, crucifixes, and vestments made it more palatable to Catholics, but offended the more radical Protestants. Those clergy who refused to conform were replaced, so that eventually appointees amenable to Elizabeth filled the ecclesial sees.

The second Parliament, 1563, reaffirmed the Act of Uniformity and passed measures for its strict enforcement. The Forty-two Articles were revised to Thirty-nine. Elizabeth was involved in this revision. The articles were designed to accommodate the major evangelical theologies, by denying transubstantiation on the one hand and Zwinglian symbolism on the other hand, and to remain open to the range of Lutheran and Calvinist interpretations. The scriptures were declared the source and norm of faith, and the creeds were accepted because they could be proved by scripture. General or ecumenical councils were declared not to be infallible in themselves. The article on predestination was presented in a masterfully ambiguous way.

The Elizabethan settlement offended the more radical Protestants, who desired to purify the church of all Roman Catholic vestiges. Those Protestants who remained within the Church of England while advocating the removal of Catholic ceremonies and forms (vestments, sign of the cross, saints' days, etc.) came to be known as Puritans. The Puritans should not be thought of in terms of later Victorian morality; they were not "puritanical" in the sense of moralistic. Those Protestants who rejected episcopal church polity and argued for clerical equality were called Presbyterians. And those who wanted all religious authority to be in local hands came to be called Congregationalists, Separatists, or Independents.

The first systematic statement of Anglicanism was presented by John Jewel (1522–1571), consecrated bishop of Salisbury in 1560, in his *Apology for the Anglican Church* (1562). Jewel's work influenced Richard Hooker (ca. 1554–1600), who became the apologist *par excellence* for the Elizabethan settlement of 1559. Hooker's masterful *Treatise on the Laws of Ecclesiastical Polity* places him among the most important theologians of the English church. In response to the Puritan conviction that whatever was not expressly commanded in scripture was unlawful, he elaborated a theory of ecclesial and civil law resting on reason and natural law that was influential on future political writers such as John Locke (1632–1704).

Another important Elizabethan was John Foxe (1516–1587), who, under Mary, had been a religious refugee in Strasbourg, Frankfurt, and Basel. His history of Christian persecutions first appeared in Latin in Strasbourg in 1554. An English translation in 1563, titled *Acts and Monuments of matters happening in the Church*, is commonly known as "Foxe's Book of Martyrs." Officially approved by the Elizabethan bishops, this work went through four editions in Foxe's lifetime. The book praised the heroism and endurance of Protestant martyrs under Mary and papist tyranny, and ranked next to the Bible in popularity. Here we read that when the fire was lit under the Protestant martyrs, Ridley and Latimer, Latimer said, "Be of good cheer, Ridley; and play the man. We shall this day, by God's grace, light up such a candle in England, as, I trust, will never be put out." Foxe's crimson martyrology helped to create a specifically Protestant, anti-Roman Catholic consciousness that blended with the nationalistic sentiment of the Protestant English-speaking world.

Although by the end of Elizabeth's reign, Roman Catholics were a small minority of mainly conservative upper nobility in England, the years from 1569 to the destruction of the Spanish Armada in 1588 were filled with perceptions of Catholic menace. A Catholic uprising in 1569 instigated by the duke of Norfolk to advance the cause of Mary Stuart was quickly put down. But the papal bull excommunicating Elizabeth in 1570 stimulated perceptions of internal and external conspiracies to overthrow the crown. Pope Pius V made it clear that his power extended over all nations and that, since Elizabeth was a slave of vice, a usurper of the pope's office, and a "Calvinist," she was cut off from the body of Christ, and all subjects were absolved from oaths of allegiance to her. The menace of Spanish invasion in 1587 led Elizabeth finally and reluctantly to execute her cousin Mary Stuart, who had been under house arrest for nineteen years.

Elizabeth's course between the extremes of Catholicism and Calvinism was politically motivated, because the former denied her legitimacy and the latter abolished the episcopacy that she believed supported monarchy. But she was not without religious sensibility. In her youth she translated Marguerite d'Angoulême's *Mirror of a Sinful Soul*, and she was always appreciative of the liturgy. She held that as long as her subjects openly observed the laws of the land, their consciences should not be examined. When she banished the Jesuits in 1585, one of her motives was to temper public outrage against foreign conspiracies and thereby to minimize public attacks on English Catholics. Like her father, Elizabeth determined the course of the Reformation in England in light of the dominant Tudor concern for royal supremacy. This concern necessitated denial of the ultramontane papacy and shaped the course of events up to the Act of Toleration in 1689.

Mary Stuart (1542–1587) and the Reformation in Scotland

The story of Mary Stuart, queen of Scots, exemplifies the Tudor struggle for royal supremacy. Mary was the daughter of James V (Stuart), king of Scotland. James's mother was Margaret Tudor, daughter of Henry VII and sister of Henry VIII. James's wife, the mother of Mary, was Mary of Lorraine from the powerful and very conservative French Guise family. These dynastic relationships explain Mary Stuart's threat to the reign of Elizabeth.

When the English defeated the Scots at the battle of Solway Moss in 1542, Henry VIII attempted to cement Scotland to England by arranging a marriage between Edward and the infant Mary Stuart. Not surprisingly, this was rejected. In 1548 Mary was sent to France, the traditional enemy of England, where she married the dauphin, soon to become Francis II. When Francis died in 1560, the queen mother, Catherine di Medici, did not want the rivalry of Mary, whose relationship to the duke of Guise and his brother, the powerful cardinal of Lorraine, gave her too much power. The Guises themselves favored Mary's return to Scotland to take up her crown, because they believed she could also claim the throne of England and thus restore Catholicism there. In the meantime, a number of Scottish lords, together with John Knox, who had returned to Scotland in 1559, rose up and expelled the French from Scotland.

Unwelcome in France and suspect in Scotland, Mary Stuart returned to Scotland to take up her crown. The men attracted to her may suggest that she was more beautiful than her surviving portraits, but do not reflect well on her reputed intelligence.

Mary's immediate concern was not religion, but dynastic politics. The cardinal of

Lorraine had suggested she turn Protestant in order to achieve her claim to the English throne. And, indeed, for a while she was conciliatory toward the Protestants, a stance no doubt difficult in light of the tactless preaching Knox directed at her. This was the man who had called her mother, Mary of Guise, regent when Mary lived in France, an "unruly cow saddled by mistake." No doubt Knox's hatred of all things French and Catholic was increased by his nineteen months as a French galley slave after the defeat of the Scottish uprising at St. Andrews in 1547. But Knox's opposition to Mary Stuart included also the fact that she was a woman. In his 1558 Genevan writing, *First Blast Against the Monstrous Regiment of Women*, Knox declared that to "promote a woman to have rule above any realm is repugnant to nature, contumely to God, a thing most contrarious to His revealed will and approved ordinance, and finally it is the subversion of good order, of all equity and justice."[2]

In 1564, Mary moved both to mollify the Scots' distaste for the rule of a woman and to strengthen her claim to the English throne. She married Henry Stuart, Lord Darnley, a grandson of Mary Stuart's own Tudor grandmother. Since Lord Darnley had been born on English soil, as Mary Stuart had not, English law enabled him to inherit England. Even better for Mary, she fell madly in love with this strikingly handsome man whose contemptible character was not yet evident.

Soon after the marriage, it became apparent that Darnley was unsuited not only for rule, but even for normal human relationships. Alienated from her husband, Mary began to put her trust in her secretary, an Italian named David Riccio. Whether or not their relationship was innocent, Darnley became enraged with jealousy and, as part of a gang, broke into the queen's chamber and stabbed Riccio to death. Mary, then pregnant with her son James, resolved to be avenged. In February 1567, Mary took her ill husband to the house of Kirk o' Field near Edinburgh. She managed to be conveniently away when the house was blown up, and Darnley, who survived the explosion, was murdered.

The conspiracy to kill Darnley was led by the Protestant James Bothwell, who took Mary to Dunbar, where they lived together until he was divorced and they could be married in a Protestant rite in May. Catholic Europe was horrified, and the Scots were thoroughly fed up with a murderous and adulterous queen tainted with Catholicism. In June, she was imprisoned in Loch Leven and forced to abdicate in favor of her son. Bothwell, himself not noted for constancy, deserted her and fled to Denmark. Although she managed to escape Loch Leven, she was unable to regain her crown. She fled to England and appealed to Elizabeth for help against the "rebels."

Mary Stuart thus put Elizabeth in an untenable position that even she could not temporize about indefinitely. Obviously, regicide was frowned on by all monarchs. Restoration of Mary to her throne would alienate Scots allies, but not to restore her would provide a focus for Catholic disaffection in England, as well as alienate other monarchs who, regardless of religion, did not wish to see people depose rulers. Elizabeth put Mary under house arrest until, finally, in 1586 the Elizabethan secret service produced documents that implicated Mary in a plot against the queen. Mary, queen of Scots, was beheaded on February 1, 1587. She went to her death with great courage. Holding her crucifix high and dressed in the red of martyrdom, she prayed for her enemies, for mercy for Elizabeth, and for grace

---

[2] Spitz, L. W., *Renaissance and Reformation Movements*, p. 465.

for England. Her dynastic ambition was realized by her son, James VI of Scotland, who on the death of Elizabeth became James I of England.

France

Into the 1520s, the French king Francis I shielded reformers and reform-minded humanists in France from ecclesial censure and punishment. The king's motivation was not evangelical but political. Since the thirteenth century, French theologians and conciliarists had argued that the French church held a privileged position in relation to the papacy. The supposed liberties of *l'Église gallicane* were reinforced in 1516 by the Concordat of Bologna between the king and Pope Leo X. The treaty increased the already considerable power of the crown over the church by, among other things, conceding the nomination of bishops and other ecclesiastics to the king. By 1516, Francis I had everything from the church that Henry VIII broke with the church to get.

However, Francis I's tolerance for reform turned to hostility when radicals indulged in violence and iconoclasm. Both ecclesial and royal authorities blamed the teachings of reformers for the actions of radicals, and men like Calvin fled abroad or went underground to escape repression. Francis's persecution of evangelicals vacillated between imprisonment and execution on the one hand, stimulated by outrages such as the affair of the placards, and moderation on the other hand, necessitated by alliances with German Lutheran princes to assist him against the emperor.

By the mid-1530s, it was clear that evangelical reform of the French church could not be carried out from within France, but would need external support. The source of this support was the Reformed church of Geneva. Once Calvin's leadership was firmly established in Geneva in 1555, he and other French exiles set up a very effective propaganda machine directed at France. Calvin was soon besieged by requests from French towns and noble families to provide them with pastors trained in Geneva.

The first evangelical congregations in France were called Huguenot, but these Calvinists preferred the term *Réformés* ("the Reformed"). Catholic satires of the time called them *la Religion Déformée*. Early congregations at Meaux (1546) and Nîmes (1547) were dispersed by persecution. The martyrdom of the Fourteen of Meaux for celebrating an evangelical communion was particularly vicious. All underwent extraordinary torture, but refused to reveal the names of other Protestants. At the stake six did submit to confessing to a priest in order to escape the penalty of having their tongues cut out, but the others remained firm even before this last mutilation.

The son of Francis I, Henry II (1547–1559), unbiased by humanist sympathies or the need to conciliate German Protestant allies, was even more severe than his father. He issued edicts decreeing harsh punishment for such heretical practices as eating meat during Lent and attending unauthorized assemblies. He also instituted a special court for heresy cases appropriately named *la Chambre Ardente* (the burning-chamber). Those accused of disseminating heresy through books or preaching were often sentenced to cruel deaths such as being drawn and quartered. Genevan pastors commissioned to France frequently signed their property over to their families because they knew they probably would not live to return.

By 1567 Geneva had sent 120 pastors into France to organize congregations, which, because of persecution, usually led a covert existence. Nevertheless, the Reformed church spread rapidly throughout France. A key to its success was the organizational genius it borrowed from Calvin's Genevan church. The first national synod of the Reformed church in France met in Paris in 1559. It set forth a confession of faith, the Gallican Confession, the first draft of which was written by Calvin. A modified form of this confession of faith containing forty articles, ratified at the synod of La Rochelle in 1571, continues to serve the French Reformed church to this day. By 1561, the national synod of France represented more than 2,000 congregations.

Calvinism in France appealed to particular social groups: skilled artisans, independent shopkeepers, and middle-class businessmen such as bankers. This phenomenon led some scholars to associate "the Protestant ethic" with "the spirit of capitalism" (usually under the heading of the "Weber thesis," after Max Weber, the nineteenth- and twentieth-century German sociologist and economist who championed the idea). There is no doubt that the Calvinist virtues of hard work and thrift motivated by a theology of vocation dovetailed nicely with a capitalist economy. As with similar theories about the Jews, however, a variety of other historical factors were involved in Calvinist business success.

The social group most significant for the Reformation in France was the nobility, especially the houses of Bourbon (after the Valois, next in line for the throne) and Montmorency. Gaspard de Coligny (1519–1572, Montmorency), the admiral of France and a major influence on the young king Charles IX, became an outstanding Huguenot leader. Other important noble families in the west and southwest of France also joined the Reformed church, and lesser nobles and peasants followed their lead, with the consequence that this area became the military bastion of the Reform movement.

The northern and eastern parts of France were in the control of an ultra-Catholic faction led by the Guise-Lorraine family. This powerful family held a strong position under Henry II and included cardinals who pressed for setting up a Spanish-style inquisition to exterminate all Calvinists. In response, a military and political Huguenot party arose to defend their power and privileges, as well as their faith. The rivalry between noble families was sharply escalated by their opposing religious commitments.

Although Henry II and his wife Catherine de Medici, niece of Pope Clement VII, detested Protestants, they were preoccupied with perpetual rivalry with Charles V in the Hapsburg–Valois wars. Furthermore, Henry did not seem to realize until the end of his reign the extent of his peoples' religious defection. With the treaty of Cateau-Cambrésis (1559), which ended the Hapsburg–Valois wars, the king was free to direct his attention to eliminating heresy in his lands. But within the year, Henry died of a wound suffered during a joust. His accidental death created a crisis in royal authority that set the stage for a rapid growth of Protestantism and a long, bitter religious conflict.

The eldest of the four Valois princes, Francis II, was only fifteen at the death of his father. During his brief eighteen-month reign (1559–1560), the ultra-Catholic party came to the fore through the domination of the government by the Guise uncles of Francis's wife, Mary, queen of Scots. Their repressive measures against Protestants caused such widespread resentment that more nobles joined those already committed to the Reformation because they both hated the Guises and had designs on the wealth of the Catholic church. The queen mother, Catherine, also sought ways to weaken the Guise faction that not only treated her disdainfully, but was trying to displace her sons in its effort to establish its own dynasty to rule France.

The intensity of anti-Guise feeling exploded in the Conspiracy of Amboise (1560), a bungled attempt by a group of Huguenot nobility to kill the Guises and remove the king from their influence. Some of these nobles were executed. The Bourbon prince Louis de Condé was implicated in the plot and sentenced to death, but was released after the death of Francis. The Conspiracy of Amboise foreshadowed the coming wars of religion, which had the nature of civil wars. Various groups, including some Calvinist pastors, joined in common, but ineffective opposition to the government. The suggestion by some Reformed leaders such as Knox and Bullinger (the successor to Zwingli) that subjects had the right to revolt against idolatrous (i.e., Catholic) rulers was firmly rejected by Calvin, who wrote to dissociate himself from the Amboise conspiracy. The involvement of Calvinist pastors in the plot has been nicely phrased by N. M. Sutherland: "Faced with a choice between resistance and extermination, they desired some solution less sublime than that of prayer alone."[3]

When Francis II died, Catherine's second son, Charles IX (ruled 1560–1574) succeeded as a minor at the age of ten. Legally, the regency could go to either the queen mother or the first prince of the blood (i.e., whoever was first in line to the throne after the reigning king's sons). The first prince of the blood was Anthony of Bourbon, king of Navarre, a Huguenot leader whose wife, Jeanne d'Albret, a convinced Calvinist, corresponded with Calvin and participated in the national synod of La Rochelle. Catherine outmaneuvered Anthony in the struggle for the regency, but that triumph entailed developing a policy favorable to the Huguenot party to counter the Guise faction.

The Colloquy of Poissy

Catherine, assisted by her chancellor Michel de L'Hôpital, created a policy of moderation toward the Protestants, suspended persecution, released Condé and other Huguenot prisoners, allowed Huguenot nobles at court to have their own services, and appointed new, liberal-leaning Catholic tutors for the young king. Anthony of Bourbon renounced his claim to the regency and accepted the title of lieutenant general of France. As a further effort to pacify her lands and, not incidentally, to provide a Gallican alternative to the Council of Trent, Catherine called for a public Protestant–Catholic dialogue. The Colloquy of Poissy, which met in September and October 1561, was a significant royal recognition of the reality and growth of Protestantism.

Chancellor L'Hôpital opened the colloquy with a speech concerning the king's gracious purpose to resolve the religious crisis by summoning this national council. The crown hoped that a mutually respectful exchange of theological views between the Catholic and Huguenot representatives might preserve peace in the Gallican church. The colloquy, L'Hôpital stated, was a place not of judgment, but of dialogue.

In immediate response, the archbishop of Lyons and primate of France, Cardinal

---

[3] N. M. Sutherland, "Calvin's Idealism and Indecision," in J. H. M. Salmon, ed., *The French Wars of Religion: How Important Were Religious Factors?* (Lexington, MA: D. C. Heath, 1967), p. 19.

Tournon, leaped to his feet to protest the very nature of the assembly. The fifty or so bishops present, for all their Gallicanism, despised a government-imposed assembly that raised heretics to their level. Heretics were to be judged, not debated.

Catherine was not interested in ultimatums and anathemas; her new policy was accommodation. At her motherly prompting, the king indicated, to the chagrin of the bishops, that the meeting would go on as scheduled. The Huguenot delegation—eleven ministers in their black Genevan robes and twenty lay representatives from various Calvinist congregations in France—was ushered into the assembly hall. Cardinal Tournon broke the tense silence with his stage whisper, "Voici ces chiens genevois!" ("Here are those Genevan dogs!").

The "Genevan dog" who stepped forth to present the Huguenot position immediately impressed his audience as a "purebred." Theodore Beza (1519–1605), born to an established Burgundian family, was a Calvinist's Calvinist and a scholar's scholar. During his thirteen-year exile in Switzerland, he had become Calvin's close friend, confidant, heir apparent, and professor of biblical studies at the new Genevan Academy. His work on the Greek New Testament is still remembered by the naming of the fifth-century Graeco-Latin manuscript of the Gospels he discovered and presented to the University of Cambridge in 1581 the Codex Bezae, and for the first critical edition of the Greek New Testament, which he published in 1565. His background of family wealth and position, similar to that of his audience, and his years of theological reflection and writing precluded any sense of intimidation from this assembly of royal and ecclesiastical dignitaries.

For the next hour, Beza eloquently and learnedly presented the Calvinist position. The queen mother was filled with hope, and even the bishops were not unmoved as Beza pledged himself to concord and elegantly surveyed doctrinal agreements between the antagonistic churches, such as the Trinity and the Incarnation. Only at the end of his speech did he make the fateful slip of stating that in the eucharist Christ's body "is as far removed from the bread and wine as is heaven from earth."[4] The prelates shattered their hitherto polite reception of Beza's address with shouts of "He blasphemes!" Catherine later called Beza's simile "absurd and offensive."

The colloquy went on for another month, but the neuralgic nerve that had already sent waves of pain through previous colloquies at Marburg (1529) and Regensburg (1541) had been inelegantly exposed by Beza. The mode of Christ's presence in the Eucharist was the rock on which accommodation foundered. For Catholic theologians, the mass was the Christian community's supreme good work of offering and receiving the corporeal Christ, whereas for Calvinist theologians, the mass was an idolatrous and blasphemous denial of the true Gospel. The Calvinists knew, as did other Protestants, that the mass was only the tip of the Catholic iceberg. The mass was upheld by a hierarchical priesthood whose ability to perform it was linked to an ordination process rooted in the successor to St. Peter and whose caste was endowed with special powers and prerogatives. From Luther on, the mass was the focal point of the Protestant Reformers' attacks on the establishment because they knew that if the mass went, the whole papal church would crumble.

When the Spanish Jesuit theologian Diego Lainez obtained permission to speak, he

---

[4]Donald Nugent, *Ecumenism in the Age of the Reformation: The Colloquy of Poissy* (Cambridge, MA: Harvard University Press, 1974), p. 100.

made it clear to the queen mother that her conciliatory intentions failed to understand that Calvinists are "serpents, wolves in sheep's clothing, and foxes." The remedy against Calvinist "venom" was not this national council of dubious ecclesial legality, but rather, the Council of Trent already in session and presided over by the pope, not the crown. Lest she did not get the point, Lainez insinuated that her crown, as well as her soul, were at stake in these matters.

The Wars of Religion: 1562–1598

The Colloquy of Poissy failed to create religious accommodation, but it did prepare the way for the first Edict of Toleration in January 1562, which provided a measure of freedom to the Huguenots. Huguenot leaders like Beza continued to have access to the court and strove for the conversion of the royal family. Huguenot public worship was allowed in private homes and outside town walls. These developments were the watershed for French Protestantism. It seemed that at the least, France might go the way of England under Henry VIII a generation earlier and adopt a national church under the control of the state.

Within a month of the Edict of Toleration, however, the situation for the Calvinists radically altered. By mid-February, Catherine came to believe that the wrath of the Guise family and the hostility of the Spanish threatened the unity of the nation and the royal future of her sons more than the Huguenots and their allies did. Her balance-of-power policy therefore shifted toward the Catholic faction. Anthony of Bourbon sensed the shift and defected from the Huguenot party for the sake of his own personal and dynastic ambitions. The Huguenot political and military resources were not sufficient to bring France into Protestantism, but they were strong enough to ensure the existence of the Huguenots as a rebellious minority. Under these conditions, civil war was inevitable. (See Figure 21.1.)

On March 1, 1562, the duke of Guise went on a hunting trip with 200 armed men. At Vassy in Champagne, they came across a large congregation of Huguenots gathered in a barn for worship and set upon them, killing some fifty and wounding many more. The incident sparked more massacres, and the religious wars were on. For more than thirty years, Huguenots and Catholics murdered and assassinated each other with increasing barbarity. In some regions, the war was endemic; elsewhere, it was sporadic or almost nonexistent and punctuated by truces. The most infamous event of all this bloodshed was the St. Bartholomew's Day Massacre (August 24, 1572).

The St. Bartholomew's Day Massacre

During one of her shifts from repression to moderation, Catherine appointed the Huguenot leader Coligny a member of the royal council. He soon became a strong influence on Charles IX. This aroused both the political and maternal anxieties of Catherine. When Coligny convinced Charles to reverse traditional foreign policy and support Protestant resistance to Spain in the Netherlands, thus risking a disastrous war, Catherine decided that Coligny must go.

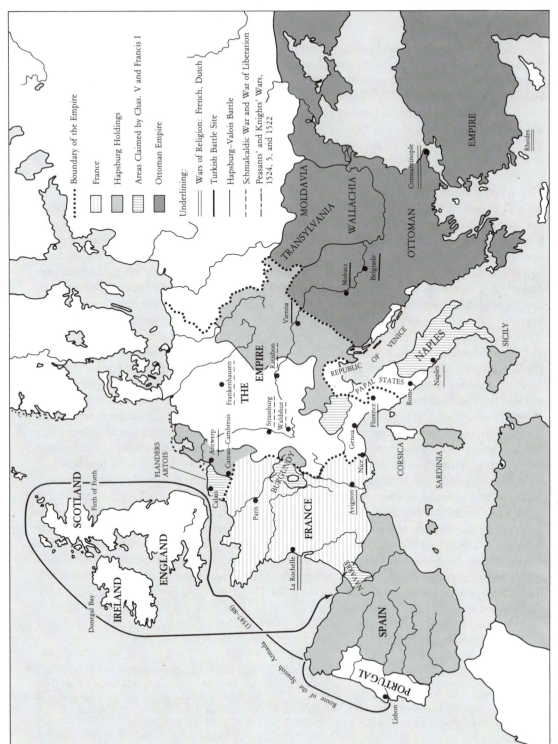

Figure 21.1 Major Battles in the Reformation Era

Knowing her son would not agree to a legal execution, Catherine opted for an assassination. She convinced herself that Coligny was an impenitent rebel who had to be killed for the peace, if not the glory, of France. In 1563, Coligny had condoned the assassination of Duke Francis of Guise. The Guise family, convinced that Coligny had ordered this deed, had long demanded revenge. Catherine conceived the cunning idea that if it appeared that the admiral was killed by the Lorraine-Guise family, then Protestant wrath would turn against the Guises, neatly eliminating both the Coligny and the Guise threats. With Coligny dead and the Guises massacred by the Protestants, the king would have a clear field. The plot had a certain brilliance and would have left the queen untouched, but for one flaw: The assassin was a poor shot and only wounded Coligny.

It is said that for the first time in her life, Catherine panicked. Charles was enraged that his esteemed father figure and counselor had been shot, and Catherine feared that Charles would learn who was behind the attack. All her concerns were now in jeopardy: the interests of state, her passion for power, and potential peril to her other son Henry, who had participated in the attack. The way out of her dilemma came with the accusation that Coligny was plotting with the Huguenots to kill the queen and her children. Whether or not the accusation was true and whether or not Catherine believed it are not known; what is known is that here was the means for influencing Charles to take steps to thwart a new Amboise conspiracy.

Catherine argued that rebels had to be executed. The crown must act quickly before the Huguenot forces were ready to strike it and, more important regarding Catherine's position, before the inquiry into the attempted murder of Coligny discovered anything. The context for the murder of Coligny and the massacre of his "rebels" was the marriage of Margaret of Valois, Catherine's daughter, and Henry of Navarre, heir to the throne since the death of his father. The marriage, negotiated as a means for creating peace between the warring religious factions by uniting the royal princess and the titular leader of the Protestants, took place in Paris on August 18. The marriage festivities filled Paris with prominent nobility, including most of the Huguenot leadership. Coligny had been shot on August 22. The plot was planned for the early morning of August 24.

The bell of the Palace of Justice gave the signal at three in the morning. To maintain order, the gates of Paris were closed, locking the Huguenot troops outside the city, in the suburbs. The king's militia was deployed in the city. One of the militia leaders, Claude Marcel, a fanatical Catholic and one of Guise's men, took it on himself to proclaim to his men that the king's orders were to kill all heretics. Lists of heretics were provided to facilitate a methodical massacre. At the signal given by the king, the unsuspecting Huguenots were slaughtered in their beds, beginning with Coligny, whose body was tossed from the window of his apartment and then mutilated. A contemporary described the savage conflagration fueled by religious hatred:

> The streets were covered with dead bodies, the rivers stained, the doors and gates of the palace bespattered with blood. Wagon loads of corpses, men, women, girls, even infants, were thrown into the Seine, while streams of blood ran in many quarters of the city. . . . One little girl was bathed in the blood of her butchered father and mother, and threatened with the same fate if she ever became a Huguenot.[5]

---

[5] Clyde Manschreck, ed., *A History of Christianity*, vol. 2 (Englewood Cliffs, NJ: Prentice-Hall, 1965), p. 144.

About 6,000 people were killed in Paris, and thousands were killed in lesser cities as the massacre spread through the land. Catherine had unleashed state terrorism.

European reactions to the massacre were mixed. Protestant leaders and royalty mourned, but took no major steps against France. Queen Elizabeth of England wore mourning to show her grief, but later agreed to serve as godmother to the daughter of the French king. The Poles ignored the massacre and elected Charles's brother, Duke Henry of Anjou, their king. Pope Gregory XIII prescribed an annual Te Deum as a special thanksgiving service that was celebrated for many years. He also had a special commemorative medal struck, *Ugonatorum Stranges*, that depicted an angel upholding the cross as prostrate Protestants are slain. It was said that the Spanish king, Philip II, laughed publicly for the first time in his life and ordered his bishops to celebrate the event with Te Deums and other ceremonies. Charles IX, however, seems to have been overcome with grief and guilt for his part in the massacre. He died less than two years later and was succeeded by his brother, at the time king of Poland, as Henry III, who reigned from 1574 to 1589.

Henry III, the last of the Valois line, refused to side with either Catholics or Protestants and moved toward a third party, the *politiques*, so called because they placed national unity before religious uniformity. Nevertheless, his ongoing conflicts with the Bourbons and Guises, known as the War of the Three Henrys because each leader had that name, led to the murders of both Henry of Guise and Henry III. In 1589 the Bourbon, Henry of Navarre, came to the throne as a Huguenot. It took Henry IV five years to subdue the Catholic League and its Spanish allies. In 1594 he converted to Catholicism under pressure from the Catholic League, which threatened to declare his succession invalid. The popular story is that Henry said, "Paris is worth a Mass." His conversion had the desired effect of securing both the legitimacy of the Bourbon succession and the unity of the nation. Since Pope Clement VIII did not insist that the decrees of the Council of Trent be enforced in France, Henry responded to the anxieties of his former coreligionists by setting forth a policy of limited toleration, the Edict of Nantes, in 1598.

The Edict of Nantes made the Catholic church the official state church with its former rights, income, and possessions. The Huguenots, about 15 percent of the population, were granted religious rights to worship on Protestant estates and in many areas, but not within five leagues of Paris. They were also granted civil rights, such as their own courts for legal protection and eligibility to hold offices, as well as political rights that included 200 fortified places. The edict did not work perfectly, but it did bring an end to the religious wars. It was revoked by Louis XIV in 1685.

Chapter 22

Catholic Renewal and the Counter-Reformation

Following Leo X's initial dismissal of the Reformation as nothing more than a drunken brawl among German monks, even the papacy began to realize that renewal and reform of the church could not be lightly brushed aside. The rapid spread of reform movements throughout Europe raised apocalyptic visions in more than one curial mind. However, the Catholic renewal movement was not merely a reaction, a Counter-Reformation, to the Reformation. Concern for renewal of the church had long been voiced by humanists such as Erasmus. And cardinals such as Gian Matteo Giberti (1495–1543) strove to upgrade the education and morality of the clergy and to restore church discipline.

However, these early renewal efforts were too little and too late to forestall the Reformation. For example, Emperor Maximilian had called for a reforming council in 1509, but he was outmaneuvered by Pope Julius II, whose Lateran Council (1512) reaffirmed the full power of the pope, condemned conciliarism, and denounced the tendency toward independence of the national churches. The gravity of the church's situation was not fully grasped by Rome until Leo's death in 1521. The cardinals then elected a Dutch cardinal of spotless reputation, Adrian of Utrecht (1459–1523), as Pope Adrian VI.

Adrian had studied with the Brethren of the Common Life and taught theology at Louvain, where he had received a doctorate in 1492. He was a friend of Erasmus, tutor of the young Charles V, and had been a bishop and inquisitor in Spain. An earnest and zealous reformer, he moved quickly toward checking Protestantism, reconciling European princes, and reforming the curia. But the times were against him: The Italians looked down on him for his rude Latin and lack of Renaissance sophistication. He was elected in January 1522 and died in September 1523. His epitaph read, "Alas! How the power of even a most righteous man depends upon the times in which he happens to live!"

Adrian was succeeded by another Medici, a cousin to Leo X, who took the title Clement VII. He was an easygoing, urbane patron of the arts. His inability to deal with Henry VIII's drive to divorce Catherine was characteristic of his ineffective efforts to conciliate all parties. He sent the moderate Cardinal Campeggio to the Diet of Nürnberg in 1524 with the offer to the Lutherans of "wine and women"—communion with both wine and bread and clerical marriage—without realizing how deep the doctrinal divisions had already become. In 1532 he consented to call the ecumenical council requested by the Protestants for the last twelve years, but he died in 1534 without convoking it.

The next pope, Alexander Farnese, Pope Paul III, was a typical Renaissance prelate. He immediately made two of his teenage grandsons cardinals, in order, as he put it, to provide for his old age. He did, however, encourage dialogue with Protestants such as Melanchthon and Bucer and made a number of humanists cardinals. In 1536, he proclaimed that the long-desired council would meet in Mantua in May 1537. In preparation for this council, he appointed a commission of nine cardinals to prepare a report on reform of the church. After two months of solid work, the commission issued the report *Advice . . . Concerning the Reform of the Church*, which scored the abuses of nepotism, simony, pluralism of benefices, absenteeism, and clerical immorality and venality. But to Protestants, the report only confirmed and substantiated their criticisms of the church. Furthermore, the commission's emphasis on *moral* reform of the church indicated that they were unable to come to grips with Luther's explicit call for *theological* reform. Luther himself published a German translation of the report with ironic glosses in the margins.

Nevertheless, there were Roman Catholic theologians who not only understood, but even shared, some of Luther's religious concerns. An outstanding example, Gasparo Contarini (1483–1542), had been present at the Diet of Worms as Venetian ambassador to the imperial court. Later (1528–1530), as ambassador to the papal court in Rome, his deep piety and diplomatic ability to negotiate and compromise differences led to his elevation to the cardinalate (1535) while still a layman. He sought to reconcile Protestant and Catholic differences and advocated an ecumenical council to heal the divisions in the church. He and his Lutheran counterpart Melanchthon did reach agreement on some significant theological issues, such as justification at the Regensburg Colloquy in 1541. But both sides rejected their mutual efforts as compromises at the expense of the truth. With the death of Contarini, the liberal Catholic reform movement also suffered a mortal blow.

One thing after another prompted the postponement of the council, and in 1542 war broke out again between Charles V and Francis I. The council, which we shall treat later, did not actually convene until 1545—twenty-five years after Luther's first calls for a council! Paul III died in 1549. After the brief reigns of Julius III and Marcellus II, Cardinal Caraffa (1476–1559) became Pope Paul IV in 1555.

Paul IV is sometimes termed the first of the Counter-Reformation popes for his dogmatic rigidity and determination to eliminate Protestantism. During his pontificate, the Catholic renewal movement shifted to repression and earned the label "Counter-Reformation." Two of its tools were the *Index of Prohibited Books* and the Inquisition.

Lists of prohibited books had been circulated since 1521, mainly by the theological faculties of Paris and Louvain. Paul IV agreed that effective thought control included burning not only authors, but also their writings, and therefore promoted a complete list of heretical works to be universally prohibited. The *Index librorum prohibitorum*, first published in 1557 by the Congregation of the Inquisition under Paul IV, was modified in 1564 by the Council of Trent. The list proscribed not only heretical Protestant works, but also humanist classics thought to be injurious to morals, such as Boccaccio's *Decameron*. Even the works of Erasmus, once offered a cardinal's hat, were forbidden and then later published in bowdlerized versions. The great majority of editions of the Bible and the church fathers were also prohibited. In 1571, Pius V established a special Congregation of the Index whose duties were transferred to the Holy Office (now titled the Congregation for the Doctrine of the Faith); the *Index* itself was abolished in 1966.

The Inquisition, juridical persecution of heresy by special ecclesial courts, has roots in the thirteenth-century proceedings against the Catharist heresy when the church secured the assistance of the secular powers. The Spanish Inquisition was closely tied to the state. In 1478, the pope granted Spanish sovereigns the right to set up and direct the Inquisition. Inquisitors had power over all religious orders and (after 1531) even over bishops. It has been suggested that the militant orthodoxy and fanatical spirit of the Spanish church resulted from the centuries of combat with Islam. Ferdinand and Isabella established powerful institutional controls against any form of deviation. By 1508 Cardinal Ximénez not only had strengthened the Spanish hierarchy by a kind of rigid moral rearmament, but had himself served as Grand Inquisitor. By the 1530s, the Inquisition was directed against Erasmians and Lutherans.

Even before becoming pope, Paul IV had been favorably impressed by the Spanish Inquisition's effectiveness and suggested it be introduced in Italy. Paul III, fearing popular hostility, was less than enthusiastic about the idea, but reluctantly allowed the then Cardinal Caraffa to introduce the Inquisition because moderate reform efforts were failing to curb the growth of Protestantism. Caraffa was so eager to begin that he set up interrogation chambers in his own house.

The judges of the Roman Tribunal were the customary Dominicans, subordinated to six cardinals appointed by the pope to serve as inquisitors general. One of these six men was Cardinal Caraffa. On July 21, 1542, Paul III formally sanctioned the Roman Inquisition and extended its authority to all Christendom. It was an effective instrument so long as the monarch cooperated with it. It was also during this period that the defensive weapon of the Inquisition was supplemented by the offensive weapon of the Jesuits.

Loyola and the Society of Jesus

Ignatius Loyola (1491–1556) was the embodiment of both the Roman Catholic church and the Counter-Reformation. The youngest of twelve children born to a Basque family of noble lineage, Loyola was trained from his youth in the ideals of the nobility. Although much taken by the romances of chivalry, his life as a courtier was less than edifying. That life took an abrupt about-face as the result of his volunteering to help defend the city of Pamplona against an advancing French army. At the siege of Pamplona in 1521, during the first of the Hapsburg–Valois wars, a cannonball broke Loyola's right leg and wounded his left. His broken leg was set by a doctor of the victorious French army, and he was taken back to the family castle to recuperate. There, doctors found that the leg had been badly set, and Loyola insisted that the leg be rebroken, reset, and a protruding bone sawed off! The ensuing discomfort and nine months of convalescence gave Loyola occasion for reflection about his life. His physical pain was compounded by his anguish at realizing that his wounds crippled his knightly ambitions. Influenced by the reading available to him in the castle, including translations of Ludolf of Saxony's *Life of Christ* and *Flowers of the Saints*, Loyola became convinced that God wanted him to become a spiritual knight. Loyola's shattered military ambitions found a new outlet: the defense of the church.

In March 1522, on the feast of the Annunciation of the Virgin Mary at Montserrat, near Barcelona, Loyola offered his sword to the service of Mary, exchanged clothes with a beggar, and, as he put it, clothed himself "with the armor of Christ." His intention to set out on a pilgrimage to Jerusalem was frustrated by an outbreak of the plague, and he remained for most of the year in ascetic retreat at the nearby cave of Manresa. During this period of intense prayer, extreme mortification, and rigorous introspection, he developed the basis for his later famous and influential *Spiritual Exercises*. Although not published until 1548, this guide for developing conformity to God's will was already in use in 1527.

The *Spiritual Exercises* are a four-part series of meditations and rules designed to strengthen and discipline the person's will to conform to and serve the will of God. The first part of the discipline is a systematic consideration of sin and its consequences. The second part presents the significance of the life and kingdom of Christ. The third part focuses on the Passion story, and the fourth part culminates the exercise with meditation on the risen and glorified Christ. The original intention was to extend the *Exercises* over four weeks. Through his exceptional insights into religious psychology, Loyola created a discipline by which he and his followers could direct themselves through progressive resolutions to detest sin, join the ranks of God's disciples, test and confirm their commitment, and actuate their wills toward the pursuit of perfection. The systematic reasoning and meditation included daily self-examination focused on cultivating a single virtue or attacking a single sinful inclination. The schedule allowed one problem area after another to be conquered in the intended process for reform of the person's life.

In contrast to Luther, Loyola perceived the problem of the church not as doctrinal aberration, but as personal aberration from the teaching and tradition of the institution. The key to reform of the church, then, for Loyola was the reform of individuals. And individual reform was to take place through self-mastery of the person's will. By complete self-mastery, the person could avoid extremes in the pursuit of service to God and the salvation of oneself and others. The orientation combined the Renaissance conception and esteem of the individual personality with the late medieval intentionality of the mystics for the perfection of the soul, which in Loyola's mind meant unquestioning submission to Christ and the church in the person of the pope.

In 1523, Loyola set out for Jerusalem to convert the Muslims, but discovered in the process that his intentions needed a solid educational foundation. At thirty years of age, he returned to Barcelona and enrolled in a school for boys. He then went on to the University of Alcalá, where his first group of followers gathered around him. Ironically, at Alcalá, he was suspected of heresy and twice imprisoned by the Spanish Inquisition. Acquitted, he went on to study at Paris in 1528 after a brief sojourn at Salamanca.

In Paris (1528–1535), Loyola earned his master's degree. There he also laid the foundations for the Society of Jesus, the Jesuits. His companions included Diego Lainez, the next general of the order, Alfonso Salmerón, and Francis Xavier, the great missionary to the Far East. With an oath reminiscent of the medieval Spanish crusades, they swore to go to the Holy Land to convert the Muslims.

In 1537 Loyola and his companions met in Venice, were consecrated as priests, and prepared to set out for Jerusalem. War between Venice and the Turks foiled these plans, so they decided to "seek their Jerusalem in Rome." In 1540, Pope Paul III sanctioned the life of service to the church that Loyola and his small group of companions envisaged. The last major medieval monastic order, the Society of Jesus was a distinct development. The older monastic ideals of contemplation and withdrawal from the world were replaced by Loyola's emphasis on action in the world. This in turn required well-educated priests, which led to the well-known rigorous training of candidates for the Society. The training interiorized monastic discipline because the Jesuits were not to be isolated in a monastery, but active in the world through mission and evangelism. Another distinctive element of the Society of Jesus was that the candidate took not only the three regular vows of poverty, chastity, and obedience, but also a fourth vow, of obedience to the pope.

The special fourth vow starkly highlights Loyola's distance from Luther on reform. To Loyola, the church was hierarchical. The authoritarian character of Loyola's understanding of one's personal relationship to the church is expressed in this vow to go without question or delay wherever the pope ordered for the work of the church. Loyola's understanding of reform was the epitome of the papalism soon to be defined by the Council of Trent. (See Figure 22.1.)

The Jesuits sought to extirpate heresy and win Protestants back to Rome by means of political influence and effective education. Jesuit political influence grew as members of the order gained access to the courts of Europe as confessors to influential persons. In this way, they were effective in inducing political rulers to suppress Protestantism. The Jesuits also placed great emphasis on education, promoting both advanced learning and strong devotion to the authority of the church. Loyola himself founded grammar schools and both the Roman College (the Gregorianum) and the German College in Rome and established missions in India, Malaya, Africa, Ethiopia, Brazil, Japan, and China. By Loyola's death in 1556 the order included more than 1,000 members, and by 1600 there were more than 8,000 Jesuits throughout the world.

The Council of Trent (1545–1563)

Loyola's understanding of reform animated the Council of Trent both in its spirit of individual renewal as the key to church renewal and in the fact that members of the Society of Jesus played key roles in the council as papal theologians. Like Loyola himself, the council illustrated the twin concerns of the Catholic church: self-renewal and opposition to what it regarded as Protestant heresy. The council was convoked in 1545 in a theoretically still-united Christendom; the council closed in 1563 with a Christendom rent by divisions that affect world Christianity down to the present.

The Council of Trent definitively ended medieval hopes for conciliarism. Indeed, Trent was so influential on the mind-set of modern Roman Catholicism, that until Vatican

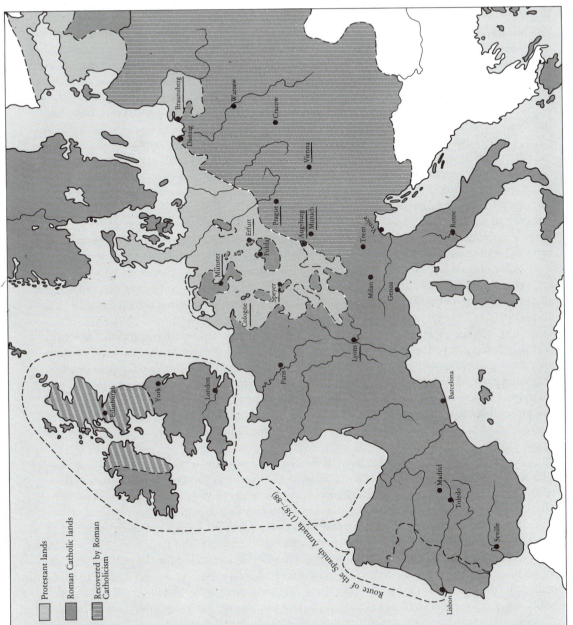

Figure 22.1   The Counter-Reformation (to 1648)

Protestant lands

Roman Catholic lands

Recovered by Roman
Catholicism

Braunsberg
Warsaw
Danzig
Cracow
Vienna
Erfurt
Prague
Münster
Fulda
Augsburg
Munich
Cologne
Speyer
Trent
Venice
Rome
Milan
Genoa
Lyons
Paris
Edinburgh
York
London
Barcelona
Madrid
Toledo
Seville
Lisbon

Route of the Spanish Armada (1587–88)

II (1962–1965), the church was known as the Tridentine (from the Latin for Trent) church. It is with the Council of Trent that the intrinsic contradiction of linking the specific with the universal in the name Roman Catholicism received meaning as a denominational term in contrast to the varieties of Protestant churches. Following the adjournment of the council, there was no other ecumenical council for 300 years, and that was Vatican I (1869–1870), which concluded one of the problem areas Trent did not resolve—papal authority and infallibility. The other problem area not treated by Trent, the person of Mary, was defined by papal decrees in 1854 (the doctrine of the Immaculate Conception: from conception, Mary was free from original sin) and 1950 (the doctrine of the Assumption: on her death, Mary was assumed bodily into heaven).

The Council of Trent itself was only reluctantly convoked after numerous delays. Papal reluctance to agree to an ecumenical council was rooted in political and theological concerns. The conciliar movement of the fifteenth century had strongly challenged papal authority when it tried to place the pope under the authority of councils. And Luther's call for a free Christian council meant a council free of papal domination, with the scriptures rather than tradition as the norm—a demand the pope obviously found offensive. The long delay in convening this council also related to the desire of every party to have the council meet in its own territory in order to control it better. The town of Trent in northern Italy was finally chosen because it was technically on German soil and therefore appeased the emperor. Political events also influenced the fact that the council as a whole did not actually meet for the entire period (1545–1563). Instead, there were three distinct assemblies: 1545–1547, 1551–1552, and 1562–1563.

The council opened on December 13, 1545, in the midst of commercial scalpers whose inflated prices for lodging and food expressed their delight at the presence of such an august gathering. On the initial crucial issues of voting and the agenda, it was decided that voting would be by individuals and that dogmatic and disciplinary reform issues would be treated concurrently. The voting decision was a specific departure from the practice of the fifteenth-century councils, which had voted by nations. The decision gave the papacy a distinct advantage, because Italians at the council outnumbered participants from other nations.

Some of the council fathers favored far-reaching reforms of the church and conciliation with the Protestants. However, the Jesuit theologians, Salmerón and Lainez, effectively countered this desire through their influence both as theological advisors and preachers at the council. Although the council did not condemn Luther in a formal, judicial sense, its doctrinal decisions were clearly intended to counter the Reformation understanding of the Gospel. Against the Reformation watchword of "scripture alone," the fourth session (April 1546) decided that the apostolic traditions must be accepted with the same reverence as scripture: "This truth and teaching are contained in the written books *and* in the unwritten traditions." Thus arose the controversial theological issue of whether scripture and tradition are two equal sources of revelation. The significance of Trent's decision is that the Magisterium—the teaching authority of the Roman church—is the final interpreter of tradition and thus of scripture. This decision was complemented by decreeing Jerome's Vulgate (old Latin) edition of the Bible as the standard for dogmatic proofs.

In response to the Reformation watchword of "grace alone," the council affirmed the role of human cooperation with grace for salvation. The sixth session, in January 1547, set forth the Catholic teaching on justification in sixteen doctrinal chapters and thirty-three canons condemning errors. In affirming free human cooperation with God's grace in salvation, the council used as proof the very text of Zechariah 1:3 ("Return to me, . . . and I will return to you") that Luther had identified as a support of salvation by human activity in his 1516 "Disputation Against Scholastic Theology."

In response to the Reformation emphasis on baptism and the Lord's Supper as the two sacraments of the Christian faith, the seventh session of the council reaffirmed the seven sacraments of baptism, confirmation, the Eucharist, penance, extreme unction, holy orders, and matrimony. These sacraments are objectively efficacious—that is, they effect grace by virtue of their administration (*ex opere operato*). With regard to Protestant communion with both bread and wine, "Holy Mother Church . . . approves of the custom of communicating under one species [i.e., the bread] and declares that this custom has the force of law." Later, in the thirteenth session (1551), the council reaffirmed the doctrine of transubstantiation.

Emperor Charles V became disturbed that the council was ignoring his demands for thoroughgoing reform and passing decrees that would imperil his concern for Protestant–Catholic reconciliation. To avoid imperial pressure on the council, Pope Paul III took advantage of the presence of a few cases of plague in Trent to induce the majority of prelates to move the council to Bologna in March 1547. Charles made it clear that he thought this was an illegal move, and he proceeded to try to settle the religious controversies in Germany on his own through the Augsburg Interim of 1548. Paul III died in 1549.

In 1551, Pope Julius III recalled the council to Trent. Protestant delegates arrived in January 1552, but they were obviously too late for any influence on the decrees already formulated against the central concerns of the reformers. A Protestant military rally against Charles led to Catholic fears that the Protestants would invade Trent; hence, this second assembly was suspended.

The third assembly of the Council of Trent, held in 1562–1563, met under the skillful diplomacy of Pope Pius IV. By this time, all hope of conciliating the Protestants had evaporated. The assembly took the earlier dogmatic decrees for granted and thereby avoided battles over whether it was a legitimate continuation of the first two assemblies. The bitter debates of this period revolved around reform proposals, especially the obligatory residence of bishops in their sees. Tendencies by the Spanish, French, and imperialists to decentralize the church and thus diminish the powers of the papacy were overcome by skillful diplomacy that won the monarchs over to the pope's position. The basis for the ultramontanism (the centralization of authority and influence in the papacy) that culminated in the declaration of papal infallibility in 1870 was thus established. The council itself became a means for renewed rejection of conciliarism by this papal triumph. Although no decree described the power and functions of the papacy, the council submitted the decrees to the pope for his confirmation. On January 26, 1564, the pope issued the bull *Benedictus Deus*, confirming the canons and decrees of the Council of Trent. The bull stated that the pope alone had the right to interpret them.

Although the Council of Trent failed to achieve all of its goals—of reformation of the faith, restoration of morality, and reunion of all Christians—it certainly restored spirit and energy to the Roman church. The decades following the council witnessed renewed theological scholarship and education, moral reform, and spiritual growth as Catholicism responded to Protestantism. Disciplinary decrees of the council stimulated biblical preaching and the establishment of seminaries to provide an educated clergy for pastoral work. A variety of moral reforms also was carried out with regard to clerical celibacy and chastity, as well as the residency and faithfulness of bishops.

The Catholic reform movement was essentially personal. The church was to be transformed by transforming its members, and its members were to be transformed by a transformed elite leadership. The emphasis on personal spiritual renewal was the emphasis of both Tridentine reforms and Loyola's Jesuits. But the renewal of prayer, penance, and spiritual and corporal works of mercy, important as it was, neglected liturgical reform. The heroic stature of individuals such as Loyola could not substitute for the centrality of public, corporate worship that Luther and other Protestant reformers had recovered. Liturgical reform and hymnody were crucial to the Protestant reformers, but the Catholic reformers remained liturgically indifferent: Late sixteenth-century Catholic worship still preserved the highly clerical complexion it had received in the Middle Ages. Of course, Catholic worship did not lack festival, drama, and artistry, but the corporate biblical emphases revived by Luther, Zwingli, Calvin, and others remained in the shadows. The spirituality of Catholic reform was the ascetical, subjective, and personal piety exemplified by such spiritual athletes as Teresa of Ávila (d. 1582) and John of the Cross (d. 1591) and the baroque artistic expressions exemplified by Bernini's striking sculpture "St. Teresa in Ecstasy" (1646) and the paintings "Christ on the Cross" and "Resurrection" by El Greco (d. 1614). Indeed, it may be argued that baroque art expressed the triumph of the Tridentine Counter-Reformation, for in its form it manifested control over seemingly turbulent forces, and in its content it focused on the emphases of the Counter-Reformation: Mary, the saints, Corpus Christi processions, and regnant popes with the keys of St. Peter.

Legacies of the Reformation

One of the consequences of the Reformation in general and the Council of Trent in particular was the splintering of western Christendom. The legacies of this fragmentation of the medieval *Corpus Christianum* have affected every aspect of modern life and thought.

The decisions of the Council of Trent on justification, scripture, and the sacraments made so definitive the divisions that had arisen in the Reformation, that hopes for a reunited Christian church would not begin flickering again until the ecumenical movement of the twentieth century. By the conclusion of the Council of Trent, there was a second generation of reformers whose memories of the "one, holy, catholic, and apostolic church" had receded behind the vivid present impressions of the martyrs and confessors of their own particular communities. Loyalty to the "fathers" of the church now came increasingly to mean loyalty to the confessions of faith of the previous generation. Conversations between, and even within, the churches too often degenerated to mutual condemnations and anathemas. The intensity and rancor of these theological and ecclesial conflicts are reflected in Philip Melanchthon's sigh on his deathbed that finally he was being delivered from the *rabies theologorum* (the "madness of the theologians").

The Reformation introduced the problem of pluralism—religious, social, and cultural—into Western culture. The modern world is still struggling with this legacy in its classrooms and courtrooms and on its streets and battlefields. It should not be surprising that the people of the sixteenth century found it exceedingly difficult to live with alternative and competing commitments.

The Reformation also affected other aspects of culture. The doctrine of justification by grace alone through faith alone released energy for this world that had hitherto been devoted to achieving the next world. With their new ethos of vocation, the Reformers undercut the medieval dualism of the sacred and the secular. In the medieval world, only the religious (priests, monks, nuns) had a sacred vocation. Those who worked in the secular world were understood to be on a lower and less God-pleasing plane. The Reformers emphasized that whatever a person did in the world that served the neighbor and helped build up the human community pleased God. All mundane tasks, from changing diapers to changing laws, were imbued with religious significance not because human works are salvational, but because God intends neighbors to be served. Nowhere was this understanding of vocation applied more explosively to medieval life than in the area of sex and marriage. According to the historian Steven Ozment, "No institutional change brought about by the Reformation was more visible, responsive to late medieval pleas for reform, and conducive to new social attitudes than the marriage of Protestant clergy. Nor was there another point in the Protestant program where theology and practice corresponded more successfully."[1] The Reformers vigorously criticized the Roman church's imposition of celibacy on priests, monks, and nuns because it removed men and women from service to their neighbor, contravened the divine order of marriage and family, and denied the created goodness of sexuality. Marriage was not just the legitimation of sexual fulfillment, but, above all, the context for creating a new awareness of human community with all its pains and joys. So Luther declared: "Marriage does not only consist of sleeping with a woman—anybody can do that—but of keeping house and bringing up children."[2] Thus, the Reformation not only saw in marriage a new, joyous appreciation for sexual drives, but also a new respect for women as companions.

Perhaps the point at which the Reformers' proclamation of vocation has received the most attention in the modern world is where religion and economics intersect. Since the publication in 1904–1905 of Max Weber's *The Protestant Ethic and the Spirit of Capitalism*, it has been popular to associate capitalism with Calvinism. Weber's thesis posited that Calvinist theology so stressed predestination, that anxious believers began to seek signs of their election in worldly success. In response to this thesis, it should be noted that the profit economy or early forms of capitalism clearly antedated the Reformation and that Calvin did not associate material success with the individual's standing before God. Calvin's understanding of predestination and providence was not individualistic, but communal and world historical. The doctrine of predestination affirms that despite evil and suffering, the ultimate destiny of the world and history rests in the good and infallible hands of God.

Calvin's theology was communal, not individualistic. Therefore, he could perceive riches as a divine blessing not in terms of endorsement of the individual, but rather as a blessing to be shared with the whole community. Conversely, poverty expresses the wrath

---

[1] Steven Ozment, *The Age of Reform: 1250–1550* (New Haven, CT: Yale University Press, 1980), p. 381.

[2] *Luther's Works*, 55 vols., ed. by Jaroslav Pelikan and Helmut T. Lehman (St. Louis: Concordia Publishing House and Minneapolis: Fortress Press, 1953–1986), vol. 54, p. 441.

of God not toward the individual, but toward the whole community for sin, and thus, the whole community should alleviate the plight of the poor. The "blame the victim, praise the achiever" ideology of modern times is a secularized and individualized kind of covenant theology. The biblical answer to this form of "Deuteronomic history," which attributes failure to intrinsic character flaws and success to moral quality, is the Book of Job. The Reformation answer is to recall the vigorous attacks Luther and Calvin made on capitalism as unrestrained greed, as well as their continual calls for government control of capitalism. On the other hand, Luther and Calvin both contributed to the development of modern social welfare. They instituted urban and state welfare programs sensitive to structural causes of unemployment and underemployment, job training, and civic responsibility for preventing, as well as alleviating poverty.

The Reformation doctrines of justification and vocation also had an impact on the development of education and the sciences. Building on the contributions of the humanists, the Reformers stressed education as the resource for preparing persons for service to the whole community. It was not accidental that universal literacy was first achieved in Scotland and the Protestant areas of Germany. As Melanchthon declared, "the ultimate end which confronts us is not private virtue alone but the interest of the public weal."

It may be argued that Luther's greatest contribution was not his tracts on such practical subjects that towns should establish schools and public libraries and that parents should make sure that their children went to school, but his initiation of a new way of thinking. In our time, it has become fashionable to call a major shift in thinking a "paradigm shift." Luther's thorough rejection of Aristotle and classical "authorities" is no less than a paradigm shift from medieval epistemology based on deduction from textual authorities to an epistemology of induction and experience. In his theological context, Luther stated, "It is not by understanding, reading, or speculation that one becomes a theologian, but through living, dying, and being damned."[3] Less dramatically, he wrote: "None of the arts can be learned without practice. What kind of physician would that be who stayed in school all the time? When he finally puts his medicine to use and deals more and more with nature, he will come to see that he hasn't as yet mastered the art."[4] Similarly, the English thinker Francis Bacon (1561–1626) compared Aristotle to the Antichrist and indicted Greek philosophers for conjuring scientific knowledge out of their heads instead of seeking it in nature.

Ironically, theological controversies after the death of Luther also contributed to the development of science. For example, Johannes Kepler (1571–1630) was not accepted for ordained ministry because his theology of the Lord's Supper was not regarded as orthodox. He then became an assistant to the Danish astronomer Tycho Brahe (1546–1601). In spite of his disappointment over being rejected for the ministry, Kepler wrote in his first publication, "I wanted to become a theologian. For a long time I was restless. Now, however, observe how through my efforts, God is being celebrated in astronomy."[5] Kepler went on to

---

[3] *Martin Luthers Werke* (Weimar, 1883), vol. 5, p. 163.

[4] *Luther's Works*, vol. 54, pp. 50–51.

[5] Bruce Wrightsman, "Lutheranism and the Protestant Synthesis: Religion and Science in America," in John E. Groh and Robert H. Smith, eds., *The Lutheran Church in North American Life* (St. Louis: Concordia Publishing House, 1979), p. 66.

influence Newton and to contribute to the triumph of the Copernican over the Ptolemaic theory of planetary motion.

Similarly, the Royal Society of London focused on scientific studies because they were free from both dogmatism and scepticism. Yet Kepler spoke for many of his scientific colleagues when he described scientists as "thinking God's thoughts after him."[6] By and large, these were religious men zealous to discover and admire the works of God in nature.

From the beginning of the Reformation, historiography played an important role. Luther used history to argue that the papacy of his day was an aberration from the early church, martyrologists such as John Foxe selectively used history to present their case for the truth and witness of Protestantism, and the dissidents argued that the entire church had fallen when it became the establishment under Constantine in the fourth century. Although these works were designed to make history serve their respective theologies, they did stimulate the development of historical criticism.

Even national literatures were influenced by great reformers. There are far too many major contributions to list them here, other than to mention the Elizabethan dramatist William Shakespeare (1564–1616), whose literary brilliance and insight into humankind remain unequaled. In music, too, the Reformation stimulated compositions that continue to enrich modern life. The Reformers' concern for making the liturgy accessible to the people was supplemented by their love for music as a glorious gift of God. Many of Luther's hymns continue to be well known and sung today, especially "A Mighty Fortress Is Our God," which informed later works by Bach and Mendelssohn. The scope and complexity of the legacies of the Reformation prompt appreciation for Thomas Carlyle's disclaimer: "Listening from the distance of centuries across the death chasms and howling kingdoms of decay, it is not easy to catch everything."[7]

[6]L. W. Spitz, *The Renaissance and Reformation Movements*, p. 588.
[7]Cited by Spitz, *ibid.*, p. 547.

The medieval ideal of the *corpus Christianum*, the union of all Christians in one body, one community, is illustrated by this twelfth-century fresco in the church St.-Pierre-le-Jeune in Strasbourg. Known as "The Procession of the Nations to the Cross," this fresco presents the solidarity of the European peoples in spite of all past conflicts. Contrast this with the fifteenth century procession of "The Hay Wagon" by Bosch, the last figure in this grouping. (Bildarchiv Foto Marburg/Art Resource)

Christ, the Judge of the World. The fourteenth-century stone relief (left) was originally on the outside wall of the Wittenberg parish church. (Bildarchiv Foto Marburg/Art Resource) Before he came to understand the righteousness of God as a gift to persons, Luther was terrified by this image of God's judgmental severity. He later recalled that he would shield his eyes as he hurried past it. The same image of Christ as Judge is portrayed in the late fifteenth-century woodcut (right). Under the lily, the word "come" (VENITE) invites the faithful to salvation; under the sword, the word "go" (ITE) commands the damned to enter the jaws of hell.

"Death and the Maiden" is from the so-called Heidelberg Dance of Death series of woodcuts (fifteenth century). Death is portrayed as a dancer whom every person has to follow. Woodcuts of the Dance of Death were widely circulated and served preachers of repentance and judgment who emphasized the transitoriness of life. Here Death claims the maiden who herself confesses that she has been preoccupied with the world and its pleasures, to the neglect of God's commandments. The popularity of these woodcuts on the eve of the Reformation is also due to their social–critical aspect: All are equal before Death, who removes the human masks of beauty, wealth, and status. At the same time, these images also express the late medieval church's hostility to life and creatureliness.

In the later Middle Ages the clergy was increasingly criticized for perceived wealth, drunkenness, and lechery. (By permission of the British Library, MS Sloane 2434, fol.44v [left]; MS Roy.10. E. IV, fol. 187r [right].)

The fourteenth-century Pieta expresses the period's emphasis upon the real, bodily suffering of Christ. Painted wood, less than life-size. German, c. 1370. (Marburg/Art Resource, NY 6.807)

"Knight, Death, and the Devil" engraving by Dürer (1513). Art historians have suggested that this engraving expresses the old theme of the Christian knight revived in humanist circles by Erasmus's *Manual of the Christian Soldier* (1504). The knight has also been identified with the martyred Dominican preacher of repentance, Savonarola (1452–1498), who thought of himself as a knight of Christ. (Fogg Art Museum, Harvard University. Bequest-Francis Calley Gray Collection)

The intense religiosity of the Catholic Baroque expression of the Catholic Reformation is superbly captured by Bernini's (1598–1680) sculpture of the Spanish Carmelite nun and mystic, Saint Theresa of Avila (1515–1582). Bernini depicts Theresa's vision of an angel who repeatedly pierced her heart with a golden arrow, producing a "pain so great that I screamed aloud; but simultaneously I felt such infinite sweetness that I wished the pain to last eternally." (Alinari/Art Resource)

Francois Dubois's depiction of the Saint Bartholomew's Day massacre. (Musee Cantonal des Beaux Arts, Lausanne)

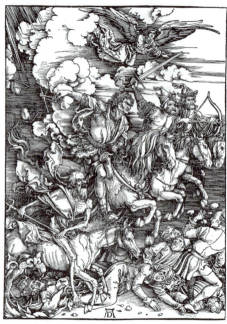

Pieter Bruegel the Elder's (c. 1525–1569) copper engraving in the style of Bosch is a variation on the theme that the big crooks hang the little crooks. The engraving also utilizes symbols of false prophets (fish), infidelity (mussel shells), and punishment of evil (knives). (Marburg/Art Resource)

The fame of Albrecht Dürer (1471–1528) continues to rest on his graphic works such as the woodcut series, *Apocalypse*, which includes the "Four Horsemen." Dürer's *Apocalypse* series appeared the same year (1498) that the Dominican preacher Savonarola was burned at the stake. People everywhere were expecting the imminent end of the world, and these prints captured and expressed this fear. The "Four Horsemen" of pestilence, war, famine, and death, which are commanded by an angel, are trampling the people before them. (Marburg/Art Resource)

"The Hay Wagon" by Hieronymous Bosch (c. 1450–1516), the central panel of a triptych now at the Prado Museum in Madrid, illustrates the Flemish proverb, "The world is a pile of hay and everyone takes from it whatever he can grab." Bosch was a moralist, here attacking greed, but his "Hay Wagon" also echoes the famous words of Isaiah (40:6): "All flesh is grass." The hay wagon, drawn by weird monsters, is headed for hell (the third panel of the triptych) while the members of a wild mob seek to grab their share of the hay, fighting and killing each other in the process. The world's powerful kings and bishops follow the wagon. The other groups illustrate the seven sins. Atop the wagon, amorous couples seem oblivious to their impending destruction. (Alinari/Art Resource)

Part IV
European Christianity Confronts the Modern Age

Carter Lindberg

Chapter 23

The Confessional Era

The Reformations shattered the medieval sense of a unified religious culture, the *Corpus Christianum*, headed by the Roman Church. The story of early modern Christianity is rooted in efforts to put Humpty-Dumpty together again. Aspirations for wholeness and stability stimulated a series of movements: Protestant Orthodoxy, Pietism, Rationalism, and the Enlightenment. These labels do not denote tidy categories or neatly discrete historical movements, but they are useful in getting a handle on the social and cultural history of modern Christianity. Such movements strove to overcome the chaos created by the several reformations by promoting a particular creed over others (Orthodoxy), promoting personal religion over dogma (Pietism), substituting reasonable religion for divisive doctrine (Rationalism), and, finally, by liberating consciences and the state from religion altogether (Enlightenment). In retrospect, it appears that one movement led logically to another, but it is important to note that their borders were permeable, and persons associated with one movement not infrequently shared aspects of another. Influences were not uni-directional, but rather dialogical. To further complicate the picture, these movements cross-fertilized each other. Also, each movement, in its own way, was an effort to contribute to the European-wide struggle for social stability that was achieved only after the last paroxysm of religious conflict ended with the Peace of Westphalia in 1648.

Each of the major Reformation movements—Lutheranism, Calvinism, Catholicism, and Anglicanism—became involved in intramural and extramural theological and political conflicts as it strove to consolidate and institutionalize its understanding of the gospel. These efforts may be described under the general rubric of "confessionalization." A confession is an explicit doctrinal statement or collection of statements that provides internal coherence and external identification of a Christian church. In the early modern period, a church received political legitimacy when the state recognized its confession. Such state churches, initially only Lutheran and Roman Catholic, are unfamiliar phenomena to Americans, who think of churches as private religious associations independent of the state. In the post-Reformation period, however, confessional churches were state establishments whose privileged positions in the society were regarded as the foundation for social integration and political stability.

Confessionalization consolidated and stabilized early modern European culture through dogmatic expressions, administrative arrangements, and the socialization of reliogiocultural life by confessional norms. The confessional era extends through the sixteenth and seventeenth centuries, although the temporal parameters of the period are not precise. Some historians date the beginning of the confessional process to the 1520s, whereas others start with the Religious Peace of Augsburg (1555). The confessional era "closes" in the seventeenth century with the convenient dates of 1648 (the Peace of Westphalia) and 1659 (the Peace of the Pyrenees).

The period is termed "confessional" because the major Reformation churches identified themselves by confessions. Hence, the Lutheran churches collectively subscribed to the Augsburg Confession (1530), supplemented by a number of other doctrinal statements incorporated into the Book of Concord (1580). The Calvinist or Reformed churches identified themselves with the Helvetic or Swiss Confessions (1536, 1566), Calvin's Geneva Catechism (1542), the Zurich Consensus (1549), the Gallican or French Confession (1559), the Scottish Confession (1560), the Belgic Confession (1561), and, especially, the Heidelberg Catechism (1563). After the dogmatic decisions of the Synod of Dort (1618–19), the last two became the generally recognized confessional writings of the Reformed churches. Among English-speaking Calvinists, the Westminster Confession and catechisms (1647–48) became normative. Catholicism held to the decrees of the Council of Trent with the Tridentine Profession of Faith (1564) and the Roman Catechism (1566). The Anglican community did not become as confessionally specific as the other Reformation churches, but rather perpetuated its identity through the Book of Common Prayer (1552, 1662), guided by the Thirty-nine Articles (1563, 1571). The various confessional writings formed the foundations of their respective communities of faith, delimited boundaries between churches, and set standards for preaching and teaching. The confessional churches allied themselves with the European states to promote confessional uniformity in their respective territories.

The word "confession" has headache potential due to its multiple meanings. Confession is an individual or communal *act* in word and deed; it has specific *contents* expressed in particular *historical contexts;* and particular confessional formulations are *authoritative* or *binding* as "confessional stands." Confessions have differing contexts, such as a confession before God (confession of sin and praise), before the congregation (baptismal confession, etc.), and before the world (doctrinal confession). The last of these often has taken the form of authoritative teaching by means of which the church emphasizes what it believes constitutes its identity.

It is important to note that the Reformation churches were not creating a new form of religious literature when they wrote confessions. Rather, they continued a tradition rooted in the Bible. Along with the earliest Christian confession that Jesus is Lord, the Bible refers to Jesus's pointed question to his disciples: "But who do you say that I am?" (Mt. 16:15). And the author of I Peter wrote, "Always be prepared to make a defense to any one who calls you to account for the hope that is in you" (I Peter 3:15). Furthermore, confessions of faith and their creedal developments are not timeless abstractions or antiquarian curiosities, but rather testimonies made, so to speak, in the dock, where the accused testifies during his trial (Mark 13:11). The Reformers, then, continued what they perceived to be the biblical mandate to defend their grasp of the gospel before hostile authorities and alternative readings of the Bible. The development of confessions did not cease in the sixteenth century. As we shall see, modern challenges—for example, totalitarianism—also stimulated confessions, such as the Barmen Confession against Hitler and National Socialism.

Confessions have the character of norms, delimiting the church and attempting to distinguish truth from error, church from counterchurch. Again, this is not just a Reformation development, but is already present in Peter's confession (Mk. 8:27–30), in the primitive confession of the incarnation (I John 4:2ff.), and in the delimitation of the community from the synagogue (John 9:22; 12:42; 16:2) and from rival religions (I Cor. 8:4ff.). Thus, the concept of confession brings in its train the concept of heresy: A confessing church opposes false teaching. As communal statements of a church's identity, confessions are fundamental political documents. For example, the Augsburg Confession, although constructed by theologians, was signed by princes, dukes, mayors, and members of city councils.

Confessionalization and Secularization

Post-Reformation confessionalization was intimately related to the process of the creation of the early modern state and, ironically, was an impetus to the secularization of the state and culture. How could this be? On the surface, it seems paradoxical that movements to intensify Christian identity could lead to just the opposite. To be sure, the modern secularized world arose from a complex of many factors, but a dominant element at the outset was the confessional church. The Reformations may have fragmented Christendom, but religion continued to be understood as the "glue" of society. It was thought that a society without a common, uniform religious basis would not be able to impose law and order or establish social harmony.

Although the confessional churches conflicted with each other, they functioned similarly in their contribution to modernization and state building as Europe shifted from a traditional and feudal social system to a modern society based on citizenship and a market economy. Churches played a significant role in the development of a unified, disciplined society of subjects. Regardless of their differences—or, more precisely, because of them—all the confessional churches entered alliances with temporal rulers in order to preserve their confessional hegemony and, if possible, extend it to other territories. A confessional church's expansion, if not its very existence, depended upon the ruler who defended it. The centrifugal forces generated by the Reformations and their accompanying violence heightened widespread desire for law and order. The antidote to the plague of religious wars was control. The French essayist Michel Montaigne (1533–1592) reflected his age when he wrote, "The worst thing I find in our state is instability."[1]

---

[1] Theodore K. Rabb, *The Struggle for Stability in Early Modern Europe* (New York: Oxford University Press, 1975), p. 54.

The development of the absolute state was not confession-specific, but was supported in its varying contexts by the confessional church of the area. Austrian Hapsburg imperialism was supported by Counter-Reformation Catholicism; the Brandenburg-Prussian state of the Hohenzollerns received its rationale from a Calvinist state religion; and the German territories were frequently buttressed by the Lutheran establishment. All the confessional churches played a fundamental role in early modern European state building.

In this process, the clergy began to acquire quasi-official status in the state. The clergy became the ecclesiastical counterpart to the developing bureaucracy of civil servants. The Reformers' rejection of clerical claims to sacral power and special status in society meant that, within Protestantism, the clergy were citizens and subjects just like their parishioners. The major Reformers themselves came from university settings, and it was not long before they and their followers began the process of professionalizing the clergy. The emphasis on preaching a biblical message required preparation in the biblical languages, which in turn presupposed formal training, professional norms, and qualifying examinations. Such professionalization also contributed to the embourgeoisement of the clergy as they shared professional training and status with lawyers, physicians, and state officials. The process of education in state-supported universities, examinations, and ordination in the state churches contributed to the clergy's acquisition of a quasi-official status as civil servant. The pastor often represented the state in his parish and, conversely, the parish to the state. The clergy, for example, provided quite practical information to the government through their maintenance of baptismal, marriage, and death records, a practice that began at the time of confessionalization. Such records assisted state planning and the inculcation of citizenship.

The tentative moves toward rationalizing and secularizing society that began to surface in the late Middle Ages were strengthened and promoted by confessionalization. The state increasingly extended its jurisdiction over areas that heretofore had been the domain of the church: marriage and the family, education, relief for the poor, and social welfare. The enactment and implementation of the innumerable church constitutions and laws necessary for overseeing these areas of the common good expanded and strengthened the jurisdiction of the state. Although this process was initially beneficial to the church, the increasing competence of the state eventually encroached upon the churches' domains. Thus, confessionalization contributed to the ideological foundation for state authority, bolstered the state's personal and economic resources, functioned as a means of integrating and stabilizing the society, and reinforced the early modern development of a system of European states.

Confessionalization and Social Discipline

Confessionalization accelerated the implementation of the rulers' definitions of the common good by legitimizing their oversight and control of the spiritual and moral lives of their subjects. Although less effective in rural areas than among urban elites and citizens, confessionalization helped reshape the public and private lives of society as a whole. Individuals and social groups, including the clergy, gradually conformed toward a relatively unified society of subjects. The churches played a significant role in advancing social discipline, for they had a legitimacy that the early modern state was still in the process of acquiring in relation to moral, political, and legal norms. Sermons, pastoral care and visitations, religious education through instruction and catechisms, religious services, and the inculcation of discipline promoted the Reformations' sense of vocation in domestic and public affairs. The values of good behavior, honesty, learning, self-discipline, work, and obedience were thereby internalized and provided a significant foundation for the social and economic transition to the modern European bourgeois society of the industrial age.

One aspect of a disciplined lifestyle that concerned all the confessions was pre- and extramarital sexual relations. Both the churches and the states wanted to strengthen marriage and the family. Moralization in the realm of marriage and the family benefited the "housefather," the *paterfamilias*. Both church and state strengthened parents' veto rights over their childrens' marital choices. Patriarchalism as the principle foundation for the family, and therefore for social order and economic stability, was strengthened. The patriarchal image of God reinforced authority, from the literal father in the local household to the metaphorical fathers of the schoolmasters, pastors, officials, magistrates, and ruler. The strengthening of partriarchalism, of course, was not a totally new phenomenon, nor were marriage and the family reduced to loveless rational–economic relationships.

The success of the confessionalization process in terms of social discipline was not due to coercion alone, but was aided by persuasion through preaching, teaching, literature, and art. The theoreticians for these endeavors were the theologians.

Orthodoxy and Neo-Scholasticism in the Confessional Era

Following the deaths of the major Reformers, and through the succeeding theological controversies over the correct interpretations of Luther, Calvin, and the Bible, there arose what is known as Protestant Orthodoxy or Scholasticism. Protestant Orthodoxy sought to think through the contributions of the Reformers and to defend those contributions by "right teaching." Ironically, the very effort to preserve the insights of the Reformers led to obscuring them; the emphasis on pure doctrine clogged the arteries of the living, dynamic faith of the Reformers. The "edifice complex" of every confessional church to construct a theological structure impregnable to alternative theological positions transmuted the initial orientation to reform the one, holy, catholic church.

Lutheran confessional theology exemplifies these developments. Theological controversies centered on the correct interpretation of Luther, extolled as the teacher of pure doctrine. Disputes between those who claimed to speak for Luther and those who followed Melanchthon precipitated a number of bitter quarrels. This *rabies theologorum*, as Melanchthon called it, was not resolved until the Formula of Concord (1577) and the comprehensive Book of Concord (1580), which then became the standard for Lutheran doctrinal teaching. From that basis, German Lutheran theologians developed ever more complex and systematic elaborations of Reformation doctrine, exemplified by Johann Gerhard's (1582–1637) *Theological Commonplaces* (nine large volumes, 1610–1622). Gerhard, the most famous of the Lutheran Orthodox theologians, coined the term "patrology" (meaning "in keeping with the doctrine of the early church fathers") as he intensively studied the early church to prove that Catholicism had strayed, but that Lutherans remained in continuity with it. His prodigious literary output included polemical attacks on Catholicism, numerous commentaries on scripture, and works on theological method, preaching, and edification.

The label of "Protestant Orthodoxy" or "Protestant Scholasticism" reflects both the theological form and method of this period, as well as its university context. The doctrinal implications of the Reformation were carefully worked out in highly rationalistic *Summas*, which reintroduced Aristotelian concepts and methods of argumentation frequently cast in polemical mold against Roman Catholic, Reformed, and even other Lutheran teachings. Unlike Luther, who not infrequently expressed his theology in German addressed "to the laity," theology became the preserve of the educated elite and was written in Latin. Much has been made—perhaps too much in light of the era's powerful musical expressions of faith by Bach—of the intellectualistic formalism and religious aridity associated with the scholastic method.

In a kind of perverse ecumenism, all the confessional churches agreed on two items: the priority of pure doctrine and a rationalistic, propositional method for achieving it. The propositional method meant that theological agreement between the confessions was impossible unless one side capitulated to the other. Whether one began with the Lutheran *Formula of Concord*, the Reformed Synod of Dort, or the Catholic Council of Trent, the resulting theological systems were mutually exclusive. Each party presupposed its possession of the unity and fullness of Christian truth and claimed that others lacked it. Each party expended rigorous efforts to construct a theological system impervious to the critiques and attacks of others. That the construction of these closed systems was no mere intellectual exercise may be inferred from the words of one of the participants, Abraham Calov (1612–1686). Calov, who produced a twelve-volume *System of Theological Themes*, expressed his zeal for orthodoxy by his morning and evening petition: "Fill me, O Lord, with hatred of heretics." Philosophical and logical distinctions entered academic and polemical theology. Where Luther spoke of faith as trust and confidence in God, the Lutheran Scholastics introduced a subject–object antithesis that distinguished what is believed (*fides quae creditur*) from faith itself (*fides qua creditur*) and stressed the objectivity of faith. Intellectual distinctions hedged out existential faith, which was presented increasingly in terms of logical assent to correct doctrine. This in turn necessitated surety of doctrine, the content of faith.

The Council of Trent had declared that scripture and oral tradition were to be regarded with "identical pious reverence and devotion." Of course, the Bible contains divine revelation as mediated by the apostles, but not in its completeness. The full truth and unity of God's revelation requires both scripture and the oral tradition passed on through the Apostles and safeguarded by the church's teaching authority, the Magisterium. In response, Protestants strove to guarantee the sole authority of scripture. In opposition to the Counter-Reformation elevation of the church over scripture, Protestants emphasized the complete material sufficiency of scripture to the point of identifying the written words with the Word of God. Hence, the Bible was increasingly viewed as a sourcebook for doctrine, all verses of which were of equal authority. Statements from scripture were described as *oracula Dei*, and the biblical authors were referred to as the "organs of the Spirit," "hands of Christ," and "amanuenses of God." The Anglican William Chillingworth (1602–1644) summed up the Protestant position: "The Bible only is the religion of Protestants." For Orthodoxy, the Bible became the "paper pope," the fundamental and infallible presupposition of all theology. In a formal, structural sense, the Protestant Orthodox and Catholic Neo-Scholastic were similar: Where the latter attached *ex opera operato* theory to the sacraments, the former attached it to the Bible.

It was, therefore, crucial that scripture be reliable. The doctrine of verbal inspiration, developed to guarantee the authority of scripture, asserted the divine inspiration of every word in the Bible. The doctrine of plenary inspiration asserted that everything in scripture was divinely revealed to the authors. The function of the exegete is to harmonize—violently if necessary—the scripture texts. Although there are apparent similarities to later American fundamentalism, Protestant Orthodoxy was not a kind of countercultural lay biblicism, but an intensive and comprehensive effort to construct a dialogue between centuries of Christian tradition and biblical interpretation.

In their polemic against the Council of Trent's authorization of the Vulgate Bible, Protestants maintained that verbal inspiration in the strict sense applied only to the original Hebrew and Greek texts. Linguistic and grammatical errors were regarded as incompatible with divine authorship. Stylistic differences among texts were explained as God's accommodation to the different writers. The doctrine of inspiration guaranteed inerrancy, authority, clarity, and efficacy of scripture in relation not only to Christian doctrine, but also to everything else in the Bible as well, including history, chronology, genealogy, and science. Biblical textual proof for inspiration included II Tim. 3:16 ("All scripture is inspired by God") and II Peter 1:21 ("No prophecy ever came by, the impulse of man, but men moved by the Holy Spirit spoke from God").

Scripture, then, is the "formal principle" for Protestant Orthodoxy. For Lutheran Orthodoxy, the "material principle" is the doctrine of justification by faith. Reformed Orthodoxy shared the Lutheran commitment to the formal principle of the authority of scripture, but was less clearly defined in terms of a material principle due to its various national confessions. Many of the confessional conflicts and theological systems in the Reformed churches related to challenges to, and expositions of its predestinarian system. A prime example is the Arminian controversy.

Arminianism

The question of predestination arises in any religion that emphasizes the priority of God in salvation. Historically, predestination becomes problematic and produces anxiety whenever it shifts from the context of pastoral care—that is, from assurance of salvation—to inquiries about divine intention. Among Catholics, the issue arose with the Jesuit Luis de Molina's *The Harmony of the Free Will with the Gift of Grace, Divine Foreknowledge, Providence, Predestination, and Reprobation* (1588). Since Molina expressly criticized Thomistic theology on this subject, the battle lines were drawn between the Dominicans and the Jesuits. The dispute dragged on through papal commissions and the Inquisition. No decision was reached other than the papal declaration that the Dominicans were not Calvinists and the Jesuits were not Pelagians. In 1611, the Inquisition decreed that future writings on grace required approbation prior to publication.

In the seventeenth-century polemical context, Reformed Orthodoxy thought it crucial to safeguard the sovereignty of God in the work of salvation from any and all challenges. If God chooses people regardless of their qualities—if God alone saves the sinner—then what role does the person play in this process?

Jacob Arminius (1560–1609), a Reformed pastor and professor at Leiden, came to question the strict Calvinist position on predestination. His effort to find a way between fatalism and Pelagianism[2] soon led to conflict with his colleague Francis Gomarus (1563–1641), a rigid Calvinist. The conflict between these two theologians led to a schism in the church of Holland.

Arminius taught that predestination is the decree of the gracious will of God in Christ through which He determined in eternity to give faith to the faithful, justifying and receiving them with the gift of eternal life. In further maintaining that Christ died for all humankind, not just the elect, and that grace is not irresistible, Arminius and his followers toned down—indeed, challenged—the Reformed doctrine of double predestination. Calvin himself had written: "We call predestination God's eternal decree, by which he himself determined what would become of each person. For all are not created equal; rather, eternal life is foreordained for some, eternal damnation for others. Therefore, as anyone has been created to one or another of these ends, we speak of that person as predestined to life or death" (*Institutes* III, 21, 5). Although Calvin regarded predestination as an inscrutable mystery best left to God, Reformed Orthodoxy did not share his modesty. Gomarus did not shrink from advancing the logical necessity of a supralapsarian position that God already had decreed double predestination before the creation. Supralapsarianism (technically, "before the fall") is the more rigorously logical Calvinist position that maintains that God decided who would be saved and who would be damned not only prior to creation, but also without consideration of humankind's fall into sin. Infralapsarianism (technically, "after the fall") is a milder perception of predestination that views God's decision in terms of his compassionate consideration of the fall.

The dispute between Arminius and Gomarus first split the student body and then spread to the pulpit and split congregations. The authorities of the new Republic of the Netherlands could not allow this controversy and its social divisions to continue.

After Arminius's death, his followers met at Gouda in 1610 and formulated his teachings in five articles, *Articuli Arminii sive Remonstrantiae*, which gave their party the name "Remonstrants." The Remonstrants hardly rejected Calvinist theology: The Articles did not promote universal salvation or require human free will for salvation, but rather affirmed God's intention to offer salvation to all, even though those to whom it is offered may reject it or fall away after initial acceptance. Nevertheless, in the charged confessional atmosphere of the time, it unleashed a firestorm of controversy. Supporters of Arminius's theology were banished from teaching posts. Hugo Grotius (1583–1645), the noted theologian, legal scholar, and pioneer of international law, advocated moderation in a parliamentary process against the Arminians and drafted his *Resolution for Peace in the Church* (1614) and *On the Satisfaction of Christ* (1617). As a reward for his efforts, Grotius was sentenced to lifelong imprisonment in 1618. Scholarship has its advantages, however, and his wife arranged his escape in a box of books. Grotius went on to an international career as theologian and lawyer in exile. He is best remembered for his *Law of War and Peace* (1625), which located the principle of justice not in theology, but in the unalterable "Law of Nature" inherent in the person as a social being, earning Grotius the title of "Father of International Law."

Unswayed by moderates such as Grotius, the Orthodox confronted Arminianism head-on at the Synod of Dort (1618–19). This international Calvinist assembly forcefully

---

[2]See Pelagius, p. 130.

rejected the arguments of the Remonstrants. The Synod is known as the "TULIP" Synod, because this Dutch meeting's articles can be arranged to form that flowery acrostic: *T*otal depravity of humankind; *U*nconditional election; *L*imited atonement; *I*rresistible grace; and *P*erseverance of the saints. The Synod also confirmed the authority of the Belgic Confession and the Heidelberg Catechism, deprived some 200 Arminian pastors of their clerical status, and sentenced Grotius to life in prison and J. van Oldenbarnevelt, leader of the republican party supported by Arminius, to death on a false charge of treason.

After 1632, the Dutch state extended toleration to the Remonstrants, whose influence extended to later English and American church history through the teachings of John Wesley and Methodism, and the struggles of New England Calvinism to construct a path between strict Calvinism and Arminianism. Arminian receptivity to more liberal and rational theology accepted the more radical Socinian and Unitarian currents of the time, influenced the Latitudinarian movement among Anglicans and British dissent, and prepared for Rationalism and the Enlightenment.

Catholic Orthodoxy

The confessional controversies of this era also influenced Roman Catholic dogmatics. Although Catholic theologians had the luxury of watching Protestants engage in seemingly endless battles of self-destruction, they, too, were involved in the veritable deluge of polemical literature between 1590 and 1620. Among the Catholics, of course, the Council of Trent formed the basis for the Neo-Scholastic retrieval of Scholasticism. In this process, Thomistic theology predominated in the spheres of theology and church politics, with the legacy focusing upon Aquinas's system rather than his spirit. Catholic dogmatics continued in this vein up to Vatican II and the encounter of the monolithic orthodoxy of Tridentine Catholicism with the modern world. Tridentine Catholicism strove to reconquer its lost territories and engaged in vigorous polemics against Protestantism, but it also had a pastoral side in striving for internal consolidation and personal renewal.

One of the ablest defenders of the faith was the Jesuit Cardinal Robert Bellarmine (1542–1621). Devoted to scholarship, he sought to overcome Protestantism by reason and argument. His major work, *Disputation on the Controversies of the Christian Faith Against the Heretics of This Time* (three volumes, 1586–93), clearly defended Tridentine Catholicism and continued to be influential among Catholic polemicists up to Vatican I. Indeed, the second volume of this work was a best-seller. The influence of the work is also evident in the some 200 Protestant responses to it in the first century after its publication. Bellarmine's participation in the revision of the Vulgate Bible, moderation in the Galileo affair, and careful limitation of papal authority in the temporal realm contributed to his effectiveness. In 1931, he was declared a Doctor of the Church.

As a member of the Holy Office (the Inquisition), Bellarmine participated in the first phase of the process against Galileo Galilei (1564–1642). Bellarmine's correspondence at the time (1611–1616) attests to his respect and good wishes for Galileo and, at the same time, his open-mindedness toward the scientist's discoveries and the heliocentric theory in general. He declared himself ready, upon provision of more evidence, to revise his interpretation of scripture. Unfortunately, others in the Inquisition did not share this perspec-

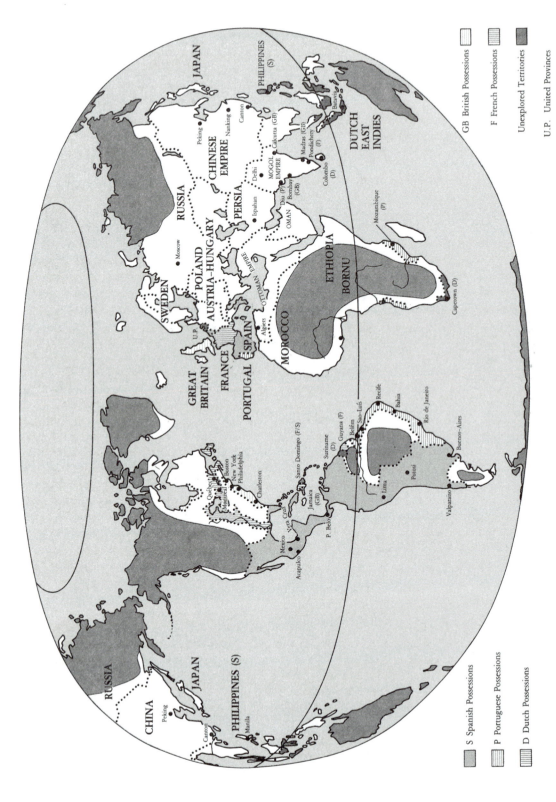

Figure 23.1 Seventeenth-Century Europe

tive, and in 1633 Galileo was condemned to life imprisonment for defending the Copernican system against objections to it from scripture (Josh 10:12f.; Psalm 103:5). Galileo recanted, and his sentence was commuted to detention on his estate. The church did not accept his mathematical–physical concept of the world facilitated by his construction of the telescope.

A major controversy within Catholicism began with the critique of the Jesuit theological hegemony associated with a Dutchman whose admission to the Jesuits was rejected: Cornelius Jansen (1585–1638). A professor of biblical studies at Louvain and then bishop of Ypres (1635), Jansen wrote an extensive study of Augustine, along with numerous commentaries on the Bible, none of which were published until after his death. The publication in 1640 of his *St. Augustine's Teaching on the Sickness, Health, and Cure of Human Nature* created a major controversy. Jansen argued that according to Augustine, sin so disabled human capability to choose the good, that salvation was possible only through the irresistible grace of Christ. Although favorably received by some of the Sorbonne theologians, the papacy responded with increasing negativity, fearing erosion of the authority of the church by this seemingly crypto-Protestant stress upon irresistible grace bestowed upon the elect. The perennial issue of divine sovereignty and human responsibility continued to be a prickly subject for Catholics as well as Calvinists.

By itself, Jansen's work would not seem to warrant its condemnation in 1643 by Pope Urban VIII. However, a school of disciples associated with the abbey of Port-Royal had taken up the Jansenist cause, the most famous of whom was Blaise Pascal (1623–1662). Pascal's *Letters to a Provincial* defended Jansenism and attacked the Jesuits for devious moral guidance and allegedly promulgating human free will to cooperate with divine grace.

The controversies over grace and free will and the Galileo affair concerning natural science and revelation raised fundamental issues for seventeenth-century Christian culture. The two major trials of the period, of Galileo and Arminius, illustrate that at the beginning of the seventeenth century Catholics as well as Protestants found themselves confronted by issues of biblical interpretation. The related questions of the teaching of primitive Christianity and the methods by which the tradition of the church may be known and applied led not to mutual toleration, but to a last effort to hang onto whatever confessional advancements had been achieved. The perils of religious and cultural insecurity were horribly realized in the last and bloodiest of the religious wars—the Thirty Years' War.

The Thirty Years' War

The theological achievements of the confessional era were, on the whole, impressive. Protestants demonstrated that Aristotelian philosophy could be used as much in service of Evangelical as of Catholic theology. The great theological systems of Protestant Scholasticism rivaled and shared the achievements of the great *Summas* of medieval Christianity: the ideal of a complete system, the development of a natural theology, truth expressed in terms of propositions, profound study of the Bible and the traditions and dogma of the early church, and reliance upon objective authority.

The deficits of the confessional era included a loss of the Reformers' preaching vitality and a growth of polemics and pedantry that spread from academic treatises to the pulpit. Sermons increasingly reflected scholastic schemas and stiff formalism and usually lasted no less than an hour. Dogmatic correctness and moral rectitude were the themes. A funeral sermon by Johannes Meinser filled 98 quarto pages—and one can only assume that by the final "amen," the congregation had begun to envy the one they came to bury. The English Puritan divine, John Howe (1630–1705), was known to tax the patience of even his most faithful hearers. One of his women parishioners once remarked that Mr. Howe was indeed a great divine, "but the dear good man spends so much time setting the table that I lose my appetite for the dinner."

Both Protestant and Catholic camps developed clichés for designating and describing adversaries. The Protestant was perceived as a heretic "whose poison is worse than the plague" and whose doctrine of justification by grace alone led to amorality. In southern Germany, Protestants were described as veritable epicureans—hedonistic lovers of carousing, drinking, and sexual pleasure. Hence, a popular proverb extolled the best of both worlds: Live as a Lutheran and die as a Catholic. Protestants directed their attacks at the Catholic Church as an institution—especially the papacy—as the source of abuses, idolatry, and dogmatic error. The papacy was said to have imposed a veritable slavery upon the faithful, and Catholic regions were perceived to be plunged into darkness and their citizens deprived of salvation. Above all, hostility was directed against the Jesuits, the mass, and the papacy.

Needless to say, such polemics did little to abate hostility between polarized confessional states. The dynamism of Calvinism as it expanded into some of the Lutheran territories of the empire and the vigorous reclaiming of territories by the Counter-Reformation progressively paralyzed imperial institutions of justice and even the Imperial Diet. In 1607, Maximillian, the hyper-Catholic Duke of Bavaria, occupied the free city of Donauwörth and expelled all the non-Catholics. In response, the Calvinist states led by the Palatinate formed a military–confessional alliance, the Evangelical Union (1608). In 1609, the Catholic states, including Bavaria, Würzburg, and others, did the same with their Catholic League. Under the direction of Maximillian, the Catholic League included nearly all the Catholic princes of the empire. Immediate war over the succession crisis of Cleves, with its Protestant and Catholic claimants, was avoided, but tensions were heightened in 1617 when the whole Protestant world commemorated the centenary of the Reformation. The jubilee highlighted the solidarity and deep-rootedness of the Lutheran and Reformed churches and reinforced their mutual antagonism toward Catholicism. Protestant sermons and prayers for the occasion stimulated strong reactions from Catholics. There was a veritable outpouring of passions and a climate conducive to civil war in cities of mixed confessional populations.

Tensions exploded in Bohemia in 1618 at the instigation of Ferdinand II of Austria, who embodied an aggressive and absolutist Catholic policy. The Bohemian estates were forced to elect Ferdinand king of Bohemia. He then set about to eradicate Protestantism and refused to consider a petition from a Protestant assembly. The charged climate of religious tension, political suspicion, and economic difficulties released its first thunderclap with the "Defenestration of Prague," a sophisticated description for the tossing of two of the imperial regents out of a high window of the palace in the city (May 23, 1618), and a revolt marked by the downfall of the king and the election of Frederick V, the Elector of the Palatinate and son-in-law of James I, on August 26, 1619, as king of Bohemia.

These events provoked the military intervention of the two confessional leagues and a war that lasted for the next thirty years which, by the 1630s, involved all the major powers of the Continent. Fed by confessional and ideological bitterness and abetted by improved military technology, the war became increasingly ferocious and brutal. Armies lived off the land, were without military discipline, and practiced unparalleled viciousness in destroying everything before them. Soldiers burned peasants alive and practiced obscene tortures upon the populace. Grimmelshausen's *Simplicius Simplicissimus* provides a gruesome contemporary account: "In short, every soldier had his favorite method of making life miserable for peasants, and every peasant had his own misery. . . . I can't say much about the captured wives, hired girls, and daughters because the soldiers didn't let me watch their doings. But I do remember hearing pitiful screams from various dark corners."[3] In Germany, the war was the most terrible catastrophe up to World War II. Between 1618 and 1648, the casualties of the German population are estimated to have been about forty percent. Losses varied, of course, from region to region, and the greatest population losses were due not directly to battles, but to the displacement of refugees, malnourishment, and epidemics caused by the constant movement of troops back and forth across the land. In some areas, whole cities were destroyed, orphans roamed the woods in packs like wild animals, and plundering was so severe that people sustained themselves on grass and at times resorted to cannibalism.

The Thirty Years' War involved political ideology, opportunism, and dynastic struggles as the great powers battled to reconfigure the map of Europe to their advantage. Reasons of state often took precedence over religious commitment, as Catholic powers such as France and even the papacy turned on the Catholic Hapsburgs, and Lutheran states refused to come to the aid of other Lutherans or Calvinists. Nevertheless, it is important to remember that in the seventeenth century intensely political issues were also religious ones: religion and politics were often cut from the same cloth. The mix of religious motives with those of politics and economics was not a contradiction for the people of the time, but a tension-filled polarity to be expressed for the greater glory of God.

The Peace of Westphalia ensured religious diversity by incorporating it into the Empire's constitution. Other than France, where bigotry was officially reinstated by Louis XIV's revocation of the Edict of Nantes (1685), the Peace of Westphalia marked something like a confessional battle fatigue. The Peace was surprisingly successful in dampening the fires of religious fanaticism and preventing widespread European conflagration for the next 150 years, until the release of nationalist fanaticism by the French Revolution. The religious aspects of this development included the rueful awareness that confessional triumphalism was not only theologically unfaithful, but personally and socially dangerous. Voices such as Grotius increasingly urged a nonconfessional, rational approach to social and political issues; even war itself should be put on a rational and legal basis. As we shall see, the next great religious movement, Pietism, stressed personal piety and inwardness over dogmatic correctness and religious compulsion.

---

[3] Rabb, T. K., *The Struggle for Stability*, p. 120.

Chapter 24

From Pietism to the Early Enlightenment

Pietism and the Enlightenment ushered in a new period of Western Christianity. Following the Peace of Westphalia, numerous religious, political, social, and intellectual indicators of a new spirit, which may be characterized by the imprecise concept, "modernity," permeated all areas of life. Politically, this is the period from the Peace of Westphalia (1648) to the end of the old Empire (1806). Within the parameters of theological and philosophical developments, it is the period from Spener's *Pious Desires* (1675) to Kant's *Religion within the Limits of Reason Alone* (1793).

Princely absolutism reached its high point in France under Louis XIV (1643–1715). A new pragmatic–rational political spirit, centered on the courts with their civil servants and standing armies, also influenced the churches and changed the entire social structure. A purposive, rational, world-immanent understanding of politics and the state consciously dispensed with religio-ethical criteria and supplanted confessional oppositions. Thomas Hobbes' (1588–1679) *Leviathan*, Machiavelli's rational goal orientation of the state, and Richelieu's concept of "reason of state" characterized the new spirit. In the face of the devastation wrought by the religious wars in all areas of life, it was necessary to begin rebuilding society, a process in which the church had a major role and from which Pietism and the Enlightenment developed.

Pietism and the Enlightenment may be viewed as siblings, with Pietism as the older sister. Scholars have characterized continental Pietism as the most significant movement of religious renewal in Protestantism since the Reformation. Arising in the seventeenth century and coming into full bloom in the eighteenth, Pietism pressed for the individualization and interiorization of religious life, developed new forms of personal piety and social life, led to far-reaching reforms in theology and the church, and left profound impressions in social and cultural life. Pietism was a transnational and trans-confessional movement.

Both Pietism and the Enlightenment arose out of the historical–religious conditions of the seventeenth century. With its stress on individualization and spiritualization, Pietism strove to overcome the spirit of the confessional era, which it saw to be creed bound, scholastic, hierarchical, spiritually sterile, and ethically lax. Pietism promoted an experiential-expressive theology against the cognitive propositionalism of orthodoxy's Aristotelian Neo-Scholasticism and advocated personal regeneration, rebirth, and sanctification against preoccupation with correct dogma and confessional controversies. Christian Hoburg (1606–1675) succinctly summed this up: "Justification is fiction, rebirth is fact." Pietists never tired of emphasizing personal sin, conversion by the Holy Spirit, and the manifestation of conversion in a holy life. At times, the stress on holy living reached the level of calls for perfection: Unless the individual's inner relationship with God issues in holiness of life (sanctification), faith is hollow and mere show. With a sloganeering skill equal to that of the best of contemporary bumper stickers, Pietists emphasized that Christian life is "a walk, not a talk," "a becoming, not being," "heart religion vs. head religion," "life over doctrine," "reality vs. the appearance of godliness," and the internalization of the faith in contrast to its externalization in font, pulpit, confessional, and altar ("the four dumb idols of the church"). Faithful living of the Christian life (*praxis pietatis*) is more important than its correct dogmatic conception. Pietists understood their movement as the continuation of the Reformation or as the "second Reformation." The Reformers made the important first step of reforming doctrine, but they did not reach the crucial second step of reforming life.

Pietism's affinity with the Enlightenment may be highlighted by sketching some of its characteristics. The ideal of Christian perfection manifest in ethical as well as spiritual renewal focused on the individual. The understanding of the church therefore shifted from the Reformers' emphasis on the "objective" Word and sacraments to the "subjective" character of the congregation. The view of the church as an association of the regenerate stimulated the tendency to separatism and the formation of conventicles known as the *ecclesiola in ecclesia* (the little church in the church). Pietist suspicion of the state church led eventually to the radical idea of the constitutional separation of church and state. The stress on moral renewal certainly stimulated a variety of efforts to renew society, but these were posited on the principle that the transformation of the world depended on the transformation of the individual. Hence, social reform rarely moved beyond private charity and free associations.

Pietism's relationship to the Enlightenment may also be seen in its incipient rationalism. In response to what it perceived to be the externalism of orthodoxy, Pietism emphasized the reception of the Holy Spirit and religious experience. But after the initial enthusiasm, how does one distinguish the Holy Spirit from other "spirits"? One answer, already proposed by Spener, the father of Pietism, is reason.

Pietism, then, is the other side of the coin of Rationalism and the Enlightenment. This also may be seen in the Pietist's abiding concern for education and the fact that the major figures of the eighteenth- and nineteenth-century Enlightenment came out of Pietism: Lessing, Kant, Schiller, Goethe, Fichte, and, of course, the "Father of Protestant Liberalism," Schleiermacher, who founded his theology on the *"feeling* of absolute dependence." Therefore, Pietism was both an effort to protect the Christian faith from the corrosives of modernity and a stimulus to that very modernity.

Because of its emphasis upon the renewed life, Pietism is often described in terms of the biographies of its leading figures such as Spener, Francke, and Zinzendorf.

Philipp Jakob Spener (1635–1705)

Spener, the "Patriarch of Pietism," was profoundly influenced by the devotional writings of the prior generation—in particular, Johann Arndt (1555–1621). Arndt, himself influenced by medieval mysticism, provided the formative classics for Pietism: *Four Books on True Christianity* (1605) and *The Little Garden of Paradise* (1610). In these and other writings, Arndt emphasized conversion, oneness with Christ, and a holy life centered on dying to the world and the self and living for God on the highest ethical plane. Although the orthodox suspected that Arndt's introspective piety would undermine Reformation doctrine, his writings were incredibly popular. By the time Spener reissued *True Christianity* in 1675, there had already been more than fifty printings in more than a dozen places, with translations into nearly every European language, including Finnish, Icelandic, Hungarian, and Slovakian. There was even a Yiddish summary.

As a youth, Spener discovered in the family library his father's well-worn copy of *True Christianity*, along with Puritan literature such as Lewis Bayly's (d. 1631) *The Practice of Piety*. In his theological studies at Strasbourg, Spener was introduced to Luther's writings. He then went to Basel, where he studied Hebrew, and then to Geneva, where he learned French and absorbed the experiential piety of the great preacher Jean de Labadie (1610–1674), the founder of a separatist Pietism in the Reformed church of the Netherlands. At Tübingen, Spener read and discussed another pietist classic, Theophil Grossgebauer's *Voice of a Watchman from Desolated Zion* (1661). Grossgebauer lamented what he perceived to be the profound decline of contemporary Christianity due to preaching that failed to promote penance and rebirth. He challenged the orthodox understanding of infant baptism and called for a datable—day and hour!—conversion experience. Returning to Strasbourg, Spener received his doctorate in 1663. In 1666, he became the senior pastor at Frankfurt-am-Main. There he made an immediate impact through his emphasis upon pastoral care and catechetical instruction, as well as preaching. In 1670 there arose the Frankfurt *collegium pietatis*, Pietist meetings that discussed the Sunday sermon, edifying literature, and ways to renew the church. The *collegium pietatis* was influenced by Labadie's idea of the *ecclesiola extra ecclesiam* (the little church outside the church). After 1675, some of this group wandered off into separatism.

Pietism's programmatic writing is Spener's *Pious Desires or the Heartfelt Yearning for God-pleasing Improvement of the True Evangelical Church* (1675), written as the foreword to a new edition of Arndt's devotions on the Gospels. Spener soon recognized the importance of his little book and translated it into Latin for international use.

The *Pious Desires* diagnosed the corrupted condition of the church, prophesied a better future for the church based on the expected conversion of the Jews and the fall of papal Rome, and presented a six-point program for reform of the church. The reform proposals included (1) increased study and discussion of the whole Bible in associations alongside of worship; (2) the realization of the priesthood of all believers through Bible study, teaching, reproving, consoling, and holy living; (3) exhortation of the clergy and the laity to move from mere knowledge of doctrine to the praxis of faith; (4) the reduction of theological controversy and confessional polemic, and the establishment of true doctrine by repentance and a holy life; (5) the reform of pastoral education as the means for renewing the church; and (6) a focusing of preaching on edification, thereby serving the demands of faith and its fruits. Spener's reform proposals exhibit both traditional and new viewpoints. What is new in relation to orthodoxy is the hope of a better time for the church on earth (a moderate chiliasm) and the reestablishment of the apostolic church according to I Cor. 14. After 1676, Spener summarized his church reform program in the formula *ecclesiola in ecclesia*. He hoped for the improvement of the church from the example and demand of pious groups.

Spener wrote in the aftermath of the Thirty Years' War. He believed that opposition between the world and salvation was so profound that it could be overcome only by rebirth, a *sui generis* event of renewal from God. Emphasis upon personal renewal through rebirth affected all aspects of Pietist theology and was the point of departure for perfectionism. The sense that only the pastor who is a true Christian can lead others to the Lord echoed donatism. However, elevation of the reborn life over doctrine promoted a certain ecumenical openness: Church unity no longer depended on doctrinal agreement, but upon a Christian lifestyle that transcended confessional lines. Later ecumenism expressed this by the slogan "Creeds divide, but deeds unite." The Pietist reading of the Bible as a record of the historical life of the early church, rather than as the source for doctrine, prompted strong historical and biographical interests. The Pietist interest in conversion and the inner life foreshadowed psycho-history. All these aspects of the Pietist theology of rebirth and renewal find echoes in the early Enlightenment emphases on ethics, the individual over the community, the shift from theology to anthropology, and history and nature as the locus for revelation.

Spener's program aroused heated opposition from the orthodox and sufficient suspicion from the authorities, that he was watched for a time by the police. He moved to Dresden as court preacher in 1686, but offended the Prince there by reproving his drunkenness. Spener's happiest and most successful years were spent as pastor in Berlin (1696–1705).

August Hermann Francke (1663–1727) and Halle Pietism

Arndt's *True Christianity* and books of English Puritan edification also influenced Francke. In his youth he excelled in languages, and in 1684 he went to Leipzig to teach Hebrew. His interest in biblical languages drew him into association with some young theologians, the *collegium philobiblicum*. His personal acquaintance with Spener occurred in the context of Spener's response to the group's inquiry about Bible study. Soon afterward, Francke had an unexpected experience that changed his life. Requested to preach on John 20:31, he attempted to distinguish between true living faith and an imagined faith built on authority and custom. His study drove him to examine his own spiritual condition, the truth of God, and the reliability of the Bible and precipitated a profound spiritual crisis. After days of anxiety, he fell to his knees, imploring God for deliverance. He recounted that all his doubt was suddenly swept away and that he experienced a rebirth of unshakable certainty.

Francke's conversion experience became prototypical for the Pietists. The Lutheran tradition had understood doubt and uncertainty as inherent in faith, as signs of divine testing. Francke now viewed doubt as a sign of unbelief. A datable conversion preceded by "penitential struggle" became signs of Halle Pietism.

In 1692, Francke became pastor in a suburban Halle church and then professor of Oriental languages and theology at Halle University. Through his work at Halle, Francke, more than Spener, gave Pietism its profile. Under his leadership, the "Francke Institutions"—a school for the poor, an orphanage, a teacher training school, a high school, a publishing house, a hospital and pharmacy, and a Bible Institute—became world famous and characterized Halle as a center for education, charity, and mission. These institutions gave concrete expression to the essential Pietist goal: transformation of the world through the transformation of persons.

In Halle, Francke also realized the reform of theological studies demanded by Spener: orientation to the *praxis pietatis*, concentration on biblical and practical theology, and the connection of study with praxis through the pedagogical insertion of theology students into the Halle institutions (an early form of modern Clinical Pastoral Education). The term "seminary" (from *seminarium*, a hothouse for young plants) came into use for the training of pastors; the church was to be the nursery and garden for the new God-obedient humanity.

The Halle Institutions flourished with the support of King Friedrich Wilhelm I of Brandenburg. Indeed, the disciplined educational program at Halle for the youth of the nobility is what gave the term "Prussianism" its connotation of discipline. Francke founded the first German Bible Institute (1710) with Carl Hildebrand von Canstein (1667–1719). By reducing the cost of printing Bibles, the two reformers effectively supported the Pietist Bible movement, which for the first time introduced Bibles into the homes of the general populace. Some two million Bibles were printed in, and distributed from, Halle in the eighteenth century.

Francke's reform impulses extended to Silesia, East Prussia, the Baltics, Scandinavia, England, America, southeast European countries, and Russia. Close cooperation with the Society for Promoting Christian Knowledge (founded in England in 1699) brought English students to Halle and Halle literature to England. Francke himself corresponded with the Puritan Cotton Mather in Boston, as well as with other church leaders in Pennsylvania and Virginia. The establishment of foreign missions spread Halle Pietism throughout the world. Bartholomäus Ziegenbalg (1682–1719) and Heinrich Plützschau (1677–1746) went to South India, and by the end of the eighteenth century eighty mission workers had been sent from Halle to India along with a printing press. The patriarch of American Lutheranism, Henry Melchior Muhlenburg (1711–1787), was Francke's missionary to Pennsylvania.

Francke's contribution to modern Protestantism may be viewed in the framework of his displacement of confessional dogmatics by Christian praxis. He placed the Bible in the center of experiential religion as the book of life, and his emphasis on the struggle of repentance and a one-time, nameable conversion reflected the modern interest in experience rather than traditional authority. The validity of Christian statements about God, humankind, and the world now rested on religious experience rather than the external authority of dogma. The anthropological–psychological point of view, also taken up by the Enlightenment, stimulated an interest in biographical writing (the whys and wherefores of conversion) and influenced the development of the psychological novel.

Zinzendorf and the Moravian Community

The most significant Pietist community that has continued up to now is the Moravians, a pre-Reformation Bohemian–Moravian Unity of the Brethren community revitalized by Nicholas Ludwig Graf von Zinzendorf (1700–1760).

The son of a minister, Zinzendorf grew up in the spirit of Arndt and Spener, but also under the influence of mystical spiritualism. From 1710 to 1716, he attended Francke's school in Halle and was permanently influenced by the missionary endeavors of Halle Pietism. He also studied law at the University of Wittenberg and travelled through western Europe, encountering the spirit of the early enlightenment, Calvinism, and Jansenism. Through these travels, Zinzendorf became acquainted with rationalism and concluded that the natural disposition of human reason was toward atheism. Thus, for him, all attempts to found the certainty of religion on proofs of God or a "natural theology" were false paths. Religion and rational thought are on different levels. In a kind of pox on both houses (Rationalism and Lutheran Orthodoxy), Zinzendorf stated, "Whoever has God in his head is an atheist." The Christian faith is a religion of the heart, and it rests not on reason, but on a personal relationship with the Savior: "Without Jesus, I would be an atheist."

In 1721, Zinzendorf entered the service of the Saxon government. Among his responsibilities was care for evangelical religious refugees from Hapsburg areas. On Sundays Zinzendorf held religious discussions in his home, gathering a community of Pietists and Separatists. In 1722, Zinzendorf permitted Moravian refugees to settle on his estate in Oberlausitz. The little group grew within five years to about 300. Called Herrnhut (the Lord's Shelter), the community included not only descendants of the Bohemian Brethren, but also Schwenkfelders from Silesia and Pietists, Separatists, Lutherans, and Reformed Protestants from various German areas. After difficult inner conflicts, the community experienced inner rebirth ("a new Pentecost") on August 13, 1727, at a common celebration of the Lord's Supper.

Zinzendorf himself provided a constitution (1727) to regulate Herrnhut as a Christian community. The communal life of brotherly love and Christian freedom was modeled on that of the early biblical community. The old traditions of the Bohemian Brethren continued, but as an *ecclesiola in ecclesia*, not as a sectarian movement. The community subscribed to the Augsburg Confession and participated in the Sunday services of the local Lutheran church. Within Herrnhut itself, there was a pronounced community consciousness based on religious experience. New forms of worship and devotion included the love feast, foot washing, and daily meditation on a word from the Bible or a verse from a hymn.

Herrnhut Pietism expressed itself in missions throughout the world. Their non-confessional style and independence of colonial powers contributed to their effectiveness in the Baltics, Holland, England, Greenland, the West Indies, and North America (missions to the Iroquois, as well as the colonies). By 1760 there were over 200 Brethren missionaries, and Zinzendorf himself established numerous daughter foundations of Herrnhut.

Although Pietism reacted to the perceived formalism and spiritual aridity of Protestant orthodoxy, it also responded to the larger cultural context. The seventeenth century began with the ideal of a uniform state church continuing the old concept of the *corpus Christianum*. But that ideal was not sustainable, if for no other reason than the religious partitions consequent upon the Reformation settlements and wars. States and cultures increasingly emancipated themselves from ecclesiastical control. The state, law, commerce, industry, science, philosophy, literature, and art were less and less aspects of an ecclesiastical civilization and were beginning to look to standards and aims supposedly derived from the nature of human life and society. Baroque music, for example, began shifting from worship settings to concert halls. And, of course, the reverse also occurred, thus raising anxieties about secular incursion into sacred space and time. In short, the pluralism initiated, although not intended, by the Reformation was becoming more and more apparent. There were now alternative modes of living and understanding life. What did this mean for Christians who had to spend a good portion of their lives in the non-churchly aspects of this developing culture? What could that "Christianity" be which was not the standard and the motive for the whole life of the Christian?

Pietism provided a provisional and, it turned out, a less-than-helpful answer: individualization and internalization of the faith. Cultural development and fragmentation could be ignored by seeking religious fellowship with the like-minded, by personal appropriation of religious truth that was no longer accepted as universal, and by subjective religious experience, personal devotion and discipline. The downside of Pietism's response to its contemporary culture involved the segregation of a certain sphere of life as peculiarly religious. The rest of life, by default, could then be seen as secular. Pietists might lament this state of affairs, but adherents of the Enlightenment rejoiced in it and sought to expand it.

Roots and General Characteristics of the Enlightenment

The Enlightenment echoed and sharpened many of Pietism's emphases, such as its orientation toward the future, nondogmatic Christianity, centrality of human experience, and historical reading of the Bible. Numerous factors in the seventeenth century influenced the rise of the Enlightenment. The merchant cities, increasingly wealthy and self-conscious, utilized rational, goal-oriented thinking in relation to economic life. A spirit of discovery grounded in practical experience ruled the natural sciences and technology. With the help of reason, people attempted to research methodically the environment of the world and to make their applications useful. Rational–pragmatic thinking was apparent also in the sociopolitical arena and in legal and constitutional work.

The Enlightenment did not look back to the golden ages of the classical period or early Christianity, but rather foresaw a continually improving future for humanity. An optimistic expectation pervaded culture and the sciences and received succinct expression in Alexander Pope's (1688–1744) dictum, "The proper study of mankind is man." The feeling arose that persons are capable of almost anything. Daniel Defoe's (1660–1731) *Robinson Crusoe* expressed the conviction that even when one is thrown back upon one's own resources, nature and life can be mastered. Hence, it is not surprising that painters and their patrons favored portraits and that landscapes reinforced the human perspective. Lessing's *The Education of the Human Race*, Rousseau's *Émile, or Treatise on Education*, and the internationally renowned Swiss reformer of education, Johann Heinrich Pestalozzi's (1746–1827) *How Gertrude Teaches her Children* expressed the conviction that the means for mastery over nature and human life resided in education. Thus arose teacher training schools. Kant himself defined the Enlightenment as the "emergence from a self-inflicted

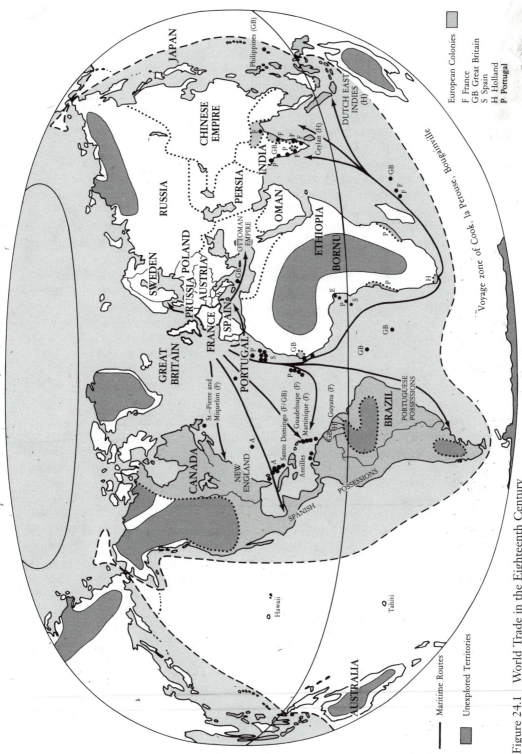

Figure 24.1 World Trade in the Eighteenth Century

Maritime Routes

Unexplored Territories

European Colonies
F France
GB Great Britain
S Spain
H Holland
P Portugal

Voyage zone of Cook, la Perouse, Bougainville

JAPAN

CHINESE EMPIRE

RUSSIA

SWEDEN

POLAND

PRUSSIA

AUSTRIA

FRANCE

GREAT BRITAIN

SPAIN

PORTUGAL

OTTOMAN EMPIRE

PERSIA

INDIA

OMAN

ETHIOPIA

BORNU

DUTCH EAST INDIES (H)

Ceylan (H)

Philippines (GB)

CANADA

NEW ENGLAND

St.-Pierre and Miquelon (F)

Santo Domingo (F/GB)

Guadeloupe (F)

Martinique (F)

Antilles

Guyana (F)

SPANISH POSSESSIONS

BRAZIL

PORTUGUESE POSSESSIONS

AUSTRALIA

Hawaii

Tahiti

state of minority" and challenged his contemporaries to think for themselves—to "have the courage to make use of your own understanding."

The first modern philosophical systems developed in Holland. The presuppositions for intellectual freedom and tolerance evolved there from the struggle for liberation from Spain, late humanism, and the economic and cultural rise of the merchant class. As the "ark of the persecuted" in Europe, Holland provided refuge and stimulation for major contributors to the Enlightenment. The Frenchman René Descartes (1596–1650), educated by the Jesuits, settled in Holland in 1629 due to his inhospitality toward his studies in Paris. He expressed the modern human self-consciousness: The self is anchored in the center of reason and understands the surrounding world as an object at the power of its disposal. Radical doubt is raised to a principle of knowledge and self-knowledge: *Cogito, ergo sum* ("I think, therefore I am"). The existence of God is rationally provable. Philosophy moves from being the "handmaid of theology" (Aquinas) to become a fundamental scientific discipline founded on empirical observations and rational principles.

In England, the "Age of Reason" and Deism had begun to make their mark already in the seventeenth century. Since confessional theology seemed to lead to never-ending conflict, a turn to reason appeared to be the better part of valor. The Rationalist and Deist agenda, emulating that of the natural sciences, sought to secure a firm foundation for the propositions of religion so that any person of sound mind and common sense could accept them. For example, Edward Lord Herbert of Cherbury (1581–1648) reduced Christianity to five points that any reasonable person could discover: (1) There is a God; (2) God is to be served; (3) such service occurs through virtue and piety, not by ritual activity; (4) mistakes are to be regretted and made good; and (5) persons may expect a divine reward here and hereafter. Obviously, any similarity between Cherbury's natural religion and the classic Christian concerns of sin and redemption are purely coincidental. Nevertheless, this characteristic presentation of "natural religion" became a popular and influential model for the whole Enlightenment. In Germany, it was often abbreviated to the three standard contents: God, moral freedom, and immortality.

John Locke (1632–1704), the classic representative of English empirical philosophy, based his understanding of Christianity on tolerance, virtue, and morality. Even theological conservatives appealed to the court of reason. John Wesley himself provides an example of the use of reason to combat rationalism when he argued for the divine authorship of the Bible: Either scripture is written by God, angels, and good men; or it is written by devils. Since devils are condemned in scripture, and "thus says the Lord" would not be said by angels or good men, the scriptures must be written by God. The introduction of rationalism into the pulpit reduced sermons to moral discourses, such as the virtue of early rising as exemplified by Mary and Martha going early to the tomb to look for Jesus.

The concern for a harmonious balance of reason and revelation reflected fatigue from religious controversy. People wanted to reduce Christianity to its essentials and thereby remove causes of conflict. On the one hand, theological reductionism resulted from introspection on the churches' diversity; and on the other hand, it reflected the growing cognizance of the diversity of world religions. The truths of faith can indeed be beyond, but not against reason. However, the English Deists advanced toward an ever-sharper biblical criticism that viewed the Bible more as a source for ancient history and morality than as the record of a revelation transcending reason and nature.

The titles of two important writings summarize this orientation: John Toland's (1670–1722) *Christianity not Mysterious* (1696) and Matthew Tindal's (1655–1733) *Christianity as Old as the Creation, or the Gospel a Republication of the Religion of Nature* (1730). The latter became the "Bible" of Deism and was translated into German. Since Christianity contains nothing mysterious in opposition to human reason, the miracle stories and resurrection reports of the Bible are open to criticism. The mathematician and eminent physicist Isaac Newton (1642–1727), a conforming churchman, denied the doctrine of the Trinity on the bases that it was inaccessible to reason and that its biblical prooftexts were inauthentic. The Toleration Act (1689) of William and Mary, although excluding Roman Catholics and Unitarians, did allow Deist thought to come out of the closet.

The most devastating criticism not only of religion, but also of the confidence in reason, came from David Hume (1711–1776). Hume was a great historian and literary figure, as well as a philosopher. The clergy of Scotland hated what he stood for, yet some of his best friends were clergymen. His opponents said that his philosophy could be summarized in the epigram "Take the 'not' out of the Decalogue and put it in the Creed." Yet his character was so good and his person so amiable, that he was honored and loved. Boswell was amazed that so godless a man could live so well and die so fearlessly.

Hume's writings on religion devastated Deist arguments for the reasonableness of Christianity: miracles, the order and harmony of nature, and the common consent of humankind. The first two, Hume said, contradict each other, and there is no historical evidence for the last. "It is," he wrote, "contrary to experience that a miracle should be true, but not contrary to experience that testimony should be false." Hume was an empiricist in believing that knowledge comes from sense experience and can be shown to be correct only when tested against further experience. In logic and mathematics, *a priori* reasoning is valid because it is limited to the relations of ideas. But questions about empirical reality must be dealt with by *a posteriori* knowledge, that is, on the basis of experience. From Hume's perspective, the alleged truths of metaphysics and theology are neither logically necessary, nor derived from experience, nor testable in experience. With regard to the Deist appeal to the *consensus gentium*, the common consent of humankind, Hume responded that the earliest forms of religion were not archetypes of English civilization, but gross anthropomorphic polytheisms. Primitive gods were mysterious, tricky beings who even fell notably short of the moral conduct of their followers.

Hume's final critique of religion was an ethical one. Religion directs human attention away from life, he said, and preoccupation with salvation is apt to make persons narrow and bigoted. He suggested that the wise person avoid the disputes of the theologians, provided that he can make himself immune to their rancor and persecution. Hume attempted to provide such immunity for himself by stating that those who defend Christianity by principles of reason are its "dangerous friends or disguised enemies," for "our most holy religion is founded on faith, not on reason." An echo of the Reformation? No, for in the climate of Deism, to say that Christianity was founded on faith was tantamount to saying it was founded on nothing at all. But with his assertion, the canny Scot exculpated himself from the charge of irreligion, while delivering a stunning attack at the same time.

In France, the close connection of the church with the Ancien Régime made it the main enemy of the French proponents of the Enlightenment. The main representative of the French Enlightenment, François-Marie Voltaire (1694–1778), had a great effect on the

French bourgeoisie as a pioneer of intellectual freedom, tolerance, and human rights. As a follower of English Deists, he used their concepts to fight against the Catholic Church (*"Écrasez l'infâme!"*—"crush the disgrace!"). Voltaire's sharp wit, expressed in essays and plays such as *La Pucelle* (a blasphemous account of Joan of Arc) and *Candide* (a rejection of theodicy), made him a controversial figure. From 1750 to 1752 he lived at the court of Frederick II of Prussia, and in his later years he resided as a country gentleman at his estate on the Swiss frontier.

Voltaire generally rejected philosophical theories of God, but he thought God remained an important presupposition for moral order and the prevention of anarchy. It is in this sense that his famous comment should be read: "If God did not exist, it would be necessary to invent him." Voltaire directed this against the conclusion of the younger generation that God is a meaningless concept and that faith in God only disturbs human life.

Fascination with the development of the natural sciences found expression in the thirty-five volume *Encyclopedia* (1751–1777) edited by Denis Diderot (1713–1784) and Jean d'Alembert (c. 1717–1783). The *Encyclopedia*, with contributors such as Rousseau, Voltaire, Holbach, and Montesquieu, was a monumental digest of eighteenth-century rationalism and mediated Enlightenment ideas about the arts, nature, and science to the French bourgeoisie. Central among these ideas was the concept formulated by the English philosopher Francis Bacon (1561–1626) that human rule over nature would advance history on the path of freedom and human happiness. Among the Encyclopedists, Marie-Jean Condorcet (1743–1794) projected unlimited human progress in his *Historical Tableau of the Progress of the Human Spirit*. He based his optimism on the advance of the natural sciences and the increasing control of nature. The future will bring, he said, the elimination of inequality between nations, the equality of peoples, and the ultimate perfectibility of humankind.

Jean Jacques Rousseau (1712–1778) desired to reach the Enlightenment goals by other means. The source for the well-being of humankind lies not in reason, but rather in the powers of feeling of the "natural man" (*ergo* Rousseau's alleged motto: "Back to nature!"). The person is born good, but society, culture, the state, and religion pervert humankind's naturally good faculties. Rousseau had a great influence through two 1762 writings: *The Social Contract*, which presented an ideal, natural order of the state as a democracy served by civil religion; and *Émile*, which offered the ideal of a rational elementary education according to nature. Thus, Rousseau is regarded as a spiritual father of the French Revolution.

The German Enlightenment

The philosophical and theological Enlightenment in Germany differed from that in Western Europe. The relationship of reason and revelation was determined not by tension-filled oppositions, but through harmonious complementarity. Enlightenment concepts in Germany were not principally different than elsewhere in Europe, but they lacked political explosiveness and critical animosity toward the church. There are general, as well as theological and historical, grounds for this distinction. The Thirty Years' War hindered German development in comparison to the rest of Europe: Confessional and political–cultural splintering tended to focus the German Enlightenment in Protestant areas, princely courts, and the universities. The main representatives of the German Enlightenment therefore were university professors and the ruling circles of enlightened absolutism. Pietism and the Enlightenment appeared in Germany at nearly the same time. Pietism's struggle against Orthodoxy essentially smoothed the way for the Enlightenment's practical goals of reform. The theological Enlightenment in Germany was less a theoretical process than a practical reform movement similar to Pietism.

Gottfried Wilhelm Leibniz (1646–1716) treated the compatibility of faith and reason, reason and revelation, philosophy and theology, and body and soul by emphasizing that they must be conceived in harmonious connections. The condition for this harmony is the distinction of necessary, eternal truths from actual truths. To the former belong the laws of geometry, but also the complete wisdom, goodness, and power of God. Here there can be no contradiction between revelation and reason, because reason establishes these truths as conceptually necessary. Although revelation is thereby subordinated to reason and theology to philosophy, a higher order can break through the natural laws.

Leibniz resolved the problem of theodicy—the justification of God in the face of evil in the world—by the thesis that our world is "the best of all possible worlds." Evil is based in the restrictedness of finite being. Reason, however, may recognize the good and the divine as the essential structure of the world. Leibniz's optimistic view of the world conceives of sin only as the imperfect good. The Lisbon earthquake (1755) that destroyed the city and tens of thousands of people also severely shook the confidence that this is the best of all worlds. Voltaire's pessimistic *Candide* (1759) ends with the advice to retire to one's garden and withdraw from the horrors of history.

Enlightenment theologians agreed with the goal of a non-dogmatic, ethical Christianity. Many of these theologians in the preaching ministry worked to present a socio-ethical interpretation of Christianity. They depicted Jesus as the great teacher of wisdom and virtue, the forerunner of the Enlightenment, who broke the bonds of error (not sin!). But the Enlightenment also raised critical issues for the churches. The radical attack on Christianity in Germany came out in the open through Gottfried Ephraim Lessing's (1729–1781) publication of the *Anonymous Fragments*, also known as the *Wolfenbüttel Fragments* after the Wolfenbüttel Library, where they were found. The material came from the Hamburg deist and biblical critic Hermann Samuel Reimarus (1694–1768). Reimarus raised questions of biblical authorship and contradictions within the Gospels and argued for the fraudulent origin of Christianity, which he attributed to the disciples. Jesus failed as a political messiah; therefore, his disciples fabricated his resurrection in order to overcome their alleged disappointment and to be able to find recognition in the world. Lessing mistakenly thought this publication would stimulate a constructive discussion about the essential meaning of Christianity. Instead, the publication unleashed a major pamphlet war that led to personal literary attacks on Lessing. In the course of this controversy, Orthodoxy was made to look ridiculous.

Lessing's own position is summarized in his famous line, "The accidental truths of history can never be the proof for the necessary truths of reason." In other words, historical testimony of revelation cannot provide certainty and assurance. Historical religions are stages for a divine process of education whose goal is the true religion of love and reason (*The Education of the Human Race*, 1780). This is also expressed in the parable of the ring in *Nathan the Wise*. Since the true ring cannot be distinguished from the two perfect imitations, each of the heirs should live as if the father's ring was given to him. The truth of the real religion is manifest in its experience and practice. For Lessing, Reimarus's sharp critique of the historicity of Christian revelation meant the possibility of bringing forth the essential religion of love and reason.

The reduction of Christianity to morality reached its high point in Immanuel Kant (1724–1804). Born of humble means and nurtured in Pietism, he received intellectual as well as spiritual encouragement from his local pastor, who persuaded Kant's parents to send him to a Pietist school at the age of eight. There he encountered the dark side of Pietism, with its zeal and hypocrisy. It has been suggested that this context instilled in him such an abhorrence of religious emotion, that he divorced himself from prayer, hymns, and church services altogether. A famous account relates that later, when he was made rector of the University of Königsberg, he led the customary academic procession to the cathedral for the inauguration of rectors, but deserted the procession at the church. His theological studies were minimal, and he never had much interest in contemporary theological writings. It is said that when at the age of seventy he wrote his main theological work, *Religion within the Limits of Reason Alone*, he turned to an old catechism to refresh his theological memory. He was born and reared in Königsberg, East Prussia, attended the university there, became professor of philosophy there, and died there without ever going outside the borders of the province.

Kant himself provided the classic definition of the Enlightenment:

> The Enlightenment represents man's emergence from a self-inflicted state of minority. A minor is one who is incapable of making use of his understanding without guidance from someone else. This minority is self-inflicted whenever its cause lies not in lack of understanding, but in a lack of the determination and courage to make use of it without the guidance of another. *Sapere aude!* ("Dare to be wise!") Have the courage to make use of your own understanding, is therefore the watchword of the Enlightenment.[1]

Kant championed autonomy, but did not mean by this doing whatever you please. Rather, true autonomy is obedience to the internal law of reason. This is what makes Kant's age, as he says, the true age of criticism. Everything must be subjected to critique. Every form of heteronomy and theonomy—that is, laws compromising autonomy imposed from outside the person whether by parents, society, church, state, or God—must be critiqued. Even reason itself must be critiqued, in order that it can be sure of itself.

Kant set forth his philosophy in three basic works: the *Critique of Pure Reason* (1781), on the validity and limits of knowledge; the *Critique of Practical Reason* (1788), on the nature of the good; and the *Critique of Judgment* (1790), on aesthetics. His distinctions of "knowing" (pure reason), "willing" (practical reason), and "feeling" (judgment) laid out the paths for theological work in the next generations: Hegel pursued knowledge as the criterion of religion, Schleiermacher took up experience, and Kant himself focused on morality.

In the *Critique of Pure Reason*, Kant concluded that no valid theoretical arguments can be given for the existence of God. Kant does not deny the existence of God, but that it can be known by reason. In a famous line, he stated, "I had to set aside knowledge in order to obtain a place for faith." Kant does not imitate Hume here. Hume contrasted reason and

---

[1]Cited in Karl Barth, *Protestant Thought: From Rousseau to Ritschl*, tr. by Brian Cozens (New York: Harper & Brothers, 1959), p. 152.

faith knowing that faith would be taken with a grain of salt. Kant however contrasts knowledge and faith because he advocates a rational faith. Rational faith is based on "practical reason," that is, on morality.

Practical reason in conjunction with moral experience—the experience of "oughtness"—leads to moral mandates: for example, "Treat every person as an end, not as a means" and "Act solely on that principle which could become a universal law governing everyone's actions." The latter is known as Kant's "categorical imperative."

Kant based religion as a moral system on his maxim, "I ought; therefore, I can." A person cannot be held responsible unless capable of doing something about his or her situation. Every sensible person will realize the truth of the categorical imperative and will set out to practice it. Duty is everything; even faith is understood in terms of the duty to fulfill one's knowledge of the good. Ecclesiastical faith, to Kant, is beyond pure reason. Pure religious faith—that is, morality—has no need for the church. The title of Kant's work on religion displaces all the "solas" of the Reformation and summarizes his own position: *Religion within the Limits of Reason Alone.*

In limiting Christianity to reason, Kant inverted the order of the Reformation. Instead of good works flowing from grace, Kant begins with good works and reads all theological subjects in this light. Hence, Christ is viewed not as the Redeemer, but as the moral archetype or model of the godly life, to be imitated by humankind. Instead of God's descent to humankind, humankind is to ascend to God's commands. Kant thereby is true to his criterion of autonomy, literally, "self-law" (*auto-nomos*), which is destroyed by anything applied from the outside, including the grace of God. If God forgives—if God has mercy on whomever He wills—then humankind is not free. The old conundrum over which Augustine and Pelagius, Luther and Erasmus, Gomarus and Arminius, among many, faced off, is resolved by Kant in favor of human autonomy. The one fly in Kant's ointment was the problem of "radical evil," which he acknowledged but could not resolve. But if evil is radical, it is also irrational, and there goes reason alone. This was shocking to Kant's Enlightenment contemporaries, whose optimistic rational concepts of God and humankind excluded wrath, sin, and evil. Hence, Goethe's pithy comment summarized the reaction of the day: In speaking of radical evil, Kant "slobbered" on his philosophical mantel.

The Catholic Church and the Enlightenment

In general, Roman Catholic theology was far less open to the Enlightenment than was Protestant theology. To Roman Catholic theologians, the Enlightenment appeared as the destruction of Christendom, if not religion in general. In the first half of the eighteenth century, there were still a few late actions in the spirit of the Counter-Reformation: The "church of the wilderness" (Camisards) was persecuted in France, and evangelicals were expelled from the Archbishopric of Salzburg in 1731. Also, the Jansenist controversy broke out again and led to another papal condemnation of Augustinianism. Jesuit influence unleashed a storm of outrage in France and other countries such as Portugal and Spain. In 1773, Pope Clement XIV finally had to suspend the Jesuit Order.

Chapter 25

The Church in the Nineteenth Century

Historians and theologians often conceptualize the nineteenth century as the "long century" that begins with the French Revolution (1789) and concludes with the outbreak of
World War I (1914). Both events mark major shifts in the fortunes of Western culture and
the Christian churches. Parallel events in the history of theology are the Romantic affirmation of liberalism in Schleiermacher's *On Religion: Speeches to Its Cultured Despisers* (1799)
and the rejection of liberalism in Barth's *Romans Commentary* (1919).

From the point of view of the history of theology and the church, the nineteenth century may be described as a series of defensive moves, some apologetic and some reactionary.
The Enlightenment and the rise of the natural sciences posed major challenges to biblical
revelation; and the social consequences of the French and the Industrial Revolutions called
into serious question the churches' relevance to society and culture. Hence, Schleiermacher's poignant question: Will Christianity henceforth be associated with obscurantism and
learning with unbelief? Will faith require the sacrifice of one's intellect?

The very possibility of theology was called into question by Feuerbach. He had the
audacity to claim that the "queen of the sciences" had no clothes when he stated that theology is nothing but anthropology. To make matters worse, the historical figure of the faith,
Jesus, was called into question by another radical Hegelian, Strauss, who described the
God–Man as a myth. And for those who heeded Marx's clarion call to socialism, that myth
was not benign, but an opiate that fogged the minds of the masses.

It appeared to both the Catholic and Protestant churches that the barbarians were indeed at the gates. In general terms, the Roman Catholic response was to lock the gates as

securely as possible. The antimodernist and ultramontanist stance of the papacy intended to shut out the modern world if it could not be destroyed. The Protestant churches were not immune to this temptation. But Protestantism, again in general terms, decided that the best defense was a strong offense and attempted to dialogue with the barbarians. Apologetic theology became preoccupied with the "essence of Christianity" in order to show that, at its core, the Christian faith was not antithetical to the modern world, but rather supported the best it had to offer. On the social level, both the Catholic and Protestant churches promoted the faith through a variety of associations that ministered to the manifold needs of those wounded by the social upheavals of the times and addressed the growing gap between the churches and the masses.

The Churches and the French Revolution

The French Revolution sparked so many changes, that one may speak of the epoch around 1800 as a profound turning point. The downfall of the absolute state and the proclamation of the Republic transferred rulership of the state from the aristocracy to the bourgeoisie and awakened the masses. The French poet François René de Chateaubriand (1768–1848) opined that the Revolution was introduced by the patricians and concluded by the masses; and Hegel termed the nineteenth century "the century of the masses." In spite of later reactions, the Revolution made it impossible to completely erase ideas of popular sovereignty and democracy. The concepts of liberty, fraternity, and equality gripped all of Europe.

The Revolution also gave birth to the new phenomenon of nationalism. For the first time in modern history, peoples engaged in life-and-death struggles for their fatherlands. Nations created standing armies and used all their human and material resources to promote their goals. The armies of the Revolution and of Napoleon spread these concepts throughout Europe. And in the wars of national liberation from the Napoleonic yoke, even the suppressed peoples perceived the religious enthusiasm that characterized revolutionary nationalism. In Prussia, for example, the war of liberation against Napoleon was waged for "God, king, and fatherland."

The revolutionary restructuring of relationships also reflected the period's economic and social changes. Technical achievements and industrialization profoundly changed the lives of people in the cities and the countryside. The rise of a worker proletariat and the rapid growth of cities created unimagined problems and, consequently, the modern mass collective that, through socialist movements, strove for political power and a share of the communal pie. By mid-century the worker movement received direction from Marx and Engels and spawned its own literature in pamphlets such as the *Proletarian Our Father* (1835): "Our Sovereign, who art in Court, highly honored be thy name; Thy tax collectors come; Thy will be done in the Lower House as in the Upper; Give us today our dry bread; Forget our demands as we also forget thy promises; Lead us not into investigation; But deliver us from revolution, For thine is the legislation, the administration, and the coercion without restriction and without distribution. Amen."

The educated encountered the French Revolution with either enthusiastic agreement or suffering rejection. On the one hand, intellectual–political aspirations going back to ideas of the Middle Ages, the Renaissance, and the European Enlightenment finally found

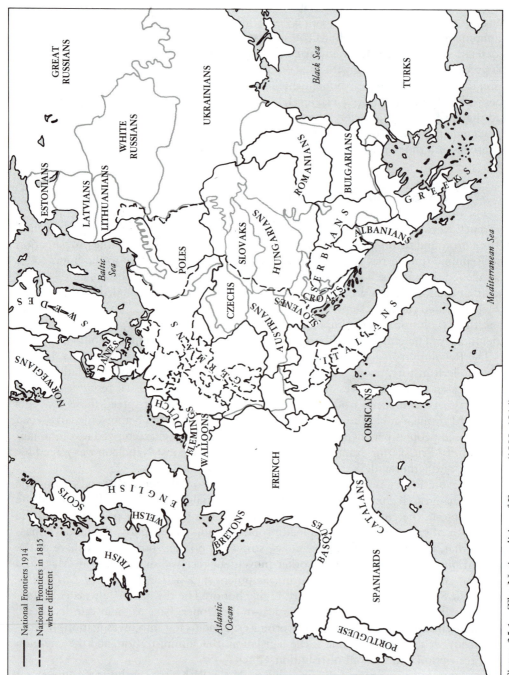

Figure 25.1   The Nationalities of Europe (1800–1914)

their sociopolitical realization. But on the other hand, the advance of the Revolution with its terrible dictatorship and the violent subjugation of European peoples to France called forth multiple counterreactions that pressed for the restoration of pre-revolutionary conditions. The struggles of the nineteenth century are thus essentially tied to the circumstances of the French Revolution.

These phenomena radically changed the conditions of the churches' existence. The French Revolution accelerated the complex process of the long dissolution of the churches' earlier domination. Of course, Pietism and the Enlightenment provided a strong practical and conceptual impetus, but it is in the nineteenth century that secularism proceeded beyond the upper middle class and created the specific modern situation of the church. The nineteenth-century surge of industrialization with its degradation of urban living conditions, vividly portrayed in social novels such as Charles Dickens's *Oliver Twist* (1838) and *David Copperfield* (1850), particularly challenged the church. Given their organizational structures, the churches provided only inadequate responses to the rapidly increasing alienation of the urban population.

The great problems in the life of the church were either directly or indirectly related to these developments. Church and state fought over schools, marriage, public morality, nationalism, and science. Nationalism and secularism desired not to kill the church, but to conform it to the rationale of the state and to establish reason over revelation for the common interest of society. Even the leaders of the Restoration who emphasized churchly authority as the guarantee of tradition and legitimacy did so for reasons of state and did not permit the church to express political interests. Monarchs throughout Europe repeatedly emphasized that, as Wilhelm II of Prussia put it, "Pastors ought to attend to the souls of the faithful and cultivate charity, but let politics alone, for it does not concern them."

The Revolution and its ideology stimulated a new orientation to history. History and tradition took their place alongside the earlier discussion of nature. Organic growth replaced earlier mechanistic conceptions of humanity and society. Revolution was identified with evolution. Historicism—the conception that all human life, individual as well as social, is understandable only by its place in historical development—was the most original contribution of the nineteenth century to the secularization process and became a mark of modern cultural consciousness. The church was thereby regarded as a phenomenon of historical culture, rather than merely the mediatrix of revelation.

The new valuation of history and the rise of historicism provided a worldview that understood events from their development and thereby led to the modern phenomena of relativism and nihilism. The fundamental problem of the eighteenth century, the relationship between faith and reason, shifted to the modern problematic of faith and history.

From the French Revolution to the Congress of Vienna

The church, profoundly tied to the old regime, shared to a great extent the fate of the absolute state in the French Revolution of 1789. For the first time in Europe, the centuries-old connection of church and state was dissolved. In contradistinction to France, the earlier American war of independence also separated church and state, but not by antagonism toward the church. There, Christianity and the free churches were rather an important factor for the people and politics.

The French National Assembly (1789–1792) secularized church property, dissolved monasteries, and provided the "Civil Constitution for the Clergy." The Civil Constitution subordinated church administration to the state, placed the election of bishops and priests with the citizens, determined clerical income, released clergy from obedience to foreign clerical authority (the papacy!), and demanded an oath of loyalty to the nation and constitution by all the clergy. In opposition to these ordinances, many bishops fled the country; and after the fall of the king in 1792, many of the lower clergy also fled. During the Reign of Terror (1793–94) dominated by Maximilien Robespierre, the government abolished the Christian calendar, prohibited Christian festivals, declared marriage a purely civil concern, and destroyed many churches and pillaged their treasures. The new cult of reason replaced worship in the churches.

After the end of the reign of terror (1795), religious freedom, for Protestants as well as Catholics, was re-established. Napoleon Bonaparte restored the Catholic Church in the concordat of July 15, 1801. The Catholic Church was recognized as the majority church of the French, but remained subordinate to the state, which provided clerical income. The pope could name new bishops, but had to accept the fact that church property was lost through the Revolution. In 1804, Napoleon, having had Pope Pius VII come to France to crown him emperor, took the crown from the Pope's hands and crowned himself! In 1809, France incorporated the Papal States. Pius responded by excommunicating Napoleon, who then imprisoned the pope. Pius's resistance during these "troubles" contributed to the enhancement of papal prestige after the fall of Napoleon in 1815.

Church Reform in Germany:
The Prussian Union and Its Consequences

In Germany, the cataclysms of the Revolution and the Napoleonic era forced a continual reorganization of the churches. While still predominantly Lutheran, Prussia now also included a number of Reformed territories whose confessional commitments had to be taken seriously. The ruling house had become Reformed in the early 1600s. On the personal level, the current ruler, Frederick Wilhelm III (1770–1840), was married to a Lutheran and wanted to share communion with her. The 300th anniversary of Luther's *95 Theses* in 1817 seemed an appropriate occasion for uniting the two Reformation churches. The king's call found a positive echo among the clergy, who were ready to drop the names "Lutheran" and "Reformed" for "Evangelical." But when the king mandated uniformity of worship according to his own liturgical creation, there was widespread opposition. This was symbolized by the Lutheran pastor Claus Harms (1778–1855), who proclaimed his own 95 theses against the Union. Thesis 78 reiterated the old issue that had divided Luther and Zwingli: "If Christ's body and blood was in the bread and wine at the Marburg Colloquy in 1529, it still is in 1817." A crucial issue became the constitutional one of justifying the king's personal intervention in the church. The opposition to the union in some congregations—above all, in Silesia—led to powerful countermeasures by the state. As a consequence, thousands of Lutherans emigrated to North America and Australia.

The controversies over the Prussian Union led finally to conciliation by the king. In a cabinet order of 1834, the confessions were guaranteed continuing existence. As a consequence, the Prussian Union brought forth three different communities: United, Lutheran, and Reformed; a unified Union Church did not develop.

Inner Mission and the Social Question

The Francke institutions at Halle, which shaped Pietism's efforts to transform the world by transforming individuals, were forerunners of the nineteenth-century Protestant efforts to respond to social issues through the Inner Mission and the deaconess movements.

These two movements soon became interrelated and addressed the same social miseries that called forth Karl Marx's famous "Manifesto." The major figures of the movements are Johann Hinrich Wichern (1808–1881), "the father of Inner Missions," and Theodore Fliedner (1800–1864), the founder of the Protestant female diaconate.

Wichern, a pastor in Hamburg, was stunned by the impoverishment of the masses and established rescue homes for neglected children. His prototype, the *Rauhe Haus* (literally, "Rough House"), opened in 1833. There, he emphasized education and job training in the context of God's forgiving grace. He then enlisted and trained assistants for this work and thereby evoked deacon and deaconess training institutes. In 1844, he began publishing a newspaper to arouse social conscience. Wichern was concerned that the future of both Christianity and society was jeopardized by the growing alienation of the urban masses from a seemingly uncaring state church. In 1848, soon after the appearance of Marx's "Communist Manifesto," he issued a "Protestant Manifesto."

In his long (two hours!) speech at the Wittenberg Kirchentag, he proclaimed that "love no less than faith is the church's indispensable mark." The church would have a future, he said, if only it would incarnate God's love in the industrialized cities. His forceful speech led to the formation of the Central Committee of Inner Missions of the German Evangelical Church.

The chief aims of the Inner Mission initially included reclaiming those who had left the church and assisting the needy, sick, and poor. Wichern advocated self-help associations for the poor and marginalized. Soon this goal broadened to include prison reform (Wichern himself became a special counselor in the Prussian Ministry of the Interior in charge of prison and welfare work), as well as care for the homeless, the mentally and physically disabled, immigrants, and seamen. The Inner Mission soon spread to other European countries and to America. It eventually became an umbrella agency for a wide variety of activities, including social welfare work and services for the elderly, children, families, and the sick.

Wichern's work was not, of course, an isolated expression of Christian faith. Throughout Europe at this time, religious renewal movements inspired social concern for the masses of people pauperized by industrialization. In England, the Methodists had long been laboring at adult education, schooling, reform of prisons, the abolition of slavery, and aid to alcoholics. Famous missions arose in Basle, London, and Paris. The YMCA (1844), the YWCA (1855), and the Salvation Army (1865) were only some of the numerous charitable organizations created to respond to the ills of modern society.

The revival of Christian service came not only through the Inner Mission, but also through the development of the deaconess movement by the German pastor Fliedner, who, among others, greatly desired the renewal of a women's ministry in the church. Fliedner's first steps toward the development of the female diaconate began with work on behalf of prisoners inspired by the English Quaker Elizabeth Fry (1780–1845) and the Mennonite deaconess movement he had observed in Holland. In 1833, a discharged woman prisoner came to the Fliedner parsonage in Kaiserswerth for help; he and his wife lodged her in their garden summer house. Thus began the famous Kaiserswerth institutions. Other discharged prisoners and women in need began arriving, and the Fliedners trained them to serve others. The first deaconess motherhouse, established in Kaiserswerth in 1836, provided a structured environment of mutual support and a training center. Soon their ministry extended beyond helping released prisoners to serving the sick, orphans, and moral outcasts. This is the origin of the Rhenish–Westphalian Deaconess Association, a model for dozens of similar associations that sprang up throughout Europe. By 1884, there were fifty-six deaconess communities with 5,653 deaconesses.

In addition to the deaconesses, the Fliedners trained salaried Christian nurses. In 1851, the pioneer English nurse Florence Nightingale (1820–1910) went to Kaiserswerth for training; later, she opened her own school of nursing. By that time, deaconesses from Kaiserswerth were serving hospitals in England, America, Jerusalem, Constantinople, and Alexandria.

The Inner Mission and diaconal movements increasingly came to understand the role that economic and social conditions such as work environments, unemployment, underemployment, and discrimination played among the people the church sought to serve. Thus, there was growing sensitivity to the view that diaconal work must encompass the political, as well as the personal and congregational, realm.

Adolf Stoecker (1835–1909), the conservative court preacher in Berlin, realized in the course of his pastoral activities that the Inner Mission and diaconal methods were not succeeding in bringing the laboring classes back to the church, and so he attempted to politicize Christian service. He organized the Christian Socialist Workers Party, whose program was to renew and reform society. He called for obligatory pensions for widows, orphans, invalids, and the elderly and for the protection of workers from unsafe and unhealthy working conditions. Both in and out of the pulpit, Stoecker vigorously advocated his conviction that the causes of human misery must be addressed and changed.

His political party, however, soon foundered on the rocks of Marxist ridicule and the opposition of landowners and industrialists. To make matters worse, his close identification of the Christian faith with German nationalism had an ugly consequence in anti-Semitic opposition to Jews, who were characterized as representatives of radical liberalism.

A country pastor, Rudolf Todt (1839–1887) took a more radical position in his *Radical German Socialism and Christian Society* (1877). Todt agreed with the socialist analyses of class struggle, industrial exploitation of workers, social alienation, and mass poverty. He viewed proletarian revolt as legitimate emancipation from oppression, but advocated reform over revolution. Although he shocked many of his clerical contemporaries, and Bismarck considered banning his writings, Todt's "National Association for Social Reform" and its newspaper did help prepare the way for later social legislation.

Another challenge to the alliance of throne and altar came from a young pastor in an industrial parish in Saxony, Friedrich Naumann (1860–1919). Naumann and his colleagues opposed any form of Christian paternalism and desired to work with social democrats to develop a party of radical reform. Bitter controversies resulted, and by the 1890s the Christian socialists of the Naumann school were denounced not only by Kaiser Wilhelm II, but also by the Prussian Protestant church. Pastors were told to stay out of politics. Naumann himself resigned from the ministry, entered politics as a left-wing liberal, and in 1919 participated in drafting the Weimar constitution as a member of the National Assembly.

Another pastor who entered politics to promote social reform was Friedrich von Bodelschwingh (1821–1910). In 1872, he accepted the directorship of the Rhenish–Westphalian home for epileptics and its associated deaconess home. Named Bethel, the center grew to include a training school for deacons, a theological school, and a home for destitute workers. Bodelschwingh's concern for rehabilitation of the sick and the outcast led him to enter politics. Elected to the Prussian Diet in 1903, he secured passage of a law in 1907 that provided homes for itinerant workers. By this time, the government began to favor such measures as means to undermine the socialist movement. Bismarck himself said, "Give the working man the right to work as long as he is healthy, assure him care when he is sick, and maintenance when he is old. . . . If the state will show a little more Christian solicitude for the working man, then the socialists will sing their siren song in vain."

Bodelschwingh's son, by the same name (1877–1946), succeeded him as administrator of Bethel. The home was further enlarged, its medical facilities improved, and its research into the treatment of epilepsy expanded. At the beginning of the German church's struggle against Hitler's effort to assimilate it into the state, Bodelschwingh was elected national bishop, but the Nazi state nullified the election. He and his friends later led the opposition to the Nazi proposal to destroy all "life not worthy of living" and thereby protected the residents of Bethel and other institutions. Bethel continues to be a model of educational, therapeutic, and ecumenical diaconal work.

By the turn of the century, a major expression of Protestant social concern was the Evangelical Social Congress. A Christian fellowship for study and action on social policy, it provided Protestant intellectuals a platform for their goal of a modern welfare state. Its president for many years was the famous theologian Adolf von Harnack (1851–1920). But evangelical social work in the nineteenth century remained a bourgeois concern; it gained little access to the industrial workers. Apart from their exemplary social engagement of individuals, the Inner Mission and diaconal movements were limited by their independence from the evangelical state churches and by Protestant attachment to the throne's opposition to socialism, communism, and democracy.

The Catholic Church in the Nineteenth Century

After Napoleon's downfall, the Bourbons were restored to the French throne, the papal states were restored to Pope Pius VII, and the Catholic convert Karl Ludwig von Haller (1768–1854) provided the restorationist ideology for counterrevolutionary regimes (*Restora-*

tion of Political Science, six vols., 1816–26). The conservatives presupposed that only a church supported by political authority could motivate and maintain the social bonds of society.

Catholicism experienced a religious renewal analogous to the contemporary Protestant Awakening. Revolutionary upheavals and the continual revision of the map of Europe fed yearnings for a unified Christian culture. The early Romantic movement had transfigured the Middle Ages into such a culture under the leadership of the papacy. Friedrich von Hardenberg (1772–1801), who took the name "Novalis," wrote a retrospective prophecy of a utopian golden age projected from the Catholic Middle Ages (*Christendom or Europe*, 1799). English Romanticism also developed a conservative orientation. Samuel Taylor Coleridge (1772–1834) and William Wordsworth (1770–1850), among others, expressed the same fervor for Anglicanism as their French and German contemporaries did for Catholicism. Sensational conversions (e.g., that of Friedrich Schlegel, a leader in the Romantic movement, in 1808) to the Roman church also promoted Catholic self-consciousness. A growing Catholic consciousness believed that only a strengthened papacy could renew the Catholic church and, thereby, Western civilization.

Pope Pius VII (1800–1823) returned to Rome in 1814 after the abdication of Napoleon. The papacy regained its political freedom, and the Curia promoted the universal church against all tendencies toward national churches. In 1814, the Pope reinstated the Jesuit Order, whose influence continually increased in the course of the nineteenth century. In a series of concordats, Rome restructured the church hierarchy in state after state.

The new centralized role of the papacy is known as ultramontanism (*ultra montes*, "beyond the mountains"). In nineteenth-century France, ultramontanism was the reaction against the Revolution and Napoleon's attempt to subjugate the church and the papacy completely to the state. Joseph de Maistre's (1753–1821) fundamental work, *The Pope* (1819), clearly expressed the infallibility of the papacy. "Christendom," he argued, "depends totally on the sovereignty of the pope . . . . There is neither public morality nor a national character without religion. In Europe there is no religion without Christendom. There is no Christendom without Catholicism. There is no Catholicism without the pope. There is no pope without the unconditional supremacy due him." The Jesuit ultramontanist offensive, abetted by an active Catholic press, expressed the antimodernist spirit through revivals of medieval piety and the systematic organization of the piety of the masses, including devotion to the Eucharist, the Sacred Heart, and Mary.

Pope Pius IX (1846–1878) and Vatican I (1869/70)

The pontificate of Pius IX focused the struggle against liberalism and nationalism. In 1854, Pius declared the first significant Marian dogma of the modern period: the immaculate conception of Mary. The dogma stated that Mary was free from all taint of original sin from the moment of her conception, through a miraculous act of the Holy Spirit. The context of this dogma was ultramontanism supported by an intensified Marian piety, such as Marian visions and miracles at Lourdes. Although a subject of medieval argument, this Marian doctrine was now proclaimed by Pius IX without consulting a council. The power of the pope to define dogma was a *fait accompli* even before it was justified by the dogma of papal infallibility.

In 1864, the "Syllabus of Errors" condemned rationalism, indifferentism, socialism, communism, Bible societies, and state independence in cultural and educational matters. Here, ultramontanist Catholicism identified with the Restoration; rejected modern society, the separation of church and state, religious liberty, and public education without clerical control; and asserted the authority of the Catholic hierarchy to regulate public affairs. Civil legislation of marriage and divorce was not valid unless it was in conformity with canon law. The church had the right to its own courts and police powers. In order that no one would miss the point, Pius began proceedings to canonize the judges of the Inquisition! The lasting impact of all this upon the public imagination is exemplified by the issue of papal power raised during the election campaign of the American Catholic John F. Kennedy, in 1960.

These developments culminated in the first Vatican Council of 1869/70, which defined the universal episcopacy of the papacy and papal infallibility. The universal episcopacy of the papacy meant the jurisdictional power of the pope over the whole church. The pope is infallible in doctrinal decisions when he speaks *"ex cathedra,"* i.e., in the exercise of his teaching office on questions of faith and morals. Such infallible decisions must be made for the whole church and the foundation of faith "preserved holy and interpreted truly." Infallibility in doctrinal decisions would have its legal ground in papal decision-making, not in the agreement of the church. Thereby, Roman Catholicism became an absolute monarchy without constitutional restraints.

From Kulturkampf *to the Modernist Oath (1871–1910)*

In general, the *Kulturkampf* refers to the clash of the Catholic church with the spirit of liberalism and nationalism in the nineteenth century. In a narrower sense, it is the struggle of the Prussian prime minister and first chancellor of the new German Reich, Otto von Bismarck (1815–1898), with the Roman Curia.

In 1870, the Catholic Center Party was founded in Germany. In light of ultramontanism, Bismarck feared pressure on the newly formed Reich from a powerful political Catholicism. The issue was not Catholicism itself; rather, it was Bismarck's desire to keep the churches, including the Protestant churches, out of state and political matters and to confine them strictly to religious matters. Anti-Catholic legislation (1871–1875) prohibited use of the pulpit for political agitation, expelled the Jesuits and related orders, and created state supervision of education. The so-called May Laws (1873), based on the supremacy of the state, limited the disciplinary power of the church, instituted a Supreme Ecclesiastical Court appointed by the emperor, mandated state control of all seminaries, and required that all clergy pass a state examination. Pius IX condemned these laws in 1875 as subversive of the constitution and rights of the church. Bismarck underestimated the extent and strength of Catholic and even Protestant opposition to these laws, and since he also desired Catholic support in his opposition to social democracy, he gradually reversed his policy.

After the death of Pius IX, tensions abated under Pope Leo XIII (1878–1903). In 1891, Leo proclaimed the encyclical *Rerum novarum*, the so-called Magna Charta for Catholic social teaching. Although beginning with a strong defense of private property and a condemnation of socialism and anarchism, the encyclical made waves by endorsing the grievances of the working class against their employers. The blame for the intolerable inequities of capitalism and the industrial age was laid at the door of the powerful and rich.

The state is responsible for the common good, including the promotion of the well-being and interests of the working class. No class is to be exploited for the advantage of another. Appropriate state intervention should deal with child labor, excessive work hours, and justice for workers, who should receive a fair wage that would provide basic subsistence for a family. The papal advocacy of justice and charity in socioeconomic issues was regarded as revolutionary, as well as subversive of the established order. Leo's application of "Christian principles" to capital–labor relations won him the title, "the working man's pope."

Nevertheless, although more conciliatory than Pius IX, Leo XIII also maintained many of the former's antagonisms to the modern world. Since the end of the nineteenth century, reform-minded Catholics had fought against reactionary curialism for greater freedom, above all in theology. Pius X (1903–1914) condemned these efforts as "modernism," and all Catholic theologians had to take the so-called antimodernist oath (1910; abrogated in 1967) before receiving a church office. Rejected as forms of "modernism" were various ideas and scientific perspectives, such as the theory of evolution, and advances in biblical studies such as textual criticism.

Nineteenth-Century Theology

German evangelical theology in the nineteenth century was particularly rich and pluralistic. Variations of Orthodoxy, Pietism, and the Enlightenment continued to exert an influence, but in competition with the new developments of "liberalism" and "culture-Protestantism." Above all, there was the towering figure of Schleiermacher.

Friedrich Daniel Ernst Schleiermacher (1768–1834)

Both sides of Schleiermacher's family included long lines of Reformed theologians. His father was a Reformed chaplain in the Prussian army who later became a convinced Moravian. Schleiermacher's education among the Moravians provided him with an abiding sense of the richness of religious individuality and religious community. In a letter to his sister in 1802 concerning his personal religious doubts and struggles, he wrote, "I can say that after everything I have again become a Moravian, only of a higher order."

He was also a pastor and professor of a higher order. Throughout his career as theology professor and dean of the theology faculty at the University of Berlin, which he helped found with Wilhelm von Humboldt, he preached nearly every Sunday at the city's Trinity Church. Next to teaching in nearly all theological disciplines except the Old Testament, he focused his lectures on the history of philosophy, dialectics, ethics, psychology, politics, aesthetics, hermeneutics, and education. His theological works ranged from his early masterpiece of apologetics (*On Religion: Speeches to its Cultured Despisers*, 1799) to a comprehensive treatise on dogmatics (*The Christian Faith*, 1821–22) that ranks with Calvin's *Institutes*. Schleiermacher took seriously the Enlightenment critiques of religion in general and Christianity in particular. He was convinced that faith loses its life when it tries to protect itself through self-defensive and self-isolating strategies. He was also a patriot who, through his forceful preaching, rallied Prussia in the war against France. His fame as a theologian was equaled by that of his person. At his death there was such a spontaneous outpouring of public mourning, that the funeral procession took several hours as tens of thousands of Berliners paid their respects.

The Enlightenment and its development in idealism stressed human freedom and autonomy. In conjunction with the natural sciences, the philosophers' turn to empirical experience reduced talk about the supernatural to talk about the natural. Traditional speech about God and revelation was therefore at best descriptions of human capabilities in otherworldly terms. Schleiermacher met this challenge on its own ground. He, too, began with experience; but in contrast to his age's infatuation with freedom, he spoke of human dependence. The experience of God is not dependent upon either intellectual abstractions or compulsions, pious or otherwise, to believe unbelievable doctrine, but rather is rooted in human experience itself as dependent experience—hence his famous description of faith as "the consciousness of being absolutely dependent, or, which is the same thing, of being in relation to God." The Christian faith does not consist of believing certain doctrines, living a certain way, or having heartwarming experiences, but rather living in relationship with God. That relationship focuses on Jesus of Nazareth as Redeemer not as the *object* of faith, but as the *mediator* of faith, which becomes real in the fellowship of believers—the church.

Schleiermacher attempted, as an apologetic theologian, to so present the truth of the gospel, that it would be understandable and credible for his contemporaries. His writings are not always easy sledding, hence the play on his name as "veil maker" (*Schleier* means "veil"), but a few epigrammatic summaries may suggest his appeal then and now: Religion is not extrinsic, but intrinsic, to human life; religion is not the object of investigation, but the subject of self-examination; Christian faith critiques not only culture, but also itself; theology is the church's "answering service," not a collection of eternal truths; and proclamation of the gospel stands over speculation about it.

The Awakening

The Awakening movement was a transconfessional religious upheaval that began in England and North America and proceeded to early nineteenth-century Germany, transcending countries and languages. In Protestant France, the Netherlands, and Switzerland, it is termed the "Réveil." The older pietist sects—above all, the Moravians—provided decisive impulses for the Awakening. The movement was multiform but had common marks: strong opposition to the Enlightenment religion of reason; the seriousness of human sin before God; the awakening to a new life only through the grace of Christ; individual, personal experience of rebirth, ultimately leading to the restructuring of society; and increased social activity and missionary efforts to spread the Christian faith. Over all these, the laity rediscovered the Bible and formed free associations for common activities.

The Awakening in England reached its high point in Methodism. The Methodist movement has been called the last great formation of the church in the history of Christianity. The founder was the Anglican clergyman John Wesley (1703–1791), next to whom in significance were George Whitfield (1714–1770) and Charles Wesley (1707–1788). The Wesley brothers founded a student association in Oxford in 1729. Their pious life according to strict rules and their emphasis upon sanctification led to the name "Methodists," mockingly applied to them.

John Wesley had his conversion on May 27, 1738 at 8:45 in the evening through his acquaintance with Moravian preaching and under the impact of Luther's preface to Romans. Wesley's conversion experience informed his outstanding preaching of the Awakening, which, abetted by his brother and Whitfield, spread throughout England, Scotland, and Ireland. Methodist preaching called for personal discipleship to Christ, aimed at conversion under penitential struggle and the experience of grace, and led to strong communal expressions. Wesley's lay preaching office is characteristic of the Methodist movement, from which came impulses that influenced English social policy. After Wesley's death, Methodism separated from the Anglican state church.

The Anglican Church also experienced an awakening, the "Low Church Movement." From these Evangelicals came essential impulses for the abolition of slavery. The free churches also made inroads on high church Anglicanism.

The Oxford Movement (1833–45) responded to the decline in church life, the spread of "liberalism" in theology, a growing interest in primitive and medieval Christianity stimulated by Romanticism, and anxiety that the Catholic Emancipation Act (1829) would facilitate conversions to Catholicism. The Oxford Movement defended the Church of England as a divine institution, the doctrine of apostolic succession, and the Book of Common Prayer as a rule of faith. These high-church directions have played an important role in Anglican theology and ecclesiology up to today.

The concerns and goals of the Oxford Movement were expressed through its *Tracts for the Times.* One of the most famous authors of these tracts was John Henry Newman (1801–1890). His *Tract No. 90* (1841) caused a major controversy by interpreting the *Thirty-Nine Articles* in congruity with the decrees of the Council of Trent. A few years later Newman was received into the Catholic Church, and in 1879 he was made a cardinal by Leo XIII. Newman's life and writings have been highly influential on both the Church of England and the restoration of Catholicism in England and elsewhere.

Currents in Evangelical Theology

The deep sea of Hegelian philosophy, which many students continue to find fathomless in every sense of the word, fed a number of currents in nineteenth-century theology. Georg Wilhelm Friedrich Hegel (1770–1831) is viewed as the most comprehensive and profound philosopher of German idealism—a view he "modestly" shared! Hegel culminated an era of supreme confidence in human rational thought. He was convinced that his philosophical system could comprehend all reality. He thought his new dynamic logic not only transcended the analytical achievements of the Enlightenment, but grasped reality itself. The division of reality into its parts provides valid knowledge, but does not grasp the whole. For example, the dissection of a frog provides knowledge of the frog's parts, but the process itself loses the total picture of "frogness" (not to mention the frog). Truth is not in particulars, but in the whole: "Die Wahrheit ist das Ganze." Rejecting the previous Aristotelian logic that "A" is not "non-A," Hegel posited the dialectical nature of reality in which everything is taken up in its opposition—thesis, antithesis, and synthesis. The synthesis itself becomes a new thesis that is opposed and transcended into a new synthesis, and on and on; reality is a historical process in which the Absolute (read "God" for the theologians) comes to its self-realization in our (read "Hegel's") reason. History is read as a dialectical process—an evolution—toward fulfillment. Boarding the train of history is to participate in its goal, whether that be the Prussian state, the classless society, or any number of ideas Hegel's students promulgated.

History, then, is an intelligible, rational order. In the preface to his *Philosophy of Right*, there is the characteristic sentence, "Everything real is rational and everything rational is real." This may not be much comfort to those who suffer the antitheses of history, but life must "suffer wounds" to be reconciled to its unity. The "cunning of reason" makes passions and reversals work on its behalf; it hides and reveals itself in its immanent empirical forms in order that the Spirit may come to self-realization through the process of estrangement and reconciliation. The appeal to theologians was the application of this system to the problem of theodicy and the overcoming of the gulf between reason and revelation. The identification of the relative with the absolute bridges Lessing's "ditch": Human freedom is accepting that what is, is right.

The nature of this text does not warrant either exploring Hegel's thought more fully or tracing his influence in more than suggestive ways. His more interesting students turned him on his head by asserting that materialism, and not idealism, is the locus of reality; hence Feuerbach's concise statement, "One is what one eats." Marx, Engels, and Lenin developed Hegel's ideas into dialectical materialism and applied it to society and politics, with the motto that our task is not to understand history, but to change it. Strauss applied Hegel's logic to the historical study of Jesus and concluded that he is a myth. And Kierkegaard, the "father of existentialism," vehemently rejected Hegel's system altogether for the sake of the solitary individual who stands before the infinitely qualitative Other, God. Kierkegaard's impact would not be fully felt until the twentieth century, but a few words can be said here about Feuerbach and Strauss.

Ludwig Feuerbach (1804–1872) and David Friedrich Strauss (1808–1874) were the *enfants terribles* of contemporary theology, who were not shy about expressing their views of the old guard. Strauss said of one of his professors that if Jesus Christ had studied theology with him, he would have abandoned Christianity before he ever started it. Both Feuerbach and Strauss were influenced by Hegel. Feuerbach, whose own influence extended to such figures as Karl Marx, Friedrich Nietzsche, Sigmund Freud, and Martin Buber, has been called the "grave digger of theology" who killed God and made humankind divine. Feuerbach caused all this excitement by his interpretation of Christianity as a projection of human fears and desires. In *The Essence of Christianity* (1841), he wrote, "The personality of God is nothing else than the projected personality of man" and "The beginning, middle, and end of religion is MAN." Having gotten his contemporaries' attention, Feuerbach went on to assert that the negation of the subject (God) does not mean negating the predicates (wisdom, love, justice). The real atheist, he said, is the person who theoretically acknowledges God and then lives as if He did not exist. But Feuerbach's positive intention to rescue faith from the abstractions of the philosophers and theologians was not well received, and he never did secure a teaching position.

Strauss also lacked the better part of valor and unleashed a storm of controversy with his *Life of Jesus* (1835). He argued that the Christ figure of the Gospels is not historical, but mythological. This was a terribly cold bath to the contemporary quest for the historical Jesus that posited an end run around critiques of Christian doctrine by historical research. For Strauss, Jesus was a human teacher of love for God and neighbor, and the idea of the God–Man was attached to the figure of Jesus by the church. Strauss advanced his point by means of Hegelian logic. The "God–Man" is the synthesis of the dialectic of God (thesis) and man (antithesis); in other words, the dialectic of the supernatural and the natural issues in the mythological. The relegation of Christology to mythology incited strong reactions from every theological quarter and also created personal hostility to Strauss.

The issue of the relationship between faith and history so sharply put by Strauss was addressed by Martin Kähler (1835–1912). His *The So-Called Historical Jesus and the Historic Biblical Christ* (1892) argued that the foundation of the Christian faith is not the historical Jesus, but rather, the Christ preached and testified to by the community. The attempt to draw a picture of the historical Jesus is an error, both methodologically and theologically. Methodologically, the Gospels are sources of the church's preaching, rather than historical sources for the biography and psychology of Jesus. Theologically, the Christian community does not focus on the dear departed Jesus, but on the present living Christ. Of course, for Kähler, the preached Christ is none other than the earthly Jesus, but the certainty of faith cannot rest upon the results of historical scholarship. By disentangling faith from historical–empirical research, Kähler provided resources for the post-War generation's response to the collapse of liberalism.

Liberal Theology

The historically oriented work of the liberal theologians had roots in the Enlightenment, but arose in the nineteenth century in a pointed form over the problem of faith and history. How is Christianity possible when the telescope, microscope, and stethoscope found no evidence of God in "the starry skies above and the moral law within"? The liberal answer posited trust in God on the encounter with Jesus. But lacking home videos by Mary and Joseph, how do we know who Jesus was and what he said? Here the centrality of historical study came to the fore. Jesus was a historical figure and therefore as accessible through historical study as any other historical figure. Hence, the liberal promotion of historical–critical study of the New Testament to find the "real" Jesus and his message behind the accretions of centuries of dogmatic developments. This enterprise is behind the liberal distinction between the religion *of* Jesus and the religion *about* Jesus and the reduction of the Christian faith to Jesus' message about the kingdom of a loving God.

Liberalism's emphasis upon historical–critical study of the Bible carried the seeds of its own destruction. But before such scholars as Johannes Weiss (1863–1914) and Albert Schweitzer (1875–1965) pointed out that Jesus was not the first-century equivalent of an English gentleman or a cultured German, but, to modern eyes, a religious fanatic who expected the imminent end of the world, liberalism was widely influential throughout the West.

Leading liberals included Albrecht Ritschl (1822–1889), Adolf von Harnack (1851–1930), and Ernst Troeltsch (1865–1923). From around 1870, Ritschl dominated the theological landscape. Influenced by Kant and Schleiermacher, Ritschl grasped Christianity as historical fact mediated by the personal experience of belief. The New Testament reliably testifies to Jesus' revelation of the kingdom of God as the ethical goal of all humankind. Jesus is the archetypal image of humanity reconciled and united in the kingdom of God. Personal redemption and the formation of community in the kingdom of God follows the transformation and turn of the human will to the will of God. Traditional dogmatic concerns such as sin, judgment, the wrath of God, the Trinity, Christology, and related expressions in the classic creeds and confessions are time-bound "husks" concealing the "kernel" of the Gospel.

Ritschl's historical orientation was carried forth by the historian of the ancient church and of the history of dogma, Adolf von Harnack. The most famous theologian of his time, Harnack demanded an undogmatic Christianity—that is, a Christianity peeled clean of the doctrinal layers added by later generations who shifted the religion *of* Jesus (the kingdom of God's love) to a religion *about* Jesus (a preexistent divine being vicariously atoning for sin). The deep well of Christian history, as Harnack colorfully put it, is choked with metaphysical garbage. In his monumental seven-volume *History of Dogma* (1886–90), he attributed the conception and development of dogma as "a work of the Greek spirit on the soil of the Gospel." By distinguishing the kernel of the Gospel from this Hellenistic husk, Harnack rescued Christianity for his contemporaries. His work is echoed today by those who call for liberation from Eurocentric theology.

In his exposition of the essence of Christianity (*What is Christianity?* 1900), Harnack addressed the possibility of Christian existence in the modern world by reducing faith to the fatherhood of God, the brotherhood of humankind, and the infinite worth of the human soul. By 1927, this volume had gone through fourteen editions and as many translations. The book ends with Harnack's personal testimony on the meaning of life: love of God and neighbor. He says, "If we then look at the course of mankind's history, follow its upward development, and search, in strenuous and patient service, for the communion of minds in it, we shall not faint in weariness and despair, but become certain of God, of the God whom Jesus Christ called his Father, and who is also our Father." Such optimism and confidence in progress, a kind of "onward and upward with the arts" theology that attempted to bring biblical proclamation into the present, became increasingly problematic as the foreignness of the biblical message in contrast to modern conceptions became clear.

The problem of the relationship between faith and history was reflected above all in the man who systematized the history-of-religions school, Ernst Troeltsch, whose impact continues in the present. Troeltsch's research focused on the questions of the relationships of Christianity to modern culture, revelation to history, and personal freedom to social conditionedness, especially in modern history. He is popularly remembered for his magisterial study of the historical relationship of Christianity to culture, *The Social Teaching of the Christian Churches* (1912). But his major legacy is his vigorous historicizing of all thinking. Nothing lies outside historical conditioning; hence his shocking comment as a young man addressing a conservative religious convention: "Gentlemen, everything wobbles." But Troeltsch was an equal-opportunity shocker, for critical historical work was as subversive of liberalism as it was of orthodoxy. The liberal hope of a firm foundation through finding the "kernel" became as suspect as the conservative claim of the absoluteness of dogma. There is no nonhistorical, eternal kernel under the husk; everything that exists exists in historical conditions. Relativism had reared its head: Troeltsch's *The Absoluteness of Christianity* (1902) made it clear that historical work as such cannot claim the superiority of one religion over another. Troeltsch realized that the historical method is a new wine that, when introduced into the old wineskins of biblical studies, church history, and theology, will burst them apart. But at that very point, European civilization itself burst apart as it descended into the unprecedented mutual slaughter of World War I.

Chapter 26

Church History and Theology since World War I

World War I convulsed all areas of life. The breakdown of social and national order, the raging hatred between the nations of Europe, and the mass death upon the battlefields of the war revealed the depths to which humankind could sink. The collapse of European civilization knocked the props out from under liberalism. The liberal optimism that had the temerity to think this was the war to end all wars evaporated before the horrors of trench warfare and gas attacks. For many theologians, especially among the younger generation, the great figures of Schleiermacher, Ritschl, and Harnack lost their theological credibility.

The war's end did little to alleviate the nightmares of humankind's dark side, for it created conditions favorable to the rise of Hitler and World War II. Psychologically unable to acknowledge defeat, and misled by their own leaders about the realities of the Versailles peace treaty, the German population reacted emotionally to the humiliating and onerous terms of reparations and the infamous "war-guilt" clause which demanded that Germany accept sole responsibility for the war. In addition to the terrible suffering visited upon the people during the war, the exactions of Versailles caused a violent nationalist reaction that, coupled with nostalgia for the monarchy and a proud Prussian military history, fueled a widespread antidemocratic bias against the new Weimar Republic. Within fifteen years, the longing for strong leadership would be met by Adolf Hitler.

The end of the monarchy also brought an end to the constitutional form of the evangelical state churches inherited from the period of the Reformation. How should the relationship between church and state be structured? The models of clear separation of church and state provided by France (1905) and Russia (October Revolution, 1917) were largely unacceptable. The Social Democrats pushed for a secular state, and thus, the Weimar constitution of 1919 declared that no state church existed and that the churches might regulate their affairs independently. But this development was received with wide-scale protests by a conservative–nationalist Protestantism. As a result, real separation of church and state was avoided. The churches were granted autonomy in regulating their affairs, but remained corporations of public law, received state support through the tax system, and were guaranteed the continuation of religious education in public schools. The significance of these controversies for the future included the suspicion that the government was riddled with secular humanists and atheists, too easily associated with democracy.

The churches did little to stem raging nationalism. Before the war, pastors and theologians, enthralled by their throne-and-altar ideology, had actively fostered nationalism. Now they preached against the "war-guilt lie" and looked to a future divine vindication of the nation and the abolition of the dictates of Versailles. The new national, antidemocratic movement, a "conservative revolution," appealed greatly to the bourgeoisie and especially the youth, and was an influential current in the Weimar Republic (1919–1933). As National Socialism began its rule, it is understandable that critical perceptions of the danger of the new ideology were hardly possible.

The major theological resource against National Socialism was the movement initiated by the young Swiss theologian Karl Barth: "dialectical theology." Its continuing influence long after World War II certainly had not a little to do with its witness in the period of National Socialism.

The interwar years were in some respects not so difficult for the Catholic Church as they were for the Protestants. The end of the German monarchy left Catholicism undisturbed in its life under the pope. Furthermore, the Catholic Center Party—next to the Social Democrats, one of the essential supports of the new Weimar Republic—represented Catholic interests in opposition to the pretensions of Prussian Protestantism. Also, in the 1920s Catholicism experienced fruitful developments in monastic and liturgical renewal.

Rebuilding the European churches after World War II was closely connected with the most significant church historical event of the twentieth century: the ecumenical movement. It, too, had its roots in the nineteenth century through the cooperative work of the churches in the mission fields and in diaconal work. Although the Roman Catholic Church still does not belong to the World Council of Churches, nevertheless, the relationship between the Catholic Church and the Reformation churches improved markedly in the twentieth century.

New Formulations in Protestant Theology

In Germany, the idealistic enthusiasm at the beginning of World War I awakened hopes of religious renewal. But the churches, which had filled in the first year of the war, were soon empty again. The expectation that materialism and socialism would be overcome and that people—especially the worker class—would return to the churches was disappointed. The "de-Christianization" begun in the nineteenth century became "dechurchification" as the war promoted, rather than halted, alienation from the church. All too frequently after the war, pastors found themselves preaching to the choir of the conservative middle class and civil servants mourning the lost monarchy.

But some voices began to pose striking alternatives to the throne-and-altar theology of a rational, moral synthesis of Christianity and culture. Rudolf Otto's (1869–1937) *The Idea of the Holy* (1917; twenty-two editions by 1930) was the prelude to a renewed understanding of God. In it, God is seen not as the extension of humankind, but as the "totally other," whom persons encounter in the *"mysterium tremendum et fascinosum."*

That same year the Berlin church historian Karl Holl (1866–1926) gave his famous lecture, "What did Luther Understand by Religion?" Here the liberal images of Luther as hero and fighter for national liberty were displaced by a totally new view of the man. On the basis of rigorous historical work and systematic analysis, a picture of Luther's theology of the cross and of justification emerged that was clearly at odds with liberalism. Holl's research initiated the so-called Luther renaissance, which also had great significance for the development of dialectical theology and understanding of the whole of Reformation theology.

The most important new theological orientation after World War I was dialectical theology, itself closely tied to Karl Barth (1886–1968). One of Harnack's prize students, Barth became a pastor in 1911 in Safenwil, a worker community of his native Switzerland, as a prelude to his expected academic career. Trained by the best liberal theologians, Barth soon discovered that his education had not prepared him for ministry in the context of the problems of real life. Shocked both by the low wages paid to area workers and that his wealthy parishioners saw no conflict between exploitation and the Christian faith, Barth became radicalized personally, politically, and theologically. He became a social democrat—that is, a Marxist without Communism—and earned the nickname "the red pastor." Required to preach, he discovered the Bible to be a "strange new world," rather than the blueprint for liberalism's great society. The next great shock came with the outbreak of World War I, when he saw, to his horror, that many of his learned professors signed the "Declaration of German Intellectuals" in support of "emperor and fatherland." It was now clear to him that liberalism was politically, socially, ethically, and religiously bankrupt.

Together with his friend Eduard Thurneysen (1888–1974), who mediated the writings of the Russian Orthodox novelist Fyodor Dostoyevski (1821–1881) to him, Barth turned his back on liberal theology and sought answers to his questions in the Bible. From intensive wrestling with the Bible, in conjunction with preaching, Barth developed his commentary on *Romans* (1919), the second, reworked edition (1922) of which, it is said, "fell like a bombshell on the playground of the theologians." It was a complete break with liberal theology that rejected every form of religious anthropocentrism and experience. The Bible is the word of the transcendent God who reveals Himself in the death and resurrection of Christ; it is a word from outside and against the world. In this light, all religion, including Christianity, is a human enterprise under God's judgment. Here Barth echoed the eminent Dane Søren Kierkegaard (1813–1855), whose attack on both Hegel and bourgeois Christendom emphasized the "infinite qualitative difference" between God and humankind. It is not in the first instance the godless world, but the religious world, including Christianity, which is challenged by the Bible.

Barth and Thurneysen were soon joined by others: (1) the Swiss Reformed theologian Emil Brunner (1889–1966), who blamed Schleiermacher above all for the misery of theology; the German Lutheran theologians (2) Friedrich Gogarten (1887–1969), who came to similar insights through an intensive study of Luther, and (3) Rudolf Bultmann, (1884–1976) who came to dialectical theology through historical research on the New Testament and the rediscovery of Reformation theology, especially Luther. The German Lutheran theologian Paul Tillich (1886–1965) shared some of their concerns, but was forced as a Religious Socialist to leave Germany in 1933. Tillich became a major theological voice in America. The movement had numerous designations—"theology of crisis," "theology of paradox," "theology of the Word of God," and "Neo-Orthodoxy"—but finally went by "dialectical theology" as the shorthand for God's "no" to the world and sin that contained His "yes" of redemption. The movement effectively spread its message through its own theological journal, *Zwischen den Zeiten* (*Between the Times*), which lasted from 1923 to 1933, by which time the leading figures were going their own ways.

Barth himself moved on to a series of German professorships until he was deported for criticism of the Nazis. At Bonn, Barth informed his students that it would be bad taste to begin a lecture on the Sermon on the Mount with "Heil Hitler." More forceful criticisms of National Socialism brought Barth before a Nazi court on the charge of seducing the minds of German students. His defense was to read Socrates' defense before the court of Athens. The judges were not amused, and Barth was expelled. He then took a professorship at Basel.

The Churches during National Socialism

In January 1933, Adolf Hitler, and with him the National Socialist Party, seized power in Germany. The party program had asserted its support for "positive Christianity," by which it meant, of course, the churches in service to the state. But few at the time had any sense of Hitler's intention to destroy the churches and to replace the Christian faith with his own brand of brutal paganism. In fact, during the twelve years of National Socialist rule, only the first steps were carried out, mainly co-option by state supervision and de-confessionalization. In spite of being persecuted, the churches never lost their legal standing; the final solution for the churches was left to be completed after the conclusion of the war.

Nazi inroads into the churches were facilitated both by the false sense of security on the part of the churches toward Nazi intentions and by the enthusiastic reception of Hitler not only by many church members, but also by many pastors. Before Hitler seized power, the Catholic bishops had warned their members of the dangers of National Socialism and forbidden Catholics from joining the party. The bishops' response to the new situation was, however, muted. As many Catholics as Protestants were attracted to the new authoritarian regime, its rapid social accomplishments, and its suppression of communism. By the end of March 1933, the conference of German bishops declared that their earlier warnings were invalid. By the next July, Hitler had removed any potential problems with Catholicism by negotiating a concordat with the Vatican. In return for the Church's giving up all German Catholic political and social organizations, the regime promised to protect Catholic schools, institutions, and clergy. Hitler, who never signed a treaty he wasn't willing to break, gained international respect, while forcing German Catholics, especially the Center Party that had supported the Weimar Republic, out of politics. Soon, however, Nazi restrictions of the Catholic press, schools, and youth organizations created conflicts that were intensified by Catholic condemnations of the paganism and totalitarian claims of National Socialism. Finally, in 1937, Pius XI's encyclical, *Mit brennender Sorge* (With profound concern), strongly condemned National Socialism and was read from Catholic pulpits. Individual bishops and priests courageously opposed the Nazi programs to exterminate the Jews and all others deemed unworthy of life, such as the mentally and physically impaired. Numerous priests were imprisoned—over 260 in the concentration camp at Dachau alone.

The Protestant churches were vulnerable to National Socialist ideology because of the nationalistic and reactionary spirit so prevalent at the time. Clergy who had proclaimed divine blessing—"Gott mit uns"—on German militarism in World War I now revised their theology to interpret defeat as a divine tribulation calling Germans to reclaim their past heroic culture and glory. The problems of the present are due to evil, external foreign forces and atheistic, internal subversion. Already in the 1920s, voices were heard advocating the purification of Christianity of its Jewish heritage. The Old Testament was objectionable, Jesus was Nordic, and the New Testament was corrupted by the "rabbi St. Paul." Church authorities certainly refuted these groups, but they were also too frequently dismissed as just the lunatic fringe of society.

Racist Protestants found a warm welcome in the National Socialist Party. In the spring of 1932, the National Socialists advanced the "German Christian Faith Movement," which united Christianity and National Socialism, vigorously promulgated a nationalistic racism, including the removal of all Jewish influences, and regulated the church by the "Führer principle." The German Christians aroused an amazing response: People who had not darkened church doors in years now came out and darkened the church itself by electing German Christians to a third of the seats in the church government; by the summer of 1933, they were the majority.

Supported by the full Nazi apparatus of press and radio propaganda, the German Christians proceeded to Nazify the church. Using the Civil Service Law (April 7, 1933) that mandated the removal of all non-Aryan, that is, Jewish, officials from every level of government, the German Christians removed all clergy of Jewish descent and also all opponents of the Nazis.

It was the German Christians' effort to insert the non-Aryan paragraph into the constitution of the church that precipitated the *Kirchenkampf* (church struggle). Opposition to the German Christians within the church was spearheaded by the World War I submarine hero and Berlin pastor, Martin Niemöller (1892–1986). In November 1933, Niemöller founded the "Pastors' Emergency League," followed by "Councils of the Brethren," as alternative church authorities at all levels of the church wherever the official administration was ruled by the German Christians. These groups quickly established contacts with the opposition and gained support from outstanding members of the theological faculties, including the not-yet-expelled Barth and the younger theologian and pastor Dietrich Bonhoeffer (1906–1945), who was later executed for his participation in an abortive plot to assassinate Hitler. Many of these theologians and pastors were later disposed of by conscripting them into the war, where they lost their lives.

Already in 1933, some two thousand pastors supported the protest against the Aryan paragraph and the Nazi use of politics and force in the church. By January 1934, the "emergency league" included nearly half (some seven thousand) of all Protestant pastors, and in

May they formed the "Confessing Church," which issued the famous Barmen Declaration. In this document, Lutheran, Reformed, and Union Church theologians rejected any and all synthesis of Christian faith with National Socialism and proclaimed exclusive allegiance to the claims of biblical revelation. Over against the German Christians, the Barmen Declaration stated, "Jesus Christ, as he is testified to us in the Holy Scripture, is the one Word of God, whom we are called to hear, whom we are to trust and obey in life and in death. We reject the false teaching, as the church can and must, that there is any other source of its teaching outside and next to this Word of God, nor do we recognize any other events, powers, figures, and truths as God's revelation." This confession, the authors made clear, was severely threatened by the German Christians; if they were to succeed, the church would cease to be the church.

A leader in drafting the Barmen Declaration was Karl Barth, for whom Nazism was a pagan revival that liberal theology was incapable of resisting. The church, if it were to remain the church of Jesus Christ, had to make a clear choice between Christ and Hitler. Later, Barth regretted that he had not made solidarity with the Jews a decisive feature of his draft text of the Barmen Declaration.

The first to make it crystal clear that racism is a denial of the gospel was Dietrich Bonhoeffer. His essay "The Church and the Jewish Question" (1933) publicly stated that the Christian community is called "not just to bandage the victims under the wheel, but to put a spoke in the wheel itself. Such action would be direct political action."[1] It is of interest that a couple of years before this, Bonhoeffer had spent a year studying theology in New York City, and American racism had made a deep impression on him.

In spite of being persecuted, the clergy and laity of the Confessing Church continued to oppose the National Socialist regime, until the outbreak of the war in 1939 ended public resistance. During that period, conflicts within the Confessing Church over theological issues—above all, the question of what makes the church the church—led Bonhoeffer to declare in 1936 that "Whoever knowingly separates himself from the Confessing Church in Germany, separates himself from salvation."

The Confessing Church was also influential in Nazi-occupied countries such as the Netherlands, Norway, and France. As a European movement, the Confessing Church contributed to the nascent ecumenical movement that would blossom after the war. The Barmen Declaration remains a model statement on faith in areas of church–state confrontation and political oppression. It influenced the *Kairos* document (1985), a theological watershed of the churches' opposition to apartheid (racial segregation) in South Africa, and the world confessional bodies of the World Alliance of Reformed Churches (1982) and the Lutheran World Federation (1977) in their condemnations of apartheid. The latter's condemnation of apartheid as a *status confessionis* echoed Bonhoeffer's statement in 1938 that where the church is "subjected by outside force to a law which is alien to the church it may not yield, but must bear witness in word and deed to its freedom from the alien law and its sole obedience to Jesus Christ. *In statu confessionis nihil est adiaphoron* [When the integrity of the church is threatened, nothing is indifferent]."[2]

National Socialism forced the Confessing Church underground. Niemöller, impris-

---

[1] John De Gruchy, ed., *Dietrich Bonhoeffer: Witness to Jesus Christ* (London: Collins, 1988), p. 127.
[2] *Ibid.*, p. 24.

oned at the Dachau concentration camp from 1938 to 1945, and Bonhoeffer, imprisoned in 1943 and executed in 1945, were among countless others—clergy and laity, Protestant and Catholic—who paid dearly for confessing their faith. The Catholic situation has already been described. The Protestant Church, too, presents a conflicted picture. On the one hand, the church was the only opposition to National Socialism that was not quickly overcome, as were the political parties and unions. It was this opposition that helped the churches regain credibility and assist the reconstruction of German life after the war. On the other hand, with the notable exception of a few figures, such as Bonhoeffer, the church's opposition was all too often focused on its own concerns. In the face of the Nazi pogrom against the Jews, there were heroic actions by individual Christians, but there was no concerted public intervention, as there was in Holland and Denmark. Immediately after the war, the Council of the German Protestant Churches acknowledged this in the "Stuttgart Declaration of Guilt" (October 1945), presented to representatives of the Ecumenical Council of Churches: "Through us unending suffering has been brought to many countries and people. What we have said many times in our congregations, we now speak in the name of the entire church: We have indeed for many years fought in the name of Jesus Christ against the spirit which in the name of National Socialism found terrifying expression; but we indict ourselves that we did not more courageously confess, more faithfully pray, more joyously believe, and more passionately love."

Developments in the Catholic Church after World War I

World War I also meant a profound turning point for the Catholic church. But the situation as a whole in the Catholic church was quite different from that of German Protestantism, due to the papal direction of the world church and its opposition to modern liberalism.

The pontificate of Pius XI (1922–1939) was especially significant. He concluded many concordats, including that with Hitler in 1933. In 1929, the Lateran treaty ended the long conflict between the Curia and the Italian state and established the full sovereignty of the Vatican city. Among Pius XI's encyclicals were *Casti connubii* (1930), which condemned contraception and sought respect for married life, and *Quadragesimo Anno* (1931), which confirmed and elaborated the points of Leo XIII's *Rerum novarum*, stressing the evils of both free capitalism and strict socialism. Pius XI was also called the "pope of Catholic Action." He held that, through activation of the laity under clerical leadership, the entire social life should be filled with Catholic impulses. Catholic Action testified to a self-conscious, powerfully active Catholicism after the war.

The living piety of modern Catholicism came especially to expression in the biblical and liturgical movements. In 1933 the Catholic Bible Work was founded to promote understanding of the Bible. The goal of the Bible movement was also shared by the "*Una Sancta* Movement," which promoted understanding of other confessions and sought to soften the positions of the Counter-Reformation. The liturgical movement desired to move from modern subjectivism back to the treasures of the ancient church, including Gregorian chants and an emphasis on the communal character of the mass.

Pius XII (1939–1958), who dealt with National Socialism by means of traditional diplomacy, has been criticized for not publicly addressing the Nazi persecution of the Jews. He did continue his predecessors' condemnation of Communism and issued a blanket excommunication of members of Communist parties and organizations. His more liberal tendencies supported the liturgical movement and biblical studies. *Divino afflante spiritu* (1943) allowed more space for scientific biblical study and limited the normative character of the Vulgate to the liturgy. On the other hand, Pius XII once again condemned modernist theological movements, especially the "new theology" in France, in his *Humani generis* (1950). More noteworthy is the dogmatizing of the ascension of Mary that concluded the development of Marian dogma since 1854 and underscored the great significance of Mariology in modern Catholicism. The occasion also was the first use of the dogma of papal infallibility since Vatican I.

The most outstanding event in twentieth-century Catholicism is certainly the Second Vatican Council (1962–1965). The largest council in church history, it began under Pope John XXIII (1958–1963) and concluded under Paul VI (1963–1978). The significance of the council is expressed in the concept *"aggiornamento,"* meaning accepting and engaging the challenges of the present time in light of the Catholic faith.

The Council's most significant achievements included the restoration of the image of the church as "the people of God," as a community of faith, sacrifice, prayer, and love; renewal of the liturgy by the introduction of vernacular languages in worship and stronger participation of the congregation, including, in exceptional cases, allowing the cup to the laity; a strengthening of the office of bishop and the college of bishops so that, in communion with the pope, the bishops work together in leading the church; a presenting of the papal office as service rather than rulership; and the promotion of ecumenism and the desire for community with separated Christians.

The Ecumenical Movement

Well before the first Assembly of the World Council of Churches in Amsterdam in 1948, there had been proposals for an international Christian association of churches. These calls for ecumenical organization reflected the late nineteenth-century missionary activities and evangelical revivals in Europe and North America. In the 1890s, the Student Volunteer Movement for Foreign Missions issued an urgent call to "evangelize the world in this generation." The tensions and divisions of confessional identities transplanted from Europe and America to the mission fields had hampered such zeal and were therefore addressed at the World Missionary Conference in Edinburgh in 1910, and again, after the intervention of World War I, at the 1927 World Conference on Faith and Order at Lausanne.

Two years earlier, in 1925, the Universal Christian Conference on Life and Work in Stockholm had encouraged the churches to address social issues cooperatively. All the delegates had been appointed by their own churches, and there was a strong Orthodox presence at the conference. The central figure there, Nathan Söderblom (1866–1931), Archbishop of Stockholm and a historian of religions, was a pioneer in bringing Orthodox and Evangelical churches together. In 1930, he was awarded the Nobel Peace Prize for his initiatives for common Christian responsibility in international peace, freedom, and justice.

The Life and Work movement itself soon began to recognize that its slogan, "doc-

trine divides and service unites," could not gloss over theological differences on the meaning of the "kingdom of God." The growing tensions over this theological issue led to mutual decisions in 1937 to plan for a merger of Faith and Order and Life and Work. The
1938 conference in Utrecht planned for an inaugural assembly of the World Council of
Churches for August 1941. The outbreak of World War II delayed this assembly until
1948.

At Utrecht, Willem A. Visser 't Hooft (1900–1985) was invited to become general
secretary of the World Council of Churches "in process of formation," a post he held un-
til his retirement in 1966. Visser 't Hooft had his formative ecumenical experience in the
Student Christian Movement. After studying theology, he joined the Geneva staff of the
YMCA. It was in this capacity that he first became involved in ecumenics and then met the
ecumenically influential American Methodist layman John R. Mott (1865–1955). Visser 't
Hooft expressed his unwavering commitment to church unity in his observation that our
Lord did not pray "that they may all enter into conversation with one another; he prayed
that they all may be one." The ecumenical task is to return to the center of the church; the
ecumenical movement is Christocentric.

The first assembly of the World Council of Churches (WCC) was held in Amsterdam
in 1948. Its theme, "Man's Disorder and God's Design," reflected the disasters of World
War II and acknowledged that the recent horrors testified in part to the churches' failures.
The concern for international order reflected not only the recent past, but also the steadily
worsening relations between East and West; hence the famous exchange between the
American Presbyterian delegate John Foster Dulles, later U.S. Secretary of State, and the
Czech theologian Josef Hromadka.

Dulles described Communism as the greatest obstacle to world peace. Hromadka
pleaded for a sympathetic understanding of Communism as a force embodying much of the
social impetus that the church and Western civilization should have been representing. In
response to the sharp exchange, the assembly insisted that no civilization can escape the
radical judgment of the Word of God and explicitly rejected the assumption that capitalism
and Communism were the only choices available. Not surprisingly, the WCC was itself affected by the struggles of the Cold War.

The years following Amsterdam focused on responding to the vast human needs created by the war. Programs of interchurch aid, service to refugees and international affairs,
loan funds, and reconstruction were major expressions of ecumenical life and work.
Through the WCC, the churches would have to show, Visser 't Hooft stated, that their
coming together "made a real difference."

In the immediate postwar years, the WCC gave priority to social and economic problems in economically underdeveloped regions; appealed to governments to prohibit all
weapons of mass destruction and abstain from aggression; described segregation based on
race, color, or ethnic origin as "contrary to the gospel and incompatible with the Christian
doctrine of man and with the nature of the church of Christ," and urged churches to abol-
ish segregation and discrimination "within their own life and society." Yet, it is not surprising, given the large Western constituency of the WCC, that it was slow to grasp the urgency of the problems facing the so-called Third World and that, like the U.N., it was
divided over how fast and how far the decolonization process should go.

The years up to 1968, when the WCC held its fourth assembly, at Uppsala, Sweden, included a number of important ecumenical events. One of the most significant of these was the rapid development of relations with the Roman Catholic Church. Only weeks after the Third Assembly in New Delhi, Pope John XXIII announced that the Second Vatican Council (1962–1965) would meet the following year and invited the WCC to send observers to the sessions of the council. It soon became evident that this pope would facilitate far-reaching changes in the Roman Catholic attitude toward other churches. The 78-year-old pope expressed his intention that the council would be a means of spiritual and apostolic renewal, an updating of the church in modern times, and a service to the unity of the church. The pope emphasized the church's duty to work actively for "the full visible unity in truth" among all Christians in a "fullness of charity" that should extend also to non-Christians.

At the same time that the WCC was developing and growing, world communions of churches (the Lutheran World Federation, World Alliance of Reformed Churches, World Methodist Council, etc.) were, and today continue to be, involved in bilateral and multilateral dialogues among each other and with other churches, such as the Roman Catholic Church and Pentecostal churches.

This striving for the reunion of separated confessions is one of the most significant aspects of modern church history. Rooted in the period of Pietism, it extended into the nineteenth-century Awakening and provided impulses to transconfessional and supranational connections in social and missionary endeavors. The ecumenical movement's conferences in the twentieth century afforded many incentives to the rapprochement of the Christian churches and essentially changed the climate between the churches in comparison to that of earlier centuries. In the history of the twentieth-century church, ecumenism has a superior place.

Galileo Galilei (1564–1642), Italian scientist who was harassed by the Inquisition because of the theological implications of his heliocentric astronomy and corpuscular physics. (The Bettmann Archive)

A Chinese mandarin. In the wake of the missionary involvement in the Celestial Empire, Confucianism was much debated among Christian theologians and philosophers. (Bibliotheque Nationale, Paris)

秦絵

The Abbey of Melk, a masterpiece of Austrian baroque architecture built on a hill overlooking the Danube by Jakob Prandtauer between 1702 and 1714. (© Wim Swann)

Gottfried Wilhelm Leibniz (1646–1716), a German mathematician, philosopher, jurist, and polymath, who pioneered the ecumenical dialogue. (The Royal Society)

A London coffeehouse around 1700. A typical place where freethinkers gathered to debate new ideas. (By permission of the Trustees of the British Museum)

A page of William Blake's grand symbolical poem, *Jerusalem: The Emanation of the Giant Albion*, written and etched between 1802 and 1820. (The Pierpont Morgan Library)

Frederick the Great of Prussia, the enlightened despot and "king-philosopher," in the company of his mentor, the French philosopher Voltaire, in the garden of Sans Souci in Postdam in the early 1750s. (The Bettmann Archive)

Vladimir Ilyich Lenin (1870–1924), the prominent Bolshevik leader, speaking in public from a motorcar. (UPI/Bettmann Newsphotos)

The bishops' procession at the installation in 1934 of the primate of the German Evangelical Church, Ludwig Müller, a leader of the German Christians and a devotee of the Führer, Adolf Hitler. (National Archives)

Friedrich Nietzsche (1844–1900), a German classical scholar and eminent philosopher, who proposed a new human type, the "superman," in *So Spoke Zarathustra* (1883–1885). (The Bettmann Archive)

Count Leo Tolstoy (1828–1910), a Russian prose writer and utopian moral and religious thinker, photographed in 1908 at his ancestral birthplace, Yasnaya Polyana. (Library of Congress)

Part V
Christianity and Culture in America

J. William Frost

Chapter 27

The New England Way

On the fourth Thursday of November, Americans celebrate their origins in the festival of Thanksgiving. The Pilgrims, the story goes, humble folk seeking to practice their religion in peace, fled persecution from the Church of England, going first to Holland and then to New England, arriving in the midst of winter. After a time of starvation in which half the men and two-thirds of the women died, the next spring the Indian Squanto showed the colonists how to plant corn. After the first harvest, Chief Massasoit and his tribe of Massachusetts Indians joined the Pilgrims in a multiday thanksgiving to God in which the Indians furnished fowl and deer for the feast. The first Thanksgiving established themes echoing through American history: gratitude for a land of abundance, God's special protection for America, the religious character of the inhabitants, freedom to worship, godliness linked with outward prosperity, and the acceptance or tolerance of pluralism, as exemplified by the native Americans.

Historians are apt to find more significance in the foundation of Jamestown, Virginia, in 1607 or Massachusetts Bay Colony in 1630 and label Plymouth a backwater. Yet it is difficult for Americans to find worthwhile mythical lessons in Jamestown, which originated to find gold and achieved prosperity through tobacco and slaves. On the other hand, the dour Puritans of Massachusetts sought godliness, but their ruthlessness to Christian and Indian opponents seemingly makes them less praiseworthy.

Even that first celebration in Plymouth may not have been a true Thanksgiving. For Pilgrim men and women, God worked through natural events to bestow his blessings and judgments. The will of God determined physical events—a chastisement by drought, war,

387

sickness, or earthquake, or, alternatively, a blessing in the birth of a child, a bounteous harvest, or victory over enemies. So for bad events the Pilgrims observed days of fasting with a church service to bewail their sins and ask God's forgiveness, and for good events they held thanksgivings at which they also attended church service, followed by a feast. Our only account of the first Thanksgiving mentions an exercise of arms and a feast, with the Indian guests furnishing deer and fowl (turkeys are not discussed), but says nothing about any church service.[1] Thus, by accident of misinterpreted history, the Pilgrims' diplomatic initiative designed to foster good relations with Indian neighbors became a Thanksgiving.

On many other occasions, Pilgrims had fasting and thanksgiving days; such events were common throughout the colonial and revolutionary period, and Lincoln proclaimed Thanksgiving a national holiday after the Battle of Gettysburg during the Civil War. Fasting and thanksgiving days expressed early Americans' belief that repentance, prayer, and moral reformation would prompt the Almighty to renew his covenant with them. Modern Americans learned to love feasting on Thanksgiving as a family gathering for remembering God's benevolence, while omitting the church service and forgetting that the Pilgrims who saw God's hand in all events observed days of fasting to bewail their sins and promise better behavior. The Thanksgiving holy day mirrors contemporary Americans' attitudes toward all religions: Americans are respectful of them, but often ignorant of their precise history, pious without confining piety to the institutional church, and happy that "God shed His grace" on their land. The theme of these next fourteen chapters is how Americans evolved from the days of the Pilgrims to our current Thanksgiving in an ostensibly secular country where overt religiosity prevails. Like the Pilgrims, modern Americans consider themselves a religious people.

European Colonization

The Thanksgiving celebration correctly stresses the importance of Christianity in the colonization of the New World. Europeans viewed the North American continent through a haze of concepts derived from the Renaissance. The Indians (misnamed in 1492 by Columbus, who thought he had arrived in India) appeared to Europeans either as Adam's offspring, perfect humans existing in a state of Edenic bliss, or as devil worshipers whose native customs should be extirpated. Ignoring immense differences in culture in the inhabitants of North America, Europeans linked all the aborigines together as "Indians," denied their right to the soil, and sought to trade with and convert them to whatever brand of Christianity the colonizers espoused. Christianity provided a rationale for settlement and conquest. Explorers planted the flag and took possession of the land for their Christian monarchs. Theologians had long declared that pagans who had a form of government had just title to lands. So after initial conquests were made, Spanish Catholic theologians rationalized conquests as necessary to protect traders and the right of trade or occupation of vacant lands. They also proclaimed the need to spread the blessings of Christianity and

---

[1] *A Relation . . . of the English Plantation setled at New Plimoth* (London: John Bellamie, 1622), pp. 60–61.

civilization to benighted peoples. Catholic religious orders took seriously their obligations to convert the Indians, and priests who came to the New World provided scathing critiques of the conquistadors' policies. Neither priests nor governor nor settlers approached the New World with appreciation for the cultures of the Indians in North, South, or Central America. The Catholic cathedral in Mexico City built upon the ruins of an Aztec holy site proved European domination over native religion, but unintentionally also symbolized the survival of Aztec religious beliefs with an overlay of Spanish Catholicism.

In order to forestall a conflict between Portugal and Spain over who owned what parts of the New World, in 1493 the pope drew a line of demarcation dividing the New World between the two countries. One result was that Portugal acquired Brazil and Spain acquired the rest of Central and South America. Other European countries claimed that discovery, settlements, and military strength granted title. So for centuries, wars among France, England, Holland, Sweden, and Spain turned out to be the final arbiter of who got what and which form of Christian religion prevailed. Spain defeated all interlopers into her empire from Florida southward, although later, France and Britain acquired islands in the West Indies. Holland defeated Sweden for the settlement on the Delaware River Valley; England defeated Holland and took New York; and eventually England drove out France from Quebec and Louisiana, only to be expelled by the American settlers who, through purchase, occupation, and war, extended their borders from "sea to shining sea." In general, in spite of the idealism and heroism of Christian missionaries, except as human material to be exploited, converted, defeated, and dispossessed, the Indian population did not count. America was created and sustained by those believing in a war God who granted success in battle to His chosen people. The belief that God was on their side fostered Europeans' ethnocentrism, assuaged qualms over their tactics, and gave Christians the confidence to dominate the New World.

Roman Catholics founded the first churches in the New World. In 1492, King Ferdinand and Queen Isabella of Spain expelled from the country all Muslims and Jews who would not convert to Catholicism, and later Spanish kings allowed no religious dissidents in their American dominions. France insisted upon the religious orthodoxy of the settlers in Canada. As in both mother countries, the church became a prop for the colonial governments, which provided military security and financial support for clergy. Religious orders sent priests to baptize Indians, build churches, and keep the settlers in the faith. Christianity seemed so essential an ingredient to civilization, that colonists feared that to lose their religion would be to revert to barbarism. Particularly in Mexico, the Catholic Church proved spectacularly successful in winning over the native population and creating new forms of piety merging traditional and Christian religious practices. Before 1600, Mexico had a university, a magnificent baroque cathedral, and a patron saint, the Virgin of Guadaloupe. Spanish Catholic friars expanded the empire by building mission stations as far north as New Mexico and California. And while initially, nineteenth-century American conquerors disdained Mexican Catholicism, in recent times the surviving mission buildings have reminded Anglos and Mexican-Americans of the Spanish Catholic influence in the American West. In time, the recent influx of migrants from Latin America will change the shape of an American Catholic Church that has evolved with little direct Spanish or Hispanic influence.

New France

Samuel Champlain's creation of Quebec in 1608 effectively initiated French colonization of the New World. The strongly Roman Catholic character of Quebec began with the first bishop, François Laval, who founded a seminary, attempted to stop sales of brandy to Indians, and became more powerful than some governors. Seeing Spanish successes, French priests sought to convert the native Americans. However, the French encountered tribes that did not live in cities, had not been subjected to Aztec overlords, and were not demoralized by conquest. In spite of heroic efforts of Jesuits who lived with the Indians while seeking to baptize them, there were no mass conversions.

French priests, the most famous of whom was Father Jacques Marquette (1637–1675), founded missions in the Midwest and explored the upper Mississippi River. Unlike English missionaries, the French did not seek to revolutionize native American life, and fur traders often adopted Indian customs. French settlements in North America spread from the St. Lawrence to New Orleans, but the total white population in 1763 was only 55,000. So the French, more interested in trade than farming, did not threaten native American lands and fought fewer major Indian wars. Instead, the French used Indian allies as a way of countering British colonial power. The close alliance between the French state and the Catholic church, together with the suspicion that Jesuit missionaries influenced Indians living in what is now northern New England to raid English settlements in Massachusetts and Connecticut, contributed to a Puritan heritage of anti-Catholicism.

The English settlers of Virginia and New England feared the French and Spanish colonies to their north and south and envied Catholic successes with the Indians. The seal of the Massachusetts Bay Company showed an Indian giving the Macedonian cry of "Come over to help us." Yet the Puritans also saw the hand of God in the diseases that had decimated the Indians and made the lands supposedly vacant and available to the colonists obeying God's command in Genesis to "be fruitful and multiply." Coming to the New World would allow English settlers to improve their outward estates, strengthen the Protestant religion, convert Indians, and counter French and Spanish power. They did not divide their reasons into religious and secular, believing that God used many kinds of means to accomplish His purposes. Not just the Puritans of New England, but many of the English who came to America in the seventeenth century, saw the New World as a promised land, a new Canaan, and also a wilderness inhabited by devil worshipers. They saw themselves as a new Israel, with the opportunity to create a holy land or a Sodom and Gomorrah. The responsibility of church and government was to guarantee that godliness prevailed.

Origins of Puritanism

Virginia has chronological priority in the story of English settlements in North America, but New England Puritans were more important for shaping the beginnings of U.S. Christian history. Puritanism began as a movement during the reign of Elizabeth I (1533–1603) to reform and to purify the Church of England from within.

During war with Spain, which began in 1588 with the defeat of the Spanish Armada,

English patriotism reinforced Protestantism and anti-Catholicism. To clergy who had become Calvinist, the Church of England needed purification—a purging of Catholic remnants and a tightening of discipline over the unregenerate. Those who sought these changes, labeled "Puritans" by their opponents, encountered royal opposition and turned to Parliament. The Puritans remained certain that the scriptures spelled out all necessary rules for faith and practice. They remained loyal to Elizabeth and hoped that her successor, James I, at the time King of Scotland and raised by Presbyterians, would bring the needed changes. In 1603, the Puritans presented their list of reforms to the new king. James granted their wish for a new translation of the Bible (now termed the Authorized or King James version), but refused their demand for changes in worship and church government. Seeing the Puritans as a potential threat to royal power, James linked his authority with the existing order in the established church and announced, "No bishop, no king."[2]

The Puritans remained as a persistent opposition group centered in Parliament through the reigns of James I and Charles I (1625–1649). One faction that gave up hope of reform from within the Church of England separated, formed its own church, and moved to Holland. In 1620, a minority of this separated congregational church left for the New World; we call them the Pilgrims. In 1630, a larger group including magistrates, ministers, and merchants, tired of enduring the persecution of the king and his bishops, and despairing of hope because of Charles's determination to rule without the aid of Parliament, gained control of the Massachusetts Bay Trading Company and used its charter as the basis for creating a virtually self-governing colony around Salem and Boston.

In the New World they found opportunity to re-create what they saw as the primitive church free from the restraints of king and church hierarchy—a church of visible saints—men and women prepared to give a public declaration of the workings of God in their lives. Puritans devoted extraordinary attention to understanding the order of conversion. They believed that all humans were born sinners, but God elected some for salvation. Through the mercy of God, some persons who prayed, read the scriptures, and attended church would experience conviction of sin, sense the promises of God, and feel the mercies of grace, which would be followed by a growth in goodness. Only those who could confess before the congregation that they had undergone conversion and whose lives showed the fruit of God's grace should be church members, i.e., visible saints.

Like other Calvinists, the Puritans insisted that sanctification could never be complete on earth, because humans remained products of original sin. Still, if the process of conversion did not lead to godliness, this showed that the person had never truly experienced grace. So a Puritan's life was filled with self-examination, seeking assurance by examining his or her inner life and external circumstances for evidence of the providence of God. In this scrutiny, the Puritan could count on help from church and neighbors. The geographic pattern of New England towns, with the central square and the church and houses close together, provided an opportunity for communal watchfulness. The New England town contained the Visible Saints, church members who could take communion and whose children could be baptized. But there were also the unregenerate, people who had not yet experienced, and perhaps never would experience, grace. They were still required to attend

---

[2] Quoted in Horton Davies, *Worship and Theology in England . . . 1603–1690* (Princeton, NJ: Princeton University Press, 1975), p. 331.

church in hopes of their conversion. Because in this life even the saints were prone to sin, Puritans insisted on rigorous enforcement of the community's standards on wrongdoers. The magistrate was a member of the church who had the responsibility of controlling sin through legislation. So the government would pass laws to enforce the morality required by the Bible and natural law, as summarized in the Ten Commandments. Allowing only male church members with some property to vote in colony elections ensured that good men would rule.

In England, Puritan ministers stressed God's entering into a covenant with his people. He promised salvation in a covenant of grace given by sending His Son to die on a cross. Without downplaying the Calvinist emphasis on predestination, covenant theology allowed ministers to stress the mercies of God and the necessity of conversion. Covenantal theology provided a metaphor to structure New England. As prospective settlers prepared to sail from England, Governor John Winthrop of Massachusetts Bay colony informed them that, by the act of migrating to New England, they had entered into a covenant to do God's will. Conversion established a covenant of grace; church members entered into a covenant when they formed a church, called a minister, or married. To accept a covenant required a person's free consent; God set the terms, but the Puritan commonwealth rested upon uncoerced adherence. Puritans examined outward events to see how their community fared with God; religious diaries or journals, as well as fasting and thanksgiving days, were by-products of the Puritan concern that the group must keep the terms of God's covenant.

The covenant placed upon authorities the responsibility of fostering truth and eradicating error. The Puritans came to New England for the freedom to follow God's will, not to tolerate error. They believed that the Bible, rightly interpreted by learned and pious ministers, provided exact guidance on fundamentals of church order and daily living. A religious toleration that allowed for diversity in faith or treated truth and error as of equal value was the devil's religion. All inhabitants had to accept the truth of the New England way.

Threats

Unfortunately for the New Englanders' peace of mind, Puritanism in old England had developed contrasting tendencies, which showed up in Massachusetts Bay. Not everybody came to the same conclusions about what the Bible required, and not everybody experienced the grace of God in the same way. Roger Williams (1603?–1683), a well-educated minister who immigrated in 1632, questioned the fundamentals of the New England way. He wanted to know upon what basis King Charles had given to the newcomers lands belonging to native Americans. Williams wanted the Puritans to repudiate the charter upon which they based their self-governance. He thought the Puritans should imitate the Plymouth Pilgrims and separate from the Church of England, an act that also might jeopardize the survival of the colony. The magistrates in New England sought to silence Williams; when he refused, they decided to send him back to England. Instead, in the middle of the winter, Williams fled and bought land from the Narragansett Indians to found Providence, Rhode Island. After he had been exiled from Massachusetts, Williams advocated complete religious freedom, denying that the Puritans had a monopoly on religious truth and suggesting that the realm of religion should be separate from that of the state, although the magistrates remained responsible for moral order; but no one should be required to attend church. In essence, Williams was a Puritan searcher after truth, becoming a Baptist for a short while and ending as a seeker.

Anne Hutchinson (1591–1643) also posed problems for New England's religious and political authorities. A very intelligent woman, Hutchinson began holding private meetings in her home to analyze sermons. She came to the conclusion that most ministers of New England preached a "works righteousness"; that is, in stressing the responsibility of the person to prepare for grace, they undercut God's free, unmerited grace. Her complaints about Puritan order of conversion potentially threatened New England's conception of how one became a Visible Saint. In 1637, first a civil and then a church court tried Hutchinson for heresy. At first she held her own, but made the mistake of claiming a direct inspiration from God. The authorities condemned Hutchinson as an antinomian—that is, a person whose false claim of a personal experience of God led her to dispense with minister, scripture, and morality. Accordingly, they exiled her from the colony. She fled in 1638 to Portsmouth, Rhode Island, where many of her supporters joined her.

Hutchinson attracted as supporters merchants who chafed under the authoritarian control of economic regulations and also men and women who hungered for a kind of ecstatic certainty in religious experience that the rigidity of Puritan theology seemingly undercut.

The third crisis involved the Pequots, a powerful tribe of native Americans dwelling in what is now northeastern Connecticut. The Puritans can be viewed as an interloping tribe engaging in power politics with other tribes, none of whom knew much about their neighbors. But there was a crucial difference between the Puritans and Indians: the New Englanders thought they had a divine mandate to control the destiny of all peoples in the area. Responding to a heavy-handed military expedition by the Massachusetts Bay Colony aimed at disciplining Pequot Indians for acts that were probably done by members of other tribes, the Pequots in 1637 attacked the dwellers in newly settled Connecticut. In answer to this attack, the Puritans allied themselves with the Mohicans, traditional enemies of the Pequots, who took the army of the Puritans to the main Pequot town, a brush-enclosed fort. When the initial surprise attack stalled, the Puritans set fire to the brush, giving the Indians, including women and children, the choice of being shot, captured, or burned alive. The "stink and scent" of burning flesh, wrote Plymouth governor William Bradford, using biblical metaphors from Leviticus, were horrible; but the victory seemed a "sweet sacrifice."[3] The Puritans disdained the fighting tactics of their Indians allies, who contented themselves with shooting a few arrows rather than striving for total victory. Instead, New Englanders molded themselves on the ancient Hebrews, whose God told them to annihilate the Amalekites, and sold Indian captives into slavery. The Pequots disappeared as a threat.

King Charles's threat to revoke the charter posed a final challenge. This threat ended with the outbreak of civil war in England in 1639, resulting in an overthrowing of monarchy and bishops and the ascendancy of English Puritans under Oliver Cromwell. Now the Church of England would be reformed, although the New Englanders were appalled at the

---

[3] William Bradford, *Of Plymouth Plantation 1620–1647* (New York: Random House, 1961), p. 296.

proliferation of religious sects and the toleration that accompanied the civil war. In essence, the war meant that for thirty years after its founding, New England would remain self-governing.

Evolution or Decline

By the 1640s, New Englanders could look over the accomplishments of their founding decade with a sense of pride. They had established colonies in Plymouth, Connecticut, New Haven, and Massachusetts, erected a church of Visible Saints, and defeated internal and external enemies. Where once had been a "howling wilderness," now there was a series of villages and farms. Each town had an unornamented meeting house and an educated minister chosen by the congregation. The law required attendance at church, although surviving meeting houses show that not everybody could fit in at one time. From sundown Saturday until sundown Sunday, Puritans observed the Sabbath, attending two church services and refraining from travel, cooking, leisure, and work. Ministers in election sermons, preached before the convening of the legislature, instructed the lawmakers on what God required of a covenanted community.

New England's triumphant orthodoxy soon encountered serious problems, however. Historians debate as to whether Puritanism evolved through new issues arising out of their successes in the new-world setting or declined because of a lack of fervor. What is certain is that the New England way changed, and many Puritans saw the change as bad. They contrasted the heroism of the first generation with the failures of their sons and daughters. One issue was crucial: The church must be composed of Visible Saints. What would happen if the children of saints did not make an open testimony to the work of God in their lives?

During the first generation, most families had at least one person who was a member of the church, who gave a public declaration of God's work in his or her life. During the 1630s, the excitement of building a new Zion in America brought a steady supply of converts into the church. But success in New England and perhaps a lack of persecution did not foster an atmosphere for the children of saints to feel confident that they had experienced grace. No one was willing to change the requirement for church membership, but it would not do for the churches to be filled with the unregenerate either. In 1648 the problem was apparent, but the ministers who came together in the Cambridge Synod to codify a pattern blending ministerial cooperation with a congregational pattern of church government did not confront the issue. In 1662 they did, however, and the resulting solution has been labeled "the halfway covenant" by historians, because the synod allowed the baptism of children whose parents had also been baptized but never became full church members. The "halfway covenant" preserved the importance of the Lord's Supper as a seal of grace rather than a means to conversion: The unconverted still could not partake of the bread and wine. Yet the "halfway covenant" also preserved the European sense of the territorial parish in which baptism incorporated children into the community. The "halfway covenant" can be interpreted as a sign of decline; after all, fewer people claimed to be regenerate. Yet it can also be seen as a sign of the strength of Puritanism: The laity resisted the new practice because they believed in the old way and wanted to avoid debasement of the church.

The Family

Disunity in the churches was only one sign of changes in the holy commonwealth. The Puritans' attempt to bring all of life under a godly discipline depended upon the family. The Puritans wanted an orderly society in which the lower orders paid deference to their superiors. Catechisms told children that "Honor thy father" included all authority: parents, ministers, and magistrates, for example. The family was a little commonwealth in which the father, in theory at least, ruled by example rather than harshness and exemplified the love of God with kindness and severity. Children learned a loving obedience. Fathers called the family, including servants and slaves, together for prayers and Bible reading on a daily basis.

Early New England probably held a larger percentage of university graduates than any country in Europe, and indeed, the Massachusetts Bay Colony founded Harvard College in 1636. Beginning in 1642, the colony created a tax-supported primary school system and required large towns to create grammar or Latin schools. Children needed to learn to read the Bible and also to memorize catechisms to understand their basic beliefs. The result of the emphasis on education was that in New England before 1700, unlike the situation in most of Europe and the southern United States, most men and women became literate. Schooling enforced the religious and deferential cast of Puritan society, but it also allowed access to new ideas.

Later generations pictured the Puritans as killjoys: In H. L. Mencken's phrase, there was always "the haunting fear that someone, somewhere, may be happy."[4] This is a false image, however. Sex outside of marriage was a sin, but sex within marriage was not, and the Puritan reputation for prudery is overstated. Adultery was harshly punished, but penalties were lessened if the couple intended to marry. The Puritans enjoyed life, but insisted that all earthly pleasures, including love of children and of husband and wife, remain subordinate to the desire for God. Young women and men married not for romantic love, lust, or money (these were unworthy motives), but from compatibility of temper, equality in station, and religious inclinations; subsequently, they learned to love each other as husband and wife. New Englanders viewed the wedding ceremony as a civil event, performed by magistrates and not ministers, and went beyond English law in allowing divorce for adultery, lack of physical consummation of the marriage, cruelty, and nonsupport. The family remained a focus of the colony, with husband and wife as helpmates with clearly defined roles in the household and in business.

The Puritans hoped to create an orderly society in which all people knew their place in the hierarchy, yet those who migrated to America wanted to improve their economic standing. Merchants living in Boston profited from their control of imported goods, and they chafed under the rules from ministers and magistrates who wanted products sold at a just price that was fair to all, rather than according to supply and demand. New England soil was stony and required much work to prepare for farming. The resulting shortage of labor meant that wages for workers rose, and the authorities complained about common people attempting to rise above their station. The abundance of land created opportunities

---

[4]H. L. Mencken, "Sententiae," in *Chrestomath* (New York: Knopf, 1949), p. 624.

for speculation and also for migration. Roger Williams complained that land became the God of New Englanders. The dispersal of settlers created conflicts between absentee owners and town residents and stresses upon the New England ideal of a closely knit community. Ministers decried the increasing emphasis upon individual self-seeking at the expense of the community.

The restoration of Charles II in 1660 brought the discrediting of Puritanism in England and the influence of a more worldly pattern of living. Charles II disliked the religious and parliamentary zeal that led to the execution of his father. The king wished to exert royal control over all colonies in America. The virtually independent existence of the Puritan colonies that allowed no freedom of worship to members of the Church of England also irritated the restored bishops. The experience of defeat affected the morale of Puritans on both sides of the ocean. Ironically, the first direct imposition of royal authority came over a group that both Puritans and Anglicans despised: the Quakers.

The Quaker Threat

The Friends, or Quakers, one of many enthusiastic religious groups including Ranters, Familists, and Muggletonians that arose during the turmoil of the Puritan revolution in England in the 1650s, insisted upon the primacy of direct, inward revelation of God. Quakers claimed that their unmediated experience of an inward Christ showed that those who had not experienced the Light (i.e., all non-Quakers) destroyed true religion. Quakers denounced an educated clergy supported by tithes as "hireling ministers" responsible for the spiritual and moral decay of England. They repudiated sacraments, hymns, and established prayers, allowed women to preach, write, and travel as ministers, and upheld strict moral standards. True worship took place in a silent meeting with no liturgy, in which men and women waited for the Lord to give them words to speak. Proclaiming that the spiritual return of the inward Christ was a sign of the approaching millennium, women and men Friends relished confrontation and vigorously proselytized. New Englanders learned of the existence of this group of "enthusiasts" from appalled Puritans in England and were determined to give the Quakers no chance to contaminate colonists.

In 1655, when two Quaker women arrived at Boston on a ship, the magistrates refused to allow them to disembark. Others who came were whipped and fined, and their books were burned. Still, Quaker traveling ministers kept coming, interrupting church services, and denouncing the New England way. To the consternation of the authorities, the Quakers converted a few people in Salem and more in the area of Plymouth. The followers of Anne Hutchinson in Rhode Island flocked to the new sect, and the magistrates in Rhode Island refused to prosecute Friends, suggesting that toleration was better policy than harshness. Prison sentences, whippings, cropping of ears, and branding seemed only to attract more Quakers. Finally, in desperation, in 1658 the Massachusetts General Court decreed that, for repeated visits, Quakers could be executed. Three Quaker men and one woman responded to the threat by returning to Boston. The court sentenced them to execution. After watching the three men hanged, the woman, Mary Dyer, a former inhabitant of Boston and follower of Anne Hutchinson, with the hood over her head and the rope on her neck, was reprieved and told not to come back. She returned and was executed. But

Massachusetts Bay had denied all appeals to King Charles II. When English Quakers brought this news to Charles, he issued a desist order, which the Bay Colony obeyed. Neither English nor Puritan authorities stopped persecuting Friends, but there were no more executions.

When Charles attempted to investigate conditions in North America and sent royal commissioners in 1663, Massachusetts Bay decided not to cooperate. A moderate party composed of merchants questioned the wisdom of this decision. These merchants, taking their cultural cues from England, challenged the strictness of the colony's behavior patterns. Rural clergymen encountered recalcitrant parishioners unwilling to pay the taxes required for the ministers' salaries. Puritan ministers created a literary form, the jeremiah sermon, in which they listed the sins of the people, recounted the chastisements of God, and listed reforms necessary to gain God's blessings. Frequent jeremiads reinforced the belief that something had gone wrong that led to the colony's straying from the founders' piety.

Time of Troubles: Indians and Witches

The late seventeenth century was a difficult time for the New England Puritans. In 1677–1679, King Phillip's War, provoked by English encroachment on Indian lands, cost the Bay Colony about 16 percent of male inhabitants of military age and led to the destruction of twelve towns and damage to one-half of the villages. In 1684, English courts revoked the charter of Massachusetts, and the new king, the Roman Catholic James II, created a Dominion of New England encompassing all the Puritan colonies and New York under the royal governor, Sir Edmund Andros. Andros attempted to levy taxes, limited town meetings, threatened land titles, jeopardized the independence of Harvard College, founded a Church of England congregation in Boston, and brought religious toleration.

When England staged the so-called Glorious Revolution in 1688 against James, Massachusetts used the pretext to overthrow Andros, claimed to be supporting the Protestant King William and Queen Mary, and obtained a new charter. The new charter used a property rather than a religious qualification for voting. New England churches remained established by law, but dissenters gained legal rights. Massachusetts was now a royal colony—a province in the British empire—rather than a holy commonwealth. Still, Puritan ministers insisted that defeat of the Indians, the overthrow of James II and Andros, and a new charter showed that God had preserved His covenant with New England.

Witchcraft

In 1692 in Salem village, seven young women began acting strangely, having fits. Medical doctors and ministers agreed that witches were tormenting the girls. The Bible declared that witches should not be allowed to live, but provided no means to decide who was a witch. New Englanders had long been concerned with witches, had investigated a few suspects, and had either brought them to self-condemnation through prayer, dismissed the charge, or tried, condemned, and executed them.

The Puritans believed that the devil had ruled New England before they arrived and now wanted to undermine the church and society. They had looked for special providence from God; now they found similar evil works of the devil, who tempted people to covenant with him to do his bidding. The devil gave to each witch a specter or imp to do her or his bidding; these specters tormented the girls, causing their strange behavior. Only the girls could see the specters and identify who controlled them. In court, and against the advice of the ministers, the judges decided that no one who was innocent would appear as a specter. So all the girls had to do was to name who was tormenting them, and those women and men would be presumed guilty.

Neighbors provided a second kind of evidence. Once a person had been accused, people recalled all sorts of omens, curses, black magic, and supernatural occurrences done by the alleged witches. Virtually anything bad that seemingly was beyond human control had been caused by witches: Children fell ill, cows died, wild beasts appeared, and prosperity came to some and misfortune to others. Searches of accused witches' homes found dolls, allegedly to torment victims. The testimony at Salem shows that, beneath the stark divide between God and the world, in the Puritan Calvinist world view lay a residue of folk beliefs about white and black magic, healing of disease, sorcery, astrology, and alchemy. God and the devil acted in daily life. Historians have used the evidence at Salem to argue that in early America, underneath the strict Reformed piety of the church lay a substratum of beliefs derived from medieval Europe.[5]

At Salem, virtually all the afflicted and the accused were female. Women who were accused were often independent, wealthy widows or those who had violated community norms by insisting on their economic rights or by quarreling with neighbors. Midwives or those who did healing were also vulnerable. Some alleged witches were church members; others defied Puritan sexual ethics. Fifty-five of those who were accused confessed, often implicating others in their testimony. Twenty who refused to confess were executed. The girls continued to cry out against more people, until eventually the governor stepped in and dismissed the court. When it reconvened, spectral evidence was no longer admissible, and no one else was convicted.

The witchcraft episode provides a revealing glimpse into the Puritan mind in the 1690s. The themes enunciated sixty years before still resonated: covenant theology, the importance of a public declaration and confession (before the court, and not the Church this time), the special promise and peril of New England, and God's and the devil's direct intervention in history. Salem witchcraft was the last instance in Massachusetts in which the governor solicited the opinion of the clergy. In 1697, concerned about several unfavorable "strokes of God," including the deaths of two children, Samuel Sewell, one of the judges of the Salem court, stood in church to ask God's forgiveness for his actions in the witchcraft trials. Providential history still remained supreme.

Early eighteenth-century New England was a divided society. Rhode Island remained different, appearing to the Puritans as either "Rogues' Island" or the "cesspool" of New England. There, Baptists and Quakers, who dominated numerically, existed alongside Jews, Anglicans, Congregationalists, and Familists. Churches existed without tax support or co-

---

[5] See Richard Weisman, *Witchcraft, Magic, and Religion in Seventeenth-Century Massachusetts* (Amherst, MA: University of Massachusetts Press, 1984); and Richard Godbeer, *The Devil's Dominion: Magic and Religion in Early New England* (New York: Cambridge University Press, 1992).

ercion, and society did not collapse. Fortunately, said the Puritans, Rhode Island remained small and isolated and would never serve as a pattern for an emergent America.

In the Puritan colonies of Connecticut, Massachusetts (including Maine), and New Hampshire (Plymouth and New Haven were no longer independent), the Congregational church remained established, and there were scattered Quaker, Baptist, and Anglican congregations. Harvard and the recently established Yale (created in 1701 because Harvard appeared too moderate) supplied an educated ministry. Clergy and magistrate together enforced a strict moral code and worried over what they perceived as growing disrespect for authority and obsession with gaining wealth. In Boston, Cotton Mather (1663–1728), the most important spokesman for third-generation Puritans, continued to exalt the founders, defend the "halfway covenant," investigate witches, and preach jeremiads to his congregations. At the same time, he showed his enthusiasm for the new learning of the Enlightenment by conducting scientific experiments and advocating inoculation for smallpox. Mather bewailed the decline of piety, but also exalted in the continuing religious fervor of the Puritans and gave thanks that God's providence had sustained New England.

Chapter 28

The Southern and Middle Colonies

The Church of England in the South

In 1607, a private trading company chartered by King James I founded Jamestown, Virginia, as an enterprise dedicated to gold, glory, and God. There was no gold, and the trading company never made a profit until it was dissolved in 1624. None of the early settlers made fortunes; few even survived. Glory, most of it posthumous, came only to John Smith, who attempted to make idle adventurers work, and to Pocahontas (1595?–1617), who as a child saved his life and, after being essentially kidnapped by the English, married John Rolfe, converted to Christianity, and died young. Trade with Indians brought little wealth, and soon the settlers spent more time attempting to dominate or kill the natives rather than convert them.

Unlike New Englanders, those who came to Virginia did not share a religious commitment, and there was no common purpose to create a close-knit community. Not religion, but the discovery of the profitability of growing tobacco shaped Virginia's history. Early Virginians engaged in the ruthless exploitation of laborers—other whites, Indians, and blacks—in an attempt to get rich from tobacco. No one confused Virginia with the biblical commonwealths of New England.

Still, the fortunes of the colony were linked with those of the Church of England. Zealous Protestants anxious to counter the influence of Catholic Spain in the New World dominated the Virginia Company, and a puritanical law code of 1612 required attendance at church services, outlawed swearing, and restricted labor on the Sabbath. For one-hundred-fifty years, the only legal form of worship in Virginia remained Anglican services conducted by ordained clergymen. Even so, the church faced a difficult situation caused by the nature of the colony. A plethora of navigable rivers flowing into the Chesapeake Bay allowed the population to disperse over a wide area in search of good land. Until late in the eighteenth century, the only city of any size in the entire South was Charleston, South Carolina, which grew because the planters attempted to flee the heat of summer by going to the shore. The rural nature of life in the South meant that parishioners had to journey a substantial distance to attend services, and the ministers and neighbors could not exercise the kind of oversight possible in a New England town. In 1724, the average parish included 550 square miles. Geography made the routine of church life difficult: visiting the sick, baptizing infants, and burying the dead. Virginia ministers read services from the Book of Common Prayer, celebrated communion infrequently, and rarely preached. The one advantage the church gained from geography was that many attended services as the best way of escaping isolation and meeting one's neighbors.

Early Virginia was not a family colony. Most of the settlers came as single men, often as indentured servants. In addition, Jamestown was located on a swampy peninsula, and the surrounding tidewater area was unhealthy. The heat, swamps, and diseases (including malaria) in Virginia resulted in the early deaths of the majority of immigrants. Not until the 1670s did native-born Virginians outnumber immigrants, most of whom came to make their fortunes and to return to England, and few of them had interest in schools or religion. Children born in early Maryland and Virginia often faced the death of one or both parents. The shortage of women and the frequency of widowhood allowed those who survived to have increased opportunities for marriage. It was said that no matter what her social station, in Virginia a woman's face was her fortune, but any improved status brought no public role in religion, nor did it result in improved educational opportunities. Throughout the colonial period there would be no tax-supported elementary or Latin schools in the South, although planters might hire tutors or send their sons to board with clergymen-teachers. Consequently, many males and most females remained illiterate. During church services prayers and creeds would be recited from memory, and the clergy announced important events and posted banns before marriage as the most effective method of communicating news.

The ratio of clergy to population in Massachusetts in 1650 was 1 to 415; in Virginia, it was 1 to 3,239.[1] There were few incentives for a clergyman to come to Virginia: The climate was bad, the pay low, and life onerous. In addition, clergymen had less power and security than in England, where a priest would be backed by a bishop and ecclesiastical courts and, once invested in a parish, had lifetime tenure. In Virginia, laymen—the governor and the assembly—fulfilled the supervisory role of bishop, and power gravitated to the socially prominent male laity who constituted the vestry. Virginia's vestries wanted annual contracts, for they wished to be able to replace a man they decided was a bad clergyman. The clergy could count on no support from higher authorities if the laity abused their power. Clergymen received most of their salaries in tobacco, which many grew on the glebe lands attached to every church. The clergy soon identified its welfare with that of the tobacco-growing planter class. In essence, the clergy became a subordinate part of the upper classes—a prop to the existing social and political order.

[1]Darrett Rutman, *American Puritanism* (New York: Norton, 1970), pp. 49–51.

Bishops in England at first neglected the church in Virginia and, during the early stages of the Puritan revolution, faced more pressing problems at home. The main political and religious issues of the Puritan Revolution did not directly affect Virginians, whose search for local autonomy continued under the monarchs and Cromwell, but who pledged fealty to whomever was in control. Because the clergy remained moderately Calvinist throughout the seventeenth century, Virginia escaped most of the religious turmoil that accompanied the Puritan Revolution and Restoration. There was no support for religious toleration, and the new religious sects were generally abhorred.

Maryland

Historians have termed Virginia and Maryland "sister colonies" in recognition of their similarities in tobacco growing, a plantation system, and slavery. Yet in the seventeenth century, their religious histories diverged. Virginia was founded and remained an outpost of anti-Catholicism. Maryland's proprietor, Cecil Calvert (1605–1675), the second Lord Baltimore, on the other hand, was a Catholic who sought to create a refuge for his coreligionists. Jesuit priests who accompanied the first settlers founded churches, and Roman Catholics became an influential minority in the colony, but there were always more Protestant colonists. In 1649, in an effort to secure religious harmony and preserve his colony from the hostility of Puritans, Lord Baltimore had the assembly pass a declaration of religious toleration, guaranteeing to all trinitarian groups the right to practice their religion in peace. Toleration failed, however: Pro-Puritan settlers opposed to proprietary power and Catholicism staged a successful revolution. The Calvert family lost control of the colony for twenty years.

The Restoration government of Charles II viewed proprietary government and Catholics favorably, and Cecil Calvert, who had become Protestant, regained control of Maryland. In the absence of Puritan and Anglican clergy to minister to a growing population, many of whom had come from Virginia, Quaker proselytizing efforts had considerable success. The Calverts relied upon political support from wealthy landowners, Roman Catholics, and Quakers to keep order. As in 1649, the success of the proprietary government depended upon the status of Stuart monarchs. The overthrow of the Catholic James II led to a revolution against the proprietary government and another takeover of the colony by Protestants. In 1704, convinced that Catholics and Quakers were dangers to the realm, the Maryland assembly established the Church of England, whose clergy were to be paid by tithe. There were only ten Anglican ministers in the colony at the time. Loyalty oaths barred Quakers and Catholics from threatening the control of the political supporters of the new Anglican establishment, and the assembly forbade public worship by Roman Catholics. Even when the Calverts regained the proprietorship in 1724, they made no effort to restore full religious liberty. In the eighteenth century dissenting Protestants had liberty to worship, and neither Catholics nor Quakers sought political power. In spite of legal prohibitions, Jesuit priests who placed titles to churches in their own names as private citizens continued to offer services. With adequate financing the Anglican Church grew slowly, while sectarians like the Friends declined. As in Virginia, the Maryland Church of England supported the power of the planter class.

Slavery

There was nothing inevitable about Virginians' commitment to slavery. Although the first shipments of slaves to Jamestown came before the *Mayflower* landed, as late as 1670 only 10% of the population was slave. By 1720, the figure was 40%. The emergence of a wealthy planter class emulating the English gentry system paralleled the growth of slavery, but at all times—even before the Civil War—a majority of Virginia planters owned no slaves. The search for great wealth by a small group of tobacco planters, who set the tone for political and religious life, resulted in large-scale importations of slaves.

Virginians unthinkingly accepted the existence of slavery. In the seventeenth century slavery was becoming rare in western Europe, but the major colonizing powers—Spain, Portugal, Holland, France, and England—engaged in the slave trade. How could these nations, all of whom created colonies in the service of God, rationalize the barbarities of the slave trade? The answer is that virtually no one had ever questioned its morality. Hebrews, Greeks, Romans, Christians, and Muslims held slaves. Historian David Brion Davis argues that, in its essential features of seeing a person as a commodity and in cruel treatment, slavery from first-century Rome to eighteenth-century Jamaica was everywhere the same.[2]

The new factor in seventeenth-century colonialism was linking slavery to a particular race. This resulted from the historical accident that Europeans began interacting with peoples from sub-Saharan Africa at the same moment that they began colonizing the New World. Europeans needed massive amounts of workers to exploit the New World. Like the Spanish, the Virginians at first sought to use native Americans, but they died out from disease, remained a potent military threat, and could easily escape into the forest. So the British began imitating the Spanish, even calling the people "Negro," after the Spanish word for black, and imported large numbers of black Africans for slavery.

Christianity contributed to the fusion of slavery and racism. In Genesis, as punishment for killing his brother, Cain was cursed and received a "mark." Noah, because Ham saw him drunk and naked, cursed his son: "A slave of slaves shall he be." Although neither of these passages mentioned race, exegetes since medieval times had applied the "mark" of Cain and the Hamitic curse to blacks. In addition, popular culture and literature identified the color black with the devil, sin, and sex—a linkage that continues in the terms "black magic" and "dirty joke." Although the Bible stated that all men were of one blood, the English created a mythology that Africans were evil, dirty, sexual, animal-like creatures destined for slavery. Southerners created special laws for controlling slaves and protecting masters, with an underlying rationale that would not change before 1860.

Virginians feared that baptizing a slave might make him or her a free person. So in 1667 the assembly declared that baptism did not require manumission, an interpretation later pronounced correct by the Church of England. In the eighteenth century Anglicans living in England provided the financial resources needed to support missionaries to Christianize slaves, and a few clergymen taught blacks how to read so that they could understand the catechism, but there were few converts. Slaveholders still resisted making blacks members of the church, because they feared the implications of even a spiritual equality. After all, the Bible denounced oppression and injustice and proclaimed that God loved the poor.

[2] See David B. Davis, *The Problem of Slavery in Western Culture* (Ithaca, NY: Cornell University Press, 1965).

In the 1670s in Bacon's Rebellion, and in the 1770s, Virginia's planters led rebellions against alleged tyranny in the name of freedom, but they remained terrified that their slaves might sometime revolt in a quest for their own freedom.

Anglican Resurgence

In the aftermath of the Glorious Revolution, the Church of England experienced a resurgence in the colonies and the motherland. Catholic France and Protestant England began a struggle for dominance that would end only in 1815. The Crown prepared for war by asserting more control over the American empire. Firmly wedded to anti-Catholicism, the government promoted a militant Church of England as an essential unifying ingredient in the battle against France. At the same time, churchmen and devout laity saw a need for moral reformation, a better educated and disciplined clergy, and a quickening of general piety. To counter weaknesses in organization of the Anglican Church in America, the Bishop of London launched two new organizations: the Society for the Propagation of the Gospel (SPG) and the Society for the Promotion of Christian Knowledge (SPCK). These missionary societies provided funds to support Anglican clergymen seeking to convert Indians, slaves, and the unchurched. The SPG became the primary vehicle for promoting the spread of the Church of England into the Middle Colonies and New England. The ideology of the SPG was militant high Anglican, viewing Congregationalists and Quakers as espousing false religion. When the SPG's missionaries settled in towns in Massachusetts rather than going out to preach to native Americans, the New Englanders concluded that the Anglicans sought to take over Harvard College and to end the Congregationalist establishment. More unsettling news came in 1724 when Yale's rector, two tutors, and four graduates in divinity became Anglicans. The Puritans had reason for their suspicions. In Maryland, North and South Carolina, and New York, efforts by royal officials aided by clergy and laity resulted in establishing the Church of England, even though dissenters always outnumbered Anglicans.

Apologists for strengthening the Church of England stressed the need for a resident bishop in the colonies. Bishops presided at the confirmation of members and invested all prospective clergy, so every candidate for ordination had to travel to London. A bishop in America would serve as a counterweight to vestry power while aiding and also supervising clergy. Parliament proved unwilling to pass the legislation to create an American bishop.

In Virginia, in the absence of a bishop, in 1693 James Blair (1655–1743) was appointed commissary, with responsibility to protect the church. That same year, he founded the College of William and Mary as a place to train Virginians in all the liberal arts, including theology. Blair's supervision improved the moral tone of the Virginia clergy and led to an increasing number of churches and the recruitment of American-born ministers, but he identified the church's interest with that of the planter class, which meant that there was no critique of slavery, only sporadic efforts to convert blacks, and little fervor. Before 1750, the Church of England in Virginia and Maryland, facing no serious opposition from dissenters, remained outwardly prosperous. Priests performed the liturgy, occasionally celebrated the Eucharist, preached rationalistic sermons stressing the ethical basis of Christian life, and enjoyed a comfortable lifestyle.

The Middle Colonies

Even in the eighteenth century, commentators did not know what to call the colonies north of Virginia and south of New England. Later, since they were in between the two geographical areas, they became known as the Middle Colonies: New York, New Jersey, Pennsylvania, and Delaware. There were two distinct regions, one along both sides of the Hudson River populated initially by the Dutch Reformed, and the other along the Delaware River settled by Quakers, with the dividing line in the middle of New Jersey. Although religious history is often written with a focus upon Virginia or New England, such an interpretation ignores the importance of the Middle Colonies. The lack of a dominant established church and a multitude of religious groups allowed this area to pioneer three distinctive elements in American religion: pluralism, the acceptance of a variety of religions; denominationalism, the recognition that there are common truths in the diversity of churches; and religious liberty, the separation of church and state and the legal equality of all denominations. The churches centered in the Middle Colonies—Presbyterians, Lutherans, German Reformed, Dutch Reformed, Quakers, and, eventually, Baptists and Methodists—have many more members than and have exerted as much influence on America as the Congregationalists and Anglicans.

The Dutch created New Amsterdam in 1624 as a trading outpost. With a weak claim to the area by right of discovery, the Dutch pioneered the process of buying land from the Indians, but showed no interest in converting them. The settlements along the Hudson River grew slowly, attracting a diverse population described as espousing many religions or none. Long Island became home to settlers from New England who sought more liberty in religion, as well as to Anabaptists and Seekers, several of whom converted to Quakerism. The Dutch Reformed Church was established, but when Peter Stuyvesant imprisoned traveling Quaker ministers, in 1657, a group of thirty-one inhabitants of Flushing insisted that the town charter "grant liberty of conscience without modification." An appeal to the directors of the West India Company brought a rebuke to Stuyvesant and a declaration that "the consciences of men ought to remain free and unshackled."[3]

The English conquest in 1664 brought formal guarantees of religious toleration and continuing tax support for the Dutch Reformed clergy. Now the Dutch settlers placed more emphasis upon their churches, seeing them as a way to preserve an ethnic identity. Anglican power showed when the royal governor interpreted a 1693 law for support of the Protestant clergy as allowing the establishment of the Church of England in New York City and three adjacent counties. So both the Dutch Reformed Church and the Church of England received state support. According to an English cleric, there were only ninety Anglican families in the whole province, with the majority of the population divided equally between Dutch Reformed and other dissenters. In the eighteenth century, an influx of French Huguenots, Presbyterians, German Lutherans, and Reformed contributed to the religious diversity of New York.

New Jersey, split off from New York in 1664 by the king to reward courtiers and then divided again into East and West Jersey, also attracted people of diverse religious persuasions. East Jersey's commerce centered on the Hudson River. In addition to Dutch settlers,

---

[3] Quoted in Rufus Jones, *Quakers in the American Colonies* (New York: Norton, 1966), p. 224.

that area attracted Presbyterians from Scotland and Ireland. Newark was founded in 1655 by Puritans from New Haven who feared contamination and disliked being absorbed into the newly chartered colony of Connecticut.

The Quaker Colonies

After Congregationalists and Anglicans, the third dominant religious group in seventeenth-century America was the Society of Friends, or Quakers, who colonized West New Jersey and Pennsylvania. Quakers also converted settlers already living in outlying areas in New England, Long Island, Maryland, Virginia, and the Carolinas. These settlers joined a movement that adapted easily to a frontier situation where the people hungered for religion, but could afford neither to pay clergy nor to build elaborate churches. Quakers worshiped in unadorned meeting houses that resembled normal dwellings. Quaker ministers from England—men and women recognized by the meeting as able to speak for God in worship services—endured the hardships of colonial travel to spread the new faith.

The members of the Society of Friends who came to dominate the Delaware River Valley area differed from the religious enthusiasts who challenged the Massachusetts Puritans. Persecution in England, a series of schisms, organization of the movement into a hierarchical structure of business meetings (with separate meetings for women), and the membership of influential men, such as William Penn, made Quakers less radical.

Quaker merchants in England, including Penn, bought the title to West Jersey and began settlements in 1672. Good, cheap land, religious liberty, and representative government promised in the West Jersey Concessions and Agreements attracted Quaker colonists, but difficulties in securing clear title to the right to government brought disorder. West Jersey became a Quaker-dominated enclave, a situation that did not change until after 1704, when the Crown unified both Jerseys under a royal governor. East Jersey's Calvinists and West Jersey's Quakers stymied efforts to establish the Church of England.

William Penn (1644–1718), son of England's great seventeenth-century naval hero, repudiated his aristocratic lifestyle by becoming a Quaker in 1662. Imprisoned four times for his beliefs, he became a leading Quaker minister and eloquent defender of his new faith. He also emerged as an advocate for religious toleration, even for Roman Catholics, insisting that only God controlled conscience, that coercion would lead to false beliefs, and that dissenters, by their hard work, increased the wealth and strength of the realm. In 1681, Charles II paid off a debt owed to Penn's father with a grant of land larger than all Ireland. Like the New England Puritans, Penn mingled economic and religious motivations. He expected to make a profit from the colony, as would those settlers who worked hard to earn a decent living. Yet Pennsylvania was also to be a "holy experiment," by which he meant a holy experience of God, whose success might portend the dawn of the millennium. The name of the capital city, Philadelphia, recalled the Greek brotherly love and the description in the book of Revelation of a place where people did God's will (Rev. 3:7–13). Migration, in theory at least, was a religious act undertaken only in response to God's will, but those who came still expected to improve their status.

Penn sought to attract godly people, not just Quakers, by guaranteeing political rights and ensuring that there would be no persecution of women and men for religious beliefs. The early laws made no provision for tithes, oaths, or a militia. Quaker pacifism meant that Indians would be conciliated, which, for Penn, meant that the royal charter must be supplemented by the purchase of lands from native Americans and that there must be justice in all dealings. Like Roger Williams, Penn genuinely respected the Indians, and they cherished his memory for the next hundred years. Pennsylvania kept peace with the Indians for seventy years.

In two brief visits to Pennsylvania, Penn moved easily in his roles as Quaker minister, proprietor with title to lands, and governor who was the source of political power. Facing challenges to his grant in England, Penn returned there, and in his absence the colony proved essentially ungovernable, with controversies over rents on land, taxes, and powers of the assembly. Quakers had not obeyed all laws in England, a practice they transferred to Pennsylvania. The first forty years of Pennsylvania history saw incessant conflict between the colonists and the proprietors.

The organization and practice of Quaker meetings transferred easily and conferred a unity upon settlers in West New Jersey and Pennsylvania; during the initial years, no other denomination held regular services. American Friends created a network of ties with Quakers in England and throughout the colonies. Royal officials and the few resident Anglicans unsuccessfully sought to end Quaker political dominance and to establish the Church of England. But Penn's publicity for his colony attracted Mennonites, Baptists, and Presbyterians who supported Quaker religious freedom in preference to Anglican toleration, which might involve paying tithes and creating a militia. Even though Quakers soon became a minority in Pennsylvania, they obtained an absolute majority of assembly seats until 1755 from an electorate that approved of their policies granting legal equality to all churches, preserving peace with the Indians, having no militia and no tithes, and keeping taxes low. Unlike their religious peers elsewhere in America and in England, Pennsylvania Friends muted their sectarian origins as they preserved political power in the British Empire.

German Sects

Penn sought to persuade other sectarian groups in Europe that they could find freedom and security in Pennsylvania. Mennonites, Amish, and Schwenckfelders shared the Quaker beliefs in inward piety, simplicity in dress and furniture, a refusal to take oaths, and pacifism. All also shared a distrust of formal theology and church establishments. Unlike the Quakers, these groups were not interested in politics or reform of the wider society, preferring to concentrate upon personal holiness. Later the German Brethren, or Dunkers, and the Moravians, churches originating in pietism, would also move to Pennsylvania. Because before migrating, the religious sects had already developed policies for creating churches, calling ministers, and controlling congregations without the aid of government, they adjusted easily to living in Pennsylvania, which they found a secure environment in which to protect their distinctive form of religious life. They approved of freedom of conscience and had to furnish neither tithes for priests, nor men or taxes for a military establishment. Their preservation of a sense of being German contributed to a desire for isolation from politics, and their hard work, simplicity of lifestyle, and communal helpfulness increased their prosperity.

German Lutherans, Reformed, and Moravians

The laity and ministers used to the power and prestige of established churches found the transition to life in the Middle Colonies difficult. Beginning in the 1720s, in response to incessant European wars, Germans began migrating to Pennsylvania in such large numbers that, before the American Revolution, about one-third of the inhabitants of the province spoke some dialect of German.

Members of the Lutheran or German Reformed churches, the Germans did not leave their homeland because of religious persecution, and they arrived in America with a tradition of cooperation. The laity, many of whom were indentured servants, arrived long before the ministers. Since the Germanic states forbade migration, the motherlands officially accepted little responsibility for their ex-countrymen's religious welfare. German arrivals in Pennsylvania felt estranged from customs of the new land and sought to preserve their ethnic identity, often through creating churches. Being German proved to be of more importance than theological consistency did, and so it mattered not at all that Lutherans and Anglicans shared a tradition of subordination to the state and respect for liturgical forms or that Presbyterians, Dutch Reformed, and German Reformed espoused Calvinist theology. In America, Germans preferred to associate with other Germans, often discovering an ethnic unity that, because of the multiplicity of German states, had not been felt in Europe.

The laity, both women and men, wished to create churches like those they had known at home. In spite of their poverty, they voluntarily attended church and contributed, by subscription or by renting pews, to support for the minister and building funds. Since there were few regularly ordained clergy who migrated, the settlers persuaded schoolmasters and others with education to read services, but these unordained men could not administer the sacraments, although a few surrendered to necessity and did so anyway. And some of the schoolmaster–pastors proved to be of dissolute moral character, abusing the trust of congregations.

Lutherans in Germany became interested in their countrymen in Pennsylvania after hearing reports about the Moravians, led by Count Zinzendorf (1700–1760). The Moravians, originally a group of Czech Brethren, experienced a resurgence after they came to live on the estate of Zinzendorf, a German who became both an ordained Lutheran minister and a Moravian bishop. Under Zinzendorf's leadership, the Moravians created a distinctive pietistic worship centering on a close identification with the suffering Jesus expressed in devotional prayers, a liturgy centering around the eucharist, and music. In Herrnhut in Germany, and in Bethlehem in Pennsylvania, the Moravians created a centrally directed communistic economy in which all labor benefited the religious society, with profits used to support missionary efforts. Moravian ministers sought to convert Indians, slaves, and other colonists who normally were not expected to practice the monasticlike disciplined life at Bethlehem. So the Moravians could either dwell in a kind of sectarian withdrawal into a separate community or participate in the world like Lutherans. Zinzendorf, who visited Pennsylvania in 1740, viewed denominational labels and theological niceties as irrelevant and, in a series of conferences, sought to create a unity of all Protestants. Moravian missionaries presented themselves as ministers for the Lutherans and Reformed. Zinzendorf's pietist ecumenism encountered opposition from Calvinists, who disliked his opposition to predestination, and from Lutherans and Reformed, who suspected that he was trying to create Moravian churches. Rather than promote unity, Zinzendorf's activities increased denominational awareness and occasioned bitter disputes. By the 1750s the Moravians had evolved into another separate denomination, concentrating their missionary activities on the native Americans.

The threat to Lutheran purity posed by the Moravians and other sectarians prompted officials at the University of Halle in Brandenburg to send ministers, the most famous of whom, Henry Melchior Muhlenberg (1711–1787), served in Pennsylvania for nearly forty-five years and helped to shape a pietist American Lutheranism. Muhlenberg willingly cooperated with Anglican, Reformed, and Presbyterian clergy who shared his emphasis upon devotional Bible study and prayer. He insisted that Lutherans learn the catechism and barred those who were dissolute from taking the sacrament.

The Halle ministers in America had to learn to accept lay authority in the church and to lead by persuasion and holy example rather than by formal authority. Neither minister nor laity could count on help from the government in case of a dispute. Members did not wish to sign long-term contracts for ministers and often would not pay the salaries of those who proved incompetent or immoral. Muhlenberg thought it took at least seven years of seasoning for a German minister to adjust to conditions described as "heaven for mechanics and farmers, and hell for government officials and clergy."[4] The poverty of congregations, geographic dispersal, and the shortage of clergy meant that Muhlenberg and other ministers had to serve several congregations and travel incessantly.

The clergy often complained of the Middle Colonies' pattern of religious liberty, seeing it as destructive of ministerial and church authority. Yet the alternative—the establishment of either Presbyterian or Anglican Churches—appeared worse. Because of their immigrant status and tradition of being aloof from politics, German churches and sects did not attempt to influence politics. Before the American Revolution, the Reformed, Lutheran, and Dutch Reformed Churches created ministerial associations, founded colleges to train ministers, and played down formal ties with the European mother churches. By being forced to adjust to a competitive situation, to find sources of finance for churches and clergy, and to accept shared authority and laity, and by providing spiritual solace to bewildered immigrants, the Lutheran and Reformed Churches prospered and reinforced the emergent pietistic emphasis in American religious life.

The Presbyterians

The Presbyterian Church became a dynamic force in the religious and political life of all the Middle Colonies early in the eighteenth century and, after the 1750s, expanded rapidly in the South. The rise of the Presbyterians came more easily because these immigrants already could understand English, even if they spoke it with a brogue, had British citizenship, and shared a Calvinist theology with New England Congregationalists and the German and Dutch Reformed in the Middle Colonies.

[4]Theodore Tappart and John Doberstein, eds., *The Journals (II) of Henry Melchior Muhlenberg* (Philadelphia: Evangelical Lutheran Ministerium of Pennsylvania and Adjacent States, 1942–48), p. 295; see also the diary (edited by Oscar Handlin and John Clive) of Gottlieb Mittelberger, *Journey to Pennsylvania* (Cambridge, MA: Harvard University Press, 1960), pp. 47–48.

Presbyterians coming to America had experiences as either independent or established churches. In Scotland, the established Presbyterian Church resisted forced Anglicization under Charles I and Charles II and regained autonomy after 1688. Seceder, or covenanting, congregations separated from the establishment. As a part of the Puritan movement, Presbyterians had ruled England from the 1640s until 1660, and the Westminster Confession of Faith and Catechisms summarized their beliefs. After 1660 English Presbyterians became dissenters, and the resulting demoralization and questioning of tradition led to some clerics' flirtation with rationalist or even Unitarian beliefs. The eighteenth-century Presbyterian Church in America contained rival religious traditions from England, Scotland, Ireland, and New England. After Cromwell's reconquest of Ireland and, later, after rebellions in 1688 in Scotland, Scots either voluntarily or by force settled in Ireland, concentrating in what is now called Northern Ireland. There they encountered opposition from Roman Catholics and discrimination from the established Church of England.

Presbyterians remained a small religious movement in the colonies until, in the first third of the eighteenth century, there was a large-scale Scots–Irish migration to the colonies, with 150,000 to 200,000 settlers by the time of the Revolution. Neither Puritans nor Virginians welcomed the Scots–Irish, who tended to move to the backcountry in Pennsylvania or to migrate south via the Shenandoah Valley. Somehow, this large mass of poor people had to be incorporated into new churches. Like the German churchgoers, Presbyterians faced a shortage of ministers and lay authority in existing congregations. The ministers' response to controlling the quality of clergy was to create local organizations, or presbyteries, for clergy and a synod whose membership covered several colonies, and also to demand subscription to all articles of faith in the Westminster Confession used in Ireland. Still, unity did not prevail, because ministers who thought that such credal statements were secondary insisted instead upon a personal experience of grace. Such an emphasis fit into pietism, as well as New England's Puritan traditions.

Before 1740, sects and churches in the Middle Colonies had learned to live with pluralism, voluntarism, and an absence of official or governmental support. The lay members of churches established in Europe approved of the religious liberty of the Middle Colonies. They showed their continuing devotion to Christianity by creating churches and seeking ministers. Ministers learned to work with the laity, while creating organizations to preserve their status and power. The importance of members of the Society of Friends in Pennsylvania's political and economic well-being gave a sectarian tinge to the Delaware River Valley settlements. For example, no other colony refused to create a militia. Since Friends rapidly became a minority, they could not have continued to dominate the assembly without the electoral support of members of churches. Because Friends had been a persecuted minority, they protected other sectarian minorities, which was one of the reasons for their initial migration to the Middle Colonies.

The favor shown to the sectarians irritated some churchmen, who complained about immorality and lack of respect and looked longingly at the Congregational and Anglican establishments in the North and South. These attitudes made the sectarians suspicious of their real intentions. No one anticipated the impact of the preaching of a twenty-five-year-old itinerant Anglican priest named George Whitefield.

Chapter 29

The Great Awakening

Awakenings, Revivals, and Revivalism

Times of heightened sensitivity or revivals of religion termed "awakenings" have marked American religion since the 1740s. Favorable and unfavorable participants, theologians, social scientists, and historians have puzzled over the causes and consequences of awakenings. Do these occasions follow or interrupt periods of religious decline, or are they the final result of the quickening of religious sensibilities? Do they show the inadequacy or the success of religious institutions? Is an awakening simply a mysterious work of God, as converts often claimed, or a work of humans using God's and their own means, as nineteenth-century revivalists argued? Or is an awakening an emotional reaction occasioned by mass hysteria and determined by external circumstances, as opponents insisted? Since social scientists have not provided a satisfactory explanation even for contemporary awakenings, the historical analysis of past awakenings in America must proceed with caution. We can describe what people say happened, but not necessarily why they happened.

In America, awakenings have so often taken the form of revivalism, that revivals and revivalism have come to be seen as almost interchangeable with awakening, although there is a distinction between them. A revival of religion is an awakening and can take many forms: an emphasis upon sacraments or moral discipline or political transformation: Revivalism is a concentration of fervor into a concise period, often during or after a worship service, in which the person undergoes a conviction of living in a state of sin, an awareness of grace, and a sense of the personal experience of God. Frequently, the process is accompanied by emotional fervor, such as crying or depression followed by joy and ecstasy. Clergy who strive to create these phenomena are termed revivalists. Revivalism after 1740 came to dominate the colonial Calvinist churches—Congregationalist, Dutch Reformed, Presbyterian, and certain Baptists.

Sources of Revivalism

Revivalism did not originate in America. As early as the 1620s, Scottish Presbyterians had religious gatherings lasting several days, beginning with repentance, confession, partaking of the sacrament, and thanksgivings. The emotional outpourings in these festivals became a continuing tradition, with itinerant clergymen conducting such sacramental revivals, holding services in barns or out-of-doors. Presbyterians of Scotland and Ireland who migrated to the Middle Colonies brought with them a tradition of protracted emotional awakenings. The awakening among German congregations in America paralleled, but was not the same as, Presbyterian and Congregational revivalism, even though ultimately pietism and revivalism reinforced each other and merged to reshape American Protestantism.

Historians emphasizing the contribution of New England to American religion find Puritanism a source of revivalism. Like pietists, Puritans emphasized devotional reading of the Bible and insisted upon a rigorous self-examination during which the person received a sense of the presence of God. That presence, first felt as law, convicted the person of sin and then, experienced as grace, brought justification. The Puritans made recounting of conversion necessary for church membership. Conversion required being made tender and surrendering one's self-will, behavior more congruent with what were considered female than male behavioral norms. The psychological barriers to conversion may be one reason why women outnumbered men church members in Puritan churches. The main differences between Puritan conversion and eighteenth-century revivalism was that the latter telescoped the process into a shorter time frame, more readily accepted emotional displays, and claimed greater assurance that the individual was truly converted.

Historians looking at eighteenth-century religion discern conflicting qualities. Jon Butler postulates a period of decline, judging by the small numbers of members who took communion, the growth of skepticism fostered by the new learning among privileged classes, and the prevalence of folk religion or magic as an alternative religious system.[1] Even the authority of the state did not compensate for institutional weakness created during the seventeenth century. Butler stresses the regional nature and varieties of theology and approach in the colonial awakenings.

Patricia Bonomi, using as a criterion not communicants, but attendance at church, pictures a robust religious life in the colonies.[2] She argues that the century marked a steady increase in the number of churches in all areas: What we encounter today as colonial churches—simple, white New England meeting houses and brick Anglican churches—date

---

[1] Jon Butler, *Awash in a Sea of Faith: Christianizing the American People* (Cambridge, MA: Harvard University Press, 1990), pp. 63–66, 98–99, 128.

[2] Patricia Bonomi, *Under the Cape of Heaven: Religion, Society, and Politics in Colonial America* (New York: Oxford, 1986), pp. 87–92.

from the eighteenth century. Lay initiative in creating and supporting churches led to a disregard of technical points of theology or church order, which prompted clerical complaints. Bonomi and Butler agree that there was discord between and within American religious communities, and both point to a sacralization of the landscape, as churches with high steeples showed the Christian orientation of towns to visitors and inhabitants.

Still being debated is whether the strength of the institutional church should be the historian's method of assessing the religiosity of the colonial peoples. Unfortunately, other kinds of evidence are fragmentary. Persons who opposed the Christian worldview could not speak freely, for laws outlawed blasphemy. Scattered comments on skepticism came from ministers. Sailors, vagrants, and travelers sitting in a tavern may have uttered atheistic sentiments; clearly, there was widespread anti-clericalism. However, for virtually the entire white population, Christianity offered a method of coping with daily events and crises: prosperity, poverty, health, illness, and death. Christianity had enormous prestige accumulated over centuries, and as yet, there was no comparable body of knowledge to challenge a population just emerging from illiteracy and lucky to have a primary school education. White colonists disdained even learning about the alternative worldviews of African slaves and Indians. The Great Awakenings could occur because Christianity already permeated the culture and revivalists could rely upon a latent belief system and the need for religious assurance.

Awakenings

Jonathan Edwards (1703–1758), Yale graduate and minister in Northampton, Massachusetts, pictured the effect of an awakening on the town in 1734. For Edwards, the revival was a miracle, a sudden outpouring of God's grace in which the community put aside secular activities to concentrate upon religion. It began when Edwards rebuked the youth for holding a dance on the Sabbath. Soon the revival spread throughout the entire population, which spent hours in prayers, Bible reading, and edifying conversation. In sermons and family visits, Edwards stressed the dangers of damnation and promises of salvation and witnessed the initial outpouring of tears of despair and final joy. Over three hundred males and females, in equal numbers, claimed to experience salvation, with an upsurge in application for church membership. The revival ended as abruptly as it began when a man despondent over his condition committed suicide. Edwards's detailed description of people undergoing conversion in a revival became a textbook for future awakenings.

Earlier, in New Jersey, the preaching of Theodore Frelinghuysen (1692–1748), a Dutch Reformed minister, prompted a revival and controversy. William Tennent, Sr. (1673–1746), a Presbyterian minister from Ireland living in Neshaminy, Pennsylvania, agreed with Frelinghuysen's emphasis upon experiential regeneration. Tennent created an academy in his home, termed by opponents the "Log College," in which he trained young men, including his son Gilbert, for the ministry. The graduates of the "Log College," whose unconventional training distressed more conservative Presbyterian ministers of the Middle Colonies, preached the necessity of being born again. So proponents and opponents of revivalism had already staked out positions before Whitefield appeared in 1740.

George Whitefield (1714–1770), a young, single, cross-eyed, ordained Anglican priest with theatrical training and a magnificent voice that Benjamin Franklin estimated could be heard by 20,000 people, had associated with Methodist revival and pioneered open-air preaching in England. In 1740, he decided to undertake a preaching tour of the colonies. Famous before disembarking in Delaware, Whitefield, whose itinerary and revival services were described in colonial newspapers, created the first media event in America. Before his death in 1770, Whitefield would complete four preaching tours of the seaboard colonies. As a skeptical young man before hearing Whitefield, Benjamin Franklin resolved to contribute only a small amount to the orphanage, but during the sermon he kept increasing his contribution until he emptied his pockets at the time of collection. The sheer size of the crowds that came to hear Whitefield created excitement. Often, he preached out-of-doors because no church was large enough to hold the mass of people who wanted to listen to him. In Philadelphia, 20,000 heard him on one occasion, and Boston, with a population of around that number, had 10,000 at Whitefield's farewell sermon. In rural and urban settings, Whitefield brought more people together in one place than had ever before happened in the colonies. The sense of anticipation and excitement of belonging to a mass religious phenomenon made people susceptible to Whitefield's eloquence.

Whitefield preached extemporaneously, and his message was clear: One had to be reborn in a conversion experience. A person who had no assurance of being saved probably had not been. Whitefield's sermons portrayed the anguish of a dying sinner finally seeking Jesus' forgiveness and stressed the necessity of beginning the process in the present. Not a profound theologian, Whitefield began preaching as an Arminian, but Gilbert Tennent and Jonathan Edwards persuaded him to favor predestinarian Calvinism, a change that meant that Congregationalists, Presbyterians, and Baptists would welcome him. The new theological orientation did not change Whitefield's basic sermon: the necessity for new birth.

Whitefield proclaimed that denomination labels had little significance: "Father Abraham, whom have you there in heaven? Any Episcopalians? No. Any Presbyterians? No . . . Whom have you there? . . . We don't know those names here. All who are here are Christians . . . Oh, is this the case? Then God help me, God help us all to forget party names and to become Christians in deed and truth."[3] Whitefield's willingness to preach in any church reinforced the pietist vision of a unity of religious experience transcending differences among Anglican, Presbyterian, Lutheran, and Congregational Churches.

In South Carolina, after Whitefield criticized what he saw as the moral deadness of the established church, the Anglican Commissary refused him permission to use the Church of England. So Whitefield preached in dissenting churches whose ministers already thought ill of Anglicans. Over time, the pattern of Anglican opposition would intensify from those who disliked the emotionalism and disorder associated with the revival and who preferred a liturgy and rational assent. Whitefield kept journals of his travels, which he published. Although Whitefield was originally welcomed in New Haven and Boston, his criticism of the colleges' failure to promote experiential religiosity turned their faculties against him.

Whitefield's successes prompted other itinerants to preach, all of whom thundered damnation, demanded new birth, and welcomed emotional signs as marks of faith. At issue

[3] Quoted in John Pollock, *George Whitefield and the Great Awakening* (London: Hodder and Stoughton, 1972), p. 118.

soon became the right of these revivalists to enter a parish without the permission of the regular minister, but with support of laity. A congregation that had listened to a clergyman for years without being converted felt him inadequate. Younger converts judged as not saved older members of the congregation who could not date their conversion experience precisely. James Davenport (1716–1757), a Yale graduate and Long Island minister, staged a burning of allegedly irreligious books and luxury items in New London, Connecticut. Davenport claimed that, upon first sight, he could distinguish Christians from the unconverted. His preaching became so extreme that a Connecticut court pronounced him mentally unbalanced.

Consequences

There were ninety-eight schisms in Congregational Churches in New England. In Connecticut, the division between supporters, termed New Lights, and opponents, or Old Lights, brought disputes over which Congregational Church enjoyed rights to tax support. After the assembly passed a law restricting itinerancy, the revival became a political issue involving the relationship of church and state, as well as religious freedom.

Whitefield and other itinerants reached only certain churches, with the Calvinist churches most susceptible. When ministers resisted the revival, some people joined the Baptists; others, deciding that revivalism brought excessive zeal, became Anglicans. While Whitefield preached to large assemblages in Maryland, Virginia, and South Carolina, the Awakening of 1740 had little immediate impact on tidewater areas, but in 1747 New Light Presbyterians in Virginia, and in 1754 Baptists in North Carolina, began revivals in the backcountry and created churches that challenged the established church. The Virginia Assembly sought to clamp down on illegal conventicles, a policy that soon brought a rebuke from England. Experiencing obstructions in Virginia made Presbyterians and Baptists question the legal rights of the Anglican establishment. The revival also threatened the complacent moralism characteristic of the Church of England in the South, creating adherents who condemned fox-hunting parsons and the ostentatious lifestyle characteristic of Virginia's gentry. Revivalists also sought to bring Christianity to the slaves, who found, in the emotional release of new birth and the indwelling of Christ, similarities to religious customs they had known in Africa.

Opponents of the revival attempted to utilize existing authority structures of the state or ministerial association to maintain order. They accused the revivalists of confusing the work of the Holy Spirit with the effects of the devil—of relying on feelings rather than intelligence and reason. They insisted that a person claiming to be saved might be confusing emotional release with new birth. Spiritual pride, misleading assurance, intolerance, and ill-thought-out zeal allegedly characterized the converts; these were not the fruits of God's grace. Above all, argued Charles Chauncy (1705–1787), of Boston's First Church, religion was a matter of intellectual assent to God's truth, and the revival exalted feeling above methodical, orderly action.

Jonathan Edwards emerged as the most perceptive defender of the revival—indeed, as sophisticated an evangelical theologian as America has produced. Edwards began with Locke's postulate that all knowledge derives from the senses. So a minister attempting to communicate eternal truths had to use images derived from experience to convey spiritual truths. In his most graphic sermon, Edwards used a metaphor drawn from nature—a spider suspended by a thread over a hot cauldron—to depict a sinner's state of risk of hellfire. Unlike Chauncy, Edwards refused to reduce religion to morality or rational judgment of evidence. Instead, he argued, religion affected the entire person—emotions, will, and intellect—and tears of terror and exaltation accompanying the revival were symptomatic of a complete reorientation of being. The only method of judging the validity of a religious experience was to examine the fruits of conversion. Persons exhibiting love, beauty, and disinterested benevolence showed the marks of God's grace. And the revival brought these on such a scale that Edwards saw in it the possibility of inaugurating a new earth in America, the dawn of a thousand-year reign of God on earth.

Edwards also resurrected the original Puritan ideal of a church composed of visible saints, with no "halfway covenanters" or open communion. When he attempted to institute this in Northampton, his parishioners threw him out, and he went as a missionary to the Stockbridge Indians. A few years later, the College of New Jersey, successor to the "Log College" and now Princeton University, selected Edwards as president, a symbol of the unity of evangelical Christians.

The history of the schism in the Presbytery of Philadelphia shows the impact of the revival. In 1743, at the time of the division, the numbers of anti- and pro-revival parties termed Old and New Light ministers were twenty-seven and twenty-two, respectively. But in 1758, when the two synods reunited, the New Lights had seventy-three ministers and the Old Lights twenty-three. By creating a core of committed young men, the revival had solved the problem of where the supply of native-born dedicated preachers would come from who could serve the churches of the newly arriving Scots–Irish. Yet the unification was not just a vindication of the revival. Gilbert Tennent had repented of the excesses of the Awakening and joined moderates in insisting that, in this life, the marks of election remained uncertain. For New England, the comparable estimates were one-third New Light, one-third Old Light, and one-third seeing virtue in both positions. Statistics on church membership tend to be unreliable, but probably are better for New England than elsewhere in America. There, the awakenings occasioned a large increase in memberships between 1740 and 1745, followed by a sharp decline to levels below what New England churches had previously experienced.

The Awakening stimulated denominational consciousness and the creation of new institutions to supply ministers. For the Presbyterians, there was the college later named Princeton; the Baptists in Rhode Island created Brown University; and Rutgers evolved from the Dutch Reformed's Queen's College. New Light Congregationalists created Dartmouth, founded as a school to teach native Americans. The Anglicans controlled King's College in New York, now Columbia, and the College of Philadelphia, now the University of Pennsylvania. Yet, paradoxically, the Awakening also contributed to a weakening of theological rigor by emphasizing a piety of the heart rather than Puritan unity of reason and faith.

The Awakening brought two changes in worship: It made respectable the preaching of sermons extemporaneously and brought a new hymnology, created by English Evangelicals Isaac Watts and Charles Wesley. The Puritans had sung the psalms by "lining out" without accompaniment, according to a few well-known tunes. That is, a leader would read out one line, and then the congregation sang the words, and so on. Now, new songs reflected Pietism and the revival, and would become standard hymns in all churches: "O for a Thousand Tongues," "Hark, the Herald Angels Sing," "Our God, Our Help in Ages Past," and "When I Survey the Wondrous Cross," among others. New Englanders hired tutors to teach four-part harmony, and a few congregations followed the Moravians' lead and installed organs.

During the revival the laity judged the qualifications of ministers, and the laity might stop attending church, separate, or refuse to pay the minister's salary. A recent history of the Presbyterian Awakening in the Middle Colonies is entitled "Triumph of the Laity."[4] Yet prestige came to ministers like Gilbert Tennent, who made hundreds repent and seek salvation. The Awakening also eroded the concept of the territorial parish. The laity joined a congregation that met their needs, even if it was only a block away from another church. So the Awakenings increased local autonomy, strengthened the voluntary nature of American churches, and, by so doing, contributed to the democratizing of the population. When laywomen and -men demonstrated that they would defy ministerial associations and governmental authority over religion, it was only one more step away from deciding political grievances on their own initiative.

Although the long-term political effects of the revival were indirect, the religious transformation was obvious: There would be a fundamental division between those who approved of the revival and those who opposed it. When they were within the same denomination, schism resulted. Among predominantly English-speaking churches, Baptists, Presbyterians, and many Congregationalists approved and increased their membership; opposed were most Anglicans. Little affected were Quakers and German-speaking sects and churches. Many converts now asserted that the only test of a minister was his ability to save souls; so there would be a conflict with denominational authorities over the educational qualifications of a minister. Proponents of revivalism also insisted that the church should be composed only of those who were visible saints and simplified the process of telling who was saved.

During the quarter century preceding the George Whitefield journey to America, England had been at peace. In 1739, Great Britain declared war on Spain. For twenty-seven of the next forty-four years, Britain and her colonies would be at war, first against Spain, then against France, and finally against each other. Religious awakenings now had to share center stage with political passion and war fever.

---

[4]Marilyn Westerkamp, *Triumph of the Laity: Scots–Irish Piety and the Great Awakening, 1625–1769* (New York: Oxford, 1988).

Chapter 30

Wars and Revolution

In America, war struck close to the bone. European monarchs did not want militias, because they feared putting guns into the hands of peasants. By contrast, all the colonies except Pennsylvania had a militia, and service was compulsory. Companies of volunteers, often with officers drawn from the same community, served during times of crisis. From 1755 to 1783, most American white males had military training at some time. Clergy preached sermons for troops going off to war, chaplains accompanied armies, and colonial governments proclaimed fasting and thanksgiving days, depending upon the events occurring in battle. The colonists, who often read their experience into the scriptures, viewed their enemies in apocalyptic tones as the Antichrist and found it easy to demonize supposedly savage Indians in alliance with popish France. In 1755 Protestant Britain represented freedom, reason, and toleration; France, tyranny, superstition, and bigotry. After 1776, these characterizations would be reversed.

In hindsight, we see the Seven Years War (1755–1763, called the French and Indian War in the colonies) as an imperial war fought by two expansionist nations to control lands occupied by an indigenous population. Both sides sought to gain the help of native Americans. When the French proved more successful, this only demonstrated to the English colonists that their opponents' alleged civilization was a mask for barbarity. Western Europeans rarely fought war to the bitter end, because that might jeopardize the monarchies and aristocracies; in America, war was fought for victory by a people who sought "regeneration through violence."[1] Success in war would prove that America was a Zion, not Babylon—that the colonists still retained special marks of God's providence.

The clergy of Episcopal, Lutheran, Presbyterian, and Congregational churches accustomed to supporting wars had little difficulty in rallying the population to the causes of Protestantism, the British Empire, and local autonomy, but the French and Indian War brought considerable soul-searching for the pacifist sects, particularly in Pennsylvania. Quakers in the assembly had previously managed to retain political power in a belligerent empire by appropriating money for nonmilitary expenditures. This strategy failed in 1755, when the French surprised General Edward Braddock's army marching overland to Fort Duquesne, now Pittsburgh, and defeated them. Indians in Pennsylvania who had watched the steadily encroaching frontier now took up arms, with the brunt of the attack borne by frontier-dwelling Scots–Irish and Germans. So the assembly created a militia and levied a war tax, though exempting conscientious objectors from serving. Devout Friends brought sufficient pressure so that most Quaker politicians withdrew from the assembly in wartime. Under the leadership of Benjamin Franklin, the assembly prosecuted the war. Questioning why God in His providence had allowed war to come to Pennsylvania, Quakers focused on injustice toward the Indians and slavery. Blaming the war upon seizures of land and unethical trading practices, and opposing the practice of giving colonists bounties for Indian scalps, Quakers sought to conciliate Indian grievances and to serve as mediators between British colonial officials and the native Americans. Believing that God was punishing them for owning slaves, Friends pronounced slavery a sin in 1755, and in 1758 they forbade any Quaker from buying or selling a slave. Committees now began working to persuade individuals to free their slaves. Anthony Benezet (1713–1784) transformed an inward-looking reform movement into the international antislavery crusade. Benezet marshaled arguments based upon religion, natural rights, reason, and sentiment to persuade all Americans that slavery was wrong. Benezet sent his pamphlets to European politicians and churchmen in an effort to persuade them to take action against slavery. Based upon his experience teaching black children, Benezet also argued that there was no difference in intelligence between whites and blacks, and that any perceived inferiority was due to environmental factors.

The Friends undertook an alternative form of religious revival, which saw the essence of religion as a disciplined obedience to sectarian norms. Their quest for purity created three reform movements destined to play a major role in American religious life: antislavery, Indian rights, and peace.

Conflict with Great Britain

In 1763, the Treaty of Paris ended France's colonies in and threat to North America, but Britain's successful imperial wars left her saddled with an immense debt and an expensive military establishment. Parliament reasoned that the debt had been incurred in defending the colonies, which were, in comparison to Britain, undertaxed. At the most basic level, the American Revolution resulted from repeated British attempts to tax colonists, who refused

---

[1] See Richard Slotheim, *Regeneration Through Violence: The Mythology of the American Frontier, 1600–1860* (Middletown, CT: Wesleyan University Press, 1973), pp. 92–93, 109, 145.

to pay and whose defiance brought a war. The slogan "No taxation without representation" meant that only the colonial legislatures had the right to tax. From 1765 through 1775, the colonists insisted upon their rights as Englishmen; only in 1776, two years after Lexington and Concord, was independence openly advocated. John Adams contrasted the war with the achievement of independence, which had, in a sense, occurred years before.[2] By this, he meant that the colonies had already achieved political autonomy and a unique culture. Thus, the war merely ratified a preexisting separation.

Compared with everyone else in Europe and with their own slave population, the colonists in 1770 were extraordinarily free and undertaxed. Why, then, did they revolt? The answer lies in their sensitivity to potential tyranny, a fear derived from history and political theory. New Englanders saw their forefathers as escaping the tyranny of a king and bishops. In 1688 and 1763, New England had again been delivered from religious and political tyranny. But events after 1763 persuaded a majority of colonists that corruption in Great Britain had destroyed freedom. If they did not resist, England would reduce the colonists to slavery—a condition of which they had firsthand knowledge.

The continuing efforts of Episcopalians in America to bring a bishop into their church contributed to the erosion of confidence in England. Anglicans insisted that without a bishop their church was incomplete, and religious freedom allowed every denomination to have its distinctive form of government. Virginians feared that a bishop would undermine the power of the vestries and that they would be taxed to pay his salary. They also opposed giving to a clerical official the kinds of civil power exercised by bishops in England. New England Congregationalists (but not Baptists) agreed. The colonists saw a bishop as a person who would increase royal authority in America by preaching passive obedience.

Without the support of Evangelicals, the American Revolution would not have been successful. The British recognized the influence of the Congregational and Presbyterian clergy, whom one loyalist termed "the black regiment" preaching "the yell of Rebellion in the Ears of an ignorant and deluded people."[3] As the crisis of 1776 drew near, evangelical clergymen, drawing upon scriptural portrayals of corrupt kings and the right of revolution, brought a passionate commitment to resistance. Congregational and Presbyterian preachers mobilized the people by preaching independence as they preached revival.

During the boycotts following the Stamp, Townshend, and Tea Acts, the clergy decried an American love of luxury dependent upon the importing of foreign goods and called upon the people to embrace a simple lifestyle in pursuit of freedom. Because being hurt economically was a spur to virtue, nonimportation allegedly liberated America from vice by encouraging home manufacturing. Patriots rejoiced after gentlewomen replaced drinking tea with spinning. When the Continental Congress decreed a day of humiliation on June 12, 1775, the rhetoric was the same as the Puritan jeremiad: An evil occurrence brought by sin required, first, humility and repentance, and then, action to improve the world. Revolutionary rhetoric reinforced the old Puritan mixture of deference before God and assertion before man.

[2] Letter from John Adams to Thomas Jefferson, August 24, 1815, *Works of John Adams*, edited by Charles F. Adams, vol. 10 (Boston: Little, Brown, 1856), p. 172.

[3] Peter Oliver, quoted in Alice Baldwin, *New England Clergy and the American Revolution* (New York: Ungar, 1968), p. 98.

Religious groups that feared the power of the Calvinists and that relied upon their influence in England resisted independence. Quakers supported colonial rights until they became convinced that the result would be war and independence. At that point, they withdrew from government, disowned any member who joined British or Revolutionary armies, and proclaimed their neutrality. After July 1776, they refused to pay taxes to or to pledge allegiance to the new state governments. The Mennonites, Amish, and Moravians followed the Quaker leadership. In 1776, the religious composition of the Pennsylvania government changed, with Quakers and Anglicans being replaced by Presbyterians, who sought to expand the new government's appeal by including Lutherans and Reformed. Pacifist sects would never again be a significant political force in the state.

Lutheran and Reformed clergy attempted to stay clear of the long controversy preceding independence, fearing that the Germans would become a scapegoat for reprisals and seeing their central task as preaching the gospel. Henry Melchior Muhlenberg complained that the war was God's punishment on the British and Americans for their arrogance. The clergy of the Church of England had taken an oath of loyalty to the Crown, the liturgy required prayers for the royal family, and many received salaries from the Society for the Propagation of the Gospel. Anglicans also feared the growing power of the Calvinists, whom they had long identified as king-killers and rebels. In New England, the Middle Colonies, and Maryland, a majority of the Anglican clergy remained loyal to England and either fled or were forced to vacate their pulpits.

The American Enlightenment

Until after the Great Awakening, the primary subject of colonial printers was religion, but after 1763 sermons, theology, and devotional literature took second place to political discourse. Newspapers and pamphlets dealt with the British constitution, justifying resistance as necessary at first to protect the colonists' equality as Englishmen and then, in 1776, to preserve the rights of a free and independent people. The rhetoric also changed, referring less to the Bible and more to natural law, seeking to persuade by invoking science and reason, rather than revelation, and showing a critical attitude towards authority. The fundamental documents of the Revolution enshrine the concepts of the American Enlightenment. For example, the Declaration of Independence rested on "self-evident truths" about "nature and nature's God" (notice that nature seems more crucial than God), who created people "equal" and bestowed the "unalienable rights of life, liberty, and the pursuit of happiness." In 1740, most colonists would have found such language unintelligible; by 1776, people communicated in the language of the Enlightenment. The founding fathers possessed the confidence that they had discovered the laws of nature. The new state and federal constitutions rested on the optimistic assumption that, with paper documents, humans could create institutions to manage society in a constructive way. Humanity could cast off monarchy and superstition and create a republic based on democracy.

Although rational Christianity remained confined to a small minority of the general population, many leaders of the revolt—Benjamin Franklin, Thomas Jefferson, John Adams, George Washington, James Madison, among others—repudiated Calvinism and evangelicalism for an enlightenment faith. The religious ideas of the revolutionary leaders originated over a century earlier. When Isaac Newton used mathematics to describe the laws of motion and gravity, he elucidated the nature of God. In the words of the Alexander Pope, "Nature and Nature's laws lay hid in night. God said, let Newton be, and All was Light."[4] Haydn's *Creation* put it even better: "The heavens are telling the glory of God and the firmament showeth his handiwork" (Psalm 19). The Bible and nature had to agree, since an unchanging God authored both. Because applying science to nature created the certainty of the laws of physics, the Enlightenment now applied science to politics, morality, and religion.

John Locke (1632–1704) became the preeminent philosopher of the new attitudes toward religion. His treatises justifying revolution, supporting religious toleration, defending rational religion, and basing knowledge upon sense experience served as a foundation for American colonial thought. For Locke, religion should not be abstruse; dogmas about the trinity, atonement, and original sin negated the essence of Christianity, which was simply "faith and repentance, i.e., believing Jesus to be the Messiah and a good life, are indispensable conditions of the new covenant, to be performed by all those who would obtain eternal life."[5]

Locke argued that the ontological argument from first cause proved the existence of God and that Jesus' miracles proved his divinity. Because of the way God created the world, right conduct increased the amount of happiness in the world. So revelation, reason, and self-interest coincided. Locke's political philosophy, which became radical in 1776, had a hundred years earlier created a kind of cosmic Toryism, that "whatever is, is right," breeding satisfaction with the Revolution of 1688, which preserved life, liberty, and property and legislated toleration for Protestants.[6]

Locke's insistence that all ideas originated from sense experience could lead in several directions. Samuel Johnson, one of the Yale students who converted to Anglicanism in 1722 and later became president of King's College, insisted that, since all humans could really know were ideas in the mind, matter was an illusion, and ultimate reality was spirit. The converse conclusion—that corporeality or matter or atoms were the only reality because all ideas derived from matter—appealed to the young Benjamin Franklin. For him, soul, mind, or spirit had no ultimate existence. In the same perspective, Jefferson believed that God was matter. Jonathan Edwards used Locke's postulates to argue that God willed the world into existence at every moment, while others insisted that the world was a self-running machine created by God, the master clock-maker. Most, however, followed the Scottish philosopher Thomas Reid, who insisted that idealism, materialism, mechanism, and skepticism were against common sense. God had so designed human minds that a few ideas, once rationally analyzed, were universally recognized as true. The existence of God, morality, and immortality were self-evident ideas. The moral sense through which thinking people understood the nature of reality provided a universal structure for the morality necessary for private and public life. So reason, revelation, and the moral sense advocated the same ethics. John Witherspoon (1723–1794), president of the College of New Jersey and signer of the Dec-

---

[4]Alexander Pope, "Epitaph Intended for Sir Isaac Newton."

[5]John Locke, *Reasonableness of Christianity*, edited by J. T. Ramsey (Stanford, CA: Stanford University Press, 1967), pp. 44–45.

[6]Alexander Pope, *An Essay on Man*, Epistle I, 1, 294.

laration of Independence, taught the Common Sense philosophy to a generation of Presbyterian ministers and to young James Madison. Jefferson's language in the preamble to the Declaration of Independence echoed Common Sense philosophy.

In France, the Enlightenment was often explicitly anti-Catholic. "With the bowels of the last priest we'll make a noose for the last King!" wrote Denis Diderot.[7] In England and America, the Enlightenment was used to support the church. Anglican bishops preached the harmony of revealed and rational religion and created a broadly comprehensive faith termed latitudinarianism that ignored theological niceties, emphasized ethics, and sought to include Calvinists, Arians, and Arminians in one church. Such emphases proved very popular in the Anglican church in the South. The Awakenings preached by Whitefield and Edwards sought to counter the first glimmerings of rational religion in America, but the leading opponents of revivalism, even in Boston, preached a rational Christianity asking for intellectual assent, good manners, and civility.

By mid-eighteenth century a few American intellectuals, termed deists, realized the potentially destructive implications for religious revelation that could be drawn from Lockean principles. The deists concluded that, because the Bible was so difficult to interpret, nature provided a more reliable guide to God. While the Bible might be necessary for the masses, intellectuals should be otherwise instructed. Deists reduced religion to a few ideas: the existence of God, ethics, and immortality.

As a young man, Benjamin Franklin flirted with deism. Yet he drew back from its skeptical implications, attending the Presbyterian church and, later, the Church of England, becoming a pewholder at Christ Church and having evening prayers with his servants. He may not have accepted the divinity of Jesus, but he remained fascinated with religion, drawing up his own prayers and liturgy. When, during a crisis at the Constitutional Convention of 1787, Franklin proposed pausing for a moment of prayer, it may have been a political ploy, but it could also have reflected a latitudinarian faith in the beneficence of God.

Political opponents called Jefferson a deist, a charge he neither admitted nor denied, believing that religion was his own business. Jefferson disliked theology and mystery in religion and distrusted all clergy. He thought Jesus a supreme ethical teacher and, seeking a way to reduce religious controversy, extracted moral passages from the New Testament, but never published them. Before 1776, a few isolated individuals in the colonies considered themselves deists, but, fearing the social implications, made no efforts to proselytize for this rational faith. In the aftermath of the Revolution, Ethan Allen of Vermont and Tom Paine identified themselves as deists, while attacking the theology of evangelical Christianity and the power of the clergy.

Religious Consequences of the Revolution

At the time of the Revolution, oaths in all colonies barred Catholics and Jews from political office. Charles Carroll, a Catholic from an influential Maryland family, was a delegate

---

[7]"Dithyrambe sur la fête des Rois," quoted in Norman Guterman, A *Book of French Quotations with English Translations* (Garden City, NY: Doubleday, 1963), p. 199.

to the Continental Congress and signer of the Declaration of Independence. Antipopery language disappeared from the patriots' rhetoric as the colonists tried to persuade the Canadians to join their cause and then concluded an alliance with France. While there were no religious tests for citizenship, most states restricted officeholding in some way. Five states reserved offices for Protestants. Delaware required a belief in the trinity, and Maryland restricted religious freedom to Christians. When Pennsylvania attempted in 1776 to broaden the loyalty oath for office in ways that might allow deists and Jews to serve, the Protestant clergy objected and persuaded the Constitutional Convention to adopt more restrictive language. Jews did not obtain full legal equality in Pennsylvania until 1792, and the new state constitution required legislators to declare their belief in a future state of rewards and punishment. The theory was that only knowledge of a future heaven and hell would bring honesty. Under the same theory, some states refused to allow atheists to testify in court. Jews could not hold office in Virginia until 1857 and in Maryland until 1867, and North Carolina restricted office holding to Protestants until 1868.

The colonists entered the Revolution insisting that they practiced religious freedom. The issue became whether the kind of toleration practiced in states with established churches or the legal equality of all churches, as in Rhode Island, New Jersey, Delaware, and Pennsylvania, would prevail. Nine states began the Revolution with an establishment. Baptists in New England complained that having to furnish a certificate of membership to avoid having their tax money go to the Congregational Church was an infringement on religious liberty. Yet in Massachusetts, Connecticut, and New Hampshire, the certificate system stayed in place, and Congregationalists remained the established church.

The Church of England lost preferred status in all colonies. The primary debate was in Virginia. The issue was not whether the Church of England deserved special treatment, since virtually all agreed that it did not, but whether all churches should receive tax support. Patrick Henry, who insisted that religion cultivated the morality necessary for a republican government, led the forces favoring an establishment of Christianity. An alliance of rationalists led by Thomas Jefferson and James Madison and joined by Baptists and Presbyterians won a bitter political battle for complete disestablishment of all churches. Each of the groups in favor of the measure had different reasons for supporting it. The rationalists argued that religion was a matter of individual opinion, God had left the mind of man free, and the exchange of ideas was the best guarantor of the emergence of truth. Religious liberty and the separation of church from government protected the state from strong religious passions and institutions. The Baptists reversed the equation, insisting that religion be protected from the state. Involving the state in religious matters led to hypocrisy and persecution. The Presbyterians rejected both of these alternatives, believing that the state and church could reinforce each other. They feared that the tax monies of those who had no religious affiliation and that the glebe lands formerly belonging to the established church would all be given to the Church of England. They preferred disestablishment to giving an allegedly unfair advantage to the Anglicans.

When Virginia disestablished Christianity and dropped religious tests for holding office, it did not repudiate the religious morality of Christianity. The new states passed laws forbidding work on Sunday, providing for the free incorporation of all churches, giving tax exemption to church property, and outlawing profane swearing. The states looked favorably on religious institutions as teaching the morality necessary to preserve republican government. Disestablishment meant that the religious orientation of the government would be unofficial, an endorsement of Christianity in general.

The federal Constitution, unlike most of the state constitutions, outlawed any religious test for office, did not mention the word "God," and rested authority upon "We the People." In response to complaints that the document needed a Bill of Rights, the new government passed the First Amendment: "Congress shall make no law establishing religion nor prohibiting the free exercise thereof." After Madison wrote the amendment, it was modified in Congress and passed the states with no debate upon the exact meaning. Rationalists and evangelicals may have interpreted it differently even then. The most plausible explanation for the lack of controversy was that the amendment applied only to the federal government and did not restrict the states. All states had legislation on religion, because churches owned property and the courts would have to decide legitimate title in disputes. But laws on religion would come at the state level. The federal government would have no jurisdiction; so it could neither "establish" nor "prohibit" any religion. In a private letter, Jefferson later referred to a "wall" between church and state, and yet the new government breached the wall by having military chaplains, paying Protestant missionaries to Indians, and proclaiming fasting and thanksgiving days.

The American Israel

Americans saw their religious and political lives prefigured in the Bible. Just as in the first century the church saw itself as a new Israel, so later religious leaders invested their political arrangements with spiritual significance. All colonists—but particularly those in New England—had utilized biblical metaphors in explaining their role in history. Puritans often saw America as the logical locality for the reign of the Antichrist or hell, rather than the site for Christ's millennial kingdom. During the French and Indian War, clerical rhetoric became more positive, exalting the British Empire and seeing America as a promised land of Christian people protected through God's special providences.

The Revolution brought the positive identification with America as a New Israel, a people specially elected by God. In 1776, Americans felt isolated, engaging in a military conflict with the world's most powerful state and espousing an untried kind of government. The patriots knew how reluctantly they had embraced independence and that they faced civil and external war. Congress, state legislators, and clergy sought to inculcate virtue in the people and the army, believing that only the righteous people would merit God's protection. Victory at Saratoga and Yorktown proved that God had vindicated Americans and bestowed on them a mission of the destruction of tyranny. As the first republican experiment in determining whether a people could govern themselves, America became a "sacred cause." Although they worried about divisions based upon class, religion, and race and even the survival of republican institutions, Americans proclaimed that God chose them to spread liberty throughout the world. Evangelicals, moderates, and rationalists all affirmed this fusion of land, republicanism, and religion. Franklin, Jefferson, and John Adams suggested that the seal of the United States depict Moses extending his hand over the sea to overwhelm Pharaoh with the motto "Rebellion to Tyrants is Obedience to God." Jefferson unknowingly echoed John Winthrop's 1630 Arabella speech about the significance of

America in world history: "The eyes of the virtuous all over the earth are turned with anxiety on us, as the only depositories of the sacred fire of liberty, that our falling into anarchy would decide forever the destinies of mankind, and seal the political heresy that man is incapable of self-government."[8] The clergy and more evangelical politicians added Christianity to the index of virtues.

Clergymen steeped in Calvinist or Lutheran theology knew the dangers of identifying any earthly realm with the kingdom of God, and rationalists wanted to create a universal standard of truth apart from any particular nation. However, the revolutionary generation reinvigorated and transformed a Christian tradition linking America with the once and future Garden of Eden, a place where flourishing churches would Christianize the social order and inaugurate the reign of Christ in a millennium of peace.

---

[8]Andrew A. Lipscomb, *The Writings of Thomas Jefferson* (Washington: Thomas Jefferson Memorial Association), chapter XIII, p. 58.

Chapter 31

The Second Great Awakening

The long revolutionary struggle had been hard on religious institutions. The political debate, a protracted war, and weaknesses in the Anglican Church meant that by 1783 less than ten percent of the population belonged to any church, although church attendance has been estimated to have been about sixty percent at the time. For nearly three million Americans, there were only 1,500 ministers and 1,900 churches. Leaders of the Calvinist churches complained about a prevailing spiritual deadness. Thomas Paine and Ethan Allen ridiculed the validity of revealed religion, holding up reason as the "Only Oracle of Man." Americans rejoiced at first and then were appalled by the French Revolution beginning in 1789, which rapidly became anti-Catholic and anti-Christian, going from a moderate constitutional program to republicanism, war, a "Reign of Terror," and conquest. Conservatives in America who feared French thought and rational religion saw in evangelical religion an antidote to French atheism.

Equally challenging was the need to bring the church to the frontier. Americans began moving into Vermont, Kentucky, Tennessee, and Ohio before the Revolution, and a major theme of the nineteenth century would be westward expansion. By 1830, one-third of the American people lived west of the Appalachian mountains. The Treaty of Paris fixed the U.S. boundary at the Mississippi River, and the Northwest Ordinance provided a mechanism for creating states and reserved some lands for schools and churches. The Louisiana Purchase, conflict with native Americans, and a war with Mexico meant that within sixty years of Washington's inauguration, the republican form of government expanded from the Atlantic to the Pacific Ocean. Clergy and politicians agreed that if the American republic

427

were to survive in such a vast expanse of territory, the churches would have to play a crucial role in civilizing frontier people.

The Second Great Awakening was an attempt to Christianize the United States population, white as well as black—a phenomenon with social and political, as well as religious
consequences. Historians have correctly described this awakening as a repudiation of European patterns and an Americanization of religion, a democratic and populist movement,
a response to the social disruption brought about by migration and the beginnings of industrialization, and an organizing movement seeking social stability for the awkward young
republic.[1] While all these interpretations have validity, our first concern must be with direct religious consequences, for at its most basic level, the Second Awakening was a
strengthening of the evangelistic and pietistic impulses initiated in the 1740s; or, to
rephrase it, revivalism became the dominant religious culture.

The denominations embracing revivalism most heartily—the Baptists and Methodists, including their various offshoots—became the largest Protestant churches, with adherents numbering two-thirds of all Protestants. Now that England was no longer a threat,
the Episcopalians gained bishops and autonomy, but, by standing apart from revivalism, lost
influence. The Awakening led to new denominations like the Disciples of Christ and Universalists, new religions like the Shakers and Mormons, numerous schisms, defenses of
Calvinism by Presbyterians, and attacks on it by other evangelicals and Unitarians. The Second Awakening also created voluntary associations for distributing Bibles and tracts,
founded Sunday schools, and supported home and foreign missions. Large numbers of
African-Americans became Christian and created their own patterns of worship. For the
first time, churches sought to enlist women in missionary and benevolent organizations.
Persons influenced by the revival sought to apply Jesus' teachings by creating public
schools, founding colleges, humanizing the treatment of the insane, solving the problems of
crime by building penitentiaries, and stopping the consumption of alcoholic beverages.
Even our now traditional form of Christmas celebrations, with decorated trees, holly, gift-
giving, and Santa Claus, originated in this period. Beginning in the 1780s and enduring until the 1840s, the Second Great Awakening was a complex phenomenon changing over time,
an explosion of energy in which Americans reshaped and applied their religion in a bewildering variety of movements. Accordingly, our treatment will be topical rather than chronological, dealing with the denominational responses to revivalism, the debate over Calvinism,
voluntary associations, new religious movements, and, finally, social consequences.

Baptists, Methodists, and Disciples of Christ

Baptist churches had heartily embraced the revivalism of the first Great Awakening and experienced steady growth in the North and the South before the Revolution. The revivals
begun by the Presbyterians in Virginia in the 1750s were continued by Baptists in the Car-

---

[1] See Nathan Hatch, *The Democratization of American Christianity* (New Haven, CT: Yale University Press,
1989); Jon Butler, *Awash in a Sea of Faith* (Cambridge, MA: Harvard University Press, 1992), chapters 8–10;
William McLoughlin, *Revivals, Awakenings and Reform* (Chicago: University of Chicago Press, 1978); and
Donald Mathews, "The Second Great Awakening as an Organizing Process, 1780–1830: A Hypothesis," *American Quarterly* (Spring 1969), pp. 23–43.

olinas and Virginia in the 1770s. Baptists emphasized lay authority and placed few restrictions upon individual congregations. After 1769 a few Baptist ministers attended the College of Rhode Island, but most had no advanced education, and the essential qualification was a conversion experience and the ability to save souls. In the early nineteenth century, Baptists tended to de-emphasize theological nuances, focusing instead on a person's responsibility to prepare himself or herself to receive grace. Adult converts received baptism by immersion and followed a pietistic lifestyle: moral discipline, Bible reading, and prayer.

During and after the Revolutionary era, Baptists criticized the planter lifestyle, supported the separation of church and state, voted for Jefferson rather than the Federalists, and preached the abolition of slavery. Like Methodists, Baptists learned that antislavery agitation killed church growth in the South and soon muted any criticism of the "peculiar institution." Their new strategy of ignoring slavery and concentrating upon church expansion and conversion was successful, and along with Methodists, Baptists became the dominant denomination throughout the South. Lay initiative, lack of planning, decentralization, democratic church polity, simple services, and a disdain for social and intellectual pretension originally marked the Baptists. By midcentury, after they had founded academies and colleges and cooperated in the benevolent empire of voluntary societies, the Baptists had become a respectable denomination.

On the surface, the Methodists could not have been more different from the Baptists. Methodists were Arminians (see pages 335–337) who opposed Calvinism, practiced infant baptism, ordained and controlled ministers and churches through annual conferences, and engaged in centralized planning. The church was hierarchical, with district superintendents and bishops who annually assigned and removed ministers from circuits, a group of congregations served by one clergyman.

Even better than Baptists, Methodists illustrate a continuity between eighteenth-century English and nineteenth-century American revivalism. As a student at Oxford, John Wesley had been a member of the Holy Club, a group dedicated to the methodical cultivation of piety. After an unsuccessful sojourn in Georgia, he returned to England in 1737, experienced conversion, and began outdoor preaching to the lower classes with great successes. When Anglicans opposed his itinerating ministry, Wesley responded, "The world is my parish." His message has been described as preaching Arminian theology with Calvinist rigor. While well educated, Wesley subordinated theology to experiential piety, remained in the Church of England all his life, and insisted that his followers take communion in Anglican services. Yet he sent out lay preachers to exhort the populace and organize classes for study, prayer, and mutual oversight. Wesley created a pietistic sect numbering nearly 90,000 within the Church of England. Only after his death in 1791 did the Wesleyan Methodists become a separate denomination in England.

In the 1760s, Wesley sent out lay preachers to America who created Methodist chapels in several cities and the South, but his defense of England's conduct with the colonies hampered the growth of the movement during the Revolution. In 1783, recognizing that the American Methodists could not remain within the Church of England, Wesley ordained superintendents (later termed "bishops") who could ordain ministers in America. Francis Asbury (1745–1816), whom Wesley sent to America in 1771, became the most influential bishop, instituting a pattern of itinerating or circuit-riding ministers in the new denomination. Before his death in 1816, Asbury traveled some 300,000 miles, crossing the

Appalachian Mountains fifty times and enduring the hardships of travel by horseback on bad roads in all kinds of weather to preach the Gospel. His single-minded pursuit of religion left no time for family life or even a sense of humor, and he complained bitterly about young circuit riders who married and wished to settle down. Methodism's revival began in Delaware, Maryland, and Virginia in the 1780s, and it replaced the Church of England as the dominant religious group in those states. Circuit riders accompanied migrants to the South and Midwest, expanding the church so that by the 1840s it claimed one million members, 4,000 itinerant ministers, and 7,700 local preachers spread over the entire nation.

Famous Methodist ministers, like Peter Cartwright (1785–1872), had, like their congregations, little formal education, relying upon the Bible and writings of Wesley, but they preached with enthusiasm the necessity of new birth and communicated to their hearers a sense of the presence of the supernatural in daily life. God, Satan, miracles, healings, and providences made religion a matter of personal commitment. Because God's forgiveness was available, the sinner had to make a decision for or against Christ. Would he stop drinking, gambling, and cursing and submit to Methodist discipline? The messengers might be rough-hewn and flamboyant, but their religious devotion and message were clear, democratic, and persuasive.

Bishops appointed ministers to serve all the churches in a circuit, the traversal of which might take weeks. Each year, ministers attended annual conferences and would be appointed to a new circuit. When the circuit rider was absent, lay preachers might speak or read services, but could not administer the sacraments. In England, Methodists at first allowed women to preach, but such freedom did not occur in America until the present century. Instead, women became Sunday school teachers and participated in Bible study classes and charitable activities. Like the Baptists, the Methodists prospered and became respectable over time, founding numerous colleges named after Asbury or Wesley, creating a publishing house for periodicals and books, and building impressive church structures.

Methodists and Baptists made effective use of a new institution pioneered in 1801 at Cane Ridge, Kentucky: the camp meeting. Several hundred families from a wide area would come to a clearing in the forest and camp there for several days. In the clearing, there would be a platform and rough-hewn benches. Several ministers, sometimes from different denominations, provided virtually nonstop preaching and hymn singing during the day, in the evening, and late into the night. Attenders anticipated and had emotional conversion experiences, with crying, trances, and exaltation. Holding camp meetings provided an effective mechanism for reaching the frontier people and continued with modifications long after the frontier disappeared. Camp-meeting religion reinforced older themes of revivalism, including a sense of cooperation among the denominations, all of which confronted individual sinners with the necessity of making a decision to be converted. For urban dwellers, the revival tent and church camps located in woods or near lakes offered an experience similar to the camp meetings' rural orientation and compression of religious fervor.

The contrasting centralized versus decentralized organizations of Methodist and Baptist show that what made them both successful were their emphases upon revivalism and morality, de-emphasis upon formal theology, clergy sharing the worldview of the frontier dwellers, and respect for common people. Still, the harmony in teachings and practices among Protestant churches should not be overstated. The various denominations would cooperate against deists and Roman Catholics, but still engaged in vigorous competition against each other and conducted acrimonious debates on infant baptism, original sin, Arminianism, communion, and church government. The revivalists' goal was not just to save a person, but to incorporate the new convert into a church community.

The revival could even be enlisted to preach intellectual assent to Christian restorationism, a movement to re-create the early church. The Disciples of Christ, or Christian Church, originated with advocates of camp meetings who found the Presbyterian emphasis upon predestination unscriptural. Alexander Campbell (1788–1866), distressed at the bickering of the different religions, sought to combine all denominations by using the Bible as the sole authority for faith and practice: "Where the Scriptures speak, we speak; where they are silent, we are also."[2] The Bible, argued Campbell, authorized faith in God and Jesus, repentance for sin, adult baptism by immersion, and celebration of communion every Sunday. Services were simple in the free-church tradition, with a ministry whose qualifications resembled Baptist and Methodist preachers. Campbell opposed mystery in religion and preached revivals to persuade people to give rational consent to the clear religious truths found in the Bible. The Disciples of Christ illustrate a major theme in early nineteenth-century religion: The revival was not an anti-intellectual repudiation of reason or common-sense philosophy. Rather, ministers and converts built upon the democratic faith in the abilities of the common person to judge for her- or himself the truth in the Bible. The result of Campbell's attempt to unify all Christians and end religious bickering was additional controversy, ending with a new denomination concentrated in the upper South and Midwest.

Presbyterian and Congregationalist Revivalists

Presbyterians initiated the earliest camp meetings, but their insistence upon an educated clergy, Calvinist orthodoxy, and decorum hampered their effectiveness in the backcountry. Frictions mounted between Presbyterians in the South and West, who embraced the new techniques, and their more theologically conservative adherents in the Philadelphia synod. Many city-dwelling Presbyterians and Congregationalists remembered the excesses of the first Great Awakening. Even so, both denominations led successful revivals in the East better described as acts of the mind than emotional outbursts. In 1801, Presbyterians and Congregationalists agreed on a Plan of Union to combine their missionary efforts in the West (which at the time included upper New York State), with each accepting the other's ministry and church polity. Under the leadership of President Timothy Dwight, Yale College, described as a "little temple," averaged an awakening every three-and-a-half years between 1795 and 1830.[3] Yale provided the intellectual leadership for the evangelical party in New England.

The Edwardean reassertion of Calvinist theology that had held sway among New England Evangelicals since the Great Awakening seemed unduly harsh in the early nine-

---

[2] Quoted in David E. Harrell, Jr., "Restorationism and the Stone–Campbell Tradition," in *Encyclopedia of the American Religious Experience* (New York: Scribner's, 1988), chapter II, p. 848.

[3] Quoted in Bernard Weisberger, *They Gathered at the River: The Story of the Great Revivalists and Their Impact upon Religion in America* (Chicago: Quadrangle, 1966), p. 64.

teenth century. Original sin and predestination appeared ill fitted for a democratic republic interested in the nobility of humankind and willing to bring the same strenuous activity to religion that was being used to tame the frontier. Edwards' God appeared remote, impersonal, immoral, and destructive of free will and human responsibility. God somehow had to be made to fit republican sensibilities without repudiating predestination.

Nathaniel William Taylor (1786–1858), professor of theology at Yale, combined commonsense realism and Calvinism by insisting that God worked in regular, intelligible ways by creating the universe and humans according to fixed moral laws and by building a moral sense into people. Sin came not because of any act of Adam, but due to each individual's acts. Taylor insisted that with God's aid, sinful humanity could help itself. The preacher, by appealing to the God-given moral traits within each person, could attempt to kindle feelings and reach the heart. Concentrating upon Jesus' suffering, humanity, and compassion would, for Taylor, awaken religious sentiments. Taylor's religious system provided a theology and an effective preaching strategy for the revival by preserving a Calvinistic flavor, the morality of God, sin, and free will.

Lyman Beecher (1775–1817), Yale graduate and successful revivalist at Litchfield, Connecticut, brought his friend Taylor's theology to Boston when he accepted a pulpit there for the purposes of doing battle against Massachusetts Unitarians. Beecher had earlier defended the alliance between the Federalist political party and the Congregationalist clergy and had opposed those who sought to separate church and state. In 1819, Connecticut ended tax support of organized religion, and in 1833 Massachusetts did the same. Beecher at first despaired, but later exulted that dis-establishment set the church free to work unhampered by the state. Beecher took his New England emphasis upon revival, voluntary associations, and social reform to Cincinnati as president of Lane Theological Seminary. When, in 1834, as part of an attempt to make Christianity relevant to social issues, Lane students began working with free blacks and debating the morality of slavery, the trustees stepped in, and Beecher supported their stance. In response, the students moved en masse to newly opened Oberlin College, which represented a more radical approach to Christian social action. The new ultra- or radical social reform grew out of the revival conduct of Samuel Grandison Finney, who would later become a professor of theology and then president of Oberlin.

If Taylor and Beecher diluted Calvinism, Samuel Grandison Finney (1792–1875) poured in gallons of republican water, becoming in the process the most important American revivalist since George Whitefield. Finney, educated as a lawyer and living in upstate New York in 1821, was a Presbyterian who decided to study the Bible and discovered that conversion was purely a matter of his "own consent." Having willed his own conversion, Finney claimed that "the Holy Spirit descended upon me in a manner that seemed to go through me, body and soul. I could feel the impression, like a wave of electricity . . . Indeed it seemed to come in waves and waves of liquid love . . . It seemed like the very breath of God."[4] Finney read a little theology with a Presbyterian minister, paid no attention to beliefs he did not like, claimed the Bible as his only doctrinal authority, and sought ordination, though confessing that he had not even studied the Presbyterian Confession of Faith. Because he was already successful at saving sinners, he gained ordination, but was essen-

---

[4] *Ibid.*, p. 92.

tially an educated layman who brought courtroom techniques to the revival—creating a "brief" for Jesus. Finney's religion was a lawyer's: God's promises of salvation were like a contract between God and the repenting sinner.

With a flair for the dramatic, Finney told sinners that accepting Jesus and going to heaven, or rejecting him and going to hell, was purely a matter of their will, and the time for decision was *now*. A person who focused all his or her energies and prayers on seeking conversion would be successful, resulting in a transformation characterized by holy living aiming at perfection. Revivalism now became a technique, not a miracle. Finney prayed for sinners by name, allowed women publicly to pray and testify in services, asked all who were saved to stand up so that the whole community could see who was not, and instituted a mourners' bench upon which those who sought conversion could sit and others could focus their prayers on them. Particularly in small towns, in services that might begin in the afternoon and last long into the night, Finney brought social pressure on sinners.

In a decade beginning in 1823, Finney conducted mass revivals first in the villages and towns of upstate New York, in a region commonly called the "Burned Over District" because of its waves of religious enthusiasm, and then in major northern cities. In spite of deep misgivings about Finney's techniques, Calvinists accepted his methods, for he brought camp-meeting techniques into the cities. A study of Finney's impact on rapidly growing and industrializing Rochester, New York, found converts from all classes, but a major impact on the industrial middle class. Revivalism united Rochester's business elite, who then imposed an ethical system on employees and the community. Workers for Christian businessmen found conversion a key to advancement, since employers approved of a religion fostering individual self-restraint, which was useful in an unregulated market economy.[5] Finney conducted major revivals until after the panic of 1837; then, as professor at Oberlin College, he created a distinctive theology which emphasized a holy life or sanctification until perfection. Oberlin became the first college in the nation to admit women and blacks, and its graduates served as missionaries and created the midwestern movement for the abolition of slavery.

Finney, whose many successors professionalized the revival, served as the prototype of later nineteenth- and twentieth-century revivalists. Neither Dwight Moody, Billy Sunday, Aimee Semple McPherson, nor Billy Graham graduated from a first-class seminary; all rested their faith on the Bible, and none cared much for theological subtlety or denominational labels. All planned their revivals carefully, created an organization to sustain their services, sought support from existing area churches, and employed music to great effect. Each brought excitement, drama, and a sense of rural or traditional values to religion, subordinated Christian community and social action to individual commitment to Christ, and received support from business classes anxious about social stability.

Reaction: Conservatives and Rationalists

Not all Calvinists accepted Taylor's theology or overlooked Finney's theological vagueness just because of his successes in the religious marketplace. Opposition centered in Presby-

---

[5] See Paul Johnson, *A Shopkeeper's Millennium: Society and Revivals in Rochester New York, 1815–1837* (New York: Hill & Wang, 1978).

terian Princeton College and Congregationalist Hartford Theological Seminary. In 1837, conservative Presbyterians (labeled the Old School) who distrusted the revival, Taylor's theology, newly founded Union Seminary in New York City, abolitionist attacks on slavery, and Congregationalist elements in Plan of Union Churches, refused to recognize union churches, thereby precipitating a major division in the Presbyterian Church. Until the Civil War, the Old School synods would defend Calvinist orthodoxy and oppose the social reform impulse stemming from revivalism. Old School Presbyterians opposed even *discussing* slavery, a stance that brought support from Southerners. The Old School's most eminent theologian, Charles Hodge (1797–1878), of Princeton, disdained what he saw as new ideas and used the Common Sense philosophy to defend the Westminster Confession of Faith. Disenchanted with the democracy of Jacksonian America, Old School Presbyterians enshrined a Federalist political theory of rule by the educated elite and deference by the masses. Old School Presbyterians disliked what they saw as the secularism of the Federal Constitution and sought passage of an amendment recognizing the existence of God and labeling America a Christian state.

Reactions against the prevalence of revivalism took place in other denominations, which, unlike the Presbyterians, avoided schisms because of decentralized power. Primitive and Landmark Baptists sought to uphold Calvinism. The Episcopal Church had acrimonious debates between "low-church" Evangelicals, who favored revivalism, temperance, and social reform, and "high-churchmen," who preferred a liturgical emphasis. Most German Lutheran and Reformed Congregations embraced evangelical emphases, but a small group of scholars at Mercersburg Seminary in Pennsylvania rejected what they saw as the simplification of religion into personal conversions. They sought to recapture a Reformation sense of the church as an organic institution, rather than to adhere to the revivalists' emphasis upon the congregation as a collection of converted individuals. Devoted to the study of church history and liturgical reform, the Mercersburg theologians sought a mystical union of Christ and the believer during the Eucharist, a view they argued was shaped by centuries of tradition. Ignored in their own time, the romantic theologians would be rediscovered at the end of the nineteenth century. Before the Civil War, the visible success of the revival drowned out the critics.

Congregational autonomy and decentralization meant that the full impact of rational religion became apparent only gradually. In 1804, Harvard rebuffed evangelicals by choosing liberals as a professor of divinity and as president. In response, the evangelicals founded Andover Newton Theological Seminary in 1808 and launched a pamphlet attack. In 1819, rationalist Congregationalism received a new name from a sermon on "Unitarian Christianity" delivered by William Ellery Channing (1780–1842), who became the spiritual leader of the movement. Churches then split, with the Unitarians controlling the church property of eighty-eight of the oldest one hundred Congregational Churches. A court decision allowing all residents of a geographic parish to vote, rather than only church members, aided the Unitarians. With evangelical Congregationalists facing the prospect of tax revenues going to churches they regarded as heretical, both groups now supported disestablishment. Unhappy with being confined by either creeds or organization, the Unitarians reluctantly created a loose denominational structure. As the comfortable creed of New England's ruling class, Unitarians refused to proselytize, and their strength remained centered in the northeastern seaboard. There is substantial accuracy in the squib description of Unitarians as believing in the "Fatherhood of God, brotherhood of man, and neighborhood of Boston."

The Unitarian label was first imposed by evangelicals furious at the questioning of trinitarian doctrine, but a more fundamental disagreement was over the liberals' rejection of original sin and affirmation of the potential goodness of humanity. According to the Unitarians, because God had installed in each person a moral sense, the essence of Christianity was ethical behavior, or a participation in the "moral perfection of the divine being." Channing refused to preach about the trinity, because the doctrine was "unintelligible," but insisted that the majority of Unitarians believed that "Jesus Christ is more than man, that he existed before the world, that he literally came from heaven to save our race . . . and is our intercessor with the Father."[6] Jesus was the perfect moral exemplar whose life showed the potential of all people.

Channing and other Unitarians insisted that they were Christians and regarded their differences with evangelicals as stemming from differences in biblical interpretation. Although valuing the Bible, Channing declared that not every word was inerrant and that humans must use reason to interpret the scriptures. In their debates with evangelicals, Unitarians introduced to America higher criticism of the Bible; that is, they used historical and textual analysis to understand the social context of the creation of scriptures. Still, Unitarianism in the 1820s seemed rather old fashioned, resembling early eighteenth-century latitudinarianism. For example, John Locke and Channing used miracles as intellectual proof of the truth of Christianity and insisted that there need be nothing mysterious about religion.

The Universalists are sometimes called poor people's Unitarians. According to popular parlance, the Universalists thought God was too good to damn them and the Unitarians thought they were too good to be damned. In the twentieth century, the two denominations would merge, but originally there were major differences. Universalism emerged in the late eighteenth century from the welter of radical sectarian and Baptist groups accompanying the Great Awakening in New England—people who did not belong to the upper classes and who fought against the established churches, whether they were Puritan or liberal. Unitarians remained rational and detached, but Universalists preached with the evangelical enthusiasm of people who had an optimistic view of humanity and millennial hopes for America. Universalists proclaimed that because original sin existed, God sent Jesus Christ so that all humanity could be saved and restored to holiness. In essence, the Universalists started from Calvinist premises and ended with democratic optimism by claiming that eternal damnation was incompatible with the loving nature of God. They could not agree whether there was any chastisement for sin after death or whether sin resulted only in punishment in this life. Universalists disliked creeds and church organization, but under evangelical attack, they created a loose association so that in New England their religious tax would not go to Congregationalist churches. By the 1830s, Universalists became less evangelical and moved closer to the Unitarians, defending universal salvation less on the basis of biblical exegesis and more on a rational and humanitarian basis.

In the 1830s, Ralph Waldo Emerson and other Transcendentalists claimed that Christianity was only one of many revealed religions. Disliking the rationalism in what they

---

[6] Quoted in David Robinson, *The Unitarians and the Universalists* (Westport, CT: Greenwood, 1985), p. 31.

termed "corpse cold" Unitarianism, the Transcendentalists brought the insights of the emergent romantic movement to religion.[7] Emerson, for example, claimed that all reality was miracle; so the gospel miracles did not prove the divinity of Christ. The Transcendentalists, named derisively because they had their heads in the clouds rather than reality, stressed intuitive knowledge of truth. Emerson, contrasting the reality of religious feelings gained by looking out a church window during a snowstorm with that gotten during a dry, rational sermon, claimed that the soul of man did not just contain the spark of divinity—it was God.

The Transcendentalist vision was aesthetic and mystical, described as combining the moral intensity of the Puritans with the sensitivity to nature of Jonathan Edwards, but dropping the pessimism associated with original sin. A movement of scholars, the Transcendentalists took selectively from Plato, Eastern religions, and the European romantic philosophy of Coleridge, Fichte, and Schleiermacher—all of whom stressed idealism over materialism—in Emerson's words, "the power of Thought and of Will, of inspiration, of miracle."[8] Every woman in her own experiences recapitulated all world history; the backyard of her house was as valid a source for knowledge of God as was the Bible.

Transcendentalism was a democratic faith, stressing the nobility of self-reliant people, denying the necessity of history or institutions, asserting that evil had no ultimate existence, and claiming that perfection was possible. A few Transcendentalists tried to reorder society by founding a communitarian settlement at Brooke Farm. Henry David Thoreau criticized the materialism in America, provided a classic defense of civil disobedience, and, at Walden Pond, sought a simplified lifestyle in tune with nature. His critique of the American obsession with progress is encapsulated in the description of the new railroad from Boston to New York as "an improved means to an unimproved end."[9] Transcendentalist Bronson Alcott sought to educate children without violence and according to their natures. His home was described by his daughter, Louisa May Alcott, in the book *Little Women*. Real religion did not come in church attendance or reading theology, but rather, "In the sublimest flights of the soul, rectitude is never surmounted, love is never outgrown."[10]

At first the Unitarians expressed outrage at the attack upon reason, miracles, and Christianity by the Transcendentalists, who seemingly denied evil and asserted pantheism. But within a generation, the Unitarians who insisted on free thought and disliked creeds began to stress their differences from Christianity and incorporated Emerson's emphases on intuition, idealism, and harmony with nature. Outside of coastal New England, the primary impact on America of Unitarians and Transcendentalists came through the literary movement termed "The Flowering of New England." The writers whom educated Americans read during the next century—poets Henry Wadsworth Longfellow, James Russell Lowell, and William Cullen Bryant; essayists Emerson and Thoreau; and novelists Margaret Fuller, Nathaniel Hawthorne, and Oliver Wendell Holmes—had all been influenced

---

[7] Joel Porte, ed., *Emerson in His Journals* (Cambridge, MA: Harvard University Press, 1982), pp. 286, 353.

[8] Quoted in Edwin Gaustad, ed., *A Documentary History of Religion in America* (Grand Rapids, MI: Eerdsmans, 1982) p. 34.

[9] Henry David Thoreau, *Walden* (New York: Modern Library, 1937), p. 46.

[10] Ralph Waldo Emerson, "The Divinity School Address," quoted in Conrad Wright, ed., *Three Prophets of Religious Liberalism: Channing, Emerson, Parker* (Boston: Beacon, 1961), p. 95.

(in Hawthorne's case, negatively) by the Unitarian–Transcendental religious movements. The distinctive themes later found in Harmonalism, Christian Science, New Thought, and New Age religious movements first appeared during the New England Renaissance.

Religions: Made in America

The people of the new nation fluctuated between sophistication and credulity, piety and crudeness, rationality and superstition. Convinced that God had a special destiny for America and that a common man or woman could judge the truth of any religious claims, they saw nothing unusual in having homegrown prophets who had discovered truths hidden from all previous Christians. Americans wanted to believe with absolute assurance and to be convinced by reason and experience. For many who thought that the triumph of republicanism during the Revolution changed the future for all governments, the wilderness or rawness of landscape reflected a protean or seemingly unshaped potential for basic institutions and offered opportunities for experiments that might reshape the family, economics, and religion. Confidence, cheap land, and millennialism inspired Americans who saw, in communal experiments, a way to create a brave new world while restoring the primitive church.

Ann Lee (1736–1784), born in the slums of Manchester, England, joined a group who claimed that the Holy Spirit inspired their practices of ecstatic dancing, singing, and trances and signified the imminent return of Christ. Lee, whose four children died in infancy, became a charismatic leader of the group and announced a new revelation: Because original sin came from sex, true followers of Christ would practice celibacy in the short interval until the end of the world. In 1779, Lee had a vision prompting her and seven followers to come to America, where they bought land in upstate New York close to Albany and continued their practices of ecstatic worship and celibacy. Ann Lee functioned as a prophetess, whose role the Bible allegedly described as "elect lady" or "woman in the wilderness."[11]

The Shakers, as Ann Lee's followers came to be known from their dancing in worship, proselytized vigorously, attracting converts from Baptists and others in New England who found themselves possessed by the Holy Spirit during worship. The sect grew, with eleven societies in 1795 and perhaps 4,000 members by 1805; by the 1830s, there were nineteen Shaker communities from Maine to Kentucky, each with several hundred members. Converts came from those whose experience of revivalism left them disillusioned and seeking greater assurance and separatism from the world. Later, the villages would attract widows and orphans, who found security in the sect.

Ann Lee's death created a crisis among the believers, who had assumed she was immortal, and resulted in the founding of a planned community in 1788 in New Lebanon, Connecticut, in which the town layout, architecture, furniture design, music, poetry, and shuffling dance during worship reflected Shaker cosmology. God, said Shakers, had dual manifestations: a Holy Father representing infinite power and a Holy Mother equaling infinite wisdom. Jesus represented the male attribute of God, Ann Lee the female. History

---

[11] II John 1; Revelation 12:6.

was the record of contention between the forces of God and evil. Revelation was progressive, with the third manifestation being Christ and the fourth and final being Ann Lee, whose mission was the restoration of primitive Christianity. Shakers had only to follow her teachings until God's work was completed on earth. The Shakers saw themselves as God's elect whose role was to create a society on earth where Christians could love in purity.

Shakers represent one of the many religious or secular communitarian attempts to reshape American life by challenging the allegedly selfish nature of capitalism or restructuring the nuclear family so that its emotional ties could be extended into the wider society. New Harmony, in Indiana, began as a pietist community following the teachings of George Rapp; later, the English socialist and freethinker Robert Owen bought the buildings and sought to erect a socialist utopia. Like Brooke Farm, New Harmony sought to create a new economic order free from individualism and capitalism. Both settlements soon failed, victims of poor business practice. More successful because they combined religious fervor with perfectionist sentiments and produced goods desired by others were Amana in Iowa and Oneida in upstate New York. Under the leadership of ex-Congregationalist minister John Humphrey Noyes (1811–1886), Oneida sought to create new family arrangements through the practice of eugenics and free love.

The Mormons, or Church of Jesus Christ of the Latter Day Saints, began as a communitarian venture, but after moving west because of persecution, evolved into a close-knit denomination. Mormon history can be used to illustrate many themes of the second Great Awakening: a disgust with religious controversy and a desire to restore primitive Christianity, a commonsense rationalism combined with supernaturalism, and a sense of both individualism and community, millennialism and optimism. The controversies surrounding the founder, Joseph Smith (1805–1844), more virulent than any squabble among the different denominations, came because he claimed that his revelations superseded the Bible and that his church was not just early Christianity rediscovered, but a new dispensation communicated by an angel. If Smith were right, all previous Christianity was obsolete.

Joseph Smith observed with dismay the competing religious claims of the revivalists. In later life, he described a conversion occurring in 1820 when he had a vision of a bodily God and Jesus, an experience that led Smith, like Jefferson, to conclude that God was material and structured the world rather than creating it *ex nihilo*. Smith's 1823 vision brought more immediate consequences, for the angel Moroni appeared to Smith and instructed him to dig up golden tablets that had been buried in Mount Cummorah, New York. Smith dug up the tablets and, while seated behind a curtain and with the aid of seer stones, translated the *Book of Mormon* to members of his family. After Smith finished compiling the *Book of Mormon*, the angel took back the golden tablets.

The Book of Mormon contained a history of the original populations of the new world, some of whom were the ten lost tribes of Israel who came to the western world before the Babylonian captivity. In the three days between his crucifixion and resurrection, Jesus appeared before and taught these peoples. Eventually, there was a conflict in which evil tribes overcame the good people. The last survivor, Mormon, buried the golden tablets, which contained a prophecy that they would be rediscovered by a prophet, Joseph, who would gather a kingdom of saints and restore the true church at the dawn of the millennium.

Almost immediately, Smith attracted followers from his family and a small group who found in these claims the religious certainty they had been seeking. After gaining the support of a Campbellite minister and his congregation, Smith moved in 1834 from New York to Kirtland, Ohio, where he created a highly organized religious settlement practicing economic communitarianism. There he reinstituted the ancient Israelite priesthoods of Aaron and Melchizedeck in a newly built temple. Economic difficulties caused by a failed bank and religious controversy within and outside the town of Kirtland brought a revelation requiring tithing instead of communal property. Many Mormons moved west to Independence, Missouri, identified as the site of Christ's return. Their Missouri neighbors saw themselves threatened by an expanding Mormon population engaged in economic cooperation and block voting, as well as welcoming free blacks. Missouri was a violent frontier area, and in response to attacks on the Mormons, Smith authorized the creation of a military force. Persecuted and defeated in Missouri, the Mormons found refuge in a new settlement across the Mississippi in Nauvoo, Illinois, which a generous charter from the legislature made virtually autonomous. Nauvoo initially had a population of around 14,000 Saints, with the lukewarm having left the movement because of the troubles in Ohio and Missouri. In Nauvoo, Smith re-created a theocracy modeled on that of ancient Israel. Controversy in the town and from non-Mormons resulted when Smith became a colonel in the militia, ran for president, and shut down a newspaper hostile to him. Rumors also circulated that Smith and other leaders advocated and practiced polygamy. Imprisoned in a jail while awaiting trial in Carthage, Illinois, Smith was murdered by a mob in 1844. After a period of disarray, the Mormons, who now numbered nearly 30,000, regrouped, with one small faction advocating dispersing among the population and following the leadership of Smith's family, while another larger group would migrate west to escape the American government and to create a self-sufficient theocracy.

Smith's revelations in Ohio, Missouri, and Illinois on church government, moral living, and social organization created a new religious synthesis, analogous to the relationship of Christianity to Judaism. Mormons repudiated original sin, predestination, and the trinity. God was material and finite, not responsible for the origin of sin and constantly struggling against evil. Adam's sin was not a curse, but a blessing, because it enabled humans to learn how to achieve salvation. Jesus' atonement made salvation possible, but each human, by act of will, could gain salvation, which enabled people to become cocreators with God. Mormonism offered endless possibility for improvement: "As man is, God once was; as God is, man may become."[12] Smith wrote that souls were eternal, a belief with far-reaching implications. In the restored Zion, salvation came through the priesthood, a status reserved for males, and so it became important for females to be included in a family. The result was a justification for plural marriage, a doctrine first secretly discussed in Kirtland, but which was openly admitted after Smith's death and never practiced by more than a small minority of Mormon men. Because Mormons believed they had re-created the true church, they vigorously proselytized not only in America, but in Europe, gaining many adherents from England and Scandinavia.

In Smith, the Mormons had a martyr prophet; in Brigham Young (1801–1877), they had a leader who presided over the institutionalization of Smith's revelations. Young organized a mass migration to a promised land in the basin of the Great Salt Lake. There, at-

---

[12] Lorenzo Snow, quoted in Jan Shipps, "The Latter Day Saints," *Encyclopedia of the American Religious Experience*, Charles Lippy and Peter Williams, eds. (New York: Scribner's 1988), p. 659.

tempting to be outside the reach of the United States government, the Mormons created a city, built their temples, and instituted a theo-democracy maintained through block voting. By 1877, when Young died, there were 150,000 members of the church. Mormons attempted to create a state of Deseret, but the U. S. government refused and passed laws, later sustained by the Supreme Court, outlawing polygamy. The courts insisted that religious freedom did not permit a practice destructive of morality and the family. In 1896, after the church president promulgated a revelation against plural marriage, Utah became a state.

Millennialism

Nineteenth-century Presbyterians, Congregationalists, Baptists, Universalists, Shakers, Campbellites, and Mormons shared a belief in the imminent second coming of Christ, or millennialism. All took seriously the prophecies contained in the books of Daniel and Revelation about the five empires, the beast from the North, the time of troubles, apocalyptic war, and the return of Christ. Those who insisted that Christ was to come to create a thousand years of peace are termed premillennialists; the alternative interpretation, termed postmillennialism, was that a thousand years of peace would precede Christ's return to earth. In general, those who despaired of America's future tended to be premillennialists, and they were also more inclined to set a date for the presumed end. Postmillennialists remained more cautious about a date, and many expressed confidence in the ability of humans to reform society to create the conditions for the reign of Christ. Because there was wavering and a multitude of interpretations of the prophecies, millennialism's significance was not in its details, but in its general tone of orientation towards the future and the expectation of a special place for America in God's plan.

Millennialism can be interpreted either as an anti-intellectual reaction to changes in American life or an attitude drawing upon general characteristics of the Second Great Awakening period, such as confidence in the reason of common man to discover the hidden meaning of the Bible. Because the religious rhetoric of America as a new Israel or of building a new Jerusalem was used in a variety of contexts, it is often difficult to distinguish an Enlightenment optimism about the future of the United States from either patriotic civil religion or millennialism. For example, Thomas Paine, Benjamin Rush, and Thomas Jefferson saw a successful Revolution and republican government as inaugurating an era of progress and perpetual peace. By contrast, in 1830, Alexander Campbell introduced a new periodical whose purpose was "the development and introduction of that political and religious order of society called The Millennium, which will be the consummation of that ultimate amelioration of society proposed in the Christian Scriptures."[13]

Millennial preaching became a staple of the Second Great Awakening used in camp meetings, churches, and colleges. Evangelical revivalists dramatized the effects that Jesus' unexpected appearance would have on unconverted sinners. Premillennial emphasis could also provide an impetus for social reforms, for humans could found voluntary associations

---

[13] Quoted in Ernest Lee Tuveson, *Redeemer Nation: The Idea of America's Millennial Role* (Chicago: University of Chicago Press), 1968, p. 81.

to cooperate with God in creating a perfect society. Millennial expectations gave a sense of urgency to the task. The perfectionist or holiness theology created by Samuel Finney in the 1840s also fit into the futurist framework, with individual and societal perfection going hand in hand.

Congregations responded warmly to ministers who provided a credible exegesis of the relevant passages. After a close study of the Bible, William Miller (1782–1849), a convert who became a Baptist preacher, became convinced around 1818 that Daniel's 2,300 days before the final days began in 457 B.C. and would end in 1843. Miller preached his timetable and gathered an enormous following as March 1843 approached. The wavering of revivalism following the Panic of 1837, which also seemed to discredit social reform, turned many to premillennial expectation. When Christ did not return, Miller's new calculations determined that October 22, 1844, was the date. That day, followers gathered in church services to await Jesus; failure again led to the "great disappointment," but not to the discrediting of either pre- or postmillennialism. Those who continued to await Christ's return now joined new religious denominations, of which the most important became the Seventh Day Adventists.

The Benevolent Empire

Lyman Beecher (1775–1863), like other New England churchmen, worried about the impact of deism and universalism, the lack of religion on the frontier, and the questioning of inherited standards of morality. Immigrants flocking to America's cities from Roman Catholic countries in Europe arrived with no previous experience of democracy and seemingly susceptible to corruption from priests or political bosses. Converting them and the masses of unchurched Americans to evangelical Protestantism, argued Beecher, was sound religion and good social policy, because those who became church members would be more inclined to accept industrial discipline without any taint of radical ideas. They would also raise their children to practice self-restraint, respect for property, and deference. In the early republic, religious social activity merged concern for spiritual and material welfare with a desire for social control of those whose presence and ideas threatened the alliance between Federalist politicians and Calvinist churches. The elite created the organizations to control the excesses of democracy, but the church women and men who volunteered to do the actual grassroots labor sought to further the work of God's kingdom on earth.

The mechanism for reform was a voluntary association with a national headquarters, a board drawn from all major evangelical denominations, and a few paid organizers and hundreds of volunteers in small towns. The interlocking nature of these organizations has led to the label "benevolent empire." Our concentration in this section will be first on those organizations devoted to proselytizing for evangelical religion and then on those which sought to change American society.

Evangelicals had a great faith in the power of the printed word, perhaps because they relied so heavily upon the Bible and saw knowledge of the scriptures as the best antidote to infidelity. In 1816, the American Bible Society determined to make economical editions of scriptures available in every home. In 1825, the American Tract Society began issuing pamphlets on a wide variety of moral and religious issues. Taking advantage of the technological revolution that made printing a nine-page tract cost only one penny, the Tract Society deluged the country with instructive literature available at little or no cost. Soon these two organizations produced more than a million Bibles and six million books and tracts a year.[14] In addition, denominations established their own tract and Bible societies and published their own weekly magazines that provided religious and secular news to subscribers.

In 1811, a few undergraduates at Williams College pledged to undertake missionary work. Their commitment led to the creation of the American Home and Foreign Missionary Society. Earlier American missionary efforts had been confined to native Americans, a task made more urgent by tepid results and westward expansion. Evangelical Protestants made their self-imposed duty of converting the native Americans more difficult by refusing to divorce white culture from Christianity and generally disdaining all things Indian. So a Shawnee or Sioux warrior would have to renounce warring and hunting and become a farmer living on a well-marked plot of private property on a reservation. He would have to abjure dancing, consulting a shaman healer, allegiance to traditional spirits, and respect for the tribal elders. The women would have to stop working in fields and confine their labor to domestic chores in wooden-frame houses. The children would attend school and learn to read in English and the newly written language of the tribe into which the missionary had translated the Bible. And, as the Cherokee experience in Georgia in the 1830s illustrated, even when a significant percentage of the tribe did accept Christianity and acculturation, this would not stop the Federal government and the state of Georgia from taking land from "savages" whom God had not intended to be farmers. The protection of missionaries, the Presbyterian Church, and the Supreme Court did not stop President Andrew Jackson's deportation policies. The narrative of the Sioux shaman Black Elk (1863–1950) shows how, after the Spirits proved powerless against white soldiers, missionaries, settlers, and rum sellers, most native Americans embraced some form of Christianity. Only since the 1920s have missionaries recognized that Christianity can be blended with traditional culture in a creative synthesis.

Evangelical Protestants saw their duty as preaching the gospel to the foreign heathen, who otherwise would be damned. With only a minimal sense of the cultures and the religious customs they would encounter, young men and women—missionary societies often sent married couples with little training except in the Christian religion—journeyed to India, China, Hawaii, Liberia, and Palestine, bringing the blessings of western civilization and evangelical Christianity. The missionaries spent years away from America (for there were no home leaves), learning to communicate Christian concepts in foreign languages into which they translated the Bible.

The missionaries and their children encountered tropical diseases, and the seasoning process killed many, but their sacrifices inspired others. Pious women who sought an adventurous escape from a confining existence found self-fulfillment in mission stations. Evangelism was the primary task, but missionaries treated illness, founded schools, taught new agricultural techniques, and sought to improve the lives of those around them. The missionary family provided a different picture of western civilization to peoples whose previous contacts were confined to adult males—traders, sailors, and government officials. In return, reports published in church periodicals gave a sense of exotic places to many church

---

[14]Jon Butler, *Awash in a Sea of Faith* (Cambridge, MA: Harvard University Press, 1990), p. 278.

members, and missionaries who returned provided valuable ethnographic information. In many congregations, women created societies, which, by donations and fund-raising activities like fairs, supported missionary work.

Traditionally, the church had relied upon catechism classes or instruction in church-sponsored schools, but, except in conjunction with schools, had created no special services or instructional material for children. The Sunday school movement, originating in England in the late eighteenth century, sought to teach poor children to read and write and instruct them in religion. Since the children worked six days a week, the schools met on Sunday. Although after the Revolution most northern states created charity schools, many poor children remained illiterate. The American Sunday School Union, founded in 1824, published materials for the use of nondenominational evangelical church schools. As states legislated for common or public schools, which included Bible reading and prayers in their curricula, Sunday schools lost their secular educational function and confined their teaching to moral and religious subjects. The American Sunday School Union published lessons for children and adults, although denominations also printed their own materials. Males exercised most authority in the Sunday School Union, but young women did most of the teaching. Genteel middle-class families considered it perfectly acceptable for a young woman to teach in a Sunday or primary school. Teachers taught children how to sing hymns, held contests to encourage the memorization of Bible verses, told stories about missionaries, gave awards for attendance, and sponsored picnics, ice cream socials, and lectures. Churches regarded a flourishing Sunday school as nearly as important as the yearly revival or attendance at worship services.

Alcohol

Early Americans consumed such prodigious quantities of alcoholic beverages, that one historian has described the United States of the time as "The Alcoholic Republic."[15] Wealthy settlers imported wine to drink at dinner, farmers drank hard cider or beer and furnished laborers or artisans with beer at lunch, and travelers and merchants found sociability and transacted business at taverns. Improvements in methods of distilling in eighteenth-century England had radically lowered the price of alcohol and made gin a poor man's drink. Colonial churches censured drunkenness, and the states tried to regulate the number of taverns, but no one showed undue concern. Alcohol, in its good and ill consequences, was a part of daily life.

In the early nineteenth century, Americans discovered an increase in the number of the poor and concluded that excessive consumption of alcohol was the cause. Intemperance also led to profanity and breaking of the Sabbath. The American Society for the Promotion of Temperance was founded in 1826 by men active in the missionary movement. This voluntary society dedicated to the eradication of drunkenness sponsored lectures and published pamphlets portraying the social cost of alcoholism in causing crime, insanity, and the breakdown of families. Songs, posters, and plays portrayed a drunken father dissipating his wages on booze while neglecting his wife and children. Individual self-will and moral dis-

---

[15] See W. J. Rorabaugh, *The Alcoholic Republic* (New York: Oxford University Press, 1979).

cipline could end drunkenness. Revivalists saw a reformed alcoholic as a testament to God's power.

Under the impact of the Finneyite revivals of the 1830s, reformers went one step further and preached total abstinence as a matter of health and holiness. They investigated the relationship between tavern culture and gambling, crime, and prostitution. Medical doctors produced tracts showing that alcohol was a menace to health, and churches introduced pledge cards that adults and children signed, promising not to drink. At first the prohibition advocates in the American Temperance Union relied on the same methods used in the revival, preaching to gain converts to total abstinence. By the 1840s, the growth of slums in cities, the increasing numbers of immigrants, and the failure to control taverns prompted reformers to consider legislative action. States allowed counties local option—the right to pass referendums to ensure that no alcoholic beverages could be sold. In 1850, Maine went one step further and restricted all sales of alcohol. Maine laws, as they were called, passed in thirteen states and provoked a vigorous debate as opponents charged evangelicals with interfering with personal liberty and attempting to control the lifestyles of immigrant populations of Germans and Irish. In the 1850s the rise of an anti-immigrant, anti-Catholic American or Know-Nothing Party and antislavery agitation eclipsed the total abstinence movement, but opposition to alcoholic beverages remained strong in evangelical Methodist, Presbyterian, and Baptist churches.

Chapter 32

The Churches and Slavery

African American Religion

By the nineteenth century, African-Americans had created a distinctive form of Christianity, a blending of rituals and beliefs derived from Africa, their experiences as slaves, Southern white religion, and their own creativity. Historians agree that there were major differences between black and white Southerners' religion, but there is an ongoing debate about the survival in, and impact of, African customs in Afro-American religion: Did slavery result in a "spiritual holocaust" that destroyed the culture brought from Africa, or did the blacks preserve an autonomous culture, keeping an identity separate from what their masters prescribed?[1] At issue is whether an African or any alternative worldview could survive the horrors of destruction of the traditional village environment, the Middle Passage to the West Indies, transshipment from the West Indies to the colonies, and the mixing of peoples from different areas with contrasting languages, customs, beliefs, and practices. To endure in America under slavery, some insist, required adopting the white man's culture. Yet the prolonged intimacy between whites and blacks during the formative period of a distinctive Southern culture and religion allowed for an interchange of beliefs, particularly those that were functionally congruent.

[1] See Albert Raboteau, *Slave Religion: The "Invisible Institution" in the Antebellum South* (New York: Oxford University Press, 1978), part I; Mechel Sobel, *Trabelin' On: The Slave Journey to an Afro-Baptist Faith* (Westport, CT: Greenwood, 1979); and Jon Butler, *Awash in a Sea of Faith* (Cambridge, MA: Harvard University Press, 1979), pp. 129–163.

445

Slaves continued to be imported through the nineteenth century, and new arrivals brought African religious beliefs with them. Because there were few whites living on plantations in South Carolina, the slaves could have preserved or relearned rites of initiation, burial customs, and conjuring. African beliefs could have provided a way to seek power over whites, i.e., by using malevolent magic or witchcraft. Moreover, there was always the possibility of reintroducing Africanisms through contacts with the Caribbean blacks. The practice of voodoo in the New Orleans area, for example, could have come directly from Africa or been derived through Haiti in the nineteenth century.

Southern white folk culture often reinforced African religion, for both races accepted magic as a force for good or ill, wore charms to ward off evil, believed in the power of spirits of the dead, and used a variety of herbal and conjuring methods to ward off illness. So what is now seen as a West African survival could have been originally brought over and been preserved by American blacks, or could have been introduced later, or could have been the result of the congruence of African and American popular religion. By late in the eighteenth century, Afro-Americans had become acculturated; that is, they spoke English, and any African beliefs and practices that survived did so within a Christian context.

The Northern states abolished slavery after the Revolution. Free blacks who had previously attended white churches encountered discrimination and either created separate congregations or organized new denominations. Richard Allen (1760–1831), an ex-slave who earned his freedom, was converted to Methodism. Beginning as an itinerant preacher and class leader, Allen founded black-owned and -supported Bethel Church, which served as mother congregation for the American Methodist Episcopal (AME) Church. Allen gained Methodist ordination, became the first AME bishop, and pioneered the merging of religious and political leadership that became characteristic of the black clergy. Arguing that the gospel had relevance to all of life, Allen spoke out in the name of Christian liberty against the slave trade, colonization, slavery, and the oppression of the blacks. Black clergy resisted seeing America, with its democracy and economic prosperity, as a new Israel. So long as racism and slavery prevailed, the United States resembled Egypt and deserved God's wrath. Slavery showed the hypocrisy in America's claim to be a Christian republic.

Slave Religion

In the colonial South, blacks learned Christianity from ministers supported by the Society for the Propagation of the Gospel, from the rare master concerned for the spiritual welfare of his slaves, or, most frequently, from revivalists. After the Revolution, Baptists and Methodists found converts among blacks who experienced a welcome release from oppression in the spiritual ecstasy encouraged by revivalists who proclaimed that Christ died to save all peoples and that conduct, not skin color, determined true virtue.

Until Reconstruction, Southern slaves attended the congregations of their white masters, where they encountered the sermons, hymns, and prayers of the Second Great Awakening. Blacks could become full members of many churches and outnumbered white congregants in some, but still had to sit in the back or balcony. After the 1830s, in response to criticism by Northerners, Southern ministers emphasized a mission to the slaves. After all, since Southerners defended slavery as a civilizing institution, they could not easily deny slaves the benefits of religion. Yet masters remained aware that allowing slaves to attend church and become members provided them a status comparable to, and standards by which to judge, white people.

White preachers presented a version of Christianity designed to foster harmony among races without addressing the crucial paradox that the slave was both a person and property. Masters learned that their responsibilities were patriarchal, to treat "slaves justly and fairly" (Col. 4:1) as members of their families and children of God. Slavery, insisted its apologists, was unlike the exploitive Northern wage labor, because owners accepted an obligation to care for the very young, as well as the old who were no longer able to work in the field. The plantation prevented grinding poverty. An owner's obligation was to foster Christianity among slaves by example. So the master and his family had to learn self-control, to "forbear threatening" (Ephesians 6:9), and never to discipline under anger.

After the 1830s, Southerners refused to countenance any discussion of the morality of slavery. Instead, they buttressed their case for the compatibility of Christianity and slavery with extensive citations from the Old and New Testaments. So the slaves attending white services heard that God had ordained slavery as the preferred pattern of society. Christianity required that servants obey their masters wholeheartedly with "fear and trembling," "rendering service with good will as to the Lord" (Ephesians 6:5–7). Rebellion against one's master was defiance of God, and the reward for being a good slave would come in the next life. It is difficult now to assess whether either race took seriously white ministerial advice or whether, instead, the mission to the slaves served only to reinforce each group's convictions about the failures of the other.

Slaves soon created their own religious observances, meeting when they would not be observed by whites. Three-fourths of whites in the South did not own slaves, and most of those who owned slaves had fewer than five. But more than half of the slaves in the South lived on plantations in groups of twenty or more, and a lack of supervision at night gave opportunities for slaves from one or several plantations to gather.

The central figure in slave religion was the preacher. He was often illiterate, because the law forbade teaching slaves to read and write; so his knowledge of theology and scripture came from memory and his influence came from his personal piety and ability through oratory to foster a sense of the presence of the Holy Spirit. Rhythmic repetitive preaching, the shout—a circular song and dance derived from Africa—and songs later termed spirituals improvised by the congregation created a distinctive and powerful liturgy.

Negro spirituals illustrate major themes in black religion. One was an identification with the people of Israel and Moses' liberation of them from Egyptian slavery to freedom: "Go down, Moses, Way down in Egypt's land, Tell ole Pharaoh, Let my people go!" A second theme contrasted a future life of glory and plenty with deprivation in this world: "I gotta shoes, you gotta shoes, All God's children gotta shoes. Oh, when I git to Heaven, gonna put on my shoes, gonna walk all over God's heaven." There was a close identification with the suffering Jesus: "Were you there, when they crucified my Lord? Were you there, when they nailed him to the tree?" Jesus' suffering was like black suffering; his resurrection prefigured the triumph of the oppressed. Moses and Jesus symbolized the coming day of liberation. The immediate experience of God provided a foretaste of deliverance ("My Lord Delibered Daniel"), the final liberation after death, "Oh, freedom." There also would come God's judgment on the wicked. Millennial expectations appeared as well:

"Blow (Gabriel) your trumpet louder, And I want dat trumpet to blow me home . . . To my new Jerusalem."[2]

Black religion provided a means of coping with slavery, a way to assert that Christ's evaluation was more important than the master's: "Nobody knows de trouble I've seen. Nobody knows but Jesus." Blacks remembered that they and their labor had been stolen; taking back ill-gotten gains from whites was not the same as stealing from black brothers and sisters. In a system where slave marriages had no legal standing and in which a family could be destroyed with the selling of husband, wife, or children ("Sometimes I feel like a motherless child"), black Christianity emphasized community cooperation, love of neighbor, and God's coming justice. Christianity gave Afro-Americans a joyful confidence that ultimately God controlled history and that right—meaning freedom—would triumph: "Go, tell it on the mountain, Over de hills an' everywhere . . . Dat Jesus Christ is born."

Churches Confront Slavery

During the late eighteenth century, Americans began to apply to black slavery the natural-rights philosophy first used to accuse Great Britain of attempting to enslave her colonists. The Second Continental Congress had not intended "all men are created equal" to apply to Negroes, but almost immediately a few colonists saw its relevance. The early anti-slavery movement also utilized humanitarian and religious sentiments. The Northern states abolished slavery in 1784. Still, at the insistence of Southern delegates, the federal Constitution acknowledged the existence of slavery, denied the humanity of blacks by giving owners added political power by the three-fifths clause, and forbade abolishing the slave trade for twenty years. When, in 1807, the slave trade was finally outlawed, the North viewed the measure as antislavery, while the South believed that cutting off additional supplies of slaves protected an investment in human capital.

In the South, although the view that slavery was an evil was widespread, there was little support for emancipation. After the Revolution, Baptists and Methodists learned that preaching antislavery doomed their expansion, and both churches jettisoned their opposition to this peculiar institution. Their defeat over slavery taught both denominations the limits on the power of evangelical religion to change Southern society and contributed to their focus on individual sin. Before the Civil War, Southern preachers condemned the North for politicizing religion and neglecting spiritual concerns.

Leading churchmen and statesman from all areas supported the American Colonization Society, founded in 1818, because sending blacks back to Africa offered a simple solution to the problems of slavery and racial animosity. As a realistic solution, colonization was nonsense because there was inadequate shipping capacity to send even the natural increase in black population to Africa. And there was no political will for the federal government to raise taxes to buy the freedom of slaves. In the South, colonization attracted those who wished to get rid of free blacks; in the North, it attracted racists as well as idealists who be-

---

[2] *Religious Folk Songs of the Negro as Sung on the Plantation* (Hampton, VA: Institute Press, 1918), pp. 9, 21, 110–111,115, 152–153, 174. Quoted in Lawrence Levine, *Black Culture and Black Consciousness* (New York: Oxford University Press, 1979), pp. 52–53.

lieved that the two peoples could not live in harmony, and it offered a politically cheap way to be antislavery. Almost no one consulted American blacks as to whether they wished to return to Africa. A few did see in the new state of Liberia a method of bringing Christianity and American civilization to Africa. Richard Allen echoed the prevailing sentiment that God had given to evangelical Christian blacks a distinct mission to convert Africa, but that home was America and no one should be coerced into leaving.

While moderates petitioned Congress and worked to end servitude gradually, slavery expanded from tidewater areas westward to the Mississippi and beyond, proving that it was not going to die out naturally. The debate over the admission of Missouri as a slave state in 1820 showed the growing divergence of North and South on the desirability of slavery or even the need to reform the "peculiar institution."

By the 1830s the failure of gradualism and a zeal for humanitarian reform and perfectionism shown in the movement from moderation to total abstinence of alcohol appeared also in antislavery. In 1831, in the first issue of his newspaper, *The Liberator,* William Lloyd Garrison announced the new credo: "On this subject, I do not wish to think, or speak, or write, with moderation. . . . AND I WILL BE HEARD."[3] Garrison, supported by the free black community, attacked colonization and demanded immediate uncompensated emancipation and enfranchisement of slaves. He denounced the federal Constitution as a "covenant with death," southerners as evil, and the churches as apostate. Welcoming women to the antislavery cause—even allowing them to participate in and speak to mixed gatherings—Garrison joined antislavery to nonresistance and the emergent women's rights movements. In time, in his request for purity, he advocated the separation of the North from the slaveholding South. Earlier, a few of the new abolitionists had become disillusioned with effects of the revival. Lucretia Mott and James G. Whittier, the poet, built upon the Quakers' longstanding opposition to slavery. Frederick Douglass (ca. 1817–1895) joined this movement after he escaped slavery in 1838 and lectured on what growing up a slave meant. Harriet Tubman, herself a runaway, courageously journeyed back into the upper South to lead other slaves to freedom. In the midwest, Theodore Dwight Weld, a Finney convert, taught his fellow Oberlin students to preach immediate emancipation like a revival. Antislavery grew rapidly, with local abolition societies attracting 250,000 members by 1838, including Unitarians like Channing and wealthy supporters of the revival, as well as the "Benevolent Empire" such as the Tappan brothers of New York City. In the North, mobs tried to silence the abolitionists, and conservatives opposed them as threats to property and union.

By the 1840s, the Northern antislavery movement splintered over Garrison's embrace of many reforms, attack upon the churches, and his disdain of politics. While the antislavery Liberty Party gathered few votes, slavery had become a political issue that would not disappear in spite of efforts of the two national parties to ignore or make contradictory pronouncements on it. In the 1850s, the newly formed Republican Party would combine opposition to slavery and fears of competition with slave labor in its slogan, "Free Soil, Free Labor, and Free Men."[4]

Major American denominations, fearing schisms, attempted to straddle the issue.

---

[3] Quoted in Louis Ruchames, ed., *The Abolitionists* (New York: Capricorn, 1964), p. 31.

[4] Eric Foner, *Free Soil, Free Labor, Free Men: The Ideology of the Republican Party before the Civil War* (New York: Oxford, 1970).

Episcopalians, Lutherans, and Roman Catholics took no stand. The Presbyterian Old School–New School split of 1837 did not involve abolition, but the Old School clearly opposed the reforms stemming from the Second Great Awakening. New School Presbyterians hoping to retain Southern members took no position on slavery until 1857, when pro- and antislavery agitation brought a separation. Charles Finney weakened the Oberlin commitment to abolition by approving of antislavery, but insisting that conversion of sinners in the revival was more important. Concerned about what they saw as temporizing on slavery by the Methodists, a small group of Primitive or Wesleyan Methodists advocating abolition left the church in the 1840s. The major division into the Methodist Episcopal Church North and South occurred in 1844 and involved the issue of whether a bishop could own slaves. For Baptists, already a decentralized denomination, the schism into separate Northern and Southern Baptists occurred in 1845 over whether missionaries could be slaveholders. The resulting animosity and continuing bitter disputes over church affiliation, particularly in the border states, helped to persuade each side of the evilness of the other and sharpened the division between slave and free states. Contemporaries saw the destruction of nationwide churches as prefiguring a possible separation of the nation.

Any hope that the South could be persuaded to give up slavery voluntarily or to drastically reform the institution ended after 1831 with the strong reaction to Garrison's newspaper and Nat Turner's Rebellion. Turner, a literate Baptist slave preacher whom his master thought had received favorable treatment, believed that God had destined him for great deeds and, after a vision of the Holy Spirit, determined to gain freedom for his people. After Turner planned and enlisted the help of fellow slaves in carrying out an insurrection that led to the deaths of fifty-seven whites, he was captured, tried, and hanged. His autobiography, dictated while he was in jail, shows the religious underpinnings of slave resistance. Southerners were already obsessed with fear of black insurrection, so they tightened laws forbidding black gatherings at night, even for religious purposes. Southerners succeeded in persuading the federal government to censor mails to screen out any antislavery materials. With abolitionists decreeing that slavery was a total evil and Southerners insisting that it was moral, there was little room for compromise.

A similar narrowing of freedom in thought occurred as the South repudiated the Jeffersonian heritage of rationalism, and Baptist and Methodist revivalism came to dominate Southern religion. Unlike the North, the South did not experience the ferment of freedom in a variety of communitarian religious experiments or humanitarian reforms. It had no movement for mass public education. The white population remained overwhelmingly Protestant Anglo-Saxon, with only a smattering of new European immigrants and, except in Louisiana, few Roman Catholics. With some exceptions—Richmond, New Orleans, and Charleston—the South remained predominantly rural, and even in 1860 most land was only one generation away from the frontier. But the South remained tied into the industrial economies of the North and Britain by using slave labor to grow for export a variety of staple crops, such as cotton, hemp, and tobacco. Britain's abolition of slavery in 1837 and growing antislavery sentiment in the North put the South in a defensive and increasingly embattled position.

The Southern clergy pictured the region as an embodiment of Christian civilization and defended slavery as a positive good. Against abolitionists who described the plantation as a brothel for women and whipping post for men, the clergy insisted upon the paternalism of masters who had accepted the burden of caring for "childlike" Negroes. Slavery was a "school" for Christianizing and civilizing Afro-Americans, who allegedly enjoyed a much better life in America than in Africa. Abolitionists ignored, said the clergy, the clear biblical evidence supporting slavery.

To Europeans, all Americans were Yankees, but Southern clergy contrasted the cavalier mentality of the Southern planters with the crass money-grubbing spirit of the Northern Yankees. Southern slaves had a better life than northern factory workers, whose bosses took no responsibility for their employees' welfare. Like the South, the great civilizations of ancient Greece and Rome, for example, had been built upon a "mudsill"[5] of slavery. As the Northern states outstripped the South in wealth and population, the clergy cried out against the aggression of abolitionists and the Republican party. Had the Southern clergy not spoken so unanimously in support of "fire-eater" or extremist politicians, the movement for secession would have failed.

The Civil War

Months of indecision following the election of Abraham Lincoln in 1860 ended with the attack upon Fort Sumter in April 1861. The hesitations and prayers for peace now ended as the clergy on both sides embraced the God of holy wars, proclaimed their cause just, blamed the war on aggression by the other side, and anticipated an easy victory. They invoked the blessings of God on the armies, saw victories as given by God, and explained defeats as due to God's chastisement for sins. The sacrifice of blood was a necessary purging so that God could create a more Christian society.

The Confederate anthem "Dixie" seems pastoral and nostalgic ("Oh, I wish I was in the land of cotton, old times there are not forgotten, Look away, look away, Dixie land") when contrasted with the Northern war song, "The Battle Hymn of the Republic." The song is infused with biblical language merging military and millennial themes: "Mine eyes have seen the glory of the coming of the Lord," who will appear in judgment, for "he is tramping out the vintage where the grapes of wrath are stored."[6] Grapes and wine were a symbol of blood used in communion services to signify sacrifice. The sin of the South deserved the wrath of a judging God who accompanied the Union armies: "I have seen him in the watch-fires" of camps and in "burnished rows of steel." Jesus as the exemplar of love and mercy was almost irrelevant. His peaceful origin was remote: "In the beauty of the lilies Christ was born across the sea." Lilies, not normally used as a Christmas flower, convey thoughts of Easter and resurrection. But Jesus' main significance was to die for a cause: "As he died to make men holy," an act equal in significance to the purpose of the war, "let us die to make them free." The chorus merged God's and the Northern army's marching, and His presence guaranteed the victory of the righteous. Although the Bible never portrayed God as marching, the chorus of Howe's "Battle Hymn" made God a soldier in the Union armies, a fighter for freedom, and a granter of victory. Americans to this day find assuring

---

[5] See Drew Gilpin Faust, *James Henry Hammond and the Old South* (Baton Rouge, LA: Louisiana State University Press, 1982), p. 346.

[6] Quoted in Henry S. Commager, ed., *The Blue and the Grey, the Story of the Civil War* (Indianapolis: Bobbs-Merrill, 1950), p. 573.

the confidence expressed in the "Battle Hymn" that God fights for freedom alongside the American armies.

Abraham Lincoln, though never a church member, knew his Bible well and summarized the moral dimensions of the war for many Northerners. Even though Lincoln believed that slavery was an evil, his aim, he originally claimed, was to preserve the union. Yet after the Emancipation Proclamation, he insisted that the North had purged the blot of slavery and could again become a chosen people. In his Gettysburg Address, Lincoln evoked a sense of fighting to preserve America's unique destiny: "that government of the people, by the people, for the people, shall not perish from the earth." His second inaugural, delivered as the war slowly ground down, was almost a sermon. Both sides, he said, prayed to the same God and expected an easy victory, but the providence of God confounded both sides. God's justice may have required that North and South shed sufficient blood to balance the blood of slavery. Yet no one should question the justice of the "Almighty," who has "His own purposes." "With malice toward none; with charity for all; with firmness in the right as God gives us to see the right, let us strive on to finish the work we are in." Our obligation, said Lincoln, was to "act in the right as God gives us to see the right."[7]

Reconstruction

Lincoln's appeal for reconciliation failed. His assassination in 1865 created a martyr president and magnified bitterness against the Confederacy. The South, while admitting defeat and rejoining the union, attempted to ensure white supremacy. This brought conflict with Northerners who, during and after the war, sought to improve the condition of the freedmen. While the fighting was still going on, slaves left the plantations, seeking freedom behind Union lines. Initially, the Northern churches had undertaken major campaigns to provide food and clothing for freedmen. Idealistic men and women, termed "carpetbaggers," who saw their Christian duty as helping blacks escape from the effects of slavery, moved to the South after the war to provide primary schooling and to train the freedmen to exercise their rights. In 1860, less than five percent of Southern blacks were literate; by 1900, nearly seventy percent were. Northern missionaries found black adults and children thirsting for knowledge so that they could read the Bible. Southern states, who for the first time were creating public schools for whites, refused to provide comparable facilities for blacks. As late as 1900, no public school in the South provided more than one year of high school education. So either on their own or with the aid of white philanthropists, blacks working through their churches created schools.

The churches also supported the creation of black academies and normal schools, some of which, like Tuskegee, Meharry, Morehouse, and Spelman, evolved into colleges that educated men for trades or the ministry and women to teach schools. The National Training School in Washington, DC, created and supported by the black Baptist Women's Convention, stressed an education centered on the three B's: "Bible, bath, broom."[8] North-

---

[7] Quoted in Richard Current, ed., *Political Thought of Abraham Lincoln* (New York: Macmillan, 1967), p. 316.

[8] Evelyn Brooks Higginbottam, *Righteous Discontent: The Women's Movement in the Black Baptist Church, 1880–1920* (Cambridge, MA: Harvard University Press, 1993), p. 216.

erners and Southern blacks sought to educate for the purpose of gaining respectability for blacks, arguing that social decorum would weaken racism and end the negative stereotypes. So the schools sought to inculcate Victorian morality and to create a black middle class, even though as late as 1900 only one percent of Southern blacks had what one might term middle-class occupations. In 1910, eighty percent of black women who were not engaged in agricultural labor were domestic servants or laundresses. The educated men and women in black churches sought to imitate white Evangelicals by opposing secular music, including ragtime and, later, jazz; dancing; smoking; and drinking alcoholic beverages.

A symbol of the new South was Confederate General Nathan Bedford Forest, an ex-slave trader and famous cavalry leader, who now became the leader of the Ku Klux Klan. The Klan, the most famous of a variety of white supremacy organizations claiming to defend Christianity and Southern civilization, used threats and violence against black voters. There was no protest from white Southern churches. Instead, the Southern Baptists and Methodists consolidated their influence and repudiated rejoining their Northern brethren, whom they charged with preaching a political religion devoid of true spirituality. The solid South, firmly committed to the Democratic party, states' rights, evangelical religion, and white supremacy, excused all failures as due to Yankee imperialism and their own defeat in the Civil War. It contrasted the sordid reality of poverty with a romanticized image of the antebellum South and a glorious war.

Experiencing a brief period of limited influence during Reconstruction, blacks soon learned that they could expect no support from Washington and would be left on their own. The one institution they could create and control was the black church. So blacks left white churches, whether Northern or Southern, and affiliated with Northern black denominations like African Methodist Episcopal or African Methodist Episcopal Zion; most became Baptists, and the National Baptist Convention, organized in 1886, had more members than the next two denominations combined. No matter how poor the congregation, the church became the religious, social, and political focus of the black community, with burial societies, fraternal organizations, and other social and charitable organizations. The church was the only public space controlled by blacks, and in local churches and national conventions they gained skills in managing finances and meetings and a sense of their worth as Christian men and women.

Particularly in the rural South, where neither preacher nor congregation was educated, as under slavery, services remained focused on an ecstatic experience of Jesus and a heavenly escape from oppression in this life. Northern black religious leaders, like Bishop Daniel Payne (1811–1893), of the AME church, saw education as the key to improving the status of their race and believed that if blacks became like whites in learning and decorum, then the white community would allow blacks more opportunity. Payne, who had attended college and who became president of Wilberforce College, sought to foster an educated ministry and more formal worship. Teachers and ministers trained in the new black schools learned to disdain shouts, improvisational preaching and singing, and dancing in worship. They denounced conjuring and folk medicine as barbaric and sought to eliminate, through education, Africanisms and superstitions from black peoples' language and culture. But the poor preferred their traditional ways of worship, and soon, with the Fiske Jubilee singers traveling in the North to raise funds, even educated blacks and whites began to appreciate the spiritual song as a major contribution to American religious hymns. At the end of the century, the major spokesman for the black community was Booker T. Washington (1856–1915), whose inspiring autobiography, *Up From Slavery* (1901), recounted his life from birth as a slave to president of Tuskegee Institute. In 1895, despairing of the pervasive racism of white culture and recognizing the dependence of his school on Northern philanthropists, Washington, in a speech in Atlanta, counseled as the way to harmony "Cast down your bucket where you are,"[9] i.e., accepting an inferior social status and working for self-improvement and economic sufficiency anyway. Washington must have felt bitter that the nation continued to betray his race as he read, for a biography he was writing, a passage from the black abolitionist Frederick Douglass' defiant 1884 speech at the Columbia Exposition in Chicago: "There is no Negro problem. The problem is whether the American people have loyalty enough, honor enough, patriotism enough to live up to their own Constitution."[10]

---

[9] The best analysis of the social context of Washington's speech is Louis B. Harlan, *Booker T. Washington: Making of a Black Leader, 1856–1901* (New York: Oxford, 1972), pp. 211–220.

[10] Quoted in William S. McFeely, *Frederick Douglass* (New York: Norton, 1991), p. 371.

Chapter 33

An American Roman Catholic Church

Republican Catholicism

Unlike all Protestant churches in America, the Roman Catholic church depended for its identity upon keeping doctrinal and administrative unity with a European-based authority. American Catholics had to convince Rome that they remained devout servants, while persuading their neighbors that they fully supported republican institutions and the separation of church and state. The papacy, reeling from a loss of power and the anticlericalism of the French Revolution, saw American democracy and religious freedom as analogous to the radical program of France and, therefore, dangerous to the faith. Identifying its interests with monarchical power in the state and hierarchical order in the church, Rome led a counter-attack against the Enlightenment. The church stood for lay obedience to the local priest, the bishop, and the pope.

At the time of the Revolution, Catholics comprised a small percentage of the American population, being concentrated in Maryland and Pennsylvania. There was no resident bishop, but Jesuit priests maintained order through the devotion of the members, whose voluntary contributions and pew rents paid expenses. Priests and elected trustees shared authority in local affairs. The laymen saw how the newly formed American Episcopal Church combined a bishop's authority with that of trustees in selecting ministers and thought that they deserved the same rights. They also knew that in Europe the patron who had built the church often obtained a right of choosing the clergyman, with the bishop's consent. The trustees of Catholic churches, often men of substance whose financial contributions supported building and priest, wished more actual authority in running their church and wanted clerics to be good preachers who would merit respect from their Protestant neighbors. The trustees wanted a church that would preserve clerical authority in spiritual matters, while giving the laity power in temporal affairs.

Charles Carroll (1737–1832), of Maryland, who was first vicar apostolate and then was consecrated in 1788 as the first American bishop, opposed the trustees' claims, but sought a means of compromise. His successors, all foreign born and educated, regarded the trustee position as making the Roman Church Protestant and democratic and so, in an effort to preserve the catholicity of the church, sought to make themselves dominant in temporal and spiritual church affairs. They wished to hold church property in their own names and to appoint all trustees. The resulting battle, termed the trustee controversy, continued intermittently from the 1780s until the 1850s. Rome supported the bishops; their republican neighbors favored the trustees. Since the disputes between trustees and bishops occurred in full view of Protestants, a side effect was to fuel fears of a Roman Catholic subversion of American government by an undemocratic hierarchy. The bishops won because they controlled the supply and loyalty of clergy and were willing to deny the sacraments to trustees and churches that defied them. The result was the creation of an American Catholic Church with the laity subordinate to priest and bishop, a pattern of church government that continued until Vatican II.

An Immigrant Church

The bishops prevailed partially because churches loyal to native-born trustees were overwhelmed by an enormous influx of migrants, chiefly from Ireland and Germany, whose new churches needed the bishops' authorization. Forty percent of the ten million immigrants to America between 1790 and 1860 came from these two lands, and most of the Irish and about one-third of the Germans were Catholics. Between 1820 and 1920 nearly 4.3 million Irish came to America, with the greatest number fleeing the prospect of mass starvation during the potato famine years of 1846–51. Previous immigrants to America were poor, but not so destitute as the Irish who stayed in cities like Boston and New York, where they landed, because they could not afford to move west. Unlike earlier Irish settlers, who were often Protestants and came with families, those who now came tended to be young and single. They would provide cheap labor for the new canals, railroads, and cotton mills.

In contrast with the Irish, the Germans who migrated tended to be artisans and farmers with some property. Many left because of the failure of the revolution of 1848 to create freedom. The Germans came as families and often journeyed to the Midwest, with large concentrations in Milwaukee, Cincinnati, and Minneapolis. Because they did not congregate in ghettos and seemed to share more values with other Americans, the Germans encountered far less hostility than the Irish did.

As a result of Irish and German migration before 1860, Roman Catholics became the single largest church in America, a position that later migration would maintain. For a hundred years, American Catholicism became a church with a majority of members who were either first- or second-generation Americans. European Catholicism was a universal faith that had taken on the flavor of different nationalities over time, but normally, there were no conflicting styles of religion in one area. Now the American church faced incorporating groups with different patron saints, festivals, and hymns, contrasting styles of church architecture and decoration, and even divergent attitudes towards the clergy and the need for frequent attendance at mass. The immigrants, however, held tightly to their traditional ways as a method of preserving their ethnic identity in a strange environment.

In post-Civil War America, particularly after 1890, added to the continuing influx of Irish and German would be the migration of Italians, Poles, Czechs, Slovenes, Lithuanians, and Hispanics, who also wished to be Catholic while preserving the religious customs of their homelands. The Lutherans formed a dozen national churches and the Eastern Orthodox groups became nine different denominations. Catholics sought to contain in one institution the animosities that splintered into national churches.[1] The Irish regarded the Italian delight in religious parades as almost pagan. Mexicans and Italians saw the clergy in their homelands as supporters of an oppressive social order and tended, therefore, to be anticlerical. The Irish and Polish had previously utilized the church as a bulwark against hated foreign domination and looked to the clergy for leadership. Poles and Germans brought their long-standing animosity to the new world. Migrants from Sicily, central, and northern Italy acted as if they were three different peoples. Ethnic rivalries complicated church government as bishops who already faced a shortage of clergy learned quickly that Irish clergy should not be appointed to an Italian parish. And these ethnic animosities continued. For example, in New England, French Canadian Catholics tended to vote Republican, while Irish Catholics supported Democrats. A study of New Haven, Connecticut, showed that as late as World War II, Italian, Irish, and German Catholics rarely intermarried. In Chicago, even though different immigrant groups dwelt in close proximity, they often did not socialize with each other and would walk a considerable distance to attend a church with their own kind of people.

The American Catholic Church faced an enormous task of finding sufficient priests, building new churches, and integrating the immigrants into parish life. The church embarked upon a massive building program, financed mostly through the contributions of American Catholics—a remarkable achievement considering the poverty of most parishioners. Historians have argued that the magnitude of benevolence of New England Catholics retarded their property accumulation and thereby hindered their social mobility. However, creating a new church dedicated to a Portuguese, Italian, or Polish saint gave a sense of stability and identity to the people in the parish.

The urgency of integrating new arrivals into the church and the rapid growth of the church helps explain why American bishops became preoccupied with "bricks and mortar" rather than theology. At first clerics came mostly from European countries, but American bishops soon created colleges with seminaries attached. From before the Civil War until the twentieth century, the Irish furnished a preponderance of priests and came to dominate the American hierarchy. Indeed, on their first arrival, Italians and Lithuanian Catholics had to worship in the basements of Irish or German churches, but soon they built their own structures. Uniate Catholic priests from eastern Europe found the American hierarchy opposed to their distinctive style of worship and right to marry, so they joined with Orthodox churches. In the late nineteenth century, fearing the destruction of their distinctive manner

[1] Carl Degler, *Out of Our Past: The Forces that Shaped Modern America* (New York: Harper, 1959), p. 292.

of worship, having failed to gain the Vatican's sanction for more autonomous ethnic parishes, a small number of Poles created the Polish National Church. The verdict of recent historians, however, is that on the whole the bishops took cognizance of ethnic diversity and responded rather sympathetically to immigrant demands.[2]

The Ghetto Church

Rome and foreign bishops saw perils for Catholics coming to a country with a tradition of anti-Catholicism and a predominance of Protestants who actively sought to convert Catholics. Also, because of the papacy's politically conservative stance, French, German, and Italian supporters of liberal democracy tended to be anticlerical, free thinking, and anti-Catholic. America offered a free press in which such radicals who immigrated could spread their ideas among the faithful. Many of the peasant migrants had been only nominally Catholic at home, and over the centuries popular or folk religion mixed originally pagan customs, superstition, and magic with Christianity. Not only in America, but in Europe, the nineteenth-century Catholic Church tried to weed out unauthorized kinds of piety and to standardize worship.

Mainstream American culture also threatened Catholic values. Shakespeare, the Puritans, Milton, and Locke represented a nation that had discriminated against English Catholics, oppressed Ireland, and destroyed religious freedom. America's heroes, such as Jefferson and Franklin, exemplified the Enlightenment, individualism, and hope for progress, contrary to nineteenth-century Catholicism's more pessimistic assessment of humanity and emphasis upon endurance, order, obedience, and hierarchy. Even religious freedom could undermine the faith, because most Americans seemed to believe that all religions were equally valid and that there was no legal ground for distinguishing between truth and error. By contrast, Catholic dogma insisted that true freedom came from both church and state's cherishing truth and suppressing falsehood.

Following the lead of the German sociologist Max Weber, historians have often emphasized that America was shaped by a Protestant or Puritan ethic in which individuals, though unsure whether they had experienced God's election (i.e., had a valid experience of saving grace), viewed material well-being as an indication of God's favor. By valuing work and individual achievement, while at the same time disdaining material display and idleness, Puritans (in spite of clerical misgivings) allegedly furthered individualist and capitalist economics. A lack of virtue brought poverty; so churches and individuals should confine charity to the "deserving" poor and use relief as a mechanism for encouraging the unfortunate to become self-supporting. The United States in the nineteenth century did conform to Weber's description of the end results of a secularized Calvinism by exalting individualism, practicing capitalism, and showing little sympathy for the poor.

Catholics who came to America brought with them and preserved a distinctive, even premodern, social ethic that questioned the value of individualism and capitalism and sought to treat the poor with compassion. Instead of accepting Luther's doctrine of work

---

[2] Charles Shanabruch, *Chicago's Catholics: The Evolution of an American Identity* (Notre Dame, IN: University of Notre Dame, 1981), pp. 226–227.

as a sacred calling, the Catholic ethic saw work as instrumental; that is, it was good because a person did it in order to live, but the primary value of work was in the person and not in what he produced. Instead of laissez-faire economics, the Church relied upon the medieval notion of just price and the obligations of employers to provide decent wages for workers. Riches were not an unmixed blessing, and the community and the wider society had claims on wealth. Charity should reflect a Christian's commitment to sharing the resources that God had temporarily entrusted to him or her to help the poor and should be given as an act of compassion rather than reform. Just as wealth did not reflect the value of the person, so poverty was not a disgrace or a result of moral failure.

Protestants affirmed that basic institutions and even human nature could be reformed through self-reliance. Catholics, on the other hand, remained skeptical of individualism's ability to change human nature. They stressed the role of the church in providing the means of grace and, consequently, respected the role of institutions in shaping human destiny. Orestes Brownson, for example, repudiated transcendentalism and became a leading American Catholic intellectual because he found an organic order and discipline in Catholicism lacking in what he saw as an individualistic Protestantism. Of course, the distinction drawn between "Protestant" and "Catholic" ethics simplifies the enormous variations within each of these religious groupings. Some Catholics practiced the "Puritan" ethic, and many Protestants criticized materialism and empathized with the poor.

The School Controversy

The new common schools illustrated the dilemma that the American common or civic piety posed for Roman Catholics. Americans supported schools because, in addition to absorbing the "three R's" and republican values, pupils also learned morality through religious exercises, prayer, hymn singing, and Bible reading. The Bible used was the King James Version rather than the Catholic Douay version (which had notes in the margins giving the "correct" interpretation), and the hymns were Protestant. When Catholics protested, a few school boards, such as those in Boston and Baltimore, sought to make the curriculum and religious exercises more nondenominationally Christian. The school authorities assumed that providing Bible reading from texts with no commentary would be sufficient, but did not recognize that reciting scriptural verses in this way would still be viewed by Catholics as pro-Protestant. The Catholic hierarchy wanted state support for parochial schools because it viewed nondenominational religion as a contradiction in terms.

Many Protestants were already suspicious of Catholic intentions. They viewed with misgivings what they saw as hordes of poor Irish, whom they blamed for increasing drunkenness and crime, living in filthy slums, lowering the wages of native-born workers, and increasing taxes for poor relief. Irish moral deficiencies, rather than poverty, were alleged to be the cause of the social pathology of the ghettos. Even worse, these people, who had no experience of democracy, soon gained the right to vote and, instructed by their priests, supported corrupt political bosses and politicians. Patrician reformers created the common school system in an attempt to remedy the "defects" of Irish parental instruction. Now they saw the hierarchy's attack on Bible reading in public schools as an attack upon the religious foundations of American democracy. Lurid tales circulated of plans of the papacy, aided by

European monarchists, to funnel money to American Catholics to undermine republican institutions and to move the papacy from Rome to the United States. By the 1830s, scholarly attacks upon Catholic doctrine and practices by leading Protestant clergy flourished alongside exposés of alleged immoral practices of priests and nuns. Americans rationalized their taste for pornography by reading about the sexual abuses performed by polygamous Mormons and celibate Catholics. Underlying the anti-Catholic literature was fear: fear of the deterioration of traditional American values under the impact of urbanization, industrialization, and immigration; fear for the future of an American democracy already weakened by debates over slavery and reform; and fear that Protestants would succumb to the pomp, ritual, and authority of Roman Catholicism.

In 1834, following a series of anti-Catholic sermons by Lyman Beecher, a mob attacked and burnt the Ursuline convent in Charlestown, Massachusetts. In 1844, after the Roman Catholic bishop had opposed requiring Catholic children to read from the King James Bible in the Philadelphia schools, representatives of all major Protestant denominations joined in an association opposing what they called the insidious inroads of Catholics who were using the openness of Americans to gain power. Portraying the bishop as demanding the end to Bible reading and prayer in schools, the clergy inspired a political movement to keep Catholics out of power, which became the dominant party in the city after a series of riots in which a church was burned, people were killed, and the militia was called out twice. In New York City, Bishop John Hughes avoided a similar riot when he threatened to station armed guards around every Catholic church and to carry the battle to the Protestants. Anti-Catholicism would be a constant feature in American politics until the eve of the Civil War. In the 1850s, the American, or Know Nothing, party came to power in several states on a platform of social reform (e.g., temperance and giving married women property rights), ignoring slavery, and anti-Catholicism. Nativism served as a tool for Protestants who made secure the right for public schools to teach a nondenominational Christianity.

As a political phenomenon, nativism temporarily vanished during the Civil War. The Catholic hierarchy's strong support for the Union and the military contribution of Catholic boys earned immense goodwill, but increased migration at the end of the century brought a revival of Protestant fears. Catholic apologists used nativism to show the fundamental incompatibility of harmony between the religions and to accentuate the need for separate Catholic institutions. Like Protestants, Catholics supported the temperance movement and created hospitals and orphanages, but they insisted that their charities remain separate. A Catholic hospital would care for Protestants, but there was no question of Catholics and Protestants providing care together in a religiously neutral or secular setting.

In the 1840s, Catholics began creating a separate or parochial school system in which children learned that religion could not be divorced from other forms of knowledge. Outside of building churches, parochial schools became the largest charitable endeavor of nineteenth-century Americans. In 1852, American bishops recommended that Catholic children should attend only schools that were under church control. The response of Catholics was far from unanimous. In New England, initially neither bishop nor parents spent much effort on parochial schools. However, in Philadelphia, Bishop John Neumann, later canonized as the first American male saint, and New York's Bishop John Hughes made building schools a top priority. German Catholics placed more priority than did the Irish, and the Irish more than the Mexican-Americans, on creating separate schools. Given the poverty of many Catholics, parochial schools could be funded only because they were staffed by lowly paid nuns in newly founded teaching orders, of which the most famous was Elizabeth Ann Seton's Sisters of Charity. (She would become the first American saint, canonized in 1975.) Because Sisters who taught school had to receive an education, they contributed to the prestige of higher education and provided an alternative role model for young women. The educational pattern for most Catholics would be to attend a public elementary or parochial school and then go to work. Low wages paid to skilled and unskilled laborers required many children to work long hours in order to contribute their pittance to keep the family from destitution.

Devotional Catholicism

Behind walls of church and school, mid-nineteenth-century American Catholics created a ghetto mentality fostering a distinctive religious culture. In the new republic, Catholics had practiced simplicity in worship, with plain buildings, mass on Sunday, and an individual ethics based on imitation of Christ. All these practices had been in general conformity with other denominations' worship and contributed to the good relations between Protestant and Catholic. By the 1840s, republican simplicity had succumbed to devotional Catholicism with more ornate structures, furnished with crucifixes, statues, pictures, incense, candles, and multiple altars, where priests (who now dressed in cassocks and were called "father") performed an elaborate liturgy not just on Sunday, but for services throughout the week. For the laity, private devotions to Mary, individual saints, or the Passion of Jesus could fill many hours, and there were special associations of laity for charity or worship. Devotional Catholicism demanded unquestioning obedience from the laity, who were expected to confess their sins in the sacrament of penance before receiving absolution or forgiveness through participating in the reenactment of the sacrifice of Jesus in the mass.

In the nineteenth century, Rome attempted to shape popular piety in America and elsewhere through granting special indulgences for devotions accentuating the centrality of the institutional church in controlling access to supernatural power. For example, the faithful engaged in devotions to the Sacred Heart of Jesus present in the Eucharist in order to counter the lack of faith of lukewarm Catholics and scoffing Protestants. The devotions receiving Rome's special imprimatur displayed the differences between Protestantism and Catholicism: prayers to special saints for the souls of the dead, contemplation of the immaculate conception of Mary, and reverence for the vicar of Christ.

Personal devotions could meet an individual's needs in a more direct manner than public worship could. So a woman seeking a special favor from Mary could recite the rosary in church, even while the priest celebrated the Latin mass. Devotions pointed the believer to a transcendent realm, while providing access to female and male saints, Mary, or Jesus, all of whom could intercede with God the Father. Compared with Protestantism, with no intermediaries between Christ and the believer and no female sacred figures, Catholicism seemingly offered greater access to the supernatural realm or at least lowered the distance between a remote God and a sinner. The Catholic Church symbolized by the pope and the bishop created unity between saints, living and dead, Mary, Jesus, and God.

By stressing certain devotions and downgrading others, the church could weed out what the bishops regarded as a superstition and what modern scholars term popular or folk religious observances of Irish, Italian, and Polish immigrants. These traditional European devotions might include heretical or ambiguous doctrines or might encourage reliance on a shrine rather than the church. Theologians insisted that prayers to the saints or Mary worked only through grace and that adoration of God underlay all devotions, but the immigrant peasant, continuing centuries-old customs, might concentrate only on her patron saint or Mary to bring good luck, heal a disease, find a good husband, allow her to bear a child, or find a job. Historian Jay Dolan termed nineteenth-century American Catholicism a sin- and guilt-obsessed culture.[3] The church sought to cultivate a believers' sentiment or emotion, rather than a reasoned assent. Except for Orestes Brownson and Isaac Hecker, founder of the Paulist brothers, who opposed the sentimentality of devotionalism and sought to encourage dialogue with main themes in democratic life, American Catholicism neither wanted nor produced intellectuals able to deal with the theological issues caused by science or industrialism and the challenges posed by a predominately Protestant civilization.

Devotional Catholicism used revivals to keep members within the faith and to convert outsiders. These revivals, conducted by traveling priests whose orders specialized in preaching, concentrated services over a few days. Churches put large crosses or other signs on their front steps advertising the revival, and services included special liturgies. Catholic revivalism was an urban ritual and did not have the rural and nostalgic flavor of Protestant revivals. Revivalists stressed the dangers of hellfire and called for personal conversion as they sought an emotional experience of God anchored in sacramental observance. The church also sought to control sin by legalism, creating rules for correct behavior during fasting or in holy seasons like Lent and forbidding a long list of moral evils.

Women dominated numerically in the revivals, as in most other activities of Catholic parish life. They constituted at least three-quarters of those who attended services, even though authority remained exclusively male and Catholics played no role in the emergent women's rights movement. Women performed the devotions and were members of the sodalities, associations organized for charity or special rituals for a saint or the Virgin. Religion was one of the few public activities open to Catholic women, and participating in the devotional societies gave women an activity outside the home that fostered a sense of purpose and self-worth. In addition, women may have found that the church's familial language—with God as Father, Jesus as Son, Mary as Mother, and the saints as Brothers and Sisters—provided an image of mutual support and patriarchal authority congruent with their life experiences. The virtues associated with the Christian life—obedience, service, love, gentleness, and self-sacrifice—were, according to the Victorians, also the characteristics in which women excelled. These terms applied to Jesus as well, and Catholic (and Protestant) representations softened or feminized him. Portraits show an ethereal person draped in soft, white, flowing robes.

The church exalted Mary, who could serve as a role model for nuns because she remained a virgin and for mothers because she bore and cared for the baby Jesus. Her patient endurance of suffering at the cross provided a model for all women. Becoming a woman re-

---

[3] Jay Dolan, *The American Catholic Experience: A History from Colonial Times to the Present* (Garden City, NY: Doubleday, 1985), pp. 225–228; see also Ann Tawes, *The Household of Faith: Roman Catholic Devotions in Mid-Nineteenth Century America* (Notre Dame, IN: University of Notre Dame, 1986).

ligious (nun) was a higher goal than marriage, but becoming a wife and mother who raised godly children was also praiseworthy. Because females were morally superior to males, God entrusted to them the roles of "moral guardian" and principal educator of children. Women also played an important role in family or domestic worship. Victorian homes often contained altars or shrines and pictures of religious subjects. Such objects allowed the children to grow up surrounded by images of piety. Poverty forced many immigrant women to work either as domestic servants or in factories, but the ideology of the church remained focused on the family, in which the father remained the authority.

The New Immigration

After the Civil War, immigration contributed to the steady growth of Catholicism. The settling of the Great Plains and the mechanization of agriculture produced enormous social dislocation among Europe's peasants. By 1900, there were more Roman Catholics in American cities than members of all other denominations combined. The church became a service agency, providing a place for identity in the impersonal city, and for arrivals, knowledge of American customs. They could see earlier immigrants who had become economically successful and now had important roles in parish affairs. The ethnic parish allowed rich and poor to participate in the same liturgy and to affirm a unity that transcended class. Before 1880, most Catholic voluntary societies dealt with spiritual subjects; but later churches also created organizations dealing with recreational, educational, and charitable activities involving people of every age. There were church-sponsored bands, drama societies, baseball clubs, and mutual-aid societies. The male-only Knights of Columbus became the most important Catholic charitable and social society.

Not all immigrants participated in parish life. Studies of different national groups in New York show that in Irish neighborhoods seventy percent belonged to the parish, in German neighborhoods forty-six percent, and in Lithuanian neighborhoods sixty-eight percent. Dolan estimates that half of European immigrants attended church regularly, although in their native lands, Mexican and Italian Catholics had much lower participation, a trend that continued, with twenty-five to thirty percent attending regularly in America.[4] Still, these two groups brought to America a tradition of making the street a focus for religion by sponsoring elaborate parades dedicated to Our Lady of Guadalupe or the Virgin Mary.

By the end of the nineteenth century, many Irish and Germans had climbed into the middle classes, and there was a small upper class whose social events duplicated those of the Protestants. "New immigrants" from southern and eastern Europe and the church as a whole retained a working-class flavor, with men employed in factories and mines and on railroads and women doing domestic work either in their own homes or as servants. As seamstresses, laundresses, and factory workers, women had wages generally two-thirds lower than men's. Employers seeking a competitive edge tried to recruit laborers from different nationalities and churches, in the belief that their antipathies would preclude union organization. All major industries remained non-union, with employers using blacklists and lockouts,

---

[4] Dolan, *The American Catholic Experience*, p. 207.

hiring replacements for strikers, using company spies or Pinkerton detectives to disrupt the organization of unions, and gaining antiunion legislation as a way of controlling labor.

The American Catholic Church was in no position to influence domestic legislation on the rights of labor, because it had little political power, at least compared with Protestant denominations. Church tradition insisted upon a just price for commodities and the dignity of labor and criticized laissez-faire capitalism, but was not sympathetic to labor unions either. Pope Leo XIII also opposed socialists and communists because of their antireligious stance and attacks upon private property. In Europe, as in America, to be a socialist in this period meant to be anti-Catholic. Unlike the Protestant churches in the cities, which tended to attract mostly middle-class masses, urban immigrant workers remained predominantly Catholic, and the church was receptive to their interests. In the 1880s, the Knights of Labor, led by Terence V. Powderly, a Catholic layman, attempted to create a large-scale industrial union. The Knights were also a secret society with elaborate rituals, however, and the church condemned all such societies. In an attempt to avoid having the Knights condemned, James Cardinal Gibbons, the highest ranking prelate in America, negotiated with the Vatican not to condemn the Knights, while seeking to persuade Powderly to stop the secrecy. Gibbons was successful on both fronts, although the Knights soon largely disappeared after being vanquished in a railroad strike in 1885.

The Americanist Movement

Gibbons became the leader of what is known as the Americanist movement. He argued that the American form of government was not anti-Catholic and that democracy and religious freedom were desirable and even a model for European Catholics. While insisting upon the priority of Catholic dogma, the Americanists sought to enter into conversation with Protestants by lecturing at Protestant colleges, appearing at the World Parliament of Religions held in conjunction with the Chicago World's Fair of 1893, and cooperating with other religious groups on temperance and charity work. Gibbons approved educating men and women, did not condemn public schools, and supported expanding government services for the poor. The liberal Catholics saw American society as basically good and sought full Catholic participation in it.

Conservative Catholics in the hierarchy complained that the Americanists were betraying the Catholic dogma and undermining obedience to the church. They saw the public schools and American democracy as anti-Catholic, using as evidence the persistence of nativism. They feared that an expansion of government services would undermine the family and thought that advanced education for women was unnecessary. Cooperation with Protestants would not lead to conversions, but only a weakening of Catholic teaching.

Both groups appealed to the papacy for support. After an investigation, the Vatican, in two encyclicals, *Testem Benevolentiae* in 1899 and *Pascendi Dominici Gregis* in 1907, supported the conservatives by condemning as heretical teaching views allegedly held by some "Americanists." Gibbons insisted that no one in the United States espoused those views, but the papal rebuke that was sent to him essentially killed the Americanist movement. The church officially would not endorse separation of church and state, religious freedom, and democracy for other countries than America. Ghetto and devotional Catholicism triumphed.

Chapter 34

Sentimentality and Science

Women and the Family

Women played a crucial role in the religious life of all churches in the nineteenth century. They made up most of those who attended worship services, supported the prayer and missionary societies, and did the work for voluntary associations. Women served as presidents and treasurers of women's organizations, both within and outside the church. However, no church ordained women, although there were female revivalist preachers.

The Quakers and the Shakers allowed women to preach, and Finney scandalized conservatives when he allowed women in mixed assemblages to pray publicly or to witness to their conversion. Oberlin became the first coeducational college and justified its action by insisting that schoolteachers and the wives of preachers needed an education. Angela and Sarah Grimké, South Carolinians whose antislavery convictions led them to move North, outraged many clergymen when they talked about their experiences in the South to audiences composed of both men and women. A daughter of Lyman Beecher, Catharine Beecher (1800–1878), founder of, and teacher in a secondary school for girls and author of best-selling books on homemaking (1841, 1846, 1865), denounced women like the Grimkés for becoming involved in political agitation and opposed the nascent women's rights campaign. Beecher defended education for women, but believed that their primary focus should remain the home, where they could create a "Pink and White Tyranny."[1] Re-

[1] Quoted in Barbara Cross, "Catharine Beecher," *Notable American Women* (Cambridge, MA: Harvard University Press, 1971), I, p. 123.

ligion provided an ideology for those who thought that women's sphere should be in the church and family, as well as for the small minority who insisted that women should have the right either to stay at home or to participate in business, law, and politics. Their subordinate position in mainline religion contrasted with their leading roles in founding two new denominations, Seventh Day Adventism and Christian Science.

To the advocates of the cult of "true womanhood," females fulfilled their God-given destiny because they were morally superior to men. Women's emotional nature made them good mothers, empathetic to their children's needs, and inclined to piety and morality. Happiest in nurturing relationships, they prevailed in the home not by domineering or reasoning their way to victory, but through subordination and self-sacrifice. So the woman's sphere became places where the finer elements of humanity could reign: the church, the family, and the arts, particularly literature. All these should express a moral vision of humanity.

The family joined gentle, loving mother with her innocent children. The church had traditionally justified baptism as covering the blot of original sin and as joining infants to the church community. A revolution in ideas about childhood occurred by 1800: Now an innocent child came into the world, in William Wordsworth's phrase, "trailing clouds of glory . . . from God."[2] The home became a place not to stamp out the untamed will of an animal-like infant, but an arena where the child's unique personality could unfold. Children's and women's natures allegedly went hand in hand because both were sweet, gentle, and loving. So woman's sacred vocation, preserving the purity in the home, created the right environment to raise moral children. The republican woman instructed mothers to shape their sons and daughters into virtuous beings because the new nation depended upon their moral character. The home became a place for religious devotions, with the family reading the Bible and saying prayers in the morning and evening and grace before meals. Now there were even special prayers for children, distinctive children's stories, and songs for Sunday schools: "Jesus loves me! This I know, for the Bible tells me so."

Sustaining a separate sphere for women could be an empowering experience. Single women could build upon their domestic nature as nurturers of the young through their role as teachers in the new common schools. And teachers received education beyond the primary level in academies, normal schools, and female-only colleges like Vassar and Mount Holyoke. Fulfilling their true character as defenders of the household and supporters of religion, married churchwomen in the early nineteenth century began forming voluntary associations for causes traditionally associated with religion, such as charity for the poor. When these predominantly middle-class women came in close contact with the destitute, they saw the need for poor relief, as well as the dangers of alcohol and prostitution. It was a small step from helping their sons and daughters avoid such dangers to petitioning for changes in laws to protect women and children and then to campaigning for reforms in asylums, temperance, and the abolition of slavery. In questioning the privileged position of men, women began advocating laws allowing divorce that did not automatically entrust children to the fathers. Also, they believed that women who married should not lose all rights to control their property.

The separate sphere that enabled women to bond together to gain a sense of their

---

[2] William Wordsworth, "Ode on Intimations of Immortality from Recollections of Early Childhood," line 64.

abilities and power also bound them to each other. Even in their spheres of child-rearing and the home, male authority prevailed. Clergymen, claiming to protect the frailty of women, denounced as unfeminine those who sought advanced education, the right to vote, or to become doctors.

Books and sermons advocating the cult of true womanhood ignored the relationship of class to gentility. Middle-class women's leisure to read novels, attend lectures, and do church work depended upon the labor of servants. Innocence and frailty did not describe the hard work of farm women, nor did such concepts help the native-born and immigrant women and children or free blacks who labored long hours for inadequate wages as servants or in the cotton mills and factories. The emphasis upon the male as breadwinner and the wife as homebody also ignored the large numbers of women, often in poverty, who lived alone either because they never married or because of the death of their husbands. The cult assumed that a woman would move from the household of her father to that of the husband. Victorian domesticity created an image of the normal family of husband, wife, and children living in a harmonious, sheltered existence. Even in its heyday, this image was more prescriptive than descriptive. Religious writers, male and female, created and sustained the image. Beginning among Protestants, it was taken up by Catholic writers after the Civil War, was brought to black women by Northern missionaries, and became universal before 1900.

Horace Bushnell (1802–1876) provided a theological rationale for the new emphasis upon the family. Neither Bushnell nor many members of his middle-class congregation ever attained an emotional conversion experience. In *Christian Nurture* (1876), Bushnell portrayed the child maturing in a religious household as gradually growing into grace in an almost imperceptible manner. The child need never experience a time of thinking of himself or herself as not a Christian. In fact, the role of the parents and the church was to provide this kind of nurturing atmosphere. The difficulty with the evangelical religion, as Bushnell saw it, was that revivalists had taken the languages of the creeds and the Bible too literally; so being born again need not require a sharp break with past life. Bushnell's theology, when utilized in Sunday School lessons, allowed a curriculum focusing upon the goodness inherent in children.

Science

Americans in the new republic remained confident that correct science and religion pointed to the same truth, because God both authored the Bible and created the world. Jefferson, for example, was the most prominent of a group of intellectuals who believed that God had created all species at one time and that no species ever became extinct. The providence of God was such, affirmed Jefferson, that there was a use for every creature and a cure for every disease. Discoveries of sea creatures' fossil remains high in the mountains could be explained by the Bible account of the flood.

Before the Civil War, college presidents, who were normally clergymen, taught courses based upon Scottish Common Sense philosophy's assertion that God had instilled in all people an innate capacity to determine right from wrong. Truth endured forever, and humans had the ability to discover it. The biblical assertion that man was created a little lower than the angels found a sympathetic audience among Americans, who had a very positive evaluation of the abilities of even common people. Humans had been specially created in God's image, an event that careful analysis of the Bible claimed to prove to have taken place in 4004 B.C. Since then, the physical characteristics of the earth had not changed. So the world, like truth, was essentially static.

Scientists who were church members, like Yale's Benjamin Silliman, confronted discoveries of dinosaur bones and a huge variety of fossils that cast doubt upon the immutability of species and seemed to show that the earth had existed for much longer than 6,000 years. Unwilling to deny the geologic evidence, Silliman essentially adjusted his interpretation of Genesis to account for the scientific data. Because the Genesis account has "days" of creation before God created night, perhaps the "day" was a long period of time, even thousands of years. Before 1860, evangelical church members reconciled science and the truth of the Bible through what is today called Creationism, the belief that God created each distinct species at different times. The last and final creations were Adam and Eve.

Evolution

Charles Darwin's *The Origin of Species* (1859) and *The Descent of Man* (1871) posed a basic threat to the belief in a static universe. Positing an evolution of all life from single cells to the animal world and mankind, Darwin denied a separate creation and the immutability of each species. Species evolved because of survival of the fittest; that is, the random mutation that best enabled the organism to cope with its environment would gradually become a dominant feature. The process of natural selection, argued Darwin, took place slowly over eons. Darwin's hypothesis ignored both a divine plan and providence and threatened natural law as espoused by rationalists, because nature operated by tooth and claw rather than by universal ethical principles. Commonsense philosophy's innate moral sense implanted by God also disappeared. Humans were not a special creation, and their ancestors included all life-forms, from protozoan to apes; now being lower than the angels meant having chimps for "cousins." Evolution jolted Americans' self-esteem.

Darwin's account provided a credible explanation for the similarities among different species and an overarching pattern by which to understand massive amounts of data, but—because genes had not yet been discovered—he could not account for why mutations could survive many generations, while acquired characteristics always had to be re-learned. Also, there were gaps in the fossil records, the most basic being between other primates and primitive and then modern humans. Such lacunae prompted some American scientists, the most famous being Louis Agassiz of Harvard, initially to reject Darwin's theories, but within a generation most biologists, including Agassiz's students, accepted evolution.

Darwinism came to stand for a conflict between science and religion, between materialism and idealism, and between harshness and love. Was the only solid foundation for knowledge science? Could nature no longer be used as a source for morality? What did evolution show about the purposes of God and the meaning of His providence? The churches had to decide whether to ignore, embrace, or confront the scientific revolution.

The first response of most American churches to evolution was to ignore it, a response that continued well into the twentieth century. American churches grew by revivals that saved souls, not by conducting intellectual debates on the relation between science and religion. The late nineteenth century's most important revivalist, Dwight L. Moody (1837–1899), when questioned about evolution, finessed the issue of science and religion. Originally a Chicago shoe salesman who, after his conversion, never even studied theology, Moody became a salesman for God. He used traditional themes—sin, hellfire, and conversion—in an unsystematic way, while stressing an individual's responsibility to make a decision. In the pulpit he became a master storyteller, so that the prodigal son became the straying boy next door. Moody provided an example for those Protestants who, throughout much of the nineteenth and twentieth centuries, solved the issue of evolution by not thinking about it.

Henry Ward Beecher (1813–1887), a son of Lyman Beecher and a contemporary of Moody, had no difficulty in accepting a sanitized version of Darwin after jettisoning most of traditional theology. Beecher proclaimed that Darwin expressed in scientific language what the Bible told more poetically. That is, evolution was creation on the installment plan, a longer working out of what the Bible summarized. Beecher pictured the growing complexity of organisms reaching fruition in human beings as a sign of progress. He had already given up belief in original sin and the creeds of the church, so it was easy to select verses in the Bible confirming what he preached and to ignore the rest.

Beecher became the most influential preacher and religious writer in America between 1840 and 1870. Through his lectures and writings for religious journals, he reached the middle classes, who sought gentility and piety without embracing either Calvinism or the revival. Beecher was a popularizer who assured these people that they could reconcile the faith of their fathers with true science. He did so by claiming that "Nature becomes to the soul a perpetual letter from God."[3] A religious person could affirm the glory of God by walking in a field, watching the sea, or smelling a rose. Here one could see God at work, and such awe could lead to an experience of grace. This conversion was not like the revivalist's saving people from sin, but more an appreciation of the God who was immanent and transcendent. The primary characteristic of Beecher's God was not judgment, but love—seen, for example, in a mother's devotion to her child. God showed love for humans by sacrificing his Son, not to satisfy justice or overcome original sin, but as a means of communication. Beecher finessed the issue posed by science by grounding religion on feelings.

Beecher's sentimental theology did not appeal to those who admired Calvinist rigor and did not wish to jettison the Bible or a judging God. While Old School Presbyterian James McCosh of Princeton endorsed Darwin, theologian Charles Hodge (1797–1878), of the same institution, denounced evolution as impiety. The Bible, declared Hodge, was inerrant in every detail, and Darwin had attacked God's word. Hodge's Bible was not an assemblage of poetry and myth conveying mystery; rather, it provided clear rational principles upon which faith rested and which the theologians explicated. Unlike Silliman and commentators who reinterpreted the Bible to conform to the latest finding of scientists, Hodge reversed the equation, demanding that the hypotheses of science support the truth

---

[3] Quoted in William G. McLoughlin, *The Meaning of Henry Ward Beecher: An Essay on the Shifting Social Values of Mid-Victorian America, 1840–1870* (New York: Knopf, 1970), pp. 60, 69.

of the Bible, which continued to require a Calvinism proclaiming original sin and predestination. In its rejection of science, exaltation of scripture, and rationalism, Hodge's theology provided a foundation for twentieth-century fundamentalism.

The Holiness Movement

There was also no sympathy for Charles Darwin from the new holiness denominations. In the eighteenth century, John Wesley had distinguished between the act of justification and the next stages in Christian life, which entailed achieving sanctification—that is, holiness or perfection.[4] In a series of prayer meetings beginning in 1837, Phoebe Palmer, a Methodist laywoman in New York City, sought to revitalize churches by advocating that members should go beyond conversion to a second act of grace, or sanctification. A similar emphasis on complete submission to God's law characterized the teaching of Charles Finney after he joined the Oberlin faculty. The fusion of the two forms of teaching perfection resulted in new denominations: Wesleyan Methodists and Free Methodists, formed in 1842 and 1860 to protest northern Methodists' temporizing on slavery. These Wesleyans who allowed women to preach and receive ordination illustrate the close relationship between radical social reform and piety. A second baptism of the spirit bestowed power for Christian service; it was "not primarily intended to make believers holy or happy but to make them useful."[5]

A revival in 1857–58, camp meetings, together with conventions and an extensive publication program, helped spread the new emphasis to other denominations. Many Americans attracted to holiness doctrines disliked what they saw as a growing worldliness in mainline denominations, as seen in services conducted by college-educated ministers in elaborate buildings in urban settings. While holiness doctrines originated in the East in cities, they spread rapidly in the Midwest and only after 1900 in the South. Tensions within Methodism emerged over the role of independent holiness associations and what some bishops saw as an overemphasis upon the need for a second act of grace. Those most committed to holiness doctrines created new denominations: The Free Methodists, Church of the Nazarene, Pilgrim Holiness, and Church of God (Anderson, Indiana). From England would come the Salvation Army. These churches illustrate the close relationship between revival piety and the social conscience, for they vigorously proselytized among the urban and agrarian poor. The holiness denominations stressed biblical truths and had little sympathy with or interest in Darwinian science.

Pentecostals and Jehovah's Witnesses

The Pentecostals acted as if Darwin had never existed. Pentecostal movements derived from the holiness emphases upon revivalism, millennialism, faith healing, and a second act

---

[4] Quoted in Jean M. Schmidt, "Holiness and Perfection," *Encyclopaedia of the American Religious Experience* (New York: Scribner's, 1988), II, p. 813.

[5] *Ibid*, p. 936.

of grace. Believers sought some visible sign that they had achieved sanctification through baptism by the spirit, for then they could, with equanimity, await the Second Coming, an event that faith healing showed would be soon. In 1900, in the midst of an emotional revival service conducted in Kansas by Charles Fox Parham, a faith healer, a woman began to speak in what observers said was a foreign language unknown to her. Her speaking in tongues was said to have proved the presence of the Holy Spirit in her. William Seymour, a black itinerant minister, carried the news into a three-year series of daily revivals at Azusa Street, Los Angeles. There, in interracial revivals—with blacks, Asians, and whites—glossolalia became a media sensation and soon spread to holiness churches in the Midwest, Southwest, and South. The disinherited, socially marginal whites and blacks became the first Pentecostals, seeking relief from poverty and the dislocation caused by the commercialization of agriculture and industrialism. Pentecostalism provided believers a comprehensive worldview, and demanded strict moral standards.

Although the movement fragmented into many denominations very early, all Pentecostal churches believe that only those who speak in tongues have received what they call the third act of grace. The Bible told of the Holy Spirit descending upon the apostles in the first Pentecost soon after Jesus' resurrection and conveying a gift of preaching in many languages (Acts 2:4). The third act of grace conveys this same ability. Some early Pentecostals claimed that they could immediately become successful missionaries using their new languages. Today, many assert that for some the tongue may be a foreign language, but for others it is a medium of communication between the speaker and God. A few persons have the gift to interpret the language to the congregation. Most insist that speaking in tongues is an involuntary act: "It seemed as if a vessel broke with me and water surged up through my being, which when it reached my mouth came out in a torrent of speech in the languages which God had given me. . . . I sang under the power of the Spirit in many languages."[6]

Pentecostal preachers continue to stress millennialism, faith healing, revivalism, and glossolalia. It is estimated that there are two million adherents in the United States and a hundred million worldwide. Major Pentecostal denominations include the Church of God (Cleveland, Tennessee), the Assemblies of God, and the Four Square Church of Aimee Semple McPherson, a flamboyant revivalist of Hollywood. Like the Jehovah's Witnesses, Pentecostals believe that the world is going to hell and that they alone will be the faithful remnant ready to welcome Christ upon his return.

The Jehovah's Witnesses were more radical than the Pentecostals in their denunciation of Darwinists, all other churches, and all states, seeing them as minions of Satan. The Witnesses followed the teachings of Charles Taze Russell (1852–1916), a haberdasher from western Pennsylvania. After long study of the Bible, Russell concluded that the millennium, by which he meant the return of a spiritual Christ to the "upper air," began in 1874 and would be followed by his reign in heaven in 1914. Soon all followers of Satan would be annihilated, but these people would not go to hell; instead, during the thousand-year reign of Christ, they would be re-created and able to convert and gain eternal life, though in a more physical form than those who accepted Russell's teaching during their first lifetime.[7]

---

[6] Reuben A. Torrey, a holiness leader, quoted in Grant Wacker, "Pentecostalism," *ibid.*, p. 938.

[7] Quoted in *ibid.*, p. 938.

Jehovah's Witnesses believe that the only correct name for God is "Jehovah" and that all are called to witness Christ's imminent return. Jesus is the son of God who died on a stake as a ransom for salvation, but he is inferior to Jehovah. Because they view all governments as evil, Witnesses refuse to salute the flag, pledge allegiance, or serve in the military. To guard against the corruption of all churches, Witnesses have no clergy and meet in Kingdom Halls. The sect grew rapidly under the leadership of Judge Joseph Rutherford (1869–1942), a lawyer, who expanded the publication of the *Watchtower* magazine and encouraged Witnesses to proselytize by home visits. Witnesses refuse to allow blood transfusions, celebrate Christmas or Mother's Day, or join other organizations. Since World War II, they have expanded rapidly in the United States and abroad, using the slogan "Millions now living will never die," a clear invoking of the second Advent.

Seventh Day Adventists

Ellen White (1827–1915) experienced her first vision shortly after the end of the world did not come on the last date named by William Miller. She concluded that, although the world would end soon and only 144,000 would be saved, God did not wish anyone to speculate upon the exact date. White joined millennial interpretation to an emphasis upon the seventh day, or Saturday, as the correct Sabbath for Christians. Claiming to have a "Spirit of prophecy," she issued some two thousand communications upon a wide variety of subjects, which, later collected in *Testimonies*, became authoritative for the Seventh Day Adventists.

When her two sons came down with critical cases of diphtheria, White, who endured ill health for years after a near-fatal accident as a child, used a prayer formula in the hope that they would not succumb to the disease. And indeed, they did not. She concluded that the medicines of doctors could not heal, for the secret to health was "God's great medicine, water, pure soft water."[8] In the 1860s, White and her husband formed an Adventist settlement and health clinic at Battle Creek, Michigan. Following the ideas of Dr. Sylvester Graham, whose flour, when made into a bread, supposedly brought health, White prescribed bland diets, promoted vegetarianism and water cures, and banned the consumption of coffee, tea, tobacco, and alcohol. She insisted that excessive stimulation brought bad health and promoted exercise and a rigorous program of self-denial to cure male masturbation, which Adventists, along with many Victorian physicians, saw as physically debilitating and causing insanity. White worked for a time with Dr. John Kellogg in the sanitarium at Battle Creek. Kellogg invented and promoted health-producing foods, of which the most famous are cornflakes and peanut butter. As she grew older, White experienced visions to preach in Europe and spent ten years in Australia proselytizing for her religion. The Adventists began as radical critics of American life, strong abolitionists, and pacifists. They rallied to the Union cause in the Civil War and, over time, became politically and religiously conservative. Today they are a rapidly growing denomination in America, Latin America, and Africa.

---

[8] Quoted in Martin Marty, *Pilgrims in Their Own Land: 500 Years of Religion in America* (Boston: Little, Brown, 1984), p. 322.

Christian Science

Christian Scientists insist that Mary Baker Eddy (1829–1910), by repudiating the tenets of transcendentalism, spiritualism, liberal Protestantism, and New Thought, created a new religious synthesis. Others see her as belonging to an American tradition stressing idealism (as against philosophical materialism), optimism, and the harmony of God, humans, and nature. She taught an alternative view of healing that drew upon the prestige of two value systems: Christianity and science.

Raised as an evangelical Calvinist, Mary Baker learned to view illness as a sign of God's punishment. Subject to bad health, she sought cure through spiritualism, seances, and the "animal magnetism" or mesmerist practices of Phineas B. Quimby, which included laying hands on a person. Soon after his death in 1866, she fell and critically injured herself. Reading the Bible the next day, she experienced healing. She then began studying the Bible to understand how Jesus healed. She concluded that Jesus was the practical demonstration of the spiritual power, a master healer who saved humans from sin, sickness, and death. His miracles were "natural demonstrations of divine power," a force available to anyone with correct knowledge. Traditional Christianity misinterpreted the nature of God. The only reality was spirit or idea; matter, illness and sin, she said, were illusions. So God created no matter. "You say a boil is painful; but that is impossible, for matter without mind is not painful. The boil simply manifests through inflammation. . . a belief in pain. Now administer mentally to your patient a high attenuation of truth of this subject, and it will soon cure the boil."[9] A person who affirms this true knowledge, gained through prayer or with the help of a practitioner of Christian Science, will bring into harmony the unreal physical body with the true spiritual existence, in which there is perfection. The result will be a healing of sin, which results in the overcoming of disease.

Eddy published a description of her beliefs in *Science and Health* in 1875, revised it many times, and four years later organized The Church of Christ, Scientist. Eddy also taught the "science" of healing to practitioners, whom she licensed, and her graduates spread Christian Science beliefs over the country. After a series of disputes with her early associates, Eddy established a centralized control over the Mother Church in Boston. She selected passages from *Science and Health*, which, with hymns, Bible readings, and lectures, constitute Christian Science worship services. Because her teachings, unlike much medical practice of the time, recognized the power of religion in healing, Christian Science grew rapidly, and by the 1930s there were nearly two thousand churches with 269,000 members. Most of the practitioners—that is, licensed healers—were middle- or upper-class women.

---

[9] Mary Baker Eddy, *Science and Health* (Boston: Trustees under the Will of Mary Baker Eddy, 1936), pp. 131, 153.

Chapter 35

Responses to the City

Protestant Evangelicalism triumphed numerically during the nineteenth century by stressing conversions and sentiment, while attempting to ignore the challenges posed by new scientific and technical knowledge. This approach succeeded among farmers and inhabitants of small towns, but by 1900 one-fourth of Americans dwelt in cities. Protestants seemed to be surrendering control of an emergent urbanized America in which city dwellers dominated politics, culture, and religion. In Chicago, an 1880 survey showed that there was only one Protestant church for every 3,601 inhabitants; in Pittsburgh, in 1888 60 percent of the Protestants came from the middle and upper classes, which made up only 10 percent of the population.[1] To be sure, there were plenty of new Catholic churches, parochial schools, colleges, and seminaries, but evangelicals viewed these with dismay as contributing to the fragmentation of society. Protestant numerical weakness might mean the end of their hegemony in American life; so immigrants and workers had to be won. In the late nineteenth and early twentieth centuries, a rural and urban middle class together attempted to preserve the close relationship between American values and evangelical religion.

Since the Civil War, American churches had confined their pronouncements on economic matters to homilies urging laborers to work hard and be honest and businessmen to treat their employees fairly. The clergy rejoiced in the "Gospel of wealth," as evidenced in new factories, an expanded middle class, and millionaires who bestowed their largesse on

---

[1] Martin Marty, *Pilgrims in Their Own Land: 500 Years of Religion in America* (Boston: Little, Brown, 1985), p. 339; Carl Degler, *Out of Our Past: The Forces That Shaped Modern America* (New York: Harper, 1962), p. 339.

universities, seminaries, museums, and churches. Catholic spokesmen like James Cardinal Gibbons, who advocated the rights of workers to join unions, faced opposition from conservative bishops who saw unions as socialistic and destructive of individual liberty. In small towns in the Midwest, where workers were known and owners were absent, Protestant and Catholic churches often identified with strikers. Jesus, after all, was a carpenter—a working man.

The ideology of the workingmen remained an amalgam of republicanism and Christianity. The Knights of Labor, which from 1880 to 1886 became the largest American union, justified its actions with biblical language and offered its members the unity of a sect. Labor leaders found linking religion with worker solidarity a means of countering differences between skilled and unskilled workers, men and women, and immigrant and native born.[2] By contrast, urban Protestant leaders like Henry Ward Beecher denounced unions and strikes, blamed poverty on the workers' moral failures, and insisted that sober workers reduce their expenditures—even support a wife and six children on bread and water for $1 a day.

A revival heritage of personal accountability and reform of society through individual transformation blinded many to the power of government to reform social evils. Leading Protestant periodicals blamed organized labor and radical immigrants for the violence that accompanied strikes in the railroad, steel, and coal industries and for the Haymarket Affair (1886), in which a bomb exploded during a police attempt to disperse a labor rally in a strike at McCormick Harvester. However, such strikes prompted many Protestants to increase their efforts to reach the workers and the poor. From 1870 to 1914, Christian economics became contested terrain as big business, organized labor, and the churches sought an ethical response to a world of uneven economic growth, depressions, poverty, and abundance.[3] Their contrasting responses, which grew out of a long tradition of American Protestant efforts to influence national policy, can be described as rescue, reform, and revolution, but there was little support for revolution, and the lines often blurred between rescue and reform.

The home mission movement and the Salvation Army represented a rescue mentality. Prosperous city churches created, financed, and controlled mission churches with Sunday schools in immigrant areas. They also built "institutional churches" by which older, downtown churches attempted to attract new members by opening their "doors every day and all day" for lectures, day nurseries, reading groups, concerts, clubs, and athletic contests in their new gymnasiums. Churchwomen visited the poor, bringing food and moral instruction and seeking to attract people to churches. Holiness preachers created industrial missions in areas where factory workers lived. A few Protestant denominations created orders of "deaconesses" in which, for the first time, churches paid women to do charity work and perform religious education.

The Salvation Army brought a distinctive holiness emphasis to the urban poor, insisting that people should act as though everything depended upon them and pray as if everything depended upon God. The Army's theology was practical: to abandon everything that did not help save souls. For example, the Army dropped the use of sacraments as po-

[2] See Paul Carter, *The Spiritual Crisis of the Gilded Age* (DeKalb, IL: Northern Illinois University Press, 1971).

[3] Kenneth Fones-Wolf, *Trade Union Gospel: Christianity and Labor in Industrial Philadelphia, 1865–1915* (Philadelphia: Temple University Press, 1989).

tentially divisive because of theological disagreements about liturgical usage. Under the leadership of Evangeline Booth (1865–1950), daughter of the English founder of the movement, the Salvation Army thrived in America with a disciplined military-style organization, evangelical fervor, and exciting services. Attracting the down-and-out through music provided by bands, the Army first provided food, shelter, and clothing as a demonstration of Christian love and then preached sin, damnation, and the saving power of Jesus. Those who were rescued could become workers to bring in others. One of the few denominations to allow women to exercise authority and preach, the Salvation Army has preserved to this day a dual emphasis upon saving souls and service to the very poor.

By contrast, Dwight Moody refused to preach about social issues. He complained that when he had offered the poor the Bible and a loaf of bread, they always looked first at the bread. Concluding that social aid distracted from his mission of proclaiming the Gospel, Moody concentrated upon the latter. He organized his revivals like mass entertainment—with advertising, huge choirs, new, catchy Gospel songs, fast-paced sermons, and an emotional altar call—but his appeal was traditional, an urban version of small-town revivals. He appealed to Americans who had come to the city and the middle classes, many of whom were already church members; but he didn't reach the immigrants. Rather than addressing problems *of* the city, Moody saved people *from* the city.

After his conversion, the young Moody saw his earliest successes come in classes he conducted for the Young Men's Christian Association (YMCA). This organization and its female counterpart (the YWCA) were established to provide low-cost housing in a safe Christian environment for rural young men and women journeying to the cities. Y's combined preaching in the streets and the distribution of religious tracts with a social ministry. Philanthropists saw them as places for wholesome recreation that would preserve youth from the temptations of alcohol, gambling, and prostitution and that would promote good citizenship. During their most influential period—from the 1870s until the 1930s—the Y's promoted evangelical Christianity in weekday and Sunday services, while promoting good sportsmanship in athletic contests in gyms (where basketball and volleyball were invented) and swimming pools. The YMCA's mixture of evangelical Christianity, exercise, and patriotism gained official recognition first during the Civil War and in later wars by providing places of recreation for the soldiers. In the twentieth century, the Y's have become interdenominational and more concerned with promoting morality and good citizenship than a distinctive interpretation of Christianity. In effect, they cut across denominational barriers to become an early ecumenical agency.

The Methodist layman and YMCA worker John R. Mott (1865–1955) sought to promote Protestant unity by creating the World Student Christian Federation in 1895 as an organization joining youth from all Protestant churches to dedicate themselves to the "evangelization of the world in this generation," by which he meant that Christianity would be preached in every culture, not that all would be converted. By 1900, there were five thousand American men and women missionaries preaching the gospel to the world. The institutional embodiment of Mott's vision of cooperation on the mission field was the World Missionary Conference, founded in 1910. Mott's journey for Christian unity resulted in his traveling throughout the world, meeting with representatives of all faiths. He welcomed contacts with Roman Catholics, as well as Greek and Russian Orthodox, and saw value in Hinduism, Buddhism, and Islam.

Mott wanted the United States to exercise moral leadership by example; but it was easy to make the transition from example to power and use American exceptionalism as a justification for empire. In the late nineteenth century, European nations partitioned Africa and created spheres of influence in China and East Asia using as justification "the white man's burden" of bringing the virtues of western civilization to the world. America's God-ordained manifest destiny, which had rationalized earlier expansion, now was updated to allow the incorporation of Hawaii and, after a war dismantling Spain's American empire, the annexation of Puerto Rico and the Philippines and a special relationship to Cuba. The churches either approved of, or kept quiet about American imperialism, even when the U.S. army bloodily suppressed a revolt against American rule in the Philippines. Roman Catholics did protest the negative stereotypes of their religion used by Protestants seeking intervention in Cuba against an allegedly decadent Spain or, later, to justify the necessity of sending missionaries to the former colonies.

Temperance Movement

The temperance, or prohibition, movement shows the blurring of the lines between efforts of rescue and political reform. In the late nineteenth century, virtually all mainline Protestant denominations and the Americanist wing of the Catholic Church supported restrictions upon the sale and consumption of alcoholic beverages, seeing the saloon as the nursery of poverty, prostitution, and political corruption. Drunkenness led to crime, abuse of wives, and accidents in factories, but reform efforts encountered an alliance of saloon keepers and big businessmen who insisted that property rights were sacred. Brewers who feared that giving women the vote would lead to prohibition financed anti-suffrage campaigns. Revivalists saw alcoholism as a personal moral failure that could be conquered by the power of Jesus, but they also knew that by 1900 nearly 40 percent of counties in the United States had voted to forbid the sale of alcoholic beverages.

Like other reform movements of the period, the temperance campaign had a hard side and a soft side. The hard side was represented by the anti-immigrant, anti-Catholic, anti-urban feelings of many rural Protestants, who saw prohibition as a way of maintaining what they defined as the American way of life. Such sentiment was always present in the movement, but was balanced by other themes until the 1920s. The soft side came from those who believed in the power of preaching and in legislation to foster morality. Ending the availability of hard liquor would diminish the frequency of alcoholism, give the poor more money to spend on necessities, and improve health. Claiming that the amount of tax revenue derived from alcohol sales did not compensate society for the ills caused by drunkenness and alcoholism, "soft-siders" hoped to lead America to virtue, to fulfill her promise as a society in covenant with God.

Women justified their temperance activities as a defense of home and family. After Frances Willard (1839–1898) became the leader of the Women's Christian Temperance Union (WCTU) in 1879, the organization grew rapidly, gaining a membership of 120,000, and combined rescue and reform motifs. Under the motto "Do Everything," the WCTU sought to protect children and women by supporting basic changes in society: women's suffrage, property and custody rights for women, raising the age of consent for sex (it was often from seven to ten), international arbitration to bring peace, free kindergartens and school lunches, reform of women's prisons, and improving labor conditions by shortening the workweek to five-and-a-half days.[4] The national convention of the WCTU supported the regulation of working conditions for women and the abolition of child labor. Willard, converted in a holiness revival, remained an evangelical Protestant, but as she grew older, she began utilizing the emergent social sciences for information. Before World War I, the policy aims of the WCTU paralleled those of the Social Gospel.

The Social Gospel

The Social Gospel was a reform movement of clerics and laymen and -women who believed that the churches should be engaged in building the kingdom of God on earth. To the revivalist emphasis upon individual transformation, advocates of the movement added a recognition of collective sin and a desire to Christianize the entire society. Not just individuals, but the society, needed to be redeemed, and a new social order should be grounded in the principles taught by Jesus. The Social Gospel advocates of the early twentieth century were neither complacent nor celebratory of the industrial growth that made the U.S. economy the largest in the world. Instead, they focused on the problems of American society: the plight of children, the squalor of the slums, and the feebleness of workers and the middle classes as contrasted with the wealth and power of John D. Rockefeller, J. P. Morgan, and the Vanderbilts—Protestant laymen whose philanthropy did not compensate for the way they exploited workers. Big business and bosses had corrupted politics at the expense of the people; now the people must insist on more democracy, regulation of business, and protection of the poor.

The Social Gospel was an optimistic creed, playing down original sin, seeing evil as a consequence of environment, and trusting that it could be known and overcome. An application of Christian ethics, derived from the scholarly study of the Bible and combined with knowledge gained from the newly professionalized social sciences—sociology, economics, history, and political science—would bring progress. So surveys would uncover the problems, and the clergy and college professors would combine their expertise in Bible ethics and economics, to make institutions express humanity's love of God and love of fellow creatures.

The Social Gospel was never a coherent and closely focused movement of people who agreed on conclusions. For example, Walter Rauschenbusch (1861–1918), a pastor of a Baptist church on the edge of New York City's Hell's Kitchen slum who became a seminary professor and primary theologian for the Social Gospel, criticized the selfishness of capitalism, wanted a more cooperative economic order, and asserted the need for labor unions. Rauschenbusch endorsed a vaguely defined socialism, but socialism in either a utopian or Marxist framework frightened the middle classes, who provided the primary support for the Social Gospel. Reformers debated the public ownership of utilities, government regulation of big business, and whether strikes were an ethical tactic. They responded favorably to the

---

[4] Quoted in Ruth Bordin, *Women and Temperance: The Quest for Power and Liberty, 1873–1900* (Philadelphia: Temple University Press, 1981), p. 95.

settlement house movement, exemplified by Jane Addams's Hull House in Chicago. The women who ran Hull House, located in a slum, provided social services and classes in domestic economy and sought to integrate the immigrants into American life while preserving their cultures. Many of the early social workers saw their profession as a religious enterprise. Seminaries began offering new courses in social ethics and required fieldwork so that prospective ministers could understand the problems of the laity. Issues of child labor, women's labor, uniform divorce and marriage laws, and immigration restriction would now be studied scientifically.

Between 1890 and 1910, the American Federation of Labor (AFL), a grouping of unions of skilled labor, grew from 80,000 to two million members. Social Gospel ministers joined with labor leaders in supporting workers' rights to organize and to gain an eight-hour day, the outlawing of child labor, and the provision of workmen's compensation for injuries sustained on the job. In a program termed Labor Forward, the AFL linked a push to organize as pro-Christianity and preached unionization like a revival. In 1915, to counter the alleged religious socialists, some of Philadelphia's leading industrialists financially underwrote the religious revival of Billy Sunday (1862–1935), a strong opponent of unions who claimed that the organized shops destroyed individual freedom. Many workmen who had joined unions also attended Sunday's revivals, showing that both reformers and conservatives sought Christianity's sanctions.

The Social Gospel was less pervasive in the South than in the Northeast, but there was strong support for prohibition and agitation to ease the conditions of farm tenancy and end convict-leased labor. Willis Weatherford's book *Negro Life in the South* (1910), which became the most widely used college text on the subject, announced, "It is not the negro that is on trial in the world, but it is we, we white men of the South."[5] Between 1889 and 1899, 1,240 black men and women were lynched in the United States. After seeing three of her friends lynched, Ida Wells (1862–1931), a black graduate of Fiske and a journalist, founded an organization to counter the mob hangings. After W. E. B. Dubois denounced the accommodationist stance of Booker T. Washington and helped create the National Association for the Advancement of Colored People, his white supporters often came from the ranks of those committed to the Social Gospel. The men and women in the National Baptist Convention, the largest black denomination, provided strong support for the Social Gospel. A few Northerners and Southern churchmen joined the leaders of black churches in denouncing the newly emergent pattern of "Jim Crow" segregation, but overall, the Social Gospel had a negligible impact on racial issues.

Because the Social Gospel was a diffuse movement, assessing its strength is difficult. Most supporters were Episcopalians, Congregationalists, and Methodists, with Baptists divided and Presbyterians lagging behind. In 1920, the Catholic bishops issued a program for social reform, with primary responsibility remaining with the states rather than the Federal government. Virtually all the mainline denominations—and they still were composed of 80 percent white Protestants—established national commissions that took liberal stands on social issues. Their cooperation on social policy fostered an ecumenical movement that led in 1910 to the creation of the Federal Council of Churches, an organization that became a

---

[5] Quoted in Ronald White, Jr., and Howard Hopkins, eds., *The Social Gospel: Religion and Reform in Changing America* (Philadelphia: Temple, 1967), p. 108.

leading advocate of progressive legislation. The Social Gospel encountered opposition from those who thought such legislation undermined individual responsibility and promoted socialism.

The animosity between Catholic and Protestant meant that there was little direct cooperation between the two groups even when they agreed on aims. Pope Leo XIII's encyclical *Rerum Novarum* (1891), condemning socialism and laissez-faire capitalism and seeking a benevolent economic order, provided a basis for Catholic participation in the Social Gospel. Leo called on governments to regulate labor conditions for women and children, guarantee decent wages, and recognize the legitimacy of trade unions. In 1906, the leading American Catholic supporter of the Social Gospel, Father John Ryan, advocated the establishment of a living wage for all workers, beginning a campaign that would succeed with the establishment of the federal minimum-wage law in the New Deal. The strong Catholic influence among the leaders of the American Federation of Labor, whose unions consisted of skilled or craft workers, contributed to the opposition of organized labor to socialism and to the more narrow focus on bread-and-butter issues. Catholics still saw themselves as a threatened minority who needed to prove their commitment to American values. Consequently, in spite of the preponderance of factory workers and poor immigrants in the American Catholic church, the hierarchy accepted Protestant leadership and the imagery set forth in the Social Gospel.

The Social Gospel provided much of the dynamism of the progressive movements that reshaped American politics in the early twentieth century. It can be viewed as the last attempt to create a Protestant America, and it influenced prominent politicians like William Jennings Bryan, Theodore Roosevelt, and Woodrow Wilson. Church leaders who supported the Social Gospel approved of progressive legislation from the states and Congress that limited business (e.g., railway regulation and the establishment of the Interstate Commerce Commission and Federal Trade Commission), promoted morality (e.g., forbidding white slavery and the transportation of alcohol into dry states), fostered democracy (e.g., the direct election of senators and the initiative and referendum), and helped workers (e.g., the outlawing of child labor, special restrictions on women's labor, the creation of the Department of Labor, and workmen's compensation). At the end of World War I, Protestant America felt vindicated by passing two constitutional amendments: prohibition and women's suffrage. Yet the way America approached and fought the war can be viewed as either a culmination or a betrayal of the Social Gospel.

World War I

The prewar peace movement drew support from conservatives, moderates, and radicals who saw increasing religious, cultural, and business ties among nations as making a major war impossible. Western civilization had reached a plateau in which diplomats and leaders knew that war was a foolish and costly way to solve international disputes. International law, treaties of arbitration, and limitations on kinds of weapons had reduced the probability of having a major war. So in August 1914, Americans expressed shock at the stupidity of European nations in going to war and resolved to be neutral in "fact as well as in name." Pacifist Christians joined with isolationists in seeking an end to hostilities, and President

Wilson offered to be a mediator. For three years Americans watched the carnage, resolving to stay out "as a man too proud to fight" and hoping for "a peace without victory."[6] As the country began to arm (just in case) and contemplated intervention, most liberal and conservative Protestants deserted the pacifist cause. In the spring of 1917, after Germany resumed unrestricted submarine warfare, Wilson asked Congress to declare war.

The churches, Catholic and Protestant, rallied to the flag, denounced German barbarism, and insisted that this war was holy, for "The world must be made safe for democracy." The Lutheran and Reformed churches, liberal clergy like Rauschenbush, and dispensational millennialist Evangelicals, all of whom saw the war as a tragedy, were drowned out by spokesmen claiming that Germans had reverted to being Huns and had betrayed the religion of Luther. Prussian autocracy must be destroyed to preserve Protestant liberty. Liberal seminary professors and revivalists proclaimed that Jesus would tell soldiers to shoot a German soldier between the eyes and approve sinking a bayonet three inches into the enemy. Patriots approved of imprisoning Jehovah's Witnesses and denounced pacifists, like Jane Addams, as un-American and un-Christian. The churches did not protest the silencing and incarceration of conscientious objectors, left-wing dissenters, and labor leaders, such as Eugene V. Debs, who opposed the war. The Federal Council of Churches and the Catholic churches demonstrated Christian patriotism by creating agencies to supply chaplains, and the YMCA and Red Cross created canteens for the recreation of soldiers. In World War I, the God of battles—who had fought in Puritan, Revolutionary, and Civil Wars—appeared again. The Social Gospel had wanted to Christianize the social order in America; the churches now insisted that without defeating Germany, the social order could not be reformed.

Wilson had committed America to a holy war to reform Europe. When the Treaty of Versailles showed that neither Europe nor America was likely to become the earthly kingdom of God, there was disillusionment with political and religious leaders, who now were charged with having led the country into war through spewing false propaganda. What good was the church, many asked, if, in a social crisis, it could neither stand apart from society to provide moral counsel nor foster peace? The election in 1920 of Warren Harding with the votes of men and the newly enfranchised women symbolized the return to normalcy and the eclipse of the Social Gospel and Progressivism. Now, at a time when, to many, the social sciences provided more objective and useful knowledge than religion, tensions that had long been present among Protestants exploded.

---

[6] Woodrow Wilson, quoted in Justin Kaplan, ed., *Bartlett's Familiar Quotations*, 16th ed. (Boston: Little, Brown, 1992), p. 572.

Chapter 36

Modernism and Fundamentalism

Modernism—or, as it is sometimes called, Liberalism—was an attempt to adjust religious ideas to the needs of contemporary society. Participants in a well-defined movement as early as 1900, liberals occupied nearly one-third of the pulpits of American Protestantism and controlled at least half of the seminaries by the 1930s. The late nineteenth century witnessed major changes in higher education, with the creation of the modern university and the attempt to apply methods of science to the study of society. The clergy now had to compete with college professors in making pronouncements on the many political issues that were susceptible to moral analysis. At same time, the authority of organized religion was called into question by those who saw the church as a relic of the past. For the first time, it became respectable in universities, as well as in the wider society, to ignore religion or to question the truthfulness of any dogma or creed because it could not be proven scientifically. Agnosticism and atheism now seemed viable and even fashionable intellectual options.

Modernism was an attempt to show that true science was compatible with, and even complementary to, religion, with each supreme in a separate sphere. For example, a scientific analysis of a Beethoven symphony or a Rembrandt painting could not do justice to its aesthetic appreciation. The same was said to be true of religious experience. Modernism was often linked to the social gospel, but there were many liberals not interested in reform, and evangelicals often supported the political reforms. Only after World War I would this division harden, as one branch of evangelicals, termed fundamentalists, condemned both the social gospel and modernism.

For modernists, advances in the study of philology, archeology, and history led to reinterpretations of the Bible. In the late nineteenth century, scholars in Germany claimed that variations in language and custom proved that Moses did not write the first five books of the Old Testament, that neither Joshua nor Judges provided an accurate account of Israel's conquest of Canaan, and that there were two or maybe three different books included in what came to be called Isaiah. Revisionism also applied to the New Testament. Neither the apostles nor eyewitnesses were said to have written the synoptic gospels, and some of the Pauline letters were thought not to have been written by Paul. Seemingly even more dangerous to revealed truth than Darwin, whose theories could be softened so that they threatened only the first chapters of Genesis, the new historical criticism seemed to undermine Protestants' faith in the certainty of the Bible. Because the Bible reflected the social, cultural, and political events of the men who wrote it down, it was not seen to be an inerrant source of timeless truth.

Modernists insisted that the Bible of the scholars was more exciting and more relevant than the Bible as it was classically interpreted, because it was more human. A historical product of people, the Bible showed men and women's struggles to comprehend God, as well as God's attempts to reach them. Filled with history, poetry, myths, and laws, the Bible now could be seen as showing a complex interplay between the divine and the human and illustrating a growth in religious consciousness from the early Hebrews to Jesus. The liberals thought absurd the expectation of the imminent end of the world (termed eschatology), proof-texting, and theological literalism. Christians should learn biblical spiritual truths, while rejecting the scripture's rudimentary understanding of science and inaccurate history. The Quran and Vedas also contained religious insights, but modernists insisted that the Bible remained unique because it portrayed God's decisive revelation in Jesus Christ.

The incarnation became the most important doctrine for modernists, because the birth of Jesus signified the presence of God in history. Jesus illustrated the nature of God, showed man at his highest, and provided a link between humanity and God. Jesus' death on the cross was not to satisfy the justice of Jehovah, but became God's way of communicating His love for and to humanity. Modernists disliked picturing God as remote and transcendent and stressed instead His immanence in nature and society. God's personality, as revealed in Jesus, proved that love was at the core of the universe. All the gospel teachings could be summarized in the two commandments to love God and one's neighbors. Stressing the infinite value of each human soul, modernists tended to ignore or de-emphasize original sin and focus upon the inevitability of progress and an exalted future for American civilization.

Liberals saw the divisions of Protestant denominations as weakening Christianity, stressed the underlying unity of the various groups, and worked to achieve denominational unification. The nascent ecumenical movement, an attempt to re-create confessional unity among churches, found an institutional focus in the Federal Council of Churches. Liberals also wanted to foster denominational cooperation in the field of missionary work because they opposed imposing tiny theological distinctions upon foreign converts. A liberal missionary program would not condemn all indigenous religious activities or seek to destroy traditional cultures. Rather, ministers should join the preaching of Christianity with education and social services, which would foster economic and political development. Even before World War I dealt a major blow to belief in progress and the perfectibility of humankind, evangelicals proclaimed that the liberals had destroyed Christianity in their quest for modernity and prepared to battle to preserve what they regarded as the essence of the faith.

Fundamentalism

Fundamentalism, a name derived from a series of pamphlets published between 1910 and 1914, was a movement cutting across denominational lines and growing out of evangelical Protestantism. What was new was not so much in content as in temper: a militant response to threats to its version of the gospel and a willingness to attack all competitors. Fundamentalists insisted that liberalism, by undercutting the authority of the Bible, denied the most important Christian doctrine: that God sent his only Son into the world to die for sin and to bring eternal life. Because the only way to gain salvation was through Jesus Christ, modernism was as dangerous as non-Christian religions in leading people to hell. The Bible was the witness to the truth of doctrine, and, following the Princeton theology of Charles Hodge, fundamentalists insisted that the Bible was inerrant, produced by men who wrote down the words dictated by God, and should not be viewed in the same manner as other historical documents. In 1925, in a rebuke to modernist influences within the church, the Northern Presbyterians summarized the five cardinal theological tenets: the inerrancy of the Bible, the virgin birth of Jesus, substitutionary atonement,[1] the authenticity of miracles, and the resurrection and physical return of Christ. All these tenets emphasized the difference between the sacred and the secular. Christianity was not a cultural artifact of the West; it was the Truth.

Fundamentalists advocated constant study of the Bible, for no part of it was irrelevant. A close analysis of the prophetic literature of Daniel and Revelation led to an emphasis on millennialism. Dwight Moody preached the imminence of the New Age (the Kingdom of God), and many of his associates successfully spread a version of millennialism termed dispensationalism. Dispensationalists insisted that an accurate exegesis of the Bible would prove that God had divided time into seven periods. At the end of each of these dispensations, He had tested humankind, found it wanting, and punished accordingly. Civilization was now in the sixth dispensation, the age of the church. However, the inroads of secularism into nations and liberalism into churches, as well as immorality of the population, proved that humanity had failed God's test once again. Very soon, a new millennial age would begin with the final battle at Armageddon; then Christ would return to begin a 1,000-year rule. The duty of Christians was to proclaim that the end of the world was at hand and to hold fast the entire gospel in the already dawning time of troubles.

In the progressive era, conservative evangelicals combined belief in the triumph of American civilization with dispensationalism. During, and especially after, World War I,

---

[1] The thesis that salvation became possible when Christ took upon himself the sins of all humans to satisfy God's justice.

however, dispensationalism contributed to a negative reassessment of the future: The war and its aftermath proved that the time of troubles forecast by millennial prophecy was now. During the war patriotic Americans, both liberals and fundamentalists, learned to hate all who might threaten their democracy. In the 1920s, fundamentalists continued that pessimistic assessment and saw a Protestant America threatened by immigrants, Catholics, Jews, blacks, communists, and modernists.

The war had proved the bankruptcy of social gospel attempts to create the Kingdom of God on earth. So during the 1920s, fundamentalists repudiated their sponsorship of progressive legislation (except for prohibition) and supported a conservative pro-business and laissez-faire policy: America must defend the gospel of Jesus against state encroachment. Fundamentalists now emphasized an individual conversion experience and identified a Christian lifestyle with opposition to drinking, smoking, playing cards, and attending movies. Against the hedonism associated with the Roaring Twenties, the fundamentalists sought to preserve what they saw as the traditional American family in which the father was the breadwinner and the wife stayed home and reared the children.

Fundamentalism cut across denominational lines. Many adherents came from what was called the Bible Belt, which included the South, and from holiness and pentecostal churches. Northern and Southern Baptists, Northern and Southern Presbyterians—all Calvinist churches—officially opposed modernism and endorsed fundamentalism. However, since the Baptists and Presbyterians also included modernists, there was a struggle for control of these denominations. Because of the Baptist belief in congregational autonomy, Fundamentalists could easily win control of local churches. This was also true of the Presbyterians. However, the fundamentalists failed when they sought to purge modernists from seminaries and the denominational boards of Northern Baptists and Presbyterians. Moderate and conservative evangelicals joined with liberals in efforts to prevent church schisms, even at the price of theological consistency. So the debate between liberals and fundamentalists, beginning before the war, becoming vituperative during the 1920s, and continuing to the present, would take place within major denominations.

Insisting upon the right of localities to control the content of public education, fundamentalists sought to forbid the teaching of evolution in many states. They succeeded in passing such a law in thirteen states, and a science teacher, John Scopes, in a staged case designed to bring in money for the little town of Dayton, Tennessee, defied the statute. The trial in 1925 became a cause célèbre, pitting two of the most famous Americans against each other: the trial lawyer Clarence Darrow for the defense and, for the prosecution, an aged William Jennings Bryan, three-time Democratic nominee for president, who always spoke for the values of small-town America. Bryan, who had no theological training, had for several years defended the Bible against evolutionary science and Modernist theology. When, during the trial, Darrow called Bryan as a biblical expert, he got the "Great Commoner" to admit that the days in Genesis might have taken years, a concession which meant that evolution might have occurred. To the fundamentalists, Bryan, who died shortly before winning the trial, was a martyr. To sophisticates, Bryan was ludicrous, and the Scopes trial proved the backwardness of small-town America. No one seemed to notice that the textbook used by Scopes insisted that evolution proved the inferiority of the black race and the superiority of whites. Intellectuals ignored fundamentalist religion, confident that it would go away. They were wrong.

Prohibition

The modernist–fundamentalist debate also weakened the impact of the social gospel. No longer could clerics take stands on contemporary issues with confidence that their church members would support them. Reform was no longer fashionable in either political party. After the Supreme Court overturned the law outlawing child labor, Congress passed a constitutional amendment, which was then sent to the states. Protestant Fundamentalists in the South and conservative Catholic bishops denounced and defeated the amendment as undermining the family and increasing the intrusiveness of the state. During the New Deal, however, Congress passed, and the Supreme Court allowed legislation against child labor.

The Protestant churches provided the driving force behind the movement to curtail the sale of intoxicating beverages. During the war, patriots pointed to the beer-drinking habits of Germans and the wasteful conversion of grain into whiskey for armies of the allies. In 1919, an extremely popular prohibition amendment was ratified by forty-six of the forty-eight states, with majorities of 80 percent in the legislatures. Even those who drank thought the reform would be good for America because proponents marshaled an impressive array of scientific and moral evidence showing the ills of alcohol and the good effects of abstinence upon personal health, business productivity (which would be increased by reducing accidents and absenteeism), and crime and poverty (which would be decreased).

The purpose of the amendment was to reduce drinking in saloons, and in this, as in the reduction of alcohol available to the working class, it was successful. Using statistics from the period, historians estimate that consumption dropped fifty to sixty-six percent, from earlier levels, and the pathology associated with alcohol also declined.[2] Why, then, was the amendment repealed in a convention in 1933? First, in the Volstead Act, proponents set the allowable limits of alcohol at .5 percent, a very stringent measure that even outlawed weak beer. Second, the government provided inadequate funds and personnel for enforcement. Jurisdiction was taken from ordinary police and entrusted to three thousand special agents who were supposed to patrol the entire nation but who were susceptible to corruption and did not always observe due process. Third, significant numbers of middle-class Americans decided that prohibition was an infringement on their personal liberties. In the cities, upper-class men and women found it fashionable to go to "speakeasies" where illegal liquor was available. Fourth, prohibition became identified with conservative Protestants who sought to impose their lifestyle on the whole nation. In the 1920s, small-town narrowness stood juxtaposed against a cosmopolitan pluralism, and those favoring the "wets" gained control of newspapers. Also, movies and magazines made drinking appear glamorous. Fifth, opponents blamed prohibition for the rise of lawlessness and organized crime, ignoring the fact that Al Capone in Chicago and the Mafia's power existed before 1919. Finally, during the depression, prohibition symbolized the excesses of the 1920s. Allowing the manufacture of beer and hard liquor would create a new market for grain for hard-pressed farmers and provide tax revenues for government. So in 1933, the Volstead Act was amended to allow 3.2-percent beer and wine. Not trusting the state legislatures, a

---

[2] J. C. Burnham, "New Perspectives on the Prohibition 'Experiment' of the 1920s," *Journal of Social History* (Fall 1968), pp. 51–68; Martin Lender and James Kirby, *Drinking in America: A History* (New York: Free Press, 1982); Norman Clark, *Deliver Us from Evil: An Interpretation of American Prohibition* (New York: Norton, 1976).

special convention passed the Twentieth Amendment that same year, repealing what became known as "the noble experiment." Yet many Americans continued to regard drinking of alcoholic beverages as a sin, and during the 1930s the average consumption of alcoholic beverages remained 50 percent below what it had been in 1918 and did not reach the levels of 1906–10 until 1975. Even so, Americans, both church members and others, drew the conclusion that morality could not be legislated.

Catholicism

Even before Pope Leo XIII had condemned Modernism in 1895, American Catholics managed to ignore Darwin and historical criticism of the Bible. Devotional Catholicism dominated worship until the 1950s. The church remained authoritarian, with the papacy as the visible symbol of a hierarchical church and bishops serving as administrators, financial managers, and builders. The archdiocese of Chicago was so dominated by Cardinal Mundelein, that it has been described as "Corporation Sole," with his legal title to all church property symbolizing his ecclesiastical power as well.[3] During his ten-year tenure beginning in 1918, Cardinal Dougherty of Philadelphia presided over the creation of ninety-two new parishes, ten new parochial schools, a new college, fourteen academies, and a seminary. However, Catholic efforts to gain any government funding for parochial schools failed, with the result that the schools were under-funded and survived only through the devoted service of nuns forced to teach large classes. The church remained a strong opponent of divorce, sexual permissiveness, and communism, and maintained an index that told Catholics which movies and books to avoid. The increasing social respectability and wealth of immigrant Catholics allowed the Democrats to nominate Al Smith for President in 1928, but the ensuing debate over whether he was subservient to the pope showed how formidable the barriers between Protestant and Catholic remained.

The rise of the Ku Klux Klan to a membership of five million was part of a rural attack upon allegedly alien values. In the 1920s, the Klan claimed to stand for traditional American Protestant virtues against the threats posed by Roman Catholics, immigrants, and blacks. In the South the Klan was primarily antiblack, but in northern states like Indiana the Klan used anti-Catholicism to become a political power. After several exposures of terror tactics and moral failings by Klan leaders, the organization declined rapidly, dropping to only nine thousand members in 1930.

The Klan also reflected popular sentiments in preaching anti-Semitism. Henry Ford denounced a Jewish financial conspiracy, while others saw Jews as fostering communism. During the depression, a Roman Catholic priest from Detroit, Father Charles Coughlin (1891–1979), attracted a national radio audience with his attacks on the New Deal and Jews. Communities and country clubs sought to keep out Jews, and colleges restricted the number of Jews they would admit.

During the 1920s, Americans no longer wanted unrestricted immigration. So a new

---

[3] Edward Kantowicz, *Corporation Sole: Cardinal Mundelein and Chicago Catholicism* (Notre Dame, IN: University of Notre Dame, 1983).

law in 1924 basing quotas on the population of 1890 served to curtail immigration from Eastern Europe, Italy, and Asia, while allowing more to come from northern Europe. The difference was racial and cultural, with Germanic and Anglo-Saxon peoples seen as preserving racial purity and more easily assimilating to American values. Stopping the flow of immigrants had a major impact on the Catholic Church. No longer would its energies be taken up with assimilating new Americans and adjusting parishes and schools to different nationalities. Indeed, second-generation Catholics often attempted to play down the heritage of the mother country. Upward mobility allowed Catholics to move to suburbs and to create parishes in which no one ethnic group dominated. Increased wealth led to demands for more schools and colleges, where ethnic identity seemed even less important.

Sociology of Religion

Scholars of the history of religion have to rely on the writings of educated classes, and consequently, there are major gaps in our knowledge of how the illiterate and poor viewed the churches. Beginning in the 1920s and continuing to the present, however, sociologists began doing field studies in which they conducted interviews and assessed the influence of religion in typical towns: "Middletown" (Muncie, Indiana), "Elmtown" and "Corn County" in Illinois, Yankee City (Newburyport, Massachusetts), and Gastonia, North Carolina.[4]

A pervasive theme was the class nature of American Protestantism. Downtown or "businessman" churches (Episcopal, Presbyterian, Methodist, and Baptist) had impressive edifices, ministers who attended divinity schools and received a salary not much lower than the merchants, and orderly services conducted with liturgy and robed choirs. However, their congregations had only a rudimentary knowledge of the Bible and theology. In Muncie, ministers of business churches lamented the decline of attendance at Sunday evening and midweek prayer services. The congregations valued ministers who were good talkers, but not too religious on social occasions. Ministers felt almost a caste apart, unable to communicate with the male members of their congregations, but valued chiefly as providers of prayer at weekly Rotary and Kiwanis meetings. Men handled the financial matters of the church; women were more likely to attend services, teach in Sunday schools, work in missionary societies, and organize their activities around the church.

Working and poor people worshiped in small, plain buildings. Their worship was informal and more overtly emotional; their ministers, paid no more than laborers, had little more education than the parishioners. The churches of the poor were more likely to

---

[4]See Robert S. Lynd and Helen Lynd, *Middletown: A Study in Modern American Culture* (1929) and *Middletown in Transition* (1937) (New York: Harcourt, Brace, 1956); Liston Pope, *Millhands and Preachers: A Study of Gastonia* (New Haven, CT: Yale, 1942); August de Belmont, *Elmtown's Youth: The Impact of Social Classes on Adolescents* (New York: Wiley, 1949); Victor Obenhaus, *The Church and Faith in Mid-America* (Philadelphia: Westminster, 1963); and W. Lloyd Warner, *The Living and the Dead: A Study of the Symbolic Life of Americans* (New Haven, CT: Yale, 1959). Modern updates are Theodore Caplow, Howard Bahr, Bruce Chadwick, Dwight Hoover, Lawrence Martin, Joseph Tammey, Margaret Williamson, *All Faithful People: Continuity and Change in Middletown's Religion* (Minneapolis: University of Minnesota, 1983); and John Earle, Dean Knudsen, Donald Shriver, Jr., *Spindles and Spires: A Re-Study of Religion and Social Change in Gastonia* (Atlanta: Knox, 1976).

demand adherence to a strict moral code denouncing playing cards, wearing lipstick, and attending movies. In both business and worker churches, women and the elderly constituted the majority of active members. Male laborers who had to be on the job six days a week working long hours claimed that they were too exhausted to attend church on Sunday.

In 1929, in Gastonia, North Carolina, there was a major strike by a newly formed union against the outside ownership of the cotton mills, which, in response to the depression, had lowered the already subsistence-level wages. Rather than investigate working conditions, the business churches condemned the strike and blamed the agitation on outside communist agitation. The only sympathy the workers received from organized religion came from their lower class churches, but even there, the clergy distinguished between temporal and spiritual needs, with the church responding only to the latter.

A major conclusion of these studies was that religious and secular values conflicted. The school board in Muncie wanted education to reinforce the Christian attitude to life: a 1925 survey of the town's high school juniors recorded that 48 percent thought evolution untrue, 26 percent thought it true, and 24 percent had no opinion.[5] The authors of the two Middletown studies contrasted dynamic forces for change with the conservatism in government, education, and church. The implication was that science and business would shape the future as religion declined in importance.

H. Richard Niebuhr's *The Social Sources of Denominationalism* (1929) put the conclusions of such sociological studies into a wider historical context.[6] Niebuhr insisted that class was what divided Protestants into sects and denominations. Sects legitimated themselves by affirming their opposition to the standards of the wider culture. They originated by following a charismatic leader. Once formed, sects maintained definite beliefs and standards, which all members accepted. Over time, the values of honesty, hard work, and simple living brought their members prosperity and made the next generation into members of the middle class. Now, as that generation sought education and respectability, its religious expectations changed, and the sect evolved into a denomination. Less concerned with enduring evil, members of the denomination sought to understand the problem of evil. Muting its opposition to the values of the culture, the denomination now cooperated with other respectable churches in seeking to shape the wider society. To Niebuhr, American Protestant denominations resembled the established churches of other countries, with two exceptions: The Catholic Church had managed to avoid schism and to incorporate different nationalities and classes: and the color line divided white from black churches, making the latter's experience unique. Unfortunately, in the Midwestern and Eastern towns portrayed by the sociologists, there were few blacks. Gastonia, on the other hand, had many blacks, but they were not studied, because the mills would not employ them and they did not attend white business or worker churches. Black churches and people remained, in Ralph Ellison's language, invisible.[7]

---

[5] Lynd and Lynd, *The Middletown*, pp. 203–205.

[6] H. Richard Niebuhr, *The Social Sources of Denominationalism* (1929) (New York: Meridian, 1960) and *Christ and Culture* (New York: Harper, 1951).

[7] Ralph Ellison, *Invisible Man* (New York: Random House, 1952); an exception to the neglect of study of African-American churches was W. E. B. Dubois, *The Souls of Black Folks* (1903) (New York: Signey, 1969), pp. 210–225.

Black Religion

Before World War I, ninety percent of blacks still lived in the South, most in an oppressive poverty compounded by sharecropping. The North remained uninterested in blacks' rights, the Supreme Court sustained legal segregation in 1896, and, through race baiting, Southern conservatives beat down Populist efforts at reform even after a prolonged agricultural depression. Disenfranchisment, Jim Crowism, vigilante violence, poverty, and discrimination kept the blacks an underclass. The Democratic party under Woodrow Wilson did nothing to stop the epidemic of lynchings or to improve the status of Negroes.

By 1940 forty percent of black Americans lived in the North, most in cities. This great migration began in World War I, when jobs became available. Because of black poverty and white racism and discrimination, blacks settled in ghettoes like Harlem, and few blacks joined white church denominations. Blacks in America remained a nation within a nation, and organized religion reflected, as well as contributed to, that separation.

In one sense, all black churches can be considered sectarian, because they have existed in tension with the larger society. As institutions created and controlled by Negroes, they remained concerned with black identity and rights and served as an inspiration for social protest and a source for political leaders. Yet even before the Civil War, in Northern cities a black middle class emerged devoted to education, economic opportunity, and integration. Stratification within the black community allows an application of a modified typology of church, sect, and cult. The sociologist Joseph Washington claimed a tripartite division: (1) black churches, which concentrated upon the next world and desired integration into white society; (2) black sects, which concentrated upon the world to come, a compensation for blacks' relative lack of power in this world; and (3) black cults, which proclaimed that a member can have it all in both this world and the next.[8] Useful primarily as a heuristic device, Washington's divisions illustrate the fragmentation in American black religion.

The black denominations, like American Episcopal Church Zion, often functioned according to Niebuhr's definition of a church religion. For example, Abyssinian Baptist Church in New York and Olivet Baptist in Chicago, each with thousands of members, created extensive social welfare programs to assist migrants. These churches tended to be reformist, to accept capitalism and democracy, and to advocate cooperation with whites in programs allowing blacks to share equally in American life. Worship services were relatively impersonal, led by educated ministers and robed choirs in imposing structures. By contrast, rural churches of the black denominations had unimpressive buildings and inadequate financial resources; their ministers concentrated upon spiritual uplift, while ignoring material needs.

The denominations did not satisfy recent migrants to the city, who found in "storefront" churches an atmosphere more like traditional Southern black religion. In 1933, a survey of 2,104 black church buildings found that 77 percent were "storefronts." One-half of these were Baptist congregations; others were Holiness and Pentecostal.[9] These congregations or "conversionist sects" emphasized an emotional worship of speaking in

---

[8] Joseph Washington, *Black Sects and Cults* (Garden City, NY: 1973), pp. 6–10.

[9] Hans Baer, *The Black Spiritual Movement: A Religious Response to Racism* (Knoxville, TN: University of Tennessee, 1984), p. 16.

tongues, trances, and ecstasy, focused on otherworldly salvation that would end the pain of living in poverty, and required adherence to rigid norms of behavior. Conversionist sects and black churches reverenced the scripture as God's truth and identified their experiences with biblical figures, but did not espouse the biblical literalism of white Fundamentalists.

Spiritualism emerged in the 1920s as an alternative form of black religion, promising a good life as a result of gaining esoteric knowledge used in magic–religious rituals. Spiritualist ministers, many of whom were women, combined spiritualism with black Protestant, Catholic, and voodoo elements in a system that provided a sense of access to power for a class that had none. Ministers, who rarely had much formal education, sought to foster in members a positive view of themselves and to show them the way to obtain prosperity through prayers and through various intermediary spirits, healings, and prophecies. Worship was unstructured, was often ecstatic, with no set times to begin or adjourn, and combined singing, prayers, offerings, sermons, testimonials, anointings, and altar calls. Frequent schisms, lack of record keeping, and the drifting of members among different small congregations made it difficult to determine the number of spiritualists.

The Father Divine Peace Missions exemplify a very different type of black sect, which may be described as "messianic–nationalist." Such sects create alternative ways of life, with members often dwelling communally; they also focus on material blessings. In a sermon in 1937, Divine preached, "I would not give five cents for a God who could not help me here on earth. . . . If God cannot prepare Heaven here for you, you are not going anywhere."[10] The Peace Missions had no formal theology. Father Divine, who did not discourage his followers from thinking of him as God, claimed to have the power to heal and kill and, initially, was thought to have conquered death.

At the height of his influence in the mid-1930s, Father Divine's basic adherents—who lived communally, devoted their earnings to the group, and worked in church-owned enterprises—may have numbered fifty thousand, with another two million sympathizers termed "Children." Divine gained adherents by inviting them to banquets at which they could eat as much as they wished. Worship in these services concentrated upon the divine figure who was present. Father Divine demanded strict moral standards from his followers, sought to build self-esteem, encouraged education, and worked to gain economic opportunities for blacks. He worked against segregation, thought racial classifications insignificant, and built an economic empire, becoming the largest property owner in Harlem. The movement began to decline in numbers in the 1950s, when Divine moved to Philadelphia and lived in seclusion.

Father Divine was one of several messianic or prophetic figures who existed on the fringes of Christianity. A supernatural leader offered an opportunity for followers to receive benefits of real power. Some cults affirmed black solidarity by rejecting the privileged position of whites and claiming a special position for blacks. For example, the Church of God (Black Jews) claimed that the original Jews were Negroes, the Moorish Science Temple of America insisted that salvation came only to Moorish-Americans, and the Black Muslims argued that the devil was white.

---

[10] Quoted in Robert Weisbrot, *Father Divine and the Struggle for Racial Equality* (Urbana, IL: University of Illinois, 1983), p. 186.

From Peace to War

The main success of advocates of the Social Gospel during the 1920s was a crusade for peace that cut across partisan lines, that could attract isolationists as well as internationalists, and that appealed to the newly enfranchised women, who wanted never again to sacrifice their sons in trench warfare. Liberal clergy, particularly in the Methodist and Congregationalist churches, concluded that Jesus' example of nonresistance called for his followers to adopt pacifism. In the disillusionment following the Treaty of Versailles, many concluded that American participation in the war had been a mistake.

Adolph Hitler's coming to power in 1933 and Japanese imperialist actions in China did not initially affect the peace movement. Isolationists who wanted to build a barrier between Americans and Europe and religious liberals who saw war as an un-Christian way of settling disputes agreed on the need for peace. The churches led campaigns to ensure peace by persuading young men to agree never to fight in a war. A poll of sixty-five thousand college students in 1935 indicated that 81 percent would not fight if the United States invaded another country and 16.5 percent would not fight even if the nation were invaded.[11] Polls showed that a majority of college males agreed. Dorothy Day (1898–1980) exemplified a Roman Catholic social gospel. A trained nurse, a social activist who as a young adult supported striking workers and associated with Communists and Socialists, and an author who lived in a common-law marriage, she converted to Catholicism, repudiated her former life, and in 1933 helped found the Catholic Worker Movement. Her newspaper advocated pacifism, racial integration, and the rights of working men and women. The laypersons in the Worker Movement who lived in voluntary poverty opened hospitality houses in many cities, where the destitute could obtain food, shelter, and clothing.

Reinhold Niebuhr (1892–1971), a brother of Richard, protested that liberal pacifism simplified Christianity and distorted politics. Niebuhr created the movement known as Christian Realism, whose principles he applied to domestic and foreign policy. The young Niebuhr came to a parish outside of Detroit as a theological liberal and advocate of the Social Gospel and gained an education in practical politics by supporting unionization against Henry Ford. He then moved to Union Theological Seminary in New York, pioneering the field of Applied Christianity, or Christian Social Ethics. Niebuhr charged the pacifists with ignoring the paradoxical nature of man as a creature of sin as well as goodness. All human activities, he insisted, are tainted with pride—an unwillingness to accept limits. Countervailing power, not love, would bring reform of domestic as well as international evils. The pacifists naively thought that Christian love could overcome sin and so could create the Kingdom of God on earth. Niebuhr insisted that an individual Christian might imitate the self-sacrificing love of Christ, but such love could not serve as a guide to political action. Christian realism valued pacifism as a model of sacrificial love, valued just-war theory for upholding a universal moral order, and valued *realpolitik* for recognizing the need for power. None, however, provided a sufficient guide to politics. Niebuhr advocated combining the best of all three, but accepted the inevitability of getting dirty hands in politics while working for, but never obtaining, justice. A prayer he wrote in 1951 summarized his faith:

---

[11] Charles Chatfield, *For Peace and Justice: Pacifism in America, 1914–1941* (Knoxville, TN: University of Tennessee, 1971), p. 259.

"God, give us the serenity to accept what cannot be changed; Give us the courage to change what should be changed; Give us the wisdom to distinguish one from the other."[12]

By the late 1930s, Niebuhr spoke for those who believed that Nazism must be opposed by political power, and even military force, if necessary. War was a scourge, but not stopping totalitarianism was worse, a betrayal of Christian responsibility for those in need. Niebuhr wrote extensively on foreign policy, seeking repeal of neutrality legislation and aid for the allies after war began in 1939. Christian realism, influential before the war mainly in eastern academic circles, would be used to justify Christian opposition to communist totalitarianism in the postwar period. Niebuhr would continue to argue that democracy was a bad system, until it was compared to all alternatives. Niebuhr offered to Americans a chastened liberalism that recognized evil, applied Christianity to society, and sought to hold the state to a standard of justice.

As events in Asia and Europe became more ominous, many liberal Christians rethought their commitment to pacifism. Except for its grudging acceptance of Dorothy Day's Christian Worker Movement, Roman Catholicism had never officially tolerated pacifism for the laity, and by the late 1930s, the papacy was disenchanted with both Fascists and Communists. Conservative evangelicals and fundamentalists had never approved of liberal pacifism. When the war came, Roosevelt, unlike Wilson, made clear where America's sympathies lay. The fall of France, the Battle of Britain, and, finally, Japan's attack on Pearl Harbor quenched Christian pacifism. There were fewer than forty-three thousand conscientious objectors out of ten million drafted. Yet the churches had learned from World War I: This time, they would support the government and provide eight thousand chaplains to minister to members of the armed forces. But at home there would be no outburst of hate, and the struggle would be viewed as an act of necessity, not a holy war or an inauguration of the Kingdom of God in America.

Organized religion in America flourished between 1920 and 1940 in prosperity and depression. The major Protestant denominations and the Roman Catholics increased their membership by sixty percent; at the same time, although they started with small numbers, pentecostal, fundamentalist, and holiness churches saw their membership rise by four hundred percent. Mainline denominations, like the Methodists, sought to end divisions that had originated before the Civil War, although initially the price for reunion of North and South was creating a separate black jurisdiction. The Federal Council of Churches provided a forum for leaders of mainline denominations to discuss issues of theology, church government, and social policy. In response, denominations that remained aloof from the council because of alleged Modernist influence formed the National Association of Evangelical Churches in 1939. The Roman Catholics remained apart from both councils, but, through force of numbers in unions and in major cities, exercised increasing influence in government policies. Proving that divided houses can sometimes not only stand, but flourish, the churches retained power in shaping American culture by providing spiritual solace for their members.

---

[12] Quoted in Richard Fox, *Reinhold Niebuhr: A Bibliography* (New York: Harper, 1985), p. 290.

Chapter 37

Religion in the Public Sphere, 1945–1996

The churches in post-World War II America sought to influence American domestic and foreign policies at the same time that they worked to provide spiritual nurture for their members in an environment of increased religious pluralism and secular alternatives. Because of the complexity of patterns of religion in recent America, our treatment is divided into two chapters, one focusing on public religion (the Cold War, separation of church and state, civil rights, Vietnam, and the new Christian Right) and a second concentrating on institutional Christianity (pluralism, patterns of religious belief, and the institutional church).

World War II left a horrifying legacy: devastation on an unprecedented scale; the Holocaust, in which a "civilized" Christian nation attempted to exterminate a people only because they were Jewish; and the atomic bombs, which were dropped upon civilian targets. Uniquely among major nations, America ended the war economically stronger than in 1939, prepared to repudiate isolationism and accept responsibility as the most powerful nation, a leader of democracies. The rivalry between the Soviet Union and the United States soon developed into the Cold War, dashing hopes that the United Nations would become a mechanism for creating a secure and peaceful world. Two systems—one atheistic, communistic, and totalitarian and the other religious, capitalistic, and democratic—contested for supremacy in all regions of the world, using military, economic, and ideological weapons. Once again, a fusion of nationalism and religion allowed Americans to see their destiny in cosmic terms as defender of the free world and to pray for God's support against the visible embodiment of the Antichrist. Eisenhower's Secretary of State, John Foster Dulles, a Presbyterian who helped create the World Council of Churches, saw the struggle as good versus evil and proclaimed that neutrality was immoral. Dulles and Americans proclaimed on coins, "In God we trust," an invocation of providential history intelligible to the Puritans—but just in case, the nation created a formidable arsenal of nuclear weapons and bombers and built a strategy based on the threat of massive retaliation.

America's religious leaders now confronted the awesome responsibility of whether to justify the use of nuclear weapons. Fundamentalist Protestants, who thought the prophecies in Revelation of a final cataclysm referred to nuclear war, expected the reappearance of Jesus and did not practice political activism, preferring to wait for God's judgment on a corrupt world. The papacy, forced to deal with hostile communist governments in Poland and Hungary and facing powerful communist parties in Italy and France, mobilized its supporters against an anti-Christian repressive ideology. In America, Catholics and conservative Protestants accepted nuclear weapons as a necessary evil and hoped that deterrence would stop the Cold War from becoming hot. Liberal Protestants wished to temper the rhetoric of the Cold War and foster peaceful competition, but did not question the necessity of a united front in a time of international peril.

The Second Disestablishment: The Supreme Court

Postwar America was very comfortable with public religious affirmations by government figures. The Congress inserted "under God" into the Pledge of Allegiance, and many members attended a weekly prayer breakfast. Eisenhower invoked religious values repeatedly and saw a vital faith as underlying democratic institutions. At the same time that politicians' profession of religion reached new heights, the Supreme Court reinterpreted the meaning of the First Amendment in a way that can be called a "Second Disestablishment." At a time when America's sense of religious identity seemed of paramount importance, the Court challenged a two-hundred-year-old tradition of fudging the alleged line between church and state. The resulting controversy over the meaning of the separation of church and state brought religious issues to the forefront of politics with an intensity not seen since the American Revolution and which shows no signs of abating even now.

The constitutional theory supporting the change was simple: Under the "due process clause" of the Fourteenth Amendment, the guarantees of the First Amendment applied now to the states as well as the federal government. So previous state laws restricting the "free exercise" of religion or favoring religion were unconstitutional. The new policies began during the Second World War. In 1943, the Court held that Jehovah's Witnesses' refusal to salute the flag was protected by the First Amendment, that towns could not restrict the Witnesses from passing out literature or proselytizing door to door, and that not saluting the flag or saying the Pledge of Allegiance was constitutionally protected behavior. But Witnesses were not exempted from child labor laws when they used minors to pass out leaflets. The Court soon protected Seventh Day Adventists' and Orthodox Jews' right not to work on Saturday and affirmed the rights of native Americans to use peyote (a narcotic) in traditional religious rites. (In 1978, during the Nixon administration, Congress legislated that the guarantees of the First Amendment applied to Indian religions.)

The Court's cases, decided upon the "free-exercise clause" or under the rubric of free speech, have involved minority religions and had little direct impact on most Americans.

The decisions show an awareness of a growing diversity in citizens' religious commitments—a recognition that the United States can no longer be described, in general, as a Christian country, as it was in 1890. In 1972, the Court decided that Amish children were exempted from attending public school after the eighth grade. The Court also determined that parents who believe in faith healing or who are practitioners of Christian Science can refuse medical care for themselves, but have no right to jeopardize the lives of their children. Further, schools have the right to require inoculation of all pupils. After the Vietnam War was over, the Court broadened the definition of "religious belief" so that those who had a strongly principled objection to all war, but did not ground that belief upon the existence of a deity, could qualify to be conscientious objectors under First Amendment provisions. Except for the ruling on the Pledge of Allegiance—which became an issue during the presidential campaign of 1988—Court rulings expanding the rights of religious exercise occasioned little comment.

Religion in Schools

Catholic parochial schools educated approximately 3.5 million children in 1965. The Catholic school system in Chicago was larger than all but four public school systems in the country, and Catholics constituted 98 percent of those who were in private schools. Hard pressed to support their schools, and a potent political force as the single largest denomination, Catholics argued that their schools served the general welfare in providing education and that forcing Catholics to pay taxes to support public schools which they did not utilize penalized their religious beliefs. After states attempted to fund parochial schools in a variety of ways, the courts intervened. The Supreme Court declared that public funds could not directly aid private schools. No money could be spent for buildings, teachers' salaries, or classroom instruction, even to subsidize those teaching secular subjects like mathematics or science. And no public school teachers could come into parochial schools.

On the other hand, granting funds was permissible if the government did not become deeply entangled in the schools, if there was a secular purpose, and if the pupils were the primary beneficiaries of the funds. This threefold test, enunciated in the Lemon Case (1971), has allowed tax dollars to be used to pay for the transportation of children to Catholic schools, to purchase laboratory equipment for and furnish (lend) state textbooks to Catholic schools, and to subsidize lunches and medical tests for Catholic school children. However, the Court has experienced difficulty in applying the Lemon test consistently. For example, the Court did not allow tax funds for special education (presumably, because such funds would have benefited the pupils directly). Further, released time for religious instruction on public school premises was illegal, but released time for religious teaching outside the school was allowed.

Court rulings about religion in public schools continue to provoke controversy. Americans created common schools in the 1830s and continue to use them to teach children values important to the wider society. As the best way to inculcate such values, the schools utilized a nondenominational, but vaguely Protestant, kind of Christianity promulgated through reading scriptures, singing hymns, teacher-led prayers, and Christmas and Easter programs. Beginning in 1962, however, the Supreme Court declared unconstitutional all teacher-led religious activities in public schools. First, the Court forbade saying a mandatory nondenominational prayer to God. Then it prohibited Bible reading, chapel services, religious pictures, a posted list of the Ten Commandments, Christmas carols sung for religious purposes, and prayers given by clergymen before athletic contests and in ceremonial occasions like graduations. The Court held that there could be no public or official religious exercise or any endorsement of religion.

The Court did not outlaw a pupil's private prayer in public schools; also, a teacher could pray privately, but not in such a fashion that students would know that the teacher was praying. In addition, the Court allowed instruction about, but not indoctrination in, or the practice of religion. States attempted to finesse the issue by legislating a moment of silence. Where the legislation's clear intent was to foster silent worship, the silence was outlawed; but the courts sustained the silence as a time for quiet reflection when the states envisaged no specific religious function.

Taking any official endorsement of religion out of the public schools proved enormously unpopular, occasioning calls for changing the composition of the court. Since the 1960s, polls have shown consistently that at least two-thirds of the American people want public prayer in public schools. Since 1980, two presidents and the Republican national platforms have regularly called for a constitutional amendment allowing such prayer. An amendment gained a majority of the Senate in 1984, but fell four votes short of the two-thirds needed for adoption.

Fundamentalist and conservative evangelical Christians claim that taking prayer and Bible reading out of the schools has allowed secularism or secular humanism to dominate, by which they mean that there is no reference to God or divine providence. They say that religious neutrality is a contradiction in terms; teaching must be either religious or secular, and the Court has enshrined secular humanism. The Court's decisions have resulted in many parents who are concerned about the lack of religion in public schools taking their children out and enrolling them in private academies. Like parochial schools, such academies want tax support, but do not want the states to regulate their curriculum. In the battle over segregation, parents who did not want their children attending racially integrated public schools helped create private schools that fostered evangelism. The courts denied tax exemption to schools and colleges refusing to admit blacks. In the 1980s parents critical of the public schools agitated for a voucher system that would utilize tax dollars to pay tuition at any school—public or private, integrated or segregated. In 1983, in a four-to-four vote, the Court allowed a voucher system in Minnesota, even though ninety percent of the benefit would aid religious schools. Because virtually all private secondary schools are religious, the voucher system would be an indirect way to gain tax support for a religiously based education.

In June 1997 the Court sent mixed signals on religious freedom. It lowered the barrier separating church and schools by allowing remedial education in religious schools by public school teachers. In reversing an earlier ruling, the Court now said that the content of the teaching would not be affected by the religious setting. Then the Court overruled a recent Act of Congress supported by virtually all religious groups asserting the primacy of the free exercise of religion except when there was a compelling state need. The Court here seemed to be saying that Americans already had enough freedom of religion.

Court decisions are rarely unanimous. Several of the church–state cases showed a polarized court in which a minority of justices was sympathetic to an accommodationist approach rather than a strict separation of church and state. Presidents Reagan and Bush sought to appoint Supreme Court justices who would be more sympathetic to the accommodationist perspective. Two recent decisions allowing student-initiated prayer on ceremonial occasions in public school and meetings of student religious groups on school property indicate that the Court may be reconsidering how intrusive it wishes to be in regulating religious activities in schools. And, of course, not all public schools obey all Supreme Court mandates, particularly when they see powerful politicians denounce and seek ways of evading or changing the rulings.

The Court and Moral Standards

Law embodies morality. That is, criminal behavior is often what the community deems immoral, whether such behavior be prostitution, polygamy, theft, or murder. As the final arbiter of law, therefore, the Supreme Court pronounces on moral issues. Although it bases its statements on the Constitution, since the 1960s the Court has encountered a fragmented public whose moral conflicts end up on the docket. The continuing political bitterness shows that the Founding Fathers' attempt to divorce church and state may work for institutional issues, but not on divisive moral questions such as abortion, homosexuality, and euthanasia. Here, decisions are based not on the First Amendment, but on inherent rights, including that of privacy.

The Court in 1965 struck down a Connecticut law forbidding the sale of contraceptive devices. Mainline Protestants had no objection, but the Catholic Church continues to maintain an opposition to all contraceptive devices, including "the pill." Officially, Catholics approve sexual abstinence and the rhythm method as the only natural methods of preventing conception. Pollsters, however, could find no differences among Catholics and Protestants in the 1970s on the acceptability and utilization of contraceptive devices. In 1967, as a part of the dismantling of laws on segregation, the Court voided a Virginia law forbidding interracial marriages.

In the 1970s, in response to the claims of newly visible gays and lesbians, homosexuality became a divisive political issue. Until then, homosexuality was a sin that the state made a crime. Homosexual students and employees could be dismissed. Even today, the Roman Catholic Church argues that homosexuality is against natural law, and many conservative Protestants insist that the Bible condemns homosexuality and see the AIDS epidemic as a sign of God's judgment on immoral activity. In 1986, the Court refused to overturn a Georgia law forbidding homosexual sex acts. Some states and cities have passed laws guaranteeing nondiscrimination against homosexuals, and recently a Supreme Court decision overturned a Colorado law denying equal-rights laws from applying to homosexuals.

By the late 1960s, professional health workers, supporters of the feminist movement, and spokespersons for liberal mainline denominations concluded that an abortion should no longer be a criminal offense. The social cost of botched back-alley abortions was too great, and civil liberties required allowing women more control of their bodies. In 1973, in *Roe* v. *Wade*, the Supreme Court ruled that the decision to abort a fetus during the first trimester could be left to the woman and her doctor; the states gained the right to regulate abortion during the second trimester and to regulate or prohibit it during the final trimester. Many Roman Catholics and evangelical and fundamentalist Protestants believe that human life became sacred from the moment of conception and regarded the Court's decision as licensed murder. The issue soon entered partisan politics, with the Republican Party endorsing overturning the decision through changing the justices of the Supreme Court or imposing statewide restrictions making abortions more difficult to obtain. Unable to reverse *Roe* v. *Wade*, opponents of abortion demonstrated in front of abortion clinics, and a few—increasingly frustrated by failure—resorted to threats and violence against doctors who performed abortions.

Abortion was the most visible of several issues pertaining to life and death that confronted the Supreme Court and the nation. The Court first restricted and then allowed capital punishment; recently, it has made executions easier by limiting appeals. Oregon passed a law allowing assistance for voluntary suicide by the terminally ill. Other issues, such as determining when and by whom life support systems can be withdrawn, the legality of doctor-assisted euthanasia, the limits to be placed on genetic engineering, and the rights of surrogate parents, continue to perplex the courts, legislatures, and churches. The religious divisions over these life-and-death issues are not consistent. Catholics and Fundamentalists oppose abortion and euthanasia, but differ on capital punishment. Protestant liberals accept abortion, oppose capital punishment, and would allow euthanasia in some cases. In the name of justice for all, Catholics bishops and liberal Protestants support a wide range of programs to aid the poor; Mormons, Fundamentalists, and conservative members of mainline Protestant denominations do not, seeing the welfare state as fostering irresponsible behavior. In the 1990s, religious commitment determines the stance of most Americans on a wide range of political and moral issues.

Civil Rights Movement

In 1950, America was a segregated society, North and South. In the South, custom and legislation required separate schools, restrooms, and sections for seats on public transportation. In the North, most hotels and restaurants refused to serve blacks, many colleges and universities denied admittance to black students, and there were only a few blacks on football teams. (There were none in the South.) Northern public schools were integrated, but residential segregation meant that there was little interaction among the races. Virtually everywhere, the churches of blacks and whites remained separate. The armed forces, desegregated by President Truman in 1948, constituted one of the few integrated national institutions in America.

In 1954, in *Brown* v. *Board of Education* (Topeka, Kansas), the Supreme Court unanimously overruled an 1893 precedent and held that segregation was illegal and should be ended with "all deliberate speed." The next year, Rosa Parks, a black woman in Montgomery, Alabama, sitting on a crowded bus, refused to give up her seat to a white rider and stand in the blacks' section. After the city arrested her to enforce segregation, blacks initiated a yearlong boycott and selected a well-educated young Baptist minister, Martin Luther King, Jr. (1929–1968), as their leader. King brought to the civil rights movement the eloquence of the most effective black preachers, a passionate commitment to social justice characteristic of the Social Gospel, and knowledge of the possibilities for nonviolent action derived from studying Gandhi's teachings and techniques in the struggle for the independence of India. Like Gandhi, King embraced nonviolence as an ethical and religious method of countering unjust laws and was willing to suffer as a way of morally countering evil. So the civil rights demonstrators did not strike back when the police clubbed and arrested them. Instead, throughout the South, young black men and women staged sit-ins at lunch counters, integrated buses and trains, and attempted to attend previously all-white public schools and universities.

Under King's leadership of the Southern Christian Leadership Conference, the civil rights movement joined blacks and whites, adults and college students, and prominent Protestant and Catholic clergymen and Jewish rabbis in a prophetic crusade against injustice. Together, activists journeyed south to integrate public transportation, hotels, and restaurants and to register voters. Southern governors led a movement, centered in the Democratic party and supported by the white churches, determined to preserve the status quo and even defy the federal government. Between 1962 and 1965, ninety-three Southern black churches were burned or bombed, an indication that segregationists feared the power of religion in the struggle. Outside Meridian, Mississippi, four civil rights workers were killed. In full view of television cameras in 1965, Sheriff Bull Connor of Selma, Alabama, unleashed an attack by police and dogs on peaceful civil rights advocates, including King, attempting to march to Montgomery.

Along with other civil rights workers, King was mobbed, threatened, and jailed. His "Letter from the Birmingham jail" defended nonviolence as a Christian strategy. In 1963, addressing several hundred thousand who had marched on Washington to support civil rights, King's "I have a dream" speech called for a color-blind America in which "all of God's children . . . [would] be able to join hands and to sing in the words of the old Negro spiritual, 'Free at last, free at last; thank God Almighty, we are free at last.'"[1] Supported by the National Council of Churches and the Catholic bishops, and aided by a series of Supreme Court decisions, President Johnson pushed through new civil rights legislation over the filibusters of Southern politicians. King's assassination in 1968 while supporting a strike of Memphis sanitation workers made him a martyr, the only black American whose birthday is celebrated as a national holiday.

Even before the assassination, the civil rights movement splintered. King retained the support of white liberals and black clergy, whose activism reinforced their position as the political leaders of their communities. Federal laws now guaranteed equal political rights, but King's 1966 campaign in Chicago seeking economic justice had little success. He had alienated President Johnson by denouncing the Vietnam War. Malcolm X (1915–1965), for a time a Black Muslim minister in Harlem, denounced Christianity as a white man's device to enslave blacks. Malcolm's diagnosis of white racism and the economic and social problems confronting the black communities resembled King's, but the Nation of Islam's cry for black pride repudiated integration and advocated self-help. The Black Panthers scorned King's nonviolent strategy as Uncle Tomism, advocated defending their rights with force, and also denounced integration as a goal. Charles Forman of CORE staged sit-ins at white

---

[1] Martin Luther King, Jr., in James Washington, ed., *I Have a Dream: Writings and Speeches That Changed the World* (San Francisco: Harper, 1992), pp. 105–106.

Northern churches to demand $500 million in reparations as payment for centuries of oppression of blacks.

In the spring of 1968, black riots in Los Angeles, Newark, and Detroit occasioned a white backlash, symbolized by Alabama governor George Wallace's receiving 10 million votes for president under the banner of his new American Party. The identification of the Democratic party with liberal social causes, including civil rights, caused a major loss of support and allowed the Republicans to become a political power in the South. Southern Baptists became a core constituency backing a conservative agenda endorsing states' rights as a way to oppose federal intervention on behalf of minorities. White Americans, from both North and South, increasingly rejected using federal power and money to improve the status of black Americans. In retrospect, the alliance that King forged among black activists and liberal and moderate Catholics, Protestants, and Jews was very fragile. Like the first Reconstruction, the second was imposed by the North on the South and sought to change society by guaranteeing political rights and educational opportunity. Although churches proclaimed that they welcomed people from all races, blacks and whites still worshiped separately.

Black churches continued to provide a political focus for a black community increasingly divided by class. A black caucus formed in Congress, and major American cities elected black mayors; in 1990, Douglas Wilder of Virginia became the first black man ever elected governor of a state. Jesse Jackson continued the tradition of ministers representing the black community in politics, becoming a powerful voice for an activist government working for the poor as he ran for president in 1984 and 1988.

Vietnam and the Bomb: Religion as Peacemaker

In the aftermath of Castro's rise to power in Cuba, America saw her mission as stopping communist subversion of poor, undeveloped, weak countries. Three presidents described South Vietnam as a stepping-stone in the communists' plot to undermine governments in Laos, Cambodia, Thailand, and then perhaps India, Indonesia, and Japan. Kennedy and then Johnson's Vietnam policy rested upon the assumptions prevalent in U.S. foreign policy since 1947 that Americans would oppose a monolithic communism. Kennedy's inaugural address promised that in the defense of freedom, a new generation of Americans "would bear any burden, pay any price." Vietnam was that price.

Ngo Dinh Diem had credentials to create a free South Vietnam: He was a patriot who had opposed the Japanese in World War II, was a Catholic supported by America's most powerful Catholic, Francis Cardinal Spellman of New York, and stood opposed to communism and ready to resist a takeover by North Vietnam. Initially, political and religious liberals and conservatives approved of what they saw as a small country's right to erect a democratic, noncommunist government. Yet when he was actually in power, Diem proved to be authoritarian, rigid, and inept. After he was assassinated in 1963, his successors were no better.

America's churches helped create a peace movement when the war was long, the governments in South Vietnam corrupt, the tactics of the American army unsuccessful, and the human cost enormous. Guerrilla war turned out to be not a crusade, but morally ambiguous. Even the peace movement itself was fractious, with old-line pacifists working with Catholic and Protestant clergy, many already active in the civil rights movement, who joined with King in proclaiming that the Vietnam war violated just war standards and betrayed basic American values. Religious doves worked uneasily with new leftists who saw the war as symptomatic of a fundamental corruption of the American political and economic system. Some new leftists attacked liberals as the enemy at hand, sought to foment revolution at home, and openly sympathized with North Vietnam. The antiwar movement, in addition to being concurrent with the civil rights and feminist movements, was identified by the press and the public with a countercultural revolution committed to hard rock music, sexual freedom, drugs, communes, and non-Western religions. While they denounced the immorality of the government, the youthful counter-cultural adherents flouted their own rejection of basic moral standards.

In 1967, after witnessing a prayer vigil on the steps of the capital led by prominent American religious leaders, Senator Eugene McCarthy concluded that the antiwar movement was here to stay and decided to challenge President Johnson for the 1968 Democratic presidential nomination. Four years later, the Democrats nominated Senator George McGovern on an antiwar platform. By 1971, surveys showed that sixty-five percent of the public thought that the war in Vietnam was "morally wrong."[2] For the first time in their history, some American churches defied the political establishment during a war. The antiwar movement made possible America's acceptance of a military defeat. Polls showed that at no time during the conflict did a majority of Americans, young or old, oppose the war, and this was true of the majority of churches as well. At the national level, the Democratic party split between doves and hawks, allowing the election of Richard Nixon in 1968 and his landslide victory in 1972, even after four more years of war. In 1980, the Republican party came to power under Ronald Reagan as a defender of the Vietnam war and military confrontation with the Soviet Union and as an opponent of the civil rights movement, women's liberation, homosexuality, and abortion. Reagan was also a defender of alleged traditional American values, small government, and evangelical religion. An essential ingredient in the conservative ascendancy was the new Christian Right.

The Moral Majority

The alliance between, and strength of the political right and religious Fundamentalists (who now called themselves Evangelicals) took the mainline churches by surprise. In the 1920s, Fundamentalists had turned their back on political involvement, being more concerned with individual salvation and the return of Christ. The South, still the Bible Belt in the 1950s, supported a strong military and unregulated capitalism as a way of opposing communism and feared that welfare programs would pave the way to socialism. To political and religious conservatives, civil rights, the Vietnam War, and feminism seemed to point up the failures of liberalism, which created people who found fault with, rather than loved, America. Then Watergate discredited President Nixon and the Republican establishment.

[2] Charles De Benedetti and Charles Chatfield, *An American Ordeal: The Antiwar Movement of the Vietnam Era* (Syracuse, NY: Syracuse University Press, 1990), pp. 298, 310, 318.

The increasing acceptance of premarital sex and of nudity in movies and magazines, the availability of drugs, and the visibility of homosexuality made Christian conservatives despair for what they saw as the growing tawdriness of American life. The national press and television fostered New York and Hollywood standards upon a "silent majority." Finally, the election in 1976 of a self-proclaimed "born-again" Southern Christian, Jimmy Carter, made evangelical religion respectable.

Fundamentalist preachers capitalized upon the use of mass communication, first radio and then television, to spread their message of anticommunism, support for capitalism, and traditional moral values. From modest beginnings, a group of independent Baptist ministers, led by Jerry Falwell, created huge churches, founded colleges, preached on television, and established a political action committee called the Moral Majority. President Reagan gained popularity by siding with the issues of the Moral Majority: prayer in schools, outlawing abortion, reducing the power of the federal government, deregulation of business, and traditional moral values. Effectively organized, well financed, and able to spread its message through the televangelists and the PTL (Praise the Lord) network, the evangelical right has become a major force in politics, particularly in the Republican party.

Whether evangelical politics will remain strong is still unclear. Americans continue to be deeply suspicious of the direct political activity of ministers. Polls show that Jerry Falwell has a two-to-one unfavorable rating, and Pat Robertson's presidential campaign in 1984 worked well only in caucus states in which a small cadre of his followers could dominate the Republican party. People claiming to be "born-again" Christians still remain a minority, and there are basic theological divisions among pentecostals and fundamentalists. The new Christian Right needs the votes of Mormons, Roman Catholics, and Orthodox Jews, but conservative Evangelicals have traditionally disapproved of these religions. In addition, the Catholic church has officially opposed major themes of the conservative platform. For example, American bishops denounced a reliance upon nuclear weapons, criticized the social cost of an unregulated pursuit of wealth, and opposed weakening social welfare.

In seeking to mobilize religion, the evangelical right will confront two basic, countervailing themes in American history: the separation of church and state and the predominance of economic concerns in voting patterns. Many lower class white evangelicals, even in the South, continue to favor social welfare programs. The Afro-American churches combine evangelical piety with conservative morality, but blacks have consistently voted for liberal social programs. Billy Graham and Robert Schuller symbolize those television preachers and a wide swath of evangelical Christians who continue to agree with Dwight Moody's position that too close an identification of Christianity with any political reform will hinder the primary task of saving souls. In addition, the Moral Majority's stance on unregulated capitalism and a morally conservative ethos do not blend easily. Americans are increasingly aware of the growing disparity between rich and poor and the risks to the environment, but their response to these problems remains uncertain.

In the 1990s, the decentralization and diversity of American churches and their inability even to agree on permissible moral conduct or the tasks of government make predicting their future political influence hazardous. As long as the American people affirm, by word and deed, the centrality of religious values, politicians will continue to seek the blessing of God for their programs. However, because of America's diversity of religious expression, applying religion in the public realm will cause controversy.

Chapter 38

Discordant Voices: Christianity in America since 1945

American society since 1945 presents a remarkable paradox, because if polls and sociologists of religion are right, the nation has become both more secular and more religious at the same time. That is, on the one hand, there are many institutions—businesses, schools, mass media—that function as if either religious beliefs or institutional religion is of marginal significance. The conventional wisdom was that as societies modernized—became better educated, more bureaucratic, economically developed, and increasingly urbanized—religion would become privatized and play a smaller role in daily life. England, Germany, France, and the Scandinavian countries seemed to prove that the major theme of western societies since the medieval period was toward secularization: Religious institutions and belief were becoming weaker. On the other hand, compared with European industrialized nations, America has *not* experienced a decline in religion in terms of either individual commitment or institutional strength, perhaps because religious and secular culture affirm common values of liberty, individualism, economic achievement, and moral decency.

In the 1950s, according to polls, sixty percent of Americans claimed church affiliation (a higher figure than church records indicated), and membership stayed between that figure and seventy percent until the 1990s. Over ninety percent of the American people tell pollsters that they believe in God, nearly as many claim to pray, seventy-six percent believe in life after death, one-third claim to be "born again" Christians, well over half believe that the Bible is either essentially true or inerrant, and forty percent attend a church in any seven-day period.[1] A higher percentage of Americans than Spaniards or Italians say that God is important in their lives; the United States shows a pervasive impact of religion comparable to Poland and Ireland. Far more people attend church on a regular basis than vote in any national election. Of course, statistics derived from polls must be carefully scrutinized: A recent study concluded that poll results are skewed because people are willing to lie about church attendance. Still, a wide variety of polls collected over a thirty-year period confirm Supreme Court Justice William O. Douglas's 1952 verdict that "we are a religious people."[2]

A follow-up survey of Middletown (Muncie, Indiana) in the 1970s found that, compared with the 1920s, more people contributed a larger percentage of their income to, and attended, church more frequently.[3] Middletown also illustrates a national trend by having far more denominations today than earlier, and most of these are small. There are thriving ethnic Protestant and Catholic churches for immigrants from Mexico, Puerto Rico, Vietnam, Cuba, and China; churches combining pentecostalism with gay rights; drive-in churches; and services in shopping centers and on the beach at Waikiki. Forty-five denominations have more than 200,000 members, but one-half of their congregations have fewer than two hundred members.[4] For most Americans, religion remains an activity in which localism predominates and to which group identity is fused.

If in government the United States went "E Pluribus Unum" (one from many), in religion it began with many and went to more. Eighty-eight percent or more Americans profess to religions that are termed Judeo-Christian. But the nation also contains practitioners of most of the religions of the world. Immigrant populations brought many varieties of their religions with them. From India came Sikhs, Jainists, and Vedantists; from China, Taoists and Confucians; from Japan, Shintoists and Nichiren Shoshu; and from Iran, the Baha'is and Shiites. So metropolitan areas can contain Buddhist shrines, Hindu temples, and Muslim mosques. Under First Amendment protection, the Supreme Court allowed animal sacrifice in the Cuban Santería cult. In airports, saffron-robed followers of the Hare Krishnas compete for donations with "Moonies," members of the Unification Church who follow the teachings of Rev. Sun Myung Moon. Gandhi's linkage of asceticism, nonviolence, and meditation appealed to many Christian pacifists who sought an ethical pattern for political action. In the 1960s, books on Zen Buddhists and Yoga became best-sellers, and pop psychologists promoted Transcendental Meditation as self-help. The very popular writings of the Trappist monk Thomas Merton (1915–1968), drawing upon Christian and Buddhist meditation, prompted a few Americans to introduce eastern contemplation techniques into mainline Christianity.

New made-in-America religions, termed cults by outsiders, echoed themes of earlier

[1] George Gallup and Sarah Jones, *100 Questions and Answers: Religion in America* (Princeton, NJ: Princeton Religion and Research Center, 1989), pp. 2–3; Barry Kosmin and Seymour P. Lachman, *One Nation under God: Religion in Contemporary Society* (New York: Harmony, 1993), pp. 2–5, 8, 289–90; David Barrett, ed., *World Christian Encyclopedia* (New York: Oxford, 1982), p. 711.

[2] "*Zorah* v. *Clauson,*" "Cases Adjudged in the Supreme Court," *United States Reports* (Washington: U.S. Printing Office, 1952), vol. 343, p. 313.

[3] Theodore Caplow et al., *All Faithful People: Continuity and Change in Middletown's Religion* (New York: Harcourt, Brace, 1956), pp. 294–297.

[4] Bureau of the Census, *Statistical Abstracts of the United States* (Washington: U.S. Department of Commerce, 1995), p. 68.

new religions. For example, Jimmy Jones of Jonestown, Guyana, and David Koresh of Waco, Texas, utilized millennial expectations to lead their followers to destruction. A combination of cosmology and health underlies L. Ron Hubbard's (1911–1986) Scientology. The Supreme Court declared that the Church of Scientology's mail-order medical devices depended upon religion and were, therefore, not subject to regulation by the Food and Drug agency. Television carried advertisements for the new "science" of Dianetics. Feminist distrust of patriarchal monotheism underlay a revival of the goddess cults and wicca (witchcraft). Ecological concern undergirded a revival of neopaganism, or "Edenic Bower," which sought to cooperate with the "life force" in nature. Spiritualism resurfaced in religions celebrating UFOs, flying saucers, séances, and telepathy.[5] In California, the home of the greatest variety of new religious movements, a poll found that one-third of the people believed in reincarnation and twenty percent practiced meditation. The visibility of the many "alternative" religions and the numbers of people who pass in and out of them reflect Americans' commitment to allow individuals to choose from a smorgasbord of religions.

Mainline Denominations

Since the second Great Awakening, a Protestant establishment—Congregationalists, Methodists, Baptists, Episcopalians, and Presbyterians—had set the tone for American society. Mormons dominated Utah, Lutherans predominated in the upper Midwest, Southern Baptists prevailed in the South, and Catholics exercised power in urban areas and through organized labor, but the Protestant establishment furnished the presidents and senators, the journalists and college presidents, and the captains of industry and wealthy landowners. In actuality, twentieth-century America had become religiously pluralistic, but authorities of the mainline denominations seemed not to realize this. They continued to make pronouncements on faith and ethics, seemingly unaware of the erosion of their base of power in individual congregations.

The strength and weakness of the mainline churches was in their close identification with American society. They had neither strong ties to a foreign authority like Rome nor its sense of tradition. They dismissed the millennialists' pessimism about the future of the United States as irrational. Confident of their ability to shape society, mainline churches welcomed a quickening of intellectual acuity provided by theologians like the Niebuhrs, Karl Barth, and Paul Tillich, the formidable scholarship behind the Revised Standard Version of the Bible, and the high quality of education in seminaries. As long as Americans felt complacent with the political and moral tone of their societies, as occurred during the 1950s, these denominations would prosper. As white Americans moved to the suburbs, mainline churches relocated with them, leaving the inner city dwellings to minorities, a phenomenon that led to what one author described as "The Suburban Captivity of the Church."[6] By this, he meant that members had become so conforming to middle-class norms and introverted, that the church could no longer provide a critique of the pursuit of

---

[5] See Robert Ellwood and Harry Partin, *Religious and Spiritual Groups in Modern America* (Englewood Cliffs, NJ: Prentice Hall, 1988).

[6] Gibson Winter, *Suburban Captivity of the Church* (Garden City, NY: Doubleday, 1961), p. 105.

wealth, the poverty of many, and the prevalent racism. Moving to the suburbs also meant that churches would be divided by class and that whites and blacks would continue to worship in separate congregations.

Norman Vincent Peale became famous for stressing the "Power of Positive Thinking," or utilizing religion for success.[7] Other clergy sought to create a new appreciation of church liturgy and tradition. Alternatively, particularly in the 1960s, the clergy emphasized the need for a new Social Gospel, focusing on civil rights, economic injustice, women's equality, or dangers of nuclear war. In general, the clerical leaders of the mainline denominations, more liberal politically than the laity and aware of the fractures in the American dream, saw speaking out as their prophetic duty. The members, by contrast, complained that they needed less socialism and more old-time gospel.

The twentieth century saw a bureaucratization of virtually all institutions: industry, education, government, and the church as well. One result was a distance between denominational authorities who set policy and local congregations. The leaders remained committed to ecumenicism. So at one level there was strong support for the National (successor to the Federal) and World Council of Churches. There were also mergers, as denominations sought to heal various nineteenth-century schisms by joining with United Methodists, the United Presbyterian Church in U.S.A., the Evangelical Lutheran Church in America, and the United Church of Christ. However, each of these amalgamations left some members irritated, and other branches, such as the Southern Baptists, Wesleyan Methodists, Missouri Synod Lutherans, and (Southern) Presbyterian Church in the U.S., refused to join. Under the auspices of the Consultation on Church Union, commissions began studying the possibilities of unions of Congregationalists, Episcopalians, Methodists, and Presbyterians, although differences in tradition and church government and the refusal to jettison long-held views of sacraments or the apostolic succession stopped the process. Such mergers began to appear top heavy with bureaucracy and irrelevant to the problems facing local congregations.

The talk of merger fostered a reduced sense of denominational consciousness. It seemingly no longer mattered if one were a Methodist, Congregationalist, Baptist, Disciple, or Presbyterian because the distinctive beliefs and polities of these denominations no longer appeared of crucial importance. So people moving to a new community would not automatically identify with the church of their childhood, but would "shop around," seeking a minister and congregation with whom they could feel comfortable. According to polls, between one-third and one-half of church members have changed denominations in their lives.[8] Since voluntarism had long been characteristic of American religion, the phenomenon was nothing new, but it meant that in the marketplace of religion, churches survived and grew by offering an attractive product.

Ministers of the mainline denominations now wore black robes, sometimes with stripes showing their academic degrees, the music came from expensive pipe organs and robed choirs, and the young attended the first thirty minutes of the service, during which they might hear a short children's sermon. Altar calls and revivals became uncommon. In-

[7] Norman Vincent Peale, *Power of Positive Thinking* (New York: Prentice Hall, 1953).

[8] See Robert Wuthnow, *The Restructuring of American Religion: Society and Faith since World War II* (Princeton, NJ: Princeton University Press, 1988), pp. 80–99.

stead, ministers proclaimed that the Christ event brought deliverance from sin and allowed the fulfilling of human destiny. Robert Schuller became a famous television preacher proclaiming that religion empowered people to become successful and feel good. Church attendance was good because "the family that prays together stays together." Mainline Protestantism was optimistic—so insistent in proclaiming God's love, that judgment seemed a relic of the past. The young studied Sunday school materials carefully tailored according to age. Churches provided child care for the very young.

Nineteenth-century revival songs like "In the Garden," "Old Rugged Cross," and "Sweet Hour of Prayer" might be sung in Sunday school, but the dignity of worship could be better conveyed by "A Mighty Fortress Is Our God," "Holy, Holy, Holy," and "Our God, Our Help in Ages Past," although "Amazing Grace" could be used on many occasions. Churches attracted new members with a staff of ministers and religious education specialists, an excellent choir, a large Sunday School, a good youth program, a multitude of weekday events, ample parking, and an imposing structure.

The postwar period saw a major boom in building new sanctuaries and educational units, often located in suburbs on large plots of land with ample parking. New structures often contained divided chancels, with the altar replacing the pulpit as the center of attention. Few of these structures were neo-Gothic or romanesque or had the imposing heavy stone or interior darkness characteristic of late nineteenth-century American churches. Instead, architecture sought to provide a friendly environment in an attempt to welcome people, to foster liturgical worship, and to offer useful space for more than Sunday morning services. In the South, churches were air-conditioned, and cushions on pews brought more comfort. By the mid-1950s, competition with television brought such a decline in attendance of Sunday evening services and midweek prayer meetings, that many congregations now abolished them.

During the 1950s, the mainline denominations thrived, continuing the pattern of constant numerical growth established during the Second Great Awakening. However, this trend ended during the 1960s, and from 1970 for the next twenty years, the mainline churches either declined absolutely in membership or lost ground because they did not keep up with increases in population. Local congregations saw contributions hold steady or decline rather than keep pace with inflation.[9]

Because there is so much variety in congregations, even within one denomination, there is no one satisfactory explanation for this decline. Sociologists of religion have hypothesized that the leadership of the churches was more ready to embrace causes of the 1960s—peace in Vietnam, civil rights, feminism—than was the laity,[10] who instead just wanted the church to provide a place of comfort and stability—of certainty in a world in which even the basic values of family, patriotism, capitalism, and morality were questioned. Charismatic worship with new Gospel songs provided a sense of power and communication with the divine that some found lacking in more formal services. Members did not wish to learn that reading the Bible required an understanding of the layers of traditions

---

[9] Peter Halvorson and William Newman, eds., *Atlas of Religious Change in America* (Atlanta: Glenmary Research Center, 1994), p. 8; Wade Clark Roof and William McKinney, *American Mainline Religion: Its Changing Shape and Future* (New Brunswick, NJ: Rutgers University Press, 1982), pp. 231–235.

[10] Caplow, *All Faithful People*, pp. 222–240; Wuthnow, *Restructuring of American Religion*, pp. 133–214.

that shaped it. There was a class element as well: The new conservatism appealed disproportionately to the lower middle-class blue-collar workers whom the new internationally competitive economy left behind.

An alternative explanation for the decline is that in the voluntaristic, competitive atmosphere of religious life in America, the mainline churches did a poorer job of proselytizing and of building new churches than evangelistic denominations did.[11] What gives this interpretation credence is the deep disagreements among conservative denominations. Mormons, Adventists, charismatics, and fundamentalists make strange bedfellows. So what may be occurring is a recurrence of earlier tendencies; after all, by defying the canons of Calvinism and identifying with the common people against an educated elite, Methodists, Baptists, and Disciples grew rapidly in the early nineteenth century. Then they became the establishment, and now they are forced to share power with Pentecostals, Missouri Synod Lutherans, and Southern Baptists.

The Evangelical Resurgence

The decline of the mainline churches was paralleled by the rise of evangelical denominations. The evangelicals shared a belief in the full authority of scripture and saw their primary task to be the conversion of sinful men and women. The denominations that rejected mergers and refused to join the National Council of Churches grew rapidly from 1945 to 1990, increasing at a rate greater than the population growth.[12] These denominations stated clearly what they believed and what they opposed. By rejecting the liberal agenda of the National Council of Churches, they could ignore or oppose the civil rights movement, peace activity, and the ordination of women—indeed, any hint of the social gospel—while concentrating upon personal piety. For example, the Southern Baptists alone among major denominations took no stand on the Vietnam War. They were pro-business and anti-Communist. All officially opposed abortion, though polls show considerable diversity on this subject. The neo-Evangelicals accepted make-up and fashionable clothes, watched television, and celebrated sexual fulfillment and prosperity.[13] Members showed their loyalty by tithing, attending prayer meetings and Sunday services, and proselytizing their neighbors.

The neo-Evangelicals conveyed a sense of being left out of a religiously and politically liberal establishment. Membership required a visible conversion experience, commitment to an inerrant gospel, and rejection of a sinful lifestyle. Fearing even a taint of historical criticism of the Bible, the Southern Baptists and Missouri Synod Lutherans purged moderate seminary professors and denominational leaders. Southern Baptists expanded their base in the nation, becoming the largest single Protestant denomination, without losing their primacy in the South or changing their Fundamentalist message.

Before emerging as a powerful force, the evangelicals spent years building institutions

---

[11] R. Lawrence Moore, *Selling God: American Religion in the Marketplace of Culture* (New York: Oxford, 1972), pp. 235–238, 251–256.

[12] *Atlas of Religious Change in the United States*, pp. 10–11.

[13] See Richard Quebedeaux, *The Worldly Evangelicals* (San Francisco: Harper & Row, 1978), pp. 77–79, 115–128.

and gaining sophistication. Their base was the South, plus a network of Bible and holiness colleges and seminaries scattered throughout the nation. The National Association of Evangelicals and the Evangelical Theological Society served as a network linking clergy and churches. *Christianity Today* became a leading periodical, and the Campus Crusade for Christ targeted young people. During the 1930s, while liberal clergy received free time from the major networks, the fundamentalists began purchasing radio time on small stations. There, they gained skill in presenting their message to mass audiences and also built a network of stations. Later on, in 1960, when the Federal Communications Commission allowed radio and television stations to count bought time as public service, the fundamentalist radio preachers had already created a style and the financial support of voluntary organizations, like the Full Gospel Business Men's Fellowship, that would make them successful.[14]

In the 1920s, there were two main streams of evangelical resurgence: a Pentecostal healing revival, which later evolved into a middle-class charismatic movement, and fundamentalism, which became neo-evangelism. These two phenomena are respectively typified by Oral Roberts and Billy Graham. Oral Roberts (1918–   ), the son of a Pentecostal minister, had only a smattering of college when he joined the revivalist circuit in 1947, preaching that the presence of Jesus could result in "miracles" of healing. To his healing ministry, he added an emphasis upon conversion, the imminent end of the world, and a link between giving and outward prosperity. By 1954, his radio ministry was presented on three hundred radio and television stations.[15] In the 1960s, believing that the stress upon gifts resulting from baptism by the Holy Spirit in the charismatic movement should not be confined to the Pentecostal churches, Roberts joined the Methodist Church. Viewing himself as a revivalist with an increased commitment to Christian higher education, he raised some $55 million to create an evangelical college, now Oral Roberts University, with a medical school.[16] Roberts's transformation of his ministry parallels changes in the major Pentecostal denominations, which seek to preserve the gifts of the Holy Spirit (glossolalia, prophecy, faith healing) in services held in substantial church buildings with educational units that reflect the growth in affluence among members.

Billy Graham (1918–   ), a graduate of Wheaton College, experienced conversion in a revival in 1934. After World War II, Graham became a preacher with the Youth for Christ organization, preaching in Europe and the United States. He emerged a celebrity after a major revival in Los Angeles in 1949. Like Roberts, Graham published many books, utilized television, and engaged in direct mail-order fund-raising. Before beginning a crusade in any city, Graham insisted on enlisting support from many churches. Using an enormous choir singing distinctive songs like "How Great Thou Art," the Graham crusades held in virtually all major American cities and in many foreign countries resulted in thousands turning to Christ.

Graham became a religious adviser to every president, from Eisenhower to Clinton, being particularly close to Johnson and Nixon. From 1949 until the 1990s, in an enormous

[14] Moore, *Selling God*, pp. 245–248.

[15] David Edwin Harrell, Jr., *All Things Are Possible: The Healing and Charismatic Revivals in Modern America* (Bloomington, IN: Indiana University Press, 1975), pp. 43–46.

[16] *Ibid.*, p. 155.

variety of contexts, Graham successfully preached his vision of evangelical Christianity: the truthfulness of the Bible; Jesus' death for sinners; postponing a decision for Christ is dangerous, since there is a future life of heaven or hell; the imminence of the millennium; the presence of the devil and evil. But accepting Jesus as Lord and Savior leads to a spiritually fulfilling life.

The evangelical subculture is spread through a variety of forms: The Campus Crusade for Christ employs 5,300 in eighty-four countries; the Billy Graham Center at Wheaton is a graduate school and media center; the Fellowship of Christian Athletes uses sports figures to witness to their faith; the Promise Keepers is for men; and the Christian Coalition, successor to the Moral Majority, focuses on politics. There are Christian businessmen's organizations, evangelical publishers, 2,400 Christian bookstores, and record companies that propagate evangelical religion through jazz, country, rock, and reggae music.[17] By the 1980s, the most visible national religious figures were the evangelical television preachers like Rex Humbard, Jerry Falwell, and Pat Robertson, who were interviewed on "Nightline" and quoted in newspapers. In the past, evangelical revivals survived scandals surrounding Aimee Semple McPherson and Marjoe; today, the cause seems destined to survive the sexual and financial misconduct of Jimmy Swaggart and Jim Bakker, because neo-Evangelicalism's strength lies in the conservative religious beliefs of thousands of local congregations.

Catholic Maturity

Catholicism in 1945 seemed little changed since 1890. The parish remained the center of religious life, with women more likely to attend services than men by a two-to-one majority. Bishops still more noted for massive building programs than theological acuteness had brought modern business practices to the managing of diocesan life and, through control of finances, had gained increasing power over school and parish. A cult of the papacy only reinforced the hierarchical nature of the church. The bishop *was* the church.

At the personal level, devotional Catholicism remained the norm, with rosary beads, novenas, sodalities, and missions. The major innovation was the spiritual retreat, at which, for a weekend or longer, a person could engage in study and meditation. In 1950, Pope Pius XIII proclaimed the bodily assumption of the Virgin Mary as infallible Catholic doctrine. The devotion to Mary and to the saints, which seemed to outsiders as detracting from Jesus' saving work, served to exacerbate Protestant suspicions of Catholicism.

Roman Catholicism remained the largest single denomination in America, with about one-quarter of all church members and no schisms. From the mid-1920s to the early 1950s, the church experienced a 42-percent growth in membership, about the same as Protestants, because the earlier high levels of European migration ceased. As the children of immigrants grew up, the church sought to incorporate them into a distinct Catholic culture through its elaborate school system, from parochial schools to colleges. In 1920, thirty-five percent of parishes had schools; by 1959, fifty-nine percent did, with the main emphasis upon elementary education and sixty percent of the teachers coming from teaching orders of reli-

---

[17] Quebedeaux, *The Worldly Evangelicals*, p. 56.

gious women.[18] The Irish bishops, who still dominated the hierarchy, generally approved of schools teaching a legalistic religion of guilt, sin, and confession and promoting the Americanization of ethnics rather than concentrating upon high academic standards. In 1955, the Catholic historian John Tracy Ellis complained about a pervasive ghetto mentality creating an intellectual desert in which Catholics did not participate in or contribute to American culture.[19] Yet by the time Ellis was writing, far-reaching changes were already making his observation obsolete.

In the 1930s, urban Catholics remained overwhelmingly blue-collar skilled or unskilled laborers whose lives after work centered on ethnic parishes, the political machine, and the neighborhood saloon. In the 1940s, two-thirds of Catholics were lower class, twenty-five percent middle class, and nine percent upper class. Catholic workers became strong supporters of the New Deal's promotion of social legislation and unionization. After World War II, Catholic soldiers benefited from the G.I. bill to finance college educations. By the 1960s, Catholics of European origins had become solidly middle class, with large numbers attending college and graduate school. Surveys showed Irish Catholics with higher economic status and more education than the members of mainline Protestant churches like the Baptists and Methodists.[20] Belying their image as rabid anti-Communists and social conservatives, Catholics—particularly those who had attended parochial school—by the 1970s were more likely than Protestants to be politically liberal on a wide range of issues, including segregation. The ethnic parish declined as newly affluent Catholics moved to the suburbs, in part as a response to blacks moving into the inner cities. In the late 1940s, bishops in the North sought to integrate Catholic schools and churches, but—except in Louisiana—there were few black members. Catholic universities, like Notre Dame and Georgetown, previously known primarily for athletic prowess, now sought to build endowments in order to become first-class teaching and research institutions. The decline of Protestant fears of Catholic subservience to Rome allowed John F. Kennedy to be elected president in 1960. Even before his assassination made him a political martyr, Kennedy, perceived as independent of the Vatican, ended the political power of American anti-Catholic nativism.

The reforms associated with Vatican II (1962–1965) can now be seen as the culmination of many changes building up over a long period. In 1943, the papacy endorsed using modern techniques to study the Bible. In the 1950s, a European liturgical reform movement emphasized the church as a mystical body, an attitude that fostered a sense of the community of priest and laity. Reformers wanted worship to focus more on Christ than on the saints and sought to promote better understanding and participation of the laity in the mass. Still, when Pope John XXIII called the Council, no one foresaw the extent of the changes.

The Council revolutionized the liturgy. Now the altar was turned so that the priest faced the congregation, the laity did less kneeling and held the host in its hand, and Latin was no longer the language of the mass; instead, the priest and the congregation spoke the psalms and responses in English (or other vernacular languages). Sin was seen in more

[18] Andrew Greeley, *American Catholic: A Social Portrait* (New York: Basic, 1977), p. 166.
[19] John Tracy Ellis, "American Catholics and the Intellectual Life," *Thought* (Autumn 1955), pp. 355–388.
[20] Greeley, *American Catholic*, pp. 41, 44, 53–63.

personal terms as alienation from God rather than as breaking a rule, and there was now less emphasis upon confession. Long-established rules, such as refraining from eating meat on Friday, were abolished. A revised liturgy reflected a theology insisting that the church, as the people of God, was called upon to be a servant. The pope stressed simplicity, concern, and humility, and bishops and priests in America sought to follow his example. Clerics no longer insisted on being called father and often wore more informal dress; nuns adopted modern habits. The bishop no longer symbolized the church, but, together with priests, women performing religious functions joined in the laity a mystical bond with Christ.

Before the Council convened, John Courtney Murray, S. J. (1904–1967) persuaded the American bishops to support a declaration on the separation of church and state, and they helped influence the Council to endorse religious freedom. Without repudiating the church's claim to truth, Rome sought to promote ecumenical friendliness, inviting Protestant churches to send observers to the Council. Soon the pope met with the Greek Orthodox Patriarch, the Archbishop of Canterbury, and evangelicals like Billy Graham. At the local level, priests might become members of the ministerium or council of churches and join with other churches in Good Friday and Thanksgiving services. Catholic scholars felt free to participate in academic conferences with Protestants, discussing issues of theology, biblical studies, and ethics. Now the church was not simply an embattled defender of a static dogma against the claims of modernity; instead, it officially recognized that revelation was historical, ongoing, and personal.

After Vatican II, dissent became a recognized part of Catholic life. In 1968 Pope Paul VI rejected the advice of his commission and issued "Humane Vitae," which condemned all artificial methods of birth control. Polls showed that ninety percent of American Catholics disagreed with this document, and there was no significant difference in the birthrate between Protestants and Catholics.[21] The papacy's stance on human sexuality alienated many Americans, and during the 1970s Catholic membership declined for the first time. The church continued to declaim against divorce and threats to the family, but many Catholics divorced and remarried and then wished to be able to partake of the eucharist, and some priests sought to relax penalties for those who had remarried. The hierarchy strongly attacked the practice of abortion, sought to reinstate a legal ban on the procedure, and disciplined those priests who dissented from the church's teachings on abortion, remarriage, and homosexuality. Most lay Catholics disapproved of abortion, but also did not want it to be a criminal act. Pope John Paul II (1978–   ) silenced some liberation theologians in Latin America and promoted to bishops and cardinals those committed to his view of the necessity of submission to the magisterium. On his several triumphal visits to America, he was welcomed as a hero by hundreds of thousands of Catholics who admired his courage and shared his faith, but did not necessarily endorse his theology.

Since Vatican II, the numbers of seminarians and women religious has dropped drastically. By the late 1980s, there were only one-fourth as many seminarians as in 1962 and an even steeper decline in the numbers of those seeking to become nuns.[22] Within the

---

[21] *Ibid.*, pp. 139–145; also, Jay Dolan, *The American Catholic Experience* (Garden City, NY: Doubleday, 1985), p. 435.

[22] Dolan, *ibid.*, pp. 436–438.

church, priests and nuns participated in a vigorous debate as to whether celibacy and maleness should be requirements for being a priest. One solution to the growing shortage of priests endorsed by many American Catholics, but opposed by the Vatican, was to allow women to become priests. The church now allows altar girls as well as boys, and laywomen and laymen to do pastoral visitations. In small parishes, a priest will perform mass on one Sunday a month, but on days when he is absent, a woman might read the service. By necessity, the laity are assuming greater roles in the conduct of church life.

Immigration is once again changing the character of American Catholicism. One-fourth of all Catholics in the United States are now Hispanics: a few are middle-class refugees from Cuba working in Florida; more are migrant workers from Mexico and Central America living in the Southwest; a third group, which has settled in New York, is from Puerto Rico; and more recently, French-speaking Haitians journeyed to Florida. One result is the creation of new ethnic parishes that require native-born priests to acquire language skills and knowledge of the host cultures. The Irish-American hierarchy confronts a mostly poor immigrant Catholic population with a long heritage of anticlericalism who are more likely to neglect attending Sunday mass in church than major festivals and whose religious life centers around the family. Catholicism also faces competition from pentecostals, who are estimated to have captured the loyalty of twenty percent of Hispanic immigrants to the United States.

Since the 1970s, Catholicism has regained its pattern of growth. It has sought to adjust to a new influx of poor immigrants, to attract blacks, and to hold onto its suburban middle- and upper-class members. Vatican II buried Tridentine Catholicism's opposition to modernity. Now Catholics and Protestants alike face the pressures of ministering to increasingly diverse congregations in a pluralistic society and confront as their common enemy a secularism that ignores or marginalizes religion.

The Black Churches

As the major institution created and supported exclusively by African-Americans without dependence upon either white philanthropy or business, the black church maintained its traditional role of reflecting the wishes of, meeting the needs of, and speaking for its constituents. As in the past, the church helped blacks to survive in an environment of racism and poverty by offering spiritual consolation, prophetic judgment on white America, and ethnic unity. In the 1960s, recognizing the need to celebrate their differences from white American standards, the clergy repudiated what they saw as complacency in Negro churches and replaced it with a more assertive black religion of liberation that would meld African and Christian themes. Using the slogan "black is beautiful" and the term "Afro-Americans," the churches sought to foster racial pride and self-identity. The civil rights movement had a major effect on the black churches. In 1961, the National Baptist Convention split over Martin Luther King's program, but by the 1980s, even churches that usually disliked mixing politics and religion offered strong support for civil rights organizations. Black churches have been described as the "NAACP on its knees." The overwhelming majority of clergy and laity in black churches insist upon their obligation to take a stand on political and economic issues.

Unlike the mainline Protestant denominations, the leading seven black denominations of Methodists, Baptists, and Pentecostals—constituting eighty percent of African-American Christians—experienced no numerical decline and enjoyed substantial growth. However, the churches reflect both the growth in, and uneven prosperity of, the black community: In 1940, eighty percent of black rural churches were wood frame; by the end of the 1980s, seventy-seven percent were of stone or brick.[23] The Church of God in Christ, a pentecostal denomination, showed the transition from poverty to working and middle class, creating better buildings, founding schools and a seminary, and establishing a bureaucracy. Yet the finances of most black churches remain inadequate. Nearly one-half of black clergy must work in another occupation to support themselves, most of the rest receive less pay than their white counterparts and no fringe benefits. The educational attainments of black clergy have improved markedly; for example, in 1938, eighty percent of black rural clergy had not attended college, and forty-five percent had no education beyond the eighth grade. Today, seventy percent have attended college, and nearly twenty percent have graduated from a seminary or a comparable institution. The minister remains the dominant figure in the church and is judged by his ability through preaching to create a communal experience of the presence of the Holy Spirit leading to conversion. Forty-four percent of black Christians claim to be born again.[24]

Next to preaching, music remains a central focus of black worship—a creative means to join congregation, choir, and minister in a quest for fellowship with God. To classic black hymns is now added music integrating rhythm, tune, and words in spirituals, gospel songs, jazz, blues, soul, and rap—although some churches dislike bringing secular music into Sunday services. The continuing quest for liberation, both physical and spiritual, is shown by the transformation of the gospel song "I'll overcome some day" into the theme song of the civil rights movement, "We shall overcome . . . . Deep in our hearts we do believe, We shall overcome someday."

The rural South continues to experience depopulation as blacks move to the cities to escape poverty. Rural churches have few members and struggle to survive, with one pastor serving many congregations. Since he is frequently absent, the laity of the church becomes more self-reliant. In the cities, North and South, black congregations average four hundred members (although there are megachurches of several thousand parishioners), ministers are more often educated and better paid, and the church is more likely to have the financial resources to support outreach programs and missionaries and to engage in social welfare projects. Most black churches continue to have weekday prayer or study services and sponsor Sunday schools, with the larger denominations producing their own instructional materials.

Thanks to the availability of jobs in World War II, the civil rights movement, and government policies, the black middle class has expanded rapidly and now includes about one-third of African-Americans. However, continued residential segregation means that eighty percent of blacks dwell in cities, where also live the one-third of the black population euphemistically termed an "underclass" of the poor, uneducated, and unskilled, who

---

[23] C. Eric Lincoln and Lawrence Mamiya, *The Black Church in the African American Experience* (Durham, NC: Duke University Press, 1990), pp. 102–103.

[24] *Ibid.*, pp. 98–100, 228.

may number as many as ten million. Middle-class black churches have a significant number of the very poor as members, and with inadequate financial resources, these churches confront daily the issues of ghetto life: lack of economic opportunity, drugs, and crime. To these are added the pressures of a sexual revolution occurring among whites and blacks, in the country as well as in cities and in America and Europe (but not Japan), that has resulted in nearly one of three children being born to a single parent and that has increased dramatically the numbers of unwed mothers, most of whom are also poor.

The major black denominations find increasing difficulty in attracting young black males, who see the church as feminine, accommodating, and insufficiently macho. Malcolm X remains a symbol of black power and defiance, a man whose conversion to Islam while he was in prison enabled him to transform his life. Because of immigration and conversions, Muslims have now replaced Jews as the second largest religion in America after Christianity, but Islam has not attracted many black women church members. Young males see in Islam a religion attracting sports figures like boxer Muhammad Ali and basketball star Kareem Abdul-Jabbar. Black Muslims offer a gospel of self-help, black solidarity, and militant opposition to drugs and crime. The black churches and the Muslims seek to provide a spiritual community for the majority of black males and to reform the small minority whose response to poverty and the social pathology of the ghetto is to embrace a nihilistic drug culture leading to crime. Because America remains a society divided by race, the black churches continue their distinctive mission as a faith community and as political spokespersons for "a nation within a nation."

Feminist Liberation

Throughout all American history, virtually all Christians—except the Shakers and Mary Baker Eddy—insisted that God had no gender and then described "Him" as "Father," "King," or "Lord." Artists always pictured God as male. Liberals emphasized "The Fatherhood of God" and "Brotherhood of Man," evangelicals sang "Onward, Christian soldiers," and the Social Gospel added "Rise Up, O Men of God"—all unconsciously emphasizing a masculine norm of correct Christian behavior. Roman Catholics agreed with liberals and fundamentalists in restricting ordination to males. Women could still do many tasks: They could serve as organists, secretaries, and missionaries; a few preached in revivals; and more sang in choirs, prepared the food for church suppers, and participated in Bible study groups. But although within their sphere women had power, effective authority in the church remained in the hands of males. The churches depended upon the *labor* of women, most of it unpaid.

Since 1945, women have participated in a social revolution by joining the paid workforce, so that now the majority of households have two wage earners. Women have also become better educated and moved from being factory workers, secretaries, nurses, and teachers into all facets of the economy. However, women's job mobility has been linked with marital instability. Since the 1960s, one out of two marriages has ended in divorce, with the result often being a decline in the women's standard of living. In the 1960s, a women's liberation or feminist movement demanded women's rights and subjected business, government, and the church to vigorous criticism.

Participants in the women's liberation movement within the church called into question the "maleness" of Christianity. Was the church a patriarchal—even misogynist—institution that helped create, and still continued, the subordination of women? By emphasizing the figures of Eve, who symbolized female weakness, and Mary, who transcended sex and personified sacrificial love, did the church foster distorted views of women as emotional, weak creatures and refuse to allow them to assert their full humanity? Did male theologians provide a warped view of female sexuality? The critics differed among themselves as to what full female humanity entailed: Was it androgynous, so that male and female equality implied spiritual sameness? Or did males and females experience life differently, with the church needing to revise its teachings to reflect that difference? Or could men and women, as humans, share a spirituality while experiencing God in distinct ways? Whatever the conclusions, the consequences for church life would be far reaching.

Feminist scholars began rethinking biblical scholarship and all of church history, seeking to understand the role of women and the structures of oppression. They concluded that God could be described as a mother, father, or friend, or even as Goddess or Wisdom (Greek *Sophia*), because all anthropomorphizing limited, as well as nourished religious life. Bible scholars emphasized that Jesus had undermined the patriarchal norms of his day by welcoming women as his followers, and these women later played major roles in the ministry of the early church, serving as prophetesses and leading congregations. The New Testament did portray conflicts over women's activity, but it was only later that the church accepted a Greco-Roman view of female inferiority. Advocates of women's religious liberation re-studied the entire history of Christianity in order to divorce the church from an alleged authoritarian, hierarchical, masculine distortion of the Gospel.

By the 1980s, one-third of the Protestant churches in the National Council of Churches allowed the ordination of women. Female students constituted one-third to one-half of the seminarians of several mainline Protestant churches. Both the Methodists and Episcopalians have ordained women bishops. Roman Catholics and many conservative Protestant denominations still refuse to ordain women, although they have opened up alternative forms of ministry. However, many congregations object to reformulating a more gender neutral or inclusive biblical and liturgical language and, while willing to have women as associate ministers, they resist employing women as senior pastors.[25] Nearly one-third of the students of the only theological seminary of the Church of God in Christ, a black Pentecostal denomination, are female, but the denomination, citing scripture, refuses to ordain women.

Continuing resistance to feminists' demands for full equality, particularly in the Roman Catholic church, has led a few women to seek spirituality outside the church as worshipers of Goddess, free thought, or neopaganism. Alternatively, feminist demands on the church have led to a backlash among fundamentalists, evangelicals, and conservative Roman Catholics, who see agitation within the church as part of a women's liberation movement that is both against nature and destructive of the family. For the first time in American history, the churches are facing a prolonged debate on the role of the women who have consistently been their most faithful supporters.

---

[25] See Anne Carr, *Transforming Grace: Christian Tradition and Women's Experience* (San Francisco: Harper, 1988), pp. 12, 43–59.

Epilogue

The theologian Paul Tillich could have been describing American history when he wrote that "religion is the substance of culture and culture is the form of religion."[26] Religion has driven reform movements—Puritanism, antislavery, Prohibition, Progressivism, and civil rights. Religious sanctions have legitimated battles with native Americans in the seventeenth century, as well as the Revolutionary War, the Civil War, two world wars, the Korean War, the war in Vietnam, and the Persian Gulf War. However, religion also fueled the protests of those who disliked dispossessing native Americans of land, expansionist wars against Mexico and Spain, and risking nuclear annihilation. Disenfranchised groups such as African-Americans, immigrants, nineteenth-century factory workers, early advocates of women's rights, and contemporary feminists also have utilized themes drawn from scripture demanding justice.

Contemporary observers of religious turmoil talk about "culture wars" fueled by religious commitment.[27] Yet in historical perspective, the current theological controversies appear less vitriolic or divisive than do past disputes; instead, religious animosity within and between churches appears a pervasive theme in American history. In the English colonies, hegemonic Anglican and Puritan churches used theology and law against dissenters. In the early nineteenth century, evangelicals denounced as dangerous to American democracy freethinkers, Roman Catholics, Unitarians, and Mormons. Before and after 1860, evangelicals who dominated the North or South accused the churches in the other section of betraying Christianity. Since the end of the nineteenth century, Modernists and Fundamentalists have debated standards for interpreting scripture and how to apply Christian ethical precepts. As in 1920, in 1997 a compromise on this deep cleavage in Christianity seems unlikely, and the vituperative debate shows no signs of ending. However, the eclipse of virulent anti-Catholicism among Protestants (and anti-Semitism as well) and the jettisoning of a ghetto mentality among Catholics have allowed Christians to focus on a new enemy, defined as secular humanism, but more accurately described as moral tawdriness and mindless materialism.

The Founding Fathers proved their genius in creating a separation of the institutions of the state from organized religion in such a way that, except in 1860, even while they competed for adherents and influence, the churches supported the basic framework of republican government and free enterprise. The separation works better because Americans have so easily blended Christianity in with basic values in the culture. For example, there are now really three great religious–secular holidays: a harvest festival at Thanksgiving, at which Americans celebrate the blessings of God; a patriotism festival on July 4, which joins freedom and America's God-given destiny; and Christmas, in which the incarnation is made to bless children and consumerism. The mass media and business exploit these holidays and make them bigger than the Christian religious event of the year: the crucifixion and Easter resurrection. Even when the holiday is linked to spring flowers, a bunny (a fertility symbol), and a fashion parade, merchants find it difficult to exploit Easter (and Passover) be-

---

[26] Paul Tillich, *Theology of Culture* (New York: Oxford, 1959), p. 42.

[27] See James Davison Hunter, *Culture Wars: The Struggle to Define America* (New York: Basic Books: Harper-Collins, 1991).

cause Lent and Good Friday are times of self-sacrifice. At Easter, good still triumphs as the devout attend services of celebration.

This section's focus on Christianity's cultural and social impact on America must not overshadow the impact of the personal spiritual nurture of the majority participating within the churches, as well as the many who refused to confine their religious search to institutional religion. Millions have participated, and still participate, in Christianity's sacred canopy by studying the Bible, reading devotional tracts, saying the rosary, singing hymns, celebrating the eucharist, listening to sermons, attending Sunday schools, and praying. Thereby, they find inward religious strength to deal with prosperity and poverty, health and sickness, and love and death. Religious festivals or rituals at baptism, conversion, first communion, marriage, and death still mark the crucial rites of passage.

Christianity shaped the United States and yet was itself reconfigured in the process. American Roman Catholics, Lutherans, Orthodox, Episcopalians, and Methodists draw their faith and practice from European mother churches, but in ecumenical gatherings their distinctive emphases mark them as sharing a new world culture. Camp meetings and Black Gospel music, the New England meetinghouses and storefront churches, the Disciples of Christ and Southern Baptists, Mormons and Christian Scientists, voluntarism and denominationalism, Great Awakenings and fundamentalism, the Social Gospel and television evangelists are a few of the uniquely American contributions to world Christianity. Measured by biblical standards, the United States is neither a success story of a chosen few creating a new Israel nor a Sodom so lacking in good people as to be cut off from God's grace. Moreover, throughout history and today, America remains, as it was in 1630, a promised land in which, through God's providence, people can dwell together in "all meekness, gentleness, patience, and liberality."[28]

---

[28]John Winthrop, "A Model of Christian Charity," in Perry Miller, ed., *The American Puritans: Their Prose and Poetry* (Garden City, NY: Doubleday, 1956), p. 83.

Elizabeth Ann Seton (1774–1821) symbolizes the major role that nuns have played in Catholic parochial education. A convert after the death of her husband, Mother Seton began a school for girls in Maryland and founded and headed the Sisters of Charity, the first Catholic American religious society. She was beatified as the first native-born American saint in 1963. (Corbis–Bettmann)

Mary Baker Eddy (1821–1910) founded Christian Science, a movement and church dedicated to obtaining health through religious certainty and contact with God. Like Mrs. Eddy, women have often played major roles in creating and sustaining new denominations. Many Americans have found a way to physical and emotional well-being through religious practices of prayer, faith-healing, positive thinking, and meditation. (Corbis–Bettman)

Lucretia Mott (1793–1880), a Quaker minister, combined nineteenth-century religious liberalism with work for many reforms: abolitionism, schools and votes for freed slaves, college education for both sexes, and equal rights including the suffrage for women. Mott, like evangelical male and female church members, joined voluntary benevolent associations seeking the improvement of American society. (Corbis–Bettman)

George Whitefield (1714–1770) (Library of Congress)

Charles Grandison Finney (1792–1875) (Library of Congress)

Billy Sunday (1862–1935) (Library of Congress)

Martin Luther King, Jr. (1929–1968) (Library of Congress)

The spellbinding "man of God" has been a fixture in American religious life. George Whitefield was the prototype, Charles Finney the embodiment of zeal in the years before the Civil War, Billy Sunday the best known preacher at the turn of the century, and Martin Luther King, Jr., a voice of conscience for all America in the 1950s and 1960s.

Christian connections with wider social and political worlds have assumed many shapes during the course of American history. Three representative specimens are illustrated here.

After the Civil War, the Northern churches supported a whole range of schools established for the freed slaves. This one was in Vicksburg, Mississippi. (Library of Congress)

D. L. Moody (1837–1899) became a well-known evangelist, but he got his start organizing Sunday school classes for urban vagabonds. Moody is the bearded man on the left in this 1876 lithograph. (Library of Congress)

A New York City parade from 1908 hints at the importance which the Roman Catholic church had assumed in the public life of Northern cities. Here Cardinal Logue and Archbishop John Murphy Farley are bracketed between the author Samuel Clemens and the politician James Farley. (Library of Congress)

While the forms have been as different as can be imagined, gathering for church has always been a permanent feature of American life.

During the nineteenth century the camp meeting was the most important vehicle for bringing the Christian message to America's rapidly expanding frontier. (Library of Congress)

This baptism from a Greek Orthodox church took place in Portland, Oregon, in 1925. It is a symbol of the continuing power of the churches to mark the transitional stages of human life. (Oregon Historical Society)

Worshippers at the Reverend George Stalling's Imani Temple (July 1989) "raise holy hands in prayer." (© Eli Reed/Magnum Photos)

Chapter 39

Christendom and Colonization

Christianity was a declining religion in the year 1450. The long centuries of Muslim rule had suppressed the voices of Christians in North Africa, the Middle East, and Asia. In Asia, Nestorianism crumbled before the conversion of central Asian tribes to Islam. In 1317, Dongola Cathedral, the pride of formerly vibrant Nubian Christianity, became a mosque. The Crusades had failed. The ultimate symbol of defeat was the Ottoman Turks' conquest of the holy city of Constantinople in 1453, with their subsequent advance through the Balkans, Hungary, and the middle of Europe. The Iberian peninsula continued its centuries-long struggle to expel the Moors. The only place in the world where Christianity remained free of Muslim control was northwestern Europe, which remained cut off from the rest of the world by the far reaches of Islam, itself a vigorous missionary religion.

Europeans—the northern "barbarians" of the Roman Empire a millennium before— were, ironically, the only ones left to uphold the Constantinian legacy of Christendom, a society in which Christianity was the religion of the government and where the state undergirded the canons of the church. The existence of Roman Catholic, European Christendom amidst a sea of Islam resulted from the vision of Pope Gregory the Great, who had launched the mission to the northern barbarians of England in 596 A.D., reportedly upon seeing blond "angels" (Angles) in the slave markets of the crumbling Roman Empire. Christian Europe witnessed the historic importance of mission, of evangelizing the geographic frontiers of Christendom. Even as the centers of Christian power declined and lost vigor, the faith grew around the margins, and yesterday's "barbarians and savages" became today's "civilized Christians." Through Christianization, yesterday's pagan enemies could also become today's political allies. European heads of state thus interpreted the process of evangelization as a public responsibility, not merely a result of the initiative of the individual believer.

The Age of Discovery

With the ability to determine latitude by the stars and with advances in mapmaking, Portugal and Spain became the first European countries to break the Muslim headlock by sailing around the Ottoman Empire, seeking gold and entering the Asian–Pacific spice trade. Portugal had arisen as a nation after the western part of the Iberian peninsula was reconquered from the Muslims in the twelfth century. The spirit of *"reconquista"* inspired Portugal to challenge Muslim strongholds in North Africa. During the fifteenth century, seventy papal bulls encouraged Portuguese attempts to reconquer formerly Christian territory and to spread the Christian religion in connection with its nascent empire. The Iberian rulers hoped to make contact with the mythic Christian kingdom of "Prester John," supposedly located somewhere in Asia. Then, in 1492, the united kingdoms of Aragon and Castile drove the Muslims out of Spain. Christopher Columbus "discovered" America for the Spanish flag the same year, and the Portuguese government sponsored Vasco da Gama, who reached India by sailing around Africa in 1497.

The "age of discovery" marked the beginning of Europe's encounter with the rest of the world, the outflanking of the Ottoman Turks, and the rise of European imperial power. Given the assumptions of Christendom, it also launched the missionary expansion of European Christianity into the cultures of Asia, Africa, and Latin America, a period of history that did not end until the Second World War. Even though the concept of Christendom gradually weakened from the sixteenth through the twentieth centuries, the tradition that Christianity was partner to the civil establishment and undergirded public values remained implicit in the missionary consciousness of European Christianity.

During the age of discovery, the concept that embodied the approach of Christendom to evangelization was "royal patronage," the *Patronatus Regalis* (*Padroado* in Portuguese and *Patronato* in Spanish). In order to encourage royal patronage of evangelization in non-Christian lands, and to continue the struggle against the Muslims, the fifteenth-century popes granted more and more control over church affairs to the Portuguese rulers. Portugal theoretically gained control over the western coast of Africa, with title of ownership, rights to collect tithes and appoint ecclesiastical leaders, the right to enslave the Africans, and the responsibility to spread the Christian faith in the territories. Once Spain leaped to the fore with the voyages of Christopher Columbus, Pope Alexander VI (1431–1503) was faced with the dilemma of how to manage the competition for ecclesiastical and political empire between the Portuguese and the Spanish. In 1493, he issued the decrees *Inter caetera* and *Dudum siquidem*, which gave control over all newly discovered lands to the Spanish monarchs. Drawing a line down the Atlantic, Pope Alexander VI upheld Portuguese control of Africa and regions to the east and granted to Spain the Americas and points west. The line was adjusted a few years later, granting Brazil to Portugal, which "discovered" it in 1500. In the papal bulls of 1493, the pope raised papal authority to new heights by claiming authority over the non-Christians of the world, and he gave Spain and Portugal power over ecclesiastical affairs in the mission territories—a loss of church control that bedeviled later popes.

From the perspective of the church, the most important aspect of royal patronage was the monopoly over missions granted to Spain and Portugal. The sovereign of each country controlled the appointment of missionaries and prelates and had the sole responsibility to evangelize all non-Catholic peoples in his or her colonial dominions. The geographical expansion of Christendom, through royal patronage, thus became a rationale for Spanish and Portuguese colonization of "newly discovered" peoples around the world.

The Iberian Encounter with Indigenous Peoples

The Portuguese in Africa

Under the auspices of Prince Henry the Navigator (1394–1460), the Portuguese became the first Europeans to colonize parts of Africa since the time of the Romans. After having gained a small foothold in Morocco, Prince Henry sent annual exploratory expeditions down the coast. Sailing around the Muslims of Morocco, the Portuguese landed on the "Gold Coast" of present-day Ghana in 1471. In 1482, they built a fort at Elmina ("The Mine") that could resupply ships and protect the Portuguese trade route from other Europeans. The Portuguese demonstrated the unity of colonization and evangelization when they asked the local chief at Elmina to be baptized, an offer he refused. Settling on the uninhabited islands of São Tomé and the Cape Verdes, Portuguese adventurers began importing slaves from the mainland to work on plantations. Portuguese exploration stretched down the Atlantic Coast of Africa, with Bartholomeu Dias (d. 1500) sailing his caravel around the Cape of Good Hope in 1487–88. Finally, Vasco da Gama (ca. 1469–1524) completed the circumnavigation of Africa in 1498 when he landed in Mozambique and then reached India the same year.

For the most part, the primary interest of the Portuguese in Africa was economic—gold and then slaves for their developing plantation economy. Given the wide expanse of the Portuguese empire and the small population of Portugal—only a million and a half—there were never enough missionaries for the colonial territories. Yet the Portuguese stranglehold on ports of entry made it difficult for missionary priests from other countries to avoid being under Portuguese control, a problem that hampered the mission of the church for centuries. Slavery soon became the major Portuguese interest in Africa, as there was a shortage of workers in the country's colonial possessions. Those who frequented the Portuguese outposts in Africa and India often took native women as wives and mistresses. The military chaplains appointed to Portuguese strongholds concentrated on providing religious services to the Portuguese and their mixed-race (*mestiço*) children.

In terms of religious practice, the worldviews of Portuguese Catholics and Africans in the fifteenth and sixteenth centuries were compatible in many ways. Ordinary Africans and pre-Enlightenment Europeans shared beliefs that the supernatural impinged on daily life—for example, in the form of dreams, visions, and witchcraft. Such things as rainfall depended on a right relationship with divine beings, and spiritual significance pervaded nature. African ancestral spirits fit easily into the pantheon of Catholic saints; both were honored and asked to protect the followers. Crucifixes, amulets, and statues could play magical roles similar to fetishes in African cultures. Portuguese and Africans shared a holistic worldview, in which the sacred and the secular, and the divine and the daily, could not easily be separated. An important difference in their religious realities, however, was that the Portuguese belonged to a world religion with a powerful hierarchy and established dogmas. In contrast, African traditional religions were more fluid than dogmatic, and they differed according to ethnic group and location.

Outside the Luso-African enclaves, the place in Africa where Portuguese evangelism was most successful was the Kongo kingdom, first encountered in 1483. The Portuguese began trading with the Kongolese. By 1491, both parties were ready to seal an alliance. A colony of artisans, priests, women, and horses landed with their implements. Two months later, the king of Kongo greeted the Portuguese and was baptized, taking as his baptismal name that of the king of Portugal. Just as in Europe, the baptism of an African king or tribal chief signified a changed religious allegiance for the entire kingdom, a political alliance with the missionary nation of Christians, and even a cultural apprenticeship on the part of the baptized. The Kongo Christians received the Portuguese as supernatural messengers. For their part, however, the Portuguese perceived the alliance as one of patron and client. They expected the Kongolese to provide slaves in exchange for the benefits of Portuguese support and the presence of a few priests. Within three years, the king of Kongo tired of the Portuguese insistence on monogamy and the burning of fetishes, and he reverted to paganism.

The story of Kongo Christianity would have been brief had it not been for the faithfulness of Mvemba Nzinga (ca. 1455–1543), one of the king's sons, who was baptized with his mother and who took the name of Afonso. When his father died in 1506, with Portuguese help Afonso won a battle for succession against a pagan brother. The Kongo ruling class continued to use Portuguese names, baptize their children, and join Catholic confraternities for hundreds of years after the initial encounter. The capital of the kingdom was renamed São Salvador and housed the cathedral, where Christian holidays became part of national life. Portuguese immigrants intermarried with the Kongolese and produced a number of children who became Catholic priests, the first of whom was ordained in 1546. Continually asking for priests and teachers, and remaining faithful to his Christian beliefs despite the cruelty and negligence of the Portuguese, Afonso I has been remembered by his people as "the apostle of the Kongo." He sent his own son, Henry, to Portugal to be educated for the priesthood. In 1521, Henry was the first African in modern times to be made a Catholic bishop—and the last chosen from his region until 1970.

Ultimately, the royal patronage became a heavy burden for the Kongo Christians. Afonso kept trying to make direct contact with the pope to request priests and help, but the Portuguese blocked his efforts. A later Kongo king managed to send information about his need for priests through a Portuguese "ambassador," and in 1596 the pope made the Kongo a diocese, with São Salvador the cathedral city, thus opening the kingdom to ecclesiastical help beyond the yoke of the Portuguese *padroado*. As the African desire for goods increased, and the Portuguese sought slaves for their colony in Brazil, rampant enslavement devastated the region. The Portuguese colonial power monopolized church, state, and a vicious slave economy. The amazing aspect of Kongo Catholicism was that it lasted for hundreds of years, priestless for the most part and despite the colonialism of the Portuguese there and in neighboring Angola.

The Spanish in the Americas and the Philippines

On October 12, 1492, Christopher Columbus (1451–1506) landed three little ships on the island of Guanahani (Hispaniola). To the end of his life, thinking he had sailed around the world and found the pathway to India, Columbus never wavered from the idea that he had reached the "Indies," whose inhabitants he called "Indians." Imbued with the medieval spirit of Christendom, Columbus marked the territories for the Spanish Crown by erecting tall crosses in strategic places. Since the people who lived on the islands were not Christians, Columbus believed that they had no human rights and were to be subjected to the Christian monarchs who first claimed them. Columbus gave the newly-discovered islands "Christian" names, an act reminiscent of baptism, but that imposed the domination inherent in being renamed against one's will.

By the time of Columbus's second voyage, Pope Alexander VI had ruled that the territories west of Africa belonged to Spain. Accordingly, Columbus took a priest with him on the second voyage to evangelize the Indians according to the *patronato*. Spanish friars accompanied the *conquistadors* on their voyages of exploration and expropriation. When Hernán Cortés (1485–1547) and six hundred soldiers arrived in Mexico in 1519, they first knelt in prayer. With them were two priests who attempted to tell the Indians about Christianity. As they moved toward the Aztec capital, Tenochtitlán (today, Mexico City), Cortés explained Catholic theology to the indigenous peoples whom he met, and he authorized baptisms of responsive tribal leaders. Carrying the cross into battle, the Spaniards destroyed the Aztec capital in a "holy war" against idolatry. Said Cortés, "My principal motive in undertaking this war and any other one I should undertake, is to bring the natives to the knowledge of our Holy Catholic faith."[1] After removing some of the images from the Aztec temple, he set up two altars. Later, the cathedral in Mexico City was built over the old Aztec temple, where human sacrifices had taken place in accordance with the traditional religion. Cortés appealed to the Crown to send Franciscan missionaries to evangelize the defeated Aztecs and the diverse peoples now "liberated" from Aztec control.

At the same time that Cortés was conquering the Aztecs with a combination of guns and crosses, Ferdinand Magellan (1480–1521) was crossing the Atlantic, sailing down the coast of South America, around Cape Horn, and across the Pacific, and, finally, landing in the Philippines in March of 1521. On Easter morning, at Limasawa, Magellan took fifty soldiers with their muskets and his chaplain ashore to say Mass. During this first Mass said in the Philippines, the fleet's artillery fired as the Host was elevated as a "sign of peace."[2] After a fencing tournament, Magellan erected a large cross on a hill, taught the people the sign of the cross, and instructed them that it would protect them from other Europeans. Over the next month on Cebu Island, Magellan told the islanders about the Christian faith and urged their baptism and the burning of their religious objects.

In 1533, Francisco Pizarro (ca. 1476–1541) captured Cuzco, center of the Inca empire in Peru. With 180 men, six of whom were Dominican friars, Pizarro looted Cuzco and destroyed its temples. Upon reaching Paraguay in 1543, Alvar Núñez Cabeza de Vaca (ca.

---

[1] Quoted in Luis N. Rivera, *A Violent Evangelism: The Political and Religious Conquest of the Americas*, foreword by Justo L. Gonzalez (Louisville, KY: John Knox, 1992), p. 48.

[2] T. Valentino Sitoy, Jr., *A History of Christianity in the Philippines. The Initial Encounter*, Vol. I (Quezon City, Philippines: New Day Publishers, 1985), p. 40.

1490–ca. 1557) immediately ordered the saying of the Mass. He had a large cross erected as a sign that he was taking possession of the land, and he required the people to swear a double oath to the Spanish king and the Catholic Church.

Clearly, the Spanish who conquered the Americas and the Philippines in the sixteenth century did not separate the evangelization of indigenous peoples from their conquest and subsequent colonization. Under the assumptions of Christendom and the legal justification of the royal patronage, Christianity became an ideology for the conquest of non-Christian peoples. Conquest involved not only exerting control over land, including the seizure of gold and other precious objects, but also forced baptism, renaming of people and places, and the destruction of outward symbols of the indigenous religions. Soon the peoples of America and the Philippines realized that baptism was not merely a ritual of friendship; rather, it was a sign of submission to the Spanish and to the religion of Christendom. Once they understood the Spanish intentions, the indigenous peoples began to resist and revolt. For example, after Magellan burned down two villages that refused to submit to the newly baptized ruler he put over them, Magellan was hacked to death in a military action at Mactan on April 27, only one month after landing in the Philippines.

After the initial encounter, native Americans wanted neither to become Christians nor to work for the Spaniards in their mines and plantations, and so they shunned the invaders. In 1503, Queen Isabella (1451–1504) dealt with the looming failure of the Spanish religious and labor policies by legalizing *encomienda*, a system whereby the Indians were divided among the Spanish colonists for work in exchange for religious instruction. Being forced into *encomienda*, the Indians would no longer be able to avoid Spanish influence. The system remained the norm throughout the colonial period in Latin America and the Philippines. In the latter, the Catholic religious orders took the place of colonists in maintaining the system, and Filipinos farmed for the Catholic church, which, over time, came to own most of the land. In practice, *encomienda* became a system of brutal slavery. Distributed like cattle to greedy fortune hunters, put to work in gold mines without adequate food, subject to European diseases, unable to escape and losing their will to live, the Indians of the Caribbean began to die off. African slaves replaced them, and the ethnic makeup of the islands changed until there were almost no indigenous Caribbean islanders left. On the mainland, within seventy-five years of their first encounter with Europeans, a native Mexican population of seventeen million had shrunk to one million.

To evangelize the shrinking population, Catholic friars such as Dominicans, Franciscans, and Augustinians sailed to the Americas and the Philippines. Often accompanied by armed guards, the missionaries went into the rural areas to preach, baptize, and catechize the Indians. As the surviving natives on the American mainland submitted to baptism, they were often gathered into villages (called *reductions,* or *reducciones* in Spanish) to live, and the Spanish built churches and schools to spread both the faith and Spanish cultural norms. Those who resisted baptism fled farther into the hills and remote areas of Central and South America. As areas became pacified and the inhabitants "Christianized," the Catholic church erected a regular diocesan structure, with bishops at the head. The first three dioceses were established in the Americas in 1511. With the founding of a diocese, a region shifted from being considered a "mission" to being considered a "church." The brutality of conquest, combined with a chronic shortage of clergy, meant that the native Americans practiced a dual religious system. While publicly professing Catholic beliefs, most continued practicing the fertility, healing, and agricultural rites of their indigenous faiths, thus creating a popular Catholicism far different from the official dogmas.

Despite the violence of the initial evangelization, sincere and pious missionaries worked within the *patronato* and made devout converts. As a form of mission, however, the state domination of religion rendered the royal patronage a moral failure, characterized as it was by violence and brutality. In Portuguese-controlled areas, royal patronage weakened mission by restricting missionaries of other nationalities, even though there were never enough Portuguese missionaries to meet the spiritual needs of the people. Because of the system that the papacy itself had decreed as official policy, the sixteenth-century popes found themselves unable to communicate directly with the emerging churches under Iberian control, to appoint church leaders, or to enforce rules for the conduct of colonists. The governing body of colonial Latin America, the Supreme Council of the Indies, founded in 1524, censored all attempts at communication between the people and the Vatican. Nevertheless, the colonization and Christianization of Latin America and coastal locations in Africa and Asia marked a turning point in the history of Christianity. A Muslim blockade no longer confined Christianity to Europe; rather, it was beginning to spread into new cultures around the globe.

Resistance to Royal Patronage: Seeking a Better Way

Internal Resistance to the *Patronato*

The first resistance to Spanish treatment of the native Americans came from the earliest missionaries to the Caribbean. The missionaries assumed that the Indians could freely choose to become Christians, and then they would gain all the rights and privileges commensurate with their status as Catholics. Yet the colonial practices resulted in the enslavement and genocide of the Indians. The goal of the church to save souls and the goal of the Spanish colonists to amass wealth were in fundamental disagreement. Clerical authority often clashed with secular authority, and the first priest in America lasted only a year before he returned to Spain. Pope Julius II tried to establish three dioceses in 1504, but the Spanish king thwarted the pope's attempt to act independently and claimed that under royal patronage, the dioceses were illegal. To establish dioceses with episcopal supervision would have reduced the power of the Spanish and Portuguese monarchs to regulate church affairs, so the kings opposed them.

The first Dominican priests arrived on Hispaniola in 1510 to find the *encomienda* system in full swing with all its abuses. Under their superior, Pedro de Córdoba, they wrote a sermon to preach to the colonists during Advent in 1511, on the scripture text John 1:23, "I am the voice of one crying in the wilderness, 'Make straight the way of the Lord.'" Father Antonio de Montesinos (d. 1545) delivered the sermon, "You are all in mortal sin! You live in it and you die in it! Why? Because of the cruelty and tyranny you use with these innocent people."[3] He chastised the colonists for their treatment of the Indians, accusing them of enslaving and murdering them to extract gold and refusing to share the gospel with

[3] Quoted in Gustavo Gutierrez, *Las Casas: In Search of the Poor of Jesus Christ*, translated by Robert R. Barr (Maryknoll, NY: Orbis, 1993), p. 29.

them. Central to the Dominicans' argument was that the Indians were human beings with souls. In another sermon, Montesinos threatened to refuse absolution to the colonists should they persist in their behavior.

Against overwhelming opposition in Spain and in Latin America, a group of missionaries in the first half of the sixteenth century, mostly Dominicans, struggled against the system of *encomienda* and the destruction of the Indians. What did evangelization mean if all the Indians were dead? Listening to Montesinos's sermon was a priest and *encomendero*, Bartolomé de Las Casas (1474–1566), who decided to give up his Indian slaves and join the Dominicans. Becoming the most prominent defender of the Indians' right to freedom and equality, he proposed a new system of evangelization whereby missionaries would found villages and preach to the Indians without the accompaniment of force. In 1515, he sailed to Spain to appeal to the king and then to the future emperor. After that, he returned to America, but when no progress was made, he went in 1517 to Spain to study the legal aspects of the enslavement of the Indians. After arguing before the court in 1519, Las Casas was granted the right to experiment in northern Venezuela with founding villages of free Indians as a means of peaceful evangelization, but the experiment failed. He was instrumental in the promulgation of the New Laws of 1542–43, which were intended to free the Indians from *encomienda*. In 1544 he became Bishop of Chiapas, but when he refused to grant absolution to the colonists for holding Indians in *encomienda*, he was driven from the area. In Guatemala, his life was also threatened, and he finally resigned from his diocese and·returned to Spain, where he continued to write on behalf of Indian rights.

After the passage of the New Laws, other bishops were appointed whose advocacy for the native Americans was outstanding, but the colonists uniformly opposed and persecuted these clerics. Antonio de Valdivieso became Bishop of Nicaragua in 1544, arriving at his diocese to discover that the governor's family controlled a third of the Indian villages. He tried to correspond with the king about the abuse and murder of the Indians, and he preached for their liberation. In 1550, however, Valdivieso was stabbed to death by one of Pizarro's soldiers. Another bishop–martyr was Juan del Valle, a college professor appointed bishop of Popayán in Colombia and Venezuela. He conducted pastoral visitations among the Indians, carrying a spear in defense against the colonists who sought to kill him. In 1555 and 1558, del Valle called two diocesan synods to draft doctrinal defenses of the rights of the Indians. In 1559, he departed for Spain to present documentation of the humans rights abuses against the Indians to the Supreme Council of the Indies. He died in 1561, trying to reach the Council of Trent with a mule loaded with evidence of abuse against the Indians.

During the sixteenth century, in the Philippines, where *conquistadors* were forcibly uniting over 7,000 islands into a country named after the king of Spain, a few dedicated missionaries similarly condemned the mode of conquest and the resulting system of *encomienda*. In 1570, the Augustinians began to speak against the abuses of the Filipinos, who were expected to pay huge amounts of tribute to the *conquistadors*. As in Latin America, the priests preached against the abusers and threatened to withhold communion from them. They prepared two memorials to present to King Philip II in 1573 and 1574, charging that the Spanish conquest involved burning villages to the ground, killing the people, raping the women, and enslaving the survivors. Given their distance from Spain and their lack of power, the missionaries had no choice but to live within the system and to ameliorate it as best they could. After a widespread uprising in 1587–89 failed to oust the Spanish, an influx of missionaries engaged in an intensified program of evangelization. Over the succeeding two hundred years, the Philippines became the first Asian country to become predominantly Christian.

Working in Portuguese territory on both sides of the Atlantic, the Capuchin order petitioned the pope in 1685 to limit the African slave trade. The Capuchins objected that African slaves had been captured in unjust wars and then treated like animals. They asked that the pope order all unjustly captured slaves released and compensated. A year before the Capuchins protested the slave trade, the head of a confraternity, an Afro-Brazilian *mestiço* of royal Kongolese blood, Lourenço da Silva, went to Rome to request that perpetual slavery be abolished. Da Silva described for the Curia the torture of Christian slaves and how even their children had no hope of gaining their freedom. Representing the Christian slaves themselves, da Silva made a great impression on the Curia, which responded by condemning the slave trade. The Vatican sent resolutions to bishops in the Iberian colonies and to its representatives in Spain and Portugal. Despite the historic condemnation, the antislavery resolutions were not enforced, because of opposition by the Council of the Indies and other vested interests.

In 1706, the Portuguese burned at the stake a twenty-year-old Kongolese woman named Vita Kimpa. Baptized Beatrice, Kimpa believed she was possessed by the spirit of St. Anthony. Preaching powerfully that Catholic crucifixes and religious objects were like pagan fetishes and should be destroyed, that Jesus was black and that God was on the side of the Kongolese, Kimpa was captured and executed for heresy. The significance of Vita Kimpa for the history of Christianity is that she was a forerunner of things to come, the "mother of black theology." Despite the state-dominated church of the Iberian royal patronage, neither the Portuguese nor the Spanish could control the Christian faith. Once introduced beyond the borders of Europe, Christianity took root in the lives and cultures of the indigenous peoples who embraced it. Regardless of the external restraints of European imperialism, the Christian faith empowered the faithful to stand up for themselves and their fellow human beings.

The *Propaganda Fide*

The papacy did not accept the state's domination of the church without fighting back. The most effective means of circumventing the *patronato* was the *Congregatio de Propaganda Fide*, established in 1622. The *Propaganda* put the missions of the church under the control of the Curia and thereby undercut such practices as the Iberian monarchs blocking communication from the New World to the pope and appointing missionaries and bishops. The first secretary of the *Propaganda* was Francesco Ingoli (1578–1649), who launched a thorough investigation into the conditions of missions around the world. What he discovered was a pathetic list of abuses, including missionaries engaged in commerce and moneymaking ventures, the absence of native ordinations, nationalist infighting among missionaries, and ignorance of indigenous languages and cultures. The Council of Mexico in 1555, for example, had forbidden Moors, Indians, *mestizos* and mulattos from joining the religious orders. How could the Catholic Church spread if nobody but Europeans could be ordained to the priesthood?

To solve the problems uncovered by his survey, Ingoli resolved to develop an indigenous clergy in mission territories. By creating more bishoprics staffed by diocesan bishops rather than members of religious orders, national churches could be established that would be accountable to Rome rather than to the Portuguese and Spanish monarchs. Ingoli recommended that in order to circumvent the Portuguese and Spanish right to appoint missionary bishops, vicars apostolic be appointed over the missions. The vicar apostolic would hold the title of a nominal episcopal see, such as one under Muslim control, and would thus not violate royal patronage. Yet the apostolic vicars would be directly accountable to the pope and could begin to ordain priests from among the local Christians, and to rebuke European missionaries who overreached their authority.

The *Propaganda* appointed the first vicars apostolic in 1637, one for Japan and one for India. Remarkably, the apostolic vicar for the interior of India was a Brahmin convert named Matthew de Castro who had studied in Rome. Ordained in 1630, he had returned to India as a missionary. But hostility to an Indian missionary, much less an Indian bishop, was so severe that the Portuguese-appointed Archbishop of Goa prevented de Castro from doing his work. De Castro died in Rome in 1677, after having been deprived of his title. Once again, the power of royal patronage, racial prejudice, and Eurocentrism undercut an effort by the papacy to create a self-sustaining national church in a mission land. It would not be until the twentieth century that the *Propaganda* reached its goals of training, ordaining, and consecrating effective indigenous leaders in mission lands.

The Jesuits

On September 27, 1540, the reforming Pope Paul III approved the founding of the Society of Jesus, soon to become the greatest missionary order in the Roman Catholic Church. The scruffy group of intellectuals from the University of Paris who became the first Jesuits were led by a Basque, Ignatius of Loyola (ca. 1495–1556). In the spirit of the Crusades, Loyola led his small band toward the Holy Land, but was blocked by the expansion of the Ottoman Turks. Stopping in Rome instead, the group solidified its principles, agreeing to strict obedience to an elected superior and to the supreme pontiff, and setting out a spiritual life based on individually performed Spiritual Exercises, rather than the usual communal chanting and prayers of most religious communities. The missionary character of the Jesuits was confirmed by the pragmatic Loyola, who told his followers to "become all things to all people," a basic missionary principle founded on the words of St. Paul. From Spanish and Portuguese Jesuits in Latin America, to Italian Jesuits in China, Japan, and India, to French Jesuits in North America and Southeast Asia, the Society was characterized by openness to other cultures. Although this openness put them at odds with the European imperial powers—especially Spain and Portugal—it created Christian communities in China, Japan, Vietnam, India, and Canada that otherwise might not have existed.

The first Jesuit missionary departed from Rome shortly before the order was approved by the pope. Francis Xavier (1506–1552) sailed from Lisbon on a voyage that lasted over a year. He settled in Goa, the Portuguese headquarters in India, as the pope's personal representative and with the support of the King of Portugal. Working among low-caste pearl fishermen, he taught them the catechism in their own language and set it to music.

As he traveled along the India coast, other groups of low-caste fishermen asked for baptism en masse and kept their faith even when local officials martyred 600 new Christians. After two years in Portuguese-controlled Malacca, he moved beyond the reaches of the Portuguese by sailing through pirate-infested waters to Japan. Having met a Japanese religious seeker in 1547, Xavier became eager to open mission work there and, from Japan, to gain a foothold in China. He and two other Jesuits with three Japanese Christians arrived at Kyushu, the southernmost major island of Japan.

The Growth and Persecution of Japanese Christianity

In Japan, Francis Xavier set the tone for a Jesuit mission that resulted in a church that has survived to the present. For example, Xavier realized that his unkempt appearance offended the Japanese, so he began dressing as a man of status—in silk. He sought out local feudal lords to gain permission to preach in their territories, and he held discussions with Buddhist monks. Most importantly, he insisted that all missionaries to Japan learn Japanese. The basic principle that missionaries should learn the language of the people to whom they minister and should indigenize their own cultural practices as much as possible became a key to the Jesuit ability to make friends and converts across deep cultural divides all around the world. Xavier died in 1552, waiting in vain for permission from the Portuguese to enter China.

In 1574, inspired by the deathbed goal of their pioneer missionary, the Society of Jesus tried to circumvent the Portuguese by sending a major mission to Japan and China composed largely of Italians and Spaniards who had not been influenced by a *conquistador* mentality. Jesuits spread into areas of Japan under sympathetic *daimyo*, local feudal lords who may have hoped that accepting a missionary would mean access to the Portuguese trade. The Jesuits translated and printed apologetic and spiritual literature in Japanese. Numerous converts came from all walks of life, although many were from the *samurai* (warrior) class who were serving Christian *daimyo*. The sincerity and motivation of the Japanese Christians was such that converts soon began to study for the priesthood, and Japanese Christians became evangelists and teachers. Japanese laypeople organized confraternities, which met for mutual support in the faith.

By 1590, nearly all of Japan had become united under General Toyotomi Hideyoshi, who began to worry that Christianity was becoming either a powerful ideology at odds with his own absolute rule or else a cover for European domination. His views seemed confirmed after Franciscans entered Japan and built Spanish-style buildings, and the crew of a ship blown off course from Manila indicated that priests were a forerunner of Spanish political control. The refusal of Christian girls to become the general's concubines and of his subordinates to repudiate Christianity at his command also angered him. In 1597, twenty-six Christians were crucified in Nagasaki; six were European Franciscans and twenty Japanese Christian leaders. Subsequent rulers increased the persecution of Christians, seeing the refusal of the Japanese people to recant under torture and humiliation as proof that Christianity was a dangerous foreign ideology. In 1614, royal edicts expelled all priests from Japan and banned Christianity, but to no avail; at that time there were 300,000 Christians in Japan, and the number kept growing. By the mid-1620s, the *shoguns* began trying to eliminate Christianity and to close Japan off from all outside influence. They used horrible tortures to force Christians to abjure the faith. The most dramatic episode in the long persecution of Japanese Christians occurred in 1637, when 37,000 Christians, both peasants and *samurai*, revolted and made a last stand from a castle at Shimabara. Inspired by millennial ideas, they fought to the death against the *shogun's* troops. The remaining Christian families in Japan went underground, where they remained under threat of execution until Christianity was legalized under Western pressure in 1873. With the historical memory of Christianity so painful, the Japanese people never again adopted it as widely as they had in the early 1600s.

Christianity and Confucianism: The Rites Controversies

Simultaneously with the remarkable spread and subsequent persecution of Christianity in Japan, Jesuits also entered China. They continuously studied Chinese culture and tried to adapt themselves to the Confucian upper classes. The Jesuit missionary who made the decisive breakthrough toward acceptance by the Chinese was Matteo Ricci (1552–1610), who entered China proper in 1583. Ricci studied Mandarin and Chinese customs. Chinese intellectuals, in turn, were fascinated by Ricci's map of the world, astronomical observations, mathematics, and knowledge of Western humanism. Ricci studied Confucianism and began to translate Chinese classics into Latin. Known as Li Madou, Ricci found acceptance for the Jesuits when he wrote two well-received books in Mandarin, *A Treatise on Friendship* and *The True Meaning of the Lord of Heaven*. The latter book attracted many literati to Christianity, including a group of Korean intellectuals who founded the Catholic Church in Korea in 1784. Ricci's greatest achievement was when the emperor's court gave him permission to reside in the capital, Beijing, and tolerated his Confucianist form of Christianity. Later, many Jesuits built on Ricci's foundation. The most important Jesuit convert, Xu Guangqi (1562–1633), served as vice president of the Ministry of Rites. Xu held a competition between Jesuit and government astronomers. When the Jesuits were able to forecast an eclipse accurately, they were put in charge of reforming the calendar for the emperor in 1629.

The Chinese Christian community that emerged around the Jesuit presence had an initial core of literati and their families, but most were ordinary people such as peasants, artisans, and merchants. Although the percentage of Christians in China never approached that of Japan, Chinese Christianity of the seventeenth century was vigorous and produced its own priests. The first Chinese bishop was consecrated in 1690, although there would not be another until the twentieth century. As in Japan, Chinese Christians kept their faith alive in lay societies. Women played a prominent role in the spread of Christianity. The granddaughter of Xu Guangqi, Xu Candida (1604–1680), devoted herself to the church after she was widowed. Through selling hand-sewn merchandise and by other means, she and a group of other women raised money to pay for church buildings, to support missionaries, to print devotional materials, and to give to the poor. In her home, Xu sponsored a group of consecrated virgins, Chinese women who refused to marry and who spent their time helping the poor, teaching religion, and serving the church. During the time when Christianity was forced underground until the mid-nineteenth century, consecrated virgins were supported by their families and acted as leaders of the underground church.

The strength of the Chinese laity was the key to the survival of Chinese Christianity over the centuries. Perhaps nowhere was Jesuit encouragement of lay initiative so pronounced as in the work of Alexander de Rhodes (1593–1660), the founder of Catholicism in Vietnam. Following the methods of the Jesuit mission in China, of which Vietnam was then a satellite, the Frenchman de Rhodes went to the upper classes in both Cochin-China and Tonkin. He did important translation work, putting the Annamite characters into romanized script and thus founding the written language used today. He produced the first dictionary and grammar of Vietnamese and wrote an important catechism. But the work for which de Rhodes is remembered most, and for which he was harassed and marginalized by the pro-patronage religious establishment, was his use of lay catechists to spread the faith. Shocked by the brutal suppression of Catholicism in Japan, de Rhodes saw clearly the need for indigenous leadership should the church fall under persecution and foreign priests be expelled. He trained lay catechists under whose ministry the conversions in Tonkin alone numbered 300,000. He also relied on the work of women, even training some as catechists. With the Portuguese and Spanish opposing his work, de Rhodes recruited additional missionaries from France; and after he died, the pope appointed vicars apostolic for Cochin-China and Tonkin, although the two were blocked from their posts by the Portuguese. The work in Vietnam marked the beginning of French Catholic missions in Asia and inspired the founding of the Paris-based Société des Missions Étrangères in 1663, a French foreign missionary society that promoted the founding of native clergies.

China, Vietnam, and Korea all had political establishments based on Confucianism, and people venerated their ancestors in traditional rituals that included kowtowing to stone tablets on which were carved the names of ancestors and offering food to the ancestors; literati similarly honored Confucius. The Jesuit success was partly because Matteo Ricci and others determined that the veneration of ancestors was not a form of worship, but rather an honoring of the dead and part of filial piety. Thus, under the Jesuits, Christianity did not challenge the most deeply held beliefs and customs of Confucian cultures. But from the beginning, the Franciscans and Dominicans resented the Jesuit monopoly in China and disagreed profoundly with Jesuit mission theory. Franciscans and Dominicans favored the royal patronage and felt that Christian missions should confront pagan cultures rather than accommodate to them. After gaining entrance to China themselves in 1632, the Mendicant orders opposed the Jesuits, believing that they had sold out the Christian faith by their use of Chinese terms for theological concepts and by permitting the rites honoring ancestors and Confucius. The Mendicants argued that, to the ordinary Chinese, veneration of ancestors was in fact seen as worship. In 1639, the archbishop of Manila condemned the Jesuit positions, as well as the Jesuit refusal to emphasize theological views offensive to the Chinese, such as the meaning of the crucifixion. As the Jesuits and their accusers appealed back and forth to the various popes, what became known as the Chinese Rites Controversies dragged on from 1693 until 1739, when Pope Benedict XIV issued the bull *Ex quo singulari*, decisively outlawing the Chinese rites.

Although the Chinese emperor Kangxi supported the ways of Matteo Ricci, the increasing Eurocentrism of the eighteenth-century church meant that Chinese views on the Rites Controversies were ignored by the popes and other European ecclesiastics. As the church in Europe grew increasingly defensive, it became less tolerant of non-Western Catholicism, and the Jesuits themselves fell under increased suspicion from the watchdogs of orthodoxy. The conclusion to the Rites Controversies made it clear that being a Christian and being a good Chinese citizen were incompatible. Persecution of Chinese Christians that had occurred intermittently during the years of the Jesuits became systematic during the eighteenth century, increasing as the century wore on and driving the Christians underground. It is estimated that by the end of the century, there were between two hundred thousand and three hundred thousand Christians in China, no more than a hundred years before.

The Jesuits in the Americas

In the Americas, the Jesuits faced thousands of different tongues and cultures based on oral traditions, as well as primal religions that lacked the forms understandable to Europeans. Another challenge to mission in the Americas was the pervasive colonial context, which sought either to harness mission for its own purposes or else to destroy it as European colonists tried to enslave the Indians and take their land. But the colonial presence in the Americas meant that most Jesuit missionaries served there rather than in Asia or Africa, with Spanish, Portuguese, and French Jesuits becoming missionaries in territories controlled by their respective countries.

As a Catholic nation, France had to abide by the royal patronage until a treaty in 1589 recognized her growing political power and gave her permission to send ships northward. The French entered the colonial sweepstakes by traveling up the St. Lawrence River and founding New France in what is now Canada, basing their economy on fur trading rather than the hunt for gold that had obsessed the Spanish a century before. When Samuel Champlain arrived at Quebec in 1615, he had with him four Recollects (strict Franciscans), who realized how huge the field under their responsibility was and so asked help of the French Jesuits, who arrived in 1625, glad finally to work as missionaries under their own government. The Recollects had tried to gather the Indian children into schools, a plan that failed dismally. Hostility against the first few Christian Indians from their neighbors was so severe, that it became necessary to found separate Christian villages for the converts.

But a sedentary policy was impossible among nomadic peoples, unused to being confined in a schoolroom or, in fact, any permanent location. The Recollect "Gray Robes" thus began going with Huron Indians in their canoes to their villages to try to learn the Indians' language. The Jesuits pursued the same policy of paying the Indians to let them accompany them hundreds of miles away to their villages. The missionaries suffered isolation, hunger, hordes of mosquitos, and the extreme physical challenges of nomadic Indian life in the far north.

The Jesuit "Black Robe" who had the most success among the Hurons, who were trading partners with the French, was Jean de Brebeuf (1592–1649), a physically powerful man who had grown up on a farm. Brebeuf believed that living as a Huron was the best way to reach these people. Traveling by canoe to Huronia, Brebeuf settled among the Bear Clan. Brebeuf and his companions tried to study and learn about Indian culture even as they attempted to attract the Indians with European technology and gadgets. Similar to St. Boniface and the conversion of the Germans, they found themselves in "power encounters," pitting Catholic rituals against those of the shamans, trying to make it rain, or to influence the elements of nature on which the Hurons were so dependent. Once the Jesuits mastered the language, they taught prayers, songs, and catechism to interested listeners.

Relics, Christian medals and rosaries, and visual images proved to be quite meaningful to the Hurons as sacred objects of mystical power. As he advanced in his knowledge of the Hurons during his two decades among them, Brebeuf took part in the oral disputations of the tribal elders, trying to convince them of the Christian truths. The greatest intellectual challenge facing the missionaries was to find adequate native terms to express abstract ideas alien to the Indians.

Conversions among the Hurons were slow, in part because their numbers declined from European diseases. Still, as they became used to the Jesuits and the threat from the warlike Iroquois increased in the 1640s, more and more Hurons turned to Catholicism. The most notable early convert was Joseph Chihwatenhwa, baptized by Brebeuf in 1637 and so spiritually advanced that the Jesuits directed him in a retreat with the Spiritual Exercises two years later. Chihwatenhwa became a lay evangelist, preaching and witnessing through his changed lifestyle until his murder in 1640. From 1632 to 1672, Jesuits baptized an estimated sixteen thousand native Americans in Canada, twelve thousand of whom were in Huronia. By the late 1600s, native converts had become famous for their piety, with lay-led prayer groups and ascetic practices such as standing in ice water, wearing hair shirts, and scourging each other with whips. Pious women gathered into celibate groups for the preservation of morality, discipline, and work among the poor.

Although the Hurons were the first Canadian tribe in which a large number took a decisive stand for Christianity, they and their early missionaries were victims of a genocidal war conducted by the Iroquois in 1648–49. The Iroquois sought to displace the Hurons as the major trading partners with the French, and they slaughtered whole villages, scattering the remnants of the nation to the four winds. Seen as the powerful shamans of the Hurons, the Jesuit priests who remained with their flocks were singled out for horrible torture by the Iroquois. The most cruelly tortured was Jean de Brebeuf, whose reputation as a powerful "sorcerer" preceded him. Despite being set on fire, scalded with boiling water, having parts of his skin stripped off and eaten, having his lips, nose, and feet cut off, and other tortures, Brebeuf kept preaching and praying without complaint until the Iroquois ripped out his heart. Along with the Huron nation, nine Jesuits met terrible deaths under the Iroquois. Over time, some of the Hurons who had survived by fleeing elsewhere became witnesses to Christianity among other groups of Indians. In the decades following the massacres, even many Iroquois, impressed by the bravery of the Jesuits under torture and by the faith of the Hurons, became Christians.

Unlike the situation in Canada, where the first Jesuits had to adapt themselves to the nomadic lifestyles of the native Americans, the opposite pattern emerged in Latin America. Here was where the Jesuits embarked on the most widespread and widely known Catholic mission of the age of exploration: gathering the Guarani Indians into fortified Christian villages known as *reductions*. In an area that included modern-day Argentina, Paraguay, Uruguay, and sections of Bolivia and Brazil, the Jesuits founded forty-eight towns that domiciled 200,000 Guarani over a period of two hundred years. Not only Spanish, but Flemish, German, Creole, and other nationalities were represented in the mission force, which numbered over 2,200 at the time the order was banned from Spanish territory in 1767. The *reductions* of "Paraguay," as the Jesuits called their "republic," inspired the philosophers of Enlightenment Europe to wax eloquent on the possibilities of utopian communities among people barely out of cannibalistic "savagery." But among the Spanish and Portuguese colonists of Latin America, the villages of Christian Indians represented an untapped labor pool—groups of Indians ripe for exploitation and enslavement. The colonists were also jealous of the financial prosperity of the *reductions*, with their careful farms and industries, in great contrast to the abusive *encomienda* system, under which production fell as the Indians were worked to death and the land was abused. Ultimately, European economic and political interests succeeded in destroying the Jesuits, thereby ending the independence and even the existence of many of the Guarani Indians.

The pioneer missionary among the Guarani was a Spanish Franciscan, Luis de Bolanos, who traveled throughout their territory and established eighteen villages between 1580 and 1593. Bolanos worked with Creole priests to produce the first grammar, catechism, vocabulary, and prayer book in Guarani. After the Jesuits decided to work among the Guarani in 1603, they built on the language and methods pioneered by Bolanos. From their beginnings in 1606, the Jesuits vigorously opposed the enslavement of the Guarani, believing that evangelization would fail if the people associated Christianity with *encomienda*. Following the relatively open approach to indigenous culture that characterized Jesuits around the world, the missionaries learned the Guarani language and based the structure of the villages on the traditional system of chiefs, or *caciques*. Walking through Guarani territory and talking with the people, the Jesuits gathered around them those Indians who saw life in the *reductions* as a viable alternative to genocide at the hands of the European colonists. The first villages were founded in 1609, with eleven founded between 1622 and 1628.

To Portuguese settlers, unrestrained by Spanish legislation that at least outlawed slavery in principle, the *reductions* became targets for slave raiding. Gangs of mixed-race thugs from São Paulo, known as *mamelucos*, specialized in capturing Indians for sale to Portuguese planters. In 1629, the *mamelucos* targeted the unarmed *reductions* and captured at least 15,000 Indians, tying them up for a brutal death march to São Paulo, where survivors would be sold. Unable to get help from the Spanish, the Jesuits evacuated 12,000 Guarani—what remained of eleven destroyed *reductions*—to a location four hundred miles away, beyond the reach of the *mamelucos*. The path to escape was harsh and dangerous, with thirty-five miles of cataracts to hike around. Only 4,000 Guarani survived the exodus, to found new villages a year later. After the evacuation, the surviving Guarani armed themselves and, by 1642, had decisively defeated all attacks by the *mamelucos*.

Under the Jesuits, the Guarani prospered, although at the cost of giving up major aspects of their traditional culture, such as their nomadic lifestyle, cannibalism, and reliance on shamans. Their houses were grouped around a church, a school, and governing council building. With the exception of the usual two Jesuits per village, the Spanish were not allowed to reside in the *reductions*, for fear they would exploit the Guarani. The Christian Indians lived a regulated life, with set hours for labor, instruction, and worship. They raised cattle and farmed, selling their excess produce to the Spanish colonists. In an attempt to eliminate the need for polygamy, each village constructed a home for widows and other women without partners. A penal system punished those who broke the rules. In their religious life, the Guarani loved music, pageantry, dancing, and ritual. They sang and played instruments in concert for Spanish officials, and they excelled even in performing the cantatas of modern composers. Their life in the *reductions* was organized around Christian feasts and processions, to which they brought an innate artistic sensibility reflected, for example, in fabulous costumes. Guarani workmen working under Jesuit architects created magnificent churches made of stone and wood.

Guarani Christian culture was doomed in 1750 when Spain ceded seven *reductions* to Portugal in the Treaty of Limits: Portuguese slave traders moved in to destroy them. Although the Jesuits led the Guarani in resistance to the colonial armies, and Spain later renounced the treaty, the damage had been done. Infuriated by, among other things, the Jesuit protection of the Indians against exploitation and the church apparently wielding power over the state, anti-Jesuit forces in Europe plotted to eliminate the fathers once and for all. In 1759, the Jesuits were expelled from Portugal and Portuguese territories; in 1762, four thousand French Jesuits were driven from France, and their work was destroyed. Then, in 1767, the coup de grace came when King Charles III of Spain issued secret orders that all Jesuits in the Spanish Empire be arrested and deported. More than 5,350 Jesuits from around the world were arrested and deported to the Papal States. All of the Jesuit missionaries to the Guarani, no matter how ill or elderly, were removed, and their ethnographic notes, maps, libraries, and music were scattered and lost. Left without their protectors, the Guarani villages declined or were destroyed. Some Guarani Christians returned to the forests, while others became integrated into colonial life or were killed. Most kept their faith intact and continued to practice their Christianity as best they could without missionaries or priests.

The suppression of the Jesuit order by the pope in 1773 underscored the decline of Roman Catholic missions from then on into the twentieth century. The largest mission force in history was destroyed, and its work could not be rebuilt even after the order was reinstated in 1814. Ultimately, the materialistic goals of colonization overrode the goals of Christianization. The ideals of Christendom had become subservient to the power of the state. The decline of Catholic missions was symptomatic of the reduced prestige of the Roman Catholic church as an institution, as subsequent anticlerical developments such as the French and Italian revolutions confirmed. The rising might of Catholic France and Protestant nations undercut the power of Spain and Portugal and, concomitantly, the royal patronage. Holland and Great Britain broke chunks off the Portuguese and Spanish empires and introduced Protestant "heresy" into formerly Catholic territories. Roman Catholic missions would not regain their potency until the highest ranks of the church learned the hard lesson that many of its missionaries had already learned: Temporal power and the growth of the faith were not the same thing.

The great irony of Catholic missions under the model of Christendom was that Christianization took place despite colonization. In fact, colonization created a context of suffering and dislocation in which baptism was seen by some as a way to negotiate the relentless pressures faced by indigenous peoples. In Japan, China, India, Southeast Asia, Africa, and the Americas, oppressed peoples found comfort and strength in the church. In places dominated by primal religions, people usually entered the Catholic Church in groups, whereas intellectuals under world religions entered the church as individuals. But no matter whether the new Christians came as members of an ethnic group or as individuals, people adhered to the church for their own reasons. Being a Christian in Paraguay became a way to survive psychically, if not physically, under brutal colonialism. Being a Christian in Japan meant maintaining a worldview alternative to that of an increasingly centralized state. Being a Christian in Huronia meant attaining a level of spiritual power greater than that of one's enemies. Being a Christian in China meant an entree into Western learning. For these and other reasons, indigenous peoples around the world began to accept the gospel despite the Eurocentric, colonial dress in which it arrived. Making it their own, they often defended it at the price of their lives.

Chapter 40

Missions in the Modern Era

From the fifteenth through the eighteenth centuries, most European governments perceived foreign missions to be an outgrowth of Christendom, a product of the unity of church and state. The Roman Catholic governments of Portugal, Spain, and France promoted missions in relation to the spread of empire. The assumption was widespread that political allegiance and religious faith went hand in hand. In northern Asia, Russian Orthodox missions to the native peoples were sponsored by the state, which saw itself as the rightful successor to the Byzantine Empire that had been destroyed by the Muslim Turks. The Russian tsars also acted as "protectors" of the Christian minorities under Muslim rule. In 1700, Tsar Peter the Great made missions part of his policy of Russian expansionism when he told the metropolitan of Kiev to send missionaries to Siberia. By the end of the century, Russian Orthodox missions reached Alaska; many Aleuts became Orthodox by the mid-nineteenth century.

The emergence of Protestantism did not immediately challenge the Christendom model of Catholic and Orthodox missions, mostly because the early Protestants were preoccupied with fighting for survival and with formulating their own theological positions. Protestants in France, Germany, England, and Eastern Europe struggled against Catholics and sometimes each other. With married clergy the norm, Protestants lacked the traditional structure for missions: that of the celibate priest or brother who was usually part of a religious community. Most Protestant countries lacked borders with non-Christian countries and so were less aware of non-European peoples than were the Catholics. A notable exception to the lack of exposure to the "heathen" were the Lutheran Swedes, who sent missionaries to the Lapps in the Arctic. Most early Lutheran and Reformed theologies did not contain a strong missionary dynamic that supported reaching beyond one's own national borders for the purpose of evangelization. In fact, the internationalization of Christianity implied by missions was seen as a defining characteristic of *Catholicism;* Protestants were initially uninterested in missions to non-Christians.

Protestants Begin Foreign Missions

When the Netherlands and England began challenging Catholic Europe for control of the sea and access to Asian and American markets, contact with non-Christians awakened Protestant interest in missions. The first Protestant theologian to argue that Jesus' command to teach all nations was still in force was Hadrian Saravia (1531–1613), whose father was Spanish and mother was Flemish. Pressure from churches caused the Dutch East India Company, founded in 1602, to send chaplains who were responsible both for Dutch spiritual life and mission to the indigenous peoples in the Dutch possessions of the East Indies (current-day Indonesia), Formosa (modern Taiwan), and Ceylon (today, Sri Lanka). The British East India Company, founded in 1600, was generally hostile to missions as interfering with trade. Over time, it nevertheless permitted chaplains to provide for the religious needs of the English in India. Although the primary purpose of most Dutch and English chaplains was to serve the military and commercial presence in those countries' territories, some played an important role in stimulating interest in missions back home.

Until they developed their own structures, early Protestant missions imitated Catholic strategies. The chaplain or missionary sponsored by the Protestant state or by a trading company typified the form of Protestant missions that most closely resembled the Catholic model of royal patronage. The most important example of Catholic models used by Protestants was that of King Frederick IV of Denmark, who decided to send missionaries to the Danish colony of Tranquebar on the coast of India. Without the existence of religious orders, the Lutheran Frederick was hard pressed to find any volunteers for missionary service. Turning to fellow Lutherans in Germany, King Frederick encountered the pietist movement, then centered at the University of Halle under August Hermann Francke (1663–1727). The pietists undertook varied ministries of good works, and their spirituality provided the first broad underpinning for Protestant missions. Francke sent two young students to Tranquebar, Bartholomaus Ziegenbalg (1682–1719) and Heinrich Plütschau (1677–ca. 1746), who arrived on July 9, 1706. Despite opposition and persecution from Danes stationed there, Ziegenbalg and Plütschau learned Tamil and Portuguese and ministered to the mixed-race progeny of the Europeans present in southern India, founding churches and schools. They translated the Lutheran catechism, prayers, and hymns into Tamil and made converts both from Catholicism and from the low castes of Hinduism. The Halle mission continued with recruits from Germany and, by the end of the century, counted between eighteen and twenty thousand converts in Tranquebar and surrounding areas.

The most striking feature of the early Protestant missions that differed from the Roman Catholic was the centrality of Bible translation. The ability to hear and to read the scriptures in one's own tongue was an essential element of the Protestant Reformation.

Martin Luther's translation of the Bible into German and Wycliffe's into English were at the heart of the mission of Protestantism. Unlike Catholic missionaries, Protestant missionaries believed that Bible translation was the key to spreading the true faith. By 1688, Dutch chaplains in Indonesia had translated the New Testament into Malay, the first translation of the scriptures into any southeast Asian language. Ziegenbalg printed his Tamil New Testament in 1714. Subsequent Halle missionaries in India translated the Bible into Telegu and Hindustani. In the Americas, Dutch settlers in northeast Brazil worked on Bible translations for the Indians in the mid-1600s, until driven out by the Portuguese in 1654. In Massachusetts, Congregationalist minister John Eliot published, in the Indian language Algonquin, the first Bible in North America: the New Testament in 1661 and the Old Testament in 1663.

Indian Missions in the English Colonies

Substantial progress in Protestant missions began to occur in the Americas when the Puritans settled New England in the 1630s. Although the charter founding the colony of Massachusetts indicated that the English colonists were to evangelize the Indians, the English king provided no money for missions. Converting the Indians was left to the initiative of individual pastors, who voluntarily took on mission work alongside their regular pastoral duties. Some Puritans believed that the native Americans were descendants of the ten lost tribes of Israel, whose conversion was part of God's plan. In 1641, Thomas Mayhew (d. 1682) bought the island of Martha's Vineyard, and the Mayhew family worked among the Indians for three generations. The early Quakers, including founder George Fox (1624–1691), preached to the Indians throughout the colonies and refused to take land from them without legal payment, believing that lifestyle was the best witness to the Christian faith. Roger Williams (d. 1683), founder of Rhode Island, as well as the first Baptist church in America, preached to the Narragansett Indians and argued that they, rather than the king of England, rightfully owned the land.

The most important Puritan missionary among the Indians was John Eliot (1604–1690), Congregational pastor in Roxbury, Massachusetts. He began preaching to the Indians in 1646 and translating prayers, the scriptures, and catechetical material into their language. Quickly gaining converts, he organized them into Christian villages, where they could live a more settled life modeled on Puritan ideals and English laws. To the "praying Indians," becoming Christian and settling into segregated villages seemed a viable alternative to destruction at the hands of greedy English colonists, who seized the Indians' land and infected them with diseases. By 1674, 1,100 "praying Indians" lived in fourteen Christian villages. Eliot's mission method reflected his Puritan theology that a sober lifestyle was a preliminary step toward acknowledging God's saving grace in one's life. It also reflected his English ethnocentrism, a factor shared by successive missionaries, many of whom founded schools to "civilize" and educate the New England Indians into English ways. Aside from the legalism of their corporate life, the lifestyle of the Christian Indians of Massachusetts was noteworthy for its emphasis on prayer and singing, in which the Indians excelled.

Eliot's success was probably due to his linguistic fluency and his emphasis on training native pastors, who then evangelized their own people. Christians from the "praying Indian" towns went to neighboring tribes and settled among them as missionaries. By the time of the American Revolution, there were at least 133 Indian pastors in southern New England. The most famous of the pre-Revolutionary Indian preachers was Samson Occom (1723–1792), a well-educated Mohegan Indian who spent twelve years as a missionary among the Montauk Indians of Long Island, New York. By 1675, an estimated twenty percent of the Indians in New England had become Christian. But then tragedy struck the "praying Indians" when a federation of native Americans under the Wampanoag sachem King Philip (Metacomet) initiated the bloodiest colonial war in U.S. history, designed to eliminate the colonists and their religion from New England. During King Philip's War of 1675–76, half of all English settlements were damaged, with six percent casualties. Although some of the "praying Indians" supported the colonists, while others remained neutral, the furious colonists rounded up the Christian Indians and put them into concentration camps on Deer Island in Boston Harbor. Suffering horribly during the New England winter, exposed and without food, many Christian Indians died. Eliot tried to supply his flock, but was nearly lynched. The number of Christian Indian villages fell to four. King Philip's War retarded the spread of Christianity among the native Americans in New England, but under Indian leadership, the churches gradually recovered and grew. By 1698, there were thirty churches served by thirty-seven full-time native American preachers and teachers.

The Moravians

Aside from the work by English settlers among the native Americans, the most important of the early Protestant missions emerged from the influence of German pietism, a movement of spiritual renewal that emphasized the importance of Bible study and lay participation for a deepened spiritual life, as well as a personal experience of "new birth" that led to a transformed, holy lifestyle. Pietism embodied a new structure for Christian discipleship, the *collegia pietatis*, or small groups in which participants could engage in prayer, Bible study, and mutual accountability in the faith. A German nobleman, Justinian von Weltz (1621–1668) died in Surinam attempting to found the first Protestant mission based on the principles of pietism, and Pietists from the University of Halle later staffed the Danish mission at Tranquebar. But the missionary potential of pietism came to fruition with the Moravians, the descendants of Hussites, Bohemian Protestants persecuted after the Thirty Years War (1618–1648) by the victorious Catholics. Emigrating to Saxony beginning in 1722, the Moravians found protection on the estate of Count Nicolaus Ludwig von Zinzendorf (1700–1760), who had been reared in the spirit of pietism. From their new home, Herrnhut, the Moravian Brethren, or Unitas Fratrum, emigrated to places around the world where they could practice their religion and engage in missions to the downtrodden.

The Moravians became the most outstanding mission body in Protestantism. In proportion to their numbers, they have supported the highest percentage of missionaries of any church. A major feature of their missionary method was that they went out in communities which established farms and handicrafts for the support of themselves and their converts. As a persecuted group, they were always ready to emigrate to a new location and build up paradise out of the wilderness. They set the pattern of using laypeople as missionaries, a break with prior Catholic models of mission. Communal solidarity and a pacifist lifestyle endeared them to indigenous peoples everywhere.

In 1731, on a visit to the Danish royal court for the coronation of King Frederick VI,

Zinzendorf met a converted black West Indian, Anthony Ulrich, who was an assistant to a Danish nobleman. The former slave was filled with passion to witness to friends and family in his native land, and he visited Herrnhut. The Moravians were enthusiastic about the possibilities he raised, and in 1732 they commissioned Leonard Dober and Tobias Leopold as missionaries to the African slaves in the West Indies. Sailing to the Danish island of St. Thomas, colonies of Moravian families began the work, only to suffer a fearful mortality rate and hostility from the white planters. But in 1736, two hundred slaves requested baptism, the beginning of remarkable Moravian success among oppressed peoples.

Besides the West Indians, during the 1730s the Unitas Fratrum began missions among the native Americans in Greenland, the Creek Indians in Georgia, the African slaves and bush Negroes of Surinam, the Khoikhoi in South Africa, and other groups of black slaves and native Americans. Everywhere they went, they faced opposition from the European colonists who enslaved the native peoples, stole their land, and did not want them empowered through education or evangelization. In 1736, for example, George Schmidt set out for Cape Town as the first missionary to the Khoikhoi, the small, light-skinned peoples who were being enslaved and killed by the Dutch and Huguenot settlers in South Africa. Having endured six years of imprisonment for preaching in Austria, Schmidt was prepared for the hostility of the Dutch, who disliked both his theology and the fact that he was evangelizing the indigenous people. Founding a school, preaching, and teaching Dutch to the natives, Schmidt gathered a congregation of forty-seven Khoikhoi. He was ousted by the Dutch authorities in 1743. In 1792, when the Moravians were again permitted to send missionaries to South Africa, they found an eighty-year-old woman who remembered Schmidt and who treasured a copy of the Dutch New Testament he had given her. Subsequently, the Moravians in South Africa founded large mission stations where converts lived, engaged in agriculture and industry, and developed a communal life.

The most famous of the early Moravian missionaries was David Zeisberger (1721–1808), who spent sixty-two years among the American Indians. Fluent in three Indian languages, he translated the Bible, hymnbook, and liturgy into Delaware. Living with his own and other Moravian families among the Indians, he guided the Delaware Christians and members of other tribes through some of the harshest times in the European colonists' ultimately successful attempt to wrest the Old Northwest (the Northwest Territory) from the native Americans. His first missionary efforts were aimed at the Mohawks, but the British arrested him and accused him of being a French spy. In 1750, he turned to the Iroquois and developed good relations to the degree of being initiated by them. But the outbreak of the French and Indian War ruined his work. In 1772, leading the refugees, converts of his early mission work, Zeisberger founded a village in the Muskingum River valley, the first organized settlement in Ohio. By 1775, nearly four hundred converts lived in several villages with farms and orchards. Most of the Christian Indians were Delawares, whose head, Chief Netawatwes, backed Zeisberger's project. The Leni Lenape, or Delaware Indians, were drawn to Zeisberger's message by its pacifism and tranquility.

But by 1777, the Moravian Indians were caught in the war zone of the American Revolution, squeezed among the British in Detroit, the colonials of the western frontier, and other groups of native Americans who fought for the British. In 1782, ninety Moravian Indians were slaughtered by American forces set on avenging the deaths of some colonists killed by hostile Indians. For seventeen years, the Moravian Indians searched for a place to settle, evacuating their villages six times and fleeing before the hostility of British, Americans, and non-Christian Indians. Finally, with their original territory secured by land grants, the Moravian Indians returned in 1798 and founded the village of Goshen, Ohio. Some of their number remained in Canada. European and native American Moravians lived in Goshen, which became known for its orchard, farms, and sugar-making. The Goshen Christians met for worship twice daily; their worship life was characterized by singing and communal celebrations, known as "love feasts." Ultimately, the War of 1812 destroyed the village in Canada. Pressured by settlers, the Goshen Indians gradually dispersed, and in 1824 the Moravians turned over the Ohio reservation to the U.S. government.

Seeing themselves as leaven, the Moravians preferred to help the powerless rather than to convert the whole world, and as a denomination they remained small. But their example of family-based mission work, church organization for self-support, and spirit of martyrdom had a profound effect on modern Protestant missions. Through the Moravians, a truly Protestant model of missions developed, supported and enacted by laypeople, rather than sponsored by monarchs and carried out by celibate clergy. John Wesley (1703–1791), the founder of Methodism, met the Moravians in 1735 and adopted some of their piety and practices, such as organizing Christians into small groups. During the nineteenth century, Methodism, with its combination of lay-led "class meetings" and itinerant ministers, became the most powerful missionary movement in North America, making up one-third of the churchgoing population of the United States by 1850. In 1790, the Moravians in England began publishing a journal that contained reports of their missionary activities around the world. A Baptist shoemaker named William Carey read some of the first issues of this paper and was inspired to launch the Baptist Missionary Society, widely considered the starting point of modern Protestant missions (p. 549). Abolitionist William Wilberforce pointed to the successful Moravian work among slaves in the West Indies as proof that slavery could be abolished peacefully in the British empire. Moravian missions among the enslaved were a sign of hope that peaceful relations could be maintained between Europeans and people of other cultures. Perhaps war, exploitation, and slavery would not be the only outcome of European interaction with non-Western peoples after all.

Voluntarism in Church and Mission

While Catholic missions operated in terms of baptizing whole societies, an exportation of the ideal of Christendom, the most mission-minded Protestants were those who believed that the church was not coterminous with the broader society, but was gathered from it. Christians would be called out individually from all nations. Similarly, the missionary was someone whom God called to the special work of spreading the faith, supported by those who chose to do so. As Protestant missions took shape from the seventeenth through the early nineteenth century, the voluntaristic principle grew in strength. The growth of voluntarism did not mean the end of Christendom, for all but the most sectarian groups retained a dream of transforming whole societies. Also, the missionary vision of European state churches—especially German Lutheran, Dutch Reformed, and Anglican—focused on founding national churches. But the cutting edge of Protestant missions emanated from principles of voluntarism and individualism, in which the church was seen as a community of individuals who had answered God's call. Missionaries were those within the community with a special mandate to spread the gospel and found individual congregations, supported by volunteer societies within the churches. With missions to the native Americans and the examples of pietism leading the way, groups of Protestants began organizing societies to support missionaries. Voluntarism and personal commitment to the gospel were hallmarks of the evangelical revival that spread across Great Britain, Germany, and the United States in the mid-eighteenth to early nineteeth century. By the 1790s, the time was ripe for an explosion of voluntary missionary societies influenced by the evangelical revival, in which committed church members gave money to support missionaries in parts of the world that had piqued their interest.

The "father" of the "modern missionary movement" was William Carey (1761–1834), a self-educated Baptist shoemaker and preacher from Northampton, England. During Carey's lifetime, Britain was becoming the major world power, with exploration and colonies around the world. Fueled by the wealth of the Industrial Revolution, the British colonial machine opened distant parts of the world to European influence. Carey followed global events with interest, and he became increasingly concerned with the need for missions to newly discovered peoples. In 1792, he wrote *An Enquiry into the Obligations of Christians to Use Means for the Conversion of the Heathens*, which surveyed the religions of the world and argued that Jesus Christ's command to preach the gospel to all nations (Matthew 28:18–20) was still incumbent upon modern Christians. Based on Carey's vision, a group of Baptists founded the Baptist Missionary Society, raised money through individual subscription, and sent Carey and his family to India as their first missionaries. Unable to minister in territory controlled by the British East India Company, which was hostile to missions, Carey and other missionaries used the Danish colony of Serampore as their base. The missionaries' first task was learning the native languages and translating the Bible into them. With native-language speakers, Carey and his group translated parts of the Bible into forty-four languages. Carey himself translated the complete Bible into Marathi, Sanskrit, and Bengali, and he established the basis for Bengali prose. Believing in the need to read the Bible and to master the knowledge of the day, the Serampore missionaries founded a college for training pastors. Hannah Marshman, the wife of one of Carey's associates, opened girls' schools, thereby launching one of the key features of Protestant missions: the education of women.

Reports from the Serampore Trio, as Carey and his associates Marshman and Ward were called, stimulated the formation of mission societies throughout Protestantism. In 1795, the nondenominational London Missionary Society (LMS) came into being, and the next year it sent its first group of missionaries to the South Pacific, a part of the world that had awakened curiosity from the exploratory journeys of Captain James Cook. In 1797 the LMS opened a mission in Sierra Leone, and in 1799 it opened one in Cape Town, South Africa. The evangelical, anti-slavery wing of the Church of England organized the Church Missionary Society (CMS) in 1799, which placed two missionaries in Sierra Leone in 1804. The CMS devoted itself to West Africa initially so as to counteract the slave trade, which was abolished by the British in 1807. The earliest settlers in Sierra Leone were led by former slaves like Baptist preacher David George, whose missionary vision involved the spread of Christianity throughout Africa by former African slaves. In 1814, the first CMS missionaries reached New Zealand.

In the United States, the first society founded to send missionaries abroad was the American Board of Commissioners for Foreign Missions (ABCFM), organized nondenominationally by Congregational ministers in New England in 1810. In 1812 the ABCFM sent its first missionaries to India, and in 1819 it sent its first to Hawaii. Among the first group of missionaries were three who were rebaptized by English Baptists in India. Upon hearing that Adoniram and Ann Judson and Luther Rice had become Baptists, American Baptists organized the General Missionary Convention of the Baptist Denomination in the United States of America for Foreign Missions to support the Judsons as missionaries in Burma (1814). Methodists organized themselves in Britain (1818) and the United States (1819). American Methodists founded their missionary society partly in response to the work of John Stewart, an African-American Methodist who began evangelizing the Wyandot Indians in 1816. The first woman's mission-sending organization in America was the Woman's Union Missionary Society, organized nondenominationally in 1860. Beginning in 1869, American women in different denominations began to found their own missionary societies, of which there were approximately forty by the end of the century.

Protestants of European origin from all over the world, including those in colonies such as Australia and South Africa, launched missionary societies. These societies represented the full-scale involvement of laypeople in planning, funding, and executing outreach to the non-Christian world. Although senior missionaries tended to be ordained clergy, many artisans, teachers, and medical doctors became missionaries as well. The involvement of laypeople, including women and families, represented a major break with the tradition of clerical missionary activity that characterized Roman Catholicism. In local churches, women founded missionary societies that met to raise money for the missions, to educate laypeople about the church around the world, and to provide fellowship. Local societies often provided the transportation, salaries, outfits, supplies, and supportive correspondence that kept the foreign missionaries going.

The suppression of the Jesuits followed by the anticlerical French Revolution had dispersed the Catholic mission force. Under Pope Pius VII, renewal in mission began, symbolized by his reinstatement of the Jesuit order in 1814 and his reorganization of the *Propaganda* after the French monarchy was restored. In 1822, the need for missionaries in Louisiana inspired a young woman from Lyons, Pauline-Marie Jaricot, to gather people into groups of ten for the regular collection of money to support Catholic missions. Her organization, the Society for the Propagation of the Faith (SPF), became the "main source of financial aid to mission" in Roman Catholicism.[1] Although Catholic missionaries continued to be sent through religious orders, the SPF marked the beginning of lay involvement in Catholic missions. Other Catholic lay societies for fund-raising and support emerged in Europe and the United States. Catholic women also began playing a more active role in missions, as a number of women's religious congregations were founded for missionary purposes. Catholic laypeople taking financial responsibility for Catholic missions was a key aspect of the missionary renewal of the nineteenth century and a step toward weaning missions from the state.

---

[1] Arnulf Camps, "The Catholic Missionary Movement from 1789 to 1962," in A. Camps, L. A. Hoedemaker, M. R. Spindler, and F. J. Verstraelen, eds., *Missiology. An Ecumenical Introduction* (Grand Rapids, MI: Wm. B. Eerdmans, 1995), p. 230.

The Great Century

Historian Kenneth Scott Latourette called the nineteenth century through the First World War "The Great Century" of Christian missions. Europeans of diverse theological persuasions introduced the Christian faith into cultures all over the world. The nineteenth-century popes promoted the spread of the Catholic Church by finally breaking the power of the royal patronage and coordinating world mission from the Vatican. New missionary vigor, particularly in France, Germany, and Belgium, gave rise to new Catholic religious societies that focused on cross-cultural mission. Russian Orthodoxy continued its missionary campaign across Northern Asia. Protestant missionary societies from every faith launched missions into Asia, Africa, and the Americas. Despite minimal support and sometimes opposition from segments of the general church population, interest in missions increased as the nineteenth century progressed.

As with any movement that operated within so many cultures and that involved men, women, and children who were themselves products of their own times, the explicit intentions and concrete activities of the missionaries had unforeseen results and implications. Missionaries could not isolate themselves from the European economic and political forces that sought raw materials and markets all over the world. Missionaries could seldom avoid operating in a context in which colonialism and imperialism were real issues for the people they had come to serve and in which missions could easily be co-opted by the powers that be. Disease and poverty greeted the missionaries wherever they went, quickly challenging any theology that spoke of future salvation with disregard for the here and now, as well as making the physical survival of the missionary a serious problem. The immensity of the world made denominational differences among Protestants seem unhelpful or even ridiculous to missionaries who were the only Christians in a sea of Hindus, Confucians, or Muslims; and yet the folks back home were sending money to build carbon copies of their own churches. Social customs such as cannibalism, infanticide, and polygamy seemed barbaric to missionaries, who then had to struggle with the appropriate role for social change within the mission of the church. Missionaries often could not escape the limitations imposed by a sense of their own racial superiority, lack of education, rigid theological formulations, or unexamined cultural assumptions. The "miracle" of the "Great Century" was not only that idealistic European Christians sent missionaries all over the world, but that so many accepted their message!

Before examining the larger context and the implications of the missionary movement as a whole, as well as the non-Western forms of Christianity that ultimately emerged, it is important to examine what the missionaries actually did. The following sketch of missionary activity during the "Great Century" is by no means comprehensive; rather, it reflects the major trends in such activity, with examples drawn largely from Anglo-American Protestantism.

Translation and Literary Work

Stemming from the principles of the Reformation, Protestant missionaries from the beginning believed that their initial task was to translate the Bible into vernacular languages. Only as people had the Bible in their own languages could they understand the gospel message and commit themselves to it. The first missionaries to an ethnic group were therefore usually ordained ministers who had studied Greek and Hebrew and were thus prepared to spend the decades it might take to reduce a language to writing, compile a dictionary, and then translate the scriptures. Under difficult circumstances, it might take several generations to produce a Bible in a given language. The translation of the Bible into Chinese typified the challenges characteristic of Bible translation. A French Catholic missionary began a translation of the New Testament in the early 1700s, but died before he could complete it. A copy of the manuscript was discovered in Canton in 1739 by a merchant, who had it reproduced and sent to the British Museum. Forty years later, a Congregational minister discovered the manuscript. When Robert Morrison (1782–1834) became a missionary with the London Missionary Society in 1806, he used the manuscript as a foundation for his own translation of the Bible. At that time, it was illegal for foreigners to learn Chinese, and Morrison's Chinese teacher carried poison to commit suicide in case his work was discovered. With Morrison's version only a beginning, others made their own translations. Bible translators have continued to disagree over which word best represents the concept of God to the Chinese, with several terms still used today by Catholics and different groups of Protestants.

Bible translation was always a collaborative affair between the missionary and the speakers of the native language. The translator relied on "language helpers" to explain the meanings of words and to find phrases that adequately represented biblical concepts. One of the most significant instances of collaboration between missionaries and native speakers was the translation of the Bible into Yoruba. The future Anglican bishop Samuel Ajayi Crowther (1807–1891), a Yoruba who had been freed from slave traders by the English, worked with the English missionary Henry Townsend. Together they produced the first translation into an African language that, at Crowther's insistence, indicated tone. Written in consultation with a linguist from Cambridge University and the German philologist Lepsius, the Yoruba translation endured the test of time and became the basis for Yoruba literature.

African mission scholar Lamin Sanneh has argued that the translatability of Christianity was the key to its success in the Third World. By adopting vernacular languages as the means of transmitting the Christian gospel, and by relying on native informants to produce Bible translations, missionaries were forced to employ indigenous modes of thought. Whether it was of the Bible and hymnal, or the catechism and liturgy, translation meant that indigenous concepts of God and human nature were carried over into Christianity. The fact of translatability gave language groups a sense of ownership over Christian theology and tradition, as well as codified and preserved many languages. By the late twentieth century, the scriptures had been translated into approximately two thousand languages, and more than one hundred Bible societies were working cooperatively on translation projects under the United Bible Societies.

Evangelism and Church Planting

Telling people about Jesus Christ and gathering them into churches required a partnership between the foreign missionary and the native Christians. A missionary might work for ten years before one or two persons became Christians, but dozens would become Christians because of the influence of the early converts. The missionary might control access to foreign funds, or to leadership training or ordination, but the indigenous Christians knew the language and the culture better than any foreigner did. Missionaries who walked through the countryside telling people about the gospel were invariably accompanied by native translators or church members who told the people what the missionary was trying to say and put the message in language the people could understand.

The part of the world with the highest percentage of church affiliation is Oceania, the island world of the South Pacific. During the nineteenth century, whole clans, villages, and kingdoms became Christian through an evangelistic process based on partnership between Westerner and islander. When the London Missionary Society arrived in the 1790s, the drastic cultural differences between the English and the Tahitians led to the failure of the first mission. But persistence by the Congregationalists finally led to the conversion of King Pomare in 1819, and from then on the Tahitian monarch supported evangelization. The Tahitians eliminated human sacrifice and adopted Christianity as a religion of peace. From the island of Raiatea, LMS missionary John Williams initiated a movement that led to the conversion of much of Polynesia. He procured a ship, named it *The Messenger of Peace*, provisioned it for 3,000 miles, and sailed across the Polynesian Islands, dropping off two missionaries from Raiatea wherever the local ruler would permit. The indigenous missionaries believed that God was leading them just as he had led the apostles in the Book of Acts. With little theological training or support, the native missionaries began to convince other islanders of the benefits of the religion of peace. Still, many of them were martyred. Nonetheless, Raiateans initiated the first big missionary movement in the South Pacific, from the Cook Islands westward through Polynesia.

In the meantime, Tonga had become Methodist under the influence of Wesleyan missionaries who converted King George (Taufaahau) in 1830. While on Tonga, Williams encountered a Samoan convert named Fouia, who wanted the gospel for the Samoans. So he joined Williams, who took him and eight Tahitians to Samoa as missionaries. Samoa became strongly Congregationalist and Tonga Methodist. Both places sent thousands of missionaries, who paddled off in deep-sea canoes and evangelized the surrounding islands. By 1834, Williams reported, every island within 2,000 miles of Tahiti had been visited by indigenous missionaries. In 1839 Williams sailed to Erromanga, off the New Hebrides. As he landed, islanders clubbed him to death and ate him. Although Williams proclaimed a religion of peace, he was slain in revenge for the brutality of white traders who were capturing people for slavery in Australia.

Tongan Methodists evangelized the cannibal islands of Fiji. One of the greatest Tongan missionaries was Joeli Bulu (1838–1877), who, after being converted, went to Fiji, where he was a missionary for 40 years. Fiji's biggest island, Viti Levu, covers 4,500 square miles. The first converts there were Tongans who lived along the coast. These Tongans moved into the mountainous interior of the country, working among the Fijians, and the island became Christian after fifty years of effort. Once Fiji became Christian, it determined to send missionaries, about the same time that it became a British Colony in 1874. Fijians entered into an agreement with the church in Australia that would supply ships and money to support Fijian missionaries. As the Fijians readied to go, a measles epidemic hit the island and killed 40,000 of them, including many pastor–teachers. Despite losing hundreds of pastors in some sections, all 84 theological students of the time volunteered to be missionaries. Walking into isolation, exile, and, in some cases, death, over 300 Fijians went to New Guinea as missionaries.

The conversion of the South Pacific to Christianity was the result of a partnership between European missionaries and indigenous Christians. Although not every place demonstrated the same degree of cooperation between the two as did Oceania, the "native evangelist" was essential to the spread of Christianity during the "Great Century." In the noteworthy instance of its Niger Mission, the Church Missionary Society put even the white missionaries under the leadership of African bishop Samuel Ajayi Crowther, although the hard realities of racial prejudice undercut his work. Thomas Birch Freeman (1810–1890), son of an African father and an English mother, spent fifty-two years as the founder of the Methodist Church in Ghana. In the late nineteenth century, women missionaries also began to train native women as "Bible women" who went into rural areas to evangelize. Once a group of converts was collected, and a few leaders were trained, indigenous pastors were put in charge of the young churches, thus freeing the missionary for other work. To the mission societies of Great Britain and the United States, their main goal during the "Great Century" was to establish self-supporting and self-governing churches capable of providing their own leadership and sending their own missionaries.

Teaching and Educational Mission

From the beginning of Protestant missions, teaching was an important corollary to the evangelistic goals of the mission. What good were vernacular Bibles if people could not read? How could indigenous pastors be trained if there was no instruction? All the major mission efforts founded schools with the goal of teaching literacy and providing a native pastorate. Schools had the dual advantage of offering a controlled setting into which new missionaries could begin as teachers until their own language capabilities improved and attracting the native population that might not be interested in Christianity, but was definitely interested in Western knowledge. In West Africa, in fact, many chiefs accepted an evangelistic mission only on the condition that the missionaries provide schools to teach reading and writing. Pressure from the indigenous people for Western learning pushed the missionaries to offer higher and higher levels of education.

Educational mission reached its highest level the earliest in India. In 1830, Alexander Duff (1806–1878) arrived in Calcutta as the first missionary from the Church of Scotland. He initiated a controversial policy of teaching English and secular Western learning at the highest levels possible; critics then and now have accused Duff of Eurocentrism in his dismissal of traditional Hindu-based learning. He believed that English thought patterns and Western science were a preparation for the gospel (*praeparatio evangelica*), and he focused on teaching Brahmins, who presumably would be leaders of society. The college he founded became affiliated with Calcutta University. The widespread adoption of teaching in English also provided India with a common language that could unite ethnic groups, a position supported by a number of Indian intellectuals. In 1835, Duff's success caused the British colonial government to support educational institutions that used English as the medium of instruction, and English became the basis for modern higher education.

For Asian women, higher education also began in India, under the American Methodist Isabella Thoburn (1840–1901), who founded the first college for women in Asia in Lucknow. American missionary women, themselves products of the emerging colleges for women in the late nineteenth century, established schools that grew into women's colleges in India, Japan, Korea, China, and South Africa. Missionary women founded a number of important secondary schools for girls in such countries as Iraq, Turkey, Iran, and Ghana. The largest women's university in the world is Ewha University in Seoul, Korea, founded in 1886 by the American Methodist Mary Scranton (1832–1909) as the "Pear Blossom" school for girls. By 1909, American missionary women were operating 3,263 schools, ranging in level from village schools to colleges.

In assessing the impact of missions on the world today, education is widely acknowledged to be one of their major contributions because, at their best, mission schools provided a bridge between the indigenous cultures and the Western learning necessary for survival in the modern world. All around the world, modern institutions of advanced education had their origins in mission schools started by denominational missionaries: the Syrian Protestant College (later American University of Beirut) (1863), Silliman University in the Philippines (1899), Robert College in Istanbul (1863), St. John's University in Shanghai (1878), Yonsei University in Korea (1885), and more. In addition, missionaries served as advisors to foreign governments as they began to institute Western secular education. For example, during the 1880s, American Presbyterian W.A.P. Martin advised the Chinese government on different models of higher education as it prepared to found state-supported Western education.

Medical Missions

Given that a large percentage of Jesus' time on earth was spent healing people, it is no surprise that modern missions engaged in medical work from an early date. German Moravians sent the first medical missionaries. The first American to become a medical missionary was John Scudder (1793–1855), who sailed to Ceylon under the American Board in 1819. Initially, medical missionaries perceived themselves to be primarily evangelists, and Scudder believed that his preaching was more important than his medical practice. But soon it became apparent that Western medicine attracted people who would otherwise have been opposed to the Gospel. By 1938, approximately 1,350 foreign and national doctors and thirteen thousand nurses were serving in mission institutions around the world. The number of mission hospitals totaled 1,092, with fourteen medical schools.

Medical missions served other purposes besides creating a positive climate for evangelism. Medical doctors found themselves competing with traditional worldviews by establishing scientific explanations for disease. Thus, medical missions served as a vehicle for modern science and Western thought. Medical missions established that Christianity was a religion of goodwill and charity, one that valued all human life on equal terms. In particular, medical care for women demonstrated that women were equal to men in importance. Women doctors used medical evidence to promote women's rights by opposing child marriage in India, foot-binding in China, and female genital mutilation in Africa. In addition to providing hospitals, dispensaries, and clinics, missions staffed other health-related social services, such as schools for the handicapped and leprosaria. In India, fourteen missions cooperated to found the leading tuberculosis sanatorium in 1915. Probably more than any other mission institutions, medical missions embodied Christian ethics in action. As late as

1940, ninety percent of nurses in India were Christians, and eighty percent had been trained in mission hospitals. By the 1930s, increasing numbers of non-Western governments began to sponsor hospitals and clinics in response to the Christian example. As Western medicine became more technical and thus more capital intensive, missions began reducing their involvement in medicine, although their interest in the larger task of healing did not abate.

Women's Work

Work for women and children was a hallmark of Protestant missions in the modern era. By taking their wives with them into foreign lands, missionaries found themselves attempting to better the situation of women around the world. Cruel practices toward women around the world pushed missionaries toward supporting social change. Social change, however, was always in tension with the desire to make as many converts as possible. Missionaries debated among themselves whether evangelism and church planting were compatible with challenging the status quo. For the most part, missionaries believed that teaching women to read and to reason in a Western fashion would help to improve the well-being of women around the world by demonstrating the potential of the female gender.

Missionary women responded to the needs of women around the globe by opening their homes and schools to teach girls the rudiments of Western sanitation and child care, domestic arts, and reading. Hostility to the education of women was so severe in most of Asia that the first schools for girls were composed of orphans. As the orphans grew up and demonstrated the Western skills they had learned, the opposition to the education of women slowly receded. Another approach to the evangelization of women was home visitation by missionaries, who engaged secluded women in conversation, teaching them reading, needlework, and Bible study. In 1852, English women pioneered organized home visitation in India when they founded the Zenana Bible and Medical Mission. The ideal of the "Christian home," in which a pious, educated wife took good care of her children and husband, who respected her in return, became a goal of missions from the 1830s onward. The concept of the "Christian home" had a powerful effect on emerging Christian cultures throughout the world. The Japanese language, for example, had no word for "home" until the arrival of missionaries in the late nineteenth century.

In 1910, the American woman's missionary movement celebrated fifty years of independent women's missionary societies. As a result of the jubilee, which was celebrated with teas and luncheons across the United States, American women collected several million dollars to support the founding of seven ecumenical women's universities and medical schools in India, China, and Japan. By 1921, when the International Missionary Council undertook a study of women in the global church, educated female elites had been formed in churches across Asia. Roughly a century of "woman's work" by Protestant missions resulted in higher literacy rates, better medical care, and more leadership roles for women in church and society.

Human Rights

An important outgrowth of missionary concern in the nineteenth century was attention to what today would be called human rights. Although most missionaries saw their work to be apolitical and centered on spiritual salvation, the injustices perpetrated on indigenous peoples either by colonial powers or by other people led a significant minority of missionaries to become advocates for human rights. Biblical principles of equality in Christ were extended into the public realm, especially in the face of glaring social injustices.

The first great social cause embraced by modern missionaries was that of the abolition of slavery. The same English evangelicals who agitated for the abolition of the slave trade and then the abolition of slavery in the British Empire founded the Church Missionary Society. They faced opposition from the traders and planters who profited from the denial of native rights to land, natural resources, and personal freedom. British evangelical Thomas Fowell Buxton (1786–1844) led the fight against the entrenched slave interests in the British Caribbean. Initiating a practice that would be widely used in human rights crusades in the twentieth century, Buxton used missionaries as informants. Relying on evidence provided by the missionaries, Buxton collected a body of information on human rights abuses under slavery. He then disseminated the information and swayed public opinion against slavery, so that in 1833 the House of Commons freed all slaves within the British empire.

But to free slaves was not enough, for other nations continued to enslave Africans. Arab slave traders based in Zanzibar continued to ravage the peoples of Africa into the twentieth century. Probably the most famous missionary who opposed the slave trade was the explorer David Livingstone (1813–1873). Livingstone believed that the introduction of "Christianity, civilization, and commerce" would provide alternative economic and social patterns that would thwart the Arab slave trade. Among Roman Catholics, Cardinal Charles Lavigerie (1825–1892) founded the White Fathers in 1868 as a missionary order in North Africa, with a specific focus on reclaiming people from slavery. African-American missionary William Sheppard (1865–1926) exposed the atrocities committed by Belgian rubber planters against laborers in the Congo. After reporting in a mission magazine about the mutilation of workers by the Belgians, Sheppard was tried for libel by the colonial government and deported.

Defense of aboriginal land rights continued to be a major challenge for missionaries around the world. The nineteenth century saw the gradual conquest and settlement of North America by European immigrants who displaced the native Americans from their ancestral lands. In the early decades of the century, the American Board spent the most effort of any mission society to evangelize the Indians. One group that was particularly responsive to the gospel message was the Cherokees, whose homeland spread across Georgia, Tennessee, and North Carolina. In the eighteenth century, they had adopted European agricultural, political, and business practices that culminated in the founding of a Cherokee republic in 1817. Presbyterian and Congregational missionaries founded schools and chapels, as did Baptists, Moravians, and Methodists. But the progress toward assimilation to American ways was destroyed when Andrew Jackson became president and supported the desire of whites to confiscate the Cherokee lands. In May 1830, the Indian Removal Bill passed through Congress and demanded that the Indians in the southeastern United States move west of the Mississippi. Missionaries remained with the Cherokees to support them in their struggle, but the state of Georgia arrested eleven white ministers and sentenced them to prison. The missionaries were confused as to what to do in the difficult situation, and most of them withdrew. But a few remained with the Cherokee people, accompaning them on the "Trail of Tears" of 1837–1838 as they walked to reservations in Oklahoma.

Missionaries often found themselves as the protectors of Christian minorities, although situations were complicated by the context of Western imperialism, in which missionaries were unavoidably involved. In 1846, after the destruction of ten thousand Nestorians by the Turks and Kurds, missionaries set up schools, churches, and clinics among the displaced refugees. The genocide of Armenians by the Turks during World War I was witnessed by missionaries, who provided documentation of the atrocities for the rest of the world to see. In 1892, in Urfa, American Board missionary Corinna Shattuck (1848–1910) hid Armenians in her home while the Turks massacred thousands outside. She single-handedly cared for 150 orphans and employed two thousand jobless Armenians who made products she sold in Europe for their support. Despite reflecting their own times, on issues ranging from slavery to land rights to western vice, nineteenth-century missionaries were the spokespersons for the viewpoints of unrepresented and otherwise unrecognized victims of social injustice.

The Maturation of the Modern Missionary Movement

The end of the "Great Century" of Christian missions was marked by the realization that the missionary movement was maturing: "Missions" were becoming "younger churches." Lands in which being a Christian was illegal in 1850 had significant Christian populations by 1900. In Korea, missions were illegal until the 1880s; but in 1907, the Korean Protestant churches had reached such a state of vigor, that they experienced a great revival and began to send their own missionaries to Koreans in distant locations. In China, an antiforeign uprising known as the Boxer Movement resulted in the martyrdom of 32,000 Chinese Christians, 181 foreign missionaries, and 52 missionary children in 1901. Yet ten years later, Chinese nationalists founded a republic with Christians at its head who had learned much of what they knew about Western government from missionaries. In India, the Sepoy Mutiny of 1857 targeted missionaries and native Christians. Individual converts from upper castes were routinely disowned or even murdered by their families. Yet by World War I, over a million Dalits (untouchable castes) had become Christian in mass movements that began in the late 1800s. In 1912, the Anglicans consecrated the first Indian bishop, V.S. Azariah (1874–1945). Despite its weaknesses, the modern missionary movement clearly succeeded in carrying the gospel message around the world by the end of the "Great Century." Although there were still many places where the gospel had never been heard, and Christians remained a small minority in most "mission lands," churches existed where Christians had been nonexistent a hundred years before.

Formal recognition of the changed realities in the world church occurred at the World Missionary Conference held in Edinburgh in 1910. The culmination of a series of missionary meetings in the nineteenth century, the Edinburgh Conference brought together 1,200 delegates from Protestant missions. Based on exhaustive correspondence and research, committees produced reports on such vital topics as "education in relation to the Christianization of national life," "the missionary message and non-Christian religions," and "cooperation and the promotion of unity." The presence of seventeen non-Western

Christians at the World Missionary Conference signified the future. Of the forty-seven addresses given at the conference, six were presented by representatives of the younger churches. Western churches began to realize that Christianity could no longer be considered their private property. Rather, the new century seemed to promise a world in which the church would be a global fellowship, gathered from the many peoples of Africa, Asia, the Americas, and Europe.

Chapter 41

World Christianity in the Twentieth Century

For American Christians, the twentieth century began in a spirit of confidence and optimism. The Protestant establishment reigned supreme, and American presidents consulted church leaders about major policy decisions. The Spanish-American War of 1898 dealt the death blow to Spanish imperialism, with the tottering Catholic power ceding its last colonies to the United States. Immigrants poured into the country and eagerly embraced the American dream. The world's fairs in Chicago in 1893 and St. Louis in 1904 demonstrated the dawning of the electric age, an era that saw the radio and the automobile transform the American lifestyle within a generation.

But from the vantage point of the rest of the world, the signs of the times looked ominous. Britain and Germany were locked in an arms race, a by-product of the contest for empire. European imperial powers had conquered much of the world, and their capitalist forces and militaries exploited the natural resources and monopolized the markets of the emerging "Third World." In 1885 at the Berlin Conference, Europe carved up Africa and distributed it among Britain, Germany, France, Portugal, Italy, and Belgium. In Latin America, although Spain and Portugal had been pushed out, entrenched gentries controlled the land and wealth of the continent. In the Far East, Japan was modernizing itself and beginning to make war on its neighbors. Then, in 1914, World War I broke out. "Christian civilization" proved to be no more than a high-sounding phrase, with war among "Christian" powers making the twentieth century the most destructive in the history of the world.

As one of the few international, cross-cultural entities at the end of the "war to end all wars," the fledgling world church stood at a crossroads. Would the church of Jesus Christ be a model for peace, reconciliation, and world unity, or would it perpetuate the "ecclesiastical colonialism" of European-based denominations? Would it support the aspirations of colonized peoples for nationhood, or would it serve as the apologist for the colonizers? Would church leadership emerge from the indigenous people, or would the Western missionaries who controlled the purse strings continue to call the shots? The history of world Christianity in the twentieth century is the story of a movement with growing pains, as the faith outgrew its European clothing and struggled to dress itself anew.

The Search for Global Community: The Ecumenical Movement

The most hopeful sign of Christian maturity at the beginning of the century was the ecumenical movement. Since the time of the Reformations, Christianity had been divided into Orthodox, Roman Catholic, and Protestant branches, with further divisions within both Orthodoxy and Protestantism. Although the division among the three major branches of the faith seemed unlikely to be healed, Protestants from the time of the pietists onward hoped for cooperation at least within Protestantism itself. Many early Protestant missionary societies began as interdenominational ventures. The nineteenth century witnessed a series of missionary conferences held by Continental mission societies, Anglo-American societies, and missionaries in specific parts of the world. For example, missionaries to China held ecumenical field conferences in 1877, 1890, and 1907 to discuss such common issues as Bible translation, education, and social change. The missionary movement became the leading source of ecumenical endeavor because the futility of denominational divisions appeared stark on the mission field, where millions of non-Christians outnumbered a tiny handful of believers. Not only did mission work require cooperation to maximize the use of resources, but Western church divisions paled into insignificance compared to the needs of the non-Western world.

During the nineteenth century, a number of nondenominational, multinational Protestant organizations emerged that concerned themselves with special ministries. For example, the Young Men's Christian Association (1844) and the Young Women's Christian Association (1854) focused on reaching urban workers and college students with varied forms of spiritual and material assistance, such as job training, recreational outlets, and Bible studies. Ecumenical conventions to promote spiritual life, Bible study, Christian social work, missionary commitment, and other causes appeared with regularity in the late nineteenth century.

A decisive moment in the ecumenical movement occurred in Edinburgh, Scotland, at the World Missionary Conference held in 1910. Inspired by that seminal meeting, Protestant leaders from around the world pushed ahead with confidence that full church cooperation and perhaps even church union would occur in the twentieth century. Out of "Edinburgh 1910" came a Continuation Committee to plan meetings approximately every ten years and to provide communication among mission agencies on such topics as labor conditions, liquor and drug traffic, relations with younger churches, and missions during wartime. The first job of the Continuation Committee under its chairman John R. Mott (1865–1955) was to organize councils of missions and, where possible, councils of churches in all the major Protestant parts of the world. Once such councils were organized, they could send representatives to an international body. Another purpose of organizing national councils was to make the transition from mission to church, as national councils gradually included more indigenous church leaders and fewer missionaries. In 1912–1913, Mott traveled through Asia and held eighteen regional and three national conferences in India, Ceylon, Malaya, Burma, China, Japan, and Korea. Out of these meetings emerged a number of national councils, as well as European mission councils, during the 1920s. The International Missionary Council was founded in 1921.

The tragedies of World War I tested the effectiveness of the fledgling ecumenical movement. Communication between German and British Christians quickly disintegrated, and massive disruption of missions occurred in colonial territories. At the beginning of the war, Germany had 1,900 missionaries, wives, and children around the world. Many of these were interned, as were British missionaries in German territories. The collapse of German missions left gaping holes that personnel and money from America, Great Britain, and Scandinavia tried to plug. John R. Mott raised $260,000,000 for the YMCA to work among prisoners of war on both sides, as well as funds to help the "orphaned" German missions. For his work during both world wars, shuttle diplomacy, and leadership of the world's YMCA, Mott received the Nobel Peace Prize in 1946. In the United Kingdom, J. H. Oldham (1874–1969) anchored the Continuation Committee. Working through the Conference of British Missionary Societies, he maintained a relationship with the British government and corresponded with missionaries and mission councils around the world. One of Oldham's greatest accomplishments was to convince the British government not to confiscate all the property of German missions at the Treaty of Versailles signed on June 28, 1919. If the British government had seized the German mission property for war reparations, then church work around the world would have been devastated. Oldham also succeeded in getting the Allies to recognize religious freedom in colonial territories after the war, thus permitting the return of German missionaries to Africa. A new ecumenical organization, the World Alliance for International Friendship through the Churches, affirmed the freedom of missions to work across national boundaries.

Following World War I, the greatest challenges faced by the ecumenical movement were to restore Christian trust and understanding across national lines and to care for the millions of refugees in Europe and Asia. One of the most acute situations was the plight of Christian minorities in the former Ottoman Empire, broken up after Turkey lost the war. During the war, Turkish genocide of Armenian Christians resulted in 600,000 deaths in 1915 alone. An estimated 100,000 each of Syrian Jacobites, Chaldeans, and Nestorians were killed. The Assyrian Nestorians lost their patriarch, most of their clergy, and over half of their members to Turkish massacre, plus thousands more to starvation and disease as the refugees fled through Muslim lines toward the British. One-fourth of all Lebanese died in World War I, almost all of them Maronite Christians. Christian businessmen in the United States founded the American Committee for Near East Relief, endorsed by Congress in 1919. The major work of Near East Relief was to care for war orphans, over 132,000 of whom were in American-sponsored orphanages. Thirty American missionaries and relief workers died from 1915 to 1918 trying to help the minorities in the Ottoman Empire, and thousands of other Americans participated in relief work after the war. During the 1920s in Europe, the YMCA and YWCA worked to assist starving, homeless students. Missionaries ran soup kitchens, clinics, and employment programs for refugees across Europe and even for Russian refugees in China.

During the 1920s, movements toward church union gained momentum. The founding of the League of Nations inspired the Ecumenical Patriarch of the Holy Synod of the Church of Constantinople to send out a letter in 1920 to all churches calling for a similar league of churches. The Orthodox churches, having suffered horribly during the world war, and now victims of political instability both in Russia and the former Ottoman Empire, felt the need for worldwide ecumenical unity. By the late 1930s, various ecumenical groups had come together and hammered out a constitution for the World Council of Churches. As missions gave way to the formation of churches in Asia, Africa, and Latin America, the young churches could become members of the global fellowship on an equal basis. Delayed by the Second World War, the World Council of Churches formally began in 1948. Only the Roman Catholic Church and fundamentalist denominations remained aloof from the World Council.

One of the most powerful impulses toward church mergers was the desire for unity among mission-founded churches in the non-Western world. As small minorities who inherited denominational divisions spawned by events in the West, non-Western Christians had little need for separate Lutheran, Anglican, Presbyterian, Methodist, and Baptist churches. The most important church mergers occurred in the "mission lands." Mergers of various Protestant denominations resulted in such union churches as the Church of Christ in China (1927); the Church of Christ in Thailand (1934); the Kyodan, the United Church of Christ in Japan (1941); the Church of South India (1947); and the United Church of Christ in the Philippines (1948). Latin American Protestants began to meet together, beginning with the Congress on Christian Work in Latin America held in 1916 in Panama. In Africa, Christians from across the continent attended the All Africa Church Conference in 1958, a meeting that gave rise to the All Africa Conference of Churches. Another feature of church cooperation in the non-Western world was the founding of ecumenical theological seminaries for the training of clergy in Singapore; Suva, Fiji; Makassar, Indonesia; Accra, Ghana; and other locations. By the 1950s, churches in Vietnam, Cambodia, China, Japan, India, Indonesia, Burma, Korea, Taiwan, and the Philippines had sent cross-cultural missionaries to other parts of Asia or to other ethnic groups within their national borders.

Christianity and Nationalism

Nationalist movements—movements for self-determination against colonialism—spread across Asia in the early twentieth century. Following the Second World War, African peoples also demanded an end to colonialism. Peoples from Algeria to China to Indonesia reacted against the political and economic domination characteristic of Western colonialism, as well as the racism explicit in "white" nations ruling "dark" ones. The world wars energized the fight to end colonialism because they laid bare the moral and political weaknesses of the West. In preparation for the Second Assembly of the World Council of Churches, leading East Asian Christians wrote a volume entitled *Christianity and the Asian Revolution,* published in 1954. As Asian Christians reflected on the social convulsions of the twentieth century, they defined the "Asian Revolution" not only as a reaction against European colonialism, but also as a search for human rights and economic and social justice, ideas obtained from the West itself. The Asian revolution involved eliminating colonialism, as well as promoting the worth of individuals and minorities against hereditary indigenous injustices. The authors noted, "As the American colonists revolted in the name of English justice against British rule, so Asians, in the name of political and social doctrines which originated in large part in Europe and America, revolted against European colonialism."[1]

The involvement of Christianity in nationalist movements was a complex phenomenon. On the one hand, missions benefited in many respects from colonialism, for the Western political presence helped them to secure land and influence and to gain military and legal protection. In their focus on the spiritual or "otherworldly," missionaries tended to avoid politics. Thus, most missionaries preferred the stability of the colonialist status quo to the uncertainties of nationalist revolution. On the other hand, missionaries helped to plant the seeds for the concepts of nationhood and the self-determination of peoples. The messages of spiritual equality, self-improvement, and individualism promoted by the mission schools and churches had a powerful, if unforeseen, impact upon oppressed peoples around the world. Mission schools were vehicles for Western learning; and post-Enlightenment ideas about geography, science, government, and the importance of individual rights resonated with the needs of peoples to modernize their own social systems and simultaneously throw off the incubus of Western domination. Missionary education awakened non-Western governments to their responsibility to educate and provide social services to their own people. Ironically, the message missions preached often set in motion a process that ultimately resulted in social upheaval and a reduction in their own power and influence. Nationalist movements were often led by indigenous Christians who both respected the missionaries as bearers of the gospel and resented them as imperialistic Westerners.

One important example of Christian leadership in nationalist revolution occurred in Korea. When the first Protestant missionary from the United States landed in Korea in 1884, King Kojong cautiously welcomed him as a representative of the United States, which could be an ally for Korea in its struggle to maintain territorial integrity in the face of Japanese, Russian, Chinese, and English aggression. Intellectuals were attracted to Christianity as a vehicle for modernization, and ordinary people appreciated the literacy training, health care, and spiritual concern of the missionaries. The churches grew rapidly in the Pyongyang area, in the northwestern part of the country.

By 1910, when Japan occupied Korea as a colony, mission schools were the only form of modern education in the country, and they became a hotbed of patriotism. In 1911, the Japanese military police accused students at a Presbyterian school of plotting to assassinate the Japanese governor-general. The police arrested 123 Koreans for conspiracy, 105 of whom were Christian nationalists. The Japanese forced the missions to stop teaching religion in their schools. Then, in 1919, the March First Independence Movement occurred, when patriots signed and circulated the Korean Declaration of Independence. Of the

---

[1] Rajah B. Manikam, ed., *Christianity and the Asian Revolution* (Madras: The Joint East Asia Secretariat of the International Missionary Council and the World Council of Churches, 1954), p. 7.

thirty-three signers, fifteen were Christians, even though Christians represented one percent of the population. Churches held rallies to support independence. The Japanese police began to persecute the Christians and destroy their churches (fifty-nine by 1920); in one case, they burned down a church with the people locked inside. Japanese colonial rule continued with great cruelty in Korea until 1945. During the latter part of the occupation, the colonial government closed many Christian schools, made the Korean churches become subservient to the Japanese church, and tortured and executed Christians who refused to bow down to pictures of the Japanese emperor. Clearly, Christianity was a powerful ideology that Koreans used to support their own aspirations for self-determination, freedom, and democracy. By the 1980s, twenty-five percent of South Koreans had become Christians.

A part of the world in which the relationship between Christianity and nationalism was extremely complex was India, a vast land populated by many ethnic groups arranged in a strict caste system, with Brahmins at the top and untouchable "outcastes" at the bottom. British colonial rule in some sense created the modern nation of India by imposing unity on the different ethnic groups, making English a universal language, and introducing Western models of government and education. Influenced by Christian missions, nineteenth-century Hindu reformers like Rammohun Roy (1772–1833) and Keshub Chunder Sen (1838–1884) embraced Jesus Christ as an ethical model and purifier of Hinduism. Yet the harsh realities of British imperialism meant that most Indians rejected the church as the institution of the oppressor, even as prominent intellectuals were attracted to the ethics of Christianity. Throughout the nineteenth century, the conversion of high-caste Hindus, Sikhs, or Muslims to Christianity was rare and occurred on an individual basis. Conversion usually involved breaking one's caste, being disowned by one's family, and often martyrdom. From the 1870s through the 1930s, the profile of Indian Christianity changed as "untouchables," later called Dalits, became Christians in large "mass movements."

By the 1880s, Christian leaders had inaugurated a nationalist movement within the churches as they protested against missionary paternalism. The idea of an Indian rather than a European church was behind the founding of Christian newspapers and organizations such as the Bengal Christian Association for the Promotion of Christian Truth and Godliness, and the Protection of the Rights of Indian Christians in 1868. Movements toward an Indian national church and the indigenization of Christian practice grew stronger, especially after political nationalism attained concrete form with the founding of the Indian National Congress in 1885. In 1887, the fifteen Christian delegates to the Indian National Congress convened to discuss the idea of a national church, the first time that Christian leaders from across the country had met together. Among the founders of the Indian National Congress were several Christians, including Kali Charan Banurji (1847–1907) who was well respected as an orator. At the Congress meeting of 1889, three of the ten women delegates were Christians, including the high-caste convert Pandita Ramabai Saraswati (1858–1922), famous for the home she founded for Hindu child widows. An advocate of women's rights, Pandita Ramabai opposed child marriage and the disfigurement and rejection of widows under Brahminism.

Although several Christians were prominent leaders of Indian nationalism in its early years, after the turn of the century that movement became increasingly connected to Hinduism. Naturally enough, since the majority of Indians were Hindus, they wanted to express their political aspirations in religio-cultural terms. The most important Christian influence on Indian nationalism was ultimately not that of the churches as institutions, but of Christian ideas espoused by nationalist leaders. In the person of the Hindu lawyer Mohandas Gandhi (1869–1948), the ideals of Christianity found expression through Hindu nationalism. During World War I, Indian nationalists saw their chance to seek "home rule" or self-government within the British Empire. The British authorities reacted with oppression. On April 13, 1919, British soldiers opened fire on protesters, killing nearly 400 and wounding 1,200. The following year Gandhi called for Indians to refuse to cooperate with the government, including boycotting elections and schools. He was arrested in 1922 and sent to prison, but in 1930 he started a massive campaign of civil disobedience authorized by the Indian Congress. Basing his program on the teachings of Christ, Gandhi steadfastly pursued a program of pacifist civil disobedience. On March 12, 1930, he marched to the sea and began to make salt, a traditional process that had been outlawed by the British. Indians all over the country participated in the salt protest, as well as boycotted British cloth and goods. The colonial government reacted by imprisoning thousands of people, but the move toward the independence of India was unstoppable, and India obtained its freedom in 1947.

Young, educated Indian Christians enthusiastically supported Gandhi, seeing in his movement the embodiment of the principles outlined by Jesus in the Sermon on the Mount. Gandhi himself had several prominent Christian friends, none of whom were closer to his heart than the Anglican missionary C. F. Andrews (1871–1940). Widely known as Deenabandhu, "friend of the poor," Andrews lived out a mission of friendship and reconciliation with the Indian people. The colonial government had tried to eliminate missionary support for nationalism after World War I by making all non-British missionaries sign a pledge of obedience to the British government as a condition of their being allowed into the country. Most missionaries went along with the British government and disapproved of any nationalist refusal to obey the authorities; but in 1930, 200 British missionaries went on record supporting Gandhi's civil disobedience campaign.

Nationalism was one of the major themes in non-Western Christianity during the first half of the twentieth century. In many Asian countries, despite the missionary partnerships with colonialism, Christianity provided some of the motivations and ethical rationales that fueled nationalist revolutions. Often, movements for the indigenization of the church spilled over into the public realm to support political nationalism. In fact, the growth of the church frequently has been related to the church's support of people's nationalistic aspirations. In Korea, for example, church support for nationalism encouraged the growth of Christianity. In India, where Christianity was connected with centuries of colonialism, there was popular resentment against Christianity despite the witness of a few prophetic Christian voices. Indonesia was another case where the Dutch held on to imperial control until violent revolution forced their hand. Under the long centuries of Dutch oppression, Islam grew faster than Christianity despite the best efforts of the Dutch missionaries.

In multiethnic situations, Christianity has frequently represented the nationalist hopes and dreams of minority peoples who have been oppressed by the majority. The Dalits of India, for example, embraced Christianity as a way to overcome their low position within the dominant Hindu worldview. Thus, they hesitated to get deeply involved in a nationalist movement fueled by Hinduism. Similarly, the rural Karen tribes in Burma (now Myanmar) have experienced Christianity as a mark of ethnic identity vis-à-vis the dominant Burmese Buddhist culture. In the early twentieth century, on the island of New Caledonia, a colonial possession of the French, the native "Kanaks" became Protestants partly in reaction to the Catholicism of the French settlers who pushed them off their lands and into reservations. The nationalist independence party of the Kanaks, the *Union Caledonienne*, had its roots in the activity of Protestant evangelists, both indigenous and missionary. The linkages between nationalism and Christianity around the world demonstrate that the gospel has not been confined to the other-worldly; rather, Christianity often acts as a powerful ideology driving social and political movements as well.

"Missionary, Go Home!"

After the end of World War II, the colonial empires of the Europeans fell apart. Some nations—e.g., Pakistan, India, Sri Lanka, Ghana, and the Philippines—obtained self-government quickly and without having to wage war against the colonizers. In other countries—e.g., Algeria, Vietnam, and Congo—independence from colonialism occurred only after wars of liberation or general uprisings. In many parts of the world, civil wars broke out as the newly freed nations fought over who would be in power, with political parties often forming along ethnic lines. More than a million people died in Hindu–Muslim violence when Pakistan was partitioned from India. The creation of Israel in 1948 meant the displacement of thousands of Palestinian Muslims and Christians, as Jews who had survived the Holocaust poured into their new nation. Korea and Indochina became battlegrounds for the Cold War. By 1970, European colonial rule had been eliminated from most of Asia and Africa, with southern Africa and parts of Oceania the most notable exceptions.

The implications of independence movements seemed dire for Christianity, as missionaries found themselves no longer welcome in new countries eager to throw off the legacy of colonialism. Newly independent nations often nationalized mission institutions such as schools and hospitals. Nationalist leaders around the world condemned Western missionaries as proselytizers, cultural imperialists, and ideologues of colonialism. Gandhi, for example, praised missions for the humanitarian aid they offered that represented the ethics of Christ, but condemned attempts to convert Indians to Christianity as "religious imperialism." India began denying visas to foreign missionaries, a practice also followed in those Muslim countries where Christian evangelism was forbidden by law. In Africa, nationalist leaders accused missions of telling the Africans to pray and then stealing their land while their heads were bowed. Jomo Kenyatta, leader of the anti-Christian, proindependence Mau-Mau rebellion in Kenya during the 1950s, and the country's first president, accused the missionaries of trying to destroy African culture. Also in the 1950s, indigenous Christian leaders who had been educated in the West, often under the sponsorship of the missions, condemned the Western missionary movement as imperialistic, racist, and destructive of the native culture.

The accusations against missionaries that poured in from Christian leaders in Asia and Africa from the 1950s through the 1970s caused radical soul-searching on the part of Western denominations. But nothing caused as much pain and shock to the Western churches as did events in China, which had been the major mission field of the world church, both Protestant and Catholic. The nationalist revolution of 1911 had brought into power a government with Christian leaders, friendly to democracy and to the West. Western missions poured in money to support Christian schools, literacy campaigns, and medical services. Even though the Chinese government insisted in the 1920s that all mission-related institutions have Chinese heads, the relationship between the nationalists and the Western missions remained cordial. But the corruption of the nationalists and their failure to meet the needs of "China's millions" provided an opening for the communists to organize under Mao Zedong. China suffered terribly at the hands of the Japanese during World War II. Then a civil war ended in communist victory and the founding of the People's Republic of China in 1949. The nationalist government fled to Taiwan, along with many Chinese Christians.

Most missionaries opposed communism because of its atheistic core and denial of individual human rights. But most Chinese Protestants attempted a rapprochement with communism in 1950 when the government forcibly organized them into the "Three-Self Patriotic Movement." In consultation with Premier Zhou Enlai, Protestant leaders under the pro-communist and American-educated theologian Y. T. Wu (1895–1979) published the "Christian Manifesto," which stated that missionary Christianity was connected with Western imperialism and that the United States used religion to support reactionary political forces. The document called for Chinese Christians immediately to become self-reliant and separate from all Western institutions. By 1952, at least 400,000 Chinese Christians had signed the manifesto. The Three-Self Movement began to hold meetings at which Christian leaders were accused of betraying the Chinese people and were sent to labor camps for "reeducation."

The outbreak of the Korean War in 1950, which pitted communist China against the United States, meant the end of the missionary movement in China. The presence of foreign missionaries threatened the security of the Chinese Christians, who were suspected of being pro-foreign, and missionaries began to leave. The communists arrested leading missionaries and accused them of being spies. Anti-Three-Self native Christians were imprisoned, sometimes for decades. The government arrested untold numbers of Chinese Catholic priests, nuns, and laypeople. For example, Father Tung Shih-chih was arrested and sent to a labor camp for speaking publicly in favor of the church, and Father Beda Chang was arrested for "counterrevolutionary activity" and tortured to death in prison. The communists arrested two American Roman Catholic bishops, both of whom were members of the leading American Catholic mission society, the Maryknolls: Bishop Francis X. Ford died of maltreatment in custody in 1952, and Bishop James E. Walsh was the last Catholic missionary in China, imprisoned in 1958 until his deportation in 1970. Because of communist harassment, the Catholic Church in China went underground and secretly ordained its own priests and bishops. The worst suffering of Chinese Christians occurred from 1966 to 1976 during the Cultural Revolution, a period in which no public worship was permitted in China. Millions of Chinese died as the government encouraged the destruction of all things religious or traditional. China watchers in the West wondered if Chinese Christianity had been destroyed—tainted in the government's eyes by its connection with things foreign.

"Missionary, Go Home!" remained a popular refrain during the 1960s and 1970s in many parts of Asia and Africa. In 1971, Christian leaders in the Philippines, Kenya, and Argentina all called for a moratorium on missionaries to end the dependence of the younger churches on the older ones. In 1974, the All Africa Conference of Churches meeting in Lusaka, Zambia, called for a moratorium on Western missionaries and money sent to Africa, because it was believed that foreign assistance created dependency and stifled African leadership. In 1968, the World Council of Churches' Assembly in Uppsala became the scene of an assault on Western imperialism and old-fashioned mission by non-Western representatives.

The response of the Western church to the attacks on Christian missions varied from group to group. Mainline Protestant mission thinking shifted to notions of partnership in mission with non-Western churches and to being present in solidarity with people, rather than engaging in outright evangelism or building institutions. The number of mainline Protestant missionaries began declining during the 1960s, and by the late 1980s, foreign missions had all but collapsed in many mainline churches. Roman Catholicism also experienced a decline in the number of Western missionaries, as fewer and fewer chose religious life as a vocation in the late 1960s. Only among independent evangelicals did the numbers of Western missionaries continue to grow, as groups like the Southern Baptists, the Mormons, and the Wycliffe Bible Translators retained a theology that focused on evangelism and ignored the critics of missionary imperialism. In the United States, the largest mission-sending nation in the world during the twentieth century, the number of independent evangelical missionaries began to surpass those from mainline churches in the late 1960s.

The Explosion of Christianity in Asia, Latin America, and Africa

In the year 1900, the "average" Christian was a European. By the year 2000, the "average" Christian was likely to be a Latin American or a sub-Saharan African. Despite the debacle of world wars and Western colonialism, by the end of the century Christianity was the largest religion in the world, encompassing one-third of the global population. Although the proportion of the world's population that was Christian remained roughly the same from the beginning to the end of the twentieth century, it did so by registering massive gains in the so-called Third World that offset decline in the West. The rapid growth in world Christianity began early in the century, but increased exponentially after the Second World War. Although Catholicism remained the branch of Christianity with by far the highest membership—approximately 980 million in 1996—the startling new reality of the late twentieth century was the existence of new, indigenous, non-Western varieties of Christianity around the world. Not only were the former mission churches being led by indigenous believers, but new religious movements and denominations flourished among people who had never seen a Western missionary. By the late twentieth century, Christianity had become a truly global religion with as much cultural variation within it as without.

The end of the European dominance of Christianity marked a paradigm shift in the history of the religion. With lower birthrates, and with secularism and prosperity both barriers to religious commitment in the West, European Christianity declined. Although the

Western church still retained the lion's share of the church's material resources, dynamic faith, worship life, and missionary commitment blossomed in the Third World.

Christianity in Asia

In Asia, home to the world's great religions, Christians remained a minority in most countries. But the vitality of Christian belief, even under dictatorial, anti-Christian regimes, meant a large increase in Christians martyred for their faith in the late twentieth century. Although the end of European colonialism in the region removed one major barrier to the growth of the church in some areas, the emergence of governments hostile to Western concepts of religious freedom made the sending of missionaries to those locations impossible. Especially in Muslim-dominated countries such as Indonesia, Malaysia, Pakistan, Iran, and nations in the Middle East, promoting Christianity or even practicing it became very difficult. The penalty for conversion to Christianity in Muslim countries under Islamic law (*sharia*) is death. Even foreign nationals working in Muslim countries were often not free to practice their religion. For example, an underground church of several hundred Filipinos met weekly in Riyadh, Saudi Arabia, until it was raided by police in 1992. A Filipino pastor was tortured and sentenced to death, but was deported under pressure from the Filipino government. In 1995, the government of Laos began to close down all churches in the northern part of the country. In 1994, three prominent Protestant pastors were murdered in Iran for supporting religious freedom. In the mid-1990s, the dictatorial Indonesian government began to prohibit missionaries to tribal areas so that there would be no more foreign witnesses to human rights abuses, and angry mobs burned dozens of churches. Already in 1975 the Indonesian government had invaded the Christian island of East Timor, an action that eventually resulted in 200,000 deaths. Ironically, the growth in Asian Christianity and its deepening roots in Asian cultures during the twentieth century resulted in greater oppression against it by tyrannical regimes.

The vitality of Asian Christianity in the late twentieth century is best illustrated by the reappearance of Christianity in China in 1979 after the Cultural Revolution. The first public worship service in China since 1966 was held at Mo En Church in Shanghai, with five thousand people present. All over the country, Christians began reclaiming buildings that had been seized during the previous decades. During the 1980s, the China Christian Council opened 13 theological seminaries. Chinese Protestant leaders began to print Bibles, create a hymnal, and provide for the pastoral needs of Christians who had been unable to worship, ordain pastors, or obtain Christian literature for fifteen years.

One of the most difficult facts to ascertain was exactly how many Christians there were in China in the late twentieth century. When the communists took over China in 1949, there were 700,000 Protestants and three million Catholics. Far from the church being destroyed during the Cultural Revolution, conservative estimates for the mid-1990s put the number of Protestants at over twelve million, gathered into 9,500 churches and 30,000 meeting points. More liberal estimates placed the number of Protestants between nineteen and thirty million. Estimates of Catholic membership, including the underground church, placed it at six million. One of the chief reasons for the growth of the church in China during the communist era was that Christianity was no longer seen as a foreign religion related to Western imperialism. By suffering under communism along with other citizens, Chinese

Christians proved they were truly Chinese. The atheism of communism made Christianity attractive for spiritual reasons, especially as people became disenchanted with communist ideology. The warmth of Christian community life and the integrity of many Christians attracted new believers.

In addition to the "official" Catholic and Protestant movements recognized by the government, millions of Chinese Christians met in "house churches," small groups of Christians who may or may not have been registered with the authorities. Those groups not registered constituted an "underground church," groups of believers afraid to register with the government or else hostile to the theologies represented by official Christianity. The house churches that appeared during and after the Cultural Revolution were often descendants of an indigenous Chinese Christianity that predated the communist era. The leaders of indigenous Chinese groups tended to prefer literalistic biblical interpretation and direct dependence on the power of the Holy Spirit, in contrast to the more educated leaders of mission-related Christianity. House churches were characterized by their emphasis on spontaneous, fervent, spoken prayer; singing and fellowship; and biblically-based teaching. Strongest in rural areas, the house churches spread the faith quietly through service and witness to their neighbors, sometimes including miraculous healings.

By the late twentieth century, Christianity in Asia exhibited surprising vitality despite its minority status and hostile contexts. Caught among the competing forces of Hindu and Islamic fundamentalism, secularism and materialism, and totalitarian governments that did not respect the rights of minorities, Asian Christians continued to struggle for the right to define themselves simultaneously as loyal citizens and Christians. Only in the Philippines and Oceania were Christians a majority and in South Korea and the Near East a substantial minority.

Christianity in Latin America

Latin American Catholicism

Judged by the number of adherents, Latin America was the most Roman Catholic part of the world at the end of the twentieth century. The Catholic Church had taken the leading role in shaping the culture and worldviews of Latin Americans since the time of the *conquistadors*. Yet in the late twentieth century, the question of Catholic identity emerged with such force that the Latin American Church became divided. On the one hand, the institutional church saw itself as the upholder of "Christian civilization," supporting authorities, cultivating a European type of piety, and opposing such ideas as popular democracy, secularism, and religious freedom. The witness of such past leaders as Bartolomé de las Casas was ignored, as were the Indian and African roots of the church.

On the other hand, after the reforms of the Second Vatican Council, Catholicism saw itself as the church of the people; for the first time in four hundred years, it supported grassroots struggles for economic, political, and social liberation. From 1962 to 1965, the bishops met in Rome to reform the doctrine and practice of the Roman Catholic Church and to bring it into the modern era. Over 600 Latin American bishops found themselves together in Rome and began to realize that, although they were numerically powerful, the Latin American Church had remained a "stepchild." Lacking their own theologies, always short of priests, the pope never visiting, and with bishops isolated from each other without a sense of corporate identity, the church had never claimed its birthright. After the end of the Vatican Council, the bishops of each region met to consider how to apply its decisions. In 1968, the Latin American bishops met at Medellín, Colombia, determined to claim a regional solidarity, to interact with the current context, and to apply conciliar themes such as the church as the people of God. Also in 1968, Pope Paul VI became the first pope to visit Latin America.

The bishops at the Medellín Conference found themselves meeting during a dark time in the continent's history: Latin America had become an arena for the Cold War and the consequent strengthening of militaries. In one country after another, military dictators seized power, with no intention of returning it to the inefficient civilian sectors. Peru experienced military coups in 1962 and 1968; Guatemala, Ecuador, and Honduras in 1963; the Dominican Republic in 1963 and 1965; Argentina in 1962 and 1966; Brazil and Bolivia in 1964; and Panama in 1968. Another shadow over the continent was the continued poverty and economic underdevelopment of the ordinary people despite some of the greatest reserves of natural resources in the world. Euro-American elites controlled most of the land, and the indigenous peasantry lived like serfs. The Catholic bishops meeting at Medellín evaluated the social context of their continent and spoke with a powerful voice against the dependence of Latin America on the industrialized north—a dependence that perpetuated the poverty of the south. Calling the church to take the side of the poor, the bishops supported a new "theology of liberation."

Liberation theology arose in the 1960s when several Latin American priests returned from their theological studies in Europe and began to analyze the Latin American situation. They evaluated it according to the Bible, Christian ethics, and Marxist class analysis, and then they proposed action to correct the inequities apparent in Latin American society. Liberation theologians argued that theology must begin in the concrete context of the people and then be developed by the people for the sake of their own liberation from structural injustice and for bringing the kingdom of God on earth. Indeed, God had a "preferential option for the poor." By the early 1970s, many Catholic priests and sisters began meeting with small groups of people to reflect on the Latin American situation, study the Bible's relevance for their lives, and act on their insights. These small groups became known as Base Christian Communities, groups of believers at the base or bottom of society—the building blocks of what would become a more just social order and a church responsive to the needs of the people. In a situation in which large parishes served thousands of people because of the severe shortage of clergy, Base Communities became a way for people to participate meaningfully in the life of the church and to improve society. Many of the missionaries who supported liberation theology and the development of Base Christian Communities had come to Latin America in the early 1960s, when Pope John XXIII called for religious orders to send missionaries to build up the Latin American church.

The ideals behind the Medellín Conference were quickly tested by the realities of military dictatorships that perceived Base Christian Communities, lay Catholic leadership, and attempts to organize the grass roots as threats to their national security. Once the Catholic church began taking the side of the people, it became a target of the military dictatorships. Just as the priests who had defended the human rights of the Indians in the early 1500s had been persecuted and killed, church leaders who took the side of the poor after

Medellín were accused of being Communists, tortured, and murdered. Militaries martyred an estimated 850 bishops, priests, and nuns in Latin America during the 1970s and early 1980s. Some of the most shocking events occurred in 1980, when El Salvador was in the middle of an undeclared civil war, with peasants struggling against an alliance of the land-holding aristocracy and the military government. The Archbishop of El Salvador, Oscar Romero, declared that the church sided with the poor. Government security forces then targeted the church, abducting and murdering catechists and active Christians, and even assassinating Archbishop Romero while he was saying Mass on March 24, 1980. North American sisters had answered Romero's request to come to El Salvador and accompany the people in their struggle for justice against the military dictatorship. They arranged food and medicine for war refugees, escorted priests into unsafe areas so they could say Mass, and documented the disappearance of persons abducted and murdered by the security forces. Also in 1980, Salvadoran security forces abducted four North American women—three sisters and one lay worker—and murdered them. Then, in 1989, the Salvadoran security forces murdered six Jesuit missionaries and two women at the University of Central America in San Salvador.

Perhaps nowhere did the church suffer as much as in Guatemala, where a thirty-year civil war between the landowners and the Indian peasants resulted in the deaths of 100,000 people. In the early 1980s, one million of Guatemala's population of nine million was displaced when the military destroyed 400 villages and slaughtered peasants accused of being Communist subversives. The military targeted Catholic lay catechists because they sought to teach the people. In 1982–83, under the rule of General Efraín Ríos-Montt, a born-again Protestant Christian, whole villages of Christians were eliminated, with leaders tortured and dismembered.

By the time the Catholic bishops met again in Puebla, Mexico, in 1979, a reaction had set in against liberation theology, which was perceived by many bishops to be an ill-disguised form of Marxism. The conference backed off from the radical critiques of capitalism it had made in Medellín, but it continued to uphold the idea of Base Christian Communities and the church as supporter of the poor. A more conservative, anticommunist Pope John Paul II began appointing more hierarchical, traditionalist bishops in Latin America, and the church retreated at an institutional level from the theology of liberation. A changing political scene in the late 1980s also dampened enthusiasm for liberation theology: Military dictatorships began handing over power to elected governments throughout Latin America. With the return of democratic institutions and the end of the Cold War, support for the theology of liberation began to decline. On the popular level, however, liberation theology had created a higher level of interest in personal spiritual growth, Bible study, and lay leadership in the Roman Catholic Church.

Becoming closer to the daily struggles of the ordinary people, the Catholic Church realized, to its surprise, that much that had passed for centuries as Catholic devotion was in fact a catholicized form of folk religion. For example, beliefs in the saints were mixed with pre-Christian sacrifices to various earth spirits. In Latin American countries with substantial African populations, such as Brazil, Cuba, and Haiti, Catholic beliefs coexisted with worship of African divinities and such practices as spirit possession and animal sacrifice. Probably because of the brutality of the initial evangelization and colonization of the region, the pre-Christian religious patterns of the native Americans and African-Americans had remained intact beneath a veneer of formal Catholicism. Thus, when the Council of Latin American Bishops met for the fourth time in 1992, one of their major concerns was the re-evangelization of the continent. By the 1990s, the Catholic church in Latin America became concerned about cultural and theological issues related to folk religion and also worried about the dynamic growth of Protestantism since the Second World War.

The Rise of Protestantism

Protestantism entered Latin America during the nineteenth century, in alliance with middle-class liberals who hoped that it might help to modernize and democratize Latin American societies. The first Protestant missionaries focused on distributing the Bible, believing that the Christendom mentality of the Catholic Church had denied the people biblical religion and freedom of conscience. Other early Protestant missionaries in Latin America came to teach in schools that supported such progressive ideas as the education of girls, individualism, and democracy. Although the numbers of Protestants remained small, the Catholic church saw them as a serious threat, and anti-Protestant agitations were frequent despite the gradual establishment of legal religious toleration. By 1900, there were eleven thousand Protestants in Brazil, but perhaps only five thousand in the rest of South America. In 1930, Protestants numbered less than one percent of the population of Latin America.

By the mid-twentieth century, most Protestant missionaries to Latin America represented theologically conservative or Pentecostal bodies. New missionary agencies like the Wycliffe Bible Translators (1934) and the New Tribes Mission (1942) conducted frontier missions and tried to reach isolated Indian tribes who did not have the Bible in their own language. Missionaries used radio to reach the masses—for example, the radio station HCJB in Quito, Ecuador, which, by the mid-1950s, was broadcasting around the clock in seven languages. Crusade evangelism arrived in 1958 when the greatest evangelist of the late-twentieth century, Billy Graham (b. 1918), conducted the "Caribbean Crusade" in eight countries. Graham's methods were imitated by Latin American evangelists, notably the Argentinian Luis Palau. Healing campaigns led to the formation of pentecostal churches, which featured spontaneous patterns of worship and music with Latin American cadences and instruments. Protestantism began expanding broadly throughout Latin America from the 1930s onward. Protestants called themselves *evangélicos*, and they excelled at preaching, Bible study, founding schools, and starting small churches, but they remained staunchly anti-Catholic and critical of the loose morality of the larger culture. When significant growth began, it took the form of pentecostalism rather than the historic missionary denominations such as Presbyterianism, Methodism, and Lutheranism. By 1994, estimates of the number of pentecostals in Brazil ranged from 10 to 35 million. Pentecostalism grew so rapidly and spontaneously through the witness of Latin Americans themselves, that by the 1990s, pentecostals represented seventy-five percent of the Protestants in Latin America.

The reasons for the growth of pentecostal Protestantism were many, beginning with the voluntaristic, indigenous nature of its leadership and worship. Whereas it took many years of study to produce a Catholic priest, who was then alienated from ordinary life and subject to hierarchical authority, a pentecostal could study the Bible and then open his own church in his home or a storefront. Pentecostalism provided opportunities for leaders who shared the worldviews and lives of the ordinary people. By the mid-1990s, scholars estimated that over fifty percent of Protestant churches in Latin America either were founded by Latin Americans without any reference to foreign missionaries or had become completely indigenous movements. The largest single indigenous congregation in Latin America was the Brazil for Christ Church in São Paulo, Brazil. Founded by Manoel de Mello, the church building seated over 20,000 people. Another large, indigenous Latin American denomination was the Universal Church of the Kingdom of God, a pentecostal group begun in the late 1970s by Edir Macedo de Bezerra. By the 1990s, this denomination had eight hundred churches with two million worshipers led by two thousand pastors throughout Latin America.

Other reasons for pentecostal Protestant growth, besides its indigenous leadership, were its strict code of personal morality, including prohibitions against drinking and adultery, and the adoption of a strong work ethic. Becoming a Protestant meant that, for the first time in many people's lives, they were choosing who they wanted to be rather than passively accepting an ascribed status as a poor peasant or oppressed worker. The Protestant work ethic helped enterprising individuals to get ahead in society. Ironically, the liberation theologies of the Catholic Base Christian Communities may have created heightened expectations for improved material lives that could not be fulfilled; and in the 1990s, many Catholics were disillusioned with liberationist ideals and became pentecostals. Instead of the intellectualism of liberation theology, pentecostalism centered on the family, with emphasis on faithfulness to one's spouse and children. Consequently, the majority of pentecostals were women attracted to the family values of the movement.

Popular Protestantism helped Latin Americans create new forms of community in an era of political and economic uncertainty and massive urbanization and dislocation. Protestantism grew so rapidly in Latin America in the late twentieth century, that scholars predicted that Protestants could constitute a third of the Latin American population by the year 2010, with their greatest strengths in Guatemala, Puerto Rico, El Salvador, Brazil, and Honduras.

African Christianity

By the end of the century, the fastest growing churches in the world were in sub-Saharan Africa, with Africa expected to become home to the most Christians on any continent in the twenty-first century. Political independence from Europe came to most African countries by the late 1960s. But with the borders of African countries determined by European administrative fiat rather than natural division, many African governments split along ethnic lines. One-party states, civil wars, military coups, famines, the AIDS epidemic, urbanization, millions of refugees, and the collapse of infrastructures plagued the continent during the late twentieth century. In the midst of some of the worst living conditions anywhere in the world, Africans organized themselves into churches. By 1984, in a remarkable process of indigenization, Africans had founded seven thousand independent, indigenous denominations in forty-three countries across the continent. In South Africa, by the 1990s, forty-seven percent of the black population were members of African-Initiated Churches, a percentage that continued to grow after the election of the first majority-rule government in 1994. Although the mission-founded denominations in Africa were largely in African hands by the 1970s, the African-Initiated Churches led the way in accommodating Christianity to African cultural forms, social structures, and traditional beliefs.

From the early days of Protestant missions to Africa during the 1800s, indigenous leaders emerged who spread the faith among their people. Among the most outstanding was the son of a Xhosa chief, Ntsikana (ca. 1780–1821). Raised as a warrior covered with red ochre, a renowned poet and orator, Ntsikana experienced a religious vision in 1815. Following the vision, he washed off his ochre, became a monogamist, and began to attend services at the London Missionary Society mission station. A pacifist who refused to fight against the British in southern Africa, Ntsikana led a group of followers in prayer and twice-daily worship. He wrote the Great Hymn that became the core of Xhosa Christian theology and worship and that represented a Xhosa understanding of God as creator and protector. In West Africa, nobody of Ntsikana's creativity and stature emerged in the early 1800s, but in the 1840s the Anglicans began to ordain Africans who had been educated in mission schools. By 1856, eleven Anglicans and several Methodists had been ordained in western Africa. A good educational system, including the founding of Fourah Bay College, as well as African leadership under men like Bishop Samuel Crowther, planted the roots of strong "historic" denominations in West Africa by the 1870s.

In eastern and central Africa, the most striking example of early African Christian leadership occurred among converts in Uganda. During the late 1870s, both the Anglican Church Missionary Society and the French Catholic White Fathers arrived at the court of Mutesa (1856–1884), the shrewd monarch of the Baganda who played them off against each other and against his Muslim Arab trading partners. By 1882, the Catholics had baptized their first converts, approximately sixteen young men who worked at the king's court. These were the early fruits of a mass conversion. Under the early Baganda Christians Mukasa Balikuddembe, Andrew Kaggwa, and Matthias Kalemba, the Catholic church began to grow as these leaders baptized the sick and provided Christian instruction to their people. Protestantism similarly grew rapidly under indigenous leadership. In the meantime, the new king of the Baganda, Mwanga, became enraged when the Christians in his court refused to engage in homosexual relations with him. After a newly baptized princess destroyed her umbilical cord, the powerful symbol of traditional religion, on June 3, 1886, Mwanga executed nearly one hundred Christians, both Catholic and Protestant. Thirty-one were burned to death and the rest tortured, hacked into pieces, and left to die. Within a few years, civil war resulted in a victory of Christians and traditionalists over the Muslims, and the mass movement into Christianity gained strength. By the time the British colonialists took over Uganda in the 1890s, the spirit of the Uganda martyrs had already created a Christianized people in East Africa. In 1894, the Baganda sent out eighty evangelists, the first of a widespread indigenous mission movement.

Ethiopianism

The systematization of European colonialism after the Berlin Conference of 1885 brought with it both an increased missionary presence in Africa and African-led resistance to European ecclesiastical and political domination. By 1910, ten thousand Western missionaries were working in Africa, of whom nearly six thousand were Catholics and the rest Protestants. In South Africa, especially, where colonialism had been preceded by white immigration and conquest of the land, Africans chafed under white leadership of the churches. In

1884, the minister Nehemiah Tile broke off from the Methodist Church to found the Tembu National Church as a denomination controlled by Africans. Similarly, African Lutheran and Baptist leaders broke off from the mission churches to found independent denominations. The early independent churches began as breakaway movements from Western churches in which racial and cultural prejudice suppressed black leadership and elements of African culture. The churches emphasized African nationalism in ecclesiastical, and sometimes political, affairs. They received the name "Ethiopian" in 1892 when a Methodist minister, Mangena Mokone, founded the Ethiopian Church in the Witwatersrand. Protesting racial segregation, Mokone found the precedent for African leadership in the Bible in Psalm 68:31, "Ethiopia shall stretch out her hands to God." Believing that Africans should lead African churches and should be responsible for the evangelization of Africa, Ethiopian or nationalist churches emerged from numerous Western denominations in southern Africa.

The emergence of Ethiopianism in African Christianity peaked from 1890 to 1920. A number of Ethiopian-type secessions also occurred in Nigeria over issues of racism in the churches and the forbidding of African customs such as polygamy. By 1920, one-third of Yoruba Christians were members of African-initiated churches. The political authorities observed Ethiopianism with alarm, for they suspected that spiritual and ecclesiastical freedom was the logical precursor of political freedom. Colonial fears of Ethiopianism, or African leadership in the churches, were so great that colonial governments quickly suppressed prophets and leaders who emerged within African Christianity. The existence of such prophets during the early twentieth century was proof both of the vitality of the growing faith and of the European paternalism that permitted little African leadership within the mission churches. One of the greatest evangelists in all of African Christianity emerged in the context of colonialism in West Africa: the Glebo prophet William Wadé Harris (ca. 1860–1929). In June of 1910, Harris had a vision of the angel Gabriel, who called him to be a prophet, wear white, destroy fetishes, and itinerate throughout West Africa, calling people to repentance and baptism. Masses of people thronged to hear him, threw away their fetishes, and began to live more orderly lives. Even though Harris counseled obedience to authorities, French colonial officials in the Ivory Coast beat and arrested him and his assistants. Harris's ministry provoked a massive revival movement that swept tens of thousands into the Methodist and Catholic churches, as well as precipitated an indigenous Harrist Church that broke off from the Methodists.

In many respects, Ethiopian churches resembled the European denominations from which they emerged, for they were founded as people's expressions of nationalism or resistance to colonial control and European racial attitudes, rather than as deliberate accommodations to African cultures. By the late twentieth century, Ethiopian movements had become more open to African cultural elements such as belief in spirits, polygamy, ritual taboos, and the veneration of ancestors.

Prophetism, Zionism, and Spirit Churches

The largest category of African-Initiated Churches was not the Ethiopian type, but a group designated as Spirit or Zionist churches. The Spirit churches were characterized by having a prophetic leader, a high emphasis on the Holy Spirit, pentecostal phenomena such as speaking in tongues and healings, and often a holy city or "Zion" as headquarters. Although many of the early leaders of Spirit churches broke off from Western denominations, by the late twentieth century the vast majority of their members had never been members of historic denominations. In short, the Zionist churches were remarkable not only for their interaction with indigenous worldviews and cultural elements, but for their missionary vigor as well. By the late twentieth century, the Zionists comprised some of the largest and most stable independent churches in southern Africa. They were led by numerous bishops who wore colorful robes and carried staffs that symbolized their high authority. In worship life, Zionists emphasized preaching, healing, singing, and vigorous dancing to drums.

One of the earliest founders of a powerful prophetic movement was the Baptist preacher Simon Kimbangu (1889–1951), a martyr to European colonialism in the Belgian Congo. In 1918, he experienced visions calling him to be an apostle. Three years later, he began to heal people and commanded them to throw away their fetishes and trust in God alone. He emphasized strict personal lifestyles, including chastity and monogamy. Fearing insurrection, pan-African nationalism, and Protestantism, the Belgian colonial authorities arrested him after a public ministry of only two months. In a military court, the authorities sentenced him to 120 lashes and death. Outraged Baptist missionaries and others asked for clemency, and Kimbangu's death sentence was commuted to life imprisonment. He was jailed thousands of miles from his home, denied visits from his family, and finally died in prison in 1951.

Kimbangu's followers were legion, spread among some groups that maintained a Christian theology and others that considered Kimbangu a "Black Messiah" and political leader who would bring in a postcolonial millennial era. The government responded to the Kimbanguist movements with persecution, deporting an estimated 37,000 heads of families into the late 1950s. Finally, in 1959, shortly before granting the Congo independence, the Belgian government permitted religious freedom and recognized the Kimbangu Church. Under the leadership of Kimbangu's three sons, especially the youngest, Joseph Diangienda, the Kimbangu Church by the 1960s grew into the largest African-Initiated Church on the continent and became the first African church to join the World Council of Churches. By 1968, the church was educating over a hundred thousand children and ran its own clinics, businesses, and farms. N'Kamba became the holy city of the Kimbanguists, and the church erected one of the largest physical structures in black Africa. The church taught obedience to the Ten Commandments, love for one's enemies, an abstemious lifestyle, care for the poor, monogamy, and the laying on of hands for healing the sick. With its own theological seminary, nurses' training school, and other institutions, the church became one of the best organized of all AICs, with eight million members in the 1990s.

In western Africa during the 1920s, a number of Anglicans began meeting in small groups for prayer and faith healing. These groups were known in Yoruba as *Aladura*, or praying people. In 1928, a road crew worker named Joseph Babalola began to have visions that he should preach the gospel. Leaving his job, he returned to his village and was baptized. In 1930, Babalola's preaching provoked a revival that resulted in a mass movement toward the *Aladura* churches. The movement split into a polygamous group that stressed divine visions and the existence of witchcraft, and another denomination, Christ Apostolic Church, with more traditional Anglican beliefs and an emphasis on education. The *Aladura* churches were the best known group of African-Initiated Churches in Nigeria.

Thousands of Spirit or Zionist indigenous churches emerged in Africa from the

1920s through the 1960s, led by male and female prophets who received divine calls through dreams and visions. The movement was notable for meeting needs that stemmed from African worldviews. For example, the Spirit churches acknowledged widespread belief in ancestral spirits, and church leaders often battled the spirits through the work of the Holy Spirit. The need of Africans for physical and spiritual healing made healing ministries important in all the churches, with women often acting as healers. Although men dominated the upper leadership of the African-Initiated Churches, women outnumbered men among the members. Spirit churches usually originated in rural areas, but spread to the cities with the migration of their members. During the late twentieth century, African-Initiated Churches were the fastest growing churches on the continent, and possibly in the world.

Christianity played a powerful role in the social organization of African peoples during the twentieth century. Both the AICs and the mission-founded denominations made important contributions to African life. The former represented the indigenization of African Christianity—the solid planting of Christianity amidst African worldviews; the latter continued to excel in providing educated leaders for the broader society. In the struggle for liberation from apartheid in Zimbabwe and South Africa, for example, the major black leaders were members of historic churches. Nobody could forget the brave stance of Anglican Archbishop Desmond Tutu against the South African government during the 1970s and 1980s, for which he was awarded the Nobel Peace Prize; or of the Dutch Reformed minister Alan Boesak, who pushed the World Alliance of Reformed Churches to condemn apartheid as heresy. After spending decades imprisoned on Robben Island, Methodist Nelson Mandela became the first democratically elected president of South Africa in 1994; and Bishop Tutu became head of the Truth and Reconciliation Commission to investigate human rights violations under the apartheid regime. Members of the historic denominations maintained wide visions of peace and justice that affected the social and political realms.

On the other hand, the fact of being Christians seemed to make little moral difference as the largely Roman Catholic Hutu and Tutsi slaughtered hundreds of thousands of each other in genocidal wars during the 1990s in Burundi and Rwanda. Despite its rapid growth in the late twentieth century, African Christianity was as human a phenomenon as its European cousins, with Christians numbered among both the oppressors and the oppressed, the sinners and the saints. The vast material poverty of the continent continued to challenge the spiritual resources of the growing churches.

The Globalization of Christianity

By the end of the second millennium A.D., the Western dominance of Christianity had ended. The fastest growing ecclesial group in the world was pentecostalism, with most of its strength in grassroots movements outside the West. Even in the "old mainline" denominations, non-Westerners came to outnumber Westerners. By 1988, for example, only thirty percent of the bishops in the Anglican Communion were from the United States or Great Britain. At a meeting of all the Anglican bishops in the decennial Lambeth Conference, the strength of the African bishops was such that they reversed a century-long ban on the baptism of polygamists. A good indicator of the seismic shift in the ethnocultural basis of Christianity was the increase in non-Western missionaries to other parts of the world. By the 1980s, at least five hundred mission societies were being led by Christians in the Third World. From South Korea alone, approximately five thousand Christians were serving as cross-cultural missionaries by 1996.

An appropriate symbol of the strength of non-Western Christianity at the end of the millennium was the Global Consultation on World Evangelization (GCOWE), held in May of 1995 in Seoul, South Korea. The evangelization of Asia by Asians, especially of those groups that did not have the opportunity to hear the gospel in their own language, was the focus of the conference. One evening, the conference met with sixty thousand Korean youth who pledged themselves to the cause of foreign missions. Whereas 17 of the 1,200 delegates at the Edinburgh 1910 conference were from the non-Western world, GCOWE '95 had 3,293 participants from 186 countries. Seven hundred forty-two Latin Americans, 690 Westerners, and 686 Asians made up the three largest blocs of delegates. The chairman of the Edinburgh 1910 conference (which had not even included Latin America on its agenda) was John Mott, a North American; the chairman of GCOWE '95 was Luis Bush, a Latin American. While the conference at the beginning of the century was concerned with the growth of nationalism in a context of European repression, delegates at GCOWE '95 repented of their own ethnic divisions and sought reconciliation. A Japanese Christian asked for forgiveness from a Korean delegate whose grandfather was killed by the Japanese. Jewish, Arab, and Palestinian Christians asked each other's forgiveness and pledged to host together the next world conference on evangelization in Jerusalem. Together, despite oppression, wars, disease, the destruction of the environment, and numerous human frailties, Christians from every land and nation ended the twentieth century still sharing the dream of the earliest disciples—that the message of Jesus Christ, the Prince of Peace, would transform the world.

Selected Bibliography

Part I: The Context, Birth, and Early Growth of Christianity

Analyses of the social and cultural history of the early Christian period down to the fourth century:

Alfoldy, Geza. *The Social History of Rome*. Baltimore: Johns Hopkins University Press, 1988.
Brown, Peter. *The World of Late Antiquity*. New York: Harcourt-Brace-Jovanovich, 1975.
Frend, W. H. C. *The Rise of Christianity*. Philadelphia: Fortress, 1984.

Analyses of Judaism in relation to the origins of Christianity:

Segal, Alan. *Rebecca's Children: Judaism and Christianity in the Roman World*. Cambridge, MA: Harvard University Press, 1986.
Neusner, Jacob. *Judaism in the Matrix of Christianity* (South Florida Studies in the History of Judaism 8). Atlanta: Scholars Press, 1991.
Collins, John J. *The Apocalyptic Imagination: An Introduction to the Jewish Matrix of Christianity*. New York: Crossroad, 1987.
Dunn, James D. G. *The Parting of the Ways: Between Christianity and Judaism and their Significance for the Character of Christianity*. Philadelphia: Trinity Press International, 1991.
Saldarini, Anthony J. *Pharisees, Scribes and Sadducees in Palestinian Society: A Sociological Approach*. Wilmington, DE: Michael Glazier, 1988.
Soulen, R. Kendall. *The God of Israel and Christian Theology*. Minneapolis: Fortress Press, 1996.

Analyses of the New Testament and its social setting:

Kee, H. C. *Understanding the New Testament* (5th ed.). Englewood Cliffs, NJ: Prentice Hall, 1993.
Meeks, Wayne A. *The First Urban Christians: The Social World of the Apostle Paul.* New Haven, CT: Yale University Press, 1983.
Kee, H. C. *The New Testament in Context: Sources and Documents.* Englewood Cliffs, NJ: Prentice-Hall, 1984.

English translations of basic ancient Jewish and Christian writings:

Charlesworth, J. H., ed. *Apocrypha and Pseudepigrapha of the Old Testament.* 2 vols. Garden City, NY: Doubleday, 1983, 1985.
Schneemelcher, W., ed., English translation edited by R. McL. Wilson. *New Testament Apocrypha.* 2 vols. Revised ed. Louisville: Westminster/John Knox, 1992.
Frend, W. H. C., ed. *The New Eusebius: Documents Illustrating the History of the Church to* A.D. *337.* London: SPCK, 1987.
Sparks, Jack, ed. *The Apostolic Fathers.* Nashville: Thomas Nelson, 1978.
Chadwick, Henry, ed. *Origen: Contra Celsum.* Cambridge: Cambridge University Press, 1965.
Chadwick, Henry, ed. *Alexandrian Christianity.* Philadelphia: Westminster, 1964.
Jurgens, W. A., ed. and trans. *The Faith of the Early Fathers.* Collegeville, MN: Liturgical Press, 1970.
Layton, Bentley, ed. *The Gnostic Scriptures.* Garden City, NY: Doubleday, 1987.

The scholarly study of Jesus:

Kee, H. C. *Jesus in History: An Approach to the Study of the Gospels* (3d ed.). Fort Worth, TX: Harcourt Brace, 1996.
Stanton, Graham. *Gospel Truth? New Light on Jesus and the Gospels.* Valley Forge, PA: Trinity Press International, 1995.
Meier, John P. *A Marginal Jew: Rethinking the Historical Jesus.* 2 vols. New York: Doubleday, 1991, 1994.

These two volumes are useful for the detailed analysis of the biblical texts that they offer, but also for the critical analysis of scholarly theories of the various subjects under examination: the sources relevant to the search for the historical Jesus (Part One); the historical background of Jesus (Part Two); Jesus' relationship with John the Baptist (Vol. Two, Chapters 12 and 13); Jesus' message (Chapters 14–16); and Jesus' miracles (Chapters 17–23). A projected section (to appear in Vol. 3) will deal with the final days of Jesus' life, his crucifixion, and his burial. The resurrection of Jesus, which Meier considers a matter of faith, not of history, will not be discussed in Vol. 3.

Part II: The Christian Empire and Early Middle Ages

Alexander, Paul J. *The Patriarch Nicephorus of Constantinople: Ecclesiastical Policy and Image Worship in the Byzantine Empire.* Oxford: Clarendon Press, 1958. A classic work on Byzantine iconoclasm.
Bolton, Brenda. *The Medieval Reformation.* London: Edward Arnold, 1983. Introduces the turmoil of twelfth-century Western Christendom and the achievements of Pope Innocent III, who recreated medieval European civilization by channeling the energy produced by religious crisis.
Bowersock, G. W. *Julian the Apostate.* Cambridge, MA: Harvard University Press, 1978. Presents and interprets the evidence for Julian's brief life and his attempted rejuvenation of paganism in the late Roman empire.

Brown, Peter. *Augustine of Hippo: A Biography.* Berkeley, CA: University of California Press, 1967. A dazzling study of Augustine and his world.

Brown, Peter. *The Cult of the Saints: Its Rise and Function in Latin Christianity.* Chicago: University of Chicago Press, 1981. A provocative essay exploring the devotion to saints in late antiquity and the battle for control of the cult.

Brown, Peter. *The World of Late Antiquity,* A.D. *150–750.* London: Thames and London Ltd., 1971. A pioneering work on Mediterranean society. Richly illustrated.

Bryer, Anthony, and Judith Herrin, eds. *Iconoclasm: Papers Given at the Ninth Spring Symposium of Byzantine Studies.* Birmingham, UK: Centre for Byzantine Studies, 1977. Groundbreaking and influential articles on Byzantine iconoclasm.

Burns, Thomas S. *A History of the Ostrogoths.* Bloomington, IN: Indiana University Press, 1984. Though somewhat spare in its consideration of Germanic religion and Ostrogothic Christianity, this book does make good use of archaeological evidence to follow changes in Ostrogothic society from the presettlement stage to the end of the kingdom in Italy.

Bynum, Caroline Walker. *Holy Feast and Holy Fast: The Religious Significance of Food to Medieval Women.* Berkeley and Los Angeles: University of California Press, 1987. Rethinks Christian asceticism and the experience of women in the later Middle Ages.

Frend, W. H. C. *The Rise of Christianity.* Philadelphia: Fortress Press, 1984. An authoritative study.

Geary, Patrick J. *Furta Sacra: Thefts of Relics in the Central Middle Ages.* Princeton, NJ: Princeton University Press, 1972; revised edition, 1990. On the cult of sacred relics and societal justifications for the theft of relics.

Herrin, Judith. *The Formation of Christendom.* Princeton, NJ: Princeton University Press, 1987. A masterful exploration of the transition from pagan antiquity to the Christian Middle Ages.

Holum, Kenneth G. *Theodosian Empresses: Women and Imperial Dominion in Late Antiquity.* Berkeley, CA: University of California Press, 1982. Sheds precious insight on the influence of imperial women, which extended even to the shaping of Christian dogma and practice.

Jones, A. H. M. *The Later Roman Empire (284–602): A Social, Economic, and Administrative Survey.* 3 vols. Oxford: Basil Blackwell, 1964. Indispensable guide to the administrative and social structures of the late Roman world.

Kazhdan, Alexander P., ed. *The Oxford Dictionary of Byzantium.* 3 vols. New York: Oxford University Press, 1991. An invaluable reference tool.

Kitzinger, Ernst. *Byzantine Art in the Making: Main Lines of Stylistic Development in Mediterranean Art, 3rd–7th Century.* Cambridge, MA: Harvard University Press, 1977. An overview of pictorial art, with over two hundred monochrome and eight color plates.

Klapisch-Zuber, ed. *A History of Women in the West;* II: *Silences of the Middle Ages.* Cambridge, MA: Belknap Press of Harvard University Press, 1992. A feminist study of women's roles in the Christian societies of the medieval West.

Mango, Cyril. *Byzantium: The Empire of New Rome.* New York: Scribner's, 1980. Surveys Byzantine Christian society, with intriguing discussions of Byzantine worldviews, monasticism, and dissenters, including pagans, Christian heretics, and Jews.

Pelikan, Jaroslav. *The Christian Tradition: A History of the Development of Doctrine;* I: *The Emergence of the Catholic Tradition (100–600);* II: *The Spirit of Eastern Christendom (600–1700);* III: *The Growth of Medieval Theology (600–1300).* Chicago: University of Chicago Press, 1971, 1974, 1978. A masterly study of dogma.

Southern, R. W. *Western Society and the Church in the Middle Ages* (The Pelican History of the Church, vol. 11). Grand Rapids, MI: Eerdmans, 1970. Briefly treats the period from 700 to 1050, but focuses on church and society from 1050 to 1550.

Strayer, Joseph R., ed. *Dictionary of the Middle Ages.* 13 vols. New York: Charles Scribner's Sons, 1982–1989. The latest scholarship on medieval subjects, from Aachen to Zwart Noc. Excellent bibliographies.

Wemple, Suzanne Fonay. *Women in Frankish Society: Marriage and the Cloister, 500–800.* Philadelphia: University of Pennsylvania Press, 1981. An important early contribution to the recent flowering of studies on medieval women.

Part III: The Late Middle Ages and the Reformations of the Sixteenth Century

Comprehensive Resources

Cross, F. L., and E. A. Livingstone, eds., *The Oxford Dictionary of the Christian Church*. New York: Oxford University Press, 1984. A one-volume encyclopedia containing over six thousand entries on all aspects of the history of Christianity.

Jedin, Herbert, and John Dolan, eds. *History of the Church*. 10 vols. New York: Crossroad, 1987. A multiauthor scholarly resource with emphasis on the theological and institutional aspects of Christianity in their cultural and political contexts; extensive bibliographies for each chapter.

The Middle Ages

Gurevich, Aaron, and trans. by Katherine Judelson. *The Origins of European Individualism*. Oxford: Blackwell, 1995. Traces the rise of individualism from Scandinavian sagas to Dante, linking intellectual, cultural, economic, and religious developments.

Hanawalt, Emily Albu, and Carter Lindberg, eds. *Through the Eye of a Needle: Judeo-Christian Roots of Social Welfare*. Kirksville, MO: The Thomas Jefferson University Press, 1994. Essays on social and religious responses to poverty and the poor from the biblical to the early modern period; comprehensive bibliography.

Le Goff, Jacques, and trans. by Teresa Fagan. *Intellectuals in the Middle Ages*. Oxford: Blackwell, 1993. Lively discussion of the creation of medieval universities, development of knowledge, and persons.

Le Goff, Jacques, and trans. by Julia Barrow. *Medieval Civilization, 400–1500*. Oxford: Blackwell, 1990. Comprehensive overview by one of the most distinguished French medievalists.

Lynch, Joseph H. *The Medieval Church: A Brief History*. London: Longman, 1992. Up-to-date readable survey.

Mollat, Michel, and trans. by Arthur Goldhammer. *The Poor in the Middle Ages: An Essay in Social History*. New Haven, CT: Yale University Press, 1986. An examination of how successive medieval generations understood poverty and responded to the poor.

Moore, R. I. *The Formation of a Persecuting Society: Power and Deviance in Western Europe, 950–1250*. Oxford: Blackwell, 1987. Stimulating exposition of the development of persecution of heretics, Jews, and lepers.

Southern, Richard W. *Western Society and the Church in the Middle Ages*. Baltimore: Penguin Books, 1973. A master scholar's view of the relations between ecclesial development and social change.

Tierney, Brian, and Sidney Painter. *Western Europe in the Middle Ages, 300–1475*. New York: Alfred A. Knopf, 1983. A standard textbook with a vigorous narrative style.

Ullmann, Walter. *A Short History of the Papacy in the Middle Ages*. London: Methuen, 1974. A historical account of the intellectual, constitutional, legal, theological, and administrative development of the papacy.

Reformation

Bouwsma, William J. *John Calvin: A Sixteenth-Century Portrait*. New York: Oxford University Press, 1988. A stimulating biography.

Brady, Thomas A., Jr., Heiko A. Oberman, and James D. Tracy, eds. *Handbook of European History, 1400–1600*. 2 vols. Leiden: E. J. Brill, 1994. Leading scholars provide comprehensive essays on all aspects of the late medieval and Reformation era.

DeMolen, Richard L., ed. *Leaders of the Reformation*. Selingsgrove, PA: Susquehanna University Press, 1984. Eleven essays on major reformers.

Dickens, A. G. *The English Reformation*. 2nd ed. University Park, PA: University of Pennsylvania Press, 1991. Lively account by a master scholar.

Diefendorf, Barbara. *Beneath the Cross: Catholics and Huguenots in Sixteenth-Century Paris.* New York: Oxford University Press, 1991. Excellent study of the French Reformation.

Edwards, Mark U., Jr. *Printing, Propaganda, and Martin Luther.* Berkeley, CA: University of California Press, 1994. Detailed analysis of the relationship of medium and message in the Reformation.

Hsia, R. Po-Chia, ed. *The German People and the Reformation.* Ithaca, NY: Cornell University Press, 1988. Twelve essays by leading Reformation scholars on such topics as cities, communication and the media, women and family, and the impact of the Reformation.

Lindberg, Carter. *Beyond Charity: Reformation Initiatives for the Poor.* Minneapolis: Fortress, 1993.

Lindberg, Carter. *The European Reformations.* Oxford: Blackwell, 1996. Comprehensive textbook; extensive bibliography.

Naphy, William G. *Calvin and the Consolidation of the Genevan Reformation.* Manchester, UK: Manchester University Press, 1994.

Oberman, Heiko A. *Luther: Man between God and the Devil.* New Haven, CT: Yale University Press, 1989. Lively biography of Luther in his medieval context.

O'Malley, John. *The First Jesuits.* Cambridge, MA: Harvard University Press, 1993. Excellent introduction to Loyola and the Society of Jesus.

Ozment, Steven. *The Age of Reform, 1250–1550.* New Haven, CT: Yale University Press, 1980. A standard, well-written textbook.

Pettegree, Andrew, ed. *The Early Reformation in Europe.* Cambridge, UK: Cambridge University Press, 1992. Essay provide a comprehensive overview of the whole of European Reformations.

Scribner, R. W. *Popular Culture and Popular Movements in Reformation Germany.* London: The Hambledon Press, 1987. Essays by a provocative social historian.

Wiesner, Merry. *Women and Gender in Early Modern Europe.* Cambridge, UK: Cambridge University Press, 1993. Introduces recent research on women's lives.

Part IV: European Christianity Confronts the Modern Age

Barth, Karl. *Protestant Theology in the Nineteenth Century.* Valley Forge, PA: Judson Press, 1973. Critical essays on Protestant thought from a neo-orthodox perspective.

Gerrish, B. A. *A Prince of the Church: Schleiermacher and the Beginnings of Modern Theology.* Philadelphia: Fortress Press, 1984. Perceptive study of Schleiermacher's relevance.

Harvey, Van A. *The Historian and the Believer: The Morality of Historical Knowledge and Christian Belief.* New York: Macmillan, 1966. Focus on the problem of faith and history in light of the work of Troeltsch.

Hsia, R. Po-Chia. *Social Discipline in the Reformation: Central Europe 1550–1750.* London: Routledge, 1989. Good introduction to confessionalization.

Lindberg, Carter. *The Third Reformation? Charismatic Movements and the Lutheran Tradition.* Macon, GA: Mercer University Press, 1983. Major sections on Pietism and charismatic movements.

Lossky, Nicholas, et al., eds. *Dictionary of the Ecumenical Movement.* Grand Rapids: Eerdmans, 1991.

Misner, Paul. *Social Catholicism in Europe: From the Onset of Industrialization to the First World War.* New York: Crossroad, 1991. Excellent, readable survey.

Rabb, Theodore K. *The Struggle for Stability in Early Modern Europe.* New York: Oxford University Press, 1975. Focuses on the "crisis" of the seventeenth century.

Stoeffler, F. Ernst. *The Rise of German Pietism during the Eighteenth Century.* Leiden: E. J. Brill, 1973.

Tillich, Paul. *Perspectives on 19th and 20th Century Protestant Theology.* New York: Harper & Row, 1967. By one of the major voices of modern theology.

Part V: Christianity and Culture in America

Anderson, Robert Mapes. *Vision of the Disinherited: The Making of American Pentecostalism.* New York: Oxford University Press, 1979. Focuses on the interaction of poverty and ecstatic religion in creating the Pentecostal movement.

Baer, Hans. *The Black Spiritual Movement: A Religious Response to Racism.* Knoxville, TN: University of Tennessee Press, 1984. The best account of many contemporary varieties of black spiritualist religion.

Balmer, Randall. *Mine Eyes Have Seen the Glory: A Journey into the Evangelical Subculture in America.* New York: Oxford University Press, 1989. An exploration of the evangelical subculture in America that became the basis for a PBS series.

Bonomi, Patricia. *Under the Cape of Heaven: Religion, Society, and Politics in Colonial America.* New York: Oxford University Press, 1986. A readable synthesis of the varieties and impact of religion in early America.

Boyer, Paul. *When Time Shall Be No More: Prophecy Belief in Modern American Culture.* Cambridge, MA: Belknap Press of Harvard University Press, 1992. An intellectual history of millennialism and apocalypticism in recent America.

Braude, Ann. *Radical Spirits: Spiritualism and Women's Rights in Nineteenth-Century America.* Boston: Beacon, 1989. Focuses on the relationship between women's communications with the dead and political reform.

Butler, Jon. *Awash in a Sea of Faith: Christianizing the American People.* Cambridge, MA: Harvard University Press, 1990. A provocative account of the reshaping and vitality of religion from the Puritans to the mid-nineteenth century.

Carey, Patrick. *People, Priests, and Prelates: Ecclesiastical Democracy and the Tensions of Trusteeism.* Notre Dame, IN: University of Notre Dame Press, 1987. The best account of the trustee controversy among American Catholics.

Cross, Robert D. *The Emergence of Liberal Catholicism in America.* Cambridge, MA: Harvard University Press, 1958. The standard source on the Americanist movement.

Curry, Thomas J. *The First Freedoms: Church and State in America to the Passage of the First Amendment.* New York: Oxford University Press, 1986. An intelligent survey of colonial and revolutionary ideas of religious freedom.

Dolan, Jay. *The American Catholic Experience: A History from Colonial Times to the Present.* Garden City, NY: Doubleday, 1985. The place to begin research on almost any topic of American Catholic history.

Ellwood, Robert S., Jr. *Alternative Altars: Unconventional and Eastern Spirituality in America.* Chicago History of American Religion Series. Chicago: University of Chicago, 1979. Seeks to understand why Americans have created new, and been attracted to, exotic religions.

Fones-Wolf, Ken. *Trade Union Gospel: Christianity and Labor in Industrial Philadelphia, 1865–1915.* Philadelphia: Temple University Press, 1989. A detailed study of factory workers' utilization of Christianity.

Gaustad, Edwin Scott. *A Documentary History of Religion in America.* 2 vols. Grand Rapids, MI: Eerdmans, 1982, 1983. A judicious selection illustrating major themes in American religious history.

Gaustad, Edwin Scott. *A Religious History of America.* San Francisco: Harper & Row, New Revised Edition, 1990. A good textbook on American religion, particularly on regional differences.

Goen, C. C. *Broken Churches, Broken Nation: Denominational Schisms and the Coming of the Civil War.* Macon, GA: Mercer University Press, 1985. Shows how the divisions of Baptists, Methodists, and Presbyterians helped harden sectional animosities leading to war.

Gottschalk, Stephen. *The Emergence of Christian Science in American Religious Life.* Berkeley, CA: University of California, 1973. A scholarly account written by an advocate.

Greeley, Andrew. *The American Catholic: A Social Portrait.* New York: Basic Books, 1977. A good use of sociological survey techniques for understanding modern Catholics.

Hall, David D. *Worlds of Wonder, Days of Judgment.* New York: Knopf, 1989. Adds to knowledge of Puritanism by showing the interaction between folk religion and orthodox piety in seventeenth-century New England.

Hambrick-Stowe, Charles E. *The Practice of Piety: Puritan Devotional Disciplines in Seventeenth-Century New England.* Chapel Hill, NC: University of North Carolina, 1982. The best account of the spiritual life of New England Puritans.

Hansen, Klaus. *Mormonism and the American Experience.* Chicago: University of Chicago, 1981. A good introduction to the relationship between basic themes of American culture and the rise of Mormons.

Harrell, David Edwin. *All Things Are Possible: The Healing and Charismatic Revivals in Modern America.* Bloomington, IN: Indiana University Press, 1975. Chronicles the rise of faith healing and Holy Spirit possession in the Pentecostal movement since the 1920s.

Hatch, Nathan O. *The Democratization of American Christianity.* New Haven, CT: Yale University Press, 1989. A vivid account of how early nineteenth-century Evangelicals helped create, and responded to, a democratic culture.

Higginbotham, Evelyn Brooks. *Righteous Discontent: The Women's Movement in the Black Baptist Church, 1880–1920.* Cambridge, MA: Harvard University Press, 1993. A pioneering study of the impact of women in the largest black denomination.

Hoffman, Ronald, and Peter J. Albert, eds. *Religion in a Revolutionary Age.* Charlottesville, VA: University Press of Virginia, 1994. Essays on the impact of religion before and during the Revolution.

Hutchinson, William R. *The Modernist Impulse in American Protestantism.* Cambridge, MA: Harvard University Press, 1976. A perceptive analysis of the rise and impact of liberal theology from the 1890s to the 1920s.

Karlsen, Carol. *The Devil in the Shape of a Woman: Witchcraft in Colonial New England.* New York: Norton, 1987. The best study of Salem witchcraft.

Kosmin, Barry A., and Lackman, Seymour P. *One Nation Under God.* New York: Harmony Books, 1993. The recent and comprehensive poll of Americans' attitudes to religion.

Kuklick, Bruce. *Churchmen and Philosophers from Jonathan Edwards to John Dewey.* New Haven, CT: Yale University Press, 1985. A clear exposition of the thought of America's most profound theologians from the 1740s to 1920s.

Lincoln, C. Eric, and Lawrence Mamiya. *The Black Church in the African American Experience.* Durham, NC: Duke University Press, 1990. A superb sociological study of the modern black church.

Lippy, Charles A., and Peter W. Williams, eds. *Encyclopedia of the American Religious Experience.* 3 vols. New York: Scribner's, 1988. The best starting place for research for anyone who wishes to go beyond a textbook. One hundred essays by specialists on many facets of American religion.

McDannell, Colleen. *The Christian Home in Victorian America, 1840–1900.* Bloomington, IN., 1986. The Christian cult of ideal women and innocent children among Catholics and Protestants.

McLoughlin, William G. *Revivals, Awakenings, and Reform: An Essay on Religion and Social Change in America, 1607–1977.* Chicago: University of Chicago Press, 1978. A provocative essay on why revivalism has been so important in American history.

Marsden, George M. *Fundamentalism and American Culture: The Shaping of Twentieth-Century American Evangelicalism, 1870–1925.* New York: Oxford University Press, 1980. The intellectual history of the rise of fundamentalism.

Marty, Martin. *Modern American Religion.* Vol. 1, *The Irony of It All, 1893–1919.* Vol. 2, *The Noise of Conflict, 1919–1941.* Chicago: University of Chicago Press, 1986, 1991. A comprehensive synthesis of early twentieth-century religion.

Marty, Martin. *Pilgrims in Their Own Land: Five Hundred Years of Religion in America.* Boston: Little, Brown, 1984. The most readable general history of American religion, filled with biographical sketches.

Mathews, Donald G. *Religion in the Old South.* Chicago: University of Chicago Press, 1977. The standard account of the triumphs and failures of evangelical religion in the South.

May, Henry F. *The Enlightenment in America.* New York: Oxford University Press, 1976. A competent survey of the impact of the Age of Reason on religious and intellectual life.

Moorhead, James H. *American Apocalypse: Yankee Protestantism and the Civil War, 1860–1869.* New Haven, CT: Yale University Press, 1978. Tells how the Northern churches viewed the war.

Raboteau, Albert. *Slave Religion: The "Invisible Institution" in the Antebellum South.* New York: Oxford University Press, 1978. A judicious account of slave religion from its arrival in America until the Civil War.

Shipps, Jan. *Mormonism: The Story of a New Religious Tradition.* Urbana, IL: University of Illinois Press, 1985. Presents the Mormons as creating a new cultural synthesis.

Stout, Harry S. *The New England Soul: Preaching and Religious Culture in Colonial New England.* New York: Oxford University Press, 1986. The New England mind as conveyed through sermons from the 1630s until the Revolution.

Taves, Ann. *Household of Faith: Roman Catholic Devotions in Mid-Nineteenth-Century America.* Notre Dame, IN: University of Notre Dame Press, 1986. The impact of devotions on Catholic piety.

Wilson, John F., eds. *Church and State in America.* 2 vols. New York: Greenwood Press, 1986, 1987. Essays and bibliography indispensable for additional research on interactions between churches and government.

Wuthnow, Robert. *The Restructuring of American Religion: Society and Faith since World War II.* Princeton, NJ: Princeton University Press, 1988. A provocative account of why Evangelicals rose and mainline denominations declined, as well as a description of the roles of religion in American life.

Part VI: Christianity in the Wider World

Anderson, Gerald H., ed. *Studies in Philippine Church History.* Ithaca and London: Cornell University Press, 1969.

Anderson, Gerald H., Robert T. Coote, Norman A. Horner, and James M. Phillips, eds. *Mission Legacies: Biographical Studies of the Leaders of the Modern Missionary Movement.* Maryknoll, NY: Orbis Books, 1994.

Axtell, James. *The Invasion Within: The Contest of Cultures in Colonial North America.* New York: Oxford University Press, 1985.

Bays, Daniel H., ed. *Christianity in China: From the Eighteenth Century to the Present.* Palo Alto, CA: Stanford University Press, 1996.

Berg, Mike, and Paul Pretiz. *The Gospel People of Latin America.* Monrovia, CA: MARC and Latin America Mission, 1992.

Betts, Robert Brenton. *Christians in the Arab East.* Atlanta: John Knox Press, 1975.

Bowden, Henry Warner. *American Indians and Christian Missions.* Chicago: University of Chicago Press, 1981.

Brown, G. Thompson. *Christianity in the People's Republic of China.* Atlanta: John Knox Press, 1983.

Caraman, Philip. *The Lost Paradise: An Account of the Jesuits in Paraguay, 1607–1768.* London: Sidgwick & Jackson, 1975.

Clark, Donald N. *Christianity in Modern Korea.* Lanham, MD: University Press of America, 1986.

Cleary, Edward L. *Crisis and Change: The Church in Latin America Today.* Maryknoll, NY: Orbis, 1985.

Cook, Guillermo, ed. *New Face of the Church in Latin America.* Maryknoll, NY: Orbis Books, 1994.

Cox, Harvey. *Fire from Heaven: The Rise of Pentecostal Spirituality and the Reshaping of Religion in the Twenty-first Century.* Reading, MA: Addison-Wesley Publishing Company, 1994.

Cragg, Kenneth. *The Arab Christian: A History in the Middle East.* Louisville, KY: Westminster/John Knox Press, 1991.

Daneel, M. L. *Quest for Belonging: Introduction to a Study of African Independent Churches.* Gweru, Zimbabwe: Mambo Press, 1987.

De Vaulx, Bernard, and translated by Reginald F. Trevett. *History of the Missions.* New York: Hawthorn Books, 1961.

Deats, Richard L. *Nationalism and Christianity in the Philippines.* Dallas: Southern Methodist University Press, 1967.

Donnelly, Joseph P. *Jean de Brebeuf, 1593–1649.* Chicago: Loyola University Press, 1975.

Drummond, Richard Henry. *A History of Christianity in Japan.* Grand Rapids, MI: William B. Eerdmans, 1971.

Dussel, Enrique, ed. *The Church in Latin America, 1492–1992.* Maryknoll, NY: Orbis Books, 1992.

———, and translated and edited by Alan Neely. *A History of the Church in Latin America.* Grand Rapids, MI: William B. Eerdmans, 1981.

Faupel, J. F. *African Holocaust: The Story of the Uganda Martyrs*. New York: P. J. Kenedy & Sons, 1962.

Firth, C. B. *An Introduction to Indian Church History*. Mysore, India: The Christian Literature Society, 1961.

Forman, Charles W. *The Island Churches of the South Pacific: Emergence in the Twentieth Century*. Maryknoll: Orbis, 1982.

Garrett, John. *To Live among the Stars: Christian Origins in Oceania*. Geneva and Suva, Fiji: World Council of Churches, 1982.

Goodpasture, H. McKennie, ed. *Cross and Sword: An Eyewitness History of Christianity in Latin America*. Maryknoll, NY: Orbis, 1989.

Gray, Richard. *Black Christians and White Missionaries*. New Haven, CT: Yale University Press, 1990.

Gutierrez, Gustavo, and translated by Robert R. Barr. *Las Casas: In Search of the Poor of Jesus Christ*. Maryknoll, NY: Orbis, 1993.

Hamilton, J. Taylor, and Kenneth G. Hamilton. *History of the Moravian Church: The Renewed* Unitas Fratrum, *1722–1957*. Bethlehem, PA: Interprovincial Board of Christian Education Moravian Church in America, 1967.

Hastings, Adrian. *The Church in Africa, 1450–1950*. Oxford History of the Christian Church. Oxford: Clarendon Press, 1994.

———. *A History of African Christianity, 1950–1975*. Cambridge, UK: Cambridge University Press, 1979.

Hefner, Robert W., ed. *Conversion to Christianity: Historical and Anthropological Perspectives on a Great Transformation*. Berkeley, CA: University of California Press, 1993.

Hickey, Edward John. *The Society for the Propagation of the Faith: Its Foundation, Organization and Success (1822–1922)*. The Catholic University of America Studies in American Church History. New York: AMS Press, 1974.

Hogg, William Richey. *Ecumenical Foundations*. New York: Harper & Brothers, 1952.

Isichei, Elizabeth. *A History of Christianity in Africa: From Antiquity to the Present*. Grand Rapids, MI: William B. Eerdmans, 1995.

Kaplan, Steven, ed. *Indigenous Responses to Western Christianity*. New York: New York University Press, 1995.

Lacouture, Jean, and translated by Jeremy Leggatt. *Jesuits: A Multibiography*. Washington, D.C.: Counterpoint, 1995.

Langer, Erick, and Robert H. Jackson, eds. *The New Latin American Mission History*. Lincoln, NE: University of Nebraska Press, 1995.

Latourette, Kenneth Scott. *A History of the Expansion of Christianity*. 7 vols. New York: Harper & Row, 1945–71.

McLoughlin, William G. *Cherokees and Missionaries, 1789–1839*. New Haven, CT: Yale University Press, 1984.

Manikam, Rajah B., ed. *Christianity and the Asian Revolution*. Madras: The Joint East Asia Secretariat of the International Missionary Council and the World Council of Churches, 1954.

Martin, David. *Tongues of Fire: The Explosion of Protestantism in Latin America*. Oxford: Blackwell, 1990.

Moffett, Samuel Hugh. *A History of Christianity in Asia. Vol. 1, Beginnings to 1500*. San Francisco: HarperSanFrancisco, 1992.

Mullins, Mark R., and Richard Fox Young, eds. *Perspectives on Christianity in Korea and Japan: The Gospel and Culture in East Asia*. Lewiston, NY: Edwin Mellen Press, 1995.

Murray, Jocelyn. *Proclaim the Good News: A Short History of the Church Missionary Society*. London: Hodder and Stoughton, 1985.

Neill, Stephen. *A History of Christian Missions*. New York: Penguin Books, 1964.

Olmstead, Earl P. *Blackcoats among the Delaware: David Zeisberger on the Ohio Frontier*. Kent, Ohio: Kent State University Press, 1991.

Pedersen, Paul. *Batak Blood and Protestant Soul: The Development of National Batak Churches in North Sumatra*. Grand Rapids, MI: William B. Eerdmans, 1970.

Rivera, Luis N. *A Violent Evangelism: The Political and Religious Conquest of the Americas*. With a foreword by Justo L. Gonzalez. Louisville, KY: Westminster/John Knox, 1992.

Robert, Dana L. *American Women in Mission: A Social History of Mission Thought and Practice*. Macon, GA.: Mercer University Press, 1997.

Ross, Andrew C. *A Vision Betrayed: The Jesuits in Japan and China, 1542–1742*. Maryknoll, NY: Orbis, 1994.

Rouse, Ruth, and Stephen Neill, eds. *A History of the Ecumenical Movement, 1517–1948*. Philadelphia: The Westminster Press, 1954.

Sanneh, Lamin. *Translating the Message: The Missionary Impact on Culture*. Maryknoll, NY: Orbis Press, 1989.

———. *West African Christianity: The Religious Impact*. Maryknoll, NY: Orbis, 1983.

Scherer, James A. *Missionary, Go Home! A Reappraisal of the Christian World Mission*. Englewood Cliffs, NJ: Prentice-Hall, 1964.

Sitoy, Jr., and T. Valentino. *A History of Christianity in the Philippines: The Initial Encounter*. Vol. 1. Quezon City, Philippines: New Day Publishers, 1985.

Stanley, Brian. *The Bible and the Flag: Protestant Missions and British Imperialism in the Nineteenth and Twentieth Centuries*. Leicester, UK: Apollos, 1990.

Tang, Edmond, and Wiest, Jean-Paul, ed. *The Catholic Church in Modern China*. Maryknoll, NY: Orbis Books, 1993.

Thomas, George. *Christian Indians and Indian Nationalism, 1885–1950*. Frankfurt, Germany: Peter D. Lang, 1979.

Tippett, Alan. *The Deep-sea Canoe: The Story of Third World Missionaries in the South Pacific*. South Pasadena, CA: William Carey Library, 1977.

Tucker, Ruth. *From Jerusalem to Irian Jaya: A Biographical History of Christian Missions*. Grand Rapids, MI: Academie Books, 1983.

Verstraelen, F. J., A. Camps, L. A. Hoedemaker, and M. R. Spindler, eds. *Missiology: An Ecumenical Introduction*. Grand Rapids, MI: William B. Eerdmans, 1995.

Visser 't Hooft, Willem A. *The Genesis and Formation of the World Council of Churches*. Geneva: World Council of Churches, 1982.

Walls, Andrew F. *The Missionary Movement in Christian History: Studies in the Transmission of Faith*. Maryknoll, NY: Orbis, 1996.

Webster, John C. B. *A History of the Dalit Christians in India*. San Francisco: Mellen Research University Press, 1992.

Whiteman, Darrell. *Melanesians and Missionaries*. Pasadena, CA: William Carey Library, 1983.

Index